The GREAT BIG BOOK *of* BABY NAMES

Cleveland Kent Evans, Ph.D.

President, American Name Society

Publications International, Ltd.

Cleveland Kent Evans, Ph.D., is one of the foremost experts on name usage in the United States. His current work on given names involves personality, social psychology, history, and popular culture. He has written many articles for scholarly and popular publications, and is frequently interviewed by print and broadcast journalists from Europe, Australia, and South America, as well as the United States and Canada. Dr. Evans is associate professor of psychology at Bellevue University and is president of the American Name Society.

ACKNOWLEDGMENTS

This book could not have been written without input from the participants on the discussion boards at babynames.com, the help of other faculty and students at Bellevue University, and other members of the American Name Society. The popularity lists for England, Wales, and Scotland were produced by Meredith Cane from data provided by the Office for National Statistics and the General Register Office for Scotland. Special thanks is due to Claudia Segger, Rajai Khanji, Victoria Stockdale, Mònica Font, Deng Reath, L. David Ladu, and Mang Thao for help with names from Japan, Jordan, South Africa, Spain, Nuer culture, Bari culture, and Hmong culture; and to the members of the Ojibwe Language Society (Miinawaa) for their help with the name Shania. Any errors in this book are the responsibility of the main author.

Louis Weber, CEO
Publications International, Ltd.
7373 North Cicero Avenue
Lincolnwood, Illinois 60712

Permission is never granted for commercial purposes.

ISBN-13: 978-1-4127-1300-9
ISBN-10: 1-4127-1300-5

Manufactured in China.

8 7 6 5 4 3 2 1

CONTENTS

naming your baby

A Revolution in Baby Naming

Over the last fifty years, American parents have radically increased the variety of names they give their children. In the 1950s, the 50 most popular names accounted for 63.4 percent of all boys born, and 52.1 percent of all girls. But by 2004, the top 50 names covered only 34.6 percent of the boys and 24.4 percent of the girls. As more people move to the United States and use popular or traditional cultural names, the variety of names increases. Also, parents from all ethnic backgrounds are now more likely to search out less common names for their children.

In this new climate for naming, it's more important than ever for parents to have good information on which to base this important decision. The Great Big Book of Baby Names provides the help you need to find the best name for your baby. The first step in this exciting process is to consider as many names as you can. In this book, you'll find thousands of names. Many of these have a brief but interesting write-up about the origin of the name and recent history of use, along with nicknames, alternate spellings, variations from around the world, and famous people with the name. You'll be especially interested in the name's origin if you want to choose a name that reflects your ethnic background. You'll want to learn about the name's history, whether you're looking for a name that is popular today or one that is more nostalgic. You'll also want to know about famous people or well-known characters from movies and literature who have had the name, because this is part of the heritage you pass on to your child. Even if you want your baby to have a unique name, you can choose one of the many you'll find in this book.

Expert Advice

Although you're free to give your baby any name you choose, deciding what to call your child shouldn't be put off until the last minute. Parents should remember that any spur-of-the-moment inspiration for their baby's name could affect that child for a lifetime. Before you choose a name, take the time to ask yourself a few questions:

Is the name easy to spell and to pronounce?

Is it easy to remember?

What nicknames can be derived from it?

Do the initials form a word? If so, is that word likely to prove embarrassing in any way?

Does the name itself resemble any words with unsuitable meanings? It's a good idea to check an unabridged dictionary, especially if you are choosing a very uncommon name, to make sure you won't inadvertently cause your child embarrassment.

It is recommended that you give your child a full name rather than a diminutive form of the name. A name that's cute for a baby may not age well. Katherine Louise is preferable to Katie Lou. You can always give a child a nickname, and the traditional form will remain his or her legal name.

Use care in naming your child after a well-known living person, such as a politician or entertainer. You cannot predict anyone's future, and your child might be stuck with a name that has a negative connotation.

Consider your last name, especially if it's hyphenated. Does the first name you've selected flow easily with the middle and last name? Also, avoid using first names that, in conjunction with your last name, are too cute, such as Crystal Glass, Candy Barr, Destiny Child, or Phil Fuller.

If possible, both parents should agree on the baby's name well in advance of the due date. Once you've decided on a name, you should try to stick with it and avoid last-minute changes. Read this book with your family, make lists of your favorite names, and discuss your reactions. Your child will appreciate your thoughtfulness.

What's in a Name?

Is it better to have a name common to your age group, one that everyone has heard, or an unusual name, one that may cause comment when people first hear it? Psychologists and sociologists have studied this question for years and still cannot agree on the answer.

On one hand, a great deal of evidence shows that when people hear a particular name, they have strong and specific stereotypes about what sort of person bears that name. For example, most Americans expect a woman named Courtney to be attractive and successful but one named Bertha to be loud and obese. Research has found that teachers may give a higher grade to a school paper by a student named Michael than to one by Hubert, even though the papers are identical. Photographs of attractive young women called Jennifer are more likely to win a beauty contest than equally attractive pictures labeled Gertrude. Employers are more likely to grant African-American job applicants interviews if they have names like Angela or James rather than Tamika or DeJuan. Much of this research has found a strong correlation between the frequency of a name in our culture and its rated desirability, especially where names for boys are concerned.

On the other hand, research that compares *actual people* with common first names to those with unusual names often shows the latter having an advantage. People with unusual first names are more likely to be listed in *Who's Who* and are more successful as psychologists. College women with uncommon first names score higher on scales of sociability and self-acceptance; they are also more likely to have a positive sense of individuality, which helps them to resist peer pressure.

Why do these different studies seem contradictory? Part of the answer is that the first set of studies forced people to form impressions based on the name alone. In contrast, recent research shows that including information about an actual person compensates for most of the negative effects of stereotypes and creates a different context in which to view a name. For example, if told we were going to meet a man named Igor, we might conjure up the image of an ugly, stupid, and evil character like Dr. Frankenstein's henchman. But if Igor turned out to be a handsome and intelligent young man who explained that his parents had admired the composer Igor Stravinsky, we would probably find his name to be intriguing and sophisticated.

Another reason for the conflicting results from this research is that uncommon names and names with negative images are not necessarily the same. Boys called Derry or Quinlan and girls called Cosima or Prairie will have a chance to create their own first impressions, free from established stereotypes. They can develop a positive, individual self-concept unhampered by the negative images that go along with names such as Adolf, Ethel, Myrtle, or Elmer.

In the final analysis, of course, your choice of a common or unusual name depends on what you believe is best for your child. After all, there are many occasions in life, such as submitting a job application or seeking admission to college, where a name *does* have a chance to create a positive image on its own. Having a popular name such as Emily or Jacob might be an advantage. If, on the other hand, individuality and creativity are especially important to you, a more unusual name might be better.

But whichever line of thought you follow, remember that a name is more than just a neutral label. The names you give your children will become lasting and important parts of their self-image. Of course, merely selecting a desirable name for your child does not guarantee happiness and success, but boys called Buckshot, Cartel, Craven, Furious, Hades, Lucifer, or Rope and girls called Density, Jealousy, Mirage, Passion, Sanity, Secret, Tyranny, or YerFancy will have a hard time overcoming the belligerent or ridiculous images names such as these evoke. (All these names were given to real children born in the United States since 1995!)

After this discussion, if you would like to ensure that your child does or does not have a very popular name, review the following list of the 40 most common names given to boys and girls born in the United States in 2004. (This list combines spellings like Hailey, Haley, and Hayley, that are normally pronounced the same.) The names are in order by column, so read down first and then over.

Top 40 Most Popular Names for Girls in the United States, 2004

Emily	Isabella	Anna	Mackenzie
Madison	Olivia	Kaylee	Jessica
Emma	Sophia	Natalie	Riley
Hailey	Jasmine	Madeline	Allison
Kaitlyn	Elizabeth	Kayla	Megan
Hannah	Alexis	Lauren	Chloe
Sarah	Samantha	Makayla	Ava
Abigail	Alyssa	Sydney	Ariana
Brianna	Katherine	Taylor	Victoria
Ashley	Grace	Kylie	Ella

Jacob	William	John	Benjamin
Michael	Joseph	James	Logan
Joshua	Anthony	Zachary	Caden
Matthew	Ryan	Jayden	Jose
Nicholas	David	Brian	Elijah
Ethan	Alexander	Nathan	Noah
Andrew	Jonathan	Brandon	Justin
Christopher	Tyler	Caleb	Cameron
Daniel	Dylan	Connor	Eric
Aidan	Christian	Samuel	Gabriel

Today, many parents in the United States want the name they choose for their baby to reflect their ethnic heritage. Although the names they pick may be unusual in this country, these parents are interested in choosing names that are popular in the country where their ancestors lived. Of course, names in other parts of the world go through fads and fashions just as they do in the United States. The names in the following lists have recently been popular in other parts of the world.

Popular Names in Victoria, Australia

Girls Names	Boys Names
Emily	Jack
Olivia	Lachlan
Jessica	Thomas
Sarah	Joshua
Georgia	James
Ella	William
Grace	Matthew
Emma	Daniel
Hannah	Benjamin
Sophie	Nicholas

Popular Names in Quebec, Canada

Girls Names	Boys Names
Lea	Samuel
Rosalie	William
Noemie	Alexis
Laurence	Gabriel
Jade	Jeremy
Megane	Xavier
Sarah	Felix
Audrey	Thomas
Camille	Antoine
Coralie	Olivier

Popular Names in England & Wales

Girls Names	Boys Names
Emily	Jack
Ellie	Joshua
Jessica	Thomas
Amy	James
Sophie	Daniel
Chloe	Samuel
Lucy	Oliver
Katie	William
Olivia	Benjamin
Charlotte	Joseph

Popular Names in France

Girls Names	Boys Names
Léa	Lucas
Manon	Théo
Emma	Matteo
Chloé	Thomas
Camille	Hugo

naming your baby   9

Clara
Inès
Océane
Sarah
Marie

Enzo
Mathis
Maxime
Clement
Léo

Popular Names in Germany

Girls Names
Marie
Sophie
Maria
Anna
Leonie
Lea
Laura
Lena
Katharina
Johanna

Boys Names
Maximilian
Alexander
Paul
Leon
Lukas
Luca
Felix
Jonas
Tim
David

Popular Names in Ireland

Girls Names
Emma
Aoife
Sarah
Ciara
Amy
Katie
Sophie
Rachel
Chloe
Leah

Boys Names
Sean
Jack
Adam
Conor
James
Daniel
Cian
Michael
Eoin
David

Girls Names
Adi
Chen
Feigel
Hallel
Maayan
Maya
Neta
Noa
Noam
Shira

Boys Names
Bar
Fishel
Gai
Ido
Nachman
Natan
Oren
Tom
Yisrael
Zalman

Popular Names in Bologna, Italy

Girls Names
Giulia
Sara
Alice
Martina
Francesca
Sofia
Anna
Elena
Chiara
Matilde

Boys Names
Alessandro
Francesco
Matteo
Filippo
Andrea
Davide
Luca
Riccardo
Lorenzo
Mattia

Popular Names in Japan

Girls Names
Momoka
Haruka
Ayaka
Misaki
Sakura

Boys Names
Yuuki
Yuuta
Haruto
Souta
Kouki

Nanami	Takumi
Yui	Kouta
Hina	Ryouta
Rin	Haruki
Haruna	Kaito

Popular Names in Jordan

Girls Names   **Boys Names**

Girls Names	Boys Names
Rawan	Sami
Suzan	Rani
Lana	Samer
Diana	Kamal
Tala	Bisher
Leena	Imad
Tamara	Raed
Reem	Hazem
Randa	Nader
Amal	Amjad

Popular Names in the Netherlands

Girls Names	Boys Names
Sanne	Sem
Lotte	Daan
Emma	Thomas
Anne	Tim
Iris	Lars
Anna	Lucas
Julia	Bram
Femke	Milan
Lisa	Max
Amber	Jesse

Girls Names	Boys Names
~~Emma~~	Mathias
Julie	Markus
Thea	Martin
Ida	Kristian
Nora	Andreas
Emilie	Jonas
Maria	Tobias
Sara	Daniel
Hanna	Sander
Ingrid	Alexander

Common Names in Russia

Girls Names	Boys Names
Anna	Aleksey
Antonina	Alexander
Elena	Ivan
Galina	Konstantin
Irina	Mikhail
Mariya	Nikolai
Olga	Pavel
Svetlana	Sergey
Tatyana	Vladimir
Valentina	Yuri

Popular Names in South Africa

Girls Names	Boys Names
Aviwe	Jabulani
Busisiwe	Khaya
Naledi	Sandiso
Nomonde	Siyabonga

Sbongile   Sizwe
Sinovuyo   Thabo
Siphokazi   Thabang
Unathi   Vuyisa
Xolelwa   Vuyo
Zanele   Xolani

Girls Names   **Boys Names**
Lucía   Alejandro
María   David
Paula   Daniel
Laura   Pablo
Marta   Adrián
Alba   Álvaro
Andrea   Javier
Claudia   Sergio
Sara   Carlos
Nerea   Marcos

Baby Names and Customs

As long as there has been language, there have been names. Naming is the first task of speech through which we differentiate one person or thing from all others. Every society has a naming system, and all these systems have certain common elements. Throughout the world, each child is assigned a sound or series of sounds that will be his or her name. Because that name is a part of the language of the child's parents, it immediately identifies the child as belonging to a particular society. So our names identify us both as individuals and as members of a group.

In many parts of Africa, a child's naming day is a festive occasion that usually occurs a week or so after the birth. Girls are named sooner than boys, but only by a day or two. An older person bestows the name, first by whispering it to the baby, because a newborn should know his or her name before anyone else does, then by announcing the name to everyone attending the ceremony.

Many Native Americans developed naming systems in which a person's individual name included the name of his or her clan. For example, all the members of a clan that has the bear as its totem animal have names relating to bears, such as Black-Bear Tracks and Black-Bear Flashing Eyes. In some groups, children are given secret names that are not revealed until the child reaches puberty or another important stage of life. In other Native American nations, an event that occurs at a child's birth may become the child's name. Today, a person living on a reservation may have one name at home but a different name when he or she is off the reservation.

In China, all given names are created out of words in the Chinese language that have an obvious, immediate meaning. Names are believed to reflect the character of the person, and great care is taken in selecting a child's name. Usually about a month after the child is born, the parents attempt to create an original name. Many girls are given names that signify beauty, such as Sweet Willow or Morning Star. Boys are given names that reflect strength and good health. In rural areas, many Chinese names still include a "generation name," a word or syllable that is the same for all children born in a family in the same generation. Three sisters, for example, might be named Yuan-Chun, Ying-Chun, and Xi-Chun, which mean "First Spring," "Welcome Spring," and "Cherish Spring." With China's one-child policy, this custom is fading in urban areas, but some Americans of Chinese descent continue this tradition by giving all their children names containing the same syllable (such as *Mar-* as seen in Marco, Marisa, Marla, Marlene, Marshall, Martha, and Marvin). Most Chinese-Americans give their children American-style first names, though they often give a Chinese-language name as the middle name, as in Brittany Ngon Lee.

Jewish names are some of the oldest names in use today. A Jewish boy is named officially when he is circumcised on the eighth day after his birth. A girl is named as soon as possible after her birth. Traditionally, an Ashkenazic Jewish child is not named for a living person for fear that the Angel of Death will mistake the child for the older person if their names are the same.

African-American Names

In the 1960s, some African-Americans began to give their children names from African cultures. Some adults also changed their names to African or Muslim names. Because slaves were often assigned the surnames of their owners and given common first names, choosing African names is a way for African-Americans to acknowledge their heritage before slavery. However, only a few genuine African names, such as Ayana, Kwame, and Jabari, have become widely popular in the African-American community. Muslim names from the Arabic language, such as Iesha, Jamal, Malik, and Aaliyah, have been more popular recently, even with African-Americans who have not adopted the Islamic religion.

Since the 1970s it has become more common for African-Americans to create new names for their children by combining their own set of fashionable sounds and syllables. Names for girls formed in this way are called "Lakeisha names" after one of the prime examples. Lakeisha names are created by linking a fashionable prefix, such as *Sha-*, *La-*, *Ka-*, *Shan-*, or *Ty-*, with a fashionable suffix, such as *-isha*, *-ika*, *-onda*, *-ae*, *-ique*, or *-ice*. The resulting names are almost always accented on the second syllable. In the 1970s and 1980s, names beginning with *La-* such as Lashonda and Lashay were most popular. In the 1990s, *Sha-* names such as Shameka, Shanae, and Shaniqua were fashionable. In 2004, names starting with *Ja-* or ending in *-iyah* such as Jakayla, Jamya, Janiyah, and Taniyah were in vogue. But the point of this custom for most parents is to create a unique name for their child, and many are successful. Even in states as large as Pennsylvania, each year the average African-American girl receives a name that no other African-American girl born in that state is given. It was not possible to include many of these unique names, such as Azanae, Kyaire, and Zaterria, in this book, but they are now the most typical kind of names for African-American girls. Names for boys that have been created similarly include DeJuan, Deonte, Jamarion, Ladarius, and Quantavious.

Hispanic-American Names

Traditionally, Hispanic-American babies were often given saints' names, and both male and female saints were considered appropriate.

Hispanic-American boys are often given religious names such as Jesus, Angel, and Salvador. Girls are often named in honor of the Virgin Mary, using words from her devotional titles such as Araceli, Rocio, Consuelo, Dolores, and Mercedes. Other traditional Spanish names popular in the Hispanic-American community include Carlos, Enrique, Fernando, Francisco, Jaime, Javier, Jorge, Jose, Juan, Julio, Luis, Marcos, and Miguel for boys and Adriana, Beatriz, Carolina, Daniela, Gabriela, Isabel, and Maria for girls. Traditional boys' names remain especially common in the Hispanic-American community, because there is still the expectation that most boys will be named after their fathers or grandfathers, a custom that is now rare in other ethnic groups.

However, not all the names popular with Hispanic-Americans are traditionally Spanish names. Hector, Oscar, and Rene have long been popular names for boys in Latin America, and non-Spanish immigrants to Central and South America, as well as the modern media, have introduced many new names. In particular, Spanish-language television programs called *telenovelas,* most of which are produced in Mexico, have popularized the names of their stars and characters wherever they are shown, including in the United States. For example, Vanessa, a very British name, is popular in the Hispanic-American community because it was the name of the title character in a television program starring Lucia Mendez, one of Mexico's most popular actresses. Other non-Spanish names more popular with Latinos than Anglos in the United States include Astrid, Daisy, Evelyn, Leslie, Lizbeth, and Yasmin for girls and Axel, Edgar, Edwin, Elmer, George, Giovanni, Omar, and Yahir for boys. Ariel and Alexis are very common names for Hispanic-American boys, while other ethnic groups now give them mostly to girls. Some Latino parents also create brand-new names for their children, especially daughters. At the moment, invented names beginning with the letter Y are in vogue, and many Hispanic girls are being given names like Yaritza, Yanelis, Yosayra, and Yuritzi.

Other Ethnic Influences

Historically, first-generation immigrants to the United States from Europe and East Asia have tried to adopt American naming customs, though since they are not completely assimilated into the culture they often give their children names that seem out of style. For example, recent immigrants from China and Korea are much more likely to name daughters Linda or Eunice than other Americans. The second generation of an immigrant group usually gives their children names that are no different from those of the majority. The third and fourth generations, however, often begin to revive names from their ancestry. Many Irish-Americans began this process in the 1940s, re-introducing traditional Irish names such as Sean, Kevin, Sheila, and Caitlin that have gone on to become generally popular. This process has now begun with Italian-Americans, who, since 1990, have strongly increased their use of traditional Italian names such as Isabella, Gianna, Lorenzo, and Leonardo.

Because of the strong influence of Islam and Hinduism, immigrants from the Middle East and South Asia don't adopt "Western" names as readily, though they do often try to choose names from their religious traditions that they think will be easier for other Americans to pronounce. Muslim-Americans give their children names such as Ali, Fatima, Zaynab, and Ziad; Hindu-Americans use names such as Aryan, Diya, Mira, and Rohan. Many names popular with East Indian–Americans, such as Arjun and Shreya, have been influenced by the stars of India's huge Bollywood film industry.

Media Influences on Naming

Many names that suddenly become popular are inspired by figures in the media, whether they are real actors or athletes, such as Ashton Kutcher or Jalen Rose, or fictional characters such as the mermaid Madison in the film *Splash*.

Of course, modern parents are not the only ones affected by the media of their day. Thelma, for example, became a popular name for English and American girls after British author Marie Corelli invented it for the beautiful heroine of her bestselling novel *Thelma*, published in 1887. But since the 1950s, television has been the most effective medium for creating new name fashions. Mallory, for example, became popular for girls when the character called Mallory appeared on *Family Ties* in the 1980s. Although a few American parents had named sons Dylan after Welsh poet Dylan Thomas or perhaps musician Bob Dylan in the 1960s, the name exploded in popularity in the 1990s after the character Dylan McKay appeared on *Beverly Hills, 90210*. Daytime soap operas also affect what Americans name their children. Kayla, now one of the top 25 names for girls in the United States, barely existed before Kayla Brady appeared on *Days of Our Lives* in 1982.

People often assume that when parents take a name from the media they want to honor the star or character who has the name. This is rarely the case. Most parents today don't want their children to have common names, but at the same time they want the names they choose to "fit in." They are therefore always on the lookout for "different but not too different" names, and when such a name gets a lot of exposure in the media, many parents discover it at the same time. This is shown by looking at the names of the characters on the hugely successful television comedy *Friends*. The names Ross and Joey weren't affected at all by the program; Monica and Rachel had very tiny increases, and Phoebe a somewhat more noticeable one. The series had the biggest impact by far on the name Chandler, which more than doubled in use just after *Friends* became a hit. This was not because viewers liked or admired the character Chandler any more than the others, but because he was the one who had the cool new name that young parents were searching for.

Even horrific characters can have a positive impact on a name's use if the name itself fits in with fashionable sounds. Gage, Peyton, and Samara are examples of scary film characters who nevertheless inspired namesakes. Names in the news can also have an effect. The number of American girls named Camille increased by 50 percent in 1969 and 1970 after Hurricane Camille hit the Gulf Coast, so it can be predicted that the number of girls named Katrina will increase in 2006 in spite of the name's association with a huge natural disaster.

Any media that is popular with people in their 20s and 30s can create a fashion for a name. Popular music inspires names both through songs, such as Rhiannon, and singers, such as Shania. Today's young parental generation is now starting to discover baby names like Raiden and Rinoa through video and computer games. Some parents are still inspired by novels, as shown by names such as Arya and Novalee. Science fiction and fantasy books, video games, and films are particularly noticeable as name sources, probably because these stories often require writers to create brand-new names.

Popularity Rankings

Before 1995, no comprehensive listing of the most popular names in the United States was readily available. Then Michael Shackleford, an employee of the Social Security Administration (SSA), created a program that uses the information from applications for Social Security numbers to create a national list of the top 1,000 names given each year. He made this data immediately accessible to anyone through the Social Security Web site. However, this list treats every different spelling as a separate name, so it underestimates the popularity of names, such as Hailey, Kaitlyn, and Caden, that have several different spellings. The popularity rankings for most names reported in this book are therefore based on a modification of the SSA list that adds together the figures for different spellings normally pronounced the same way. There are, of course, many unusual spellings that do not make the top 1,000 list in a given year. When one is considering a very popular name such as Madison or Zachary, the number of children given spellings below the top 1,000 list would not greatly affect their final ranking. However, for names near the bottom of the list, it's quite possible that the rank could be affected by the unknown number of children given unusual, unranked spellings. Therefore it's more accurate for the less popular names to continue to use the original SSA rank in reporting their popularity. In interpreting the entries in this book, when a 2004 popularity ranking is given, it is from the modified "spellings added together list" unless it specifically states the ranking is "on the SSA list," in which case the original list where each spelling is counted separately has been used.

Picking the Perfect Name

The choice of your baby's name is a very important decision, and this book is designed to help you select a name that both you and your child will enjoy for a lifetime. *The Great Big Book of Baby Names* presents a comprehensive selection of names from around the world and gives you detailed information about each name. It will help make the adventure of naming your baby a fun and fascinating one. Enjoy!

fun lists

If you'd like to choose a name with special meaning, the following lists can help. Each has a different theme—some are fun, some are serious, and many are of famous people. All the names in these lists are detailed later in this book, so you can look them up for more information. This is just a sampling of the thousands of names inside. So dive in, and enjoy!

New Again: Names that Just Changed from Dorky to Cool

Boys Names

Ajax	Leo
Atticus	Milo
Augustus	Oliver
Elliott	Oscar
Hugo	Silas
Jasper	Simeon
Julian	Tobias

Girls Names

Ada	Ivy
Adeline	Lucille
Bella	Luna
Clara	Rhea
Eleanor	Sadie
Greta	Stella
Hazel	Violet

Off the Beaten Path: Names for People Who Don't Follow the Crowd

Boys Names

Actassi	Pershing
Angus	Reverdy
Fountain	Rupert
Galway	Sinclair
Inigo	Tecumseh
Jotham	Tighe
Knox	Topher
Ogden	Ving
Ormond	Winthrop
Pascal	Yelberton

Girls Names

Aphra	Milbry
Beta	Orpah
Bliss	Psyche
Drusilla	Romaine
Easter	Seraphina
Fairuza	Undine
Garnet	Vashti
Iola	Verity
Lenuta	Xanthe
March	Zanazan

Boys Names

Ansel	Lucian
Brice	Pablo
Claude	Paul
Diego	Pierre
Gerhard	Piet
Jackson	Raphael
Jacques	Salvador
Leonardo	Vincent

Girls Names

Camille	Judith
Cindy	Kara
Frida	Louise
Georgia	Marisol
Giovanna	Mary
Hannah	Maya
Helen	Rosa
Imogen	Sally

Diva Names:
For Opera Lovers

Boys Names

Arturo	Marcelo
Ettore	Placido
Giacomo	Richard
Giuseppe	Rolando
Jose	Tristan
Luciano	Vincenzo

Girls Names

Aida	Kathleen
Aria	Leonora
Beverly	Marilyn
Carmen	Mimi
Cecilia	Renata
Gilda	Renee

Orchestral Names:
For Fans of Classical Music

Boys Names

Andres	Johann
Franz	Leonard
Frederic	Ludwig
Gustav	Maurice
Hector	Neville
Igor	Wolfgang
Itzhak	Zubin

Girls Names

Arabella	Harmony
Bella	Jennifer
Blanca	Joelle
Cadence	Leila
Elodie	Melody
Fantasia	Victoria
Giselle	Yoko

Boys Names

Archie	Marcus
Branford	Miles
Coleman	Mingus
Dexter	Nestor
Herbie	Sonny
Lonnie	Wynton

Girls Names

Alberta	Ella
Billie	Etta
Cassandra	Jazzmyn
Christiana	Marian
Cleo	Patricia
Eartha	Shirley

Boys Names

Armani	Halston
Bill	Karl
Calvin	Perry
Carson	Ralph
Christian	Tommy
Esteban	Yves
Gianni	Zac

Girls Names

Carolina	Gisele
Chanel	Heidi
Claudia	Kimora
Coco	Naomi
Cynthia	Nicole
Donna	Stella
Essence	Vera

Boys Names

Adriel	Jaheim
Axel	Jairo
Beck	Jermaine
Chad	Jude
DeVante	Lennon
Donovan	Tarkan
Dylan	Tyrese
Elvis	Zion

Girls Names

Aaliyah	Mandy
Ashanti	Mariah
Celine	Rhiannon
Deja	Selena
Jewel	Shania
Julissa	Shanice
Layla	Shreya
Leilani	Whitney

Country Names:
For Parents Who Like Country Music

Boys Names

Clint	Porter
Dallas	Randy
Dwight	Ronnie
Garth	Toby
Hank	Trace
Hoyt	Travis
Kenny	Vince
Marty	Waylon

Girls Names

Aubrey	Naomi
Faith	Reba
Gretchen	Shania
Kathy	Stacey
Lacy	Tammy
LeAnn	Tanya
Loretta	Trisha
Martina	Wynonna

Names in the News:
Journalists and Newscasters

Boys Names

Anderson	Morley
Bill	Paul
Bryant	Peter
Dan	Stone
Forrest	Ted
Joseph	Tom
Matt	Walter
Mike	Wolf

Girls Names

Barbara	Hannah
Campbell	Katie
Candy	Lesley
Christiane	Natalie
Connie	Nina
Deborah	Paula
Diane	Soledad
Fredricka	Willow

Names in Space:
Astronomical People and Terms

Boys Names

Draco	Rigel
Edwin	Rodolfo
Giovanni	Sirius
Guion	Tycho
Neil	Virgil

Girls Names

Andromeda	Mae
Eileen	Merope
Judith	Nova
Kalpana	Sally
Larissa	Valentina

Comic Genius: For Parents Who Like Comedy

Boys Names

Billy	Jackie
Craig	Jerry
Dana	Keenan
Don	Milton
Drew	Mort
Eddie	Rodney
Gilbert	Rowan
Howie	Stan

Girls Names

Bonnie	Patricia
Ellen	Phyllis
Ernestine	Roseanne
Fannie	Saffron
Gracie	Thalia
Imogene	Vicki
Lily	Vivian
Lucy	Wanda

Starstruck Names: Popularized by Actors/Actresses

Boys Names

Alec	Keanu
Ashton	Kiefer
Brandon	Leonardo
Cary	Marlon
Corbin	Mekhi
Denzel	Orlando
Dustin	Parker
Gary	Troy
Jameson	Tyrone
Joaquin	Viggo

Girls Names

Camryn	Lauren
Charlize	Mackenzie
Diya	Marisa
Greer	Marlene
Gwyneth	Mia
Ingrid	Quinn
Jada	Raquel
Keira	Reese
Kim	Simone
Lana	Talia

Names of the Future: For Science Fiction Fans

Boys Names

Anakin	Neal
Gene	Neo
Hal	Piers
Jules	Ryker

Girls Names

Deanna	Ripley
Justina	Rowan
Moya	Trinity
Octavia	Ursula

Boys Names

Atticus	Max
Declan	Neo
Draven	Nico
Ethan	Shane
Gage	Sincere
Jody	Tanner
Maverick	Tristan

Girls Names

Ariel	Melanie
Ayla	Peyton
Chelsea	Samara
Elle	Savannah
Lara	Shelby
Lyric	Tammy
Madison	Tracy

From the Halls of Hogwarts: Harry Potter Names

Boys Names

Albus	Neville
Argus	Norbert
Cedric	Percy
Draco	Ron
Harry	Rufus
Horace	Salazar
Kingsley	Sirius
Lucius	Vernon

Girls Names

Araminta	Nymphadora
Bellatrix	Olympe
Celestina	Penelope
Dilys	Phyllida
Ginevra	Pomona
Hermione	Rosmerta
Hestia	Rowena
Myrtle	Sybille

The Play's the Thing: Shakespearean Names

Boys Names

Clarence	Iago
Curtis	Malcolm
Douglas	Oberon
Duncan	Orlando
Edgar	Othello
Edmund	Richard
Ferdinand	Romeo
Hal	Sebastian
Hector	Titus

Girls Names

Beatrice	Katherine
Bianca	Marina
Cordelia	Miranda
Gertrude	Olivia
Helen	Ophelia
Imogen	Portia
Jessica	Regan
Juliet	Rosalind
Kate	Viola

Boys Names

Adonis	Linus
Ajax	Orion
Apollo	Phoenix
Brage	Raiden
Jason	Thor

Girls Names

Athena	Leda
Daphne	Minerva
Electra	Pandora
Galatea	Persephone
Hera	Phaedra

Nielsen Names: Popularized by TV Characters

Boys Names

Avery	Dylan
Bailey	Hayden
Brandon	Heath
Bret	Holden
Carter	Jared
Chandler	Luka
Chase	Nash
Colby	Nicholas
Corey	Ricky
Dawson	Wesley

Girls Names

Alexis	Kristen
Allie	Mallory
Audra	Piper
Blair	Sabrina
Erica	Samantha
Felicity	Sierra
Jaime	Skye
Jaleesa	Trista
Jenna	Whitley
Kayla	Zaria

Geography Test: Place Names

Boys Names

Austin	London
Boston	Raleigh
Chad	Richmond
Cuba	Santiago
Dallas	Trenton
Denver	Utah
Israel	York
Kanye	Zaire
Kobe	Zion

Girls Names

Adelaide	India
Alexandria	Ireland
Asia	Jamaica
Atlanta	Kenya
Brittany	Mecca
Brooklyn	Monserrat
Florence	Paris
Geneva	Sedona
Georgia	Sydney

In the Lab: Scientific Names (Includes Nobel Prize Winners)

Boys Names

Albert	Kelvin
Aldo	Konrad
Darwin	Luis
Enrico	Masatoshi
Frederick	Niels
Isaac	Santiago
Kary	Stephen

Girls Names

Barbara	Maria
Christiane	Marie
Dorothy	Mildred
Gertrude	Rachel
Irene	Rita
Jane	Rosalyn
Margaret	Sylvia

The "Write" Names: Authors and Poets

Boys Names

Ambrose	Ernest
Armistead	Geoffrey
Augusten	Irving
Byron	Langston
Charles	Milton
Dalton	Rudyard
Dante	Sinclair
Elmore	Upton
Emerson	William

Girls Names

Alice	Gwendolyn
Anais	Harper
Anne	Katherine
Bronte	Madeleine
Charlotte	Maeve
Danielle	May
Edith	Maya
Edna	Virginia
Emily	Willa

Read All About It: Nobel Prize Winners in Literature

Boys Names

Dario	Miguel
Elias	Octavio
Gabriel	Pablo
Kenzaburo	Saul
Knut	Seamus

Girls Names

Elfriede	Pearl
Gabriela	Selma
Grazia	Sigrid
Nadine	Toni
Nelly	Wislawa

Boys Names

Adolfo	Jimmy
Cordell	Jose
Desmond	Nelson
Elie	Woodrow

Girls Names

Alva	Jody
Bertha	Mairead
Betty	Shirin
Jane	Wangari

Medical Names:
For Parents Who Want a Future Doctor

Boys Names

Asa	Jonas
Damian	Louis
Galen	Luke
Jason	Sanjay

Girls Names

Alyssa	Isis
Clara	Jordan
Fabiola	Michaela
Florence	Ruta

What's Old Is New Again: Victorian Names
Likely to Return to Popularity Soon

Boys Names

Arthur	Henry
Ellis	Leon
Ephraim	Lewis
Fred	Otto
Harvey	Walter

Girls Names

Dora	Louisa
Elsie	Mabel
Flora	Olive
Ida	Selma
Lena	Zora

Crowning Glory: Royal Names

Boys Names

Cesar	George
Charles	Louis
Edward	Philip
Ferdinand	William

Girls Names

Alexandra	Elizabeth
Augusta	Josephine
Caroline	Mary
Diana	Victoria

The Sporting Life: Names of Athletes

Boys Names

Aramis	Michael
Boris	Mickey
Braylon	Moises
Brett	Nolan
Evander	Pedro
Fernando	Peyton
Gehrig	Randall
Hideo	Reggie
Jackie	Roberto
Jalen	Ronaldo
Jesse	Ryne
Kareem	Santino
Keyshawn	Shaquille
Kirby	Troy
Lance	Tyson
Marquis	Xavier

Girls Names

Althea	Lisa
Annika	Malia
Brandi	Martina
Briana	Meseret
Carly	Mia
Chamique	Michelle
Cheryl	Monique
Dominique	Nadia
Gabrielle	Nancy
Jackie	Olga
Janet	Rebecca
Katarina	Serena
Kerri	Shannon
Kylie	Tracy
Laila	Venus
Lauren	Wilma

Bright and Beautiful: Color Names

Boys Names

Albus	Green
Blaine	Kieran
Blake	Reid
Canaan	Roy
Cole	Rusty

Girls Names

Azure	Lavender
Blue	Magenta
Cyan	Sapphire
Ebony	Scarlett
Indigo	Sienna

Yee-Haw!: Names for Future Cowhands

Boys Names

Branson	Maverick
Chance	Montana
Cody	Trace

Girls Names

Audra	Kitty
Belle	Lucille
Cheyenne	Minnie

Dakota	Ty	Dakota	Sedona
Jesse	Utah	Dusty	Sonora
Lafe	Wyatt	Kayla	Stormy

Boys Names

Birch	Nature
Canyon	Ridge
Cedar	River
Eagle	Rock
Falcon	Sage
Hawk	Sky
Lake	Stone
Moss	Yarran

Girls Names

Aspen	Prairie
Breeze	Rainbow
Brook	Sage
Denali	Sequoia
Fern	Shasta
Laurel	Shenandoah
Meadow	Sunshine
Ocean	Willow

Boys Names

Bjorn	Davin
Braxton	Felix
Bruno	Francis
Caleb	Koda
Cullen	Wolf

Girls Names

Birdy	Lark
Fawn	Leona
Gazelle	Raven
Kiara	Reem
Kitty	Velvet

Boys Names

Acton	Obadiah
Bion	Paxton
Ewan	Quinlan
Fintan	Reno
Grennan	Thane
Lathan	Theron
Lowen	Vaden
Nevin	Velten

Girls Names

Adria	Lavinia
Arabella	Lucinda
Aurelia	Octavia
Della	Olympia
Emerence	Oriana
Flannery	Thea
Gemma	Viveca
Jerusha	Zelda

Aaron

Hebrew *Aharon,* perhaps "teaching" or "shining." Aaron was the older brother of Moses. Because Aaron was born during the Israelite bondage in Egypt, his name may also be derived from an Egyptian word meaning "mountain," referring to an exalted religious leader. In the 1980s, this biblical name suddenly became more popular than it had been in years. After reaching a peak around 1994, it began to fall off, but Aaron was still the 59th most popular boys name in 2004.

Famous names: Aaron Burr (U.S. vice president)
 Aaron Copland (composer)

Nicknames: **Ronnie, Ronny**

Other spelling: **Arron**

Variations: **Aarao** (Portuguese), **Aaro** (Finnish), **Aaronas** (Latvian), **Aron** (Romanian), **Aronne** (Italian), **Haroun** (Arabic)

Abbot, Abbott

Aramaic *abba,* "father." *Abba* was a title of respect in Aramaic, the language Jesus and the disciples used. In the sense of "father," Christians used it as a title for the head, or supervisor, of a monastery.

Abdullah

Arabic *Abd-Allah,* "servant of God." This has long been one of the most popular names in the Muslim world and has been among the 1,000 most common boys names in the United States since 1996. Abdullah's popularity stems from its having been the name of the prophet Muhammad's father, as well as from its meaning.

Abel

Hebrew *hebel,* "breath" or "evanescent"; also, possibly connected with Assyrian *ablu,* "son." Abel was the second son of Adam and

Eve. He was killed by his brother, Cain, in the first murder, as recorded in the Book of Genesis.

Abner

Hebrew "father of light." In the Bible, Abner was the uncle of King Saul and commander of his army. Al Capp used the name for the title character of his long-running comic strip, *Li'l Abner*.
Famous name: Abner Doubleday (inventor of baseball)
Variation: **Avner** (Hebrew)

Abraham

Hebrew "father of many." In the Book of Genesis, the founder of the Hebrew people was originally named **Abram,** but his name was changed at God's command: "Neither shall thy name any more be called Abram, but thy name shall be Abraham; for a father of many nations I have made thee." Like most Old Testament names, this name was not widely used until the time of the Protestant Reformation in the 16th century. Abraham has been slowly but steadily rising in use in the United States for more than 30 years as Old Testament names for boys have come into vogue. Almost 2,000 boys were named Abraham in 2004, ranking it 184th.
Famous name: Abraham Lincoln (16th U.S. president)
Nicknames: **Abe, Abie, Bram**
Variations: **Abramo** (Italian), **Ibrahim** (Arabic)

Abram

Abraham's original name meant "high father," but in English it's often considered just a short form of his later name. Abram has been brought back into use as Abraham's popularity has risen, though there were only 374 born in the United States in 2004.

Actassi

Chamoru (Guam) "share the sea."

Acton

Old English *actun*, "town by the oaks."

Adair

Scottish form of **Edgar.**
Famous name: Adair Elizalde (Mexican singer)

Adam

Hebrew *adama*, "earth, clay." As the first masculine name in the Bible, it is one of the oldest recorded names. Because of Adam's fall from grace, the name was seldom used by Jewish families until the 20th century. As a Christian name, it was often used in England and Scotland during the Middle Ages and until the 18th century. It became popular again in the 1970s, and though it's now receding, Adam was still among the top 100 boys names in 2004.

Famous name: Adam Smith (economist and philosopher)

Nicknames: **Ad, Ade, Addy**

Variations: **Adamo** (Italian), **Adan** (Spanish), **Adao** (Portuguese), **Adhamh** (Irish and Scottish)

Adan

As the Spanish form of **Adam**, *Adán* (pronounced "ah-DAHN") has been found on the lower half of the SSA list since the 1940s. But its recent sharp increase (doubling in use between 2002 and 2004) probably means that many non-Hispanic parents are using it as another spelling of **Aidan**. If Adan and Aidan were counted together, Aidan would rise from tenth to seventh place for 2004. (See also **Aidan**.)

Addison

Middle English *Addisone*, "son of Addy"(see **Adam**). Addison burst onto the scene as a boys name in 1986 at 513th on the SSA list, and such sudden appearances usually imply some pop culture influence. In this case it might have been the television series *Moonlighting*, which began in 1985 and featured Bruce Willis as detective David Addison. Though it's unusual for a character's surname to be immediately taken up by parents as a first name, there are other examples (see **Ryker**). Addison has stayed fairly steady in use ever since, with more than 400 boys given the name each year. However, parents considering it for a son need to be aware that around 1994 other parents began to see Addison as the perfect alternative to **Madison** as a girls name, and in 2004 there were five times as many girls as boys named Addison in the United States.

Aditya

Sanskrit *Aditya*, "belonging to the goddess Aditi." Aditi is the Hindu sky goddess, and her name means "free from bonds." Aditya is one of the more popular boys names in the American Hindu community; almost 250 were born in 2004.

Adlai

Hebrew "Yahweh is justice." This name occurs once in the Bible for the father of Shaphat, the shepherd for King David. But it has become well known through the Stevenson family, in which members of three generations have had this unusual name: Adlai Ewing Stevenson (U.S. vice president), Adlai Ewing Stevenson, Jr. (statesman, diplomat, ambassador, and twice a candidate for president of the United States), and Adlai Ewing Stevenson III (U.S. senator).

Adler

Old German "eagle."

Adolfo

Spanish form of **Adolf,** Old German "noble wolf." Adolph was once a favorite German name, but since World War II, few parents have chosen this name because of its association with Adolf Hitler. However, the traditionalism of Hispanic parents has kept Adolfo common in that community even while Adolf has disappeared. The number of Adolfos born in the United States has generally been increasing for the past 25 years along with the Hispanic population. More than 400 were born in 2004. Argentine architect and sculptor Adolfo Pérez Esquivel won the Nobel Peace Prize in 1980 for his human rights work.

Adonis

Greek form of Semitic *Adonai,* "lord." The derivation of this name shows that the Greeks borrowed the myth of Adonis from cultures to their east. Adonis was a beautiful youth who was the beloved of Aphrodite, the goddess of love. His name has become a general term for an extremely handsome man and is one of the most popular names taken from classical mythology in use today. It's been on the SSA list for boys since 1993; 230 Adonises were born in 2004.

Adrian

Latin *Hadrianus,* "from the Adriatic." To the Romans, this name indicated that a person was from Adria, or Atri, on the Adriatic Sea. The famous Roman emperor Hadrian, a military genius, built a wall of defense in the Roman province of Britain between Solway Firth and the mouth of the Tyne. Six popes have taken the name, including Adrian IV, the only English pope. Adrian has boomed in popularity in the United States since 1960. In 2004 there were more than 6,000 Adrians born, and the name ranked 76th.

Nicknames: **Ade, Adry, Hadrian**

Variations: **Adriano** (Italian), **Adrien** (French), **Andreian** (Russian), **Arrian** (Scandinavian)

Adriel

Hebrew "flock of God." There is one minor character in the Bible named Adriel (the husband of King Saul's daughter Merab), but the name has rarely been used until recently. It entered the SSA top 1,000 list in 2002 and has been rising slowly. At least part of its support is in the Hispanic-American community, possibly as a result of the recent success of the salsa singer Adriel. But by blending the sounds of names like **Adrian** and **Daniel,** Adriel may also be appealing to non-Hispanic parents looking for a "different but not too different" name.

Agustin

Spanish *Agustín*, form of **Augustine.** Agustin has risen in use since the 1940s as the Hispanic-American population has grown. It ranked 650th on the SSA list in 2004.

Ahmad, Ahmed

These are both common forms in English of Arabic *Ahmad,* "more praiseworthy." It is one of the most popular Muslim names all around the world. If both forms are counted together, 951 boys were given the name in the United States in 2004, ranking it among the top 300 American names.

Famous name: Ahmad Rashad (sportscaster)

Aidan

Gaelic *Aedan,* form of *Aed,* "fire." St. Aidan was an Irish-born monk sent from Iona in Scotland to convert the then-heathen English to Christianity. Though this name was well known to church historians and Episcopal priests, hardly any American boys were named Aidan before 1990, the first year it ever appeared in the SSA top 1,000 list, at 889th place. Aidan then exploded to tenth place in 2004, about the fastest boom ever for any boys name. This success is because Aidan combines the popular sounds parents are looking for along with an ancient Celtic past that legitimized it for those who wouldn't

think of using a recent invention like **Jayden.** But the sound is the more important factor, which is shown by **Aiden, Aden, Aydan, Ayden,** and **Aydin** all separately being among the top 1,000 names of 2004 on the SSA list (and see also **Adan**).
Famous name: Aidan Quinn (actor)

Ajax

Greek *Aias,* the name of two different Greek heroes of the Trojan War, the greater of which was noted for his size, strength, and bravery. Many older Americans may have a hard time disassociating this name from the brand name of a household cleanser, but by blending the sounds of other names like **Aidan, Jack,** and **Max,** Ajax is starting to sound "cool" to adventurous young parents.

Akinyele

Yoruba (Nigeria) "valor benefits this house."

Alan

Celtic, uncertain meaning, perhaps "rock." The name was introduced into England in 1066 by the Norman leader, Alain, earl of Brittany. After it entered Britain, it also became popular in Scotland and Wales. The name also became standard in English ballads.
Famous names: Alan B. Shepard, Jr. (astronaut)
                 Alan Thicke (television host and actor)
                 Alan Greenspan (economist)
Nicknames: **Al, Allie**
Other spellings: **Allan, Allen, Alyn**
Variations: **Alain** (French), **Alano** (Spanish), **Alanus** (Latin)

Alastair, Alistair

Gaelic form of **Alexander.** Few American parents name their babies Alastair, in spite of the present huge popularity of Alexander.
Famous name: Alistair Cooke (journalist)
Nicknames: **Al, Alec**
Other spelling: **Alasdair**
Variations: **Alaster** (English and Scottish), **Alastor**

Alban

Latin *Albanus,* the name of the first Christian martyr in Britain. The name may be a Latinization of the Celtic name *Alp,* "crag," influenced by the Latin word *alba,* "white."

Albert

Old German *Adalbert,* "noble and bright," from *athal* [noble] + *berhta* [bright]. Several saints, including St. Albert the Great, a 13th-century monk known for his study of natural sciences, have this name. It became popular after Prince Albert married Queen Victoria in 1840. But it only ranked 305th in the United States in 2004.
Famous name: Albert Einstein (physicist)
Nicknames: **Al, Bert, Bertie, Beto, Tito**
Variations: **Adelbert** (Dutch), **Albertko** (Slovakian), **Alberto** (Portuguese, Spanish, and Italian), **Albertok** (Polish), **Albertukas** (Latvian), **Albrecht, Alpo** (Finnish), **Alvertos** (Greek), **Aubert** (French), **Bechtel** (German), **Delbert**

Alberto

Spanish, Italian, and Portuguese form of **Albert.** This name continues to be common in the Hispanic-American community.
Famous name: Alberto Gonzalez (U.S. attorney general)

Albus

Latin *albus,* "white." It's been suggested that J. K. Rowling chose this as the first name of Hogwarts' Headmaster Dumbledore in the *Harry Potter* series because of his long white beard and his status as one of the most respected and ethical wizards in the world.

Alden

English surname, form of either Old Norse *Halfdanr,* "half-Dane," or Old English *Ealdwine,* "old friend." Alden was reasonably popular in the 1920s, and since 1995 it's been increasing in use again as parents rediscover two-syllable forms ending in *–n*. Alden ranked 735th on the SSA list in 2004, with 250 American boys given the name.

Aldo

Italian and German from Germanic *alda,* "old and wise." Forestry scientist Aldo Leopold (1887–1948) is considered the founder of the discipline of wildlife ecology.

Alec

Scottish form of **Alexander.** This name rapidly increased in use during the 1990s, with some parents undoubtedly being inspired by the recent fame of actor Alec Baldwin. Parents didn't seem to mind

that "smart aleck" has been a common term for a know-it-all since the 1870s. However, use of the name is now receding again.
Famous name: Sir Alec Guinness (actor)
Other spelling: **Aleck**

Alejandro

Spanish form of **Alexander**. In 2004, Alejandro was the number-one name for newborn boys in Spain, and it's increasing in use in the United States as well. More than 4,600 Alejandros were born in the United States in 2004, making it the 99th most popular name for American boys that year.
Other spelling: **Alexandro**

Alessandro

Italian form of **Alexander**. About 300 Alessandros were born in the United States in 2004, ranking it 673rd on the SSA list.
Famous name: Alessandro Scarlatti (composer)

Alex

This short form of **Alexander** is now popular as a first name in its own right, having been among the top 100 names for American boys since 1984. It is also an extremely popular nickname for girls.
Famous name: Alex Rodriguez (baseball player)
Variation: **Alika** (Hawaiian)

Alexander

Greek "defender of men." Alexander the Great was a Macedonian king and general who conquered vast amounts of territory around the Mediterranean and established an empire that spread Greek culture throughout the ancient world. For 700 years his name has been especially popular in Scotland, and it is enjoying a strong revival elsewhere, now being one of the 20 most popular names for boys in both England and the United States.
Famous names: Alexander Graham Bell (inventor of the telephone)
             Alexander Pope (poet)
Nicknames: **Al, Alec, Alek, Alex, Sandy, Xander**
Variations: **Alastair** (Gaelic), **Alejandro** (Spanish), **Aleksander** (Polish), **Alessandro** (Italian), **Alexandr** (Czech), **Alexandre** (French), **Sandor** (Hungarian)

Alexis

Greek "defender, helper." Like **Angel** and **Ariel,** this was originally a male name. While still often used for boys by Hispanics, it is now almost exclusively a girls name in other American communities. Its popularity for Hispanic boys is actually booming: More than 4,000 boys named Alexis were born in the United States in 2004. Alexis de Tocqueville was a 19th-century French author whose books are prized for their insights into American character and values.

Alfie

This pet form of **Alfred** has suddenly become quite popular with parents in England and Wales, where it's been among the top 50 names since 2002. So far American parents are ignoring it, in spite of the 2004 remake of the classic film *Alfie* starring Jude Law.

Alfonso

Old German *Adolfuns,* "noble and eager," from *athal* [noble] + *funsa* [ready]. This Spanish royal name was brought to Spain by the Visigoths, and several kings of Spain and Portugal have had this name.
Nicknames: **Al, Alf, Alfie, Foncho, Fonz, Fonzie, Fonzo, Poncho, Ponso**
Variations: **Afonso** (Portuguese), **Alfa** (Czech), **Alfonsin** (Spanish), **Alfonz** (Slovakian), **Alifonzo, Alonso, Alonzo** (Spanish), **Alphons** (German), **Alphonse, Alphonsus** (Latin)

Alfred

Old English *Aelfred* from *aelf* [elf] + *raed* [counsel]. In the mythology and traditions of Germanic and English countries, elves are considered to be wise and good counselors. This belief is reflected in the name of Alfred the Great, the last major king of England before the Norman Conquest. Other English kings before him also had the name. It was in common use until the 16th century and came back into fashion in the 18th century when Old English names became popular. However, it is rarely given to American boys today.
Famous names: Alfred Hitchcock (movie director)
Alfred Nobel (inventor and initiator of the Nobel Prize)
Nicknames: **Al, Alf, Alfie, Alfy, Fito, Fred, Freddie, Freddy, Fredo**
Variations: **Alfredas** (Lithuanian), **Alfredo** (Spanish and Italian), **Alfredos** (Greek), **Avery, Elfred, Lafredo**

Alfredo

Spanish, Italian, and Portuguese form of **Alfred.** This name is still fairly popular with Hispanic-Americans.
Nicknames: **Feyo, Fito, Fredo**
Variation: **Lafredo**

Algernon

(See **Grennan.**)

Ali

Arabic *ali*, "sublime, elevated." The Shiite branch of Islam originated from a movement that supported Ali, Mohammed's son-in-law, as the rightful leader of the Islamic state. Used today both by Muslim immigrants and African-Americans, Ali was the 346th most popular American male name of 2004.

Allen

Variation of **Alan.**

Alonso, Alonzo

Spanish short forms of **Alfonso.** This was a fairly popular name with Anglo-Americans in the United States during the 19th century. It is mostly used in the African-American community today.
Nicknames: **Lon, Lonnie, Lonny**

Alton

Old English *ald-tun*, "old town," or *aewiell-tun*, "town at the head of the stream."

Alvaro

Spanish *Álvaro*, from the Visigothic *al*, "all," and *war*, "guard." This is one of the many Spanish names that has increased in use in the United States during the last 50 years along with the Hispanic-American population. Alvaro was 509th on the SSA list in 2004.

Alvin

Old English *Aethelwine*, "noble friend," from *aethel* [noble] + *wine* [friend]; or *Aelfwine* from *aelf* [elf] + *wine* [friend]. Alvin was one of the top 100 names for American boys born in the first four decades of the 20th century, but it has fallen away since. Its popularity may have been reinforced a bit by the heroism of Sergeant Alvin York in World War I.

Modern Americans are likely to associate the name with the mischievous cartoon character Alvin the Chipmunk. The name is now more popular with African-Americans than with other ethnic groups.
Famous name: Alvin Ailey (choreographer)
Nicknames: **Al, Alv, Alvy**
Variations: **Aluin** (French), **Aluino, Alvino** (Italian and Spanish), **Alwin** (German), **Alwyn, Aylwin, Elvin, Elwin**

Amadeus

Latin "lover of God." Several saints have been named Amadeus, and Amadis of Gaul was a legendary medieval knight whose exploits form the center of a cycle of romances. The name received considerable publicity in the 1980s through the movie *Amadeus,* which is a fictional version of the life of composer Wolfgang Amadeus Mozart.
Variations: **Amadee** (French), **Amadeo** (Italian), **Amadis** (Spanish), **Amias, Amyas, Amyot**

Amari

Perhaps a Swahili or Berber form of Arabic *ammar,* "long-lived." Amari is one of several boys names ending in *–mari* that have recently become popular in the African-American community. There were 632 Amaris born in the United States in 2004, which made it one of the 400 most popular names for American boys.

Amarion

Just as **Jamari** led to **Jamarion, Amari** has been expanded to Amarion in the African-American community, and the use of this new name is growing even faster than that of the original form. Amarion ranked 423rd in 2004, with 501 American babies given the name.

Ambrose

Greek *Ambrosios,* "immortal." Ambrose was the name of several early Christian saints, and as a result it was fairly popular in Ireland during the 19th century. Irish-Americans kept the name in the top 1,000 in the United States until the 1930s, but it's been rare since.
Famous name: Ambrose Bierce (short story writer)

Amery, Amory

Norman French form of Germanic *Amalrich* from *amal,* "bravery," and *ric,* "power."

Amir

Arabic "local ruler, prince." This is now one of the more common Muslim names in the African-American community.
Other spelling: **Ameer**

Ammon

In the Old Testament, Ammon is the name of a country northeast of the Dead Sea. The city of Amman, Jordan, is built on the site of Ammon's ancient capital. The Ammonites were bitter enemies of the Israelites, but in the *Book of Mormon*, Ammon is the name of two different admirable characters. The name Ammon is regularly used in Utah.

Amos

Hebrew "burden" or "burden carrier." Amos was a shepherd, and when he listened to the Lord, he became a prophet. The name Amos was still fairly common in the United States in the late 19th century, but it steadily decreased in use until it finally fell off the SSA top 1,000 list in 1998. With the recent revival of other Old Testament names for boys, adventurous parents looking for uncommon names might be wise to consider Amos as a possibility.

Anakin

Annakin is a form of *Anketin*, itself a Norman French form of Old Norse *Asketill* from *oss* [god] + *ketill* [sacrificial cauldron]. Many Celtic and Germanic myths mention a divine cauldron where warriors who have been slain in battle can be brought back to life by the gods. George Lucas named the character Anakin Skywalker for his friend Ken Annakin, a British film director. Even though Anakin Skywalker eventually becomes the villain Darth Vader in the *Star Wars* films, several instances of American boys named Anakin have been noted in the last few years.

Anderson

English and Scandinavian "son of **Andrew**." Anderson is one of the ten most common last names in the United States, and during the late 19th century it was often used as a given name. It fell away during the 20th century but has gotten some renewed interest from American parents recently, more than doubling in use since 1998, though it was still only 594th on the SSA list in 2004. The increase may be linked to newscaster Anderson Cooper's work on CNN. Recently, Anderson has also been a popular name for boys in Brazil.

Andon

A form of **Anthony** in the southern Balkans (Bulgaria, Macedonia, and Albania) as well as in Micronesia in the South Pacific, but it may have other origins as well. Andon suddenly jumped onto the SSA list in 2004 at 857th place.

Andre

French form of **Andrew.** This name has become popular with African-Americans, and it ranked 189th in use in 2004.
Famous names: Andre Agassi (tennis player)
Andre Braugher (actor)

Andreas

German and Greek form of **Andrew.** For more than 30 years Andreas has been present on the SSA top 1,000 list but has never risen above 800th place, making it a good choice for those who want a name that is neither very common nor very eccentric.

Andres

Spanish form of **Andrew.** This name continues to be popular with Hispanic-Americans.
Famous name: Andres Segovia (classical guitarist)

Andrew

Greek *andreas* or *andreios,* "man, manly, strong." This is one of the top ten names for boys in the United States. St. Andrew was the first disciple of Jesus and the brother of St. Simon Peter. St. Andrew is the patron saint of Scotland and Russia. During the Middle Ages, the saint was so popular in England that several hundred churches were named for him.
Famous names: Andrew Carnegie (industrialist)
Andrew Jackson (7th U.S. president)
Andrew Johnson (17th U.S. president)
Nicknames: **Andie, Andy, Dandie, Dandy, Drew, Tandy, Tito**
Other spellings: **Andrue, Andruw**
Variations: **Anders** (Scandinavian), **Andor** (Hungarian), **Andre** (French), **Andrea** (Italian), **Andreas** (German and Greek), **Andrei** (Russian and Ukrainian), **Andrejc** (Slovenian),

Andrejko (Slovakian), **Andres** (Spanish), **Andrius** (Lithuanian), **Andrzej** (Polish), **Andzs** (Latvian), **Antti** (Finnish), **Drew, Ondrej** (Czech)

Andy

Form of **Andrew.** This nickname is sometimes used as an official given name, especially in the American South.
Famous name: Andy Warhol (artist)

Angel

Spanish form of **Angelo.** In previous centuries, this was a male name in England, especially in Cornwall. Angel Clare is the most prominent male in Thomas Hardy's novel *Tess of the D'Urbervilles.* Angel has been booming in use during the last decade, reaching 54th on the national popularity chart for boys. However, more than 90 percent of these boys have Hispanic-American parents. Other groups generally only use Angel as a name for girls, in spite of the success of the television series *Angel,* where the title character, played by David Boreanaz, was a vampire trying to redeem himself.

Angelo

Italian form of Greek *Angelos,* "a messenger"; originally from Hebrew "a messenger of God." Italians brought the name Angelo to the United States, and it is popular among Italian-Americans. It is also popular with Hispanic-Americans, although they like **Angel** even more.
Famous name: Angelo Dundee (boxing trainer)
Nicknames: **Ange, Angie, Gelo, Lito**
Variations: **Andel** (Czech), **Angel** (Spanish and Cornish), **Angelyar** (Russian), **Angyal** (Hungarian), **Aniol** (Polish), **Anzhel** (Russian)

Angus

Gaelic *Aonghus,* "one choice," originally the name of an ancient Celtic god. Traditionally associated with Scotland, Angus has been a very popular name in Australia recently.

Ansel

A short form of **Anselm,** Old German *ans* [divine] + *helm* [helmet]. Ansel is given occasionally to American boys today, perhaps in honor of 20th-century American photographer Ansel Adams.

Anson

English surname, "Agnes" or "Ann's son." Like **Nelson** and **Rodney,** the use of Anson as a first name originally honored a British naval hero: in this case Lord George Anson (1697–1762), an admiral who had famous victories over both the Spanish and French fleets in the 1740s. Although Anson reached its peak of popularity around 1810, it has never completely died out. Between 1974 and 1984 it was kept in the public eye by actor Anson Williams, featured as Potsie on the television series *Happy Days.*

Anthony

Latin *Antonius,* a Roman family name of no specific meaning but sometimes translated as "inestimable, priceless one." This name has long been popular in Western Europe and in the Americas because of St. Anthony, the ascetic and founder of Christian monasticism. Shakespeare's plays *Julius Caesar* and *Antony and Cleopatra,* in which Mark Antony is a major character, helped increase the popularity of this name. In the United States, it is usually spelled with an *h,* changing the pronunciation from its traditional one. The older pronunciation is retained in the nickname Tony. Anthony has been among the 20 most popular American names for 20 years and has even been drifting upward in use lately, reaching 11th place in 2004.
Famous name: Sir Anthony Hopkins (actor)
Nicknames: **Nico, Toncho, Tonek, Toni, Tonico, Tonio, Tony**
Variations: **Akoni** (Hawaiian), **Andon, Andonios** (Greek), **Antal** (Hungarian), **Antek** (Polish), **Antoine** (French), **Anton** (Czech, German, Norwegian, Romanian, Russian, Serbian, Slovenian, Swedish, and Ukrainian), **Antonio** (Spanish and Italian), **Antony**

Antoine

French form of **Anthony.** Like **Andre,** this French name has been very popular in the 20th century with African-American parents. Antoine de Saint-Exupery was the French aviator who wrote the classic children's story *The Little Prince.* Ironically, the name Antoine was out of fashion in France itself during much of the 20th century, and the French took to using the English form **Anthony** to name their sons. Antoine did revive strongly in France during the 1990s, however.
Other spellings: **Antjuan, Antwan, Antwon**

Anton

Slavic and Germanic form of **Anthony.**
Famous name: Anton Chekhov (writer)

Antonin

Latin *Antoninus*, diminutive of **Anthony,** first made famous by Roman emperor Antoninus Pius (86–161).
Famous name: Antonin Scalia (U.S. Supreme Court associate justice)

Antonio

Spanish and Italian form of **Anthony.** This form is extremely popular in the United States with both Hispanic-Americans and African-Americans and is among the 100 most-often-used names for boys. Antonio is the merchant in Shakespeare's *The Merchant of Venice.*
Famous names: Antonio Banderas (actor)
          Antonio Vivaldi (composer)

Antony

In Great Britain, where **Anthony** is pronounced with a "t" rather than a "th" sound in the middle, this is merely a spelling variation. In the United States, however, it is a separate name as it forces people to use the "British" pronunciation. Although there were 81 times more Anthonys born in the United States in 2004 than Antonys, the 238 Antonys were enough for the name to make the SSA top 1,000 list in 761st place.

Apollo

Greek *Apóllon,* perhaps from a pre-Hellenic word meaning "the dispeller." Apollo was the ancient Greek god of reason, prophecy, healing, archery, dance, and music.

Aram

Armenian "royal highness."

Aramis

This name was made famous by Alexandre Dumas's 1844 novel *The Three Musketeers.* Dumas based his book on a semi-fictional account of life as a musketeer by Gatien de Courtilz; de Courtilz in turn based the character Aramis on the real musketeer Henri d'Aramitz. His family was from the village of Aramitz in the French Pyrenees; though the original meaning of the place name is unknown, it is

probably from the Basque language. Dumas's story depicted Aramis as the most amorous of the musketeers, and the name still has romantic connotations, reinforced by its use as a brand name for colognes and similar products. Though Aramis has always been a rare name, a few imaginative parents choose it every year.
Famous name: Aramis Ramirez (baseball player)

Archer

Old French *archier*, "bowman." If American parents revive **Archie** anytime soon, they may prefer to use Archer as the official name.

Archie

Short form of **Archibald,** a Norman French name composed from the Old Germanic *ercan*, "genuine," and *bald*, "bold," traditionally common especially in Scotland. In this case the pet form has been more popular than the full form as an official name in the United States for well over a century. Archie was one of the top 100 names for American boys in 1900, but then it steadily fell away until it almost vanished around 1990. Like **Alfie,** Archie has become quite popular in England during the last decade, and it is now among the top 50 names for boys there. Perhaps this will get American parents to reconsider Archie as a name for their own sons, though the image of Archie Bunker from television's *All in the Family* may still be too strong. The other image of Archie most Americans have is that of the red-headed all-American teenager from the comic books that first appeared in December 1941. That Archie is certainly more admirable than Archie Bunker but does add another set of humorous connotations that make it hard for some parents to take the name seriously.
Famous name: Archie Shepp (free jazz saxophonist)

Argus

Greek *argós*, "shining." In Greek mythology, Argos was a giant who guarded the cow Io, and so *argus* has come to mean "guardian" in literary English. This makes it a good name for Argus Filch, the suspicious and vigilant Hogwarts caretaker in the *Harry Potter* novels.

Ari

Hebrew "lion," an Israeli name now frequently used by Jewish families in the United States.

Ariel

Hebrew "lion of God." In the Book of Ezra, Ariel is listed as one of Ezra's chiefs and is sent to Iddo to obtain ministers for the house of God. Shakespeare made Ariel the witty, light, and graceful spirit in *The Tempest*. Milton used the name in *Paradise Lost* for one of the rebel angels. As a name for boys, Ariel is still fairly popular with Hispanic-Americans, but other Americans now generally use the name only for girls. It is quite popular as a name for men in modern Israel because of the fame of Ariel Sharon, the former general who became prime minister.

Variations: **Arel, Arik** (Israeli)

Aries

Latin "ram," one of the 12 constellations of the zodiac.

Arjun

Sanskrit *Arjuna*, "made of silver" or "peacock." Arjun is one of the most popular names now for sons of Hindu immigrants to the United States and ranked 741st on the SSA list in 2004. Arjun Rampal is a former fashion model who has become one of the most famous actors in Bollywood, India's counterpart to Hollywood.

Arlo

Evidently invented by the 16th-century English poet Edmund Spenser in his epic poem *The Faerie Queene* as the name of a hill where the gods debate; perhaps related to **Harlow.** Arlo was regularly used in the early 20th century in the United States, but today it's known primarily because of the singer Arlo Guthrie. If other names ending in –o like **Leo** and **Enzo** continue to rise in usage, Arlo may soon start to sound "cool" to young parents.

Armand

French form of **Herman.** Armand is much rarer than **Armando** in the United States.

Famous names: Armand Assante (actor)
Armand Hammer (industrialist)

Armando

Spanish and Italian form of **Herman.** Its enduring popularity with parents of Hispanic descent makes this by far the most common derivative of Herman in the modern United States. It ranked 228th for American boys born in 2004.

Armani

Italian surname, "son of **Armando.**" Armani is the most common given name for boys in the United States today that is derived from a trade name; in this case the brand name for luxury fashion items founded by Italian designer Giorgio Armani. Armani has been among the top 1,000 names for American boys since 1994, and it is one of the few names given to an almost equal number of boys and girls over the last decade.

Armin

Form of **Herman.** This is actually a short form of *Arminius,* the Latin form of Herman. The original Arminius was a leader of the ancient Germanic tribes who defeated the Roman armies in A.D. 9 and thus prevented the Roman Empire from extending east of the Rhine.

Armistead

English surname, "dweller at the hermitage." As a given name Armistead is most often found in North Carolina, where it honors Lewis Armistead, a Confederate general from that state.
Famous name: Armistead Maupin (author)

Arnav

Sanskrit *Arnava,* "ocean." This name is popular enough with parents of South Asian descent to rank 880th on the SSA list in 2004.

Arnold

Old German *Arenvald* from *arn* [eagle] + *wald* [ruler]. Arnold was a popular name in 12th- and 13th-century England. The version of the name brought to England by the Normans was Arnaut. From the 17th to the 19th centuries, the name disappeared, but it was revived in the late 19th century. It appeals to few parents today. In spite of Arnold Schwarzenegger being a governor of California as well as a macho film star, the name was only 904th on the SSA list in 2004.
Famous name: Arnold Palmer (golfer)
Nicknames: **Arn, Arnie, Noldy**
Variations: **Arnaldo** (Italian), **Arnaud** (French), **Arne** (Czech), **Arnoldo** (Spanish), **Arnolds** (Latvian), **Arnot** (Hungarian)

Arthur

Probably Latin *Artorius,* a family name; also, possibly Celtic *artos,* "a bear," or Irish *art,* "a stone." Long associated with the name of one of the earliest kings in Britain, King Arthur of the Round Table, the name first occurs in a short Latin chronicle written by a Breton monk, Nennius. The legend is believed to have originated in the Celtic region of what is now Wales and Cornwall, England. The romance of Arthur began to develop piecemeal, a poem here and another there, until a composite of Arthur and the Knights of the Round Table was formed into an integrated whole, *Morte d'Arthur* by Sir Thomas Malory, in 1485. The legend became a symbol of the spirit of England and inspired many poetic writings, including Edmund Spenser's *The Faerie Queene* and Alfred, Lord Tennyson's *Idylls of the King.* Matthew Arnold, William Morris, Mark Twain, and Edwin Arlington Robinson also wrote about the Arthurian legend. Thus King Arthur became a popular symbol of manliness and chivalry for Victorian parents, and his name was popular for American boys born between 1875 and 1930. Since then its popularity has fallen, and it's now not even among the top 300 names for boys.
Famous names: Arthur Ashe (tennis player)
Arthur Schlesinger (historian)
Nicknames: **Art, Artek, Artie, Arty, Turi, Tuto**
Variations: **Artair** (Scottish Gaelic), **Arthuro, Artur** (Bulgarian, Czech, German, Hungarian, Swedish, and Portuguese), **Arturo** (Italian and Spanish), **Artus** (French)

Arturo

Spanish and Italian form of **Arthur,** still popular enough with Hispanic-Americans to rank 269th for boys born in 2004.
Famous name: Arturo Toscanini (composer of operas)

Asa

Hebrew "healer." In the Bible, Asa was a king of Judah who attempted to reform his people by destroying images of false gods. Today Asa is well known to fans of the soap opera *One Life to Live* through the character Asa Buchanan, a rich, powerful, unscrupulous businessman. Asa has been inching up in use lately; perhaps parents see it as a masculine counterpart to the popular girls name **Ava.**

Asher

Hebrew "fortunate." In the Bible, Asher is the eighth son of Jacob and the founder of one of the 12 tribes of Israel. Asher was a rare name before the 1990s, but American parents have recently discovered it as a masculine alternative for **Ashley** and **Ashton**. It's now one of the fastest-growing boys names, with five times more Ashers born in 2004, when it was the 302nd most popular name for boys, than in 1994.

Famous names: Asher B. Durand (painter)

Ashley

Old English "ash tree meadow" from *aesc* [ash tree] + *leah* [field]; a surname often used as a first name. In the United States, this name is almost exclusively given to girls. Before 1960, it was a name for boys in the United States, and it was still popular for boys in the 1990s in England and Australia, only falling out of the top 100 list in England in 2003. In those countries, the spelling of the name is related to gender, with Ashley being a male name and Ashleigh a female form.

Famous name: Ashley Montagu (author)

Nicknames: **Ash, Lee**

Other spellings: **Ashleigh, Ashlie**

Ashton

English place name and surname, "ash tree farm." Like most surnames, Ashton has occasionally been given as a first name since the 19th century, but it wasn't until 1982 that it first made the SSA top 1,000 list for boys. Over the next four years the name's usage gradually increased. Then in November 1985 the television miniseries *North and South* aired, featuring a female character called Ashton. In 1986 the name leapt onto the list of popular names for girls, with five times more girls than boys being named Ashton that year. For the next 11 years, there were more girls than boys named Ashton every year in the United States, and, as had been the case with some other names given to both genders, such as **Courtney,** African-American parents were much more likely to give it to sons than were parents from other ethnic groups. Then an amazing thing happened: In 1998, there were more boys named Ashton than girls, and the name took off for boys while sinking for girls. In 2004, Ashton was the 84th most common name for boys, with 5,368 born, while it was only the 383rd name for girls, with 652 born (and that includes girls with the name spelled **Ashtyn**). It may be significant that 1998 was the year that actor Ashton Kutcher first came to wide notice on television's *That '70s Show*. His fame, combined with the fashion for boys names ending in –*n,* prepared parents to see Ashton as an appropriate masculine form again. This history makes Ashton the first name since **Dana** to have switched gender from male to female and then reversed that gender change.

Atreyu

English form of *Atreju,* the name of the young warrior hero in German author Michael Ende's children's novel *The Neverending Story,* which has been translated into more than 40 languages and has inspired several popular movies. It is possible, but unconfirmed, that Ende may have created the name by modifying *Atreya,* a Sanskrit name meaning "son of Atri" or "receptacle of glory." Though it's still a rare name, several American boys have been named Atreyu recently. That Atreyu could easily have **Trey** as a nickname may be part of what gives parents the courage to bestow it on their sons.

Atticus

Latin "man from Attica," the region of Greece where Athens is located. Most Americans will have read Harper Lee's classic novel *To Kill a Mockingbird* in a high school or college literature class. The hero of that story is Atticus Finch, a southern lawyer who takes on an unpopular case defending a black man falsely accused of rape in a Southern town. The 1962 film based on this novel starring Gregory Peck is considered one of the classics of American cinema. Atticus was too far out as a name to make an impact with parents in the 1960s, but it has gotten some notice the last few years. In 2004 Atticus first appeared on the SSA top 1,000 list, in 938th place. It will be interesting to see if Atticus and **Maximus** will be the forerunners of a new fashion for classical boys names ending in –*us.*

August

German form of **Augustus.** August's popularity with German-Americans made it one of the top 100 American names in the 1880s. It has never completely died out and was 671st on the SSA list in 2004. African-American playwright August Wilson won the Pulitzer Prize for drama in both 1987 and 1990.

Auguste

French form of **Augustus.**

Famous name: Auguste Rodin (sculptor)

Augusten

Form of **Augustine.**

Famous name: Augusten Burroughs (writer)

Augustine

Latin *Augustinus*, diminutive of **Augustus.** The name Augustine was common in England during the Middle Ages because of the adulation of St. Augustine, the author of *The Confessions* and *The City of God.* Today its own short form **Austin** has eclipsed it, but the long version is still occasionally found.

Variations: **Agostinho** (Portuguese), **Agostino** (Italian), **Agustín** (Spanish), **Augusten, Augustyn** (Polish), **Austin**

Augustus

Latin "venerable." The name of the first Roman emperor was introduced into England directly from Germany when the House of Hanover became the royal family. The name Augustus almost disappeared in the United States during the 1970s, but it has been slowly coming back since 1991, ranking 846th on the SSA list in 2004.

Nicknames: **Augie, Chucho, Gus**

Variations: **August** (German), **Auguste** (French)

Austin

Middle English form of **Augustine.** This became a surname in medieval England and later was taken up again as a first name. Formerly, it was used most often in Texas in honor of Stephen F. Austin, a leader in the Texas war for independence from Mexico and for whom the city of Austin, Texas, was named. During the 1990s, however, the name became fashionable all across the United States as parents searched for alternatives to the previously faddish **Justin** and **Dustin.** Between 1995 and 1998, Austin was one of the ten most popular names for American boys, but its popularity is now falling almost as quickly as it rose, and it was only the 42nd most common name in 2004.

Other spelling: **Austen**

Avery

Norman French form of **Alfred.** Avery, always in use but never very common, began a slow erratic rise in the late 1980s, then suddenly doubled in use in 1993 after it was used for the baby on the hit television series *Murphy Brown.* It slowly continued to rise and ranked 217th among boys names in 2004, with about 1,500 born. However, it will probably start to fall away soon since there are now almost three times as many girls as boys receiving the name.
Famous names: Avery Brooks (actor)
Avery Schreiber (comedian)

Axel

Danish form of **Absalom,** a biblical Hebrew name meaning "father of peace." That meaning is somewhat ironic because Absalom was the son of King David who started a civil war against his father and whose death caused David great anguish. Thus, Absalom has never been a popular name in English-speaking countries, but Axel was very popular in both Denmark and Sweden in the early 20th century. A few American parents began to name their sons Axel in the 1990s, perhaps because of the fame of Axl Rose of the rock music group Guns N' Roses. Axel exploded in popularity in the Hispanic community between 1999 and 2000, probably due to a character named Axel Harris (played by Patricio Borghetti) in the Spanish-language television series *DKDA.* The series was about a group of young friends who formed a rock band, and it was so popular that the actors later toured as the band throughout Latin America. The name's cachet with Hispanics is now being reinforced by the young Argentine singer and guitarist Axel Fernando, who has begun to bill himself as just "Axel."
Other spellings: **Aksel, Axl**

Aydin

This can be a Turkish name (pronounced "EYE-din") meaning "moonlit night" or, metaphorically, "intellectual man," which has spread throughout the Muslim world. But in the modern United States it is probably still another spelling variation for **Aidan.**

Babao

Chamoru (Guam) "battle flag."

Bailey

Old English *beg-leah,* "wood or clearing where berries grow"; also, English *bailiff,* which comes from the Old French *baillis,* "porter." But in Middle English, *baile* meant "outside the castle wall," so it's impossible to determine the exact derivation of the name. Bailey had almost completely switched to being a girls name in the United States when, in 1994, the television series *Party of Five* premiered. The heartthrob character of Bailey Salinger, played by actor Scott Wolf, immediately inspired many parents to name sons Bailey again. Bailey was among the top 200 names for boys between 1996 and 2000. But it fell back to 381st in 2004 and seems on its way once again to becoming primarily a female name.

Variations: **Baillie** (English and Scottish), **Baily, Bayley**

Bakari

Swahili (East Africa) "promise."

Baldwin

Old Germanic "bold friend." This was a popular name in the Middle Ages in both Flanders and England.

Variation: **Baudouin** (French)

Balthasar, Balthazar

Medieval variant of *Belshazzar,* "Baal protect the king." This Babylonian name was used in medieval Europe as one of the names of the three Wise Men who brought gifts to the infant Jesus in the New Testament. It has never been common in England or the United States, but with today's search for new names, the publicity being given to it by the career of actor Balthazar Getty, and the recent interest in **Jasper,** the name of another Wise Man, there's some chance that parents may finally notice it within the next few years.

Barden

Old English "barley valley."

Barnaby

Greek from Aramaic *Barnabas,* "son of consolation." The prefix *bar-* means "son of" in Aramaic. Barnabas was a companion and aid to St. Paul in his missionary work. The name has been used in England since the Middle Ages. Charles Dickens used the name for the title character of *Barnaby Rudge,* and *Barnaby Jones* was the name of a long-running television series.

Nicknames: **Barn, Barney**

Variations: **Barna** (Hungarian), **Barnaba** (Italian and Polish), **Barnabe** (French and Portuguese), **Bernabé** (Spanish), **Varnava** (Russian)

Barney

Form of **Barnaby** or **Bernard.** This name may bring to mind the purple dinosaur on the popular television program for preschoolers.

Famous name: Barney Frank (member of Congress)

Other spelling: **Barnie**

Barrett

Middle English *barrat,* "quarrelsome person," from Old French *barat,* "haggler." Barrett has been on the SSA top 1,000 list since 1954. Its use was fading, but since 2002 it's shown signs of renewed vitality.

Barrington

British place name from one of several towns whose name originally meant "estate of a man called *Bara* or *Beorn.*"

Barron

Old German "a free man." Spelled baron, this name is a royal title.

Variation: **Baron**

Barry

Irish *bearach,* "spear." This name was exclusively Irish until the 20th century, when it became popular in England and the United States. The large number of Irish immigrants to those two countries probably influenced the spread of the name.

Famous name: Barry Goldwater (politician)
Variation: **Barrie**

Bart

Form of **Bartholomew** or **Barton.** This name is now identified with the television cartoon character Bart Simpson. His creator, Matt Groening, named him Bart because it's an anagram for "brat."

Bartholomew

Hebrew "son of Talmai" from Aramaic *telem,* "furrow." This name contains the prefix *bar-,* which means "son of." Little is known of St. Bartholomew; the only reference to him is in the Gospel of Mark, where he is listed as one of the apostles. He preached in India and in Armenia, where he is said to have been skinned alive and then crucified head down. The name became popular in England after the 12th century, with almost 200 churches dedicated to the saint, but it is rarely given in any English-speaking country today.

Nicknames: **Bart, Barth, Bartie, Bartle, Bat, Tola, Toli**

Variations: **Bartal** (Hungarian), **Barthelemy** (French), **Bartholomaus** (German), **Bartollo, Bartolo** (Italian and Spanish), **Bartolomé** (Spanish), **Bartolomej** (Czech), **Bartolomeu** (Portuguese), **Bartos** (Czech), **Bertalan** (Hungarian), **Vartolomej** (Bulgarian), **Vartolomeu** (Romanian)

Barton

Old English *Beretun* from *bere* [barley or corn] + *tun* [farm]. Barton is known primarily as a surname, with several famous people carrying the name, including Clara Barton, who organized the American Red Cross and worked to reform women's prisons.

Nickname: **Bart**

Basil

Greek *basileios,* "royal." Several saints had this name, including St. Basil the Great, founder of the Eastern Orthodox Church. His father was St. Basil; his mother, St. Emmelia.

Famous name: Basil Rathbone (actor)

Nicknames: **Bas, Vas**

Variations: **Basileus** (Dutch), **Basilio** (Spanish, Portuguese, and Italian), **Basilius** (Swedish), **Bazyli** (Polish), **Vasili, Vassily, Vasska** (Russian), **Vasilios** (Greek), **Vazul** (Hungarian)

Bastian

This short form of **Sebastian** is familiar to many children as the name of the boy who reads *The Neverending Story* in the fantasy novel by Michael Ende and the films based on it.

Baxter

Old English *bæcestre,* "baker." Though the suffix *–ster* was originally only used for words designating women in Old English, by the 12th century words such as *baxter* could refer to bakers of either sex.

Baylor

Perhaps a form of Middle English *bailor,* "one who delivers goods." This name is well known in Texas because of Baylor University.

Beau

French "handsome." Originally a nickname for a good-looking or well-dressed young man, this name is associated with the American South because it was the short form of **Beauregard,** a French sur-name meaning "handsome-look." This was used as a first name in honor of Pierre Beauregard, a Confederate general. Today Beau is used nearly equally by parents in all parts of the United States and was the 308th most popular name for boys in 2004. (See also **Bo.**)
Famous name: Beau Bridges (actor)
Other spelling: **Bo**

Beck

This English surname can have several origins, including Middle English *bekke,* "brook"; Old English *becca,* "pick axe"; or Old French *bec,* "beak," the last being a nickname for someone with a prominent nose. Rock singer Beck's full name is Beck David Campbell.

Ben

Usually a form of **Benedict, Benjamin, Bennett,** or **Bernard;** also, from Scots *beann,* "peak," or Hebrew *ben,* "son of." Ben has been popular as a separate name in both Great Britain and Australia recently, but only 440 parents in the United States chose to put Ben on a birth certificate in 2004, as opposed to 13,567 who used Benjamin and 635 who used Bennett. Actors Ben Affleck, Ben Browder, and Ben Stiller certainly make sure that Ben is frequently mentioned in entertainment news reports.
Famous name: Ben Shahn (painter)

Benedict

Latin *benedictus,* "blessed." The name connotes holiness and auster-
ity. St. Benedict of Nursia, the father of Western monasticism and
founder of the Benedictine Order, was so strict and insisted on such
a high level of asceticism while he was an abbot that his monks tried
to poison him. The name did not occur in England before the Norman Conquest. It will be interesting to see if the reign of Pope
Benedict XVI leads to an increase in the use of this rare name; it
would make a good alternative for the popular name **Benjamin.**
Famous name: Benedict Arnold (American Revolutionary traitor)
Nicknames: **Ben, Benito, Benny, Betto, Dick**
Variations: **Bendek** (Polish), **Benedetto** (Italian), **Benediktas** (Latvian),
Benito (Spanish), **Benedikt** (Bulgarian, Czech, and Ger-
man), **Bengt** (Swedish), **Bennett, Benoit** (French), **Pentti**
(Finnish), **Venediktos** (Greek)

Benjamin

Hebrew "son of the south" or "son of the right hand." This name is
found in three places in the Bible. In Genesis, Benjamin is the
youngest son of Jacob. He was originally named Benoni, "son of my
sorrow," because of the pain he caused his mother as she was dying
giving birth to him. Jacob renamed him. In Chronicles, the sons of
Benjamin are listed, and a grandson named Benjamin is noted. A
Benjamin also appears as the son of Hiram in the Book of Ezra. The
name was common in England during the 17th century and stayed
popular until the late 19th century, when use of biblical names
declined. Recently, the name has made a strong recovery, ranking
among the 40 most-used names for American boys since 1990.
Famous names: Benjamin Britten (composer)
Benjamin Franklin (statesman and inventor)
Benjamin Spock (pediatrician)
Nicknames: **Ben, Benjy, Bennie, Benny, Mincho**
Variations: **Beniamin** (Polish), **Beniamino** (Italian), **Benjaminas**
(Lithuanian), **Beniek** (Polish), **Binyamin** (Hebrew), **Veni-
amin, Venya, Venyamin** (Russian)

Bennett

Middle English form of **Benedict.** The use of this name has been
increasing lately as an alternative for **Benjamin.**

Benny

Form of **Benedict, Benjamin,** or **Bernard.** This name has been used in literature for mentally handicapped characters, such as Benjy in William Faulkner's *The Sound and the Fury,* Benny in John Steinbeck's *Of Mice and Men,* and Benny on the television series *L.A. Law.*
Variation: **Benjy**

Bentley

Old English *beonet-leah,* "bent-grass meadow." Americans over age 50 may remember this name from the television series *Bachelor Father,* which originally aired from 1957 to 1962. In this comedy, John Forsythe played Bentley Gregg, a playboy attorney who became the guardian for his orphaned teenage niece.
Other spelling: **Bently**

Bernard

Old German *Berinhard,* "brave as a bear," from *berin* [a bear] + *hard* [firm]. This name came to England at the time of the Norman Conquest and has been popular since the 12th century. In the United States, it is usually accented on the second syllable, but in Britain it's pronounced "BURR-nerd." Several saints have had this name. St. Bernard of Montjoux, the patron saint of mountaineers, did missionary work in the Alps, where two passes, as well as a breed of lifesaving dogs, are named for him.
Famous name: Bernard M. Baruch (economist)
Nicknames: **Barn, Barney, Ben, Benny, Bernie, Berny, Dino, Nado, Nayo**
Variations: **Barnard, Bernal, Bernaldino, Bernardin** (French), **Bernardino** (Italian, Spanish, and Portuguese), **Bernardo, Bernat** (Hungarian), **Vernaldo, Vernardino** (Latin American), **Vernardinos** (Greek)

Bernardo

Spanish form of **Bernard.** Bernardo O'Higgins (1778–1842) was the revolutionary general who won Chile's fight for independence from Spain and became that country's first president.

Bert

Form of **Albert, Bertram, Delbert, Herbert, Hubert, Norbert,** or **Robert;** from Old German *berhta,* "bright."

Bertram

Old German *Berahtraben* from *berhta* [bright] + *hraben* [raven]. This name came into England at the time of the Norman Conquest. It was regularly used until the 1930s, but it's unusual today. Shakespeare used the name for the Count of Rousillon in *All's Well That Ends Well,* and Sir Walter Scott used it in *Castle Dangerous.*

Nicknames: **Bert, Bertie**

Variations: **Bartram** (English), **Bechtel** (German), **Beltrán** (Spanish), **Bertrand** (French), **Bertrando** (Italian), **Bertrao** (Portuguese)

Bertrand

French form of **Bertram.**

Famous name: Bertrand Russell (philosopher)

Bill

Form of **William.** Bill almost never occurs as an official name, but of course it's how many Williams prefer to be known.

Famous names: Bill Blass (fashion designer)
Bill Clinton (42nd U.S. president)
Bill Cosby (actor)
Bill Gates (software mogul)
Bill Moyers (journalist)

Billy

Form of **William.** Sometimes this name is chosen by entertainers or men in occupations in which a nickname seems more appropriate than a formal name. As a separate given name, its rank was exactly 400th for boys born in the United States in 2004. Like most pet forms of masculine names, it is more often given as an official form by parents in the South than in other parts of the country.

Famous names: William Franklin "Billy" Graham (evangelist)
Billy Crystal (comedian)

Other spelling: **Billie**

Variations: **Bili** (Romanian), **Vila** (Czech), **Vili** (Hungarian)

Bion

Derivative of Greek *bios,* "life." Bion was the name of an ancient Greek pastoral poet who lived around 100 B.C., and his name was occasionally used in the early 19th century when American parents were

attracted to the names of other Classical Greek and Latin poets like
Homer and **Virgil**. With its similarity in sound to names like **Brian,
Ryan,** and **Zion,** it's a bit surprising that it hasn't yet been rediscovered.

Birch

Old English *birce*, "birch tree." This name is gaining interest from
parents who like "nature names."
Famous name: Birch Bayh (U.S. senator)

Bishop

Old English *Biscop*. As a surname it was originally a nickname for
someone who looked like a bishop to his neighbors, or for someone
who had been elected as the "boy bishop" in a medieval pageant.

Bjorn

Swedish, from Old Norse "bear."
Famous name: Bjorn Borg (tennis player)
Other spelling: **Bjorne**
Variation: **Bjarne** (Danish and Norwegian)

Blade

In spite of its somewhat aggressive image, some parents are starting
to use this word as an alternative for names like **Cade** and **Blake.**

Bladen

Surname from **Blaydon,** a place name from Old Scandinavian *blár,*
"cold" and Old English *dun,* "hill." This name is just being discovered
as a further addition to the popular list of rhyming names that
includes **Aidan, Brayden, Caden,** and **Jayden.**
Other spellings: **Blaiden, Blayden**

Blaine

Scots Gaelic *Blaan,* "yellow." This surname is used as a given name,
especially in the United States, where Celtic names are in vogue.
Other spellings: **Blain, Blane**
Variation: **Blaan**

Blair

Gaelic *blar,* "plain, battlefield." Although still given to some boys, this
surname is more common as a girls first name in the United States.
Famous name: Blair Underwood (actor)

Blaise

French form of Latin *Blasius,* probably from *blaesus,* "lisping." St. Blaise was a fourth-century Armenian martyr. Not surprisingly, this name often gets respelled as **Blaze,** which in 2004 was actually slightly more common than the original spelling.

Famous name: Blaise Pascal (philosopher and mathematician)

Blake

Old English *blac,* "pale," "loss of color," or "shining white"; also, Old English *blaec,* "black" or "dark." Confusion between these two similar-sounding Old English words means that this name can be said to mean its own opposite. Until the 20th century, this was almost always a surname. As a given name it now ranks among the 100 most common names for American boys. Blake Carrington, the wealthy oil baron played by John Forsythe in the 1980s television series *Dynasty,* probably helped increase parents' awareness of the name. It also fits in with the current vogue for short names starting with *B,* including **Brad, Braden, Brent, Brett, Brock,** and **Bryce.**

Famous name: Blake Edwards (movie director/writer)

Blaze

(See **Blaise.**)

Bo

In Sweden and Denmark, this is a popular name derived from Old Norse *bua,* "householder"; in the United States, it's usually considered a respelling of **Beau.** Bo Bice, the rock singer from Alabama who was runner-up on the 2005 season of *American Idol,* is Harold Elwin Bice, Jr. on his birth certificate.

Famous name: Bo Jackson (athlete)

Bob

Form of **Robert.** Bob is actually quite rare as an official form on birth certificates, but it's how many Roberts prefer to be known.

Famous names: Bob Dylan (singer)
Bob Hope (comedian)

Bobby

Form of **Robert.** This nickname is often combined with another name, as in Bobby Joe, Bobby John, and Bobby Lee. Like Billy,

Bobby is used as an official name in the southern part of the United States, and it ranks among the 400 most commonly used names for American boys. Bobby is also a popular nickname for politicians, entertainers, and athletes.
Famous names: Bobby Darin (singer)
Bobby Fischer (chess champion)

Bodog

Hungarian "happy"; used in Hungary as a "translation" of **Felix.**

Bomani

Ngoni (Malawi) "warrior." This name is occasionally used by African-Americans who want to give their children an African first name.

Boris

Tartar *Bogoris,* "small"; later associated in Russia with the Slavic word *bor,* "battle." The ninth-century King Boris of Bulgaria was the first Slavic ruler to accept Christianity. Recently, Boris has been a popular name for German boys because of the fame of tennis player Boris Becker.
Famous names: Boris Godunov (tsar of Russia)
Boris Karloff (actor)
Nicknames: **Boba, Borenka, Borisik, Borka, Borya**
Variations: **Borys** (Polish), **Borysko** (Ukrainian)

Boston

The city in Massachusetts is named after a town in England whose name was *Botuluestan* in Middle English, meaning "Botwulf's stone." This referred either to a boundary marker or a meeting place in medieval England. Boston is one of the new "place names" that's gotten a lot of discussion for several years, but 2004 was the first year it actually appeared on the SSA top 1,000 list, at 902nd place. Actor Kurt Russell named his son Boston in 1980.

Boyden

Old French *Bodin,* probably a contracted form of **Baldwin.**

Brad

Old English *brad,* "broad"; also, a shortened form of **Bradley** or **Bradford.** Many Americans born in the 1950s and 1960s will associate this name with the "overly normal" character played by Barry Bostwick in the cult film *The Rocky Horror Picture Show.* Although still usually a nickname, Brad is occasionally given as an independent first name to American boys.

Famous name: Brad Pitt (actor)

Braden

Irish Gaelic *Bradain*, "salmon." Braden was rare as a first name until the 1980s, when it rapidly began growing in popularity as parents discovered it as an alternative for **Brandon** and **Brian.** It has continued to rise in the rankings ever since, though it has been overtaken by its own alternatives, **Aidan, Jayden,** and **Caden.** The sound of the name is the most important factor for most parents in choosing it, as is shown by the fact that **Brayden** is now the most common spelling, having overtaken the original in 2000. All the main spellings taken together were the 56th most common boys name of 2004.

Other spellings: **Bradyn, Braeden, Braedon, Braiden, Braydon**

Bradford

Old English "broad ford." This place name developed first into a surname, but now it's often used as a first name. Such use probably originally honored William Bradford (1590–1657), the first governor of the Plymouth Colony in Massachusetts.

Nickname: **Brad**

Bradley

Old English "broad meadow." This place name that became a surname is now common as a first name. Its popularity may have been influenced by the fame of Omar Bradley, a World War II general. Bradley was especially popular in the late 1970s and was still among the top 200 names for boys in 2004.

Nicknames: **Brad, Lee**

Other spellings: **Bradlee, Bradly**

Brady

Irish Gaelic *Bradaigh*, perhaps from *bradach*, "spirited"; also, Old English *brad eage*, "broad or wide-set eyes," or *brad eg*, "broad island." This surname is another name for boys starting with *Br-* that is fashionable today. It's hard for many younger baby boomers not to think of the television series *The Brady Bunch* when they hear this name.

Other spelling: **Bradie**

Brage

Old Norse *bragr,* "most excellent." Brage was the Norse god of poetry.

Bram

Short form of **Abraham,** best known as the name of Bram Stoker (1847–1912), the author of *Dracula.*

Brandon

English place name, "hill covered with broom," although in Ireland sometimes a form of **Brendan.** This aristocratic British surname first gained notice in 1953 when Brandon DeWilde played the young boy in the classic Western film *Shane.* The name really took off, however, when another child actor, Brandon Cruz, played Eddie on television's *The Courtship of Eddie's Father* in the late 1960s to early 1970s. By 1985, Brandon was second only to Michael as a name for African-American boys and was hovering just below the top ten list for whites. There were signs that the name was starting to fade when it suddenly surged back into the top ten for boys of all races in 1991. This was undoubtedly caused by Brandon Walsh, the high school heartthrob played by Jason Priestley on *Beverly Hills, 90210;* the same show generated a flood of babies named **Dylan.** By 2004 its popularity was slowly dropping off again, but it was still among the top 30 names for American boys.

Branford

English surname and place name, Old English *Bregnesford,* "ford by the hill."
Famous name: Branford Marsalis (jazz saxophonist)

Branson

Middle English *Brantestone,* "Brant's farmstead." Branson is another name starting with *Br-* that American parents have taken up lately. It will remind many people of country music because of the popular tourist destination of Branson, Missouri.

Brant

Old Norse *Brandr* or Germanic *brand,* "firebrand, sword." This word came to mean "sword" to ancient Germanic tribes because of legends where saints or heroes held flaming swords. The alternative spelling **Brandt** is frequently found.

Braulio

St. Braulio was a bishop of Zaragoza, Spain, in the seventh century. The derivation of his name is unclear, but authorities believe it comes from the Germanic word *brand,* "firebrand" or "sword." This ancient Spanish name has been given new life in the Hispanic-American community recently through a character in a television series called *Corazones al Limite,* where handsome young actor Aarón Diaz plays Braulio, a teenage heartthrob character who is the male lead in a story about the trials and tribulations of high school seniors.

Braxton

English surname, perhaps meaning "hunting dog farm." Parents began to discover Braxton as an alternative for **Brandon** in the 1980s, and in 2004 more than 1,500 Braxtons were born in the United States, ranking it 207th.
Famous name: Braxton Bragg (Confederate general)

Brayan

This spelling of **Brian** is frequently used by Hispanic parents in the United States, because the sound of English *eye* is spelled *ay* in Spanish, and many want their Spanish-speaking relatives to easily know how to pronounce the name in the proper "American" way.

Brayden

(See **Braden.**)

Braylon

Probably a recent African-American creation. Football wide receiver Braylon Edwards saw his name make the SSA top 1,000 list for the first time, in 700th place, in 2004 while he was still playing for the University of Michigan. He is therefore following in the footsteps of another Michigan athlete, basketball player **Jalen** Rose, in having a significant impact on African-American names even before joining a professional team. The fact that Braylon and Jalen rhyme is undoubtedly a factor in the name's quick success.

Brecken, Breckin

Probably spelling variations of either **Brecon,** the name of a district of Wales noted for its beautiful mountains, the Brecon Beacons, or **Breckan,** an Irish surname from Gaelic *Breacán,* an ancient personal name meaning "speckled." Since the Welsh district was named after **Brychan,** a fifth-century Welsh prince whose name is probably a Welsh form of the same Celtic word, Breckin could be considered a particularly good name for a boy expected to have a lot of freckles. Parents should be warned, however, that the spelling Brecken turns up frequently as a girls name.

Famous name: Breckin Meyer (actor)

Brendan

Irish Gaelic *Breanainn,* itself a form of Welsh *breenhin,* "prince." This name is revered in Ireland because of St. Brendan the Navigator, a sixth-century monk whose extensive travels gave rise to the legend that he discovered the New World years before Christopher Columbus. Long popular in Ireland, Brendan is gaining renewed interest from American parents because of the great popularity of **Brandon.** Since 1991 the name has held a place just below the top 100 names given to newborn boys in the United States.

Brennan, Brennen

Irish Gaelic *Braonain,* "moisture, drop of water, tear." This Irish surname is being used as a modern first name as some parents search for alternatives to **Brandon** or **Brendan.** Some parents who give this name to their sons might think of it as honoring Supreme Court Associate Justice William J. Brennan, Jr.

Brent

Celtic "high," or Old English "burnt," as in a burned place or field. Brent recently became popular in the United States after **Brett** had paved the way, and it was one of the top 100 names of the 1970s. In turn, Brent's vogue led to the more recent use of similar names such as **Brant** and **Brenton.** By 2004, however, Brent had fallen off to only 362nd on the popularity chart. Brent Spiner is the actor who played Lt. Commander Data on the popular television series *Star Trek: The Next Generation.*

Famous name: Brent Musburger (sports announcer)

Brenton

Old English place name and surname meaning "Bryni's homestead." Brenton has been among the top 1,000 names on the SSA list since 1966, rising steadily to its peak at 260th in 1984 and then falling back to 872nd in 2004. It owes its use as a given name primarily to parents who wanted to call their sons **Brent** but were reluctant to put a one-syllable name on a birth certificate.

Bret, Brett

Celtic *Breton* from Old French *Briton,* "a person from Brittany." Brett became popular in the United States during the 1960s and at its peak in the 1980s ranked about 70th among the most-often-used names. It was brought to the attention of Americans by the hit television series *Maverick,* which originally ran from 1957 to 1962. Its gambler hero, Bret Maverick, made actor James Garner famous, and he briefly revived the character in 1982 in a series called *Bret Maverick.* Later, the popularity of baseball player George Brett may have also contributed to the name's success. It's rapidly falling away today, though, ranking only 212th in 2004.

Famous name: Brett Favre (football player)

Brevin

This appears to be simply an African-American creation blending the sounds of **Brian** and **Kevin,** but there is another possible origin. Brevin is the French form of *Bregwin,* the name of the 12th Archbishop of Canterbury in England who died in 764. Bregwin is an old Saxon name; the meaning of the first syllable is unknown, but the second is probably *wine,* "friend," a common ending for Germanic and Anglo-Saxon names also found in **Edwin, Alwin, Baldwin,** etc.

Famous name: Brevin Knight (basketball player)

Brian

Probably from Celtic *Brigonos,* "high, noble." This name is popular in Ireland because of the legendary Irish hero King Brian Boroimhe, who lived in the tenth century. The name Brian was introduced to England with the Norman Conquest by Breton vassals of William the Conqueror. It dropped from use as a given name outside of Ireland during the 18th and 19th centuries, but it made a strong return and ranked among the top ten names in the United States during the 1970s and 1980s. Its popularity is now slowly receding, but it was still among the top 30 American names in 2004.

Famous names: Brian Boitano (figure skater)
                 Brian Dennehy (actor)

Variations: **Brayan** (modern Hispanic), **Briano** (Italian), **Bryant**

Brice

Fewer than 10 percent of parents choosing this name today use this original spelling of **Bryce.**
Famous name: Brice Marden (artist)

Brock

Old English *brocc*, "badger," or *broc*, "brook." This may have originally been a nickname for someone who was accused of "badgering" or pestering his neighbors. Brock was 236th on the list of names given to American boys in 2004.
Famous name: Brock Peters (actor)

Broderick

Welsh *ap Rhydderch*, "son of **Rhydderch.**" Rhydderch is an ancient Welsh name meaning "ascending king." Broderick was 978th on the SSA list for boys in 2004.

Brodie, Brody

Brodie is a Scottish place name and surname, probably from Gaelic *brothach*, "muddy place." Brody is a Jewish surname indicating that one's ancestors came from a Ukrainian town whose name meant "ford." As a first name, parents prefer Brody over Brodie six to one, which makes it the first Jewish surname to become generally popular as a first name. The name has risen rapidly since first being seen on the SSA list in 1980. In 2004 more than 2,000 boys were given this name, making it 179th on the popularity chart.

Bronson

Middle English *Brunson*, "son of the brown man." For unknown reasons, this was a fairly popular name in Hawaii during the 1980s. A few parents who give this name may be thinking of actor Charles Bronson, star of action movies such as *Death Wish*. His original last name was Buchinski.
Famous names: Bronson Arroyo (baseball pitcher and singer)
Bronson Pinchot (actor and comedian)

Brooks

English "dweller by the brook." This name has been increasing in use a bit lately. Parents evidently accept it as a masculine counterpart for **Brooke.**

Bruce

French *Braose,* a place name, possibly meaning "muddy" or "from the brush thicket." The Bruces of Scotland were originally Normans and came from Bruys, France, during the Norman Conquest. The most famous member of the family, Robert "the Bruce," was king of Scotland in the 14th century. Bruce was rare as a first name outside Scotland until the 1930s, but it was extremely fashionable in the United States from 1940 until 1970. Its popularity is now receding, and it was only the 415th most common name for American boys born in 2004.
Famous name: Bruce Springsteen (singer)
Nickname: **Brucie**
Variations: **Bruhs, Bruis** (French), **Bruys** (Scottish)

Bruno

Old German *brun,* "brown," usually associated with bears. This name is not as popular in the United States as it is in Germany, where it is associated with the 11th-century St. Bruno of Cologne. After a brilliant career as a professor of theology and philosophy, he founded the Carthusian Order at Grenoble. He was made a saint in 1623, and his day is October 6. In the 1960s, Bruno was a popular name in France, and it is also used in Italy and Poland.
Nicknames: **Bru, Bruni, Bruny**
Variation: **Brunonas** (Lithuanian)

Bryant

Form of **Brian.** This name has been especially popular with African-Americans due to the fame of television newscaster Bryant Gumbel. It is also regularly used by white parents.

Bryce

Form of **Brice,** Celtic name of unknown meaning. The original Brice was a medieval bishop of Tours, France, who was venerated as a saint after being unjustly accused of adultery. The name Bryce began its rise to popularity around 1965. Its vogue began in the Southwest, perhaps being influenced by Utah's spectacular Bryce Canyon National Park, but by 2004 Bryce was most common in the Mid-western and Mid-Atlantic regions. Nationally it was the 108th most common male name of 2004.
Other spelling: **Brice**

Bryson

Middle English *Briceson,* "son of **Brice**." The reluctance to put one-syllable names on a birth certificate made the rise of this longer version of **Bryce** predictable. Parents discovered it in the 1980s, and by 2004 it was 176th on the list. Bryson was also the name of an ancient Greek mathematician, born around 450 B.C., but it's unlikely many modern American parents are naming children after him. The ancient Greek name was derived from the verb *vryo,* "to blossom."

Burt

Short form of **Burton.**
Famous name: Burt Reynolds (actor)

Burton

Old English *burhton,* "farmstead near a fortress," from *burh* [fortified place] + *tun* [town].
Nickname: **Burt**

Byron

Old English *byrum,* "at the cattle sheds." This homely name was originally given to "the person who lives in the cow barn." It was first used as a given name in honor of one of the great English poets, George Noel Gordon, better known as Lord Byron, the author of *Don Juan* and *Childe Harold's Pilgrimage.*
Famous name: Byron Raymond White (football player and U.S. Supreme Court associate justice)
Variation: **Biron**

Cade

Old English *Cada*, "lumpy," or Middle English "pet." Cade first appeared on the SSA list in 1983. It may be a coincidence, but in 1983 Ralph Macchio played the character Johnny Cade in the film *The Outsiders*, based on the classic teenage novel by S. E. Hinton. The use of Cade sparked the even greater success of **Caden.** Cade climbed in use throughout the 1990s, but it may have peaked in 2002 as parents came to see Caden as its "full form." Still, nearly 2,000 Cades were born in 2004, making it the 181st most common boys name.

Caden

Form of *MacAdáin*, "son of Adam," Irish and Scottish surname. (See also **Kaden.**) Like **Jayden,** Caden is a formerly rare name that has exploded in popularity because it blends the sounds of other popular names like **Caleb** and **Hayden.** Caden's frequent use began in Rocky Mountain states like Utah in the late 1980s. Caden first made the SSA top 1,000 list in 1992; Kaden followed in 1993, and they since have been joined by **Caiden, Cayden, Kadin, Kaeden,** and **Kayden.** Taken together, these spellings were the 33rd most common boys name of 2004. Though Caden is still a good bit more common in states west of the Mississippi, its use is fast spreading eastward.

Cal

Short form of **Calvin.**
Famous name: Cal Ripken, Jr. (baseball player)

Cale

Short form of **Caleb.** Like Caleb, Cale is increasing in use and is now among the top 400 names for American boys.
Famous name: Cale Yarborough (NASCAR driver)
Other spellings: **Cael, Kale**

Caleb

Hebrew *kalebh,* "dog." In the Bible, Caleb is one of the 12 spies sent by Moses to scout the land of Canaan before the Israelites enter it. Because he and Joshua are the only ones of the 12 who urge the people to have faith in God's promise that they will overcome the Canaanites, Caleb and his family are given the city of Hebron when the Israelites conquer it years later. Caleb was a popular name with the Puritans, and it never died out. Since the 1970s Caleb has been enjoying a revival; it was the 28th most common name given to American boys in 2004, its highest rank ever. Some of its recent popularity may be linked to the character Caleb Snyder on the television soap opera *As the World Turns,* but the "long *a*" vowel in its first syllable as well as its long history helps to make it fashionable.
Nickname: **Cale**

Callum, Calum

Scottish Gaelic form of Late Latin *Columba,* "dove." St. Columba or Calum was an Irish-born monk who converted the Scots to Christianity in the sixth century. His name has been popular in Scotland and England since 1990, but it is still rare in the United States.

Calvin

Latin *calvinus,* "bald." This French surname was turned into a first name in honor of John Calvin, a Protestant reformer and theologian and the founder of the Calvinist movement. During the presidency of Calvin Coolidge, many parents named their baby boys Calvin. Today, the name is more popular with African-Americans than with other parents in the United States.
Famous name: Calvin Klein (fashion designer)
Nicknames: **Cal, Calv**
Variation: **Calvino** (Spanish and Italian)

Cambridge

English place name, Old English *Grontabricc,* "bridge over the river Granta." The modern name is Cambridge rather than Grantbridge because the Normans found the former easier to say.

Camden

Middle English *Campeden,* "valley with enclosures." As **Camryn** has become common for girls, parents have discovered Camden as a masculine alternative. Since entering the SSA top 1,000 list in 1990, Camden has multiplied in use by 12, reaching 204th place in 2004.

Cameron

Scots Gaelic *camsron*, "bent nose," or *cambrun*, "bent hill." This name is popular in Scotland, where it's the name of a great clan. Two great Scottish theologians, John Cameron and Richard Cameron, are commemorated when Scottish boys are given this name. Cameron became more popular as a first name in the United States during the 1990s. The use of the name for girls may have helped it to start falling away for boys, but it was still 38th on the boys list in 2004.
Famous name: Cameron Crowe (filmmaker)
Nickname: **Cam**

Campbell

See this name in the girls section of the book. Campbell just barely made the SSA top 1,000 for boys in 2003 and 2004, but it may not do so again, considering it's now three times more popular for girls.

Canaan

Hebrew "purplish red," name of the land conquered by the Israelites.

Cannon

Another surname of multiple origins, Cannon can be from Manx *Cannanan*, "white head"; Irish Gaelic *Canán*, "wolf cub"; or, most often, Middle English *canun*, "clergyman," a much more peaceful meaning than the modern military associations of the word. Cannon is another surname ending in −n that's lately entered the top 1,000 SSA list for boys; 211 were born in 2004.

Canyon

Though not yet common enough to make the SSA top 1,000 list, Canyon is a "nature name" that has been regularly used in the United States for several years. Its similarity in sound to other presently fashionable names may give it a bright future.

Carl

Form of German **Karl**, itself a variation of **Charles**. Carl was brought to the United States by German immigrants in the 19th century and had become one of the top 30 names for American boys from all ethnic backgrounds by 1900. The name remained popular until about 1950, but its use has since fallen steadily. During the 1960s, after the name began to go out of fashion in America, Carl became a common name in Great Britain.

Famous names: Carl Jung (psychoanalyst)
Carl Lewis (Olympic track athlete)
Carl Sandburg (poet)

Variation: **Karl** (German, Russian, Serbian, Swedish, and Norwegian)

Carlo

Italian form of **Charles.** Carlo Collodi is renowned the world over as the writer of *Pinocchio.*

Carlos

Spanish form of **Charles.** This is an extremely popular name with Hispanic parents in the United States, and it has sometimes been used by non-Hispanic-Americans, especially in Appalachia.

Famous names: Carlos Santana (musician)
Carlos Valderrama (soccer player)

Variations: **Calicho, Calo, Carlino, Carlucho**

Carlton, Carleton

Variation of **Charlton.** Although these two names have the same origin, Carlton is a great deal more popular than Charlton as a first name in the United States.

Carmelo

Italian form of Hebrew "the garden." This name has suddenly become popular in the African-American community out of admiration for basketball star Carmelo Anthony.

Carrington

English surname and place name, "place of Cara's people."

Carson

Medieval Scottish *de Acarson,* referring to some unknown place name. Carson has had continuous if limited use as a given name since 1880, perhaps because of admiration for the Western scout Kit Carson. Its use ballooned after 1980 as parents discovered it as another "two syllables ending in *–n*" name for boys. Carson reached 98th on the popularity list in 2004. Though it may originally have had a Western flavor, it probably has a more urbane image today due to talk show host Carson Daly and fashion expert Carson Kressley.

Carter

Norman French *cartier*, "cart driver." This name had been inching up in popularity until 1994, when it quickened its rate of increase considerably. This may be related to the character of Dr. John Carter (often addressed as "Carter") on the successful television drama *ER*, which began that year. The name also fit in with the fashion for surnames ending in *–er* as boys names. Carter was the 92nd most popular name for boys in 2004.

Cary

Middle English *Kari,* perhaps "pleasant stream"; or Irish Gaelic *O Ciardha,* "son of the dark one." Actor Cary Grant (born Archibald Leach) was solely responsible for the name's minor popularity from 1950 through 1970.
Other spellings: **Carey, Kary**

Casey

Irish Gaelic *Cathasach,* "watchful." As a name for boys this brings to mind J. L. "Casey" Jones, the train engineer whose sacrifice of his own life to save those of his passengers in a 1900 wreck near Monroe, Virginia, is immortalized in the famous ballad. He received his nickname because he was born in Cayce, Kentucky. Casey was a popular name in the 1980s and 1990s, but it has now begun to fall off. Remarkably, Casey has maintained almost an equal use for boys and girls in the United States for a generation.

Cash

Old French *casse,* "box, chest," originally a surname for a maker of these. Of course it's impossible for most Americans to not think of money when they hear this name. Cash is a recent but fast-growing deposit onto the SSA top 1,000 list; there were 223 boys given the name in the United States in 2004.

Cason

As an English surname, Cason comes from a local dialect pronunciation of Cawston, a town in Norfolk whose name means "Kalfr's homestead." Parents have only recently discovered Cason as a name that fits in with the vogue for similar-sounding names like **Caden** and **Mason**. Cason entered the SSA top 1,000 list in 2002, and its spelling variation **Kason** appeared in 2004. With both forms added together, almost 400 boys were given the name in 2004.

Casper

Danish and English variation of **Jasper**. Casper was regularly used in the United States until the 1920s, but its association with the friendly cartoon ghost has kept the name from sharing in the recent increased interest in Jasper.

Cecil

Latin *Caecilius*, a Roman family name from *caecus*, "blind." Cecil was popular 100 years ago but is now not even one of the top 1,000 names given to boys in the United States.
Famous name: Cecil B. DeMille (movie producer)
Nicknames: **Cece, Ces**
Variations: **Cecilio** (Italian and Spanish), **Cecilius** (Dutch), **Celio** (Portuguese), **Sessylt** (Welsh)

Cedar

The name of an evergreen tree.

Cedric

This name first appeared in *Ivanhoe* by Sir Walter Scott, who may have mistaken it for *Cerdic*, the mythical founder of West Saxony; *Cerdic* may derive from Welsh *Caradawg*, "amiable." The central character in Frances Hodgson Burnett's *The Little Lord Fauntleroy*, published in 1886, is also named Cedric. Surprisingly, this very English name made the top ten in France during the 1970s. In the United States, the name is now used primarily by African-Americans. *Harry Potter* readers will remember Cedric Diggory, captain of the Hufflepuff quidditch team who is Harry's rival for the affections of Cho Chang.
Nicknames: **Ced, Rick, Rickie, Ricky**
Variation: **Cerdic**

Cesar

Spanish form of *Caesar*, a Roman family name of uncertain meaning. The name has a royal sound because it was the family name of the first dynasty of Roman emperors, and the Russian word *czar* is

derived from it. Cesar has long been common in Latin America and
with Hispanics in the United States.

Famous name: Cesar Chavez (farm labor leader)

Chad

Old English *Ceadda,* perhaps based on Welsh *cad,* "battle." Also the
name of a country in Africa. St. Chad was a seventh-century bishop of
Lichfield, England, who was noted for being extraordinarily humble
and devout. Chad was a rare name, used mostly by Roman Catholics
in England, until it was brought to the attention of Americans by
singer Chad Mitchell in the 1960s. It was given more impetus by actor
Chad Everett when he appeared as Dr. Joe Gannon on the television
series *Medical Center* in the early 1970s. Chad was among the top 50
names for American boys from 1975 through 1984; by 2004, it had
slipped to 313th place.

Famous name: Chad Lowe (actor)

Chaim

Hebrew *chayim,* "life." The Orthodox Jewish community in the
United States is so small that very few of the names they favor have
a chance of making the SSA top 1,000 list. Chaim is the exception;
its huge popularity within that group has kept Chaim on the list
continuously since 1972. Admiration for Chaim Weizmann
(1874–1952), the first President of Israel, probably has a lot to do
with the success of this name.

Chalmers

Scottish form of Old French *chaumbre,* "bedchamber" or "private
servant."

Nickname: **Chal**

Chance

Originally a nickname for **Chauncey,** which was fairly common as a
given name in the northern United States during the 19th century
in honor of Charles Chauncey, the second president of Harvard
University. Chauncey was originally a Norman French place name
meaning "Cantius's estate." Americans in general (and those in
Hollywood in particular) began to notice Chance as a boys name in
the 1960s. The meaning of the word *chance* led screenwriters to
give the name to risk-taking adventurers in Westerns. Though it

seems to have peaked in use around 1996, Chance was still the 240th most popular name for American boys in 2004.

Chandler

Anglo-French *chandeler*, "maker or seller of candles." Parents looking for new names began to discover Chandler in the 1980s. It fit in with the fashion for occupational surname forms ending in *-er* and had a "preppy" image that appealed to many. It increased steadily but slowly until the television comedy *Friends* appeared in 1994. There were 703 boys named Chandler in 1993, but 1,854 in 1995, which shows that parents looking for new names found one while viewing the character Chandler Bing, played by Matthew Perry. As with many media-influenced names, the extra boost Chandler got from the show didn't last long: The name peaked in 1999 and then rapidly receded. In 2004 there were 1,104 Chandlers born in the United States, making it the 262nd most common boys name.

Channing

English surname of uncertain meaning, but perhaps a variation of Middle English *chanun*, "clergyman."

Charles

Old German *carl*, "a man," through Latin *Carolus*. Charles has remained a consistently popular name from the time of Charlemagne (Charles the Great), the king of the Franks and emperor of the West. The name came to England with the Norman Conquest but did not become popular until the royal Stuart family began to use it. Its popularity continues today, with Charles, Prince of Wales, the heir apparent to the throne of England. In the United States, it was one of the top ten names for boys between 1830 and 1950 and still ranked 66th in 2004, although like most traditional names it is more popular east than west of the Mississippi.

Famous names: Charles Barkley (basketball player)
　　　　　　　Charles Darwin (naturalist)
　　　　　　　Charles Dickens (novelist)
　　　　　　　Charles Lindbergh (aviator)
Nicknames: **Charley, Charlie, Charly, Chick, Chuck, Chucky, Lito**
Variations: **Carl, Carlo** (Italian), **Carlos** (Portuguese and Spanish),
　　　　　　Carol (Romanian), **Carroll** (English), **Karel** (Czech), **Karl**

(German and Russian), **Karlis** (Latvian), **Karol, Karolek** (Polish), **Karolis** (Lithuanian), **Karoly** (Hungarian)

Charlie

Form of **Charles**. Charlie has always turned up regularly as an official form as well as a nickname for Charles, and during the last few years its use has been increasing. In 2004 there were 804 sons named Charlie in the United States, which made it the 317th most common boys name.
Famous name: Charlie Sheen (actor)

Charlton

Old English *Ceorlatun*, "town of freemen," from *ceorl* [freeman] + *tun* [town].
Famous name: Charlton Heston (actor and former NRA president)
Variations: **Carleton, Carlton**

Chase

Old French *chaceur*, "hunter." This surname became a popular American first name in the 1980s when Robert Foxworth played the character Chase Gioberti on the television drama *Falcon Crest*. It may have been helped by its similarity in sound to **Jason**. The name has been holding its own near the bottom of the 100 most popular names for boys since the early 1990s.

Chaz

This snappy short form of **Charles** had a minor boom as an independent given name in the late 1980s, but it's been falling since and seems destined to disappear again soon.

Chester

Old English *ceaster*, "walled town" or "fortress." As a place name, Chester dates to the Roman occupation of England, when it referred to people who lived in the *castra*, or camp.
Famous name: Chester A. Arthur (21st U.S. president)
Nicknames: **Ches, Chet**

China

The name of the country. Though most children called China in the United States are girls, award-winning British fantasy author China Miéville is definitely a man.

Chioke

Ibo (Nigeria) "gift of God." African children are traditionally seen as welcome gifts by their parents. Chioke reflects this belief, as do names from other cultures, including the Hebrew name **Jonathan,** "gift of the Lord (God)."

Chris

Shortened form of **Christian** or **Christopher.** Although Chris qualifies as a pet name, it appears independently often enough to be among the top 400 names for boys. The continued popularity of both Christopher and Christian means that Chris will be one of the most-heard male names for years to come.
Famous names: Chris Martin (rock singer)
                  Chris Rock (comedian)

Christian

Greek *kristos*, "anointed one," through Latin *Christianus*, "Christian." In England, Christian was first frequently used in the late 17th century because it is the name of the central allegorical character in John Bunyan's *Pilgrim's Progress*. The name continued to be popular throughout the 18th century, but its use declined during the 19th century. Christian boomed during the 1980s when parents in the United States rediscovered it as an alternative to **Christopher,** and since 1995 it has consistently ranked around 20th on national popularity charts. Basketball player Christian Laettner and actors Christian Bale and Christian Slater are helping to keep this name in the public eye.
Famous names: Christiaan Barnard (heart surgeon)
                  Christian Dior (fashion designer)
Nicknames: **Chris, Christ, Christy, Kit, Kris, Krys**
Variations: **Chretien** (French), **Christino, Crisciano** (Portuguese), **Cristian** (Spanish and Romanian), **Cristiano** (Italian), **Hristo** (Bulgarian), **Karsten** (Danish), **Khristian, Kristian, Kristjanis** (Latvian), **Krizas** (Lithuanian), **Krystian** (Polish)

Christopher

Greek *Kristophoros*, "Christ bearing" (one who carries Christ in his heart), through Latin *Christopherus*. The name comes from a legend of a huge, ugly, strong man named Christopher who offered to carry a small boy across a river. The child grew heavier and heavier until

Christopher thought he would drown. As the man was beginning to despair, the child revealed himself to be the Christ Child, who was carrying the world on his shoulders. No historic saint by this name exists, only the allegorical legend. Christopher is the patron saint of travelers and car drivers. In the United States, this has been one of the top ten names for boys since 1967, and it was still the eighth most common name in 2004.

Famous names: Christopher Columbus (navigator)
Christopher Reeve (actor)

Nicknames: **Chris, Christ, Christy, Kester, Kit, Kris, Kriss, Stoffel, Tobal, Tobalito, Topher**

Variations: **Christoforus** (Dutch), **Christoph** (German), **Christophe** (French), **Cristobal** (Spanish), **Cristoforo** (Italian), **Cristovao** (Portuguese), **Hristofor** (Macedonian), **Kristaps** (Latvian), **Kristof** (Slovakian and Hungarian), **Kristoffer** (Swedish)

Chuck

Pet form of **Charles**. Chuck is primarily a nickname, but it's occasionally used as a given name.

Famous name: Chuck Berry (singer)

Clarence

English, from the title of the duke of Clarence, itself from Clare, a place name in Suffolk, England, from Celtic "bright or warm stream." In Shakespeare's *Richard III,* George, duke of Clarence, is executed by his brother Edward IV and the duke of Gloucester, later Richard III. The play was often performed in the United States during the 19th century. *Clarence* was also the title of the 1830 novel by American author Catharine Maria Sedgwick, which was one of the first best-sellers written by a woman. As a result, Clarence became a popular first name and was among the top 20 names for American boys born between 1870 and 1910. Clarence maintained its popularity with African-Americans years after it had gone out of fashion with other parents, but it's rapidly going out of style with them as well; there were only 245 Clarences born in the United States in 2004.

Famous names: Clarence Darrow (lawyer)
Clarence Thomas (U.S. Supreme Court associate justice)

Nicknames: **Clair, Clare**

Clark

Greek *kleros* and Latin *clericus,* "religious person, clergyman," through English *clerk,* "scholar" or "a man of learning." When this occupational name is spelled Clark, it reflects the British pronunciation of the word "clerk." Over the centuries, the word has changed its meaning from "religious scholar" to "an employee in a shop or store." Today Clark brings to mind Clark Kent, Superman's alter ego.
Famous name: Clark Gable (actor)
Variation: **Clarke**

Claud, Claude

Latin *claudus,* "lame." This Roman family name originally described a disability. Claud was a popular name in late 19th-century America, but it's been almost completely out of fashion since then, possibly because it's too close in sound to the word *clod.* The adaptation of Robert Graves's two novels *I, Claudius* and *Claudius the God,* which became a PBS television series, made the original form of the name familiar to many Americans during the 1970s and 1980s.
Famous names: Claude Debussy (composer)
                   Claude Monet (painter)
Nicknames: **Claudy, Cloyo**
Variations: **Claudicio, Claudino, Claudio** (Portuguese, Spanish, and Italian), **Claudiu** (Romanian), **Claudius** (Dutch and English), **Klaudiusz** (Polish), **Klavdii** (Russian), **Kolos** (Hungarian)

Clay

Old English *claeg,* "clay." This surname was initially used as a first name to honor Henry Clay, a 19th-century American statesman who was the chief designer of the Missouri Compromise of 1850. In spite of the fame of Clay Aiken, from the 2003 season of *American Idol,* the number of Clays born in the United States fell by more than 25 percent between 2003 and 2004, showing that even well-liked sudden celebrities don't always have a positive effect on what new parents think of a name.

Clayton

English place name, "farm on clayey ground." This surname has been regularly used as a first name in the United States since the 1850s and is still often used today, remaining in the top 200 names for American boys.

Cleanth

Probably from the Greek proper name *Cleanthes*. Cleanthes was a stoic philosopher and the successor to Zeno. The name is rarely used today.

Clement

Latin *clemens*, "kind, gentle, mild, merciful." St. Clement was the third pope. He was martyred by drowning with an anchor tied to his neck and is the patron saint of sailors. Clement Moore was the author of the famous poem "A Visit from St. Nicholas." The name Clement is very rare in the United States, but it was a top ten name in France between 1994 and 2003.

Nicknames: **Clem, Clemmie, Menz, Te, Tente**

Variations: **Clemencio** (Spanish), **Clemente** (Italian, Spanish, and Portuguese), **Kelemen** (Hungarian), **Klemens** (German, Latvian, and Polish), **Klemensas** (Lithuanian), **Klement** (Czech and Slovakian), **Klementos** (Greek), **Kliment** (Bulgarian and Russian), **Klymentiy** (Ukrainian)

Cleve

Form of **Cleveland** or **Clive.** In the United States, Cleve is almost always short for Cleveland. Cleve Jones founded the NAMES AIDS Memorial Quilt.

Cleveland

Old English "cliff land." This surname became an American first name in honor of Grover Cleveland, the 22nd and 24th president of the United States.

Famous name: Cleveland Amory (animal rights activist)

Nickname: **Cleve**

Clifford

Old English "a stream-crossing near a cliff." Clifford became a popular name in the latter part of the 19th century, but its use has fallen off considerably during the past decade. Its image may not have been helped by Cliff Clavin, the know-it-all mail carrier character on the TV series *Cheers*.

Nicknames: **Cliff, Cliffy**

Clint

Short form of **Clinton,** which itself boomed as an official name during the 1970s, perhaps due to the fame of actor and director Clint East-wood. Clint fell off even quicker than Clinton in the 1990s, however, and in 2004 wasn't even among the top 1,000 names on the SSA list.
Famous name: Clint Black (country singer)

Clinton

English place name, "hill town," from Old Norse *klettr* [hill] + Old English *tun* [town]. The use of Clinton as a first name originally honored DeWitt Clinton, a governor of New York who helped to open up the West by building the Erie Canal. Clinton has been fairly common in the United States ever since. It rose sharply in use during the 1970s but fell off just as sharply during the 1990s because of its association with President Bill Clinton. Even those who admire Clinton now believe that names associated with politicians are a bit gauche. Only 250 boys named Clinton were born in the United States in 2004, ranking it 731st on the SSA list.
Nickname: **Clint**

Clive

Old English *clif,* "cliff." After Robert Clive conquered India, this sur-name became a well-used given name in England, but it has never caught on in the United States.
Famous names: Clive Barker (horror novelist and film producer)
Clive Owen (actor)
Variations: **Cleve, Clyve**

Clovis

(See **Louis.**)

Clyde

Celtic "river" or Welsh "heard from far away"; also, "cleansing," in reference to *Clota,* a river goddess. There is a River Clyde in Scot-land, and the Firth of Clyde is an estuary formed by that river. Clyde was a popular first name in the late 19th century, while the similar-sounding **Claud** was even more popular, but it is rarely used today.
Famous name: Clyde Cessna (airplane manufacturer)

Cody

Irish surname either from Gaelic *Cuidightheach,* "helpful person," or *Mac Oda,* "son of Otto." Cody became a first name in the American West in honor of Buffalo Bill Cody, the famous Western showman. It became fashionable west of the Mississippi in the early 1980s and rapidly spread eastward when television talk show host Kathie Lee Gifford gave birth to her son Cody in 1990 and made him a main topic of conversation on *Live with Regis and Kathie Lee.* Cody was among the top 25 names for American boys during the 1990s and, though fast decreasing, was still 81st in 2004.
Other spellings: **Kodie, Kody**

Cohen

Hebrew *kohen,* "priest." American parents have suddenly begun to use Cohen as a given name in large numbers. The name was given to 310 boys in 2004, which catapulted it onto the SSA top 1,000 list in 647th place, a very high initial entry point. Cohen therefore becomes the second Jewish surname after **Brody** to make the shift into becoming a common first name.

Colby

Old Norse "Koli's farm," English place name. Koli was an Old Norse nickname for a swarthy person. This last name came into frequent use as a first name after 1970, probably because it sounds so similar to the previously faddish **Cody** and **Colton.** Its use peaked around 1992, but it then had another sharp increase in 2001, which briefly made it one the top 100 names for American boys. This may have been due to Colby Donaldson, the photogenic runner-up on the television reality show *Survivor: The Australian Outback.* Though now receding in use again, Colby was still more popular in 2004 than it had been during the late 1990s.

Cole

Old English *col,* "coal-black"; or a form of **Nicholas.** Like **Colby,** this name rapidly increased in use as parents began to search for alternatives to popular names such as **Kyle** and **Cody,** and it's been a top 100 boys name in the United States since 1997.
Famous name: Cole Porter (musician and composer)

Coleman

Irish Gaelic *Colmán*, derived from Latin *columba*, "dove." Coleman is a name that has never been very popular but is still given with some regularity. It was absent from the SSA top 1,000 list during the 1970s, but it reappeared in the 1980s and has been steadily used ever since, with a mild peak around 1997.

Famous name: Coleman Hawkins (jazz saxophonist)

Colin

Scottish from Gaelic *Cailean*, "youth" or "cadet"; also, a medieval shortened form of **Nicholas.** A Celtic variation of the Gaelic name yields Old King Cole, a mythical king of Britain. The chief origin of Colin, however, is France, where it was a form of **Nicol.** It came to England either during or just after the Norman Conquest, and it's been in use there ever since. The breed name "collie" originated from a real Middle English dog's name, **Colle,** an old pet form of Colin. Colin has been increasing in use in the United States and was 61st on the popularity list in 2004; more than a third of parents use the spelling **Collin** to try to prevent people from pronouncing the name like "colon."

Famous names: Colin Farrell (actor)
                 Colin Powell (U.S. secretary of state)

Variations: **Col, Colan, Collie, Collin**

Colm

This is the Irish Gaelic form of *Columba,* the same Latin name that became **Callum** in Scotland. Fans of *Star Trek* will associate this name with actor Colm Meaney, who played Chief Miles O'Brien on both *The Next Generation* and *Deep Space Nine.*

Colton

Old English *colt-tun*, "town where colts are bred"; also, "Cola's or Koli's town." Colton became surprisingly popular during the 1990s, when it was among the 100 most common names for American boys. Some parents may have seen it as a more formal version of Colt, a name that received much exposure during the 1980s when Lee Majors played stuntman Colt Seavers on the television series *The Fall Guy.* Colton ranked 119th in 2004.

Nickname: **Colt**

Columbus

Anglicized form of *Colón,* Spanish surname from Latin "dove." Admiration for the explorer Christopher Columbus made this a fairly common boys name in the late 19th century, but it's been hard to find examples of boys named Columbus born since the 1950s.

Conan

Irish Gaelic *Conán,* "hound, wolf," the name of six Irish saints. This rare name brings to mind the contrasting images of Conan the Barbarian and late-night television host Conan O'Brien.

Conor, Connor

Irish Gaelic *Conchobar,* "wolf-lover." This has been a popular name in Ireland since the Middle Ages and was borne by several early Irish kings. Connor's popularity is soaring in the United States; it rose from 191st to 29th place as a name for American boys between 1989 and 2004, but the reasons for this are obscure. It certainly appeals to parents looking for a name with a romantic Irish history. Connor Trinneer is the actor who played Commander Charles "Trip" Tucker III on *Enterprise,* the most recent series in the *Star Trek* television empire. Famous name: Conor Cruise O'Brien (Irish statesman and author) Other spelling: **Conner**

Conrad

Form of **Konrad.**
Famous name: Conrad Anker (mountain climber)

Cooper

Middle English *couper,* "maker of barrels and vats." This occupational surname first entered the SSA top 1,000 list in 1983 and has been steadily rising since, reaching 136th place in 2004, when more than 3,000 Coopers were born.

Corbin

Old French "little raven." There is little doubt that actor Corbin Bernsen introduced this name to American parents. He became well known when television's *L.A. Law* began in the fall of 1986, and Corbin jumped onto the SSA top 1,000 list at 590th place in 1987. The name stagnated for about five years after the show ended in 1994, but then it began to rise again with the present fashion for boys names ending in *–n*. More than 1,400 Corbins were born in 2004, ranking it 220th.

Cordell

English surname from Old French *Cordele,* "little cord," perhaps originally a nickname for a maker or wearer of strings or ribbons. Cordell Hull was the U.S. secretary of state from 1933 until 1945, and he won the Nobel Peace Prize in 1945 for his work in helping to found the United Nations. Cordell first entered the SSA top 1,000 list for boys in 1933, and it has been on and off that list ever since, never becoming very common but never vanishing for any lengthy period. Cordell's accent on the second syllable has contributed to its being especially popular with African-Americans.

Corentin

Breton *Kaourintin,* name of a medieval saint and bishop in Brittany; the meaning of his name is unknown. There is a legend that St. Corentin possessed a magic fish that he cut a slice from every day and ate, and that the fish was found whole again every morning. Corentin was a popular name throughout France in the late 1990s.

Corey, Cory

Old Norse *Kori* or Irish Gaelic *Comhraide,* both of unknown meaning. Corey became common as a first name for African-American boys in the late 1960s because of Corey Baker (played by Marc Copage), the title character's son on *Julia,* and probably the first African-American child featured on an American television series. In 1991, Corey was 33rd on the list of names given to American boys, but it had fallen to 148th by 2004.

Famous names: Corey Feldman (actor)
                  Corey Pavin (golfer)

Other spellings: **Korey, Kory**

Cornelius

From an old Roman family name, possibly from Latin *cornu,* "horn." Cornelius used to be especially common among Irish-Americans, because in Ireland it was the traditional substitute for *Conchobar* (see **Connor**) during the centuries when the English rulers of Ireland frowned on the use of Gaelic names. Most Irish-Americans stopped using the name around 1970, but for a while it was saved from obscurity by being taken up strongly in the African-American community. Today it's swiftly vanishing. The most famous Cornelius today is still the 19th-century railroad magnate Cornelius Vanderbilt.

Cortez

Spanish *cortés,* "courteous," the Spanish counterpart to **Curtis.** Cortez is one of the few Spanish surnames ever to become a well-used first name in the United States. Its vogue began, especially in the African-American community, in the 1980s, and it peaked around 1990. Today it is receding and may disappear soon.

Courtney

Middle English *de Curtenay* from *Courtenay,* Norman French place name, "short one's manor." Although Courtney is now an extremely popular name for girls, it has also regularly been given to African-American boys. An example is Harvard graduate Courtney B. Vance, who plays assistant district attorney Ron Carver on *Law & Order: Criminal Intent.*

Craig

Celtic *creag,* "crag." This Scottish surname became popular as a given name during the 1950s. It remained quite popular through the 1970s but is now rapidly going out of style. Since Craig Ferguson followed Craig Kilborn as the host of *The Late, Late Show* in 2005, Craig may be the favorite name of insomniacs.
Variation: **Cragg**

Creed

English surname from *Creoda,* a rare Old English name of unknown meaning; Creoda was the first king of Mercia in central England. Some modern parents may interpret this name as being from the vocabulary word, from Latin *credo,* "I believe."

Creek

It was inevitable that this word would show up as a "nature name" once **River** and **Lake** were well established.

Creighton

Variation of **Crichton,** name of a town in Scotland, possibly from Gaelic *crioch,* "boundary," and Old English *tun,* "farm, settlement." Creighton is starting to get a bit of notice as a "different but not too different" alternative for names like **Dayton** and **Brayden.** The name is perhaps best known through Creighton University.

Crispin

Latin *Crispinus,* derived from *Crispus,* "curly-haired." St. Crispin was a third-century Christian martyr of Rome who was popular in England in the Middle Ages.
Famous name: Crispin Glover (actor)

Cruz

Spanish "cross." Though this name is sometimes used for girls in Spain, Hispanic-Americans overwhelmingly prefer it for boys. Lately the name has been on a decided upswing.
Famous name: Cruz Bustamante (California politician)

Cuba

Name of the largest Caribbean island, perhaps from a Taino (Native American) word meaning "central place."
Famous name: Cuba Gooding, Jr. (actor)

Cullen

This name has several distinct origins. In Ireland it's a surname from either *Cuileann,* "holly," or *Coileán,* "little dog." In Scotland it's from a place name meaning "little nook," and in England it's a surname meaning one's ancestors came from the German city of Cologne. As a first name, Cullen entered the SSA top 1,000 list in 1974 and rose slowly and steadily until it hit a mild peak in 1997, when it began to slowly fall away again.

Curt

Form of **Curtis** or **Kurt.**
Famous name: Curt Schilling (baseball pitcher)

Curtis

Old French *corteis,* "courteous." Shakespeare used this name for one of the characters in *Taming of the Shrew.* Curtis was fairly common during the 1950s and 1960s, but it has now fallen away dramatically to rank at 290th place in 2004.
Famous name: Curtis Strange (golfer)
Nicknames: **Curt, Kurt**
Other spelling: **Curtiss**

Cy

Nickname for **Cyril** or **Cyrus**. This nickname has become a name in its own right, possibly because of its association with Cy Young, an outstanding baseball pitcher whose name was given to an annual award for the best pitcher in both the American and National Leagues.
Famous name: Cy Twombly (artist)

Cyril

Greek *kyrios*, "lord, master." There have been several saints with this name. The most famous St. Cyril, "Apostle to the Slavs," is credited with inventing the Cyrillic alphabet that is still used in Russia and other Slavic countries.
Nicknames: **Cy, Cyrek** (Czech), **Lilo**
Variations: **Kiril** (Bulgarian), **Kirill** (Russian), **Kyrylo** (Ukrainian)

Cyrus

Persian *Kurush*, perhaps from *kuru*, "throne," through Greek *Kyros*, referring to the great Persian king mentioned in the Old Testament. King Cyrus befriended the Israelites and issued a proclamation allowing them to return to the Holy Land. The name Cyrus rose from 829th to 511th on the SSA list between 1990 and 2004. It may appeal to parents looking for an alternative to names like **Tyler** and **Kyle** with more historical depth.
Famous name: Cyrus McCormick (inventor)
Nickname: **Cy**
Variations: **Ciro** (Portuguese, Italian, and Spanish), **Kyros** (Greek)

Dakarai

Shona (Zimbabwe) "Rejoice!" This African name parallels English names such as **Joy.**

Dakota

Name of an American Indian nation; later the name of two states in the northern Great Plains. The names of almost all the American states have been used as given names from time to time, but Dakota is the first one to become generally popular. Although its *–a* ending would normally make it thought of as a girls name by most English speakers, the masculine image of the West overshadows this; the name sounds as if it were originally a nickname for a cowboy from the Dakotas. Dakota flourished all over the United States during the 1990s, and though now starting to recede it was still among the top 150 names given to American boys in 2004. More than twice as many boys than girls are given this name each year.

Dale

Old English *dael,* "valley, hollow." This place name first became a surname and then a given name. Dale is still primarily a male name in the United States, though it is now becoming unusual, falling to 602nd on the SSA list in 2004.
Famous names: Dale Chihuly (blown-glass sculptor)
　　　　　　Dale Earnhardt Sr. & Jr. (NASCAR drivers)
Other Spelling: **Dayle**

Dallas

Old English *dalhous,* "house in the valley"; also, Scottish place name, "meadow house." As a boys first name Dallas peaked in both 1935 and 1995, an unusual pattern. It ranked 323rd in 2004. Because of Dallas, Texas (named for George Mifflin Dallas, vice president of the United States under James K. Polk) the name evokes the Old West.

Famous name: Dallas Wayne (country singer)

Dallin

Form of *Dalling*, English place name and surname, "Dalla's people's place." Dallin is one of the few names on the top 1,000 list that owes its ranking to a religious community. It is extremely popular in Utah and other areas with large Mormon populations because of admiration for Dallin H. Oaks, a former president of Brigham Young University who became a member of the Council of Twelve, the ruling body of the Church of Jesus Christ of Latter-day Saints, in 1984. Dallin entered the SSA list in 1993, and though it is receding in popularity, it may have a greater future if non-Mormons discover it as another fashionable "two syllables ending in *–n*" name for boys.

Dalton

Old English *daeltun*, "valley farm." This place name developed first into a surname and later into a first name. Dalton quickly became common during the 1990s, when it was among the top 100 names for boys in the United States, but by 2004 it had fallen to 163rd.

Famous name: Dalton Trumbo (novelist)

Damian, Damien

Greek *damazein*, "to tame." Several saints were named Damian, including St. Damian, who became widely known for his healing powers and medical skills. Along with his brother, St. Cosmas, he is the patron saint of doctors. This made it an appropriate name for Father Damien, the famous missionary to Hawaiian lepers. Damian also appears in Sir Walter Scott's *Ivanhoe*, in which Scott gave the name to a young man studying for Holy Orders. Damian has been steadily rising in use in the United States since around 1975 and was one of the top 100 names of 2004, despite its use as the name of the Antichrist in the *Omen* film series.

Nicknames: **Dame, Damek** (Polish)

Variations: **Damiano** (Italian), **Damon, Demyan** (Russian and Ukrainian)

Damon

Classical Greek form of **Damian**. Damon is best known from the ancient Greek legend of Damon and Pythias, two friends who were

willing to lay down their lives for each other. Their story has been retold many times in books and plays as the finest example of human loyalty. The name Damon became popular in the late 1960s, especially with African-American parents, and it was still among the top 300 names overall in the United States in 2004.
Famous name: Damon Runyon (writer)
Variations: **Dame, Damian, Damien** (English)

Dan

Hebrew "judge"; also, a form of **Daniel.** In the Old Testament, Dan is the son of Jacob; his mother was Bilhah, Rachel's maid. Because of this biblical character, Dan has sometimes been used as a separate name since Puritan times and is not always thought of as a nickname for Daniel. The most famous Dan today is undoubtedly Dan Brown, author of the best-selling novel *The Da Vinci Code.*
Famous name: Dan Rather (TV newscaster)
Nicknames: **Dannie, Danny**

Dana

Perhaps Old English "a Dane." This rare surname became a male given name in the 19th century in honor of Richard Henry Dana, Jr., author of *Two Years Before the Mast.* Because it ends in *–a,* Dana had already become more common for girls than boys in the early 1940s when the fame of Hollywood leading man Dana Andrews reversed that. Between 1947 and 1954, more boys than girls were named Dana, and it took another four decades for Dana to disappear from the SSA top 1,000 list for boys.
Famous name: Dana Carvey (comedian)

Dane

Middle English, "a dane," or Old English, "a valley."
Famous name: Dane Clark (actor)

Daniel

Hebrew "God is my judge." In the Old Testament, Daniel refused to obey an order of Darius of Persia and so was thrown into a den of lions. He was saved through the intercession of God. This well-known biblical story has assured the popularity of the name, especially in Protestant countries. In the United States, Daniel has ranked in or near the top ten names given to boys for the last 20 years.

Famous names: Daniel Boone (pioneer)
Daniel K. Inouye (U.S. senator)
Daniel Webster (statesman)
Nicknames: **Dan, Dannie, Danny**
Variations: **Danielek** (Polish), **Danielus** (Lithuanian), **Daniil** (Greek and Romanian), **Danilo** (Serbian), **Danko** (Czech), **Danylo** (Ukrainian)

Dannie, Danny

Forms of **Dan** or **Daniel**. Danny is frequently given as an official name in its own right, especially in the American South.
Famous names: Danny DeVito (actor)
Danny Glover (actor)

Dante

Italian *durante*, "lasting." This Italian name is closely associated with Dante Alighieri, the author of the *Divina Commedia*. Today it is a popular name with African-Americans, who often spell it Donte or Dontay.
Famous name: Dante Gabriel Rossetti (artist)
Variations: **Dontay, Donte, Durand, Durante**

Daquan, Dequan

Probably an African-American creation, although both of these spellings turn up frequently as Chinese names. Without knowing the Chinese characters the names are written with, it's impossible to give a meaning. Both spellings have been in regular use in the African-American community since at least 1978.

Darian, Darien, Darion

Darien is the name of the eastern part of Panama; the name comes from the Spanish designation for a Native American tribe now called the Chucunaques, and its original meaning is unknown. Though Darien was the most common spelling of the given name when it first appeared on the SSA list in 1965, Darian quickly eclipsed it, showing that the sound of the name is more important to parents than any geographical connection. It has probably been seen as a slightly more sophisticated version of **Darren**. The name peaked in use in the mid-1990s and has receded a bit since, but when the three spellings are counted together it was still the 304th most common boys name of 2004.

Dario

Spanish *Darío* and Italian *Dàrio,* forms of **Darius.** Italian playwright Dàrio Fo won the 1997 Nobel Prize for literature. In spite of his Italian name, Indy racecar driver Dario Franchitti is a Scotsman. Dario has been increasing in use lately in both Hispanic-American and Italian-American families.

Darius

Latin form of Persian *Darayavahush,* "he who upholds the good." Darius the Great, ruler of the Persian empire (522–486 B.C.), allowed the Jews to rebuild the temple in Jerusalem. His prominence in the Old Testament led some of the early Puritans to give this name to their sons. In the 20th century, Darius has been most popular in the African-American community. Though that popularity peaked around 1991, the name was given frequently enough in 2004 to rank among the top 300 names for boys in the United States.
Famous names: Darius Kasparaitis (hockey player)
                  Darius Rucker (singer)
Variation: **Darío** (Spanish), **Dàrio** (Italian)

Darl

Form of **Darryl,** or masculine form of **Darlene.**

Darnell

English surname from Old French *darnel,* a type of grass, perhaps for someone who lived by a field where it grew. It may be a coincidence, but Darnell first entered the SSA top 1,000 list in 1939, the same year the film actress Linda Darnell (1923–1965) made her first picture. Parents may have seen the name as an updated version of **Darrell.** Like most male names accented on the second syllable, Darnell has been especially common in the African-American community. The name slowly rose and declined regularly in use, peaking in 1984 when 740 boys were given the name. In 2004, only 267 American boys were named Darnell, ranking it 707th on the SSA list.

Darrell

Form of **Darryl,** now the most common spelling.
Famous names: Darrell Hammond (comedian)
                  Darrell Waltrip (NASCAR driver)

Darren

Probably from Irish Gaelic *Dubhdara,* perhaps meaning "black oak"; this would have originally been a nickname for a strong or stouthearted person. This name was virtually unheard of until actor Darren McGavin began appearing in movies and on television during the 1950s. Between 1964 and 1972, the name was also featured as that of Darrin Stephens, the mortal husband on the television series *Bewitched.* The program and the name were soon exported to England, where Darren became much more popular than it had ever been in the United States; it was a top ten name in England and Wales throughout the 1970s. Although Darren has been a well-used name in the United States since the 1960s, it had fallen to 249th place by 2004.
Other spellings: **Daren, Darin, Darrin, Darron**

Darryl, Daryl

Middle English *deAyrel,* "from Airelle," a town in northern France. Darrel was originally a Norman French surname that was often used by English and American novelists around 1900 because of its aristocratic air. When Darryl F. Zanuck later helped found 20th Century Fox and became Hollywood's most famous movie producer, he inspired thousands of other parents to give his name to their sons. Darryl became especially popular with African-American parents, and it was second only to Michael as a black male name in the 1960s. In the 1980s, the mute brothers Darryl and Darryl got lots of laughs on *Newhart.* However, their name is rapidly vanishing from the list of popular baby names today.
Famous name: Darryl Worley (country music singer)
Other spellings: **Darrel, Darrell, Daryle**
Variation: **Darl**

Darwin

Old English *Deorwine,* "dear friend." Charles Darwin published his classic work *The Origin of the Species* in 1859, but his surname did not develop any frequency as a given name in the United States until after 1910. It rose quickly over the next two decades and peaked in use in 1938 at 297th place on the SSA list. After that it fell steadily until it briefly dropped off the list in 1995. Since 2001, however, it looks likes Darwin has been starting to slowly come back into fashion.

Dave

Short form of **David.**

Famous name: Dave Barry (humorist)

David

Hebrew *Dodavehu,* "darling or beloved of God"; originally a lullaby word. David fell below the American top ten list for boys in 1990 after being there for more than 50 years, but it was still 15th in 2004. In the Bible, David was the second king of Israel and the author of many of the Psalms. While he was still a boy, he killed the giant Goliath. Charles Dickens used the name for the title character of *David Copperfield.* David Duchovny, David Hasselhoff, David Hyde Pierce, and David Schwimmer are all actors who've made names for themselves on American television programs.

Famous names: David Letterman (late-night TV host)

David Livingstone (explorer)

Nicknames: **Dave, Davey**

Variations: **Davide** (Italian), **Davyd** (Russian and Ukranian), **Dawid** (Polish and Yiddish), **Dewey, Dovydas** (Lithuanian), **Taavetti** (Finnish)

Davin

Irish Gaelic *Daimíne,* "deer," or *Damán,* "little stag." It's also possible that Davin is sometimes used as a modern invention blending **David** and **Kevin.** Davin entered the SSA top 1,000 list in 1969 and stayed at the same low level of use until it increased by about 50 percent in the last few years. Still, there were fewer than 400 Davins born in the United States in 2004, so the name is far from being overused.

Davion, Davian

Davion is a rare French surname based on a medieval pet form of **David,** but this name has probably been re-created by modern parents blending David and **Darian.** Davion first entered the SSA top 1,000 list in 1991 and has steadily grown more popular, ranking 318th in 2004 with almost 800 boys given the name.

Dawson

Middle English *Daweson,* "son of **David.**" A few American parents discovered Dawson as a "different but not too different" name in the early 1990s as the trend for boys names ending in –n began, and it first entered the SSA top 1,000 list in 1994. By 1997 it had increased by 30 percent, but then in 1998 there were suddenly nine times the number of Dawsons born, which made it 175th on the SSA list that year. The engines of this rise were the film *Titanic*, which opened in December 1997 with Leonardo DiCaprio playing Jack Dawson, and the television series *Dawson's Creek*, which began in January 1998 with James Van Der Beek in the role of Dawson Leery. The name peaked in 1999 and by 2004 had fallen back 40 percent, to 196th place, with about 1,750 babies given the name.

Dayton

English surname, probably a variation of the place name *Deighton*, "farmstead surrounded by a ditch." Like **Trenton** and **Camden,** Dayton is another example of a midsize American city that has inspired many parents to name sons after it because the name fits in with the sound patterns now in vogue. It first entered the SSA top 1,000 in 1990 and has slowly risen; it ranked 504th on the list in 2004, with nearly 500 American newborn boys given the name.

Deacon

Old English *deacon*, "church deacon." Until recently, Deacon was more often a nickname for a pious person than a given name. But the search for boys names that fit the "two syllables ending in *—n*" pattern led to its discovery by modern parents, and it showed up on the SSA top 1,000 list for the first time in 2004, in 892nd place.
Famous name: Deacon Jones (football player)

Dean

Greek *deka*, "ten," through Middle English *deen*, "leader of ten" (from which dean of a college derives); also, Old English *dene*, "valley." Famous name: Dean Koontz (horror writer)
Nickname: **Dino**
Other spelling: **Deane**

DeAndre

This is the most common of the many African-American names for boys formed by putting the prefix *De-* in front of another name. Such forms began to occur regularly in the 1970s and were at their height of popularity in the 1980s. They have receded today, but DeAndre was still among the top 350 names for all American boys

born in 2004. Other popular *De-* forms include DeAngelo, DeJuan, DeMarco, DeMarcus, DeMario, DeMarion, and DeShawn.
Other spellings: **Deondray, Deondre**

Declan

Irish Gaelic *Declán,* meaning unknown. This was the name of a saint who founded the monastery of Ardmore in Ireland. The name Declan was popular in Ireland a generation ago but is out of fashion there now. However, Irish-Americans have recently discovered it, and it entered the SSA list for the first time in 1998. This was the year after Richard Gere had played Declan Mulqueen in the thriller film *The Jackal,* but that might be a coincidence. Declan was the 382nd most common name of 2004, and its similarity to other fashionable names like **Donovan** and **Dylan** bodes well for its future popularity.

Dee

Welsh "holy one." Dee is also often a nickname for names that begin with the letter *D*. Dee Brown is the author of the classic work on American Indian history *Bury My Heart at Wounded Knee.*

Delbert

Variation of *Adelbert,* the Dutch form of **Albert.** This American name first developed in upstate New York among descendants of the original Dutch settlers of New Netherland. It was fairly popular between 1900 and 1940 but is very rare today.
Nicknames: **Bert, Del**

Demetrius

Greek "belonging to Demeter, the Earth Mother, goddess of fertility." This name was extremely popular with African-Americans in the 1980s and 1990s and was still among the top 400 boys names in the United States in 2004.
Variations: **Demetrio** (Spanish and Italian), **Dimitri, Dmitri** (Russian), **Dumitru** (Romanian)

Dennis

French *Denys* from Latin *Dionysius* and Greek *Dionusios,* the god of Nysa, a Greek mountain, and the god of wine. St. Dennis is first mentioned in the Book of Acts as Dionysius the Areopagite. According to tradition, he was the first bishop of Athens and was martyred during the persecution of Christians in A.D. 95. The name also belonged to several other saints and a pope. As a first name, Dennis was extremely popular in the United States during the 1940s and 1950s, but its use has since faded, perhaps because of its identification with the mischievous comic strip character Dennis the Menace.

Famous names: Dennis Hastert (speaker, U.S. House of Rep.)
Dennis Hopper (actor)

Nicknames: **Den, Denny**

Other spelling: **Denys**

Variations: **Denes** (Hungarian), **Denis** (French), **Dion, Dionisio** (Spanish and Portuguese), **Dionigi** (Italian), **Dionisiy** (Russian), **Dionizy** (Polish), **Dionys** (German), **Dionysios** (Greek), **Dwight**

Denver

English surname and place name, "ford of the Danes." Denver, Colorado, was named after James Denver, who was governor of the Kansas territory (where the site was then located) at the city's founding in 1858. As a first name, Denver was most popular in the 1920s; it fell off the SSA top 1,000 list in 2002 after a long decline.

Famous name: Denver Pyle (actor)

Denzel

Either from *Denzell,* a Cornish place name of obscure meaning, or from a German surname meaning "dancer." There's little doubt that the modern vogue for this name is associated with the career of Denzel Washington. The name first entered the SSA top 1,000 list in 1990, the year after Washington earned his first Oscar nomination for the film *Glory.* Denzel was most common in the early 1990s, but it was still 751st on the SSA list in 2004.

Deon

Form of **Dion.**

Derek

Dutch *Diederick* or *Direk* from Old German *Theodoric, theuda* [people] + *ricja* [rule]. This name came to England during the 15th century when there was an increased flow of trade with the Dutch. It was used only sporadically until the late 20th century, when it suddenly became very popular.

Famous name: Derek Walcott (winner of the 1992 Nobel Prize for literature)

Variations: **Dederick, Dereck, Derrick, Dieter, Dietrich** (German), **Dirk** (Dutch), **Theodorick**

Dermot

Irish Gaelic *Diarmait,* name of an ancient hero considered the "greatest lover in Irish literature."

Famous name: Dermot Mulroney (actor)

Variation: **Derry**

Derrick

Form of **Derek.** This spelling is particularly popular with African-Americans.

Famous name: Derrick Coleman (basketball player)

Derry

Short form of **Dermot;** also, an Irish place name, perhaps meaning "oaks."

Desmond

Irish Gaelic *Desmumhnach,* "man from South Munster." Desmond Tutu, Anglican archbishop of Cape Town, South Africa, won the Nobel Peace Prize in 1984. His name had been rising in use in the United States since the 1950s; it peaked in 1992 and has fallen off since. It was the 406th most popular boys name of 2004, with more than 500 Desmonds born that year.

Famous name: Desmond Morris (zoologist and ethologist)

Destin

American surname of unknown origin. The Gulf Coast resort city of Destin, Florida, is named after Leonard Destin, who moved to the area around 1845 from New London, Connecticut. Perhaps his surname is a variation of **Destan,** a French surname from Old French *d'estang,* "by the pond." Destin first entered the SSA list in 1994. Parents may have seen it as an updated version of **Dustin** or perhaps a male form of the very popular girls name **Destiny.** But Destin's time in the sun was short-lived; after peaking at 706th on the SSA list in 1999, it dropped to 992nd in 2004.

Devin, Devon

Irish Gaelic *daimine*, "fawn"; Old French *devin*, "excellent"; or an English county name, "land of the Dumnonii tribe." Both spellings are pronounced the same by white Americans as they are in Britain, but African-Americans often accent Devon on the second syllable. Both spellings are now used for boys and girls in the United States.
Variation: **Davon**

DeVonte

African-American creation blending **Devon** and **Dante.** In 1991 the R&B singing group Jodeci burst upon the scene. Between 1991 and 1995 they had ten Top Ten hits. The lead singer of the group, Donald DeGrate, Jr., was known by his stage name, DeVante Swing. His name was as much of a sudden hit as his songs; in 1992 the forms **DeVante,** DeVonte, **DaVante,** and **DaVonte** were all in the SSA top 1,000 and together were one of the top ten names for African-American boys. Like many names that are such sudden successes, however, DeVante immediately began to recede from its initial high point, and by 2004 DeVonte was the only spelling still on the SSA top 1,000 list. In the future, it will be easier to correctly guess the age of a DeVonte than that of a man with almost any other name.

Dewey

Perhaps a form of *Dewi*, Welsh variation of **David.** This name was often used in the 19th century, but it is now known mostly as the name of one of Donald Duck's nephews.
Nickname: **Dew**

Dexter

Old English *deghstre*, "dyer." By pure coincidence, this English surname has the same form as Latin *dexter*, meaning "right-handed" or "skillful," and occasionally parents who know Latin may choose it for that reason.
Famous name: Dexter Gordon (jazz saxophonist)
Nickname: **Dex**

Dick

Form of **Benedict or Richard.** Dick Whittington was the orphan boy who became the mayor of London.
Famous name: Dick Butkus (football player)

Diego

Originally a medieval Spanish form of *Didakos,* a Greek name meaning "student," but interpreted in Spain for centuries as a form of **Santiago.** Diego has been climbing in popularity with Hispanic-Americans recently. It was the 80th most popular boys name in the United States in 2004.

Famous names: Diego Maradona (soccer player)
                   Diego Rivera (muralist)

Dieter, Dietrich

(See **Derek.**)

Dillon

(See **Dylan.**)

Dimitri

Russian form of **Demetrius.** This may be a soap-opera-influenced name, as both the nighttime *Knots Landing* and daytime *All My Children* introduced characters named Dimitri in the early 1990s, just when American parents first really started to use the name. It's been falling in use rapidly since 1997, however, and may disappear again soon. Dmitri Mendeleev (1834–1907) was the chemist who created the periodic table of the elements.

Dion

Form of **Dennis.** This is now a fairly popular name with African-Americans, although the spelling **Deon** is slightly more common. Dion was one of Plato's students who became the ruler of Syracuse in 356 B.C.

Famous name: Dion (musician)

Diro

Armenian "gift of God."

Dodge

(See **Roger.**)

Dominic

Latin *dominicus,* "of the Lord"; usually refers to the Lord's day, Sunday, and was given to children born on that day. This name began to be used in England in the 13th century, influenced by the fame of

St. Dominic, founder of the Order of Preachers, known now as the Dominican Order. Dominic has been rising in use lately and ranked 70th among the names given to boys in the United States in 2004. It remains especially popular with Italian-Americans.

Nicknames: **Dom, Mingo, Nick, Nicki, Nickie, Nicky, Nik**

Variations: **Domenico** (Italian), **Domingo** (Spanish), **Domingos** (Portuguese), **Dominick** (English), **Dominik** (Polish and Russian), **Dominiks** (Latvian), **Dominique** (French), **Domonkos** (Hungarian)

Dominique

French form of **Dominic**. This became a popular name with African-Americans because of basketball player Dominique Wilkins, who was born in France while his father was stationed there with the U.S. Army and was named by his French nanny.

Don

Form of **Donald**. This name is primarily a nickname, but occasionally it may refer to the Spanish title, which is the equivalent of "mister" in English, or to the Italian title, which is the equivalent of "lord."

Famous name: Don Rickles (comedian)

Donald

Scots Gaelic *Domhnall* and Old Irish *Domnall,* "world mighty." This name was popular in both England and the United States between 1915 and 1965. King Donald was the first Christian king of Scotland. Wealthy real estate developer Donald Trump increased his considerable fame with the reality television show *The Apprentice*.

Famous name: Donald Sutherland (actor)

Nicknames: **Don, Donnie**

Variations: **Donaldas** (Lithuanian), **Donaldo** (Italian), **Donnell** (Irish)

Donnell

Irish form of **Donald,** very popular with African-American parents between 1960 and 1990.

Donovan

Irish Gaelic *Donndubán,* "dark brown swarthy one." This Irish surname was used as a first name by the now-forgotten British author Edna Lyall in her 1882 novel *Donovan* and its best-selling 1884 sequel *We Two*. As a result, Donovan was established as an infrequent but regularly used name in the United States from 1900 onward. The name had an upswing in use at the height of Scottish singer Donovan's fame in the late 1960s. It drifted downward a bit in the 1970s until it was about the 500th most common name and then started a slow but steady climb up the popularity charts in 1983, leading to its position at 170th for boys born in 2004. It's probable that many young parents today are using Donovan as a way to name sons after older relatives called **Donald** while updating that name's image.

Other spelling: **Donavan**

Dorian

This name was invented by Oscar Wilde for the tragic hero of his 1891 novel *The Portrait of Dorian Gray*. He undoubtedly took it from the adjective "Dorian," referring to the earliest Greek-speaking settlers of what is now southern Greece. Dorian is a "stealth" name, never very popular but among the top 1,000 names on the SSA list since 1961. Its use jumped sharply in 2000, perhaps because of the character Dorian on the television series *Moesha*. There were 583 Dorians born in the United States in 2004, ranking it 388th.

Famous name: Dorian Yates (bodybuilder)

Doug

Form of **Douglas,** given fairly often as an independent name in the 1960s but very rare today.

Famous name: Doug Flutie (football player)

Douglas

Gaelic *Dubhglas,* "dark blue stream." Douglas was originally the name of a river and later of a Scottish clan. The Douglas clan in Scotland dates back to at least the eighth century. Shakespeare depicts Archibald, the earl of Douglas, as one of the Scottish conspirators against Henry IV in *Henry the Fourth, Part One*. The name was used for both boys and girls in England during the 17th century, and it only became widely popular for boys after 1920.

Famous names: Douglas Fairbanks, Jr. (actor)
Douglas MacArthur (general)

Nicknames: **Doug, Dougie**
Other spelling: **Douglass**

Doyle

Irish Gaelic *Ó Dubhghaill*, "descendant of the dark stranger."

Draco

Latin "dragon" from Greek *drákon*. The name of a circumpolar constellation, but also the name of an ancient Athenian who, around 620 B.C., wrote a code of laws for the city mandating extremely severe penalties; this is where the modern word "draconian" comes from. Of course modern children will identify the name with Draco Malfoy, Harry Potter's chief persecutor.

Drake

Old English *draca*, "dragon." Drake has been steadily increasing in popularity for more than 20 years, reaching 246th place for American boys born in 2004.

Draven

The 1994 film *The Crow* has become one of the biggest "cult movie" successes of all time, in part because its star, Brandon Lee, was accidentally killed during its filming. The film itself was based on a series of underground comic books by James O'Barr about a man named Eric who is resurrected by a magical crow after his murder to become an invulnerable avenging superhero. The screenwriters of the film gave Eric the surname Draven, undoubtedly created from the words "dark raven" to reinforce the theme of the film. The coolness factor of the character combined with how the name fit in with the fashionable sounds of the time immediately caused parents to begin using the name for their sons. Draven flew onto the SSA top 1,000 list in 1995 and has never left, and, unlike many other celebrity-inspired names, it continues to grow in use.

Drew

Old German *Drogo*, "carry" or "ghost"; also, French *Dru*, "favorite"; also, a form of **Andrew**. This name was first introduced in England at the time of the Norman Conquest by Dru, a companion of William the Conqueror, and it has been in use ever since. In spite of Andrew's continued popularity, Drew has been drifting downward recently. It was the 200th most common name for boys in 2004.
Famous name: Drew Carey (comedian)
Other spelling: **Dru**

Dryden

English surname meaning "dry valley." Dryden probably became a given name first in honor of the English poet John Dryden (1631–1700).

Drystan

(See **Tristram.**)

Duane

Irish Gaelic *Dubhain,* form of *dubh,* "black." This name was moderately popular in the United States from 1945 through 1965, but it has since developed a working-class image and has fallen out of fashion.
Famous name: Duane Eddy (musician)
Other spellings: **Dwain, Dwayne**
Variations: **DeWayne, Doane**

Dumisani

IsiZulu (South Africa) "give praises."

Duncan

Scottish form of Old Irish *Dunecan,* "brown warrior." This name has always been associated with the Scots, although it has figured prominently in Icelandic sagas. King Duncan I of Scotland is best known outside Scotland as the king who is assassinated by the power-hungry Macbeth in Shakespeare's tragedy. In the mid-1990s, it seemed briefly that Duncan might become fashionable in the United States, but since 1998 its minor vogue has been fading.
Famous name: Duncan Hines (gourmet)
Nicknames: **Dun, Dunc**
Variation: **Dunkanas** (Lithuanian)

Dustin

Perhaps a Norman French form of Old Norse *Thorsteinn,* "Thor's stone." Dustin was a top 50 name in the United States from the late 1970s until 1990, undoubtedly because of the fame of actor Dustin Hoffman, who was himself named after Dustin Farnum, a silent-movie star who acted mostly in Westerns. Since 1990 the name's popularity has quickly faded, and Dustin was only the 213th most common name in 2004.

Dwight

Probably Middle English *Diot,* a form of *Dionysus* (see **Dennis**). This name has never been popular in England. As a surname, it emigrated to the United States from England in the 17th century and became an American first name in honor of Timothy Dwight, an early president of Yale University. It received its greatest use in the 1950s because of the popularity of Dwight D. Eisenhower (the 34th U.S. president), but use of this name has fallen greatly in recent years.
Famous name: Dwight Yoakam (country music singer)

Dylan

Welsh "of the sea." Dylan was the Welsh god of the ocean waves. A popular name in Wales, it only began to be used in the United States in the 1950s, mostly through the influence of the singer Bob Dylan, who took his name from the Welsh poet Dylan Thomas. Its popularity had been slowly increasing until 1991, when the number of Dylans born in the United States suddenly tripled in two years. This was undoubtedly due to the character Dylan McKay on the popular television series *Beverly Hills, 90210.* However, about 15 percent of parents use the spelling **Dillon,** which may mean that baby boomers are also remembering the character of Marshal Matt Dillon from *Gunsmoke.* (Dillon is an English and Irish surname with at least five different origins.) In any event, Dylan in all its spellings has continued to increase in use, if at a somewhat slower rate, and it was the 19th most common name for American boys born in 2004.
Famous name: Dylan McDermott (actor)
Nickname: **Dyl**
Variations: **Dillon, Dylon**

Dyson

Medieval English "son of *Dye,*" a pet form of Dionysia, the medieval female form of **Dennis.** This is one of the few surnames based on a mother's rather than a father's name.

Eagle

Middle English *egle*, the name of the bird. This name qualifies as both a "patriotic name" and a "nature name."

Eamon

(See **Edmond.**)

Earl

Old English *Eorl*, "noble man or warrior." This royal title was often used as a given name in the United States between 1870 and 1940, but it is now out of fashion, ranking only 943rd on the SSA list in 2004. Among English nobility, the title indicates a rank between marquis and viscount and corresponds to the title of count in other countries.

Famous name: Earl Warren (U.S. Supreme Court chief justice)

Variations: **Earle, Erl, Erle**

Easton

English place name and surname, "eastern farmstead or village." As **Weston** became a popular name, American parents inevitably discovered Easton as an alternative. The number of Eastons born in the United States has more than quadrupled since 1990, and by 2004 it was among the top 400 names for sons.

Eaton

English surname from one of many place names meaning either "farm on a river" or "farm on an island." The alternative spelling **Eton** has upper-crust associations because of the famous British boarding school.

Ed

Nickname of **Edmond, Edward, Edwin,** or **Edgar.** Ed is rarely used as a separate name.

Famous names: Ed McMahon (TV personality)
      Ed Sullivan (TV personality)

Eddie

Form of names beginning with *Ed-,* including **Edgar, Edmond, Edward,** and **Edwin.** Often given as a first name, especially in the American South. Originally a nickname, it became a favorite with entertainers.
Famous names: Eddie Albert (actor)
　　　　　　　Eddie Murphy (comedian)

Edgar

Old English *Eadgar,* "prosperous spearman," from *ead* [wealth] + *gar* [spear]. This name has been popular since the tenth-century reign of Edgar of England, a respected, successful, and influential ruler. Shakespeare used the name for the loyal son of the duke of Gloucester in *King Lear.* Edgar is a popular name with Hispanic-Americans today.
Famous names: Edgar Allan Poe (writer)
　　　　　　　Edgar Renteria (baseball player)
Nicknames: **Ed, Eddie**
Variations: **Edgard** (French and Portuguese), **Edgardo** (Italian and Spanish), **Edgars** (Latvian), **Garek** (Czech)

Edmond, Edmund

Old English *Eadmund,* "prosperous protector," from *ead* [wealth] + *mund* [protection]. Before the Norman Conquest, several English kings and two saints, St. Edmund of Abingdon and St. Edmund the Martyr, were named Edmund. The name has been used continuously by royalty in England. Edmund was the bastard and disloyal son of the duke of Gloucester in Shakespeare's *King Lear.*
Famous names: Edmund Burke (statesman)
　　　　　　　Sir Edmund Hillary (mountaineer)
Nicknames: **Ed, Eddie, Mundy**
Variations: **Eamon** (Irish), **Edmondo** (Italian), **Edmundo** (Spanish and Portuguese), **Edmunds** (Latvian), **Mundek** (Polish), **Odon** (Hungarian)

Eduardo

Spanish form of **Edward,** frequently used by Hispanic-Americans.
Famous name: Eduardo Chillida (sculptor)

Edward

Old English *Eadweard,* "wealthy guardian," from *ead* [wealth] + *weard* [guardian]. This ancient name has often been the name of the

king of England. Several King Edwards ruled West Saxony and England before the Norman Conquest, and eight have ruled since. The latest was Edward VIII, who abdicated after less than a year on the throne to marry Wallis Simpson. Edward VII, who succeeded his mother, Queen Victoria, gave his name to the Edwardian era, which corresponds to his reign from 1901 to 1910. That decade was when Edward was at its high point of use in the United States, ranking among the top ten names. It has been drifting downward ever since, ranking 133rd in 2004 with about 3,100 boys given the name.
Famous names: Edward R. Murrow (TV reporter)
　　　　　　　　Edward Norton (actor)
Nicknames: **Duardo, Ed, Eddie, Eddy, Edo, Ned, Ted**
Variations: **Edouard** (French), **Eduard** (German, Estonian, Romanian, Russian, Ukrainian, and Yiddish), **Eduardo** (Spanish), **Eduardos** (Greek), **Edvard** (Danish, Norwegian, and Slovenian), **Edvardas** (Lithuanian), **Ewart, Odoardo** (Italian)

Edwin

Old English *Eadwine*, "rich friend," from *ead* [wealth] + *wine* [friend]. The first Edwin of historical record was the king of Northumbria, who converted to Christianity in 627. After he was killed at the battle of Heathfield, he was canonized St. Edwin. Like **Edgar,** Edwin is a popular name with Hispanic-Americans today but is out of fashion with other ethnic groups. Coincidentally, in 2004 Edgar and Edwin were the 167th and 168th most popular names for boys born in the United States.
Famous name: Edwin Hubble (astronomer)
Nicknames: **Ed, Eddie, Eddy, Ned, Ted**
Variations: **Eduino** (Spanish), **Edvino** (Italian), **Edvins** (Latvian)

Efraín, Efren

Both of these Spanish forms of **Ephraim** have been common in Latin America even though they are unusual in Spain. If these spellings are counted as one name, they were the 404th most common boys name in the United States in 2004.

Ekoka

Bakwerri (Cameroon) "great chief."

Eldon

Old English "Ella's hill."

Eli

Hebrew "height"; also, a short form of **Elijah** or **Elisha.** Eli was the high priest who advised Hannah, the barren wife of Elkanah, that God would grant her petition to have a child. The child was Samuel, who Eli trained in the ways of the Lord. The name Eli did not come into general use until the 17th century, when the Puritans turned to the Old Testament for names. It never completely disappeared as an American name and since 1990 has been boosted by the same tide of fashion that's lifted **Elijah** and **Elias.** Eli was the 158th most common boys name of 2004.

Famous names: Eli Wallach (actor)

Eli Whitney (inventor)

Other spelling: **Ely**

Elián

In December 1993, Elizabeth and Juan Miguel Gonzalez of Cardenas, Cuba, had a son who they named Elián, a name they created by combining the first three letters of **Elizabeth** with the last two of **Juan.** In spite of that romantic naming, the couple separated in 1997. In November 1999, Elián's mother, without his father's knowledge, fled from Cuba with him and 12 others in a small boat. The boat sank, and Elián's mother drowned, but he was rescued and turned over to a great-uncle in Miami. His father then sued for him to be returned to Cuba. The case created a national furor, with many in the Cuban-American community insisting that Elián not be sent back to Cuba. However, the courts ruled in favor of his father, and Elián flew to Cuba with him in June 2000. This sad case will live on for years in American nomenclature; 576 families named sons Elián in 2000, catapulting the name onto the SSA top 1,000 list in 428th place. The name hasn't left the list since, and 204 Eliáns were born in the United States in 2004.

Elias

This alternate form of **Elijah** has been drawn up in that name's wake. Though Elias is the traditional Spanish form, it occurs in many other languages, and the majority of its recent increase in use has been among non-Hispanics. There were more than 1,700 Eliases born in 2004, giving it a popularity rank of 197th. Elias Canetti won the Nobel Prize for literature in 1981.

Elie

French form of **Elijah**. Author Elie Wiesel, a Holocaust survivor, won the Nobel Peace Prize in 1986. His work to combat intolerance and injustice worldwide has continued through the Elie Wiesel Foundation for Humanity.

Elijah

Hebrew "Yahweh is my God." Elijah was the Hebrew prophet who appeared before Ahab, the king of Israel, and predicted that God would punish his people with a great drought because the king practiced idolatry. Later, Elijah ended the famine by praying to God and denouncing Ahab for having murdered Naboth. At the end of his life, Elijah was carried to heaven in a chariot of fire. The name was popular during the Middle Ages but then dropped from use. It was revived in the 17th century by the Puritans, and it has boomed in use recently, soaring from being the 243rd to the 31st most common boys name in the last 15 years. Elijah Wood gave his name a lot of positive publicity by playing Frodo in the *Lord of the Rings* film trilogy.

Variations: **Eli, Elia** (Italian), **Elias** (Czech, English, German, Greek, Hungarian, Portuguese, Spanish, and Yiddish), **Eliasz** (Polish), **Elie** (French), **Elliot, Elliott, Ellis, Illes** (Hungarian)

Elisha

Hebrew "God is salvation." Elisha was the Hebrew prophet who succeeded Elijah. He performed many miracles, including raising a person from the dead, causing an axe to float in water, curing lepers, and predicting the conclusions of sieges.

Variations: **Eli, Elisee** (French), **Eliseo** (Spanish and Italian)

Elliot, Elliott

Middle English form of **Elijah**; or Old English *Athelgeat*, "noble Geat (a Germanic tribe)," or *Aelfweald*, "elf rule"; or Scots Gaelic *eileach*, "mound." This British surname of many origins has long been used as a first name in the United States. Eliot Ness, real-life leader of a squad of Treasury agents in the 1930s, had his struggle with gangster Al Capone dramatized in several films, in the late 1950s to early 1960s television series *The Untouchables*, and in the contemporary version of that series. Elliott was also the name of the young hero of Steven Spielberg's 1982 movie *E.T. the Extra-Terrestrial*. However, this did not prevent Elliott from falling in popularity until 2002, when it began to slowly inch up again. Perhaps those who first saw *E.T.* as a child are starting to have sons of their own.

Famous name: Elliott Gould (actor)

Other spellings: **Eliot, Eliott**

Ellis

Medieval English form of **Elijah.**

Elmer

Old English *Aethelmaer* from *aethel* [noble] + *maer* [famous]. This name almost never occurs in England; it is strictly American. The name has become unpopular in recent years because it conjures a backwoods country feel for most people. The cartoon character Elmer Fudd does not improve the name's image; neither does the preacher Elmer Gantry in Sinclair Lewis's novel of that same name.

Variations: **Edelmar** (German), **Elmar** (Hungarian), **Elmers** (Latvian)

Elmore

Middle English *Elmour,* "river bank where elms grow," English place name and surname. Elmore Leonard is one of America's most respected and loved authors of crime fiction. Many of his books, including *Get Shorty, Touch, Maximum Bob,* and *Be Cool,* have been made into movies or television programs.

Elon

Hebrew "oak tree," the name of three minor characters in the Bible, and a university in North Carolina.

Elroy

Old French "the king." This name is very rare in the United States, but it's familiar to fans of the television cartoon series *The Jetsons* as the name of the young son in the family.

Variation: **Leroy**

Elsdon

Old English *Ellis's dene,* "Ellis's valley."

Elton

English place name *Aeltun,* "eel town" or "Ella's village or farm."

Famous name: Elton John (singer/songwriter)

Elvin

Form of **Alvin.**

Elvis

Perhaps a Welsh version of *Ailbhe,* an Irish name from Celtic *albho,* "white," although as likely to be a Southern invention blending the names **Alvin** and **Ellis.** It's surprising that Elvis is still a fairly rare name despite the great hero worship of Elvis Presley. However, Irish singer Declan Patrick McManus did rename himself Elvis Costello in honor of "The King," and around 300 American families choose this name every year for a son.

Emerick

This is a more "Germanic" form of the same name meaning "bravery-power" that also became **Amery.** As **Emerson** has moved toward becoming a girls name, some parents are turning to Emerick as a more "masculine" alternative.

Emerson

Middle English "son of **Amery.**" This surname became a first name in the United States during the 19th century in honor of Ralph Waldo Emerson, the famous poet and essayist. It is not very popular for boys today, but it has recently started to be used for girls.

Emil, Emile

German and French forms of Latin *Aemilius,* a Roman family name, possibly connoting "rival." Jean-Jacques Rousseau presented his treatise on education in *Emile,* in which he advised parents to bring up their children according to the laws of nature.
Famous name: Emile Zola (novelist)
Nicknames: **Em, Emilek** (Czech and Polish)
Variations: **Eemeli** (Finnish), **Emilio** (Spanish and Italian)

Emiliano

Spanish form of Latin *Aemilianus,* a longer form of *Aemilius* (see **Emil**). Emiliano Zapata (1879–1919) is one of the great revolutionary heroes in Mexican history. In spite of that, Emiliano was a rare name until recently, even in the Hispanic community, but it suddenly began to surge in popularity around 1999. By 2004 it was the 332nd most popular name for boys born in the United States.

Emilio

Spanish and Italian form of **Emil.** This name is regularly used by Hispanic-Americans and has become well known through the fame of actor Emilio Estevez. He is the son of actor Martin Sheen, whose original name was Ramon Estevez.

Emmanuel

Hebrew "God is with us." This is the name of the future Messiah prophesied in the Old Testament Book of Isaiah and identified with Jesus in the Gospel of Matthew in the New Testament. The name Emmanuel has long been more common in continental Europe than in any English-speaking country, but in the United States today it is popular with Hispanic-Americans and African-Americans.
Famous name: Emmanuel Lewis (actor)
Variations: **Emanoil** (Romanian), **Emanuel** (Czech, Polish, and Scandi-
navian), **Emanuele** (Italian), **Emanuelis** (Lithuanian),
Emmanuil (Russian), **Immanuel** (Dutch), **Manu** (Basque
and Finnish), **Manuel** (Spanish)

Emmet, Emmett

Middle English "son of **Emma.**" This is one of the few British sur-names based on a woman's, rather than a man's, first name. Irish-Americans began to use Emmett as a name for boys in the 19th century in honor of Robert Emmet, a hero in the Irish struggle for independence who was executed by the British in 1803. The first name then spread to other ethnic groups and was fairly popular in the United States in the 1890s. Though it fell off greatly after that, it never completely disappeared from the SSA list. With the rise of **Emma** as a girls name, adventurous parents have rediscovered Emmett as its male counterpart, and its use quadrupled between 1985 and 2004, though at this point it's still somewhat rare.
Famous name: Emmett Kelly (clown)

Enoch

Hebrew "experienced, educated." Enoch was the eldest son of Cain, although some biblical scholars suggest that he may have been Abel's son, because Enoch is listed in the Book of Genesis only as a grandson of Adam. The name was popular with the Puritans.
Variation: **Hanoch** (Hebrew)

Enos

Hebrew "man." Enos was the son of Seth and a grandson of Adam. Although nothing more is written about Enos in the Bible, the name has been used in England, Ireland, and the United States since Puritan times. However, Enos is a very uncommon name today.
Famous name: Enos Slaughter (baseball player)

Enrico

Italian form of **Henry.** Enrico Fermi won the 1938 Nobel Prize in physics for his work on nuclear fission.

Enrique

Spanish form of **Henry.** This name is still quite popular in the Hispanic-American community. Almost 1,300 Enriques were born in the United States in 2004, ranking it 243rd that year.
Famous name: Enrique Iglesias (singer)

Enzo

This is usually explained as being a short form of **Lorenzo** or **Vincenzo,** but Italian experts on names say it may also be an "Italianization" of the German name **Heinz** (see **Henry**). Enzo has recently boomed in popularity in France and is now one of the top ten names there. It's also rapidly increasing in the United States as Italian-Americans begin to return to their roots for baby names. It entered the SSA top 1,000 list in 2003 and in 2004 ranked 790th, with 225 boys given the name. Enzo Ferrari (1898–1988) founded the Ferrari automobile company.

Ephraim

Hebrew "fruitfulness," in the Old Testament the name of one of the sons of Joseph, founder of one of the tribes of Israel. This name was regularly used in the United States during the 19th century but has been almost nonexistent during the 20th and early 21st. It shows no signs of revival in spite of the increased popularity of other Old Testament names such as **Asher** and **Ethan.**
Variations: **Efraín** (Spanish), **Efrem** (Russian), **Efren** (Spanish)

Equator

This is one of the more interesting place or word names that American parents have come up with lately.

Eric

Old Norse, possibly from *ei* [always] + *rikr* [ruler]. In England, this name is a result of Danish colonization, but Eric is popular in the United States because it is a common name in all Scandinavian countries. The name has been quite fashionable since the 1960s. Though it's slowly decreasing in use, it was still the 39th most common name for American boys born in 2004.

Famous names: Eric Clapton (singer and guitarist)
Eric Lindros (hockey player)
Eric the Red (Norwegian explorer)

Nicknames: **Ric, Rick, Rickie, Ricky**

Variations: **Erich** (German and Slovakian), **Erico** (Portuguese and Italian), **Erik** (Danish and Swedish), **Eriks** (Latvian), **Erkki** (Finnish)

Erich

German and Slovakian form of **Eric**.

Famous name: Erich Maria Remarque (author)

Erik

Scandinavian form of **Eric**.

Famous names: Erik Erikson (psychologist)
Erik Estrada (actor)

Erle

Variation of **Earl**. As the creator of Perry Mason, Erle Stanley Gardner may be the most famous American mystery writer.

Ernest

German *Ernst,* "serious, earnest." This name was introduced to England in the 18th century by the royal family of Hanover. Edward Bulwer Lytton published his novel *Ernest Maltravers* in 1827. Oscar Wilde used the name to launch one pun after another in his play *The Importance of Being Earnest.* Popular in the United States during the Victorian era, Ernest has fallen out of fashion since 1930.

Famous name: Ernest Hemingway (novelist)

Nicknames: **Ern, Ernie**

Variations: **Ernek** (Czech), **Ernestas** (Lithuanian), **Ernesto** (Portuguese, Italian, and Spanish), **Erno** (Hungarian), **Ernst** (German, Russian, Slovakian, Swedish, and Ukrainian)

Ernesto

Spanish and Italian form of **Ernest.** Ernesto is still common enough in the Hispanic-American community that there were twice as many newborn boys named Ernesto in the United States in 2004 as there were boys named Ernest; it ranked 315th on the popularity chart. Ernesto Zedillo was President of Mexico from 1994 to 2000.
Famous name: Ernesto Lecuona (composer and pianist)

Ernie

Form of **Ernest.** Today this name is best known as half of the puppet duo Bert and Ernie on *Sesame Street.*
Famous name: Ernie Els (professional golfer)

Erwin

Old English *Eoforwine* from *eofor* [boar] + *wine* [friend]. This name is sometimes mistaken as a variation of Irvin or Irving, but Erwin is an entirely different name.
Nicknames: **Ern, Erwinek** (Polish)
Variations: **Ervin** (Czech and Slovakian), **Ervins** (Latvian), **Irwin, Irwyn**

Esenam

Ewe (Togo) "he has heard my prayer," a name for a much-wanted child. In Togo this name is used for both boys and girls.

Espen

This is the Norwegian form of a name that is **Esben** in Danish and **Esbjörn** in Swedish; all are derived from Old Norse *Ássbjörn,* "divine bear." Espen was quite popular in Norway during the 1980s. Since 2002 two different fathers in the United States have received nation-wide publicity for naming their sons after ESPN, the cable television sports network. One of their wives, however, wisely insisted that the child's name actually be listed as Espen on the birth certificate.

Esteban

Spanish form of **Stephen.**
Famous name: Esteban Cortazar (fashion designer)

Ethan

Hebrew "strength, permanence, and firmness." There are four men named Ethan in the Old Testament, but all of them are obscure characters, though Ethan, son of Mahol, is mentioned as having been

almost as wise as Solomon. The name was not used until the 18th century, when it was taken up by the Puritans. Ethan Allen was an American Revolutionary War hero who had many boys named after him in the early 18th century, and later Edith Wharton used this name for the hero of her tragic novella *Ethan Frome*. But Ethan was a rare name until the end of the 1980s, when it suddenly leapt into the top 100 names for boys in the United States. Some of this increase was probably because Ethan was the name of Elliot and Nancy's son on the late-1980s television series *thirtysomething*. During the same period, Ethan Allen Cord (played by actor Lee Horsley) was the chief character on the television Western *Paradise*. When those programs went off the air, Ethan lost popularity for a few years until 1996, when Tom Cruise played Ethan Hunt in the first *Mission: Impossible* movie. Ethan then exploded in use and became a top ten name in the United States in 2002. The name has been even more successful in Canada, where it's been the number-one name in most provinces since 2002. The total number of characters called Ethan in films and television programs mentioned on the Internet Move Database shows the same pattern, rising in the 1980s, then falling in the middle 1990s, and soaring thereafter. Of all the popular names of the last decade, Ethan's success with average American parents has most paralleled its Hollywood publicity.
Famous names: Ethan Coen (film director)
Ethan Hawke (actor)

Etienne

French form of **Stephen.**

Ettore

Italian form of **Hector.**
Famous name: Ettore Bastianini (operatic baritone)

Eugene

Greek *Eugenios*, "well born"; Latin *Eugenius*. Popes and princes have chosen this name because of its connotation of nobility, and their choice has increased its popularity with the general public. St. Eugenius of Carthage was noted for his piety and goodness. Pope Eugene III helped unite the Eastern Church with the Church of Rome. Prince Eugene de Savoie Carignan was a great Austrian general; he led the Second Crusade and helped the duke of Marlborough to victory over Louis XIV and contributed more to the popularity of this name than anyone else.

Famous names: Eugene V. Debs (political activist)
               Eugene O'Neill (playwright)
               Eugene Ormandy (conductor)

Nicknames: **Gene, Geno**

Variations: **Eugen** (German and Romanian), **Eugenio** (Portuguese, Italian, and Spanish), **Eugeniusz** (Polish), **Evgen** (Slovenian), **Evgenije** (Serbian), **Owen** (Welsh), **Yevgeni** (Russian)

Evan

Welsh form of **John.** The name Evan is becoming steadily more popular, especially in the eastern United States, and ranked 49th nationwide for American boys born in 2004.

Nicknames: **Ev, Van**

Variation: **Yvaine** (English)

Evander

Latin form of Greek *Euandros,* "good man." In Roman legend, Evander was a prince from Arcadia in Greece who founded a town on Rome's Palatine Hill. The name Evander has always been rare, but some American parents are starting to consider it as an alternative for **Evan.** The most famous bearer of the name is undoubtedly the boxer Evander Holyfield.

Ever

Though this could be thought of as a short form of **Everett,** many parents today interpret it as a "word name" that indicates the steadfastness of their love for the child and for each other.

Everett

Old German *Eburhart,* "brave as a boar," from *ebur* [wild boar] + *hartu* [strong]. This name entered England at the time of the Norman Conquest. Then, as now, it rarely appeared as a first name.

Famous name: C. Everett Koop (U.S. surgeon general)

Nickname: **Ev, Ever**

Variations: **Ebert** (German), **Evarardo** (Italian and Spanish), **Everhard** (German), **Evert** (Swedish), **Evrard** (French)

Ewan

Ewan is a modern Scottish form of the ancient Gaelic name *Eóghan*. Experts are divided as to whether this was simply the Gaelic form of **Eugene** or whether it is a separate Celtic name meaning "born of the yew." The same disagreement exists about the name's Welsh counterpart, **Owen.** Whatever its derivation, Ewan is a popular name in Scotland, though Scots now prefer the spelling Euan over Ewan by a ratio of about three to two. Ewan is still quite rare in the United States, though with the present fashion for Owen and the fame of Scottish actor Ewan McGregor, it would make a good "different but not too different" choice.
Other spellings: **Euan, Ewen**

Ewart

Norman French form of **Edward** or Middle English *ewehirde,* "shepherd of ewes."

Ezekiel

Hebrew "the strength of God." The biblical prophet Ezekiel wrote during the Babylonian exile around 580 B.C. He is famous for his vision of God riding in a chariot carried by four fantastic creatures. Ezekiel was often found as a first name in colonial New England, but during the 20th century it was most popular with Hispanic-Americans. There are signs, however, that Ezekiel is starting to catch on with all ethnic groups today as an alternative to other popular biblical names like **Elijah** and **Zachary.**
Nickname: **Zeke**
Variation: **Ezequiel** (Spanish and Portuguese)

Ezra

Hebrew "help." With permission from King Artaxerxes, Ezra, a Hebrew scribe and priest, led the Israelites out of exile to rebuild the temple in Jerusalem. Ezra authored the Book of Ezra and is believed to have written other books in the Bible as well. Like **Ezekiel,** Ezra is a biblical name on the rise; its use tripled over the last decade, and it reached 350th place on the SSA list in 2004.
Famous name: Ezra Pound (poet)
Nicknames: **Ez, Ezzie**
Variations: **Esdras** (Spanish), **Esra** (Finnish)

Fabian

Late Latin *Fabianus,* derived from Latin *faba,* "bean." This Roman family name may have originally designated a farmer's favorite crop. St. Fabian was a pope who was martyred in A.D. 250 during a persecution of Christians by the emperor Decius. This name hasn't been very popular in English-speaking countries, but it does receive regular use from Hispanic-Americans. Many Americans will remember Fabian, the Philadelphia teenager who was an overnight singing sensation in the late 1950s. Perhaps because it fits the popular "long *a* in the first syllable, ends in *–n*" sound pattern, Fabian's use has increased a bit lately. It was 251st on the popularity chart in 2004.

Fairfield

Middle English *Feirfeld,* "beautiful field."
Famous name: Fairfield Porter (painter and art critic)

Falcon

Old French *falcun,* the name of the bird.

Fariji

Swahili "consolation." This African abstract name has been chosen by a few African-American families.

Farrell

Irish Gaelic *fearghal,* "brave." This name was common in medieval Ireland and was brought to the United States by Irish immigrants in the 19th century.

Felipe

Spanish and Portuguese form of **Philip.** The present heir to the throne of Spain is Felipe de Borbón, Prince of Asturias. Felipe's use in the United States has risen along with the Hispanic population, and it's now among the top 400 names for American boys.

Felix

Latin *felix*, "happy." Felix was once a very popular name and was the name of four popes and many saints. In the Bible, Felix was a procurator of Judea who was influenced by St. Paul's preaching, but when Felix was removed from his post, he left Paul in prison. It follows that popes chose the name for its Latin meaning, not to honor the historic Felix. On the television comedy *The Odd Couple*, based on a play by Neil Simon, Tony Randall played the fastidious Felix Unger. Felix the Cat lives up to his name with his jovial attitude toward life. The name is given to about 700 American boys every year.
Famous name: Felix Mendelssohn (composer)
Nicknames: **Fee, Fele, Feles, Pito**
Variations: **Bodog** (Hungarian), **Felice** (Italian), **Feliks** (Polish and
Russian), **Feliksas** (Lithuanian)

Ferdinand

Gothic "daring adventurer" from *fard* [journey] + *nand* [ready]. This royal name has belonged to kings of Aragon, Austria, Leon, Castile, Spain, the Holy Roman Empire, Naples, Portugal, and the two Sicilies—some 23 in all—making Ferdinand the all-time most popular name for kings. Ferdinand II of Spain helped launch Christopher Columbus on his voyage to the Americas. Shakespeare used the name for Miranda's suitor in *The Tempest* and for the king of Navarre in *Love's Labour's Lost*.
Nicknames: **Ferd, Ferdie**
Variations: **Ferdek** (Polish), **Ferdinando** (Italian), **Ferdinandos**
(Greek), **Ferdys** (Czech), **Fernand** (French), **Fernando**
(Spanish), **Nandor** (Hungarian)

Fergus

Old Irish "manly vigor" from *fer* [man] + *gus* [vigor]. Although this name is associated with Ireland, Fergus was the king of Scotland who repelled invasions of the Picts and Britons in 330 B.C. He was later drowned; the town of Carrickfergus was named to honor him.
Nicknames: **Ferg, Fergy, Gus**
Variations: **Ferghus, Ferris**

Fernando

Spanish form of **Ferdinand.** Although the name Ferdinand is almost never found in the modern United States, Fernando is still quite popular within the Hispanic-American community. It ranked 253rd in use in the United States in 2004.

Famous name: Fernando Valenzuela (baseball player)

Nicknames: **Ferni, Nando, Nano**

Variations: **Fernandino, Hernando**

Ferris

Irish surname based on **Fergus.** In Scotland, this name is associated with the Ferguson clan, formerly MacFergus. In the United States, it is occasionally used by Irish-Americans. The 1986 movie *Ferris Bueller's Day Off* didn't inspire many of its fans to use the name.

Variation: **Farris**

Fidel

Spanish form of Late Latin *Fidelis,* "faithful." It's hard not to think of Fidel Castro when hearing this name, and it is not at all popular with Cuban-Americans. However, the traditionalism of Hispanic-Americans in general, who are the segment of the American population most likely to name sons after their fathers or grandfathers, means that Fidel was still being given to babies often enough in 2004 to retain a place on the SSA top 1,000 list—though it was 999th place! Fidel Ramos was instrumental in toppling the corrupt regime of Ferdinand Marcos in the Philippines and went on to serve as his country's president between 1992 and 1998.

Fife

Though theoretically this could be a new "word name" from the musical instrument, parents who give it are more likely thinking of the Scottish surname and place name. This is a very old name, originally of an ancient kingdom said to have been founded by Fib, one of the seven sons of Cruithe, the founder of the Picts, who were the original inhabitants of Scotland. Its meaning is unknown.

Finlay, Finley

Gaelic *Fionnlagh,* "fair-haired warrior." This Scottish name is only used occasionally in the United States, but since 2001 it has become very fashionable in England. With Americans now discovering **Finn** as a boys name, little Finlays will probably be turning up in the United States very soon.

Finn

Gaelic *Fionn,* "bright, white." Finn MacCool is a hero of ancient Irish legend. He is described as a warrior king noted for his strength, generosity, justice, and loyalty. Recently Finn has become popular in Ireland itself, and American parents are starting to notice it; the name was 571st on the SSA list in 2004. It is poised to become a new Irish-American favorite when parents tire of names like **Connor** and **Liam.** Of course, Finn could also be a favorite with Americans of Scandinavian descent, since it can also be derived from Old Norse *Finnr,* "person from Finland."

Fintan

Gaelic, either "the white ancient one" or "white fire." In Irish mythology Fintan was the only survivor of Ireland's original human settlers. He lived for thousands of years and became the patron of storytelling. Later there were 74 Christian saints named Fintan in Ireland.

Fisher

Old English *fiscere,* "fisherman." With **Hunter** being a popular name, it was inevitable that some parents would use Fisher as an alternative. It entered the SSA top 1,000 list for boys in 2004 in last place. Famous name: Fisher Stevens (actor)

Fletcher

Old French "a maker of arrows." This occupational surname was moderately common as a given name a century ago. It almost vanished after 1970, but the fashion for using surnames ending in *–er* as boys names has just begun to revive it, though there were still only 171 Fletchers born in the entire United States in 2004.
Nickname: **Fletch**

Flint

Old English "rock." This name probably began as a nickname, meaning "hard as a rock." It is both a surname and a given name, and even though it is very rare now, the popularity of similar-sounding male names such as **Clint** and **Trent** may bring it more use.

Florian

Latin "blooming." This name has a similar derivation to the girls name **Florence.** Although it was introduced into England just after

the Norman Conquest, it's been much more common in Germany and Poland than it has ever been in any English-speaking country. Florian was also quite common in France during the 1990s.
Famous name: Florian Mayer (tennis player)
Variations: **Floren, Flory**

Floyd

English variation of Welsh **Lloyd,** "gray." The change in spelling resulted when native English speakers tried to pronounce the Welsh *Ll-,* a sound that exists in few other languages besides Welsh. Floyd was popular in the United States during the late 19th century, but most parents today find it old-fashioned. Many Americans identify this name with the character Floyd Lawson, the Mayberry barber on *The Andy Griffith Show,* who was played by actor Howard McNear.
Other spelling: **Floyde**

Forrest

Old English "forest" or "forester." Forrest started out as a place name or an occupational name. As a given name, it became popular in the late 19th century in the American South, where it was chosen to commemorate the exploits of Confederate general Nathan Bedford Forrest during and after the Civil War.
Famous name: Forrest Sawyer (newscaster)
Nickname: **Foss**
Variations: **Forester, Foster**

Foster

This English surname has four possible derivations from Middle English words for "foster parent," "keeper of the woods," "sheep-shearer," or "saddle-tree maker."
Famous name: Foster Brooks (entertainer)
Nickname: **Foss**
Variations: **Forester, Forrest, Forrester, Forster**

Fountain

Old French *fontane* from Latin *fontanus,* "of a spring."

Francis

Latin *Franciscus,* "Frenchman," from Old German *franc,* "free." Francis has been the name of several kings and many saints. St. Francis of Assisi, the patron saint of animals and ecology, is the most famous saint with this name. Born Giovanni, he is said to have been given the name Francesco because of his fluency in French. His father called him a madman and brutally disinherited the future saint. Francis's life of poverty and devotion caused many disciples to follow him. The name became popular in England in the 16th century and has been in use ever since, though its use has been receding for years. It lost half of its remaining popularity between 1990 and 2004 and was only 525th on the SSA list that year.

Famous names: Francis Bacon (modern artist)
                  Sir Francis Drake (admiral)

Nicknames: **Fran, Franek, Frank, Frannie, Franny**

Variations: **Ferenc** (Hungarian), **Francesco** (Italian), **Francisco** (Portuguese and Spanish), **Franciszek** (Polish), **François** (French), **Franjo** (Serbian), **Frans** (Swedish), **Frantisek** (Czech), **Frantiskos** (Greek), **Franz** (German)

Francisco

Spanish and Portuguese form of **Francis.** This name has retained popularity with Hispanic-Americans. Though not used as often as it once was, there were still six times as many Franciscos born in the United States in 2004 than there were boys named Francis.

Nicknames: **Chico, Cisco, Paco, Pancho**

Franco

Italian form of **Frank** that ranked 893rd on the SSA list in 2004.

François

French form of **Francis.**

Famous name: François Truffaut (film director)

Frank

Old French *franc*, "free man"; also, a form of **Francis** or **Franklin.** Frank was one of the most popular names for American boys in the late 19th century. During the 1890s there were more than 12,000 Franks born in the United States every year; in 2004 there were fewer than 1,500.

Famous names: Frank Capra (film director)
                  Frank Sinatra (singer)
                  Frank Lloyd Wright (architect)
                  Frank Zappa (musician)

Nicknames: **Fran, Frankie, Franky**

Variations: **Franc** (Bulgarian), **Franco** (Italian), **Franjo** (Serbian), **Franz** (German), **Pranas** (Lithuanian)

Frankie, Franky

Pet forms of **Frank** or **Franklin.**

Famous name: Frankie Avalon (singer)

Franklin

Middle English *frankeleyn*, "a free landowner." In England in the 14th and 15th centuries, Franklin was a title that designated a landlord who was of free but not noble birth. This name is still associated with statesman and inventor Benjamin Franklin.

Famous names: Franklin Pierce (14th U.S. president)

Franklin Delano Roosevelt (32nd U.S. president)

Nicknames: **Frank, Frankie, Franky, Linn**

Franz

German form of **Francis** or **Frank.**

Famous name: Franz Josef Haydn (composer)

Fred

Form of **Alfred** or **Frederick.** This name has been used in its own right in both England and the United States since the middle of the 19th century and was among the top 20 names for American boys born from 1875 through 1900. By 2004, however, it was not even among the top 1,000 names on the SSA list and showed no sign of revival. Fred is the name of Ebenezer Scrooge's nephew in Charles Dickens's novel *A Christmas Carol,* but most modern Americans will better remember the cartoon character Fred Flintstone.

Famous names: Fred Astaire (dancer and actor)

Fred Dryer (football player and actor)

Fred MacMurray (actor)

Freddie, Freddy

Forms of **Alfred** or **Frederick.** On official birth certificates in the United States this name is now more common than **Fred,** especially in the South.

Famous names: Freddie Mercury (rock musician)

Freddy Fender (country singer)

Frederic

French form of **Frederick.**

Famous names: Frederic Chopin (composer and pianist)
Frederic Remington (painter)

Frederick

Old German *Frithuric* from *frithu* [peace] + *ricja* [rule]. Frederick has long been a royal name in Germany. When Hanover became the royal house of England, the name came along with it. Frederick, the Prince of Wales, was the son of George II of England. This name has been declining in use in both England and the United States since the 1930s. More than 25 percent of American parents who give the name now use the spelling Fredrick. Frederick Banting won the Nobel Prize in medicine in 1923 for discovering insulin, which has since saved the lives of millions of diabetics.

Famous name: Frederick Douglass (anti-slavery crusader)

Nicknames: **Fede, Fico, Fred, Freddie, Freddy, Fredek** (Polish), **Fredi, Frico, Fritz, Fritzchen, Ikoy, Ric, Rick, Rickie, Ricky, Riki**

Variations: **Federico** (Portuguese, Spanish, and Italian), **Frederic** (French), **Frederik** (Danish), **Fredrick, Fredrik** (Swedish), **Friderik** (Serbian), **Friedrich** (German), **Frigyes** (Hungarian)

Freeman

Old English *Frēoman,* "free-born man." Freeman was fairly common as a first name a century ago but has been hard to find since 1970.

Fritz

German pet form of **Frederick.**

Famous name: Fritz Lang (film director)

Fulton

Old English "place with birds" from *fugol* [bird, fowl] + *tun* [enclosure]. The modern use of this name honors Robert Fulton, a 19th-century American inventor and civil engineer, whose many patents include the commercial steamboat.

Fyodor

Russian form of **Theodore.** Russian author Fyodor Dostoevsky's 1866 novel *Crime and Punishment* is still considered one of the greatest fictional presentations of the criminal psyche ever written.

Gabriel

Hebrew "man of God," the name of an archangel. This angel first appeared to Daniel in the Old Testament and then to Mary in the New Testament, when he announced the impending birth of Jesus. Because of Gabriel's association with messages from God, in 1921 Pope Benedict XV declared him the patron saint of letter carriers and telephone operators. The name Gabriel was rare in the United States before the 20th century because many Anglo-Saxon Protestants thought it was sacrilegious to name children after angels. But the huge popularity of **Michael** has encouraged American parents to reconsider the names of other angels, and Gabriel rose from 92nd to 40th on the list of names given to newborn sons between 1991 and 2004.

Famous names: Gabriel Byrne (actor)
Gabriel Garcia Marquez (1982 Nobel Prize winner for literature)

Nickname: **Gabe**

Variations: **Gabor** (Hungarian), **Gabriele** (Italian), **Gavrylo** (Ukrainian), **Kaapo** (Finnish)

Gage

Old Norman French *gauge,* used as a name for an official who checked legal weights and measures in medieval times. Two different media phenomena brought this name to the attention of modern parents. First, between 1972 and 1977 the television series *Emergency!* featured a paramedic named John Gage (played by actor Randolph Mantooth) who was normally called "Gage" on the show. Probably a bigger influence, though, was Stephen King's 1983 novel *Pet Sematary,* made into a movie in 1989. Its most horrific character was a dead three-year-old named Gage, who, after being buried in the evil pet cemetery, comes back from the dead to murder his mother. In spite of that, many young women found Miko Hughes, the child actor who played Gage, to be so cute they were inspired to give the name to their own sons. Of course neither *Emergency!* nor *Pet Sematary* would have started a vogue for the name if it didn't fit in with the sounds of popular names such as **Jake** and **Kaden**. Gage is now among the 150 most common names for American boys.

Gahigi, Gahiji

Rwandan "small hunter." This African warrior's name is sometimes chosen by African-American parents.

Galen

Probably a Latin form of Greek *galene*, "calm." Galen was a highly respected second-century Greek physician.

Galvin

Irish Gaelic *Gealbhán*, "bright white."

Galway

Irish Gaelic *galimh*, "stony." Galway Bay, along with the county and city of Galway, is a place that many Irish-Americans think of with nostalgia. However, as a first name, Galway is extremely rare.

Gamaliel

Hebrew "God is my reward." In the Old Testament, Gamaliel was the son of Pedahzur and prince of Manasseh. In the New Testament, he was the rabbi who taught Saul of Tarsus (St. Paul).

Gannon

Irish Gaelic *Mac Fhionnáin*, ultimately from *fionn*, "fair."

Gareth

This name first occurs as the name of the younger brother of Gawain (see **Gavin**) in Thomas Malory's *Morte D'Arthur*, the version of the legends of King Arthur on which most modern treatments of the story have been based. It's unclear how Malory invented the name, but it may be from Welsh *gwaredd*, "gentle." Gareth has always been rare in the United States, though it was frequently used in Wales during the last century and would make a good "different but not too different" twist on **Garrett**.

Garner

Form of **Warner,** or Old French *gerner*, "storehouse for grain."

Garrett

Middle English form of both **Gerald** and **Gerard.** Garrett was the 1990s replacement for **Gary.** Throughout the 1990s it was one of the 100 most-used names for boys in the United States, though since 2001 its high point seems to have passed.
Nicknames: **Gar, Garry, Gary**
Other spelling: **Garret**
Variation: **Jarrett**

Garrison

Middle English *Garardson,* "son of **Gerard.**" Garrison Keillor, born Gary Keillor, lengthened his name because he thought Garrison would look more distinguished as an author's name. Keillor's famous radio program *A Prairie Home Companion* first appeared in 1974. He and the program were widely known by 1978, but the name Garrison didn't show up on the SSA top 1,000 list for boys until 1986. Since 1995 Garrison has been well established as a minor alternative for **Garrett** and **Harrison,** never being lower than 775th or higher than 650th on the SSA list.

Garth

Old Norse *garthr,* "enclosure," through Middle English *garth,* "garden, yard." This surname has been used as a first name since the early 19th century, but it has never been especially popular, even though Garth has been a well-used name for fictional characters. There is a Garth in Maxwell Anderson's play *Winterset.* Garth was the name of the character played by actor Martin Mull in the television series *Mary Hartman, Mary Hartman* as well as the name of the popular character played by Dana Carvey in the movie *Wayne's World,* based on sketches from *Saturday Night Live.* The popularity of country singer Garth Brooks saw the name inch upward in use during the early 1990s, but it has since become rare again.
Nickname: **Gar**

Gary

Old English *gari,* "spear," or a short form of **Garrett.** This name was one of the top ten names for boys during the 1940s and 1950s in the United States. It owed its popularity to Gary Cooper, two-time Oscar winner for *Sergeant York* and *High Noon.* His original name was

Frank Cooper; the name Gary was suggested to him by his agent, Nan Collins, who had been born in Gary, Indiana. For a time, Gary was also used to Americanize such European names as Garibaldi. As an official name, Gary has receded in popularity, but it will often be heard as a nickname for **Garrett** among boys born in the 1990s.
Famous names: Gary Larson (cartoonist)
Gary Sinise (actor)
Other spelling: **Garry**

Gatbel

Nuer (southern Sudan) "son of corn," a name given to a boy born during the year his family has a successful harvest.

Gatlin

Surname, possibly a form of Old English *gædeling,* "kinsman, companion."

Gautam

Sanskrit *Gautama,* meaning uncertain. "Descendant of the best ox" and "remover of darkness" have been suggested by Indian scholars as possible meanings. As the family name of Gautama Siddhartha, who became the Buddha, this name is used by both Hindus and Buddhists in southern Asia today.

Gavin

Scottish form of Welsh *Gwalchgwyn,* "white hawk." Gavin, or Gawain, was the first—and most courteous—knight of King Arthur's Round Table. Gawain is the hero of "Sir Gawayne and the Grene Knight," the finest of the Arthurian romances. William Faulkner's character Gavin Stevens plays an integral part in several of his novels. This name has been rising in use for the last 20 years; in 2004 it was 55th on the American popularity list. Rock singers Gavin Rossdale and Gavin DeGraw are keeping this name in the minds of young parents.
Famous name: Gavin McLeod (actor)
Nickname: **Gav**
Variations: **Gaven, Gawain, Gawayne**

Gaylord

Norman French *Gailhard* from Germanic *gail* [gay, joyous] + *hard* [hardy, strong]. Senator Gaylord Nelson founded Earth Day in 1970.
Variations: **Gallard**

Gehrig

German surname, probably meaning "son of *Geri*," an old Germanic name meaning "spear." Gehrig has occasionally been given as a first name in the United States to honor Lou Gehrig (1903–1941), whose huge success as a baseball player combined with his tragic early death from Amyotrophic Lateral Sclerosis (now often called "Lou Gehrig's disease") made him one of the greatest legends of the sport.

Gene

Form of **Eugene.** Gene began to be thought of as a separate name at the beginning of the 20th century. It was fairly popular between 1920 and 1950 but is now out of fashion.
Famous names: Gene Autry (singer and actor)
               Gene Kelly (entertainer)
               Gene Wolfe (science fiction and fantasy author)

Geoffrey

Old German *Guafrid,* "peaceful land"; or *Walahfrid,* "peaceful traveler"; or *Gisfrid,* "pledge of peace"; in Norman French, all three of these names became *Jeufroi,* which was taken into Middle English as *Geffrey.* Geoffrey Chaucer, author of *The Canterbury Tales,* is the best-known literary Geoffrey. Geoffrey is the traditional British spelling of this name, but in the United States Jeffrey is the more popular form; fewer than 10 percent of American parents use the British spelling.
Nicknames: **Geoff, Jeff**
Variations: **Geoffroi** (French), **Geoffroy** (French), **Jeffrey**

George

Greek *georgos,* "farmer." This name dates back to ancient Greece. Virgil celebrated the pleasures of farming in *The Georgics,* a poetic treatise on agriculture. St. George, a Roman military tribune who was martyred at Lydda, Palestine, was the favorite saint of Edward III of England. In 1349, the king dedicated the Order of the Garter to St. George, thereby making him the patron saint of England. The name, however, did not move into common use in England until the royal house of Hanover ascended the throne of Great Britain; there have been four kings named George since then. In the United States, George remained a popular name after the Revolution because of the first president, George Washington. It was one of the top ten

names for American boys until 1938. But it has steadily lost ground since and was only 145th on the popularity list in 2004. Hispanic-Americans and Greek-Americans are fondest of the name today.
Famous names: George Clooney (actor)
George Lopez (comedian)
George Stephanopoulos (political analyst)
Nicknames: **Geordie** (Scottish), **Georgie, Orito, Yoyi, Yoyo**
Variations: **Georges** (French), **Georgios** (Greek), **Göran** (Swedish), **Gyorgy** (Hungarian), **Jerzy** (Polish), **Jorge** (Portuguese and Spanish), **Jurgen** (German), **Yrjo** (Finnish), **Yuri** (Russian and Ukrainian)

Gerald

Old German *Gairovald,* "spear ruler," from *ger* [spear] + *vald* [rule]. This name existed in England before the Norman Conquest. In the eighth century, St. Gerald founded monasteries and a convent. This was a popular American name during the first half of the 20th century. But only 544 Geralds were born in the United States in 2004, making it the 405th most common boys name. Its nickname, Jerry, is now given more often as a first name than is Gerald itself.
Famous name: Gerald Ford (38th U.S. president)
Nicknames: **Gerry, Jerry**
Variations: **Garrelt** (Dutch), **Garrett** (English), **Geralde** (French), **Geraldo** (Portuguese, Italian, and Spanish), **Geraldos** (Greek), **Geralds** (Latvian), **Geraud** (French), **Gerhold** (Dutch and German), **Gerold** (German), **Giraldo** (Italian), **Giraud** (French), **Jerrold**

Geraldo

Spanish and Italian form of **Gerald.**
Famous name: Geraldo Rivera (talk-show host)

Gerard

Old German *Gairhard,* "spear-brave," from *ger* [spear] + *hardu* [hard]. This name arrived in England with the Norman Conquest. Seven saints have been named Gerard, and three other Gerards have been blessed but not canonized. This name had a mild peak of popularity in the 1950s, when it was among the top 200 names for American boys. It vanished from the SSA top 1,000 list after 2002.

Famous name: Gerard Depardieu (actor)

Nicknames: **Gerry, Jerry**

Variations: **Garrett, Gellert** (Hungarian), **Gerardo** (Portuguese, Italian, and Spanish), **Gerhard** (German and Swedish)

Gerardo

Spanish, Italian, and Portuguese form of **Gerard.** Gerardo is used more by Hispanic-Americans than by other groups. It was the 225th most common name given to boys in the United States in 2004.

Gerhard

German form of **Gerard.**

Famous name: Gerhard Richter (artist)

German

Spanish *Germán,* form of Latin *Germanus,* "brother." This name rose in use along with the Hispanic population during the 1980s but has been receding since 1996. The Spanish pronunciation of German results in confusion with **Herman,** but they are two different names.

Variation: **Jermaine**

Gerry

Form of **Gerald, Gerard,** or **Jeremiah**; variation of **Jerry.** This spelling is much less common than Jerry.

Other spelling: **Gerrie**

Giacomo

Italian form of **James.**

Famous name: Giacomo Puccini (opera composer)

Giancarlo

Italian blend of **Gianni** and **Carlo.** Like **Giovanni,** this name is now frequently used by Hispanic-Americans as well as Italian-Americans.

Gianni

Short form of **Giovanni,** now being revived by Italian-Americans. Gianni ranked 622nd on the SSA list for boys in 2004.

Famous name: Gianni Versace (fashion designer)

Gideon

Hebrew "hewer"; the original meaning may have referred to one who cuts wood or to a warrior who cuts down the enemy in battle.

In the Bible's Book of Judges, Gideon is the leader of the Israelites in their victory over the Midianites. The name was taken up by the Puritans in the 17th century but was largely absent during the 20th century. Since the year 2000 it has reappeared on the SSA top 1,000 list and is steadily increasing in use, ranking 692nd in 2004. Variation: **Gidon** (modern Israeli)

Gil

Spanish and Portuguese form of **Giles,** or short form of **Gilbert** or **Gilberto.**

Gilbert

Old German *Gisilbert,* from *gisil* "pledge" + *berth* "bright." Brought to England by the Normans, the name Gilbert was fairly common during the Middle Ages. Gilbert was among the top 100 names for American boys born in the 1920s, but it's been falling away ever since and ranked 560th on the SSA list in 2004.
Famous name: Gilbert Gottfried (comedian)
Nicknames: **Gib, Gil**
Variations: **Gielbert** (Dutch), **Gilberto** (Italian, Portuguese, and
Spanish)

Gilberto

Spanish form of **Gilbert,** now slightly more common than Gilbert itself in the United States.

Giles

Greek *aigidion,* "kid (young goat)," through Latin *Aegidius* and French *Gide, Gilles;* associated with soldiers because shields were made of goatskin. St. Giles, a seventh-century Greek monk, left his homeland to avoid the publicity that his miracles had caused and went to France where he became a hermit. His asceticism won him renown there as well. He is the patron saint of beggars and the disabled.
Variations: **Egidio** (Italian), **Egidius** (German), **Gide** (Provencal), **Gil**
(Portuguese and Spanish), **Gill** (Norwegian), **Gilles**
(French), **Gillis** (Danish), **Gyles** (English)

Gino

Italian pet form of many names ending in *–gino,* including Giorgino and Luigino. Gino has been given often enough as an independent

name in the United States to have been on the SSA top 1,000 list
for boys since 1954, though it looks like it may fall off that list soon.
Famous name: Gino Quilico (operatic tenor)

Giovanni

Italian form of **John.** This Italian name is now popular with Hispanic-
Americans. It reached 135th place on the list of names given to
American boys in 2004. This is partly because of Latin-American
actors such as Giovanni Mendez and Giovanni Ciccia, who have
been popular with viewers of Spanish-language television programs.
Famous name: Giovanni Schiaparelli (astronomer)
Variations: **Gianni, Jovani, Jovanni, Jovanny, Jovany**

Giulio

Italian form of **Julius.**

Giuseppe

Italian form of **Joseph.**
Famous name: Giuseppe Verdi (opera composer)

Glenn

Celtic *gleann,* "wooded valley, dale, glen." This place name and sur-
name became a popular given name in the 19th century, perhaps
because Sir Walter Scott used it often in his novels, especially in *The
Monastery,* which chronicles the Glendenning family. Glenn was well
used in the 1950s and 1960s, but by 2004, it was only the 678th
most popular name for American boys on the SSA list.
Famous names: Glenn Ford (actor)
Glenn Gould (pianist)
Other spelling: **Glen**
Variations: **Glyn** (Welsh), **Glynn** (Scottish)

Godfrey

Norman French from Germanic *god* [God] + *fred* [peace]. This
name was brought to England during the Norman Conquest.
Godfrey is almost never chosen by parents in the United States.
Variation: **Gottfried** (German)

Gonzalo

Spanish, a Visigothic name with a first syllable from Germanic *gund*
[strife]. The meaning of the second part of the name is disputed;

"disposed to," "elf," and "safe" are all possibilities. Gonzalo was an extremely common name in medieval Spain, and **Gonzalez** ("son of Gonzalo") is one of the top ten Hispanic surnames in the United States today. Gonzalo is no longer one of the top Spanish first names, but it is still used in the Hispanic-American community.
Nickname: **Gonzi**
Variations: **Goncalvo** (Portuguese), **Gonzaleo, Gonzoyo**

Goran

Since most American books leave out umlauts, one might assume this name is the same as **Göran,** the Swedish form of **George.** But without those two little dots over the *o,* this is a completely separate Serbo-Croatian name, probably based on the word *gora,* "mountain." It has become well known to Americans recently because of the fame of tennis player Goran Ivanisevic and actor Goran Visnjic, both of whom were born in Croatia.

Gordon

Uncertain origin, but may come from a French place name, *Gourdon,* or from Celtic *gor* [spacious] + *din* [fort]. Gordon became a popular name in England in the 19th century because of the exploits of Charles George Gordon, a general and adventurer known as "Chinese Gordon" and "Gordon Pasha." Gordon's Gin is named after him. During the 1950s, Gordon was a popular name in Canada, undoubtedly due to admiration for hockey star Gordie Howe.
Famous name: Gordon Lightfoot (musician)
Nicknames: **Gordie, Gordy**

Grady

Irish *Grada,* "noble" or "illustrious." This name was first used in the southern part of the United States, partly in honor of Henry W. Grady, a Georgia journalist and orator who coined the phrase "The New South" and was instrumental in the rise of Atlanta as a major city. Probably because it rhymes with **Brady,** American parents are starting to notice it; Grady tripled in use between 1997 and 2004.
Nickname: **Grade**

Graeme

This spelling of **Graham** is almost never seen in the United States but is common in England and Australia.

Graham

Old English *Grantham* from *grand* [gravel] + *ham* [home or village]. This name was taken from England to Scotland in the 12th century by William de Graham, a Norman baron, and became the name of a major Scottish clan. Graham was extremely popular as a first name in Great Britain and Australia during the 1950s and 1960s. Although not very popular with American parents, it still holds steady at around 375th place on the popularity list, with about 600 boys given the name every year in the United States.
Famous names: Graham Greene (novelist)
Graham Nash (musician)
Variations: **Graeme, Gram**

Granger

English surname from Old French *grangier,* "one in charge of a granary or an outlying farm." Though probably best known today as the surname of Hermione Granger in the *Harry Potter* series, this name has been given as a first name occasionally in the United States.

Grant

Norman French *graunt,* "tall, large." Like **Graham,** Grant is a surname that migrated from England to Scotland in medieval times, becoming much more common in Scotland than it had been in England. In the 19th century, Grant became a first name in the United States when parents began to name their sons in honor of Ulysses S. Grant, commander of the Union Army during the Civil War and the 18th president of the United States. The name still gets steady use; it was 139th on the popularity list in 2004.
Famous names: Grant Tinker (television producer)
Grant Wood (painter)

Gratian

Latin *Gratiānus,* ultimately derived from *gratus,* "pleasing, good-looking." Gratian was the name of an emperor of the western Roman empire who ruled from A.D. 375 to 383. Almost 800 years later, an Italian monk called Gratian founded the science of canon law. In modern times Gratian seems to have been most used in Romania. It's been rare in the United States but might be considered a masculine form of the now-popular female name **Grace.**

Grayson

Middle English *Grayveson*, "son of the steward." The surname Grayson is growing in popularity as a first name. Almost 1,500 were born in 2004, ranking it 218th on the SSA list.

Green

Old English *grēne*, the color. As a surname, this usually indicates that one's ancestor lived by the village green. Green was regularly given as a first name in the United States during the latter half of the 19th century, though it seems to have disappeared after World War I. Some young parents today consider it a "color name" for children.

Greg, Gregg

Forms of **Gregory.**
Famous names: Gregg Allman (rock singer)
Greg Louganis (Olympic diver)

Gregory

Greek *Gregorios*, "watchful." Sixteen popes and many saints have been named Gregory. Gregory I "the Great" was pope for 14 years in the sixth century; he was instrumental in converting the English to the Christian faith. In 1582, Pope Gregory VIII established the Gregorian calendar, which we still use. Gregory held a spot among the top 50 names in the United States between 1947 and 1988. But 21st-century parents are abandoning it, and it was only 185th in 2004.
Famous names: Gregory Hines (dancer and actor)
Gregory Peck (actor)
Nicknames: **Greg, Gregg**
Variations: **Goyo** (Spanish), **Gregoire** (French), **Gregor** (Czech, German, and Norwegian), **Grigor** (Bulgarian)

Grennan

English surname from Old French *grenon* or *gernon*, "mustache," originally a nickname for a man who wore one. This would make an excellent modernization for **Algernon,** a name with the same derivation that has developed a namby-pamby image.

Griffin

Form of Welsh *Gruffudd*, perhaps "strong prince"; or Middle English *griffin*, "gryphon." A gryphon is a mythical animal with the head and wings of an eagle and the body of a lion; many medieval coats of arms included gryphons. The number of Griffins born in the United States quintupled between 1991 and 2004, when it was the 230th most common boys name.

Famous name: Griffin Dunne (actor)

Nickname: **Griff**

Grover

Old English "one who lives by a grove." The fame of President Grover Cleveland made this one of the top 50 names for American boys for a few years around 1890, but now it's given primarily to boys named after a father or grandfather. A blue muppet named Grover, a member of the cast of *Sesame Street,* has made parents fondly aware of the name even if they don't choose to use it.

Nickname: **Grove**

Guadalupe

Though it's more common for girls, this name, given by devout Mexican Roman Catholics in honor of the Virgin of Guadalupe, is also sometimes bestowed on boys.

Guido

Italian form of **Guy.** Because of the way this name has been used in American gangster movies, it has somewhat of a "Mafia henchman" image. That makes Guido less attractive than other Italian male names to Americans. But in Italy, Guido has no such connotations.

Guillermo

Spanish form of **William.** It was the 368th most common name given to boys born in the United States in 2004.

Guion

Old French *Guyon,* a pet form of **Guy.** In 1983, astronaut Guion Bluford, Jr., became the first African-American in space.

Gunnar

Old Norse *Gunnarr,* "battle warrior"; or Old German *Gundher,* "battle army." In the Germanic saga *The Nibelungenlied,* Gunnar is Brunhild's husband and Kriemhild's brother. The name was primarily used in the United States by Scandinavian-Americans until 1993, but since then other parents have been noticing it, perhaps because of the fame of rock singer Gunnar Nelson. Almost half of the parents who give the name use the somewhat militaristic spelling **Gunner.**

Variations: **Gontier** (French), **Gunder** (Danish)

Gus

Form of **Augustus, Fergus,** or **Gustav.** With the increasing use of **August** and Augustus and the popularity of **Gustavo** with Hispanic-American parents, this rare name may be heard more in the future.

Famous name: Gus Van Sant (film director)

Gustav

Old Norse from *Gautr* [a tribal name] + *stafr* [staff]. This Scandinavian name spread to other countries during the reign of Gustavus Adolphus (Gustaf II) of Sweden, who ascended to the throne in 1611.

Famous name: Gustav Mahler (composer)

Nicknames: **Gus, Gust, Gusti, Tabo, Tavito, Tavo**

Variations: **Gustaf** (Swedish), **Gustave** (French), **Gustavo** (Italian, Portuguese, and Spanish), **Gustavus** (Latin), **Gusts** (Latvian), **Kustaa** (Finnish)

Gustavo

Spanish form of **Gustav,** increasingly popular among the Hispanic-American community. More than 1,000 Gustavos were born in the United States in 2004, ranking it 265th on the SSA list.

Guy

Old German *Wido,* either "wood" or "wide," through French *Guy.* The name Guy came to England during the time of the Norman Conquest and was in common use until 1605 when Guy Fawkes decided to kill King James I and members of Parliament by blowing up the Parliament building. He and his fellow conspirators filled a cellar with gunpowder, but before anything blew up, they were caught and executed. Guy Fawkes Day is still celebrated in England. The name Guy went out of fashion until 1815 when Sir Walter Scott revived it for his novel *Guy Mannering.* Guy was among the top 50 names for American boys in the 1880s, but it went out of fashion when "guy" became a slang term for "man."

Famous name: Guy de Maupassant (short story writer)

Variations: **Guido** (Italian, Spanish, and Portuguese), **Gvidas** (Lithuanian), **Gvidon** (Bulgarian, Croatian, and Russian), **Wyatt**

Hadrian

(See **Adrian.**)

Hakeem

Arabic *Abd al Hakim*, "servant of the wise."

Hal

Originally a medieval form of **Harry** or **Henry;** later also a form of **Harold.** Prince Hal, the rakish son of Henry IV of England and the companion of Falstaff, is depicted in Shakespeare's *Henry IV, Part I* and *Henry IV, Part II*. But in *Henry V,* he has grown up to become a courageous, responsible king. Many today will think of HAL, the computer in the 1968 film *2001: A Space Odyssey,* when they hear this name. Famous name: Hal Linden (actor)

Halston

English surname from a place name, possibly meaning "farm on a neck of land." Since the fashion designer Halston turned his name into a symbol of elegance and sophistication, a few parents have given this name to their sons every year.

Hamilton

Old English "bare or cleared hill" from *hamel* [scarred] + *dun* [hill]. This place name and surname became a first name in the United States in honor of Alexander Hamilton, the first Secretary of the Treasury of the United States and one of the most popular political figures during George Washington's presidency.
Nicknames: **Ham, Tony**

Hamish

Scottish form of **James.** Hamish is very rare in the United States, but it is the name of the little boy in the comic strip *Baby Blues,* though he's usually called **Hammie** by his parents.

Hamisi

Swahili "born on Thursday." Day names are common in many cultures. In Daniel Defoe's novel *Robinson Crusoe,* Friday is the native man who assists Crusoe. In Spanish-speaking countries, Dominic and its many variations mean "born on Sunday."

Hamlin

Norman French *Hamblin,* a diminutive form of Germanic *Haimo,* "home." The name arrived in England after the Norman Conquest and soon became popular as **Hamblen, Hamblin, Hambling, Hamlen,** and **Hamlyn.** All these forms died out as first names around 1500 but survive as surnames today.
Nickname: **Ham**

Hamza

Possibly from Arabic *hamuza,* "to be steadfast." Hamza is a pre-Islamic name from ancient Arabia that has continued to be popular because it was the name of the prophet Muhammad's uncle, one of his more courageous and loyal followers. It is one of the more common names used by Muslims living in the United States today.
Famous name: Hamza Yusuf (scholar of Islam)

Hank

This name existed in medieval England as a short form of *Jehankin,* itself from *Jehan,* a Middle English form of **John.** The name died out in England, but in America it is now used as a nickname for **Henry.** This probably came about when English speakers had contact with the early Dutch settlers in New Netherland (New York), because *Hannek* and *Henk* are common pet forms of **Hendrik,** the Dutch version of Henry.
Famous names: Henry "Hank" Aaron (baseball player)
Hank Williams (country musician)

Hannibal

Phoenician "one favored by the god Baal." Hannibal, a Carthaginian general, crossed the Alps in 218 B.C. and defeated the Romans. He did not follow up his victory by sacking Rome, but returned to Carthage. Some parents might be swayed away from this name because of the character Hannibal Lecter in the movie *The Silence of the Lambs.*
Variations: **Anibal, Hanibal**

Hans

Danish, Dutch, and German form of **John.** Many Americans will recall the story of the Dutch boy Hans Brinker and his silver skates. Famous name: Hans Christian Andersen (writer)

Harding

Old English *Hearding,* "son or follower of *Heard.*" Heard was an Old English name meaning "hardy, strong, brave." This surname was first used as a given name to honor President Warren Harding.

Harlan

Old English *Harland,* "gray land." This surname most likely became a given name originally in honor of the Harlan family of Kentucky, the most prominent member of which, John Marshall Harlan, served on the U.S. Supreme Court from 1877 until 1911 and cast dissenting votes against racial segregation. His grandson, John Marshall Harlan II, also served on the Supreme Court between 1955 and 1971. The most famous man with this first name, Harlan Sanders, maintained the Kentucky connection by founding Kentucky Fried Chicken. Famous name: Harlan Ellison (science fiction writer)

Harley

Old English "hares' glade." Harley was fairly common as a male given name in the late 19th century, and though it receded during the 20th, it never completely vanished. After a low point in the 1960s it rose in use during the 1990s, but it's falling off again as parents realize the name is now twice as common for girls as it is for boys.

Harlow

Old English "army hill."

Harold

Old English *Hereweald* from *here* [army] + *weald* [power]; also, Old Norse *Harivald.* Harold II was the last Saxon king of England. He reigned for only a few months because he broke the oath he had made to William the Conqueror, duke of Normandy. Harold's army met William's at the battle of Hastings on October 14, 1066, where the Saxons were defeated and Harold was killed. The story is retold by Tennyson in his poem *Harold.* Lord Byron used the name in his long poem *Childe Harold,* on which Berlioz based his opera *Harold in Italy.* Harold was a very popular name in the early part of the 20th century, but it's been falling out of fashion for decades and is no longer even among the top 500 names for American boys.

Famous names: Harold Lloyd (silent film comedian)

Harold Ramis (actor, director, and writer)

Nicknames: **Hal, Harry**

Variations: **Garald** (Russian), **Harald** (German and Scandinavian), **Haraldo** (Portuguese and Spanish), **Haralds** (Latvian)

Haroun

(See **Aaron.**)

Harrison

Middle English *Herryson*, "son of **Henry.**" This name increased substantially in use during the 1980s and 1990s, but it may have peaked in 1998. There were more than 1,700 Harrisons born in the United States in 2004, and it ranked 199th that year.

Famous name: Harrison Ford (actor)

Harry

Originally a form of **Henry;** in modern times, also a form of **Harold.** In Elizabethan England, the name Henry was pronounced Harry, but when spelling became more uniform, Harry became a separate name. The combined effects of Prince Harry and Harry Potter have led to a strong revival of the name in England, where it has been 11th most popular since 2002. No such increase has occurred in the United States, where the number of Harrys has fallen 30 percent since 1990 until it was only the 460th most popular name in 2004.

Famous names: Harry Belafonte (singer)

Harry Houdini (magician)

Harry S. Truman (33rd U.S. president)

Variations: **Arrigo** (Italian), **Hal**

Harvey

Breton *Haerveu*, "battle-worthy." This warrior's name came to England during the Norman Invasion. Today, however, Harvey is not associated with fierceness but with the gentle, imaginary rabbit in Mary Chase's play *Harvey*, which was made into a movie starring James Stewart. St. Harvey lived during the sixth century and was known for his piety. Because he was blind, he is invoked for eye trouble. Though the name Harvey is now completely out of fashion in the United States, it has come back strongly in England and Wales, where it was among the top 40 names of 2004.

Famous name: Harvey Fierstein (playwright and actor)

Variations: **Herve** (French), **Hervey**

Hassan

Arabic "good." This was the name of a grandson of the prophet Muhammad who is venerated as a martyr by the Shi'ite branch of Islam. The name has been among the top 1,000 names for American boys on the SSA list since 1971.

Hatcher

Middle English *Hetchere*, "dweller by the gate."

Hawk

Old English *Hafoc*, "hawk." Unlike **Eagle** and **Falcon,** Hawk was used as a first name in ancient Anglo-Saxon society. The fact that all three of them are being used as "nature names" for boys today shows the great respect that many nature lovers have for raptors or hunting birds.

Hayden

Old English *heg denu*, "hay valley," English place name; or Irish Gaelic *Eideain*, "armor." This name came out of nowhere in 1990, reaching 221st place on the popularity chart in 1991. That means that in the first three years of the 1990s alone at least 4,000 American boys were named Hayden, many more than had been so-named in the previous three decades. This explosion must have been inspired by Hayden Fox, the title character of the television series *Coach,* which debuted in February 1989. As one of the rhyming forms of **Aidan** and **Jaden,** Hayden has continued its climb and was the 85th most popular name of 2004, with more than 5,300 born that year.

Famous name: Hayden Christensen (actor)

Other spellings: **Haden, Haiden**

Heath

Old English *hæth*, "heath," a surname for someone who lived on the heath. The frequent use of Heath as a given name was no doubt inspired by the character of Heath Barkley (played by Lee Majors) on the television Western *The Big Valley*. The show premiered in the fall of 1965, and in 1966 Heath catapulted onto the SSA top 1,000 list in 359th place, an amazing initial position. Unlike some television-inspired names, however, the use of Heath did not decline when the series left the primetime airwaves in 1969. Heath's highest years of use were during the middle 1970s, which probably shows that parents had accepted it as a masculine counterpart for **Heather,** which was at its highest point of use during the same years. But since the late 1970s, Heath has been steadily fading away. It did have a minor upturn in 2001 and 2002, just after the Australian actor Heath Ledger became a star through the film *A Knight's Tale,* but the name is already receding once again. There were 280 boys named Heath born in the United States in 2004, ranking it 690th on the SSA list.

Hector

Greek *Hektor,* "one who holds fast" or "restrainer." In Homer's *Iliad,* Hector, the brave son of Priam, was killed by Achilles, and his body was dragged three times around the wall of Troy. In England, the name is part of the legend of King Arthur. Sir Hector was the foster father of the king, and Sir Hector de Mares was a knight of the Round Table. Shakespeare depicted Hector as the sensible older brother of Paris and Troilus in his play *Troilus and Cressida.* In the United States today, Hector is a very popular name with Hispanic-Americans but is only rarely found in other ethnic groups. Almost 2,000 Hectors were born in 2004, ranking it 182nd on the SSA list.
Famous name: Hector Berlioz (composer)
Nickname: **Heck**
Variations: **Ector** (Greek), **Ettore** (Italian), **Heitor** (Portuguese), **Hektor** (Polish, Czech, and Scandinavian), **Hektoras** (Lithuanian)

Henri

French form of **Henry.**
Famous names: Henri Matisse (painter)
Henri Nouwen (writer on spirituality)

Henry

Old German *Haimirich* from *haimi* [home] + *ric* [ruler, protector]. Henry is a royal name in England, France, and Germany. Henry I of England, the fourth son of William the Conqueror, ruled for more than 30 years. His grandson Henry II established English common law. Henry VIII is said to be the founder of the modern English state. In the United States, Henry was a top ten name in the 19th century but then fell steadily in use until about 1994, when it bottomed out at around 150th. It then began a slow rise back up the popularity curve to 110th place in 2004. Henry today is perhaps the boys name whose use is most marked by educational status; physicians and lawyers seem to think Henry is a great name for a son, while blue-collar parents still seem to think the name sounds a bit wimpy.

Famous names: Henry Fonda (actor)
Henry Ford (industrialist)
Henry Wadsworth Longfellow (poet)
Henry David Thoreau (author)

Nicknames: **Hal, Hank, Harry**

Other spelling: **Henrey**

Variations: **Andrique, Eanraig** (Scottish), **Enrico** (Italian), **Enrique** (Spanish), **Heinrich, Heinz** (German), **Hendrik** (Danish and Dutch), **Henri** (French), **Henrico, Henrik** (Swedish), **Henryk** (Polish), **Jindrich** (Czech), **Kiki, Kiko, Quico, Quiqui**

Herbert

Old German *Hariberct* from *harja* [army] + *berhta* [bright]. Herbert was one of the top 50 names for American boys until 1933. It then slid downward until it fell out of the SSA top 1,000 list in 2003.

Famous name: Herbert Hoover (31st U.S. president)

Nicknames: **Bert, Bertie, Herb, Herbie**

Variations: **Erberto** (Italian), **Harbert** (Dutch), **Hebert** (French), **Herberto** (Spanish), **Heribert** (German and Slovakian), **Heriberto** (Spanish), **Hoireabard** (Irish)

Herbie

Form of **Herbert.** For more than 35 years the Disney studios have been making movies about a Volkswagen Beetle called Herbie, from *The Love Bug* in 1968 to 2005's *Herbie: Fully Loaded.*

Famous name: Herbie Hancock (jazz pianist and composer)

Heriberto

Spanish form of **Herbert,** still well used by Hispanic-Americans.

Herman

Old German *Harimann* from *harja* [army] + *mann* [man]. This name was common around 1900 but declined throughout the 20th century, finally vanishing from the SSA top 1,000 list in the year 2000.

Famous name: Herman Melville (novelist)

Nicknames: **Herm, Hermie, Hermy**

Variations: **Armand** (French), **Armando** (Spanish and Italian), **Armant, Armin, Armond, Erman** (Romanian), **Ermanno** (Italian), **Harman, Harmon, Hermann** (Danish and German)

Herschel

German and Yiddish "deer."

Famous name: Hershel Walker (football player)

Nicknames: **Hersch, Hersh, Hirsch, Hirsh**

Other spelling: **Hershel**

Hideki

Japanese "excellent tree."

Hideo

Japanese "excellent male."

Famous name: Hideo Nomo (baseball player)

Hillman

English surname that can mean either "dweller by the slope" or "servant of *Hild*." Hild was an Old English name meaning "battle."

Hiram

Perhaps a form of Hebrew *Ahiram*, "brother of the exalted." In the Bible, Hiram is the king of Tyre. He sent cedar trees, as well as carpenters and masons, to King David to build him a house. Later, Hiram cut down the cedars of Lebanon to build David's son, Solomon, a palace. The name was in regular use in the northern United States from the 17th century to the late 19th century. The form Hyrum is still regularly given to boys in Utah in honor of Hyrum Smith, brother of the Mormon prophet Joseph Smith, who was martyred in Illinois in 1844.

Nickname: **Hi**

Variation: **Hyrum**

Hobart

Variation of **Hubert.**

Hogan

Irish surname, Anglicized form of Gaelic *Ó hÓgáin*, "descendant of *Ogán*, an ancient Gaelic name meaning "young."

Holden

Old English *Holedene*, "deep valley," from *hol* [hollow] + *denu* [valley]. This unusual name was chosen by J. D. Salinger for the teenage antihero of *The Catcher in the Rye*. But even though that book, published in 1951, became a favorite of teenagers, the name Holden didn't really catch on with American parents until the darkly handsome character Holden Snyder debuted on the daytime soap opera *As the World Turns* in 1985. Holden first appeared on the SSA top 1,000 list in 1987 and has steadily risen since, ranking 338th in 2004.

Hollis

Old English *holegn*, "holly." This name could be thought of as a masculine form of **Holly** and given to boys born around Christmas.

Homer

Greek *Homeros*, meaning uncertain, perhaps "hostage" or "blind." Homer became a fairly popular American name in the early 19th century when names from classical Greek and Roman literature were in vogue. The name is rarely found in the United States now. Homer is best known as the name of the father of the television cartoon family *The Simpsons*. This should ensure that American boys named Homer will remain scarce for at least another generation.
Famous name: Homer (Greek poet)
Variations: **Homere** (French), **Homero** (Spanish), **Homeros** (Greek), **Omero** (Italian)

Hood

Old English *hod*, "hood," originally a nickname for someone who made hoods or who wore a distinctive hood. This surname goes at least as far back as Robin Hood, the legendary English outlaw. Hood is extremely rare as a first name.

Hooper

Old English "one who fits hoops on barrels." Hooper is a rare given name in spite of similar popular names like **Cooper** and **Hunter**.
Nickname: **Hoop**

Horace

Latin *Horatius*, a Roman family name, which may be related to *hora*, "time." The Roman poet Horatius Flaccus is known as Horace.

Horace Slughorn is the new teacher of Potions in *Harry Potter and the Half-Blood Prince*.

Variations: **Horacio** (Spanish), **Horatio, Horatius** (Estonian and German), **Oracio, Orasio, Orazio** (Italian), **Racho**

Horatio

Variation of **Horace**. Captain Horatio Hornblower is the hero of the well-known stories by C. S. Forester.

Famous names: Horatio Alger (author)

Horatio Nelson (British admiral)

Houston

Old English and Scottish "Hugh's town." Samuel Houston was president of the Republic of Texas. Originally Houston was bestowed as a first name to honor him. During the 1980s it seemed as if Houston might become a popular name, but it peaked in use around 1994 at only 632nd on the SSA list and had fallen back to 822nd by 2004.

Howard

Old German *Huguard* from *hug* [heart, mind] + *hard* [hardy, brave]; or Old Norse *Haward* from *ha* [high] + *vard* [guardian]. This aristocratic English surname became a popular first name in wealthy American families during the 1870s and by 1900 had spread to all social classes. Howard has been going out of fashion since 1950, but a few parents are still choosing it for their sons; it was 779th on the SSA list in 2004. Howard Hughes, the wealthy industrialist, was in the public eye throughout his life. As a young man, he was a dashing playboy; as an old man, a bizarre recluse.

Nicknames: **Howie, Ward**

Variations: **Hewart**

Howie

Pet form of **Howard**.

Famous name: Howie Mandel (comedian)

Hoyt

Middle English *hoit*, "long stick," originally a nickname for a very tall and thin man.

Famous name: Hoyt Axton (country singer)

Other spelling: **Hoyte**

Hubert

Old German *Hugubert* from *hug* [heart, mind] + *berht* [bright, famous]. Eighth-century St. Hubert is the patron saint of hunters.
Famous name: Hubert Humphrey (U.S. vice president)
Nicknames: **Bert, Hub, Hube, Hubi, Hubie**
Variations: **Hobart, Hoibeard** (Irish), **Hubbard, Huberto** (Spanish), **Hugbert** (German), **Uberto** (Italian)

Hudson

Middle English "son of **Hud**"; Hud being a common medieval pet form of **Hugh**. The name Hudson is best known today as the name of New York's Hudson River, which was named after English explorer Henry Hudson, who discovered it for his Dutch employers in 1609. Hudson had some minor popularity as a given name a century ago. It re-entered the SSA top 1,000 list in 1995, and by 2004 it had increased by a factor of seven to be the 295th most common boys name.

Huey

Pet form of **Hugh**.
Famous name: Huey Lewis (rock musician)

Hugh

Probably Old German *huga*, "heart, mind, spirit." This name was popular in England and France during the Middle Ages because of St. Hugh of England, a medieval bishop noted for his charity and his defense of the Church against the crown, and because of Hugh Capet, founder of the Capetian dynasty in France. A top 100 name in the United States in the 19th century, Hugh then went into a long decline. Its rank of 918th on the SSA list in 2004 was its lowest ever.
Famous name: Hugh Grant (actor)
Nicknames: **Hewie, Huey, Hughie, Hughy**
Variations: **Hud, Huet, Hugo** (Danish, Dutch, German, Spanish, and Swedish), **Hugon** (Polish and Spanish), **Hugonas** (Lithuanian), **Hugues** (French), **Hutch, Huugo** (Finnish), **Ugo** (Italian), **Ugon** (Greek)

Hugo

Form of **Hugh**. Hugo has been steadily rising in use since the 1960s. It is now more popular than ever in the United States, ranking 336th for boys born in 2004. This is partly because it's a name used by the growing Hispanic population, but also because Hugo's image has shifted from being geeky to being quirky.

Famous name: Hugo Chávez (president of Venezuela)

Humberto

Spanish form of *Humbert,* from Germanic *hun,* "bear cub" or "warrior" and *bert,* "bright." Though **Humbert** is generally an unpopular name, the Hispanic-American use of Humberto has kept it among the top 1,000 names for boys born in the United States since 1944.

Humphrey, Humphry

Norman French *Humfrey;* form of Old German *Hunfrid* from *hun* [bear cub, young warrior] + *frid* [peace]. Even the well-loved actor Humphrey Bogart wasn't able to attract many parents to this little-used name. It dates to at least the 12th century in England and was the name of the unfortunate duke of Gloucester, the son of Henry IV, who founded one of the first libraries at Oxford University and later was starved to death in the Tower of London.

Variations: **Onfredo** (Italian), **Onfroy** (French)

Hunter

Middle English *huntere,* "huntsman." Hunter increased in popularity rather rapidly during the 1990s, rising from 255th place in 1989 to 39th place in 2000 on the list of names for newborn boys in the United States. Perhaps some of its success can be traced to the 1980s television series *Hunter,* which starred former professional football player Fred Dryer as Rick Hunter, a sergeant in the Los Angeles Police Department. The rugged outdoor associations of the word *hunter* also contribute to the name's image. Hunter's peak may have passed, though, because it slipped to 57th place in 2004.

Famous name: Hunter S. Thompson (journalist)

Huntington

Middle English *Huntindune,* "hill where hunting occurs."

Hyatt

English surname, perhaps "dweller by the high gate."

Hyrum

(See **Hiram.**)

Iago

Italian and Welsh form of **James.** In Shakespeare's *Othello,* the villain-ous Iago convinces the Moor that his wife has been unfaithful.

Ian

This Scottish form of **John** was rare in the United States before 1970 and usually indicated Scottish ancestry. Since then it has steadily ascended in popularity, reaching 73rd place in 2004. Sir Ian McKellen's distinguished acting career has been enhanced by his performance as Gandalf in the *Lord of the Rings* film trilogy.
Famous names: Ian Fleming (writer)
                    Ian Thorpe (Olympic swimmer)
Other spelling: **Iain**

Ibrahim

Arabic form of **Abraham.** The use of Ibrahim by both Muslim immi-grants and African-Americans has led to a recent increase in the number of boys given this name in the United States.

Ichabod

Hebrew *Ikabhoth,* "where is the glory?" In the Old Testament, the wife of Phinehas goes into labor when she learns that her husband has been killed in battle; she then dies in childbirth after naming her son Ichabod. Because of this story, it became the custom among the Puritans in colonial New England to name boys Ichabod whose mothers died in childbirth. The name had almost died out by the 19th century when Washington Irving wrote *The Legend of Sleepy Hollow* and named its comic schoolmaster hero Ichabod Crane.

Iggy

Pet form of **Ignatius.**
Famous name: Iggy Pop (punk rocker)

Ignacio

Modern Spanish form of **Ignatius,** still used by Mexican-Americans today in honor of Ignacio Zaragoza, the general whose defeat of invading French forces at Puebla on May 5, 1862, is celebrated every year as Cinco de Mayo.

Ignatius

Form of *Egnatius,* Roman family name of Etruscan origin and unknown meaning, but altered to resemble Latin *ignis,* "fire." Several saints were named Ignatius, including St. Ignatius of Antioch, who was killed by lions in the Roman arena, and St. Ignatius Loyola, who founded the Society of Jesus, the Jesuits.
Nickname: **Iggy**
Variations: **Ignacio** (Spanish), **Íñigo** (medieval Spanish)

Igor

Russian form of Scandinavian *Ivar* from Old Norse *yr* [yew] + *herr* [army].
Famous name: Igor Stravinsky (composer)

Ikaika

Hawaiian "strength" or "power." Ikaika has been one of the most common native Hawaiian names given by Hawaiian parents over the last 30 years.

Ike

Short form of **Isaac.**
Famous name: Ike Turner (rock musician and record producer)

Ingmar

Scandinavian from *Ing* [a Norse fertility god] + *maerr* [famous]. This name has become known in the United States through movie director Ingmar Bergman.

Inigo

From *Íñigo,* an old Spanish form of **Ignatius,** blending it with Basque *Eneko,* possibly "place on a slope." This name is known because of Inigo Jones, a 17th-century English architect whose buildings are still widely admired today. Though this name is almost never used, if other male names ending in –o like **Leo** and **Enzo** continue to rise in popularity, Inigo might catch the eye of a few bold namers.

Ira

Hebrew "watchful" or "young ass."
Famous name: Ira Gershwin (lyricist)

Irvin

Form of **Irving.** In 2004 there were actually 305 Irvins and only 180 Irvings born in the United States.

Irving

Scottish place name and surname, probably meaning "green river." Like **Byron, Emerson,** and **Milton,** Irving is a surname that became a first name out of admiration for a famous author: Washington Irving, the early-19th-century American writer most remembered for *The Legend of Sleepy Hollow.* In the 19th century, Jewish immigrant parents gave their son or daughter a Hebrew name, usually in honor of a deceased relative, to be used in the synagogue. The parents also gave the child an "American" name on their birth certificate to help them assimilate into the larger society. It was the custom, however, to pick an "American" name that started with the same letter as the Hebrew name. There are many biblical Hebrew names starting with *I,* such as **Isaiah, Israel,** and **Isaac,** but when most Jews first came to the United States, the only obviously "American" name starting with *I* was Irving. Thus, Irving quickly became a predominantly Jewish name in the United States, which, ironically, defeated the purpose of parents who wanted to give their son an American name that wouldn't immediately type him as Jewish.
Famous name: Irving Berlin (composer)
Nicknames: **Irv, Ving**
Variations: **Irvin, Irvine, Irwin**

Irwin

Variation of **Irving** or **Erwin.**
Other spelling: **Irwyn**

Isaac

Hebrew "laughter." In the Old Testament, Isaac was cherished by his mother, Sarah, because the Lord granted her wish to have a child when she feared she was too old to bear children. But after giving Sarah and her husband, Abraham, this child, the Lord demanded that Abraham sacrifice his son to show his faith. Just before he was about to slay Isaac, the Lord appeared and spared the boy, explaining that Abraham's willingness to obey was testimony enough. The name Isaac has steadily become more popular; it rose from 118th on the list of names given to American boys in 1991 to 50th in 2004.

Famous names: Isaac Asimov (author)

Isaac Newton (mathematician and physicist)

Isaac Stern (violinist)

Nicknames: **Ike, Ikey, Ikie, Zac, Zak**

Other spellings: **Isac, Isacc, Ysaac, Ysac**

Variations: **Isaak** (German, Greek, and Russian), **Isacco** (Italian), **Itzhak, Izaak** (Dutch and Polish), **Yitzchak, Yitzhak** (modern Hebrew)

Isaiah

Hebrew "Yahweh is salvation." The Book of Isaiah was written by a prophet who lived seven centuries before Jesus. In the 1980s Isaiah was already popular with African-American parents, but since then it has soared in use among all ethnic groups. Isaiah was the 46th most popular boys name in the United States in 2004.

Other spelling: **Isiah**

Variations: **Esaias** (Danish and Swedish), **Isaia** (Italian and Romanian), **Isaías** (Spanish and Portuguese)

Isaias

Spanish *Isaías,* form of **Isaiah.** As Isaiah has boomed in use in the general population, Isaias has done the same with Hispanic parents and was 502nd on the SSA list in 2004.

Isamu

Japanese "brave." Japanese-American sculptor Isamu Noguchi (1904–1988) is considered one of the most influential artists and designers of the 20th century.

Ismael

Spanish form of *Ishmael,* Hebrew "God hears," the name of Abraham's son by Hagar, said to be the ancestor of the Arabs. Though **Ishmael** is rare in the United States, Ismael is increasingly popular among Hispanics and ranked 297th among newborn males in 2004.

Israel

Hebrew *Yisrael*, "God perseveres" or "wrestling with God." This name was given to Jacob after he successfully wrestled with an angel, and his descendants were called the people of Israel. The name Israel has been rising in use since the 1960s; it ranked 205th for American boys born in 2004.

Variations: **Israele** (Italian), **Izrael** (Polish and Hungarian), **Izraelis** (Lithuanian), **Srul** (Yiddish)

Issa

Arabic and Swahili form of **Jesus.**

Itzhak

Variation of **Isaac.**
Famous name: Itzhak Perlman (violinist)

Ivan

Russian variation of **John.** Ivan was the name of six Russian tsars. The 15th-century Ivan III, called Ivan the Great, helped unify Russia by preventing the Tartars from overrunning the country. The 16th-century Ivan IV, known as Ivan the Terrible, was the first tsar of unified Russia. Although he brought order to the central government, he was known for his personal cruelty. As similar-sounding names like **Evan** and **Isaac** have boomed, Ivan has been drawn up in their wake, reaching 122nd place in 2004, with more than 3,000 American boys given the name. **Iván** is also a popular name in Spain.
Famous names: Ivan Lendl (tennis player)
Ivan Reitman (film director)
Nickname: **Van**

Ives

(See **Yves.**)

Ivor

English form of an Old Norse name from *ȳn*, "yew, bow" and *herr* "army, warrior." Ivor has always been quite rare in the United States, but it is well known in Britain because of the memory of Ivor Novello (1893–1951), one of the most popular singers and songwriters in British history. The Ivor Novello Award is given in the United Kingdom every year to the writer of the best song.

Jabari

Swahili "brave" or "martyr for the cause." Jabari is one of the few African-language names that has become generally popular in the African-American community. It ranked 613th on the SSA list in 2004.

Jabulani

IsuZulu (South Africa) "celebrate."

Jace

This short form of **Jason** has become more common as a name in its own right as Jason itself has fallen away. Jace was the 172nd most common boys name of 2004.

Jack

Form of **John**, from Middle English *Jankin, Jackin.* Jack was considered an independent name in England as early as the 14th century. The name abounds in folktales and children's nursery rhymes, including "Jack and the Beanstalk," "Jack Sprat," "Jack and Jill," and "Little Jack Horner," which shows that Jack had already become the name for the typical "every-man" in England centuries ago. It is once again the typical name in England, where Jack has been the number-one name for boys since 1995. Jack quintupled in use in the United States between 1990 and 2004, when it reached 52nd on the popularity chart. The name's success in the United States is masked by the reluctance of many American parents to use one-syllable names for boys; if Jack and **Jackson** were counted together, they would have been the 11th most popular name for American boys born in 2004.

Famous names: Jack London (novelist)
Jack Nicholson (actor)
Jack Nicklaus (golfer)

Nickname: **Jackie**
Variation: **Jock** (Scottish)

Jackie

Form of **Jack.**

Famous names: Jackie Gleason (comedian)
Jackie Robinson (baseball player)

Other spelling: **Jacky**

Jackson

Middle English *Jakson,* "son of **Jack.**" When the alternative spellings **Jaxon** and **Jaxson** are counted in, there were over 1,000 more boys named Jackson in the United States in 2004 than there were boys officially named Jack. Jackson has exploded even faster than Jack; there were more than 11 times as many Jacksons born in 2004 as there were in 1990. Interestingly, the Jack vs. Jackson contest in 2004 paralleled the political divide: Parents in states that voted Republican tended to favor Jackson, while in Democratic states Jack was the winner. There were only six states where the pattern did not hold. This may be connected to the contrasting media images of the names; many women feel that Jack has a sophisticated "preppy" image today, while Jackson reminds them more of a cowboy.

Famous names: Jackson Browne (singer)
Jackson Pollock (painter)

Jacob

Ancient Semitic *Ya'aqob,* "may God protect," later interpreted as Hebrew "supplanter." In the Book of Genesis, Jacob was the son of Isaac and Rebecca. He tricked his father into giving him the inheritance that rightfully belonged to his brother, Esau. Jacob later became the founder of the Israelite nation. He is also remembered for his vision of a stairway to heaven, called Jacob's ladder. In 1999, Jacob performed the amazing feat of knocking Michael out of the number-one spot it had held for 45 years, and it's remained the most popular boys name in the United States since. Jacob's success probably came by combining the popular "long *a*" sound with a solid historical pedigree, and it was the only obvious traditional name starting with *J* left for revival after **Jason, Jeremy, Justin, Jonathan, Jordan,** and **Joshua** seemed overused to many young parents.

Nicknames: **Jake, Jakie**

Variations: **Giacobbe** (Italian), **Jacobo** (Spanish), **Jacques** (French), **Jakob** (German), **James**

Jacques

French form of **Jacob** or **James.**

Famous names: Jacques Cousteau (explorer)
Jacques Louis David (painter)

Jaden

See **Jayden.** Until 2002 this was the most common spelling of this very popular name.

Jaheim

African-American creation blending the name **Jamal** and the word *Raheem*, Arabic "compassionate." The fame of the hip-hop artist Jaheim catapulted his name into the SSA top 1,000 list in 2001, but it may already be receding in use again.

Jaime

Spanish form of **James,** ranking 255th for American boys born in 2004.

Jair

Hebrew "enlightened," the name of five minor biblical characters. This name entered the SSA top 1,000 list in 1996 when Jair Lynch became the first African-American to win an Olympic medal in gymnastics by attaining the silver on parallel bars. Jair ranked 604th on the SSA list in 2004.

Jairo

Spanish form of **Jair,** coincidentally ranking 605th on the SSA list in 2004, just below Jair. Jairo, however, has been among the top 1,000 names on that list since 1985. Part of the name's recent success in the Hispanic community may be due to the Argentine singer Jairo, whose full name is Jairo González.

Jake

Usually a form of **Jacob** or **James,** but the football quarterback Jake Plummer was born a **Jason.** More than 4,000 American boys were given Jake as their official name in 2004.

Famous names: Jake Gyllenhaal (actor)
Jake Steinfeld (fitness expert)

Jaleel

Arabic *Jalil,* "grand, exalted."

Jalen

When Jalen Rose was born in 1973, his mother created his name by blending the names of his father and uncle, **James** and **Lenny.** Rose went on to become hugely famous as a college basketball player at the University of Michigan, and African-American parents immediately began to name sons after him. The popularity of the name has increased with Rose's professional basketball career. More than 5,000 Jalens were born in the United States in 2004, making it 86th on the popularity list.

Other spellings: **Jaylan, Jaylen, Jaylin, Jaylon**

Jamal

Arabic "beauty, handsomeness." This name, popular in most of the Arab world, also became the most popular Muslim name in the African-American community during the 1990s. The similar Arabic names **Jamel** and **Jamil** (meaning "handsome") are also well used.

Other spellings: **Jamaal, Jamahl**

Jamar

This is a very rare Muslim name used in Pakistan from the Arabic word for "sparks," but it is not used as a name in the Arabic-speaking world. In the United States, Jamar has been a popular African-American name since the 1970s. It was probably created by combining the sounds of **Jamal** and **Lamar.** Since 1997 **Jamari** has also become popular with African-Americans; this looks like a Swahili version of Jamar, and examples of men with this name exist in both Tanzania and Indonesia, but it is not related to any known Swahili word. However, it is the sound rather than the derivation that is driving these names' popularity, which is shown by the fact that **Jamarcus** and **Jamarion** are also common enough in the African-American community to make the SSA top 1,000 list in 2004. It seems best to see these names as creative African-American forms that imitate African names, rather than being truly African themselves.

James

English form of **Jacob.** This name developed from late Latin *Iacomus,* a form of the original Latin *Iacobus.* In the New Testament, two of Jesus' apostles were named James. Another James was a brother of Jesus and the first bishop of Jerusalem; he is thought to be the author of the Epistle of St. James. James I of England, also James VI of Scotland, was the son of the executed Mary Queen of Scots. James II reigned for only three years. When he was suspected of trying to return the country to Roman Catholicism, his daughter Mary and her husband, William of Orange, were encouraged to take over the British throne, which they did in the Glorious Revolution. Two literary giants also share this name: James Joyce of Ireland and American James Baldwin. In American history, the name is presidential. James Madison, the father of the Constitution and one of the authors of the Federalist papers, was the fourth president. James Monroe was the fifth president and the author of the Monroe Doctrine. James Polk was the 11th president and designed the doctrine of manifest destiny. James Buchanan was the 15th president, and James Garfield was the 29th president. The fictional spy James Bond and actor James Dean, who gained fame with the movie *Rebel Without a Cause,* provide dashing images for this traditional name. Though nowhere near as common as it used to be, James was still 22nd on the popularity list in 2004, with more than 16,000 American boys given the name that year.

Famous names: James Earl Jones (actor)

James Stewart (actor)

James Taylor (singer)

Nicknames: **Jake, Jamey, Jamie, Jamy, Jay, Jem, Jemmy, Jim, Jimmy**

Variations: **Giacomo** (Italian), **Hamish** (Scottish), **Iago** (Italian and Welsh), **Jacques** (French), **Jago** (Cornish), **Jaime** (Spanish), **Jayme** (Portuguese), **Santiago** (Spanish), **Seamas, Shamus** (Irish)

Jameson

Middle English *Jamesson,* "son of **James.**" American parents who like James but want to name their sons something slightly unusual began choosing this name during the 1980s while actor Jameson Parker was starring in the television series *Simon & Simon.* It has remained in steady use since, showing signs recently of increasing popularity.

Other spelling: **Jamison**

Jamie

Pet form of **James,** traditionally popular especially in Scotland. Jamie was one of the top 100 names for boys born in the United States in the 1970s, until *The Bionic Woman* came along in 1976 and made

many Americans think of Jamie as being primarily a female name. Though it's fallen away drastically since then, Jamie hasn't completely vanished as a boys name, being 541st on the SSA list in 2004.
Famous name: Jamie Foxx (actor)
Other spelling: **Jamey**

Jamil

Arabic "handsome."

Jamir

Possibly a South Asian variation of **Jamil,** or an African-American creation.

Jan

Dutch, Scandinavian, Polish, and Czech form of **John.**
Famous name: Jan Vermeer (painter)

Jaquan

African-American creation combining the syllables *Ja-* from names like **Jamal** and *–quan,* also found in **Quantavious.** Jaquan has been one of the more successful such creations, especially considering that there aren't any particular celebrities contributing to its use. Jaquan has been in the SSA top 1,000 list since 1988 and was 496th on that list in 2004.

Jared

Perhaps Hebrew "descent" or Akkadian "servant." In the Book of Genesis, Jared is the father of Enoch and grandfather of Methuselah. The only other information given about him is that he lived to age 962, making him second only to his grandson in longevity. Puritan parents in the 17th century began calling sons Jared to express the hope that they would have long and healthy lives. There is also a Jared in the Book of Mormon who has a nameless brother—always referred to as "the Brother of Jared"—who is an even more important person; he receives a vision of Christ and is told about Jesus' future coming in the flesh. This kept the name well used in Utah for years after it almost disappeared from the rest of the United States. Jared revived strongly all over the United States in the late 1960s when Jarrod Barkley (played by actor Richard Long) appeared as the self-controlled lawyer son on the television Western *The Big Valley.*

Many parents probably saw Jared as an updated version of **Gerald;** indeed, **Jarrod** is a rare English surname based on Gerald. Jared, and not Jarrod, became the more common spelling because parents were familiar with that version. American parents have felt free to respell this name, and forms such as **Jarod, Jarred, Jerad, Jerod, Jerrid, Jerrod,** and the like have been well used alongside the two main spellings. The name remained fairly common throughout the 1980s and had an increase of about 25 percent between 1996 and 2000 while Michael T. Weiss was playing Jarod on the television series *The Pretender*. This put Jared among the top 50 names for American boys, but since 2000 the name has fallen rapidly, landing at 128th place in 2004.

Jaron

This name is often pronounced differently depending on the bearer's ethnicity. African-Americans often accent the name on the second syllable, while others are more likely to rhyme it with **Darren.** For both groups it is probably an invented name blending the sounds of names like **Jared, Jamal, Darren,** and **Javon.** Jaron and **Jaren** counted together made this the 421st most popular boys name of 2004.

Jarrett

Form of **Garret.**

Jarvis

English form of French *Gervaise,* a medieval saint's name of unknown origin.

Jason

Greek "the healer"; used in New Testament times as a Greek form of **Joshua.** In Greek mythology, Jason led the Argonauts on their quest for the Golden Fleece. He later married the sorceress Medea, who helped him fulfill his quest. His life turned to tragedy when Medea, suspecting Jason of infidelity, killed their children. Jason was a rare name until it suddenly boomed in the late 1960s. It rapidly became one of the most popular names for boys in the United States, being the second most common in the 1970s. But Jason's popularity began to recede around 1980, and it was only 51st on the list for newborn boys in 1991. The murdering monster character called Jason in the *Friday the 13th* series of "slasher" films may have contributed to this quick fall. After 1992, Jason had a slight rise in use, which may have been due to boys named

"Jason II" after fathers born during the name's 1970s heyday. Jason was the 48th most common name in 2004.

Famous name: Jason Robards (actor)

Nicknames: **Jace, Jake, Jay**

Jasper

Possibly from a Persian word meaning "treasurer." Traditionally, Jasper was one of the three kings who came to Bethlehem to worship the baby Jesus, but there is no biblical mention of the name. Moderately common in the United States in the late 19th century, Jasper then fell away from use somewhat but never disappeared as a name for boys. Recently it's been inching up in popularity as parents search for J names that have not been overused.

Variations: **Caspar** (Dutch), **Casper** (Danish and English), **Gaspar** (Spain), **Gaspare** (Italian), **Kaspar** (German)

Javen

Probably an alternate spelling of *Javan,* an Old Testament name meaning "Greece." American parents have just begun to discover Javen as another alternative for **Jason** and **Jayden.** The name first entered the SSA list in 2002. It's probably not a coincidence that gospel singer Javen Campbell released an album titled *Javen* that same year.

Javier

Spanish form of **Xavier.** There were 2,500 Javiers born in the United States in 2004, making it the 157th most common name.

Famous name: Javier Bardem (actor)

Javon

This African-American creation, normally accented on the second syllable, has been one of the more successful new names for black males since the 1980s. It was the 365th most common boys name in the United States in 2004. Recently the fashion for the "long *a*" vowel has also led many African-American parents to name sons **Jayvon.**

Other spellings: **Javonne, Jevon, Jivon**

Jay

Old French *jai,* "blue jay," from Latin *gaius,* "rejoiced in"; also, a form of **James, Jason,** or other names beginning with J.

Famous name: Jay Leno (comedian)

Jayden

A man named **Jadon** (Hebrew "God will judge") is barely mentioned in the Book of Nehemiah in the Old Testament, but as the biblical spelling only started to advance after **Jaden** and Jayden were already popular, it's unlikely to be the real source of this modern name. Rather, Jayden is an example of a name invented from other popular sounds, probably by blending **Jason** and **Braden.** The name was in evidence in Utah by 1990. Jaden and Jayden first made the national SSA top 1,000 list in 1994; **Jadon** in 1998; **Jaiden** and **Jaydon** in 1999; **Jaeden** in 2000; **Jadyn** in 2001; and **Jaidyn** and **Jaydin** in 2004. When all nine spellings are added together, Jayden was the 24th most common boys name of 2004, with only its rhyming twin **Caden** among the top 50 names rivaling it in the speed of its rise.

Jean

French variation of **John.**

Jeff

Form of **Jeffrey, Geoffrey.**
Famous name: Jeff Gordon (NASCAR driver)

Jefferson

English surname, "son of **Geoffrey.**" This name honors Thomas Jefferson, the third president of the United States, still considered one of the greatest American historical figures. The name Jefferson has never been extremely popular, but it's been among the top 800 boys names in the United States for the past two centuries. Its most famous bearer was Jefferson Davis, president of the Confederate States of America.

Jeffrey

Variation of **Geoffrey.** This spelling is much more popular in the United States than the original English form, Geoffrey.
Nickname: **Jeff**
Other spellings: **Jeffery, Jeffry**
Variations: **Joffre, Joffrey** (French)

Jeremiah

Hebrew "may God raise up, exalt." Jeremiah was a biblical prophet who wrote the Book of Lamentations as well as the Old Testament book named after him. As **Isaiah** and **Elijah** have risen in use, Jeremiah has also begun to enjoy a revival, leaping to 82nd in popularity in 2004, an increase of 15 places in only one year.

Nicknames: **Gerry, Jerrie, Jerry**

Variations: **Geremia** (Italian), **Jeremías** (Spanish), **Jeremie** (French), **Jeremio, Jeremy** (English), **Yirmeya** (modern Hebrew)

Jeremy

English form of **Jeremiah.** This version of the name dates to at least the 13th century in England. Jeremy became a top 30 American name in the 1970s, but since then its popularity has slowly faded. It was only 116th on the SSA list for boys born in 2004.

Famous name: Jeremy Irons (actor)

Other spelling: **Jeremie**

Jermaine

English surname, form of **German.** This name had one of the biggest explosions of use ever. The Jackson Five released their first album in 1969; Jermaine entered the SSA top 1,000 list at 623rd in 1970 and by 1974 ranked 127th. Most of the boys whose names were inspired by Jermaine Jackson were African-American, making Jermaine a top ten boys names in that community. The 557 Jermaines born in the United States in 2004 ranked it 399th overall for boys.

Jerome

Greek *Hieronymos*, "holy name." The fourth-century St. Jerome translated the Old Testament from Hebrew into Latin. Composer Jerome Kern is remembered for his musical *Showboat.*

Famous name: Jerome Robbins (choreographer)

Nicknames: **Jerrie, Jerry**

Other spelling: **Gerome**

Variations: **Gerònimo, Girolamo** (Italian), **Hieronymus** (German, Dutch, and Scandinavian), **Jeroen** (Dutch), **Jerónimo** (Spanish)

Jerry

Form of **Gerald, Gerard, Jeremiah,** or **Jerome.**

Famous names: Jerry Falwell (televangelist)
Jerry Lewis (comedian)
Jerry Seinfeld (comedian)

Other spellings: **Gerrie, Gerry, Jerrie**

Jerzy

Polish form of **George**.

Jesse

Hebrew "God exists." In the Bible, Jesse was the father of David, who became king of Israel. In the 19th century, the famous outlaw Jesse James plundered the West. In the 1936 Olympics in Berlin, African-American athlete Jesse Owens won four gold medals for the United States, disputing Adolf Hitler's theory of Aryan superiority. In the 1980s, civil rights leader Jesse Jackson became the first African-American to run for president.

Other spellings: **Jessie, Jessy**

Variations: **Jess, Yishai** (modern Hebrew)

Jesus

Aramaic and Greek form of **Joshua,** Hebrew "God saves." People in many cultures have considered this name to be too sacred for general use, but it has always been popular in Spanish-speaking countries. The rise in the Hispanic-American population has led to a 30 percent increase in the number of boys named Jesus in the last decade, and the name was the 70th most popular nationally in 2004.

Variations: **Jesús** (Spanish), **Issa, Jesito**

Jett

Evidently a respelling of the word *jet* as in "jet plane." John Travolta's son Jett was born in 1992, and George Lucas's son Jett was born in 1993. The name, however, didn't enter the SSA top 1,000 list until 1999. In 2004 there were 349 American newborn boys named Jett.

Jim

Form of **James**.

Famous name: Jim Carrey (actor)

Jimmy

Form of **James**. Although his legal name is James Earl Carter, the 39th president of the United States is more comfortable with his nickname, Jimmy. He won the Nobel Peace Prize in 2002. Though use of Jimmy as an official name is now receding, even in the South, there were still more than 1,000 boys given the name in 2004.

Other spellings: **Jimi, Jimmie**

Joachim

Probably from Hebrew *Johoiachin,* "established by God." In medieval Christian tradition, Joachim was the name of the Virgin Mary's father. As such it became a common name in many European countries, though it never caught on much in England, perhaps because people weren't sure of its pronunciation. (It should be JO-ah-kim.) Joachim has never been a common name in the United States, though it has been used on rare occasions by devout Roman Catholic families.
Variations: **Achim** (German), **Gioachino** (Italian), **Jáchym** (Czech), **Joaquín** (Spanish), **Jokum** (Danish and Norwegian)

Joaquin

Spanish *Joaquín,* form of **Joachim.** This name has long been in regular use in Spanish-speaking countries, and it continues to be popular with Hispanic-Americans. Since 2000 its use has been increasing in the United States at a particularly good rate, which perhaps means that some non-Hispanic parents are also now using it, inspired by the fame of actor Joaquin Phoenix. Joaquin was the 352nd most common boys name of 2004.

Jock

Scottish form of **Jack** or **John.**

Jody

Form of **Joseph.** This name owes its use as an official form to the 1946 film based on Marjorie Kinnan Rawlings's 1938 novel *The Yearling,* where Jody is a boy who raises a pet fawn and then is told to shoot the deer once it becomes a buck. Jody's career as a boys and girls name almost exactly paralleled each other, though there have always been more girls than boys given the name.

Joe

Form of **Joseph.**
Famous names: Joe DiMaggio (baseball player)
Joe Louis (boxer)

Joel

Hebrew "the Lord is God." In the Bible, Joel was a Hebrew prophet. The name is steadily used without being overly popular.
Famous name: Joel Grey (actor)
Variations: **Ioel, Yoel** (Hebrew)

Joey

Form of **Joseph.** Almost 500 American boys were given Joey as their official name in 2004.

Johann, Johannes

German forms of **John.** Two of the world's great composers share this name: Johann Sebastian Bach and Johannes Brahms.

John

Hebrew *Johanan,* "God has favored" or "God is gracious." For the last six centuries, this has been one of the most popular names for boys in the majority of European countries. In the Bible, John the Baptist was a cousin of Jesus. He was imprisoned for denouncing King Herod, and he was beheaded at the request of the king's step-daughter, Salome. St. John the Evangelist was a brother of James and one of the apostles. He is probably the author of the Gospel of John and three of the Epistles. Among Christians, the name has always been revered. It is the name of more than 20 popes and more than 80 saints. John XXIII, who was elected pope in 1958, called the Second Vatican Council, which radically changed the Roman Catholic church. Pope John Paul II, formerly Karol Jozef Wojtyla, was the first non-Italian pontiff to be chosen as pope in more than 450 years. Only one John has sat on the English throne: King John, a son of Henry II and Eleanor of Aquitaine, was crowned following the death of his brother Richard in 1199. He was forced to sign the Magna Carta, paving the way for a representational government in Great Britain. Four of England's greatest poets are John Milton, John Donne, John Keats, and John Dryden. The name also has great presidential connections through John Adams, John Quincy Adams, John Tyler, and John F. Kennedy. Astronaut John Glenn was the first American to orbit the earth, and musician John Lennon is considered to be one of the finest composers of rock music.

Famous names: John Brown (abolitionist)
John McCain (U.S. senator)
John Wayne (actor)

Nicknames: **Jack, Jackie, Jacky, Johnnie, Johnny**
Other spelling: **Jon**
Variations: **Eoin** (Irish), **Evan** (Welsh), **Gian, Gianni, Giovanni** (Italian), **Hannes** (Afrikaans), **Hans** (Danish, Dutch, and German),

Hansel (Bavarian), **Iain, Ian** (Scottish), **Ioan** (Romanian),
Ioannes (Greek), **Ivan** (Slavic), **Jaan** (Estonian), **Jan** (Czech,
Danish, and Dutch), **Janek** (Czech), **Janis** (Latvian), **Janne**
(Finnish), **Janos** (Hungarian), **Jasius** (Lithuanian), **Jean**
(French), **Jehan** (Belgian), **Jen, Jens** (Danish, Norwegian,
and Swedish), **Joao** (Portuguese), **Jock** (Scottish), **Johan**
(Danish), **Johann, Johannes** (German), **Jovan** (Serbian),
Juan (Spanish), **Juha** (Finnish), **Seainin, Sean, Shane** (Irish),
Vanni (Italian), **Vanya** (Russian), **Yahya** (Arabic), **Yeho-
chanan** (modern Hebrew), **Yochanan** (Yiddish)

Johnny

Form of **John.** Almost 1,300 boys were given Johnny as their official
name in 2004, ranking it 241st.
Famous names: Johnny Depp (actor)
Johnny Mathis (singer)
Other spelling: **Johnnie**

Jon

Form of **John** or **Jonathan.**
Famous names: Jon Stewart (political satirist)
Jon Voight (actor)

Jonah

Hebrew "dove." Most people remember the prophet Jonah because
he was swallowed by a big fish and regurgitated still alive three days
later. He taught that Yahweh was the God of the Gentiles as well as
of the Israelites. The name Jonah is climbing the charts as parents
discover it as an alternative for **Joshua** and **Jonathan.** Its use has
increased tenfold since 1992, and in 2004 Jonah was the 173rd most
common name for American newborn boys.
Variation: **Jonas**

Jonas

Form of **Jonah.** Jonas Salk, a 20th-century medical researcher, discovered the polio vaccine.

Jonathan

Hebrew "God has given" or "God's gift." In the Old Testament,
Jonathan is the son of King Saul who swears to remain David's closest

friend, even though Saul hates David and wants to kill him. When Jonathan falls in battle, a grieving David utters the famous lament, "Your love to me was wonderful, passing the love of women." David and Jonathan therefore became the biblical symbol of true friendship. Nevertheless, Jonathan was a rare name until the Puritans began to use it in colonial New England. Indeed, it was such a common name around Boston in 1776 that the British called all American Revolutionary soldiers "Brother Jonathan." The name then went out of fashion until the 1950s, when parents looking for alternatives to **John** began to make it popular again. Jonathan peaked in use around 1985 but since 1992 has held steady at around 17th on the list for American boys, with around 17,000 Jonathans born each year. Surprisingly, the name has recently been especially popular with Hispanic-Americans, in spite of its having almost no tradition of use in Spanish-speaking countries.

Famous names: Jonathan Swift (political satirist)

Jonathan Winters (comedian)

Nickname: **Jon**

Other spellings: **Johnathan, Johnathon, Jonathon**

Variation: **Jonatán** (Spanish)

Jordan

Hebrew *Yarden,* from *yarad,* "to descend," the name of the river that flows from the Sea of Galilee to the Dead Sea. This became a first name in the 12th century when soldiers returning from the Crusades brought home vials of water from the Jordan that were later used in the baptism of their children. As a result, Jordan became a popular name for children of both sexes in several western European countries. In the United States, use of the name began to revive around 1970 for both sexes. In 2004 about ten boys received the name for every six girls. The name's peak for both genders has just passed, but Jordan was still ranked 47th for American boys born in 2004. As a boys name, Jordan has been somewhat more popular with African-American parents than with others, which may mean that basketball star Michael Jordan's incredible popularity inspired some people to give his last name as a first name to their sons.

Other spellings: **Jorden, Jordon**

Variations: **Giordano** (Italian), **Iordache** (Romanian), **Iordanos** (Greek), **Jourdain** (French)

Jorge

Spanish form of **George.** More than 3,000 Jorges were born in the United States in 2004, ranking it 124th that year.
Famous name: Jorge Luis Borges (writer)

Jose

Spanish and Portuguese *José,* form of **Joseph.** This has been the overwhelmingly most popular boys name in all Spanish-speaking countries for centuries, and it retains that place with Hispanic-Americans. Almost 12,000 Joses were born in the United States in 2004, making it the 34th most common name for boys, and it was the top boys name in Texas and Arizona. Two Joses from Portuguese-speaking countries have won Nobel Prizes in the last decade: Jose Saramago of Portugal won the Literature Prize in 1998, and Jose Ramos-Horta of East Timor shared the Peace Prize in 1996.
Famous names: Jose Carreras (operatic tenor)
              Jose Feliciano (singer and guitarist)

Joseph

Hebrew "the Lord shall add (children)." In the Old Testament, Joseph was the favorite son of Jacob. He was sold into slavery in Egypt by his brothers, but by interpreting the dreams of the pharaoh, he gained authority and rose to a position of power. In the New Testament, Joseph was the husband of Mary, the mother of Jesus. Two Holy Roman emperors, Joseph I and Joseph II, reigned in the 18th century. In North America, Chief Joseph of the Nez Perce tribe rebelled against a treaty that would have forced his people to be resettled. In 1877, he led them on a long, harrowing march from Oregon toward Canada, but they were stopped within miles of the border. The term *yellow journalism* reflects the aggressive newspaper style of publisher Joseph Pulitzer, who introduced tabloids to the United States. Pulitzer is even better remembered for his endowment of the Pulitzer Prizes. Joseph remains one of most-used names in the United States, ranking between seventh and twelfth every year since 1990; its popularity has held up better than that of either **John** or **James.**
Famous names: Joseph Conrad (author)
              Joseph Mankiewicz (movie producer and director)
              Joseph Smith (founder of the Mormons)
Nicknames: **Jody, Joe, Joey**

Variations: **Giuseppe** (Italian), **Iosef** (Greek), **Jose** (Spanish), **Joseba** (Basque), **Josef** (Czech, Dutch, German, and Scandinavian), **Jozef** (Polish), **Juozas** (Lithuanian), **Juuso** (Finnish), **Osip** (Russian), **Seosamh** (Irish), **Yosef** (Hebrew), **Yusuf** (Arabic)

Josh

Short form of **Joshua,** occasionally used as an official given name. Hollywood is starting to fill up with young actors called Josh, including Hartnett, Duhamel, Brolin, Holloway, and Lucas.

Joshua

Hebrew "God saves." Joshua was Moses' successor as the leader of the Israelites and led the nation into the Land of Promise. The Book of Joshua recounts the settling of Canaan. This name was regularly used by the Puritans in colonial New England. Joshua was revived in the 1970s and is now one of the most popular American names; in 1991, it reached third place on the list of names given to boys in the United States, and it has not been out of the top five since.
Famous name: Sir Joshua Reynolds (painter)
Nickname: **Josh**
Variations: **Giosue** (Italian), **Jason, Jesus, Josua** (German), **Josue** (French and Spanish), **Yehoshua** (modern Hebrew)

Josiah

Hebrew "God heals." Josiah, the king of Judah, destroyed idols and other evidence of the worship of false gods. The name was popular among the Puritans from the 17th century through the 19th century. Josiah is enjoying a slow revival now that similar names such as **Joshua** are fashionable again. It reached 142nd on the popularity list in 2004, when more than 2,700 Josiahs were born in the United States. Josiah Wedgewood founded the famous china business.
Variations: **Josia** (Swedish), **Josias** (French, German, and Spanish), **Jozsias** (Hungarian), **Giosia** (Italian)

Josue

Spanish *Josué,* form of **Joshua,** recently enjoying an increase in use by Hispanic-Americans. It ranked 198th in 2004.

Jotham

Hebrew "God is upright."

Jovan

This Serbian form of **John** has been on the lower half of the SSA top 1,000 list since 1976. Jovan's popularity as a boys name may be linked to its use as a brand name for cologne.

Juan

Spanish form of **John,** traditionally the second most popular name for Hispanic males after **Jose.**
Famous names: Juan Carlos de Borbón (king of Spain)
Juan Gris (Cubist painter and sculptor)

Judah

Hebrew "praise." Judah was the fourth son of Jacob and Leah and was the founder of the tribe of Judah, the most powerful of the 12 tribes of Israel. This name was used somewhat by the Puritans in the 17th century, but it has never been generally popular.
Variations: **Giuda** (Italian), **Iuda** (Bulgarian), **Jude**

Jude

Form of **Judah.** There was a minor vogue for Jude in the late 1950s and early 1960s. This was on the downswing when the Beatles released the popular song "Hey Jude" in 1968, which revived the name for about nine years before it began to fall away again. Its use started to increase again around 1996. In 2004 Jude reached its highest point ever, ranking as the 342nd most popular name.
Famous name: Jude Law (actor)

Jules

French form of **Julius.** Some people consider French author Jules Verne the father of science fiction.

Julian

Latin *Julianus,* "belonging to Julius." Julian was a common name among early Christians. Several saints are named Julian, including Julian the Hospitaller, medieval patron of both innkeepers and travelers. Julian has grown increasingly popular and is now among the 100 most common boys names in the United States.
Famous name: Julian Lennon (singer)
Variations: **Giuliano** (Italian), **Julianus** (Finnish and German), **Juliao** (Portuguese), **Julien** (French), **Julion**

Julio

Spanish form of **Julius,** well used by Hispanic-Americans.
Famous name: Julio Iglesias (singer)

Julius

Roman clan name, perhaps from *Jovilios,* "descended from Jove
(Jupiter)." Of all the ancient Romans, Julius Caesar is the best known.
Pope Julius II was the patron of the artists Michelangelo and
Raphael. Julius Marx found success as comedian Groucho Marx.
Famous name: Julius Erving (basketball player)
Variations: **Giulio** (Italian), **Jule, Jules** (French), **Julio** (Spanish), **Yul**

Junior

This word was quite common as a given name in the 1920s. In 2004
there were still 310 American boys given Junior as their first name.

Justice

This is one of the most common "word names" today. In this spelling
the name is being given almost equally to boys and girls, but enough
boys are being named **Justus** (a Roman name with the same meaning) that the total of both spellings together is 34 percent higher
than that for the girls. Together Justice and Justus ranked 299th for
American boys born in 2004.

Justin

Latin *Justinus,* derivative of *Justus,* "the just." St. Justin Martyr, who was
executed at Rome in A.D. 165, is often credited with being the first
Christian philosopher. He was known for holding public debates with
non-Christians where he defended his faith from charges of
immorality and atheism because Christians refused to sacrifice to
the emperor. Before 1970, Ireland was the only country where the
name Justin was frequently found, but it then exploded in use all
over the English-speaking world. Justin was among the top 15 names
given to American boys between 1982 and 1991, but it fell to 37th
place by 2004. Singer and actor Justin Timberlake is undoubtedly the
best-known bearer of the name today.
Variations: **Giustino** (Italian), **Gustino, Husto, Justinas** (Lithuanian),
Justino (Spanish and Portuguese), **Justinus** (Dutch and
Scandinavian), **Justyn** (Czech and Ukrainian), **Jusztin**
(Hungarian)

Kaden

German surname indicating one's ancestors lived in one of several villages called Kaaden or Kaden in Bohemia or Germany. As a modern American first name, it's one of the many spelling variations of **Caden.**

Kai

Danish and Frisian form of *Gaius,* Roman given name of uncertain origin; or Hawaiian "sea." Kai first entered the SSA top 1,000 list in 1979, and since about 1993 it has been rising at an accelerated pace. In 2004 there were 1,300 boys given the name, ranking it 238th.
Other spellings: **Kaj, Ky, Kye**

Kainalu

Hawaiian "sea wave."

Kamari

Perhaps a Swahili version of Arabic *Qamar,* "full moon." Kamari has recently become popular in the African-American community along with other names that rhyme with it such as **Jamari** and **Omari.**

Kane

Irish Gaelic *Cathain,* "battle"; also, Old French *cane,* "reed," or *Caen,* "battle plain." In the 1980s this surname became quite popular as a first name in Australia, but it's only had modest success in the United States, perhaps because it sounds like Cain, the name of the first murderer in the Bible.
Other spellings: **Cain, Kain, Kaine, Kayne**

Kanye

Record producer and rapper Kanye West's parents probably named him for the town of Kanye in Botswana. That name means "hill of the chief" in the Tswana language. In 2004 there were 499 newborn boys named Kanye in the United States, ranking it 424th.

Kareem

Arabic "noble." This name was made famous by Kareem Abdul-Jabbar, the long-reigning king of the basketball courts, and it's still used enough by African-Americans to rank 617th on the SSA list. Other spellings: **Karim, Karime**

Karl

German variation of **Charles.**
Famous names: Karl Lagerfeld (fashion designer)
                     Karl Marx (political philosopher)
Variation: **Carl**

Karsten

Low German or Danish form of **Christian.**

Kary

Variant spelling of **Cary.** In 1993 American biochemist Kary Mullis was co-winner of the Nobel Prize in chemistry for his 1983 invention of a way to make copies of strands of DNA, which is the basis for all modern genetic testing.

Keanu

Hawaiian "the coolness," usually referring to a cool breeze. This formerly unique name was bestowed upon actor Keanu Reeves by his father, who was partly of Hawaiian descent. Though Reeves became well known after *Bill & Ted's Excellent Adventure* in 1989, the name Keanu didn't appear on the SSA list until 1994, the year *Speed* was released, showing that it helps to be a big name "action" star to have babies given your name. Keanu's high point of use was in 1995, but it has been on the SSA top 1,000 list ever since, and it got another boost right after Reeves starred in the cult-classic film *The Matrix*. In 2004 Keanu was 863rd on the SSA list, with exactly 200 born in the United States. The name is also now being used all over Europe due to Reeves's fame.

Keaton

English place name, perhaps partly based on Celtic *cēd*, "wood." American parents discovered Keaton as a slightly different twist on names like **Keith** and **Keegan** in the 1980s, and the name has been slowly increasing in use ever since. It ranked 324th in 2004. Though it may be a coincidence, the rise of Keaton does somewhat parallel the career of actor Michael Keaton and so may be an example of a celebrity's surname affecting parents' choices of a first name.

Keegan

Irish Gaelic *MacAodhagáin,* "son of *Aeducan,"* a diminutive of *Aed* (see **Aidan**). As another fashionable surname ending in *–n,* Keegan was discovered in the late 1970s and steadily rose in use for more than 20 years. Though there are signs the name may have peaked, there were more than 1,500 Keegans born in the United States in 2004, ranking it 209th that year.

Keenan, Keenen

Irish Gaelic *Cianáin,* a form of *Cian,* "enduring." This name had a minor vogue during the 1980s, reaching 244th place on the list of names given to American boys in 1991, but it's been fading since. Famous name: Keenen Ivory Wayans (comedian and producer)

Keith

Scottish place name; origin and meaning unknown but may come from Celtic "the forest." Keith was a very popular name in the 1960s and, although its peak is now far in the past, there were still more than 1,200 boys given the name in 2004.
Famous names: Keith Hernandez (baseball player)
　　　　　　 Keith Richards (musician)

Kelemen

(See **Clement.**)

Kell

English surname, form of *Ketill,* Old Norse "sacrificial cauldron." (See **Anakin.**) This could also be a short form of **Kellen** or **Kelly.**

Kellen

German surname from place names meaning "swamp." Kellen first appeared on the SSA top 1,000 list in 1981, two years after tight end Kellen Winslow began his career with the San Diego Chargers. Parents enthusiastically accepted his name as a more "masculine" form of **Kelly,** and it's been on the SSA list ever since. Though its use seemed to be fading a few years ago, it's been growing in use again recently as the fashion for boys names ending in *–n* becomes stronger. Kellen was the 440th most common boys name of 2004.

Kelly

Irish Gaelic *Ceallagh,* uncertain meaning, perhaps "churchgoer," "bright-headed," or "strife." Although Kelly has been hugely popular as a female name in the United States since the 1960s, it slowly disappeared as a boys name, remaining among the top 1,000 names on the SSA list until 2003.

Famous name: Kelly Slater (surfing champion)

Kelsey

Probably Old English *Ceolsige* from *ceol* [ship] + *sige* [victory]. This was originally a name for boys, but after 1980 Kelsey became popular for girls and now has almost died out as a masculine form.

Famous name: Kelsey Grammer (actor)

Other spelling: **Kelsie**

Kelson

Probably invented by author Katherine Kurtz for one of the main characters in her *Deryni* series of fantasy novels. Several instances of fans naming sons Kelson have been noted.

Kelton

Scottish surname from a place name of undetermined meaning. Since the early 1990s some parents have discovered Kelton as a more "masculine" version of **Kelly** or **Kelsey.** Between 200 and 300 American boys are given this name every year.

Kelvin

Perhaps Gaelic *caol abhuinn,* "narrow water." The Kelvin is a river running through the grounds of the University of Glasgow, Scotland. In 1892 Queen Victoria named William Thomson, a Scottish physicist, as the first Baron Kelvin for his scientific achievements. Later the scientific scale of temperature that starts at absolute zero was named after Baron Kelvin. Around 1950 American parents seem to have taken up Kelvin as a variation of **Calvin.** Though use of Kelvin peaked at around 207th in 1965, it has receded slowly and was still the 369th most common boys name of 2004.

Ken

Form of **Kenneth.** In Japanese, Ken is also a boys name meaning "fist" and is featured in the Street Fighter series of video games.

Famous names: Ken Kesey (writer)
Ken Watanabe (actor)

Kendall

English surname from a place name, "valley of the River Kent." Kendall has been regularly used as a first name by parents searching for alternatives to **Kenneth** since the early 20th century. The name slowly rose in use until around 1993, which was the first year that more girls than boys were named Kendall in the United States. Since then, as more parents noticed the new gender ambiguity of the name, it's been dropping away swiftly for boys.

Kendrick

British surname from either Welsh *Cynwrig*, "chief hero," or Old English *Cyneric*, "family ruler." Parents discovered Kendrick as an alternative for **Kenneth** around 1964. It was among the 400 top names on the SSA list between 1976 and 1994 but has been receding since.

Kennedy

Irish Gaelic *Cinnéidigh*, "helmeted head" or "ugly head." Kennedy had a time during the 1960s when it was in regular use as a boys name because of John F. Kennedy's presidency; its high point then was 1964, just after Kennedy was assassinated, when 229 boys were given the name. Since 1994 Kennedy has once again been among the top 1,000 names for American boys on the SSA list, but now it is much more popular for girls.

Kenneth

Scots Gaelic *Coinneach*, "handsome," or *Cinaed*, "fire-born." In the ninth century, Kenneth McAlpine was the first king to rule both the Picts and the Scots in the area now known as Scotland. Kenneth was a top 50 name from about 1900 until 1980, and it was still 125th in 2004.
Famous name: Sir Kenneth Clark (art critic)
Nicknames: **Ken, Kenney, Kennie, Kenny**

Kenny

Form of **Kenneth.**
Famous names: Kenny Chesney (country music singer)
Kenny Loggins (musician)
Kenny Rogers (singer)

Kensington

Old English "farm of Cynesige's people." Cynesige was an Anglo-Saxon name meaning "royal victory."

Kent

Name of a county in southeastern England, probably from Celtic "coast" or "border." This English place name and surname has been much more popular as a first name in the United States and Canada than it has been in England itself.

Kenyon

English surname, from a place name probably from Old Welsh *Cruc Einion,* "Einion's mound." Kenyon had an upswing in popularity during the 1970s, then started to fade. But it has returned to the SSA top 1,000 list since 1997. Budding writers will associate this name with the *Kenyon Review,* a literary magazine published at Kenyon College that has given many American writers their start.

Kenzaburo

Japanese "healthy third son." Japanese novelist Kenzaburo Oe won the 1994 Nobel Prize in literature. Many of his books are autobiographical and deal with the problems of raising a handicapped child, a topic that was taboo in Japan before his work. His own autistic son, Hikari Oe, who was born with severe physical and mental disabilities, has become a well-known composer in Japan.

Keon, Keyon

Keon is a form of the Irish surname *McKeon,* "son of **Ewan,**" but it was probably in many cases also an African-American rhyming creation based on **Deon** or **Leon.** It also has occasionally been used as an Americanized spelling of *Kiyan,* a Farsi (Iranian) name meaning "leader" or "tent of a nomad." Keon has been on the SSA top 1,000 list since 1978 and has gradually increased in use. When the two main spellings are counted together, there were 489 Keons born in the United States in 2004, ranking it 431st that year among all names given to American boys.

Keshawn, Keyshawn

Both spellings of this African-American creation, blending names like **Keon** with **Shawn,** have been on the SSA top 1,000 list since 1996. If both names are taken together, there were 570 boys given the name in 2004.

Famous name: Keyshawn Johnson (football player)

Kester

(See **Christopher.**)

Kevin

Irish *Caemgen,* "comely birth, beloved child." The sixth-century St. Kevin was known as a hermit and is one of the patron saints of Dublin. This common Irish name has been one of the top 50 most popular names for boys in the United States since 1953. Its status as the name of a typical American male was reinforced by Kevin Arnold, the chief character on *The Wonder Years,* the nostalgic television series that helped many baby boomers relive their childhood during its run from 1988 to 1993. The name is particularly common among American actors: Kevin Bacon, Kevin Costner, Kevin Dillon, Kevin Dobson, Kevin James, Kevin Kline, Kevin Smith, Kevin Sorbo, and Kevin Spacey are all successful. With American films and television being some of our most important exports, it's not surprising that during the 1990s Kevin became a popular name throughout western Europe and was the number-one name for boys born in France between 1989 and 1994.

Other spelling: **Keven**

Khalil

Arabic *khalil,* "friend." This is now one of the most popular Muslim names with African-American parents; it ranked 373rd among names given to American boys in 2004. It should be noted, though, that baseball player Khalil Greene is neither African-American nor Muslim, but is a member of the Baha'i faith, for whose followers the name Khalil implies the concept "friend of God."

Kian

Irish Gaelic *Cian,* "ancient, enduring," the name of several heroes in ancient Irish legend. This is not the same name as either **Keon** or **Kyan** and should be pronounced to rhyme with **Ian.** The use of Kian has been slowly rising since 2000. There were 261 born in the United States in 2004, ranking it 721st on the SSA list.

Kiefer

German "barrel maker" or "pine tree." When actors Donald Sutherland and Shirley Douglas had a son in 1966, they decided that the last name of their friend—novelist, screenwriter, and film producer Warren Kiefer—would be perfect as a first name for their son. Now Kiefer Sutherland has grown up and made a name for himself as an actor. Other spellings: **Keefer, Keifer**

Kieran

Irish Gaelic *Ciarán*, from *ciar*, "black." This name of 26 Irish saints has been on the SSA top 1,000 list in the United States since 1992. Famous name: Kieran Culkin (actor)

Kim

Form of **Kimball**, Old English *Cynebeal* from *cyne* [royal] + *beald* [bold], or Welsh *Cynbel* from *cyn* [chief] + *bel* [war] or **Kimberly.** The best-known Kim is the title character of Rudyard Kipling's novel about an Irish boy growing up in India, whose full name is Kimball O'Hara. Famous name: Kim Stanley Robinson (science fiction author)

King

Old English *cyning*, "king, tribal leader." Famous name: King Vidor (film director)

Kingsley

Old English "king's meadow." To *Harry Potter* fans, Kingsley Shacklebolt is the Black Wizard in charge of hunting down Sirius Black. Famous name: Kingsley Amis (author)

Kirby

Old English "church village" from *ciric* [church] + *by* [village]. Famous name: Kirby Puckett (baseball player) Other spelling: **Kerby**

Kirk

Scottish form of Old English *ciric*, "church." Famous name: Kirk Douglas (actor)

Kit

Form of **Christian** or **Christopher.** Famous name: Kit Carson (scout)

Knox

Scottish surname, from a place name based on Old English *cnocc*, "round-topped hill." This name has sometimes been given to honor John Knox, the follower of John Calvin who helped to establish Protestantism in Scotland.

Knut, Knute

Danish, from Old Norse *Knutr*, "knot," originally a nickname for a short but tough Viking. A Danish invader named Cnut, or Canute, ruled England in the 11th century. He is the king who tested his power by commanding the waves to be still. Knute Rockne, the famous University of Notre Dame football coach, modernized the game by stressing the forward pass. Norwegian writer Knut Hamsun won the 1920 Nobel Prize in literature.
Variations: **Canute, Cnut**

Kobe

Basketball star Kobe Bryant was supposedly given his name after his parents saw Kobe steaks on a restaurant menu. The steaks are named after Kōbe, Japan, and the city's name means "door of the gods." Kobe is pronounced just like **Coby** and **Koby,** which were originally short forms of **Jacob** and were already somewhat in use when Bryant became famous. But Bryant's formerly unusual spelling has now become more popular than the other forms. Though the name did take a sharp drop in 2004, with the three spellings added together it was still among the top 300 boys names of 2004, with more than 1,000 born in the United States.

Koda

In 2004 there were 178 boys born in the United States named Koda, ranking it 930th on the SSA list. The explanation seems to be the character in the 2003 Disney/Pixar animated film *Brother Bear*. In the film an Inuit boy named Kenai is magically transformed into a bear and must learn how to survive by befriending a real grizzly bear cub named Koda. Parents probably saw Koda as an alternate version of **Cody** or **Dakota;** the screenwriters probably meant the name to be a short form of **Kodiak** (Inuit "island"), the name of the Alaskan island where the largest grizzly bears are found. Kodiak itself has occasionally been used as a boys name in the United States.

Koichi

Japanese "cultivate first," implying "growing first son."

Konrad

Old German *Conrad,* "bold counsel."
Famous name: Konrad Lorenz (ethologist)
Nicknames: **Con, Conny, Kurt**
Other spelling: **Conrad**

Kramer

German surname *Krämer,* "street vendor, shopkeeper."
Other spelling: **Cramer**

Kris

Form of **Christian** or **Christopher.** Kris Kringle is the Bavarian
equivalent of Santa Claus, or St. Nicholas.
Famous name: Kris Kristofferson (singer and actor)

Krishna

Hindi from Sanskrit "dark, black." In Hindu teachings, Krishna is an
incarnation of the god Vishnu and a proponent of selfless actions.
He is usually pictured playing a flute.

Kristian

Form of **Christian.**

Kumar

Hindi "youth" from Sanskrit *kumara,* "boy, son."

Kurt

Form of **Curtis** or **Konrad.**
Famous names: Kurt Russell (actor)
Kurt Vonnegut (writer)
Kurt Weill (composer)
Other spelling: **Curt**

Kwame

Akan (Ghana) "born on Saturday." Kwame Nkrumah led the West
African nation of Ghana to independence in 1957. It was the first
African colony to receive its freedom from a European power.
Kwame was one of the first genuinely African names to be regularly
used by African-American parents.

Kyan

When hairdresser Hugh Douglas was meditating one day, the thought came to him that he should change his name to Kyan. Evidently his subconscious mind thought that a blend of the sounds of **Kyle** and **Ryan** would be perfect as a "different but not too different" celebrity name. That must be right, because since Kyan Douglas has been appearing on *Queer Eye for the Straight Guy* his name has caught the eye of lots of parents. There were 374 Kyans born in the United States in 2004, ranking it 589th on the SSA top 1,000 list. (In Ireland Kyan is also a rare surname deriving ultimately from Gaelic *Cathán*, "battle.")

Kylan

This name seems to be a modern invention; no instances of it have yet been noted before 1972. It was probably inevitable that some parents who liked the sound of **Kyle** but were reluctant to use a one-syllable form as an official name would come up with Kylan as their solution. The name first entered the SSA top 1,000 list in 1998 and its use has been growing slowly.

Kyle

Scots Gaelic *caol*, "narrows, strait." This Scottish surname was only occasionally given as a first name before the 1950s, but it was among the top 25 names for boys in the United States between 1986 and 1999. Its peak has now passed, and it was only the 64th most common name in 2004.
Famous name: Kyle MacLachlan (actor)
Other spelling: **Kile**

Kyler

Dutch *Cuyler*, "archer," or German *Keiler*, "wild boar." The success of this name is due to its blending the sounds of **Kyle** and **Tyler**, making it a perfect example of a "different but not too different" alternative. Kyler first entered the SSA top 1,000 in 1986 and has continued to rise even as Kyle and Tyler have both now passed their peaks. In 2004 it was the 256th most common name for American boys, with more than 1,000 born.

Kyros

(See **Cyrus**.)

Lachlan

Gaelic *Lochlann,* "land of lochs; Norway," originally given to Norwegian settlers in Scotland. This is a popular name in Australia because of Lachlan Macquarie (1762–1824), a British colonial governor who led Australia's transition from a penal colony to a free settlement.

Lafayette

French place name and surname, "beech tree grove." This name honors the memory of Marie Jean Paul Roch Yves Gilbert Motrier, the Marquis de Lafayette. At the age of 20, Lafayette was granted the rank of major general in the American Revolutionary Forces. He served throughout the war as a leader of troops and as an aide to General George Washington. For his services, he was honored as an American hero. Many counties and towns were named for him.
Nicknames: **Fay, Lafe**
Variation: **Fayette**

Lafe

Originally a nickname for **Lafayette,** Lafe had some independent use during the 19th century. Lafe McKee was an actor who appeared in hundreds of Western films between 1912 and 1949. Though today this name is somewhat confused with **Leif,** it retains a cowboy image and would go well around a campfire with **Ty, Chance, Maverick,** and **Clint.**

Laird

Scottish "lord," in the sense of "landowner."

Lake

This is one of the more common "nature names" for boys today.

Lal

Hindi "beloved boy" from Sanskrit "to play, caress."

Lamar

French *la mare*, "the pool or pond."
Variation: **LaMarr**

Lamont

Medieval Scottish *Lagman*, from Old Norse *Logmadr*, "law man." The resemblance of this name to French *le mont*, "the mountain," is accidental. Many Americans will remember this name from Lamont Sanford, the son on the 1970s television series *Sanford and Son*.

Lance

Old German *Lanzo*, "land," later associated with French *lance*, "light spear"; also, a short form of **Lancelot**.
Famous name: Lance Armstrong (bicyclist)

Lancelot

Origin uncertain, but perhaps from Old Norman French *Ancelot*, "young servant." In the Arthurian romances, Sir Lancelot was a French knight who came to King Arthur's court. Although he fell in love with the king's wife, Guinevere, he rallied to Arthur's side to battle Mordred.
Nickname: **Lance**

Landon

Probably a form of *Langdon*, Old English "long hill." The use of Landon as a first name in the United States is steadily increasing, perhaps in honor of Michael Landon, the actor and television producer who died in 1991. In 2004, the name reached 75th place in popularity, a gain of ten ranks in only one year.

Lane

English "path" or "roadway."
Other spelling: **Laine**

Langston

Old English "long or tall stone," originally a place name indicating the presence of an ancient stone monument.
Famous name: Langston Hughes (poet)

Lanny

Form of **Lawrence**.

Larkin

Middle English pet form of **Lawrence.**

Larry

Form of **Lawrence.** This name started out as a nickname for Lawrence, but it became a popular independent name in the 1940s. Although it is now much less fashionable, Larry was still given by American parents more often than Lawrence on birth certificates in 2004.

Famous names: Larry Bird (basketball player)

Larry King (commentator)

Larry McMurtry (novelist)

Lars

Scandinavian form of **Lawrence.** Parents showed some minor interest in Lars as a baby name from about 1958 through 1976, around the same time its Scandinavian cousin **Leif** was also in evidence. Given the love at the present moment for two-syllable forms, perhaps **Larson** will soon be seen as a good alternative.

Famous name: Lars Ulrich (heavy metal rock drummer)

Lathan

Probably a form of **Latham,** from Old Norse "place of barns."

Lawrence

Latin *Laurentius* from *Laurentum,* an ancient Roman town that may have derived its name from *laurus,* "laurel or bay tree." The ancient Greeks revered the laurel tree and used its leaves for wreaths to celebrate victory. There were three St. Lawrences. The first lived during the third century and suffered a terrible martyrdom by being roasted to death. Lawrence was one of the top 50 names for American boys between 1890 and 1958. Since then it has receded, falling to 330th place by 2004.

Famous name: Lawrence Welk (bandleader and musician)

Nicknames: **Lanny, Larrie, Larry, Lauren, Laurie, Law, Lawry, Lon, Lonnie, Lonny, Loren, Lorin, Lorry**

Other spellings: **Laurance, Laurence, Lawrance**

Variations: **Labhrainn** (Scottish), **Labhras** (Irish), **Larkin, Lars** (Scandinavian), **Laurenco** (Portuguese), **Laurens** (Dutch), **Laurent** (French), **Laurentius** (Latin), **Laurenz** (German), **Lauri** (Finnish), **Laurits** (Danish), **Lavrentij** (Russian), **Lenz**

(Swiss), **Lorens** (Scandinavian), **Lorenz** (German), **Lorenzo** (Italian and Spanish), **Lorinc** (Hungarian), **Lovre** (Croatian), **Wawrzyniec** (Polish)

Lawson

Medieval English *Lawisson,* "son of **Law,**" a pet form of **Lawrence.** Lawson was regularly used as a first name in the United States during the 19th century and retained a good bit of use until the 1940s. Then it vanished as a first name until the modern vogue for two-syllable boys names ending in *–n* led to its rediscovery. It reappeared on the SSA top 1,000 list in 2000 and has been growing rapidly in use. More than 250 boys were named Lawson in 2004, ranking it 726th on the SSA list.

Lawyer

The word used as a name.

Layton, Leighton

Both of these English surnames, which are pronounced the same, trace back to English villages whose names originally meant "leek enclosure" or "herb garden." Layton is the more popular spelling today because it makes the pronunciation clearer. As similar names such as **Dayton** and **Peyton** become more popular, parents are also being attracted to Layton.

Lee

Old English *leah,* "meadow." Lee was formerly popular in the U.S. South, where it honors both General Robert E. Lee and his father Henry "Light Horse Harry" Lee. Surprisingly, this very American name was one of the top ten names for boys born in England in the early 1980s. It is quickly fading as a first name in the United States today, though it's still frequently found as a middle name.
Famous names: Lee Iacocca (industrialist)
        Lee Marvin (actor)
Other spelling: **Leigh**

Leif

Old Norse *leifr,* "heir, descendant." Most Americans will remember learning about Leif Ericsson and his discovery of Vinland, probably somewhere in North America, almost 500 years before Columbus's voyage. There was a minor vogue for the name Leif during the 1960s and 1970s, but it has since faded. Part of Leif's lack of success was confusion over its pronunciation; "Lafe" would be closer to the original Scandinavian, but there's a natural tendency for Americans to look at the name and want to say "Leaf."

Famous name: Leif Garrett (singer and actor)

Leith

Scots Gaelic *lite*, "wet," originally the name of a river near Edinburgh, Scotland. This Scottish surname occurs occasionally as a first name in the American South, where many people from Scotland settled.

Leland

Old English "fallow land." This British place name and surname became a given name that symbolized professionalism, good taste, and wealth in the 19th century because of A. Leland Stanford, the railroad magnate and philanthropist who founded Stanford University in California. Despite this, Leland steadily fell from its high point in the 1920s, and today it is no longer among the top 1,000 names on the SSA list.

Lemuel

Hebrew, probably meaning "belonging to the Lord." Although parts of the Book of Proverbs are credited to Lemuel, nothing else is known about him. Jonathan Swift used this name for the central character of *Gulliver's Travels*. Lemuel is a very rare name today.

Len

Form of **Leonard.**

Lennie, Lenny

Forms of **Leonard.** There was a brief period in the 1960s and 1970s when Lenny showed up regularly as an official given name, but its fashionable period has now passed.

Famous names: Lenny Bruce (comedian)
Lenny Kravitz (rock singer)

Lennon

Irish surname from either *Leannáin*, "little cloak," or *Lonán*, "blackbird." Many parents who give this name are consciously honoring the memory of singer John Lennon.

Lennox

Scottish *Leunaichs,* "place of elms," from Gaelic *leamhanach.*
Famous name: Lennox Lewis (heavyweight boxing champion)
Other spelling: **Lenox**

Leo

Latin "lion." Thirteen popes were named Leo, including Leo the
Great, who prevented the Huns from sacking Rome. Six emperors
of Constantinople were also called Leo. Perhaps because of the
constellation Leo, the association of this name with the lion, the king
of beasts, is obvious even to those who don't know Latin. Russian
author Leo Tolstoy is certainly considered a lion of the literary
world. His novels include *War and Peace* and *Anna Karenina.* Leo is
having an international upswing in the early 21st century. Léo is now
one of the top 20 names for newborns in France, and in the United
States Leo has almost tripled in use since 1990. It is now among the
250 most common boys names.
Famous name: Leo Buscaglia (author)
Variations: **Leao** (Portuguese), **Leon** (French, Slavic, Spanish, and
Irish), **Leonas** (Lithuanian), **Leone** (Italian), **Leonon, Leos**
(Czech and Slovakian), **Lionel, Lowen**

Leon

Form of **Leo.** Parents with an ear for unusual music might like this
name, which is shared by musicians Leon Redbone and Leon Russell.

Leonard

Old German "lion hard." In the sixth century, St. Leonard converted
his master, Clovis, a powerful Frank king. This may explain why the
name was formerly common in parts of France. Leonard was a
popular name in both Britain and the United States during the first
half of the 20th century, but its fashionable period was over by 1950.
Famous names: Leonard Bernstein (composer and conductor)
Leonard Nimoy (actor and director)
Nicknames: **Len, Lennie, Lenny**
Other spelling: **Lennard**
Variations: **Lenard** (Hungarian), **Lennart** (Scandinavian), **Leonardo**
(Italian, Portuguese, and Spanish), **Leonardus** (Dutch),
Leonhard (German), **Lienhard** (Swiss)

Leonardo

Italian, Spanish, and Portuguese form of **Leonard.** Most adults will recognize this name as that of one of the greatest artists of all time. Italian-born Leonardo da Vinci is remembered for his majestic paintings, including the "Mona Lisa" and "The Last Supper," but he is also the epitome of the Renaissance man. He was not only a painter but also a sculptor, an architect, and an engineer. His sketches and engineering plans brought him renown in his own time, and 500 years after his death, his models for airplanes and designs for engines are still being studied. Since the film *Titanic* came out in 1997, the most famous Leonardo around the world has been actor Leonardo DiCaprio. DiCaprio's publicity agents claim that his mother chose the name Leonardo because the baby kicked strongly when she viewed a da Vinci painting while pregnant. DiCaprio's fame has probably been instrumental in his name's steady rise on the popularity list, and Leonardo is now among the top 200 names for boys born in the United States.

Leonel

Spanish form of **Lionel,** extremely rare in Spain but growing more popular with Hispanic-Americans since the 1960s. There were 526 Leonels born in the United States in 2004, making it the 411th most common boys name that year.

Leonid

Russian form of *Leonidas,* an ancient Greek name meaning "son of the lion."
Famous name: Leonid Brezhnev (Soviet statesman)

Leopold

Germanic *liut* [people] + *bold* [brave], altered so that the first syllable resembles Latin *Leo,* "lion." As the name of Queen Victoria's uncle, who became the first King of the Belgians, this name has aristocratic associations. If **Leo** and **Leonardo** continue to grow in popularity, Leopold may also have a bright future.

Leroy, LeRoy

Old French *le roi,* "the king." This name was generally popular in the United States during the late 19th century, but since 1920 it has been primarily used only in the African-American community.

Nicknames: **Lee, Roy**
Variations: **Elroy, Leeroy, LeRoi**

Leslie

Scottish clan name of uncertain origin; possible meanings include "garden by the pool" and "court of hollies." This once-popular name for boys is now used primarily for girls.
Famous name: Leslie Nielsen (actor)
Nickname: **Les**
Other spellings: **Lesley, Lesly**

Lester

Old English form of *Leicester* from *Ligore* [a tribal name of uncertain meaning] + *cester* [from Latin *castra*, "city"]. This aristocratic British surname has been used as a first name in England since about 1840. In the United States, it was popular in the late 19th century, but its use has since faded. In the 20th century, it seems to have appealed more to parents in the South than the North. William Faulkner used the name for a farm boy in *The Sound and the Fury*.
Nickname: **Les**

Levi

Hebrew "joined in harmony." In the Old Testament, Levi was a son of Jacob and Leah. Levi Eshkol was the prime minister of Israel from 1963 to 1969 and led the Six-Day War. Levi is slowly becoming more fashionable and is especially popular with parents in rural areas of the western United States.
Other spelling: **Levy**

Lewis

Variation of **Louis.** Lewis Carroll is remembered for his books *Alice in Wonderland* and *Through the Looking-Glass*. The name Lewis has revived strongly in Great Britain the last few years, especially in Scotland, where it was the number-one name for boys born in 2004. So far there is no sign of this revival in the United States, where the use of Lewis continues to decline.

Liam

This Irish short form of **William** was first noticed by American parents in the late 1970s and has been steadily rising in use ever since. Though the actor Liam Neeson has helped to make the name known, the name's popularity seems more linked to the general search for "new" Irish names rather than any effect of his career. Liam was the 117th most common boys name of 2004.

Lincoln

English place name *Lindocolonia* from Celtic "lake" and Latin "colony." This surname became an American first name during the Civil War in honor of Abraham Lincoln, the 16th president of the United States. Parents have recently rediscovered the name Lincoln, and it more than doubled in use between 1996 and 2004, ranking 549th on the SSA list that year, higher than at any time since the 1870s.
Nicknames: **Lin, Linc, Link**

Link

This is usually considered a pet form of **Lincoln** but is also gaining notice as the name of the hero in the very popular Legend of Zelda video game series.

Linus

Latin form of Greek *Linos,* in mythology a musician who was one of the tutors of Hercules. St. Linus, the second pope, was martyred in A.D. 76. The name is best known through Linus, the brother of Lucy, in the popular comic strip "Peanuts" by Charles Schultz, but computer buffs will associate it with Linus Torvalds, the Finnish-born creator of the Linux operating system.
Famous name: Linus Pauling (chemist)

Lionel

Medieval French and English form of **Leo.**
Famous names: Lionel Barrymore (actor)
　　　　　　　Lionel Richie (musician)
　　　　　　　Lionel Trilling (literary critic)
Variations: **Leonel** (Spanish), **Lionello** (Italian)

Llewellyn

Form of Welsh *Llywelyn,* an ancient name of uncertain origin, possibly meaning "resembling the god of light." The modern Welsh spelling has been altered to include the word *llew,* "lion." Llewellyn I and Llewellyn II ruled Wales in the 13th century. The English royal title Prince of Wales originated with them. Llywelyn ab Gruffydd supported Simon de Monfort against Henry III of England and was defeated in 1265. When he refused to pay homage to Edward I, the English captured Wales and killed Llywelyn. The Welsh have kept the name alive as a statement of their independent spirit.

Nickname: **Lew**

Variations: **Lewelyn, Llewelyn**

Lloyd

Welsh *Llwyd*, "gray" or "holy." This name was popular in the United States between 1900 and 1940 but is now out of fashion. David Lloyd George, who is usually referred to as Lloyd George, was prime minister of Great Britain during World War I.

Famous names: Lloyd Bridges (actor)
     Lloyd Cole (rock musician)

Variations: **Floyd, Loyd**

Logan

Scots Gaelic "little hollow." This Scottish place name and surname has ballooned in popularity as a first name. Though its vogue began in the western United States, it has now spread to all parts of the country. In 2004 Logan was the 32nd most common name given to American boys, with more than 13,000 born that year. Perhaps the most famous bearer of this Scottish name in American history was an American Indian. The Cayuga chief Tahgahjute (perhaps meaning "long eyelashes") adopted the name Logan around 1750 in honor of James Logan, a Pennsylvania Quaker known as a friend of American Indians. Chief Logan later moved to Ohio, where his family was massacred by settlers in 1774. This caused him to go to war against the British. He refused to attend the signing of the peace treaty, ending this minor war in 1775, but he sent a letter so eloquent in its description of the injustices done to Native Americans that he became a heroic figure to many of the same settlers he had been fighting. The towns of Logansport, Indiana, and Logan, West Virginia, were named for Chief Logan.

Lon

Form of **Alonso, Lawrence,** or **Mahlon.**

Famous name: Lon Chaney (actor)

London

The name of the capital of England is so ancient no one is sure what it originally meant, though at this time the best guess is that it's from pre-Celtic words meaning "place on the navigable river." Modern parents' search for new names has lead them to use many place names, and London fits in with the sound of other popular ones like **Boston** and **Dayton.** It's been on the SSA top 1,000 list since 2000, and in 2004 exactly 200 American boys were given the name.

Lonnie, Lonny

Form of **Alonso** or **Lawrence.** In 1995 Dr. Lonnie R. Bristow became the first African-American elected President of the American Medical Association. Lonnie seems to be a particularly lucky name for musicians, with Lonnie Johnson, Lonnie Mack, Lonnie Brooks, and Lonnie Plaxico all well known to fans of blues and jazz.

Loren

Form of **Lawrence.**

Lorenzo

Spanish and Italian form of **Lawrence.** In the 15th century, Lorenzo de Medici was the ruler of Florence and a patron of the arts. Lorenzo was established as a first name for Americans in the early 19th century because of traveling evangelist Lorenzo Dow (1777–1834). Though forgotten today, he drew incredible crowds and was idolized then as rock stars are today. Thousands of boys were named after him. The recent influx of Hispanic immigrants has given Lorenzo another boost; it was among the top 300 names for boys in 2004.
Famous name: Lorenzo Lamas (actor)
Short forms: **Enzo, Loren**
Variations: **Lencho** (Mexican), **Lorenzino, Renzo**

Lorin

Form of **Lawrence.**

Lorn, Lorne

From *Lorn,* a Scottish place name of unknown meaning. Lorne Michaels was the producer of television's *Saturday Night Live* between 1975 and 1980 and has been again since 1985.
Famous name: Lorne Greene (actor)

Lothair

Old German from *hlud* [fame] + *heri* [army]. This was the name of two Holy Roman Emperors; the French province of Lorraine was named after Lothair I in the early Middle Ages. This name has always been quite rare in English-speaking countries, although Lothar has been common in Germany.

Variations: **Lotario** (Spanish and Italian), **Lothaire** (French), **Lothar** (German), **Lothario**

Lou

Form of **Louis**.

Famous names: Lou Costello (comedian)
Lou Gehrig (baseball player)

Louis

French form of Old German *Hludwig*, "famous warrior," through Latin *Ludovicus*. Many prominent Frenchmen, including 18 kings, share this name. Louis I was a ninth-century Holy Roman Emperor who divided his kingdom and paved the way for the nation of France. Louis IX was canonized as a saint for his efforts on behalf of the Crusades. Louis XIV, the Sun King, who reigned from 1643 to 1715, built the palace of Versailles. Louis XVI, who inherited the financial problems caused by the wars his father had fought, died on the guillotine during the French Revolution. French chemist Louis Pasteur is noted for his many contributions to science and medicine, including the lifesaving theory that diseases are spread by bacteria. Louis Braille invented an alphabet for blind readers like himself. Louis (and its alternate spelling, Lewis) became very popular in the United States during the last half of the 19th century, but it was only the 232nd most common name given to American boys in 2004.

Famous names: Louis Armstrong (musician)
Louis Leakey (paleontologist)
Louis Sullivan (architect)
Louis Comfort Tiffany (glass manufacturer)

Nicknames: **Lew, Lewie, Lou, Louie**

Other spelling: **Lewis**

Variations: **Alois, Aloisius** (Latin), **Aloys** (French), **Aloysius, Clodoveo** (Spanish), **Clovis** (Latin), **Ljudvig** (Russian and Ukrainian), **Lodewijk** (Dutch), **Lodovico** (Italian), **Ludis** (Latvian),

Ludovic (Scottish), **Ludvig** (Scandinavian), **Ludvik** (Czech), **Ludwig** (German), **Ludwik** (Polish), **Luigi** (Italian), **Luis** (Spanish), **Luiz** (Portuguese), **Luthais** (Scots Gaelic)

Lowell

Norman French *lovel*, "wolf cub." The use of this surname as a first name probably originally honored the 19th-century American poet and essayist James Russell Lowell. At that time, it was common for parents to name sons after their favorite authors; see **Byron, Homer, Irving,** and **Milton** for other examples.

Variations: **Lovell, Lowe**

Lowen

Danish-American form of **Leo** or **Leon.** This name has been used for several generations in families of Danish descent living in Nebraska. *Løve* or *Løwe* was a nickname meaning "lion" that was used in 18th-century Denmark, though Lutheran church authorities did not allow it as an official name. Danes who emigrated to Nebraska in the 19th century evidently created Lowen as their own version of Leon, because the name's bearers have always been told it meant "lion." As an English surname, however, Lowen goes back to Old English *Lēofwine*, "beloved friend."

Luca

Italian form of **Luke.** This name has suddenly become popular outside of Italy. Luca was the sixth most common name given to German boys in 2004 and is now among the top 100 names given to boys in England and Wales. In a sense, Luca is even more success-ful in France; though **Lucas** is technically the top name there, in French the –s in Lucas is not pronounced, so the French count Luca and Lucas as two different spellings of the same name. In the United States, Luca first entered the SSA top 1,000 list for boys in 2000 and more than doubled in use by 2004. (See also **Luka.**)

Lucas

Latin form of **Luke.** Lucas was the 65th most common name given to American boys in 2004. Most are probably called Luke in everyday life, however. If Lucas and Luke were counted together, they would be among the top 20 names for boys born in the United States. In 2001, Lucas was the top name given to boys born in France.

Lucian

Form of Latin *Lucianus*, "bringing light." Lucian was a second-century satirist, and St. Lucian was a third-century martyr. Lucian Freud, a grandson of Sigmund Freud, the founder of psychoanalysis, is considered one of the greatest modern artists in Great Britain.
Variations: **Luciano** (Italian and Spanish), **Lucien** (French)

Luciano

Italian and Spanish form of **Lucian.** Luciano entered the SSA top 1,000 list in 1996 and by 2004 was 757th, perhaps another example of Italian-Americans returning to their ancestral culture for names.
Famous name: Luciano Pavarotti (operatic tenor)

Lucius

Latin *lux*, "light." Children growing up today may develop a very different image of this name than that origin would suggest because of the sinister character Lucius Malfoy in the *Harry Potter* novels.
Variation: **Lucio** (Italian, Spanish, and Portuguese)
Nickname: **Luke**

Ludovic

This Scottish form of **Louis** was fashionable in France during the 1970s. It will be interesting to see if American parents eventually discover it as an alternative to **Luca, Lucas,** and **Luke.**

Ludwig

German form of **Louis.** This name has never been popular outside of Austria, Switzerland, and Germany, despite the admiration for one of the world's greatest composers, Ludwig van Beethoven.
Nicknames: **Ludi, Lutz**

Ludy

German surname, probably a form of **Ludwig.**

Luigi

Italian form of **Louis.**

Luis

Spanish form of **Louis.** Luis is one of the most popular traditional Spanish names with Hispanic parents in the United States. The American physicist Luis W. Alvarez won the Nobel Prize in physics in 1968. He later developed the now widely accepted theory that a meteor impact caused the extinction of the dinosaurs.

Famous name: Luis Buñuel (movie director)

Nicknames: **Licho, Lucho**

Luka

This is the form of **Luke** used in the southern Slavic languages of the Balkans. As **Luca** has become popular, Americans have naturally taken up Luka as an alternative spelling, which has undoubtedly been encouraged by the presence of the character Dr. Luka Kovac on the television drama *ER* since 1999. Luka first entered the SSA top 1,000 in 2004; when Luca and Luka are counted together, they were the 301st most popular name given to American boys that year.

Luke

Greek *Loukas*, "a person from Lucania"; in the United States, also used as a nickname for **Lucius** or **Luther.** The original popularity of Luke was based almost entirely on St. Luke, who wrote the third Gospel. He is the patron saint of physicians and painters. The most famous modern Luke is undoubtedly Luke Skywalker, hero of the original *Star Wars* movie trilogy. Luke has been an extremely popular name in both Australia and England since about 1975. The name's rise in the United States has been steady but gradual, and Luke was 53rd on the list of names given to American boys born in 2004.

Famous names: Luke Perry (actor)

Luke Wilson (actor)

Variations: **Luc** (French), **Luca** (Italian and Romanian), **Lucas** (Latin and Dutch), **Luka** (Bulgarian, Macedonian, Slovenian, and Serbo-Croatian), **Lukas** (German, Scandinavian, and Czech)

Lukudu

Bari (southern Sudan) "boy born during rain."

Lutalo

Luganda (Uganda) "warrior."

Luther

Old German from *liut* [people] + *heri* [army]. Parents who choose this name usually wish to honor Martin Luther, the originator of Protestantism.

Famous name: Luther Vandross (singer)
Nicknames: **Luke, Lute**
Variations: **Luither** (German), **Lutero** (Spanish), **Lutherio, Luto**

Lyle

French *l'isle,* "the island."
Famous names: Lyle Alzado (football player)
Lyle Lovett (musician)
Other spellings: **Lile, Lyel, Lyell**
Variations: **Delisle, Lisle**

Lyman

Old English "man living at the pasture." Lyman Beecher was one of the leading proponents of the abolition of slavery and presumably a strong influence on his daughter, Harriet Beecher Stowe, who wrote *Uncle Tom's Cabin.* Lyman Frank Baum created Dorothy, her mismatched crew, and the Yellow Brick Road in his book *The Wonderful Wizard of Oz.*

Lyndon

Old English "hill of linden trees." Lyndon Baines Johnson was the 36th U.S. president. There was an increase in the number of boys named Lyndon during his presidency (1963–1968), making him one of the last politicians to positively influence the use of his name while he was in office. Lyndon has been off the radar screen as a baby name since 1990, though.
Other spellings: **Linden, Lindon**
Nickname: **Lyn**

Lynn

Celtic "stream, pool." This English place name and surname began to be used as a first name for boys around 1880. It was very popular in the 1940s, but its shift to use for girls has now driven Lynn completely off the boys list.
Famous name: Lynn Swann (football player)
Other spellings: **Lin, Linn, Lyn, Lynne**

Macaulay

Irish and Scottish "son of *Amalgaid* or **Olaf.**" Macaulay is very rare as a first name.

Famous name: Macaulay Culkin (actor)

Nicknames: **Mac, Mack**

Maddox

Surname meaning "son of *Madog,*" which is a Welsh given name meaning "goodly, fortunate." Actress Angelina Jolie adopted a Cambodian boy in 2002 and named him Maddox. The name, which had been very rare, immediately leapt onto the SSA top 1,000 list in 2003 and almost doubled again in 2004. That year 721 boys were given the name Maddox, ranking it 345th among all boys names. Maddox blends the sounds of **Madison** and **Max,** giving a masculine twist to the former, which is what makes this name so appealing.

Madison

Middle English "son of **Matthew**" or "son of **Maud.**" James Madison, the fourth president of the United States, is the source of this name. He was president during the War of 1812. Madison is now quite rare as a boys name, but it is very popular for girls.

Mahlon

Hebrew "illness." In the Bible, Mahlon was the eldest son of Elimelech and Naomi and was the husband of Ruth. The name began to appear in the 17th century under the influence of the Puritans and retained some use through the 1940s, but it is very rare today.

Malachi

Hebrew "my messenger." This name of the last book of the Old Testament was frequently used in Ireland as an English equivalent of various Gaelic names starting with *Mael,* meaning "servant of." The recent upsurge in the use of this name is hard to explain. Not even on the SSA top 1,000 list in 1989, Malachi soared to 152nd place in 2004, with almost 2,600 American boys given the name. Certainly its combined associations with Israel and Ireland appeal to parents from a wide variety of religious backgrounds, and it may be seen as an alternative for previously popular Old Testament names like **Isaiah, Isaac,** and **Caleb.**

Malcolm

Gaelic *maol-Columb,* "servant of Columb," from Latin *columba,* "dove." This was the name of four Scottish kings. In Shakespeare's play *Macbeth,* Malcolm III joined with Macduff to defeat Macbeth. Recently many African-American parents have chosen the name Malcolm to honor slain civil rights leader Malcolm X, so it's now among the top 500 names for boys.
Famous names: Malcolm Forbes (publisher)
      Malcolm Jamal Warner (actor)
Nickname: **Mal**

Malik

Arabic "king, sovereign." This is now the most common male Muslim name in the African-American community, partly because Malcolm X's official name after his conversion to orthodox Islam was El-Hajj Malik El-Shabazz.
Famous name: Malik Yoba (actor)
Other spellings: **Maleek, Maliek, Malique**

Manabu

Japanese "to learn," a popular name for Japanese boys born in the 1970s and 1980s. Most Japanese families put a high value on education and success in school, a value that this name reflects.

Manu

This Basque and Finnish form of **Emmanuel** has recently become well known as the nickname of basketball star Emanuel "Manu" Ginobili, who was born in Argentina.

Manuel

Spanish form of **Emmanuel.**
Nickname: **Manny**

Marc

French form of **Mark.**
Famous name: Marc Chagall (painter)

Marcel

French form of Latin *Marcellus,* a diminutive form of **Marcus.** Marcel was formerly popular in France because of St. Marcel, a Christian missionary to Gaul (now modern France) who became a martyr for his faith in the third century. Though it's never been very popular, Marcel has remained on the SSA top 1,000 list in the United States since 1911. The most famous Marcels have an artistic French image, including writer Marcel Proust, painter Marcel Duchamp, and mime Marcel Marceau.
Variations: **Marcello** (Italian), **Marcelo** (Spanish and Portuguese)

Marcelo

Spanish form of **Marcel,** recently increasing among the Hispanic-American population.
Famous name: Marcelo Álvarez (operatic tenor)

Marco

Italian form of **Mark.** The American use of this name has been slowly increasing since the 1940s. In 2004 almost 2,000 Marcos were born in the United States, ranking it 183rd that year. Venetian Marco Polo explored the Far East in the 13th century and introduced spaghetti and gunpowder to European culture.

Marcos

Spanish form of **Mark,** tied with **Malik** at 234th place in 2004.

Marcus

Roman forename probably derived from Mars, god of war. Marcus Antonius and Marcus Brutus had opposite opinions about Julius Caesar. Marcus Aurelius, the Roman emperor, was a Stoic philosopher as well as a persecutor of Christians. This original Latin form of **Mark** has long been common among African-Americans, undoubtedly because of admiration for Marcus Garvey, the Jamaican-born civil rights leader who founded a back-to-Africa movement in the early 20th century and promoted the idea of black pride.
Famous name: Marcus Roberts (jazz pianist)

Mario

Italian and Spanish form of *Marius*, a Roman clan name probably related to Mars, the god of war, but in modern times often used as a masculine form of **Maria.** Many young Americans will associate this name with the video games starring the Super Mario Brothers.
Famous name: Mario Cuomo (politician)

Mark

Form of **Marcus.** St. Mark is the author of the second Gospel. Venice, Italy, is the home of the famous St. Mark's Cathedral. When writer Samuel Clemens wanted a pen name, he found inspiration not in any historical Marks but in an expression often heard along the Mississippi: "mark twain." Twain is the minimum safe depth of two fathoms. Mark was a top ten name during the baby boom; in 2004 it fell below the top 100 names for the first time in 60 years.
Famous names: Mark Rothko (painter)
Mark Wahlberg (actor and singer)
Variations: **Marc** (French), **Marco** (Italian), **Marcos** (Spanish), **Marcus, Marek** (Czech and Polish), **Markku** (Finnish), **Marko** (Serbo-Croatian and Ukrainian), **Markos** (Greek), **Markus** (Danish, Dutch, German, and Swedish), **Marques** (Portuguese), **Morkus** (Lithuanian)

Marlon

Actor Marlon Brando (1924–2004) was named after his father. It's unknown how his grandparents chose his father's name. It may simply be a respelling of the surname *Marlin,* which is itself a form of **Merlin,** perhaps under the influence of **Mahlon.** Whatever its origin, there's little doubt that the use of Marlon as a first name is a tribute to Brando's fame. Both his film career and the rise of the name on the SSA top 1,000 list began in 1950. Though the name peaked in use in 1972, its slippage down the popularity charts has been very gradual. There were still 454 Marlons born in the United States in 2004, ranking it 521st on the SSA list that year.

Marques, Marquez

Marqués is a Spanish surname with the same meaning as **Marquis;** *Márquez* is a Spanish surname meaning "son of **Marcos.**" Both of them have become well-used given names in the African-American community as alternative versions of Marquis. The fashion for Marques began around 1975 and peaked in the late 1980s; Marquez didn't enter the SSA top 1,000 until 1988 and peaked in 1998. Both were still in the SSA top 1,000 in 2004.

Marquis

Medieval Latin *marchensis*, "count of a borderland," an English and French title of nobility. Marquis was used occasionally as a first name by white Americans in the early 20th century, but now it is almost exclusively an African-American name. In 2004, it was among the top 500 names on the SSA list. African-Americans also give the name **Marquise** to their sons, although technically that is the title for a woman who holds the rank of a marquis.

Famous name: Marquis Grissom (baseball player)

Marshall

Old French *marshal*, "horse groom" and later "a leader of men." This name's military sound has perhaps contributed to its decline, but it was still among the top 350 names for American boys born in 2004.

Famous names: Marshall Field (merchant)
          Marshall McLuhan (writer)

Nickname: **Marsh**
Other spelling: **Marshal**

Martin

Latin *Martinus*, form of *Martius*, "of Mars." Among Roman Catholics, Martin was a popular name in the Middle Ages. Four popes took this name, perhaps in honor of the fourth-century St. Martin, the bishop of Tours and the patron saint of France. The name is revered by Protestants because of Martin Luther, who inspired the Reformation. Charles Dickens used the name for the title character of *Martin Chuzzlewit*.

Famous names: Martin Buber (philosopher)
          Martin Luther King, Jr. (civil rights activist)
          Martin Short (comedian)
          Martin Van Buren (8th U.S. president)

Nicknames: **Mart, Martie, Marty**
Other spellings: **Marten, Marton**
Variations: **Martainn** (Scots Gaelic), **Martijn** (Dutch), **Martino** (Italian), **Morten** (Danish and Norwegian)

Marty

Form of **Martin.**

Famous name: Marty Robbins (country singer)

Marvin

Old English *Maerwine* from *maer* [famous] + *wine* [friend].

Famous name: Marvin Gaye (musician)

Nickname: **Marv**

Variations: **Marve, Mervyn, Merwyn**

Masatoshi

Japanese "bright talent." It seems that the parents of Masatoshi Koshiba were being prophetic when they chose this name for their son, who was co-winner of the Nobel Prize in physics in 2002 for his work on the detection of cosmic neutrinos.

Mason

Old French *masson,* "a stonecutter." There were almost six times as many Masons born in the United States in 2004 as there were in 1990, making it the 60th most common boys name. Its fashionable sound fits in with other popular names such as **Aidan, Jayden,** and **Caden.** Parents would not name a son "Maiden" for obvious reasons.

Nickname: **Mace**

Mateo

Spanish form of **Matthew,** 250th most common boys name of 2004.

Mathias

New Testament Greek form of **Matthew.** This more formal variation of Matthew is suddenly in use again more than a century after it seemed to vanish as an American name. The spelling Mathias is only slightly more common than **Matthias.** Together they were the 360th most common boys name of 2004, and they're poised to keep rising as parents keep searching for biblical names that don't seem overused. Mathias was the number-one boys name in Norway in 2004.

Matt

Form of **Matthew.** Actor James Arness played the Western marshal Matt Dillon on the television series *Gunsmoke.*

Famous names: Matt Dillon (actor)
Matt Lauer (newscaster)

Matthew

Hebrew *Matisyahu*, "gift of the Lord." St. Matthew, a former tax collector and one of the 12 apostles, was the author of the first Gospel. The name has enduring popularity in England and the United States. In the 19th century, Admiral Matthew Perry opened Japan to trade to the West. Matthew has been among the top five names given to American boys since 1980.

Famous names: Mathew Brady (Civil War photographer)
Matthew Broderick (actor)

Nicknames: **Mat, Matt, Mattie, Matty**

Variations: **Mata** (Scottish), **Matej** (Bulgarian and Slovenian), **Mateo** (Spanish), **Mateusz** (Polish), **Mathew, Mathias, Mathieu** (French), **Mats** (Swedish), **Mattaus** (German), **Matteo** (Italian), **Matthaeus** (Danish), **Mattheus** (Dutch), **Matthias, Matti** (Finnish), **Mattias** (Swedish), **Matvei** (Russian), **Matyas** (Czech and Hungarian)

Maurice

Latin *Mauricius*, form of *Maurus*, "a Moor." St. Moritz, the fashionable Swiss ski resort, is named for St. Maurice, a third-century martyr. Though this name hasn't been generally popular for some time, it has been fairly common in the African-American community.

Famous names: Maurice Chevalier (entertainer)
Maurice Ravel (composer)
Maurice Sendak (illustrator)

Nicknames: **Maurie, Maury**

Variations: **Mauri** (Finnish), **Mauricio** (Spanish), **Maurits** (Danish and Dutch), **Maurizio** (Italian), **Maurycy** (Polish), **Mavriki** (Russian), **Meurig** (Welsh), **Moric** (Hungarian), **Moritz** (German), **Morris, Morse**

Mauricio

Spanish form of **Maurice.** The number of Mauricios born in the United States has been rising sharply. It was the 337th most common boys name of 2004, with 743 born that year.

Maverick

English surname, probably a form of *Matherick*, but the original meaning is as yet undiscovered. The modern English word "maverick," meaning "someone who exhibits great independence in thought and action" came about because of Samuel A. Maverick (1803–1870) who, between 1847 and 1854, kept a herd of cattle he refused to brand. Unbranded calves came to be known as "mavericks," and that meaning was expanded to independent people. That use of the word as well as the Western connection was what attracted the creators of the tongue-in-cheek television Western series *Maverick,* which originally ran from 1957 to 1962 and starred James Garner as Bret Maverick, a traveling gambler. The series became a cult favorite in reruns, and so the movie *Maverick* was released in 1994 starring Mel Gibson as Bret Maverick, Jr. The name Maverick fit in more with the tastes of the 1990s than the 1950s; it immediately entered the SSA top 1,000 in 1994 and has kept rising since. In 2004 there were 235 boys named Maverick born in the United States, ranking it 763rd on the SSA list.

Max

Form of **Maximilian, Maximus,** or **Maxwell.** Max was originally brought to the United States by German and Jewish immigrants, having its first peak of use in 1914, when it was 99th on the SSA list. It then fell off, but around 1985 it began to rise in popularity again. Several things happened about that time that made Max seem cool to new parents: the three *Mad Max* movies starring Mel Gibson came out between 1979 and 1985 and achieved cult status; the even more avant-garde character Max Headroom appeared in movies and television in the late 1980s; and the slang phrase "to the max" became current. Perhaps most importantly, the late 1980s were just the time when children who had grown up with Maurice Sendak's classic picture book *Where The Wild Things Are* began to have kids of their own, and it's hard for anyone who's read that book not to see Max as being a great name for a little boy. The reluctance of many Americans to put a one-syllable form on a birth certificate masks the extent of Max's popularity. Max was only the 161st most common name of 2004 on its own, but if all the boys named **Maxim,** Maximilian, **Maximo,** Maximus, and Maxwell are added in, Max becomes the 70th most popular name.

Famous names: Max Ernst (painter)

Max Schmeling (heavyweight boxing champion)

Max von Sydow (actor)

Maxim

This Russian form of **Maximus** is also used by the Germans, Dutch, Czechs, Slovaks, and Hungarians. Like Maximus, it has been on the SSA top 1,000 list since 2000. Many will associate this name with the men's magazine launched in 1997.

Maximilian

Latin *Maximilianus,* a diminutive of **Maximus.** The Romans bestowed the title Maximus on their great warriors. Ironically, St. Maximilian was martyred in the third century because he refused to be drafted into the Roman army. In France, Maximilien Robespierre was one of the leaders of the French Revolution. A few decades later, Austrian Archduke Maximilian was quite popular at home, but the Mexicans did not appreciate his being given the title of Emperor of Mexico by Napoleon, and they executed him. More than 1,000 Maximilians were born in the United States in 2004, making it the 275th most popular boys name.

Famous name: Maximilian Schell (actor)

Nicknames: **Mac, Mack, Max, Maxie, Maxy**

Variations: **Maksymilian** (Polish and Ukrainian), **Massimiliano** (Italian), **Maximiliano** (Spanish), **Maximilianus** (Dutch), **Maximilien** (French), **Miksa** (Hungarian)

Maximo

This Spanish form of **Maximus** first appeared on the SSA top 1,000 list in 2002, showing that Hispanic parents are also affected by the vogue for **Max.**

Maximus

Latin "the greatest." This Roman family name was unheard of in modern times until Russell Crowe appeared in the Oscar-winning role of Maximus in the 2000 film *Gladiator.* It immediately appealed to parents looking for longer versions of **Max** and has been on the SSA top 1,000 list ever since.

Nickname: **Max**

Variations: **Maksym** (Polish and Ukrainian), **Massimo** (Italian), **Maxim** (Russian), **Maxime** (French), **Maximo** (Spanish)

Maxton

Scottish place name, "Magnus's farmstead."

Maxwell

Scottish place name, "Magnus's salmon pool." This surname became a first name in Scotland in the 19th century. Maxwell has been the chief beneficiary of the feeling of many modern parents who love Max that it's inappropriate to put a single-syllable name on a birth certificate. In 2004 it was the most common name in the Max family, reaching 137th on the popularity chart.

Nickname: **Max**

McKinley

Scottish surname, form of Gaelic *Mac Fhionnlaoich,* "son of **Finley.**" At the end of the 19th century, Americans were still naming children after politicians. William McKinley (1843–1901) started getting boys named after him while he was governor of Ohio, and when he ran for President in 1896, McKinley became one of the 200 most common boys names, a position it held all during his presidency. Its decline was quite gradual, and it didn't leave the SSA top 1,000 list until 1967. Today a few parents who are attracted to *Mc-* names are looking at McKinley again, though its similarity to **Mackenzie** may mean that parents of daughters as well as sons will rediscover it.

Mekhi

Use of this name is due solely to the career of actor Mekhi Phifer, who was born in Harlem in 1975. Unfortunately, no information is readily available on how his parents chose this name. It doesn't seem to be mentioned in any work on African, Muslim, or Hebrew names, and it's probable that it is newly invented, perhaps based on **Mikhail,** since it's pronounced "Meck-high." It is growing in use in the African-American community; 812 boys were named Mekhi in the United States in 2004, making it the 314th most popular name overall.

Mel

Usually a form of **Melvin** or **Samuel,** but this is not the case for the Australian actor Mel Gibson. He was named after St. Mel, a nephew of St. Patrick. The original meaning of the name is unknown.

Famous name: Mel Brooks (producer)

Melquíades

Spanish form of **Melchiades.** This was the name of an African-born bishop, also known as Miltiades, who was Pope from 310 to 314.

Experts disagree, but the best guess seems to be that his name originally meant something like "belonging to the red-haired family."

Melvin

Perhaps a masculine form of **Malvina,** a name invented by Scottish poet James Macpherson in the 1700s; or, less likely, from Irish Gaelic *maoillmhin,* "gentle chief."
Nicknames: **Mel, Vinnie, Vinny**

Merlin

Latinized version of Welsh *Myrddin,* a given name from the Romano-Celtic place name *Moridunum,* "sea fort." Merlin is, of course, best known as the name of the wizard in the countless retellings of the legends of King Arthur. As a given name it was used fairly often in the United States in the 1920s and 1930s, but it's hard to find any Merlins born since the early 1970s.
Famous name: Merlin Olsen (football player and actor)

Merrill

Gaelic "sea-bright," related to the girls name **Muriel;** or from Old English *myrige* [merry] + *hyll* [hill], a British place name.

Micah

Hebrew "who is like Yahweh?" Micah is considered one of the minor prophets in the Old Testament. This name has hardly been used in English-speaking countries until recently, but some American parents began to discover Micah as an alternative to the popular **Michael** in the 1970s. The name has enjoyed a slow, steady rise in use ever since, and in 2004 it reached 160th place on the list of boys names.

Michael

Hebrew "who is like the Lord?" The Archangel Michael leads the great battle described in the Revelation of St. John the Divine. The name of the Italian painter Michelangelo refers to the archangel. Emperors of Constantinople, Romanian kings, and the first Romanov tsar of Russia shared this name. Between 1953 and 1998, Michael was the most popular name for boys in the United States. Even though **Jacob** has now surpassed it, Michael was still a strong second on the popularity list in 2004, with nearly 26,000 American boys given the name. Michael is popular with Americans from all ethnic, racial, and religious backgrounds. Fully 5 percent of the members of the United States House of Representatives in 2004 were called Michael or Mike. Mickaël recently replaced Michel as the common form of this name in France. Michael is also replacing Miguel in Brazil.

Famous names: Michael J. Fox (actor)
Michael Jordan (basketball player)
Michael Moore (filmmaker)

Nicknames: **Mick, Mickey, Mickie, Micky, Mike, Mikey**

Variations: **Meical** (Welsh), **Micah, Michail** (Russian), **Michal** (Polish), **Micheal** (Irish and Scottish), **Michel** (French), **Michele** (Italian), **Mickaël** (modern French), **Miguel** (Spanish and Portuguese), **Mihael** (Greek), **Mihai** (Romanian), **Mihaly** (Hungarian), **Mihhail** (Estonian), **Mikael** (Swedish), **Mikel** (Basque), **Mikelis** (Latvian), **Mikhail** (Russian), **Mikko** (Finnish), **Mitchell, Mykolas** (Lithuanian)

Mickey, Mickie, Micky

Form of **Michael.** This nickname for Michael may be best known through Walt Disney's cartoon creation Mickey Mouse, but this association isn't exclusive, thanks to baseball player Mickey Mantle, writer Mickey Spillane, and actors Mickey Rooney and Mickey Rourke.

Miguel

Spanish and Portuguese form of **Michael.** Spanish writer Miguel de Cervantes Saavedra wrote *Don Quixote.* Another famous author with the name is Miguel Angel Asturias, a Guatemalan who won the Nobel Prize for literature in 1967. Miguel is popular with Hispanic parents and was 104th on the list of names given to all boys born in the United States in 2004. American children today will be familiar with the name because of the animated series *Maya and Miguel.*

Mike

Form of **Michael.** Just over 330 boys born in the United States in 2004 were given Mike as their official birth-certificate name.

Famous name: Mike Wallace (broadcast journalist)

Mikhail

Russian form of **Michael.** This name has long been extremely popular in Russia. Americans are now familiar with it because of two famous Mikhails: Baryshnikov, the ballet dancer and choreographer, and Gorbachev, leader of the Soviet Union before its collapse. As a result, a few American boys are now being named Mikhail each year. Nicknames: **Mischa, Misha, Mishenka**

Milan

Czech and Hungarian, from Slavic *mil,* "mercy."
Famous name: Milan Kundera (author)

Miles

Norman French *Milo* possibly from Slavic *mil,* "mercy," or Latin *miles,* "soldier." Miles Standish was a leader in the founding of New England, but he is better known through Henry Wadsworth Longfellow's poem "The Courtship of Miles Standish." Miles was the 150th most common American boys name in 2004; 40 percent of parents choosing this name today use the alternative spelling **Myles.**
Famous name: Miles Davis (jazz musician)
Variations: **Milan** (Czech and Hungarian), **Mille** (French), **Milo, Milos** (Czech, Slovenian, and Romanian)

Milo

This was originally the Latin written form of **Miles** in medieval records. Milo came to be used on its own in the 19th century when the Victorians revived many medieval names, and it was also used in Ireland to Anglicize *Mael Muire,* a Gaelic name meaning "devotee of Mary." It was used fairly often, especially in Irish-American families, through the 1920s, but then it fell away and almost vanished by 1960. Around 2000 it was taken up as a "cool" name by the avant garde, and it reached 770th place on the SSA list in 2004.

Milos

Another form of Slavic *mil,* "mercy." (See **Milan** and **Miles.**)
Famous name: Milos Forman (film director)

Milton

Old English "mill town" or "middle town." This surname became a first name in honor of John Milton, the 17th-century English poet who wrote *Paradise Lost.* In television's early years, comedian Milton Berle made this name familiar but didn't increase its popularity.
Famous name: Milton Friedman (economist)
Nickname: **Milt**

Mingus

Alternative spelling of *Menzies,* a Scottish surname ultimately from the Norman French place name *Mesnières,* itself from Latin *manēre,* "to reside." Mingus is still rare as a given name, but parents looking for longer names that could give **Gus** as a short form are starting to consider it. Parents who use it can find an admirable namesake in Charles Mingus (1922–1979), a jazz bassist, composer, and bandleader who was active in the fight to end racial segregation.

Misael

Spanish form of *Mishael,* Hebrew "who belongs to God." There are three Mishaels in the Old Testament, the first being an uncle of Moses and Aaron, and the second being one of the three young men thrown into the fiery furnace in the Book of Daniel. That Mishael is usually referred to as **Meshach,** his Babylonian name, when the story is retold. **Mishael** is almost never used, but Misael is regularly given in the Hispanic-American community, and more than 300 newborns in the United States were given the name in 2004.

Mitch

Form of **Mitchell.** Though Mitch is rarely found as an official name on birth certificates, most men named Mitchell in the United States use the short form in almost all contexts. This seems to be the case for Mitch Albom, author of the bestseller *Tuesdays with Morrie.* Famous name: Mitch Miller (singer)

Mitchell

Middle English form of **Michael.** Mitchell was fairly common between 1988 and 1997, when it was among the top 100 names, but it is now dropping in use and was only 202nd on the popularity list in 2004. Nickname: **Mitch**

Mohamed

Arabic "praiseworthy." Many experts believe that Mohamed is the most common male given name in the world, as in many Muslim cultures the majority of families name a son after their prophet. The immigration of Muslims to the United States has led to a steady increase in the use of this name since the 1980s. In 2004, more than 1,400 American boys were given the name.

Other spellings: **Mohammad, Mohammed, Muhammad**

Moises

Spanish form of **Moses,** steadily increasing in use along with the Hispanic population. Moises ranked 329th on the boys names list in the United States in 2004.

Famous name: Moises Alou (baseball player)

Monroe

Gaelic *mun-Rotha,* "mouth of the Roe" (a river in Ireland). James Monroe was the fifth president of the United States. His surname was frequently used as a given name during the 19th century, but it practically disappeared in that role around 1960 and has not yet been revived in spite of today's fondness for other presidential names such as **Jackson, Lincoln, Carter,** and **Reagan.**

Other spellings: **Monro, Munroe, Munrow**

Montague

A place name from Montaigu, France, that means "pointed hill." Drogo de Montacute brought the name to England in 1066.

Montana

Latin or Spanish word for "mountainous," the name of the American state. In the early 1990s after **Dakota** became popular, parents started considering the names of other Western states as boys names. Montana was the only one to be used enough to reach the SSA top 1,000 list. However, the *—ana* ending of the name attracted even more parents of girls than boys, so Montana's time in the sun as a boys name was brief, lasting only between 1992 and 1999.

Monte, Monty

Form of **Montgomery.**

Famous name: Monty Hall (television game show host)

Montgomery

French place name, "Gumric's hill." Gumric itself is an Old Germanic name from *gum* [man] + *ric* [powerful].

Famous name: Montgomery Ward (merchant)

Nicknames: **Monte, Monty**

Morgan

Welsh, either *mor* [sea] or *mawr* [great] + *can* [bright]. As often happens when a formerly male name becomes common for girls,

Morgan has been dropping in use for boys for more than a decade. There are now about seven girls being named Morgan for every one boy. However, there were still nearly 1,000 boys given the name in the United States in 2004.
Famous name: Morgan Freeman (actor)

Morley

Old English "marsh meadow."
Famous name: Morley Safer (journalist)

Morrie

Form of **Morris** or **Seymour**. Because of the best-selling book *Tuesdays with Morrie,* the late philosophy professor Morrie Schwartz is undoubtedly now the most famous man with this name.

Morris

Form of **Maurice**.
Nickname: **Morrie**

Morrison

Middle English *Morisson,* "son of **Maurice**."

Mort

Form of **Mortimer** or **Morton**.
Famous name: Mort Sahl (comedian)

Mortimer

French place name *Mortemer* in Normandy, "dead sea."
Famous name: Mortimer Adler (philosopher and educator)
Nicknames: **Mort, Mortie**

Morton

Old English "marshy farmstead."
Nickname: **Mort**

Moses

Probably Egyptian "child." As an infant, Moses was taken from the Nile River by the daughter of Pharoah. Because the ancient Hebrews didn't understand the meaning of the Egyptian name he was given, they interpreted it as meaning "saved, drawn out of the water." In the Old Testament, Moses was the lawgiver of the Israelites and led them to the promised land, which he could not enter. He died after having viewed it. This name was used by Jews throughout the Middle Ages. In the 17th century, the Puritans made it popular. But in the late 19th century it, along with other Puritan names, fell into disuse. It is still fairly rare today despite the revival of many other biblical names.

Famous name: Moses Malone (basketball player)

Nicknames: **Moe, Moke, Monchi** (Spanish), **Mose, Mosie, Moss**

Variations: **Moise** (French and Romanian), **Moisei** (Bulgarian), **Moises** (Spanish), **Moisis** (Greek), **Mojzesz** (Polish), **Mojzis** (Slovakian), **Mooses** (Estonian and Finnish), **Moshe** (Hebrew), **Moyses** (Portuguese), **Moze** (Lithuanian), **Mozes** (Dutch and Hungarian)

Moshe

Original Hebrew form of **Moses.** Along with **Chaim,** Moshe is a name that makes the SSA top 1,000 list because of its use by Orthodox Jews. Over 300 Moshes were born in the United States in 2004.

Moss

Form of **Moses.** Also considered a "nature name."

Muhammad

Alternate spelling of **Mohamed.**

Famous name: Muhammad Ali (boxer)

Murray

Celtic "sea settlement" or from Irish Gaelic *Giolla Mhuire,* "servant of the Virgin Mary." Though fairly common during the first third of the 20th century, Murray has not been among the top 1,000 names on the SSA list since 1976.

Myron

Greek "myrrh, perfume." The original Myron was an ancient Greek sculptor who lived around 450 B.C. His statue "The Discus Thrower" is still one of the world's most famous works of art. Myron became a boys name in the United States during the early 19th century classical revival when other classical names like **Homer** and **Virgil** were also taken up. Myron was fairly common in the early 20th century, but it developed an unfortunate nebbishy image and completely disappeared from the SSA top 1,000 list in 2004.

Variation: **Miron** (Slavic and Spanish)

Najeh

Probably an African-American form of *Nājī,* Arabic "safe, survivor."
Famous name: Najeh Davenport (football player)

Nandor

Hungarian form of **Ferdinand.**

Nash

English surname from Old English *aten asche,* "by the ash tree." At
this point Nash looks like it's going to be one of the best examples
of a name with "flash in the pan" popularity inspired by television.
The series *Nash Bridges,* starring Don Johnson as a San Francisco
police inspector, premiered in 1996, and Nash jumped onto the SSA
top 1,000 list for boys names the same year in 759th place. Since
the series ended in 2001, the name has been receding, and it was
only 984th on the list in 2004. Perhaps its one-syllable form doesn't
fit in with the tastes of many parents today.

Nasir

Arabic *nāsir,* "helper" or "supporter." This is now one of the faster-
growing Muslim names in the United States, popular with both
African-Americans and with Muslim immigrants from India and Pakistan. More than 500 American boys were named Nasir in 2004,
ranking it 420th. Nasir Hussain (1926–2002) was one of the most
prolific and successful producers in India's Bollywood film industry, the
largest movie industry in the world.

Nathan

Hebrew "the given." In the Old Testament, the prophet Nathan was
the one man who could stand up to King David. He chastised him
for sending Bathsheba's husband into battle. Nathan has been a
popular Jewish name for centuries. Nathan Hale was the often-

quoted American Revolutionary hero who said on the gallows, "I only regret that I have but one life to lose for my country." Nathan rose quickly to popularity during the early 1970s and has been one of the 50 most common names for newborn boys since 1975. Though it seemed its vogue might be receding in the early 1990s, since 1992 Nathan has risen in use by over 40 percent, and it was the 26th most common boys name of 2004. Its resemblance in sound to other recent favorites such as **Caden** and **Mason** has given Nathan more staying power than many other 1970s favorites.
Famous name: Nathan Lane (actor)
Nicknames: **Nat, Nate, Natty**
Variation: **Natan** (Polish, Spanish, and Italian)

Nathaniel

Hebrew "the Lord has given." Nathaniel was a popular name in New England during the 18th and 19th centuries. Along with **Nathan,** it has recently been revived and is now well within the top 100 names for boys. The trend has been for Nathan to be more somewhat more popular with white parents while Nathaniel is used more by Hispanic-Americans and African-Americans.
Famous name: Nathaniel Hawthorne (novelist)
Variations: **Nataneal** (Spanish), **Nataniel** (Polish), **Nathanael**

Nation

Perhaps the ultimate "patriotic name." Several instances of parents using this "word name" have been noted lately. Its similarity in sound to **Nathan** makes it a good "different but not too different" choice.

Nature

Perhaps the ultimate "nature name." It's interesting that most of the examples of children given this name so far have been boys, in spite of the well-known concept of "Mother Nature."

Neal

Alternate spelling of **Neil.**
Famous name: Neal Stephenson (science fiction novelist)

Ned

Form of **Edward** or **Edwin.**
Famous name: Ned Beatty (actor)

Nehemiah

Hebrew "God has consoled." In the Bible, Nehemiah, cupbearer to Artaxerxes I of the Persian empire, persuades that king to let him return to Jerusalem and organize the rebuilding of the city and its walls. The name Nehemiah was not used outside of the Jewish community until the Puritans started searching the Old Testament for names in the 17th century. Like many such names, it slowly died out during the 19th century and had almost vanished as a name for American newborns by 1887. But the modern fashion for other Old Testament names such as **Isaiah** and **Malachi** has given new life to Nehemiah. It re-entered the SSA list of the top 1,000 names in 1998 after an absence of more than a century and has steadily ascended since. There were 378 Nehemiahs born in the United States in 2004, ranking it 584th on the SSA list.

Neil

Irish Gaelic *Niall,* uncertain meaning, perhaps "champion," "passionate," or "cloud." Neil is a name that has never been hugely popular in the United States, and it has fallen in use by two-thirds since 1990. Though it is still a solid, unfaddish name, its one-syllable status may be causing it to lose out given contemporary tastes.

Famous names: Neil Armstrong (astronaut)

Neil Diamond (singer)

Neil Simon (playwright)

Neil Young (rock musician)

Other spellings: **Neal, Neale, Neall, Neel, Neill, Niel**

Variations: **Nial, Niall** (Irish and Scottish), **Nigel, Niles, Njal** (Scandinavian)

Nelson

English "son of **Neil.**" South African civil rights activist Nelson Mandela, jailed for more than 25 years, has given this first name worldwide recognition. He won the Nobel Peace Prize in 1993.

Variations: **Niles**

Neo

The creators of the film trilogy *The Matrix* say that the name of the hero Neo (played by Keanu Reeves) is an anagram of the word "one," but critics have noted that the Greek prefix *neo-*, meaning "new," also contributes to the many symbolic meanings fans find in these movies. There have been several hundred boys named Neo in the United States since the first of the *Matrix* films premiered in 1999, though not quite enough in any one year for the name to make the SSA top 1,000 list. In Sweden, Neo was among the top 100 names for boys born in 2004. If **Leo** continues to grow in popularity, American parents may turn to Neo as an alternative.

Nestor

Spanish *Néstor*, an ancient Greek name perhaps based on *néomai*, "I return." The original Nestor was the elderly king of Pylos, one of the leaders of the Greeks in the war against Troy who had a reputation for wisdom. His name has historically been well used in both Spain and Italy because it was also the name of several early Christian martyrs. Like many traditional Hispanic names, Nestor grew in use during the 1970s and 1980s as the Hispanic population increased. However, it's been receding in the United States since 1992, so it must be going out of fashion even with tradition-minded Hispanic parents. Nestor was the 876th name on the SSA list in 2004. Famous name: Nestor Torres (jazz flutist)

Neville

French *Neuville*, "the new town." The image of this name for children of the 21st century will be dominated by the clumsy but loyal character Neville Longbottom in the *Harry Potter* films and novels. Famous name: Neville Marriner (conductor)

Nevin

Irish Gaelic *Naomhan*, form of *naomh*, "holy"; or *cnaimhin*, "bone."

Nhiakou

Green Hmong (Laos) "golden money." This is a common name among Hmong refugees living in the United States.

Niccolo

Italian form of **Nicholas.** Famous Italians with this name include Niccolo Machiavelli, author of *The Prince*, a philosophy of politics, and violinist Niccolo Paganini.

Nicholas

Greek *Nikolaos* from *nike* [victory] + *laos* [people] through Latin *Nicolaus*. So many miracles are credited to the fourth-century St.

Nicholas that he has become the patron of Russian schoolchildren, sailors, and pawnbrokers. Nicholas has long been a popular name in Europe. It was the name of five popes and two Russian emperors. In England, the name goes back to before the Norman Invasion. Its long-established roots have given rise to many variations, including Cole and Colin, which are now popular independent names. Charles Dickens used the name for the title character of *Nicholas Nickleby*. Although Nicholas has enjoyed only moderate popularity in the past, it became very fashionable in the late 1970s and has been among the top ten names given to American boys since 1991. Nicholas Bradford, a character on the family-oriented television series *Eight Is Enough* played by Adam Rich starting in 1977, may have had a strong impact on the name's increased use, but the way for it had already been paved by the previous rise of **Nicole** for girls.

Famous names: Nicholas D. Kristof (columnist)

Nicholas Poussin (painter)

Nicholas Sparks (novelist)

Nicknames: **Nick, Nicki, Nickie, Nicky, Nicol, Nik, Nikky**

Variations: **Claus, Cole, Colin, Klaus** (Danish and German), **Kolya** (Russian), **Launo** (Finnish), **Miklos** (Hungarian), **Mikolaj** (Polish), **Mikolas** (Czech), **Mykola** (Ukrainian), **Neacail** (Scots Gaelic), **Niccolo** (Italian), **Nico** (Greek and Italian), **Nicola** (Italian), **Nicolaas** (Dutch), **Nicolao** (Portuguese), **Nicolas** (French and Spanish), **Nicolaus, Nicolo** (Italian), **Nidzo** (Serbian), **Niels** (Danish), **Niilo** (Finnish), **Niklas** (Scandinavian), **Niko** (Dutch and Slovenian), **Nikolai** (Russian), **Nikolaos** (Greek), **Nikolaus** (German), **Nils** (Swedish and Norwegian)

Nick

Form of **Dominic** or **Nicholas.**

Famous name: Nick Nolte (actor)

Nico

This short form of **Nicholas** first entered the SSA top 1,000 list in 1988 and reached its high point the very next year at 546th place. It was in 1988 that actor Steven Seagal starred in his first megahit action film, *Above the Law,* where his character was called Nico Toscani. Nico was certainly a name in the Hollywood air at the time, because the soap operas *All My Children* and *Days of Our Lives* both introduced characters called Nico in 1987 or 1988. Of course, to put this in perspective, even though Nico has never been out of the SSA top 1,000 since 1988, even at its highest point fewer than 500 boys per year received the name.

Nicolas

French and Spanish spelling of **Nicholas.**
Famous name: Nicolas Cage (actor)

Niels

Danish form of **Nicholas.** There is a natural tendency for Americans to confuse this name with **Neil,** but the true Scandinavian form of Neil is **Njal.** Niels Bohr, the Danish physicist who won the Nobel Prize in 1922, was a leading figure in the development of quantum theory, which led to the atomic age.
Variations: **Nels** (Swedish), **Nils** (Norwegian and Swedish)

Nigel

This name was created by a medieval mistake; clerks writing in Latin a thousand years ago wrongly associated **Neil** with Latin *niger,* "black," and so inserted the g. Nigel has never been very common in the United States. Most Americans think of it as a typically British name, which indeed it is, having been popular in England and Wales for boys born in the 1960s and 1970s. Its minor period of American popularity in the 1980s and 1990s was largely confined to the African-American community. Nigel ranked 764th on the 2004 SSA list.
Famous name: Sir Nigel Hawthorne (actor)

Nikhil

Sanskrit *Nikhila,* "complete, whole, entire." Nikhil is one of the more common names being given by Hindu immigrants to their sons in the United States, possibly because it yields the popular American nickname **Nik** and so allows the child to easily fit in with American culture. There were 203 boys named Nikhil born in the United States in 2004.

Nikita

Russian form of Greek *Aniketos,* "unconquerable."
Famous name: Nikita Khrushchev (Soviet statesman)

Niles

Another form of **Neil** or **Nelson,** now well known because of the character Niles Crane on the long-running television comedy *Frasier*. This name is still rare in spite of the continued popularity of **Miles.**

Noah

Hebrew, perhaps "rest." The story of Noah and his ark is probably the best-known tale in Western civilization, although essentially the same story occurs in most other cultures. Because of Noah's goodness and righteousness, God favored him and let him in on the secret that the world was going to be destroyed by a flood. Noah was given directions on building a boat and told how to select those who were to be saved from the flood. After the flood, the descendants of Noah repopulated the world. The name came into vogue in the 17th century when it was used by the Puritans. It went out of fashion in the 19th century, but during the 1980s it began a slow revival in the United States that greatly accelerated after 1993. More than 11,000 American boys born in 2004 were named Noah, which made it the 36th most popular name.

Famous names: Noah Webster (lexicographer)
Noah Wyle (actor)

Variation: **Noe** (French and Spanish)

Noe

Spanish and French form of **Noah,** steadily increasing since the 1940s along with the Hispanic-American population. It ranked 386th among American boys names in 2004.

Noel

Latin *natalis,* "birth," through Old French *noel* or *nowel;* traditionally used as a name for children born on Christmas Day.

Famous name: Sir Noel Coward (playwright)

Other spellings: **Nowel, Nowell**

Variations: **Natal** (Spanish), **Natale** (Italian)

Nolan

Irish Gaelic *Nuallain* from *nuall,* "shouter, chariot-fighter, champion." With a sound that fits in with today's fashions, Nolan has almost quintupled in use over the last 20 years, being given to almost 2,500 American boys born in 2004.

Famous name: Nolan Ryan (baseball pitcher)
Variation: **Noland**

Norbert

Old German, perhaps "aurora borealis" from *nord* [north] + *berht* [bright]. St. Norbert was struck by lightning and began to hear the words of God. He reformed his life, became a monk, and established the Order of Premonstrants. Norbert is a very unusual name in the modern United States, but it's well known to many youngsters as the name of Hagrid's Norwegian Ridgeback dragon in the *Harry Potter* books.
Nicknames: **Bert, Bertie, Nobby, Norb, Norby**

Norm

Form of **Norman.** Many Americans still associate this name with Norm Peterson, the jovial character played by George Wendt on the long-lived comedy series *Cheers.*

Norman

Old English "North man." Norman was one of the top 50 names in the United States between 1915 and 1941, but today it has largely disappeared from use.
Famous names: Norman Lear (television producer)
Norman Mailer (writer)
Norman Rockwell (painter)
Nicknames: **Norm, Normie, Normy**
Variation: **Normand**

Norris

Old Norman French *norreis,* "person from the north."

Norton

Old English "north town." Norton had a bit of use in the early 20th century but has been invisible since 1940. The character Norton on the old *Honeymooners* television skits may inhibit parents from using this name in spite of the fashion for **Easton** and **Weston.**

Oba

Yoruba (Nigeria) "king."

Obadiah

Hebrew "servant of God," name of one of the prophetic books of the Old Testament. Though it was used by the Puritans in the 18th century, Obadiah has been extremely rare for at least 150 years. With similar biblical names such as **Isaiah** and **Nehemiah** becoming fashionable, and with Ewan McGregor having given the pet form **Obi** a younger positive image in the *Star Wars* prequel trilogy, this name would make an excellent "different but not too different" choice.

Oberon

Name of the king of the fairies in William Shakespeare's *A Midsummer Night's Dream*, and an alternate form of *Auberon*, a Norman French name that may have originally meant "noble bear."

Octavio

Spanish form of Latin *Octavius*, a Roman family name from Latin *octāvus*, "eighth." Octavio is one of the traditional Spanish names that's been growing in use along with the Hispanic-American population. More than 300 Octavios were born in the United States in 2004. Mexican writer Octavio Paz won the Nobel Prize in literature in 1990.

Odo

Form of **Otto.** Fans of *Star Trek* will associate this name with Odo the shapeshifter and security chief on the space station *Deep Space Nine*.

Odon

(See **Edmond, Otto.**)

Ogden

Old English "from the oak valley" from *ac* [oak] + *denu* [dale or valley]. If it had a more attractive initial syllable, the fashionable *-den* ending of this name might lead more new parents to be enthusiastic about choosing it for their sons.

Famous name: Ogden Nash (poet)

Olaf

Old Norse *Anleifr* from *anu* [ancestor] + *leifr* [heir, descendant]. St. Olaf was the first Christian king of Norway and the first of many royal Olafs, which probably accounts for the name's enduring popularity throughout Scandinavia. Most American Olafs have Scandinavian ancestors.

Variations: **Amblaoibh** (Irish), **Olav** (Norse), **Oliver**

Oldak

Palauan "unifying."

Olin

French and Dutch surname from a pet form of Old German *Odal*, "prosperity."

Olino

Hawaiian *'ōlino*, "brilliant, bright, dazzling."

Oliver

Uncertain meaning; perhaps Old German *Alfihar*, "elf-host"; a French form of **Olaf**; or Old French "olive tree." Whatever its origin, the name spread throughout northern Europe during medieval times and England more than 900 years ago. Shakespeare used the name for the brother of Orlando in his play *As You Like It*, but in the 17th century, Oliver Cromwell's ruthless reign tainted the name. In the 18th century, one of the few instances of the name is that of novelist Oliver Goldsmith. In the 19th century, Charles Dickens brought a new image to the name with his novel *Oliver Twist*, about an orphan boy who finds happiness. Oliver has been enjoying a strong revival in England and Wales, where it was the seventh most common name for boys in 2004. Americans are beginning to notice it; Oliver more than doubled in use between 1997 and 2004, when it was 221st on the U.S. popularity chart. The recent success of **Olivia** as a female name may predict a bright future for Oliver.

Famous names: Oliver Wendell Holmes (U.S. Supreme Court associate justice)
Oliver Stone (movie director)

Nicknames: **Noll, Nolly, Olley, Ollie, Olly**
Variations: **Oliva** (French Canadian), **Oliverio** (Italian and Spanish), **Olivier** (French), **Olivo**

Omar

Arabic "thriving, prospering, long-lived" or Hebrew "speaker." This name had a literal application for at least two men who prospered in their chosen professions and whose reputations have been long-lived: 12th-century Persian poet Omar Khayyam and U.S. Army General Omar Bradley, commander of the Normandy invasion. With support from the Hispanic- and African-American communities as well as from recent Muslim immigrants, Omar has been among the top 200 names for boys in the United States since 1988.
Famous name: Omar Sharif (actor)
Variations: **Amar, Omari** (Swahili)

Omari

Swahili form of **Omar.** Boys names ending in –*mari* are now in vogue in the African-American community, and Omari is part of this upswing. The name ranked 573rd on the SSA list for boys in 2004, with 388 born that year.

Omarion

When Omari Grandberry became part of the youthful R&B group B2K, he adopted Omarion as his stage name. When the group's first album became a runaway hit in 2002, many parents adopted Omarion as a name for their own sons. In 2004, when Omarion launched his solo career, there were 573 American boys named Omarion, making it one of the top 400 names of the year.

Onterrio

Respelling of **Ontario,** the name of the Great Lake and Canadian province, from Iroquoian words meaning "fine lake."
Famous name: Onterrio Smith (football player)

Oral

Latin *oral,* "spoken," from *os,* "mouth." This seems to be an appropriate name for preacher and television evangelist Oral Roberts, who was named by an aunt who simply liked the sound of the word.
Famous name: Oral Clyde Hildebrand (baseball pitcher)

Orban

(See **Urban.**)

Orel

From a Czech surname meaning "eagle." In 1988, Orel Hershisher, a baseball pitcher, won the Most Valuable Player Award in the World Series, the Cy Young Award, and many other top honors.

Orion

Greek "son of light." In Greek mythology, Orion was a mighty hunter. The constellation Orion is easily recognized by the row of stars that make up Orion's belt.

Variation: **Orien**

Orland

Form of **Roland**.

Orlando

Italian form of **Roland**. Orlando is the hero of Shakespeare's play *As You Like It* and the name Virginia Woolf chose for the title character of her fictional biography of her friend Vita Sackville-West. Although originally an Italian name, this name is now popular with Hispanic-Americans. Orlando had been receding in use after 1987, but since 2000 it's been increasing a bit, which may be due to the fame of actor Orlando Bloom. There were 774 Orlandos born in the United States in 2004, ranking it 327th that year.

Famous name: Orlando Cepeda (baseball player)

Ormond

Irish Gaelic surname *Ó Ruaidh,* "descendant of the red one"; or Irish place name *Ur Mhumhain,* "eastern Munster." Experts believe that the surname took this form since the family coincidentally lived in the region called Ormond.

Orson

Old Norman French "bear cub" from Latin *ursus,* "bear." The prominence of movie director and actor Orson Welles, whose credits include *Citizen Kane* and *The Magnificent Ambersons* as well as his famous "War of the Worlds" radio broadcast, did nothing to increase the popularity of this unusual name.

Famous name: Orson Bean (actor)

Variations: **Orsino, Ursin** (Danish, French, Russian, and Romanian), **Ursino** (Italian and Spanish), **Urson, Ursyn** (Ukrainian)

Orville

French "gold town." This name was invented by Fanny Burney for the hero of her 1778 novel *Evelina*. The name was made popular in the United States by Orville Wright, who with his brother Wilbur flew the first motor-driven airplane.
Famous name: Orville Redenbacher (entrepreneur)
Nicknames: **Orv, Orvie**

Osborn

Old English *Osbeorn* from *os* [god] + *beorn* [bear, warrior]. This is an old name in England that is found mostly in Northumberland. It has been in general use since long before the Norman Conquest.
Nicknames: **Oz, Ozzie**
Variations: **Osborne, Ozburn**

Oscar

Irish Gaelic from *os* [deer] + *cara* [friend]. Scottish researcher James Macpherson revived this name in the 18th century through his supposed translations of the third-century poems by Ossian. (Most modern scholars believe that Macpherson wrote the poems himself and merely claimed that they were translations of ancient writings.) These works were popular throughout Western Europe, and Napoleon Bonaparte insisted that his godson, Oscar Bernadotte, be given the name. When Bernadotte later became king of Sweden, Oscar became a common name throughout Scandinavia. Oscar is the pet name for the awards given by the Academy of Motion Picture Arts and Sciences. The gold-covered statuettes supposedly got this name in 1931 when the librarian of the Academy, Margaret Herrick, said that the trophies looked like her uncle Oscar. Oscar has long been a popular name throughout Latin America, and most boys given the name in the United States today are of Hispanic ancestry. However, there are signs that Oscar is beginning to sound "cool" to avant garde parents.
Famous names: Oscar de la Hoya (boxer)
　　　　　　　Oscar Hammerstein (librettist)
　　　　　　　Oscar Wilde (playwright)

Nicknames: **Ossie, Ozzie**
Other spelling: **Oskar**

Osman

Turkish form of Arabic *Uthman*, "young bustard." A bustard is a Middle Eastern bird similar to a crane. The Turkish sultan Osman founded the Ottoman Empire in 1517.

Ossie

Form of **Oscar** or **Oswald**.
Famous name: Ossie Davis (actor)

Osvaldo, Oswaldo

These Spanish forms of **Oswald** have been well used in Latin America and by Hispanics in the United States since 1970, when the popular telenovela *Yesenia* featured a handsome military officer named Oswaldo as its hero.

Oswald

Old English *Osweald*, "divinely powerful," from *os* [god] + *weald* [power]. This name dates back to at least the seventh century through the king of Northumbria, who was killed in a battle with the Welsh army. The name is unusual in the United States, although the nickname Ozzie became well known through Ozzie Nelson in the 1950s television comedy *The Adventures of Ozzie and Harriet*. Rock singer Ozzy Osborne made it a name for the 1980s and then revived his fame as the star of his own reality television series starting in 2002.
Famous name: Oswald Spengler (philosopher)
Nicknames: **Ossie, Oz, Ozzie, Ozzy, Wallie, Wally**
Variations: **Osvaldo, Oswaldo** (Spanish)

Othello

Name of the tragic hero of Shakespeare's play *Othello*, written around 1602. Shakespeare probably invented this name to sound suitably exotic to his audience. It's possible he expanded **Otho** or based it on "Ottoman" (see **Osman**). Some Shakespearean scholars have suggested that it is a pun on the phrase "Oh, tell," since it's likely that when Shakespeare wrote the play he was expecting the name to be pronounced as "Otello" rather than with the *th* sound normally heard today.

Otho

Though usually listed as a form of **Otto,** Otho was also the name of a Roman emperor who ruled for a few months in A.D. 69 during the chaotic time after Nero was overthrown. In his case, Otho is a name of ancient Etruscan derivation and unknown meaning.

Otis

Middle English *Otes, Odes,* "son of **Otto** or *Odo,*" the latter from Old Norse *odd,* "point of a weapon." This surname became a first name in the United States in honor of James Otis, an 18th-century Massachusetts patriot thought to have been the first to use the phrase "taxation without representation."
Famous name: Otis Redding (singer)

Otto

Old German *asdo,* "rich." Otto von Bismarck, chancellor of the German empire, is known for engineering the unification of Germany in the 19th century.
Variations: **Odo** (Latin and Polish), **Odón** (Spanish), **Otao** (Portuguese), **Otho, Oto** (Bulgarian and Croatian), **Otone** (Italian), **Otti** (Estonian), **Otton** (French, Greek, and Russian)

Owen

Usually a Welsh form of **Eugene,** though in Ireland sometimes an Anglicization of *Eógan,* "born of the yew." This name is known in Welsh history through the 12th-century general Owen of Gwynedd and the 15th-century rebel Owen Glendower, who failed to achieve his bid for Welsh independence. Since 1994, Owen's use has skyrocketed. There were more than 6,600 Owens born in the United States in 2004, a nearly 14-fold increase in a decade.
Famous name: Owen Wilson (actor)
Variations: **Ewan, Ewen, Owain**

Owodunni

Yoruban (Nigeria) "it's nice to have money."

Ozburn

(See **Osborn.**)

Pablo

Spanish form of **Paul.** This name has grown increasingly popular as the Hispanic-American population has increased. It was ranked 273rd for boys born in the United States in 2004. Chilean author Pablo Neruda won the Nobel Prize in literature in 1971.
Famous name: Pablo Picasso (painter)

Paco

Pet form of **Francisco.**

Palasan

Armenian "balsam."

Pancho

Spanish form of **Francisco.**
Famous name: Pancho Villa (bandit)
Variations: **Panchito, Pancholo, Panzo**

Paolo

Italian form of **Paul.**
Famous name: Paolo Veronese (painter)

Park

Middle English *Parc,* surname for one who lived by a game park, or a form of **Parker.**

Parker

Old English "a gamekeeper." This is an occupational surname, like Baker. As with many common surnames, Parker has been occasionally used as a first name since the 19th century. It had almost completely disappeared, though, before 1978, when actor Parker Stevenson began appearing on the television series *The Hardy Boys Mysteries.* After Stevenson initially influenced use of the name, it seems to have risen steadily without much added help from Hollywood. Parker may have hit its high point from 1999 to 2003, when it was about 125th on the popularity list each year; in 2004 it slipped to 134th place.

Nickname: **Park**

Parmenion

From the Greek verb *parménein,* "to persevere, be constant, be faithful." This was the name of one of Alexander the Great's most important generals, and like other classical names, it was given on rare occasions to boys in the United States in the early 19th century. It could be updated today with the shorter form **Parmen.**

Parnell

A Norman French contraction of Latin *Petronilla,* perhaps "little rock," the name of an early Christian martyr who was said to be the daughter of St. Peter. Parnell is one of the few European surnames from medieval times based on a woman's rather than a man's first name. Charles Stewart Parnell was an Irish nationalist leader, and some Irish-Americans choose to name their sons after him.

Pascal

French form of Latin *Paschalis,* "relating to Easter or the Hebrew Passover." This name honors Good Friday, and boys born on that day traditionally were named Pascal. The Sunday following Good Friday is Easter, the day for hunting eggs, which used to be called Pascal eggs. The name Pascal is hardly used in English-speaking countries, but it was very popular in France during the 1960s.

Variations: **Paschal, Pascoe** (Cornish), **Pascual** (Spanish), **Pasquale** (Italian)

Pat

Form of **Patrick.** Former football star Pat Tillman became an American hero when he joined the Army Rangers and was killed by friendly fire in Afghanistan in April 2004.

Patricio

Spanish form of **Patrick.**

Patrick

Latin *patricius,* "member of the nobility." St. Patrick, the patron saint of Ireland, was born in England and educated in France. In A.D. 432

he went to Ireland to preach the gospel. Until the 17th century, most people in Ireland held St. Patrick in such high esteem that his name wasn't used. In the United States, the statesman and orator Patrick Henry urged the declaration of war against the English crown with his famous line, "Give me liberty or give me death." The name was popular in England, Scotland, and the United States during the 20th century. It became one of the 50 most common names for boys in the United States in 1948 and didn't lose that status until 1997. By 2004 it had fallen to 107th place.

Famous names: Patrick Ewing (basketball player)
               Patrick J. Leahy (U.S. senator)
               Patrick Stewart (actor)

Nicknames: **Paddy, Pat, Patsy, Patty, Ticho** (Spanish)

Variations: **Padraig** (Irish Gaelic), **Padrig** (Welsh), **Patrice** (French), **Patricio** (Spanish and Portuguese), **Patricius** (Dutch), **Patrik** (Czech, Finnish, Swedish, and Hungarian), **Patriss** (Latvian), **Patrizio** (Italian), **Patryk** (Polish)

Patton

English surname from *Paton*, a pet form of **Patrick.**

Paul

Greek *paulos*, "small." St. Paul, a Jew who had persecuted Christians, became one of Christianity's most ardent advocates after his conversion. Through his epistles, Paul's presentation of Christian beliefs became one of the main foundations of the faith. Paul was also the name of six popes. Paul was not a common name in England before the 20th century, but it was very popular in Russia, Italy, Spain, and France. Painters Paul Cezanne, Paul Gauguin, and Paul Klee lent the name artistic roots, while the American Revolutionary hero Paul Revere gave the name stature in the United States. The name has been particularly popular among actors, including Paul Muni, Paul Newman, Paul Robeson, Paul Scofield, and Paul Winfield. Paul also seems to be a lucky name for biochemists recently: Paul Nurse was cowinner of the Nobel Prize in medicine in 2001, and Paul C. Lauterbur shared the same prize in 2003. Though the modern search for newer names and the reluctance to use one-syllable forms has led to a drop in Paul's use, it was still the 132nd most common boys name given in the United States in 2004.

Famous names: Paul Harvey (commentator)

Paul McCartney (musician)

Nickname: **Paulie, Pava** (Russian)

Variations: **Paal** (Estonian), **Paavo** (Finnish), **Pablo** (Spanish), **Pal** (Hungarian, Scots Gaelic, and Swedish), **Paolo** (Italian), **Pau** (Catalan), **Paulo** (Portuguese), **Paulos** (Greek), **Paulus** (Latin and Dutch), **Paval** (Bulgarian and Slovenian), **Pavao** (Serbo-Croatian), **Pavel** (Czech and Russian), **Pavlo** (Ukrainian), **Pawel** (Polish), **Pol** (Irish Gaelic), **Polo** (Italian), **Poul** (Danish), **Povilas** (Lithuanian), **Powell**

Paxton

English surname from a place name, "farmstead of a man called *Pæcc*." Since it blends the sounds of **Max** and **Peyton,** a few parents have recently discovered Paxton as a "different but not too different" alternative. It's been on the SSA top 1,000 list since 1997 but is still uncommon, with fewer than 200 boys given the name each year.

Payne

Old French *paien,* from Latin *paganus,* "rural dweller," later "non-Christian." Despite its meaning, this was a fairly common given name in the Middle Ages.

Famous name: Payne Stewart (golfer)

Pedro

Spanish form of **Peter.** This name is still often used by Hispanic-Americans, and it ranked 216th among names given to boys in the United States in 2004.

Famous names: Pedro Almodovar (film director)

Pedro Guerrero (baseball player)

Variations: **Perico, Pero, Peyo, Pico**

Peerless

The word, meaning "incomparable," used as a name.

Pello

(See **Peter.**)

Penrhyn

Welsh "promontory."

Percival

Origin uncertain, but may come from French *perce-val*, "valley piercer." This name was invented by writer Chretien de Troyes in the 12th century. He used it for a knight who was on a quest for the Holy Grail. The story is retold in Sir Thomas Malory's *Morte d'Arthur* and also in Alfred, Lord Tennyson's *Idylls of the King*.
Nicknames: **Perce, Percy**
Other spelling: **Perceval**
Variations: **Parcifal** (Dutch), **Parsifal** (Italian, Polish, and Czech),
          Parzival (German and Hungarian)

Percy

French place name "Persius's estate" or a form of **Percival.** In medieval England, this was considered a good name for a rugged masculine knight, but in modern times Percy has lost its macho image. Children who hear the name today may think of Percy Weasley, Ron's rule-abiding older brother from the *Harry Potter* books.
Famous name: Percy Bysshe Shelley (poet)

Peregrine

Latin *Peregrinus*, "foreigner, stranger," related to the word "pilgrim." There were several saints of this name, and it was fairly common in the Middle Ages, but today it is mostly known through Peregrine Took, the hobbit generally called "Pippin" by his friends in J.R.R. Tolkien's *The Lord of the Rings* series.

Perkin

Medieval pet form of **Peter.** This name is known in British history through Perkin Warbeck (1474–1499), a Flemish commoner who convinced many that he was the rightful heir to the English throne.

Perrin

Middle English *Peryn,* a pet form of **Peter.**

Perry

Old English *pyrige*, "pear tree." The many books, television shows, and movies about the exploits of defense attorney Perry Mason overshadow most other connotations of this name.
Famous names: Perry Como (singer)
          Perry Ellis (fashion designer)

Pershing

American form of German *Pfoersching,* "a person who grows or sells peaches." This name is very unusual today. It honors General John Joseph "Blackjack" Pershing, commander of the U.S. Expeditionary Forces in World War I. The name was given to sons of soldiers who fought under his command.

Pete

Short form of **Peter.**
Famous name: Pete Seeger (musician)

Peter

Greek *petros,* "rock." St. Peter was a fisherman called to be one of the 12 apostles and regarded as the first pope, which is why so many churches have been named after him. In Russia, three tsars were named Peter. Peter I, called Peter the Great, attempted to westernize his country in the 18th century. Peter Ilyich Tchaikovsky is known as one of the world's great composers. In the 20th century, the name became very popular in England and Australia, perhaps because of James Barrie's *Peter Pan.* Peter was also popular in the United States between 1940 and 1975. Although now going out of fashion, it was still 140th on the list of names given to American boys born in 2004.
Famous names: Peter Jennings (broadcast journalist)
　　　　　　　　Peter O'Toole (actor)
　　　　　　　　Peter Paul Rubens (artist)
　　　　　　　　Peter Sellers (actor)
Nicknames: **Pete, Petey, Petie**
Variations: **Par** (Swedish), **Peadar** (Gaelic), **Peder** (Danish), **Pedro** (Spanish), **Pekka** (Finnish), **Pello** (Basque), **Per** (Scandinavian), **Perkin, Petar** (Bulgarian), **Peto** (Hungarian), **Petr** (Czech), **Petras** (Lithuanian), **Petro** (Ukrainian), **Petros** (Greek), **Petru** (Romanian), **Petrus** (Dutch and German), **Petter** (Norwegian), **Pierce, Piero** (Italian), **Pierre** (French), **Piers, Piet, Pieter** (Dutch), **Pietro** (Italian), **Piotr** (Polish), **Pyotr** (Russian)

Peyton

Old English "Paega's farm." Peyton Randolph of Virginia was the first president of the Continental Congress in 1774, and that kept the name Peyton in steady—if rare—use in the southern United States throughout the 19th century. Around 1988 Americans in all regions began to notice the name, and it quickly rose in use. Though the fame of football player Peyton Manning certainly hasn't hurt the name, he didn't start the vogue for it since he wasn't even a college freshman until 1994. Peyton was the 114th most common boys name in 2004; about a third of the parents who give it spell it **Payton.** If new parents notice how common the name is also getting for girls, however, its fall in use for boys may be as swift as its rise.

Phil

Short form of **Philip.**
Famous names: Phil Collins (singer)
               Phil Donahue (talk show host)
               Phil McGraw (psychotherapist and talk-show host)

Philip, Phillip

Greek *Philippos,* "horse lover." In the New Testament, Philip was one of the apostles. Philip of Macedon was the father of Alexander the Great. In both France and Spain, the name has a long association with royalty, including six French and five Spanish kings. The most famous was Philip II, who united the Iberian peninsula and ruled over an empire that also included Milan, Naples, Sicily, the Netherlands, and much of the New World. In England, Philip Mountbatten, consort of Queen Elizabeth II, was also given the title of duke of Edinburgh. The name peaked in use during the 1940s and 1950s and was the 169th most common name in 2004.
Famous names: Philip Johnson (architect)
               Philip Roth (writer)
Nicknames: **Flip, Phil, Pip**
Variations: **Felipe** (Spanish), **Felippe** (Portuguese), **Filib** (Scots Gaelic), **Filip** (Scandinavian, Polish, and Czech), **Filippino, Filippo** (Italian), **Filippos** (modern Greek), **Fulop** (Hungarian), **Philipp** (German), **Philippe** (French), **Philippus** (Dutch), **Pilib** (Irish), **Pilypas** (Lithuanian), **Pylyp** (Ukrainian)

Phinehas

The name of two minor characters in the Bible, the first a grandson of Aaron. This is one of the few Old Testament names that is not originally Hebrew; it derives from the ancient Egyptian word *Panhsj,* meaning "man from Nubia," the African country immediately to the south of Egypt. Like many Old Testament names, Phinehas was first used by the Puritans in colonial New England, but even back then its spelling was uncertain. This is shown by the most famous bearer of the name, showman **Phineas** T. Barnum. Actress Julia Roberts recently gave the name publicity by naming her son **Phinnaeus,** a "Latinized" spelling of the name used on rare occasions in the 19th century. Though many criticized her for this, if names like **Finn** and **Finley** continue to grow in popularity, Phinehas may soon fit in perfectly with modern tastes.

Phoenix

The name of the mythical bird that sets its own nest on fire and is reborn from the ashes. The legend of the Phoenix was originally Egyptian, and the ancient Greeks reinterpreted the Egyptian word for the bird, *benu,* as *phoinix,* derived from their own word for "crimson." The early Christians used the phoenix as a symbol of resurrection. Americans today are most likely to associate the word with the city in Arizona, so it's hard to say if Phoenix is more of a geographical or mythical name to the parents using it today. Phoenix first entered the SSA top 1,000 list for boys in 1995 and has steadily increased in use. In 2004 there were 403 American boys given the name Phoenix, ranking it 558th on the SSA list that year.

Pierce

Middle English variation of **Peter.**
Famous name: Pierce Brosnan (actor)

Pierre

French form of **Peter.**
Famous name: Pierre Renoir (painter)

Piers

Middle English form of **Peter.** The long poem *Piers Plowman* by William Langland is one of the few pieces of medieval English literature that has survived to be widely read today. Its title character exhibits a work ethic and sense of fair play that is still admired in the modern world.
Famous name: Piers Anthony (science fiction and fantasy author)

Piet

Dutch form of **Pete** or **Peter.**

Famous name: Piet Mondrian (artist)

Pilot

The word used as a name. Actor Jason Lee, a former professional skateboarder, has probably gotten more publicity for naming his son Pilot Inspektor than for any of his film roles or skateboarding successes.

Placido

Italian, Spanish, and Portuguese form of Latin *Placidus,* "untroubled, unworried, faithful." Technically, the correct spelling of this name in Italian is *Plàcido* and in Spanish, *Plácido.* Though such accent marks are almost always ignored in the United States, Europeans often feel that to leave them out creates a serious misspelling.

Famous name: Placido Domingo (opera singer)

Nicknames: **Placi, Plasio**

Variations: **Placid** (English and Russian), **Placide** (French), **Placyd** (Polish and Ukrainian), **Plakidos** (Greek)

Plato

English form of Greek *Platon,* "broad shouldered." Greek philosopher Plato was a student of Socrates and the teacher of Aristotle.

Porter

Middle English *porter* from Old French *portier,* "gatekeeper, doorkeeper." This occupational surname has been sporadically used as a given name since the 19th century. There are signs that it is about to join names like **Parker, Tanner,** and **Tucker** as a fashionable "former surname ending in *–er*" for boys in the United States.

Famous name: Porter Wagoner (country singer)

Poul

Danish form of **Paul.**

Powell

British surname with three different origins. If English, it can either be a form of **Paul** or an indication that one's ancestor lived by a pond or pool. If Welsh, it's from *ap Hywel,* "son of Hywel," a Welsh name meaning "eminent, noticeable." Powell is very rare as a first name, but a few instances have been noted since the 19th century.

Pranav

Sanskrit *Pranava*, "humming; mystical syllable." When a Hindu or Buddhist chants using the word "om," they are repeating the "pranava." Pranav is now one of the more fashionable boys names in the U.S. Hindu community, ranking 762nd on the SSA list in 2004.

Prentice, Prentiss

English surnames from Old French *aprentis*, "apprentice," a young man learning a trade.

Prescott

English place name from Old English *preost* [priest] + *cot* [cottage, dwelling]. This surname became a first name in New England in honor of William Prescott, a Connecticut leader in the Revolutionary War. It is still occasionally used today. Prescott Bush, a U.S. senator from Connecticut in the early 20th century, was the father of George H. W. Bush and the grandfather of George W. Bush.

Preston

Old English "priest's town." Preston had been in steady, regular use as an American first name for more than a century when it began to increase around 1985. By 2004 it was the 149th most common name given to boys born in the United States.
Famous name: Preston Sturges (director and screenwriter)

Prince

Latin *princeps*, "the first." Prince was a fairly common name among slaves before the Civil War and has been traditionally passed down in a few African-American families, including that of singer Prince. His original full name was Prince Rogers Nelson.

Princeton

American place name, "prince's town." Princeton, New Jersey, was named in 1724 to honor the British royal family. (There was already a "Kingston" nearby.) Although today the name is most associated with Princeton University, the College of New Jersey did not change its name to honor the town it was located in until 1896, 150 years after it was founded.

Pulan

Chamoru (Guam) "moon."

Quaashie

Ewe (Ghana) "born on Sunday."

Quade, Quaid

This surname can either be German, in which case it derives from the medieval word *quāt*, "malicious," originally given to a quarrelsome neighbor, or it can be Irish or Manx from *MacUaid*, "son of **Walter**." Perhaps because of the fame of actors Dennis and Randy Quaid, this name is starting to show up occasionally as a first name in the United States. There are reports that some parents are reinterpreting Quade as "quad" and thinking it's a perfect name for a fourth child.

Quantavious, Quantavius

This African-American creation, which seems to blend the sounds of African names such as **Quaashie** with an ending from the Latin name *Octavius*, "eighth son," is fairly popular in the African-American community in the southeastern United States.
Variation: **Quintavious**

Quartus

Latin "the fourth."

Quentin

Latin "the fifth." This was a popular name with the Romans, who traditionally used it for a fifth son. St. Quentin was martyred in the fifth century. The movies have made most Americans familiar with San Quentin, the maximum security prison in California. Quentin had a minor revival in the United States during the 1980s and 1990s, but its popularity may have peaked around 1998. It was the 296th most common boys name of 2004.
Famous names: Quentin Burdick (U.S. senator)
                 Quentin Tarantino (film director)
Variations: **Quintin, Quinton**

Quincy

French "fifth son's place." This surname became a first name in honor of John Quincy Adams, the sixth U.S. president.
Famous name: Quincy Jones (musician)
Nickname: **Quinn**

Quinlan

Irish surname, from either Gaelic *Caoindealbhán,* "comely form," or *Conaillán,* "little brave hound."

Quinn

Usually from Irish Gaelic *O Cuinn,* "descendant of *Conn*"; Conn may have meant "wise." It can also be a rare English surname from the Norman French word for "monkey." Like **Quentin** and **Quinton,** Quinn trended upward in use during the 1990s but may have just passed its peak. It was 277th on the 2004 list of most common names.

Quint

Short form of **Quinton.** Fans of old television Westerns may remember that Burt Reynolds played the blacksmith Quint Asper on *Gunsmoke* between 1962 and 1965.

Quinton

Form of **Quentin** or English place name, "queen's manor." When the alternative spellings Quintin and Quinten are added in, this is the most common Q- name today. Quinton was 258th on the list of names given to American boys born in 2004.
Variations: **Quinn, Quint, Quinten, Quintin**

Quran

Arabic *qurān,* "recitation," name of the Holy Book of the Islamic faith, sometimes given as a name to the sons of devout Muslims.

Rafael

Spanish and Portuguese form of **Raphael.** This name is quite common among Hispanic-Americans and reached 193rd on the list of names given to boys in the United States in 2004.

Rafe

This represents the pronunciation of **Ralph** still used by the upper classes in England, though in the United States it's also sometimes a pet form for **Raphael.** Rafe has always been quite rare as an official birth certificate form.

Rahul

Sanskrit *rāhula,* "able, efficient." Like **Rishi,** this name is being given often enough by Americans of East Indian descent to be among the top 1,000 boys names in the United States. The cricket player Rahul Dravid is hugely famous in India, where the game of cricket may be more popular than it is in its English homeland.

Raiden

Japanese "thunder and lightning." Originally the name of an ancient Japanese god, Raiden was introduced to Americans in 1992 by the video game Mortal Kombat. When the movie based on this game came out in 1995, the character's name was spelled **Rayden.** Both spellings are turning up for boys in the United States as parents search for more variations on names like **Caden, Jayden,** and **Aidan.**

Raistlin

A name invented by Tracy Hickman for a cynical, morally complex character in his *Dragonlance* series of fantasy books (coauthored with Margaret Weis), which are set in the universe of the role-playing game Dungeons & Dragons. Fans of these books and games have named quite a few sons Raistlin in the last 20 years.

Raleigh

English place name and surname from Old English "red clearing." Raleigh, North Carolina, was named for the famous English explorer and colonizer Sir Walter Raleigh (1552–1618).

Ralph

Norman French *Raulf,* form of Old German *Radulf* from *rat* [counsel] + *wulf* [wolf]. This name was common in the United States between 1870 and 1920 and remained fairly popular until 1950. Ralph has now lost much of its popularity and was only 581st on the SSA list of boys names in 2004. Television didn't help the name: Ralph Kramden of *The Honeymooners* and Ralph Malph of *Happy Days* may have been lovable in their own way, but few parents want to name their sons after these characters.

Famous names: Ralph Waldo Emerson (essayist)
　　　　　　Ralph Lauren (fashion designer)
　　　　　　Ralph Nader (consumer advocate and presidential candidate)
Nicknames: **Rafe, Ralphie**
Other spelling: **Ralf**
Variations: **Radolf** (German), **Ralfs** (Latvian), **Raoul** (French), **Raúl** (Spanish), **Rauli** (Finnish)

Ramiro

Spanish name of Visigothic origin, probably from Germanic *ragin,* "advice," and *māri,* "famous." Ramiro was a popular name in medieval Spain, as shown by the common surname Ramirez, "son of Ramiro." It is still frequently used by Hispanic-Americans today.

Ramon

Spanish *Ramón,* form of **Raymond.** Though receding a bit in use, it is still a fairly common name in the Hispanic-American community. Ramon ranked 312th for boys born in the United States in 2004.

Ramsey

Old English *Hramesege,* "wild-garlic island."

Randall

Middle English form of Old English *Randwulf* from *rand* [shield-rim] + *wulf* [wolf]. This name was only rarely used before the 20th cen-

tury, but it became very popular in the United States during the 1940s. Randall's popularity has been fading since 1965; it was only 494th on the SSA list of names in 2004. The short form Randy is now two-and-a-half times more common than Randall itself.
Famous name: Randall Cunningham (football player)
Nicknames: **Rand, Randey, Randi, Randie, Randy**
Variations: **Randell, Randle, Randolf, Randolfo** (Italian and Spanish), **Randolph**

Randolph

This form of **Randall** died out as a first name after the Middle Ages but survived as a surname. It was revived again as an American first name in the late 18th century, probably in honor of the aristocratic Randolph family of Virginia. The Randolphs spawned many prominent politicians, including Edmund Randolph, the first attorney general of the United States. As a first name, Randolph was much rarer than Randall during the 20th century. Its time of popularity during the 1950s both began and ended sooner than Randall's.
Famous name: Randolph Scott (actor)

Randy

Form of **Randall.** Though its popularity has also fallen off since the 1950s, Randy is now much more popular as an official form than Randall, being the 285th most common name given to American boys in 2004. Randy is almost never used as a first name in England because the British commonly use the word *randy* to mean "oversexed" or "lecherous," and are therefore amazed that Americans consider it an appropriate name for a baby.
Famous names: Randy Newman (musician)
Randy Quaid (actor)
Randy Travis (country singer)
Other spellings: **Randey, Randi, Randie**

Raphael

Hebrew "God cures" or "God has healed." In Jewish literature, Raphael is an archangel and the teacher of Tobias. In his narrative poem *Paradise Lost,* John Milton made Raphael the representative that God sent to instruct Adam and to warn him not to eat fruit from the Tree of Knowledge.

Famous name: Raphael Sanzio (Italian Renaissance painter)
Variations: **Rafael** (Spanish and Portuguese), **Rafail** (Russian), **Rafal**
(Polish), **Rafe, Raffaello** (Italian)

Rashad

Arabic "good spiritual guidance." Rashad was the second most commonly given Islamic name in the African-American community (after **Jamal**) during the 1990s, though its use has now faded somewhat.

Rasheed

Arabic "rightly guided, mature." Although not as popular as **Rashad,** this name is also now frequently found among African-Americans.

Raul

Spanish *Raúl,* form of **Ralph,** still used regularly by Hispanic-Americans.

Raven

Old English *hraefn,* "raven." This is now primarily a feminine name in the United States, but it is still used rarely for boys.

Ray

Short form of **Raymond.** Common in the early 20th century, Ray was only the 402nd most used boys name of 2004.
Famous names: Ray Bradbury (writer)
Ray Charles (musician)
Ray Romano (actor and comedian)

Raymond

Old German *Raginmund* from *ragan* [advice] + *mund* [guardian or protector]. This name dates back to the Crusades. Raymond was a common name in England and the United States through the 1950s. Although its use is now fading, it was still the 180th most used name for American boys in 2004, with 2,000 Raymonds born that year. Many Americans today will identify the name with the title character of the television comedy *Everybody Loves Raymond.*
Famous names: Raymond Burr (actor)
Raymond Chandler (novelist)
Nickname: **Ray**
Variations: **Raimo** (Finnish), **Raimondo** (Italian), **Raimund** (German),
Raimundo (Spanish and Portuguese), **Ramón** (Spanish),
Raymundo, Reamonn (Irish)

Reagan

Form of Irish Gaelic *Riagán,* uncertain meaning, but perhaps related to *ríodhgach,* "impulsive." During the last decade, American parents have shown more interest in giving sons the surnames of U.S. presidents as first names than at any time since the 19th century: **Jackson, Lincoln, Truman, Kennedy, Carter,** and Reagan are all on the rise. Reagan entered the SSA top 1,000 list for boys in 1996, three years after it did the same for girls. In 2004, there were 357 newborn American boys named Reagan, but 2,249 girls were given the name in that spelling, along with many other girls named **Raegan** and **Regan.** Reagan continues to increase in use for boys as well as girls, though that will probably change when new parents realize just how many girls there are out there who've been given the name.

Reath

Nuer (southern Sudan) "season of drought."

Reece, Reese

Welsh *Rhys,* "ardor." These two spellings are equally used, and when the original **Rhys** is added in, more than 1,500 boys were given the name in 2004, ranking it 210th. However, parents should be advised that the spelling Reese is now more often given to girls than boys.

Reggie

Form of **Reginald.**
Famous names: Reggie Jackson (baseball player)
　　　　　　　Reggie Miller (basketball player)

Reginald

Old English *Regenweald* from *ragan* [advice] + *weald* [power]. Reginald has never been a popular name with white Americans, who much prefer its Scottish variation, Ronald. It was, however, extremely popular between 1940 and 1980 in the African-American community.
Nicknames: **Reg, Reggie, Reggy, Ryne**
Variations: **Raghnall** (Irish), **Ragnvald** (Scandinavian), **Reinald** (Dutch and German), **Reinaldo** (Spanish), **Reinhold** (Danish and Swedish), **Reino** (Finnish), **Reinold** (Dutch and German), **Reinwald** (German), **Renald, Renaldo** (Spanish), **Renaud, Renault** (French), **Reynold, Rinaldo** (Italian), **Rinold, Ronald** (Scottish)

Regis

Old Provencal "ruler." Regis originally became a first name in France in honor of St. Jean-François Regis, a 17th-century French Jesuit known for his work with prostitutes and the poor. This is a very rare name in America, but it is nevertheless well known because of television talk-show host Regis Philbin.

Reid

Old English *hreod*, "reeds"; also, Old English *read*, "red."
Other spellings: **Read, Reade, Rede, Reed**

Reinaldo

Spanish form of **Reginald.**
Variations: **Naldo, Reynaldo**

Remington

Old English *Rimingtun*, "town on the boundary stream." This old English place name was used for the central character of the 1980s television series *Remington Steele*. However, the show's writers were probably thinking about Remington firearms rather than the English heritage of this name. Even though the series ended its original run in 1987, use of the name Remington for American boys didn't peak until 1998, which may imply that it was a name "stored" for future use by teenagers who watched the program.

Rene

French *René*, form of Latin *Renatus*, "reborn." In the United States, this name is mainly used by Hispanic parents. More than 560 American boys were named Rene in 2004, ranking it 454th on the SSA list.
Famous names: René Descartes (philosopher)
René Magritte (surrealist painter)

Reno

This name is an Americanized spelling of the French surname *Renault*, a French form of **Reginald.** Both Reno, Nevada, and El Reno, Oklahoma, were named for Jesse Lee Reno, a Union general in the Civil War who died in battle in 1862. His surname has been used as a first name on rare occasions ever since, and some parents are giving it a second look now that similar-sounding names like **Leo** and **Enzo** are rising in use.

Reuben

(See **Ruben.**)

Reuel

Hebrew "God is my friend;" the name of four different minor characters in the Bible.

Reverdy

French surname from Old French *reverdir*, possibly either "maltreated" or "renewed."

Rex

Latin "king." This was not used as a name in English-speaking countries before the 19th century. Though fairly common during the 1940s and 1950s, the name is very rare today.
Famous names: Rex Harrison (actor)
Rex Reed (drama critic)
Variations: **Rey** (Spanish), **Roi, Roy**

Rhett

This is an Americanization of the Dutch surname *de Raedt,* from Middle Dutch *raet,* "advice." Many people assume that Margaret Mitchell invented this name for her romantic character Rhett Butler in *Gone With the Wind,* but she actually took it from the surname of Robert Barnwell Rhett, a prominent secessionist figure in South Carolina history. Though the film based on that novel was fantastically successful when it was released in 1939, Rhett didn't enter the SSA top 1,000 list for boys until 1955. It's been on that list ever since, not rising higher than 595th or falling lower than 895th since 1961, which makes it one of the most consistent boys names of the last 40 years. In 2004 it ranked 712th.

Ricardo

Spanish form of **Richard.** The 141st most used boys name of 2004.
Famous name: Ricardo Montalban (actor)

Richard

Old English "strong ruler." **Ricard** is the Old English version of this name, but the French spelling Richard became popular in England after Eleanor of Aquitaine gave that name to her second son. He is famous as the crusader King Richard I (Richard the Lionhearted). For a king who reigned only slightly more than two years, Richard III is also quite well known. Shakespeare's play by the same name depicts him as a monster directly responsible for the murder of his two young nephews, who were heirs to the throne. Richard III was slain at the Battle of Bosworth, and Henry VII became king, establishing the Tudor dynasty. The Tudors encouraged the evil portrayal of Richard III to strengthen their position. The name thus became unpopular in England for several centuries. By the 18th century, the name was back in fashion, as evidenced by English playwright Richard Sheridan, American admiral Richard Byrd, and many other historically well-known Richards. In the 20th century, Richard Nixon, the 37th president of the United States, blighted the name when he resigned in dishonor over the Watergate scandal. Richard's popularity is again falling away, but it was still the 98th most common name given to American boys in 2004, with a total of more than 4,700 born.

Famous names: Richard Burton (actor)
Richard Rogers (American composer)
Richard Wagner (German composer)

Nicknames: **Dick, Dickie, Dicky, Rich, Richie, Rick, Rickie, Ricky, Ritchie**

Variations: **Rhisiart** (Welsh), **Ricardo** (Spanish), **Riccardo, Ricciardo** (Italian), **Rickert** (German), **Rico, Rikard** (Scandinavian), **Riku** (Finnish), **Risteard** (Irish Gaelic), **Ryszard** (Polish)

Richmond

Norman French *Richemund,* "strong hill." This became both a place name and a surname in England. Richmond, Virginia, was named after Richmond in Surrey, England, because founder William Byrd said its site on the James River reminded him of how the Thames looked in Surrey. Both Richmond and **Raleigh** were regularly used as boys names in the early 20th century, just as **Trenton** is today.

Rick

Form of **Cedric, Eric, Frederick, Richard,** or **Roderick.**
Famous name: Rick Moranis (actor)

Rickie, Ricky

Usually a short form of **Richard,** but can also be from **Cedric, Eric, Frederick, Roderick,** or any other name containing the syllable *-ric.*

Ricky suddenly became common as a separate name in the 1950s, probably because television featured two cute kids named Ricky: the character Ricky Ricardo, Jr., of *I Love Lucy* and Ricky Nelson of *The Adventures of Ozzie and Harriet*. Ricky still has some use as an official name, especially in the South, but it was only 328th on the list for American boys born in 2004.

Famous name: Ricky Van Shelton (country singer)

Ridge

English surname from Old English *hrycg*, "ridge"; also an Irish surname, used to translate Gaelic *Cú Iomaire*, "hound of the ridge." Modern parents, however, often consider this to be a "nature name." Some of its popularity can be traced to the character Ridge Forrester on the television soap opera *The Bold and the Beautiful*.

Rigel

Arabic *rijl*, "foot," name of a blue supergiant star in the left foot of the constellation Orion. Rigel is one of the brightest stars, sending out over 47,000 times the amount of light that the sun produces.

Rigoberto

Spanish form of Germanic *Rigoberht*, from words meaning "power" and "bright." There were medieval saints of this name in both France and Germany, but the part of the world it's most common in today is Latin America. It ranked 687th on the SSA list in 2004.

Riku

Though this is a Finnish form of **Richard,** its use in the United States today is probably more from its Japanese origin, where it means "land" or "continent." The name has recently been very popular in Japan itself and is being introduced to Americans as one of the three main characters in the popular video game Kingdom Hearts.

Riley

Irish Gaelic *Raghailligh*, perhaps "valiant"; or Middle English *Ryeley*, "rye field," a place name. This surname boomed in popularity as an American first name during the 1990s as parents searched for alternatives to the extremely popular name **Ryan.** Riley was the 102nd most common name for boys in 2004, with about 4,500 born. However, just as happened with **Ashley** during the 1970s,

Americans began to use Riley extensively for girls only a few years after it became popular for boys. By 2004 there were twice as many girls as boys being given the name.

Other spellings: **Reilly, Rylee, Ryley**

Rishi

Sanskrit *rsi,* "singer of sacred hymns," the name for the sages who wrote down the sacred Vedic scriptures. This is one of the more popular boys names now being used in the East Indian immigrant community in the United States. Rishi Kapoor is a successful Bollywood actor in Indian films.

River

This is one of the more popular "nature names." The tragic death of actor River Phoenix didn't hurt his name; in fact, River first entered the SSA top 1,000 list in 1994, the year after Phoenix died. There were 413 Rivers born in the United States in 2004, which ranked it 550th on the SSA list that year.

Roald

Norwegian from Old Norse *hrothr* [fame] + *valdr* [ruler]. Children's author Roald Dahl is famous for writing *Charlie and the Chocolate Factory, James and the Giant Peach,* and *The Witches,* all of which have been made into popular films.

Rob

Short form of **Robert.**

Famous name: Rob Lowe (actor)

Robby

Pet form of **Robert.**

Famous name: Robby Benson (actor, writer, and director)

Robert

Old English *Hreodbeorht,* "shining in fame," from *hrothi* [fame] + *berhta* [bright]. After the Norman Conquest, the Old English name was replaced by the Norman-French version, Robert. It's been a popular name ever since, particularly in Scotland, where the national hero Robert the Bruce and the poet Robert Burns are honored. Writer Robert Louis Stevenson, American general Robert E. Lee, American poets Robert Frost and Robert Lowell, and politician Robert Kennedy all add distinction to the name. Many famous actors have also been named Robert, including Robert De Niro, Robert Downey, Jr., Robert Duvall, Robert Redford, and Robert Wagner. Though Robert's use has dropped recently, it was still among the top 50 names given to American boys in 2004. Like other traditional names, it's now more common in the eastern part of the United States.

Nicknames: **Bert, Bob, Bobbie, Bobby, Rabbie, Rob, Robb, Robbie, Robby, Robin**

Variations: **Beto, Rab** (Scottish), **Robart** (Bulgarian), **Robat** (Welsh), **Robertas** (Lithuanian), **Roberto** (Italian, Portuguese, and Spanish), **Robrecht** (Dutch), **Roibeard** (Irish Gaelic), **Roope** (Finnish), **Rovertos** (Greek), **Rupert, Rupprecht** (German)

Roberto

Spanish and Italian form of **Robert.** This name is very popular with Hispanic-American parents. More than 1,800 Robertos were born in the United States in 2004, ranking it 191st.

Famous name: Roberto Clemente (baseball player)

Robin

Form of **Robert.** Although Robin began as a diminutive of Robert, it has been an independent name for centuries, kept alive by the legend of Robin Hood. Even though Robin has been used more for girls than boys since at least 1940, it did not disappear completely from the top 1,000 boys names on the SSA list until the year 2000.

Famous name: Robin Williams (actor and comedian)

Rocco

Italian from Old German *hrok*, "rest." This name became popular in Italy because of St. Rocco, a 14th-century Frenchman who abandoned a pilgrimage to Rome to care for plague victims in Lombardy. Most Italian-Americans named Rocco are actually called **Rocky.**

Variations: **Roch** (French), **Roque** (Spanish and Portuguese)

Rock

When actor Roy Fitzgerald began his Hollywood career, his agent renamed him Rock Hudson after the Rock of Gibraltar. Even at the height of Hudson's fame, however, Rock was always a rarer name on American birth certificates than **Rocky.**

Rockwell

Old English *Hrocwella,* "rocky spring," a place name.
Nickname: **Rocky**

Rocky

Usually a form of **Rocco** (or, rarely, **Rockwell**) in the modern United States. Though fairly common in the 1950s, Rocky is rare today.
Famous name: Rocky Marciano (boxer)
Nickname: **Rock**

Rod

Short form of **Roderick** or **Rodney.**
Famous names: Rod Serling (writer)
Rod Steiger (actor)

Roddy

Form of **Roderick** or **Rodney.**
Famous name: Roddy McDowall (actor)

Roderick

Old German *Hrodric,* "famous ruler," from *hrod* [fame] + *ric* [power]. This name was brought to England in medieval times by Scandinavian settlers and was revived there in the 19th century. Roderick was fairly common in the African-American community until the 1990s, but it is falling away rapidly today.
Nicknames: **Rick, Rickie, Ricky, Rod, Roddy**
Other spellings: **Roderic, Rodrick**
Variations: **Gigo, Roderich** (German), **Roderyk** (Polish and Ukrainian), **Rodrigo** (Spanish, Italian, and Portuguese), **Rodrigue** (French), **Rurik** (Russian)

Rodney

Old English "Hroda's island," a place name. Rodney is falling in use; it was 383rd on the popularity list in 2004.
Famous name: Rodney Dangerfield (comedian)
Nicknames: **Rod, Roddy**

Rodolfo

Spanish and Italian form of **Rudolph,** still frequently used by Hispanic-Americans. In 1985 Rodolfo Neri Vela became the first Mexican astronaut to fly in space.

Rodrigo

Spanish, Italian, and Portuguese form of **Roderick.** Rodrigo was hugely popular in medieval Spain, which is why *Rodriguez,* "son of Rodrigo," is the most common Spanish surname in the United States. Although its period of top status is long past, Rodrigo is still regularly used in the Hispanic-American community.

Nicknames: **Gigo, Ruy**

Rogelio

This is the main Spanish form of **Roger,** and it is still often used by Hispanic-American parents. Rogelio was the 410th most common boys name for newborns in the United States in 2004.

Roger

Old English *Hrothgar* from *hrothi* [fame] + *gar* [spear]. This name dates to the Domesday Book and was a favorite in medieval England, but it almost disappeared during the 1700s. Revived in Victorian times, Roger was very popular during the 1930s and 1940s, but it began to fall in use at the start of the baby boom in 1946. It was only 370th on the list of names given to American boys in 2004. Roger Williams was the founder of Rhode Island and an advocate of religious freedom and universal democracy.

Famous names: Roger Ebert (film critic)
　　　　　　　Roger Moore (actor)

Nicknames: **Rog, Rodge**

Other spelling: **Rodger**

Variations: **Dodge, Geyo, Rodzers** (Latvian), **Rogelio, Rogerio** (Spanish), **Rogero** (Portuguese), **Rojelio, Rudiger** (German), **Ruggiero** (Italian), **Rutger** (Dutch)

Rogers

Middle English *Rogeres,* "son of **Roger.**" There are many common English surnames formed by adding -s to a first name, such as Williams, Roberts, and Daniels, but Rogers is the only one of these that has ever been regularly turned back into a first name in the United States. The reasons for this are obscure, as Rogers was already increasing as a first name before baseball player Rogers Hornsby became famous in 1917. Rogers remained in use through the 1960s, but today it has basically disappeared.

Rohan

This is a name with four very different origins. It can be a Hindu name from Sanskrit *rohana,* "ascending"; a Norman French surname from a place name in Brittany; or a variation of the Irish surname **Rowan.** Lastly, a few parents may be attracted to the name because of the Plains of Rohan in J.R.R. Tolkien's *The Lord of the Rings* trilogy. It's hard to say which of these derivations is the most important, but it's probable that many Hindu families in the United States are using this name because they know it fits in with American tastes better than many other East Indian names. Rohan was the 413th most common name given to American boys in 2004, coincidentally placing it one spot below Rowan on the list.

Roland

Old German *Hrodland,* "famous throughout the country," from *hrodi* [fame] + *landa* [land]. The story of Roland, the most famous knight of Charlemagne, is retold in the French classic *Chanson de Roland.* Roland was a popular American name in the 1920s but has steadily declined in use since then. Only 230 Rolands were born in the United States in 2004, ranking it 780th on the SSA list that year.
Famous name: Roland Martin (professional angler)
Nicknames: **Rollie, Rolly, Rowe**
Variations: **Orland, Orlando** (Italian), **Roeland** (Dutch), **Rolando** (Spanish and Italian), **Rolann** (Irish Gaelic), **Rolant** (Welsh), **Roldán** (Spanish), **Roldao** (Portuguese), **Rowland**

Rolando

Spanish and Italian form of **Roland.** Rolando is another example of a traditional name that is much more common among Hispanic-Americans than it is with other groups. Twice as many Rolandos as Rolands were born in the United States in 2004. Rolando has also been used frequently in the African-American community.
Famous name: Rolando Villazon (operatic tenor)

Rolf

Old German *Hrodulf,* "famous wolf," from *hrod* [fame] + *wulf* [wolf]. This name, which is often confused with **Ralph,** is actually a medieval Norman French version of **Rudolf.**
Variations: **Rolfe, Rollo, Rolph**

Rollo

Latin form of **Rolf**. Viking Rollo, a Norman duke, brought this name to England.

Roman

Latin *Romanus*, "a Roman." This name, which has long been common in Latin and Slavic countries, began to rapidly grow in use in the United States during the 1980s. This may be partly due to Roman Brady, a popular character on the daytime soap opera *Days of Our Lives*. Roman was the 227th most used boys name of 2004.

Variations: **Romain** (French), **Román** (Spanish), **Romano** (Italian), **Romanos** (Greek), **Romanus** (Dutch), **Romo** (Finnish)

Romeo

Italian form of Latin *Romaeus*, "pilgrim to Rome." Shakespeare immortalized this name in *Romeo and Juliet*. Romeo had some minor use as a given name in the United States during the early 20th century. It then disappeared until the late 1990s, when it started to seem cool to the avant garde on both sides of the Atlantic. Though there were only 352 Romeos born in the United States in 2004, that's at least three times as many as a decade ago.

Ron

Short form of **Ronald**. Ron's image has been positively affected lately by the character Ron Weasley, Harry Potter's best friend. Famous name: Ron Howard (actor and movie director)

Ronald

Scottish form of **Reginald**. This form of Reginald has long been the most popular variation of that name in English-speaking countries. In the United States, it was especially well used from 1930 to 1960. In 1980, Ronald Reagan was elected the 40th president of the United States, but this didn't stop the name from continuing its fall in popularity throughout the 1980s. By 2004 it was only 224th on the list of most used names for boys. The clown Ronald McDonald, spokesperson for the fast-food chain, is the second most recognized fictional character by American children, surpassed only by Santa Claus.

Nicknames: **Ron, Ronnie, Ronny**

Variations: **Raghnall** (Irish), **Renaud** (French), **Ronaldo** (Portuguese, Spanish, and Italian)

Ronaldo

This form of **Ronald** is becoming increasingly popular in the Hispanic-American community, probably because of the fame of Brazilian-born soccer star Ronaldo Luíz Nazário de Lima, who is usually known simply as Ronaldo.

Ronan

Irish Gaelic *Rónán,* "little seal (the animal)." American parents searching out "different but not too different" names have recently discovered Ronan; it entered the SSA top 1,000 list in 2001 and had doubled in use by 2004, when 318 Ronans were born in the United States. Ronan seems to be a particularly good name for Irishmen with successful musical careers. Irish tenor Ronan Tynan sang at Ronald Reagan's funeral in 2004; Ronan Keating is one of the most successful pop singers in Europe; and Ronan Browne is reviving the ancient Irish tradition of playing the Uilleann pipes, bringing that music to a mass audience.

Ronnie, Ronny

Pet forms of **Aaron** or **Ronald.**
Famous names: Ronnie Milsap (country music pianist)
Ronny Cox (actor, singer, and songwriter)

Roosevelt

Dutch "field of roses." In the 18th and 19th centuries, surnames of presidents, such as Washington, **Jefferson,** and **Madison,** were commonly used as first names. In the 20th century, both Theodore Roosevelt and Franklin Delano Roosevelt inspired many parents while they were in office to use their surname to name their sons.
Famous name: Roosevelt "Rosey" Grier (football player)
Nicknames: **Rosey, Rosie**

Rory

Irish Gaelic *Ruaidri,* "red king." This name had a sharp upswing in use during the late 1970s but has been falling away since.

Ross

Form of Old German *Rozzo,* "fame," or *hros,* "horse"; also, Celtic *rhos,* "moorland." Ross was somewhat fashionable in the 1980s, but its use has been fading since. The character played by David

Schwimmer on the television series *Friends* briefly slowed the name's decline. Ross was only 614th on the SSA list in 2004.

Rowan

Irish surname from Gaelic *Ruadhán,* "little red one." Many parents think of this as a nature name from the word for the tree also known as the mountain ash, which is noted for its bright red berries. The name is being given to both boys and girls, but in 2004 the boys were still 40 percent ahead. Rowan first entered the SSA top 1,000 list for boys in 1999 and has risen considerably since, to 412th place in 2004. Fans of British comedy will associate this name with Rowan Atkinson, the British physical comedian whose characters Blackadder and Mr. Bean are famous in their own right.

Variation: **Rohan**

Rowdy

The word, meaning "disorderly, rough." In spite of its meaning and the fact that it is only a nickname for its most famous bearer, former Olympic swimmer and motivational speaker Rowdy Gaines (his real name is Ambrose Gaines IV), a few parents in the United States tempt fate every year by naming their sons Rowdy.

Roy

Gaelic *ruadh,* "red," later also interpreted as Old French *roi,* "king." Extremely common a century ago, Roy has been fading ever since. In 2004 there were only 530 Roys born in the United States, and most of them were probably named after older male relatives.

Famous names: Roy Blount, Jr. (writer)
Roy Lichtenstein (artist)
Roy Rogers (actor)

Variations: **Rex, Rey** (Spanish), **Roi** (French)

Royal

The idea of turning dictionary words with positive meanings into names is not confined to either Puritan or modern times; Royal is an example from the 19th century. Many parents were evidently inspired by the popularity of **Roy** to use this adjective as a given name for their sons. Royal was fairly common during the first half of the 20th century, but it dropped off the SSA top 1,000 list of boys names in 1972.

Royce

Middle English *Royse,* form of Germanic *Rothais* from *hrod* [fame] + *haidis* [type, sort].

Ruben, Reuben

Hebrew "behold a son." In the Old Testament, Reuben is Jacob's oldest son. This name was popular with the Puritans, but today it is used most often by Americans of Hispanic ancestry. Ruben was among the top 200 boys names in 2004, but it's been drifting downward in use and doesn't seem to have been helped by Ruben Studdard's win on the 2003 season of *American Idol.*

Nickname: **Rube**

Variations: **Reuven, Rubén** (Spanish), **Ruvim** (Russian and Romanian)

Rudolf, Rudolph

German "famous wolf." This name was a favorite of Austrian nobility. Rodolfo is the hero of Puccini's opera *La Boheme,* and Rudolf Rassendyll is the hero of *The Prisoner of Zenda* by Anthony Hope. Modern Americans will immediately associate this name with the Christmas song "Rudolph the Red-Nosed Reindeer," which may be why it's almost nonexistent as a baby name today.

Famous names: Rudolph Nureyev (ballet dancer)
　　　　　　　Rudolph Valentino (silent film star)

Nickname: **Rudy**

Variations: **Rezso** (Hungarian), **Rodolfo** (Italian and Spanish), **Rodolphe** (French), **Roelof** (Dutch), **Rolf** (English and Scandinavian)

Rudy

Form of **Rudolf.** Though its use is slowly fading, the name Rudy is still given to about 400 American boys every year.

Rudyard

Old English "pond with red carp."

Famous name: Rudyard Kipling (novelist and poet)

Rufus

Latin *Rufus,* "man with red hair." At the end of his Letter to the Romans, St. Paul wrote, "Greet Rufus, chosen in the Lord." This positive biblical reference led to Rufus being used as a name by the

Puritans in colonial New England. The name stayed in frequent use until World War I, but today it has almost vanished in spite of the fame of singer Rufus Wainwright. Rufus Scrimgeour is the Minister of Magic in J. K. Rowling's *Harry Potter and the Half-Blood Prince*.
Variations: **Ruf** (French and Bulgarian), **Rufe, Ruffo** (Italian), **Rufo** (Spanish, Portuguese, and Croatian), **Rufusz** (Hungarian), **Ryffe** (Finnish)

Rull

Palauan "sting ray."

Runako

Shona (Zimbabwe) "handsome."

Rune

Old Norse *Rúni*, "secret lore." This name was quite common in Scandinavia in the 20th century and is occasionally found in the United States today.

Rupert

Low German and Dutch variation of **Robert,** brought to England by Prince Rupert of the Rhine, who was a general for his uncle Charles I during the English civil war in the 1600s. Rupert Boneham won a million dollars for being the most popular contestant on television's *Survivor: All Stars* in May 2004, but it's unlikely that he'll give the boost to his first name that fellow contestant Colby Donaldson gave to his. However, the young actor Rupert Grint, who plays Ron Weasley in the *Harry Potter* films, may have more luck in that department.
Famous names: Rupert Everett (actor)
Rupert Murdoch (publisher)
Variation: **Ruperto** (Italian)

Rush

Middle English *rush,* originally a surname for someone who lived near a pond or marsh covered by rushes.
Famous name: Rush Limbaugh (radio talk-show host)

Russell

Norman French *Rousel,* "one with red hair." This aristocratic English surname began to be used as a first name in the United States before 1800. Russell was among the top 100 names for American boys born

between 1889 and 1982, but it had fallen to 331st place by 2004. Actor Russell Crowe's fame has done nothing to help the name.
Famous name: Russell Simmons (recording executive)
Nicknames: **Russ, Rusty**

Rusty

Nickname for a man with red hair, or a pet form of **Russell.**
Famous name: Rusty Wallace (NASCAR driver)

Rutger

Dutch form of **Roger.**
Famous name: Rutger Hauer (actor)

Rutherford

Old English "cattle ford." Rutherford B. Hayes was elected 19th president of the United States by a margin of only one vote in the electoral college.

Ryan

Probably Irish Gaelic *Rigan,* "little king." This name began a swift rise to prominence in the 1960s. Its rise paralleled the career of actor Ryan O'Neal, but this may be coincidental because the name has had much more staying power than the actor's career. Ryan has been among the top 20 names given to American boys since 1976, and its rank has even gone up a bit lately, to 14th in 2004. Ryan has managed the feat of maintaining its rank among the most popular names while the actual proportion of boys given the name has gone down by 40 percent since its high point in 1985.
Famous name: Ryan Seacrest (television host)

Ryder

English surname, Old English *ridere,* "mounted warrior." One of several names starting with *Ry-* that have risen in use lately because they contain fashionable sounds, Ryder first entered the SSA list in 1994. It rose in use fairly slowly until it suddenly increased by 170 percent between 2003 and 2004 and jumped to 311th place.

Ryker

Dutch surname from Middle Dutch *riken* "to become powerful or rich." Ryker has two competing associations for many Americans. First, there's Riker's Island, the New York City jail featured on countless television crime dramas. Second, there's Commander Riker of *Star Trek: The Next Generation*. Both of these create tough masculine images, though the latter is certainly much more positive than the former. **Riker** is a German surname derived from the same word as Ryker. Ryker has lately been taken up as another twist on **Ryan**. It first made the SSA top 1,000 list in 2003 and in 2004 was in 782nd place, with 229 boys given the name.

Rylan

This is probably a modern creation based on **Ryan** or even a name arising from a mishearing of **Ryland.** Isolated examples of the name exist in public records of the late 19th century, but they are so rare that misprints of Ryland are a possible explanation. Whatever its origin, many parents obviously find Rylan to be a perfect "different but not too different" alternative for Ryan. It's one of the fastest-growing boys names today, having entered the SSA top 1,000 list for the first time in 1997, then shooting up to 340th place by 2004, when 736 newborns were given the name.

Ryland

Middle English *Riland,* "land where rye is grown," English surname. Though historically Ryland is much older than **Rylan,** this form didn't enter the SSA top 1,000 list until 2003. It was 899th in 2004.

Ryne

Ryne Sandberg was one of the most successful professional baseball players of the 1980s and 1990s, generally considered one of the best second basemen of all time. He was named after Ryne Duren, a well-known baseball relief pitcher of the 1950s and 1960s. Ryne was actually Duren's nickname; his given named was Rinold, an Americanized spelling of **Reinold,** the German form of **Reginald.** Sandberg spent almost his entire professional career between 1981 and 1997 with the Chicago Cubs, and though the Cubs are baseball's perpetually heartbreaking team, that didn't prevent fans from naming their sons Ryne. Ryne was among the top 1,000 names on the SSA list between 1984 and 1996, following Sandberg's career almost exactly. Many parents probably saw it as a one-syllable variation of **Ryan.**

Ryoji

Japanese "good, peace."

Sage

As a surname this is from Old French *sage*, "wise," but like **Stone** it's often interpreted as a "nature name," in this case from the name of the plant. It entered the SSA top 1,000 list as a boys name in 1991. At first, parents probably associated the name with western sagebrush. But associations with the spice may have taken over, because parents began giving the name to daughters in great numbers. As early as 1993 there were more newborn girls than boys named Sage, and around 1998 the name began to fall off for boys as parents noticed how female-dominated the name was becoming. In 2004 Sage was the 666th name on the SSA list.

Sal

Short form of **Salvador.**
Famous name: Sal Mineo (actor)

Salazar

Spanish surname from Latin *sala* [hall] + Basque *zahar* [old], originally indicating the family who lived in the oldest house in the area. It's known to *Harry Potter* fans as the first name of Salazar Slytherin, one of the founders of Hogwarts School.

Salvador

Spanish form of Latin *salvator*, "savior." Like **Jesus,** this name is also popular in Spanish-speaking countries and with Hispanic-Americans.
Famous name: Salvador Dali (surrealist painter)
Nicknames: **Chavo, Sal, Sallie**
Variations: **Salvadore, Salvatore** (Italian), **Spas** (Russian), **Spejus** (Lithuanian)

Salvatore

Italian form of **Salvador.** This name used to be very popular in Sicily and Calabria, parts of Italy that were once ruled by Spain. In the

United States, Salvatore is now being used by Hispanic-Americans as well as Italian-Americans.

Sam

Short form of **Samuel.** Uncle Sam, the symbol for the United States that became popular during World War II, is the best-known Sam in history. As an official name, Sam enjoyed a small increase in use while Ted Danson was playing the character Sam Malone on the television series *Cheers.* American parents' resistance to using one-syllable forms, however, means that over the last decade Sam has been declining in use while Samuel has increased by 27 percent.
Famous names: Sam Neill (actor)
                  Sam Shepard (playwright)

Sami

Arabic "elevated, sublime"; or a form of **Samuel.**

Samir

Arabic *samir,* "one who regales with nighttime conversation," or Sanskrit *samira,* "set in motion." With both Muslim and Hindu derivations, this is a common name for sons of South Asian immigrants in the United States.

Sammy

Form of **Samuel.**
Famous name: Sammy Davis, Jr. (actor and singer)

Samson

Hebrew *Shimshon,* "man of the sun," hero of the famous biblical story in which the incredibly strong man Samson is betrayed by his Philistine lover Delilah when he reveals that he will lose his strength if his head is shaved. The Philistines shave his head while he is sleeping, and Samson is captured and blinded. But when his hair grows out again, he gets his revenge by destroying a Philistine temple by bringing down the pillars with his superhuman strength. This dramatic story has always been a favorite with both Jews and Christians, and as a result Samson was one of the few Old Testament names to be regularly used in medieval times. In the modern United States, Samson has been drifting in and out of the SSA list since 1977, with between 100 and 200 boys given the name each year.

Samuel

Hebrew "name of the Lord." The prophet Samuel wrote two books of the Old Testament that cover an important era in the early history of Israel. Like other biblical names, Samuel came into frequent use after the Protestant Reformation. Men of letters named Samuel include author Samuel Butler, lexicographer and essayist Samuel Johnson; diarist Samuel Pepys; and Samuel Clemens, who wrote under the pen name Mark Twain. Samuel Adams was a leader of the American Revolution, and Samuel Houston was president of the Republic of Texas. Samuel has slowly but steadily returned to popularity in the United States during the last generation; it was 30th on the list of names given to American boys born in 2004.

Famous names: Samuel Beckett (Irish playwright)

Samuel L. Jackson (actor)

Samuel Morse (inventor)

Nicknames: **Mel, Sam, Sammie, Sammy**

Variations: **Sami** (Arabic), **Samu** (Hungarian), **Samuele** (Italian), **Samuelo, Samuil** (Russian, Greek, and Bulgarian), **Sawel** (Welsh), **Shmuel** (modern Hebrew)

Sandor

Hungarian form of **Alexander.**

Sandy

Form of **Alexander** and names beginning with *San-*.

Famous name: Sandy Koufax (baseball player)

Sanjay

Sanskrit *Sañjaya,* "completely victorious."

Famous name: Dr. Sanjay Gupta (television medical reporter)

Santiago

Spanish for "Saint James," popular in Spain because of veneration for the shrine of Santiago de Compostela in Galicia, an important destination for medieval Christian pilgrims. Santiago was the 291st most used name for American boys born in 2004. Santiago Ramón y Cajal, who won the Nobel Prize for medicine in 1906, is deemed the founder of modern neuroscience because of his discoveries about how the brain and nervous system work on the cellular level.

Variations: **Diego, Tiago**

Santino

Spanish form of Latin *Sanctinus*, "son of the saint." This name has recently been increasing in use in the Hispanic community, perhaps because of the influence of soccer star Santino Quaranta.

Santos

Spanish "saints," originally a name given to boys born on All Saints' Day, November 1; the Spanish counterpart to the French name Toussaint. In 2004 there were almost equal numbers of boys named Santos and **Santino** in the United States, but Santos has a long history in the Hispanic community, having been on the SSA top 1,000 list since 1900, while Santino only arrived on the list in 2002.

Sargent

Latin *servient*, "server" or "attendant," through Old French *serjant*. The same word later became English *sergeant*, an enlisted person's rank in the army. This unusual name became better known during the Kennedy presidency; the president's brother-in-law, Sargent Shriver, was the first director of the Peace Corps and later unsuccessfully ran for the vice presidency in 1972. Today he is best known for being Arnold Schwarzenegger's father-in-law.

Saul

Hebrew "loaned." This may seem like an odd meaning for a name, but it probably signified the idea that the child was "on loan" from God. Saul was the first king of ancient Israel. Though the name has been used somewhat by both Jews and Protestants in the past, today Saul is by far most popular in the Hispanic community. The name has been increasing in use there. More than 1,000 Sauls were born in the United States in 2004, which ranked it 268th for the year. American novelist Saul Bellow, who died in April 2005, won the Nobel Prize in literature in 1976.

Savion

Probably an African-American creation, perhaps based on Italian *Saviàno*, itself either meaning "of the Sabine people" or a derivative of Latin *sapius*, "wise." Whatever its origin, the name is well known because of the award-winning tap dancer, choreographer, and stage director Savion Glover. The name Savion entered the SSA top 1,000 list for boys in 1998. In 2004, it was in 897th place on that list.

Sawyer

Middle English *saghier*, "sawer of timber." This is another one of the "occupational surnames" ending in -er that parents have taken up since 1990. Sawyer first entered the SSA top 1,000 list in 1991 and increased sporadically until it ranked 385th among newborn American boys born in 2004.

Schuyler

Dutch "teacher." This name was first used as a given name in honor of Philip John Schuyler, a soldier and statesman who served in the French and Indian Wars and the American Revolution, participated in the Continental Congress, and became a U.S. senator from New York. The alternative spellings **Skylar** and **Skyler** have now completely eclipsed the original Dutch form.

Scott

Old English "a Scotsman." This was the middle name of two famous Americans, Francis Scott Key, author of the national anthem, and writer F. Scott Fitzgerald. The name was popular in the 1960s and 1970s. African-Americans, however, avoided naming their sons Scott, in spite of the fame of African-American composer Scott Joplin. The name's popularity is now plummeting; it was only 203rd on the list for American boys born in 2004.

Famous names: Scott Carpenter (astronaut)
Scott Turow (author)
Nicknames: **Scottie, Scotty**
Other spelling: **Scot**

Scotty

Pet form of **Scott**. *Star Trek* fans will associate this name with the starship *Enterprise*'s chief engineer, whose official name was Lt. Commander Montgomery Scott.

Seamus

Irish Gaelic form of **James.** Irish-American parents seem to have been reminded of this name when Irish poet Seamus Heaney won the Nobel Prize in literature in 1995. That was the first year that Seamus ever made the SSA top 1,000 list, and it's been slowly increasing in use ever since, reaching 783rd place in 2004.

Other spelling: **Shamus**

Sean

Irish form of **John.** Sean became extremely popular with Americans from all ethnic and racial backgrounds in the 1970s. Sean's popularity is now falling; it was the 51st most common name given to American boys in 2004. Not surprisingly, Sean was the number-one name for boys born in Ireland in 2003.

Famous names: Sean Connery (actor)
　　　　　　　 Sean Penn (actor)
Other spellings: **Seann, Shaun, Shawn**
Variation: **Shane**

Sebastian

Greek *sebastos*, "old, venerable," through Latin *Sebastianus*, "man from Sebastia." St. Sebastian was a Roman who was martyred in the third century by being shot with arrows; this became a favorite subject for religious art. In Shakespeare's *Twelfth Night*, Sebastian is Viola's twin. This name was rare in the United States until recently, but it is fast becoming popular; Sebastian rose from 335th to 103rd on the list of names for boys between 1989 and 2004.

Famous name: Sebastian Cabot (actor)
Variations: **Bastian, Bastien** (French), **Passi** (Estonian), **Seb, Sebastián** (Spanish), **Sebastiano** (Italian), **Sebastien** (French), **Sevastian** (Romanian and Russian), **Sevastianos** (Greek)

Seithon

Fon (Togo) "God is my owner." Since this name nearly rhymes with **Nathan,** it's a good addition to American parents' list of choices.

Sem

Dutch form of *Shem,* Hebrew "reputation," the name of Noah's eldest son in the Old Testament story of the flood. The Dutch have traditionally been especially fond of short names, and Sem was the number-one name given to boys born in the Netherlands in 2004.

Semaj

Though this name looks vaguely like it could be Muslim or Hindu, it seems to be a modern invention created by spelling **James** backward. Almost all of the examples found of such names are African-American, the most prominent being Dr. Leahcim Semaj, a leader of the Rastafarian movement in Jamaica and the United States who was born Michael James. The recent success of **Nevaeh** as a girls name shows that some American parents find reverse spelling a "cool" way to create a new baby name. There were 246 boys named Semaj born in the United States in 2004.

Sergio

Spanish, Italian, and Portuguese form of *Sergius,* a Roman clan name perhaps from an Etruscan word for "servant." This name, well used in the Hispanic-American community, was the 190th most common for boys born in 2004.

Famous names: Sergio Leone (film director)

Sergio Mendes (musician)

Variations: **Serge** (French and Finnish), **Sergei, Sergey** (Russian)

Seth

Hebrew "appointed." Seth was the third son of Adam and Eve. This name is gradually becoming more common and reached 91st place among American boys born in 2004. It's certainly used much more often than Cain or **Abel,** the names of Seth's older brothers.

Shamar, Shemar

Probably a recent African-American creation blending the sounds of names like **Shaquille** and **Jamar.** Even though parents prefer the Shamar spelling, the use of this name seems linked to the career of actor Shemar Moore, who has played Malcolm Winters on the daytime soap opera *The Young and the Restless* since 1994.

Shane

Variation of **Sean.** This name was practically nonexistent until the classic Western film *Shane* was released in 1953. Parents in both Great Britain and the United States then began giving the name to their sons. But Shane's popularity is falling off now, with fewer than half the number born in 2004 as there were in 1990. In 2004 Shane was the 151st most common name given to American boys.

Shannon

Irish Gaelic, probably related to *sean,* "old"; both an Irish surname and the name of Ireland's longest river. Ever since Shannon first entered the SSA top 1,000 list in the late 1930s, it has been more commonly given to girls than boys. However, a substantial number of parents have continued to use it for sons. Its peak year for boys was

1972, only four years before its peak use for girls, at which point more than three girls were being named Shannon for every one boy given the name. In the 1980s and 1990s this ratio was more like twelve to one, but in 2004 it was back down to six to one; in that year there were only 197 male Shannons born in the United States, which ranked it 873rd on the male SSA list.

Shaquille

French-influenced respelling of **Shakil,** Arabic *shakil,* "well-formed, handsome." This name was extremely popular in the African-American community in the early 1990s because of basketball superstar Shaquille O'Neal, so much so that in 1993 it was among the top 200 names for all boys born in the United States. But, unlike some other basketball-inspired names, the vogue for Shaquille didn't last very long, and it had vanished from the SSA list by 1997.

Shaun, Shawn

Alternate spellings of **Sean.**

Shea

Irish Gaelic *séaghdha,* "hawklike, stately." This Irish surname has been on the SSA top 1,000 list for boys since 1982. It's never been common and, except for a brief time in the late 1980s, it has been used more often for girls than for boys. There were 191 male Sheas born in the United States in 2004, ranking it 890th on the SSA list.

Shel

Short form of **Sheldon.** Prospective parents should familiarize themselves with Shel Silverstein's delightful poetry books. His *Where the Sidewalk Ends* is one of the best-selling children's books of all time.

Sheldon

Old English *scylf-dun,* "flat or slightly sloping hill." This name was most popular in the 1930s. In spite of a somewhat nerdy image, it hadn't quite disappeared from the SSA top 1,000 list in 2004.
Nickname: **Shel**

Sherman

Old English *scearramann,* "man who shears cloth or sheep." This first name that is derived from a surname often honors Civil War General William Tecumseh Sherman. Sherman's peak of popularity was

in the 1890s, so it's not surprising that, in spite of having an image similar to **Sheldon**'s, it disappeared from the SSA list after 1994.
Famous name: Sherman Alexie (author)

Shigeru

Japanese "to grow or flourish."

Sidney

Old English *sidenieg,* "wide, well-watered land," English place name. Algernon Sidney was an English aristocrat who opposed King Charles II. He was executed in 1683 after being convicted of treason in a rigged trial. In 1776 American orators used Sidney's fate as an example of the tyranny of British royalty, and so Sidney became a fairly popular given name in the United States in the early 19th century. This popularity was later reinforced by Sydney Carton, the hero of Charles Dickens's *A Tale of Two Cities.* Today Sidney is fast disappearing as a name for American boys, as it has become quite fashionable for girls, but there were still 261 newborn boys named Sidney in 2004.
Famous names: Sidney Poitier (actor)
　　　　　　　 Sidney Sheldon (writer)
Nicknames: **Sid, Syd**
Other spelling: **Sydney**

Sigmund

Old German *Sigumund,* "victorious protector." This name is still synonymous with Sigmund Freud, the founder of psychoanalysis.
Nicknames: **Siggy, Ziggy**

Silas

A New Testament name, probably a Greek contraction of Latin *Silvanus,* "from the woods," but originally it may have also represented an Aramaic form of **Saul.** In the New Testament, Silas was the companion of the Apostle Paul, and there are many spirituals that speak of "Paul and Silas." The name Silas was rare in England until the Puritans took it up after the Reformation, and then it was fairly common in the United States in the 19th century. It fell off considerably and almost disappeared by the 1960s, but then it slowly began to rise again. The pace of this rise has greatly quickened since 1990 as parents have discovered Silas as part of their search for historical names that have a fresh sound. There were more than 600 Silases born in the United States in 2004, which ranked it as the 377th most popular name. Silas has several literary associations, including George Eliot's *Silas Marner*, and *The Rise of Silas Lapham* by William Dean Howells.

Simeon

This is the original Old Testament version of the Hebrew name that became **Simon** in the New Testament. The first Simeon in the Bible was the second son of Jacob; one of the 12 tribes of ancient Israel bore his name. The Puritans revived Simeon as a first name in the 17th century. It disappeared at the start of the 20th century, but around 1996 a few adventurous parents rediscovered the name. It has been present on the SSA top 1,000 list since, ranking 845th in 2004.

Simon

Hebrew *Shimeon,* "he listens"; also, Greek *Simon,* "snub nose" (a nickname). Simon is a name with a very different history in the United Kingdom and the United States over the last 50 years. The name began to rise in use in Britain after 1950, and this increased popularity was reinforced when a British television series called *The Saint* premiered in 1962 featuring a suave, sophisticated, handsome secret agent called Simon Templar played by Roger Moore. This helped Simon rise to huge popularity in Britain during the 1960s and 1970s. Meanwhile in the United States, Simon was out of style and developed the image of an overeducated egghead, partly due to the character Simon in the 1980s animated cartoon *Alvin & The Chipmunks.* Hispanic parents sometimes used it because of the fame of Simon Bolivar, the liberator of South America, but others avoided it. As Simon was going out of style in Britain during the 1980s, Americans in the creative community began to notice it. That led, in 1996, to the name being given to a teenage heartthrob character in the family-oriented series *7th Heaven,* and it continued a slow, steady rise. But in 2002 the image of Simon abruptly changed for many Americans when Simon Cowell (born in 1959 in England at the start of the fashion for the name there) began his reign as a judge on *American Idol.* Many young viewers quickly developed the image of a Simon as being harshly critical and sarcastic, like Cowell's onscreen persona. But as the name fits the fashionable sound pattern so many are looking for today (two syllables ending in -*n*), any setback because of Mr. Cowell may well be temporary.

Famous name: Simon LeBon (pop singer)

Nicknames: **Si, Sy**

Variations: **Shimon** (modern Hebrew), **Siemen** (Dutch), **Sim** (Scots Gaelic), **Simao** (Portuguese), **Simone** (Italian), **Szymon** (Polish), **Ximon**

Sincere

The success of this word as a boys name will probably surprise a lot of Americans who don't live in African-American neighborhoods. It comes from a 1998 film called *Belly* in which the character Sincere, played by the rapper Nas, is a wealthy gangster who decides to give up his life of crime and get in touch with his African roots. This story of redemption obviously appealed to many African-American parents; Sincere has been on the SSA top 1,000 list since 2000, and in 2004 more than 250 boys were given the name in the United States.

Sinclair

English form of *Saint Clair,* a French place name.

Famous name: Sinclair Lewis (novelist)

Sirius

Greek *seirios,* "glowing," the name of the brightest star in the sky, called the Dog Star because of its location in the constellation Canis Major. It is an appropriate name for Sirius Black, Harry Potter's godfather in J. K. Rowling's novels.

Siyabonga

IsiZulu (South Africa) "we give thanks."

Sizwe

IsiZulu (South Africa) "nation."

Sky

Originally a short form of **Skyler,** though today often interpreted as a "nature name."

Skyler, Skylar

When **Tyler** became popular in the 1980s, American parents rediscovered **Schuyler** as a "different but not too different" alternative. Skyler quickly became the most common spelling of the name, and 21st-century parents often think of it as a "nature name" based on the word *sky.* The name has been among the top 200 names for boys since about 1990, but it may have peaked around 1996 as parents noticed that it had become an even more popular name for girls. Though the trend is for Skyler to be the more common spelling for boys and Skylar for girls, about a third of each gender are given the other's main spelling.

Nickname: **Sky**

Solomon

Hebrew *Shlomo* from *shalom,* "peace." King Solomon, the son of David and Bathsheba, was the ruler of Israel about 3,000 years ago. He built palaces and temples and had a reputation for great wisdom. The Song of Solomon, considered to be one of the most beautiful Hebrew poems, is attributed to him. The revival of biblical names has begun to affect Solomon, which doubled in use between 1990 and 2004, though it was still only 481st on the SSA list that year.

Nicknames: **Sol, Sollie, Solly**

Variations: **Salomo** (Dutch and German), **Salomon** (French, Polish, and Spanish), **Salomone** (Italian), **Shlomo** (Hebrew), **Solamh** (Gaelic), **Sulayman** (Arabic), **Zalman** (Yiddish)

Solon

Greek, perhaps from *sólos,* "cylinder of iron."

Sonny

Originally a nickname for a small boy, Sonny has been surprisingly common as an official birth-certificate name. It's been in the SSA top 1,000 list continuously since 1927. Though it's most associated today with the entertainer and politician Salvatore "Sonny" Bono (1935–1998), slide guitarist Sonny Landreth, jazz tenor saxophonist Sonny Rollins, country singer Sonny Burgess, blues harmonica player Sonny Terry, and rock singer Sonny Sandoval, among others, show that this may be one of the best names for success in popular music, no matter what the genre.

Soren

Danish *Søren,* form of Latin *Severinus,* a Roman family name originally meaning "stern." Forms of the name spread throughout Western Europe because Severinus was the name of several well-loved medieval saints. Soren has just been noticed by American parents looking for a "different but not too different" boys name ending in

-n. It first entered the SSA top 1,000 list in 2003 and increased more than 20 percent to be ranked 849th on that list in 2004. The most famous Soren is the Danish philosopher Søren Kierkegaard, who is considered the founder of the modern existentialist movement. His reputation as a melancholy, isolated individual perhaps fits the original meaning of the name.

Spencer

Middle English "steward" or "storekeeper." This surname became a first name in the 19th century, perhaps in honor of Herbert Spencer, a celebrated philosopher who applied Darwin's theory of evolution to social problems and coined the phrase "survival of the fittest." The name Spencer rose in popularity during the 1980s and 1990s, but there are signs that its vogue may be starting to fade.
Famous name: Spencer Tracy (actor)
Nickname: **Spence**
Other spelling: **Spenser**

Stan

Short form of **Stanley.**
Famous name: Stan Laurel (comedian)

Stanley

Old English "rocky meadow." This surname began to be used as a first name about 200 years ago. It was quite popular during the early 20th century but is fast vanishing as a name for newborns today.
Famous name: Stanley Kubrick (movie director)
Nickname: **Stan**

Stefan

Scandinavian, German, and Polish form of **Stephen.** With all spellings combined, this was the 372nd most popular boys name of 2004.
Other spellings: **Stephan, Stephon**

Stellan

A Swedish name of mysterious origin; Stellan has been used in Sweden since the 16th century. Swedish experts think it was originally a German name, but nothing similar to it occurs in recent German name dictionaries. It's been suggested that it's related to the Germanic root word *still,* "calm, quiet," but that is just a guess. Whatever its origin, the name is now receiving positive notice in the

United States because of Swedish actor Stellan Skarsgård. With the increasing popularity of **Stella** as a girls name, it will be interesting to see if American parents take up Stellan as a masculine equivalent.

Stephen

Greek *stephanos,* "crown." The Book of Acts relates the stoning of St. Stephen, who is considered the first Christian martyr. Many Stephens are well known to modern Americans, including composer Stephen Foster, who wrote "Oh! Susannah"; writer Stephen Crane, author of *The Red Badge of Courage;* Stephen Biko, the slain South African civil rights activist; American composer Stephen Sondheim, who is known for *Sweeney Todd, West Side Story,* and *Into the Woods;* horror writer Stephen King; and English physicist Stephen Hawking. Either spelled Stephen or Steven, this was a top ten name for American boys between 1955 and 1980, but it's now receding and was only 62nd on the list for newborns in 2004.

Nicknames: **Steve, Stevie**

Other spelling: **Steven**

Variations: **Esteban** (Spanish), **Estephano** (Portuguese), **Estevan** (Spanish), **Etienne** (French), **Staffan** (Swedish), **Steef** (Dutch), **Stefan** (Scandinavian, German, and Polish), **Stefano** (Italian), **Stefanos** (Greek), **Steffan** (Welsh), **Stepan** (Russian), **Stephan** (French), **Stiofan** (Irish Gaelic), **Szczepan** (Polish)

Sterling

Old English *stearling,* "a starling"; Middle English *sterrling,* "little star, pure silver coin"; or from a Scottish place name.

Other spelling: **Stirling**

Steve

Short form of **Stephen.**

Famous names: Steve Martin (comedian)
Steve Young (football player)

Nickname: **Stevie**

Steven

Variation of **Stephen.** This has been the more common spelling of the name in the United States since the 1950s.

Famous name: Steven Spielberg (movie producer and director)

Stevie

Form of **Stephen** or **Steve.**

Famous name: Stevie Wonder (musician)

Stone

English surname meaning "dweller among the rocks," though some modern parents interpret it as a "nature name" taken directly from the modern word. This name first entered the SSA top 1,000 list for boys in 1995. It reached a minor peak in 1999, and since then has been slowly receding. The name's public image is dominated by that of the television newscaster Stone Phillips.

Stuart

Old English *stigweard,* "steward of the manor," from *stig* [hall] + *ward* [guard]. Stuart was common in the United States between 1935 and 1965, but it has now fallen off the SSA top 1,000 list. The vogue for Stuart came later in England, where the name was popular in the 1970s and 1980s. So the typical British Stuart is now a young father, while American Stuarts are more likely to be grandfathers.

Nicknames: **Stew, Stu**

Variation: **Stewart**

Sullivan

Irish Gaelic "descendant of *Súileabhán,*" a name that meant "dark-colored eyes." This is one of the most common Irish surnames, but until recently it was rare as a first name. In the late 1990s it became a fashionable name for boys in northern France. It entered the SSA top 1,000 list in the United States in 2002. There were only 175 American boys named Sullivan born in 2004, but the name is poised to make a major move upward if it gets positive media mention.

Sylvester

Latin "of the woods." Many Americans are likely to think of the cartoon cat who can't catch Tweety Bird when they hear this name.

Famous name: Sylvester Stallone (actor)

Nicknames: **Sly, Sy**

Other spelling: **Silvester**

Tabor

English surname from Old French *tabour,* "drummer."

Tad

Short form of **Thaddeus.** There was a minor vogue for Tad as a separate name in the 1960s and 1970s, but the name has disappeared from use today.

Talon

The word meaning "claw of a bird of prey." It is probably significant that dragons are also said to have talons, because this name seems to be a favorite for characters in fantasy role-playing or video games. Indeed, the first prominent use of Talon as a given name seems to have been for Prince Talon, the hero in a 1982 fantasy film called *The Sword and the Sorcerer.* The name entered the SSA top 1,000 list in 1990 and has been given to more than 200 boys every year for the past decade.

Tanner

Old English *tannere,* "tanner of hides." In the early 1980s Tanner shot up seemingly from nowhere to become common, especially in the western United States. It may be significant that 1976, the first year Tanner appeared among the top 1,000 boys names on the SSA list, was also the release year of the film *The Bad News Bears,* which featured a feisty Little League baseball player called Tanner Boyle. But the simultaneous increase in Tanner, **Taylor, Trevor, Tucker,** and **Tyler** also shows that a certain sound pattern in names had become popular with American parents. Tanner rose to around 80th place on the national list for American boys in 1998 but slipped back to 129th by 2004. Throughout its career, Tanner has appealed mostly to white parents and has been practically ignored by the African-American community.

Tariq

Arabic *tāriq*, "morning star" or "nocturnal visitor." Tariq is popular with Muslims because of Tāriq ibn-Ziyad, the Berber leader who conquered Spain in the eighth century. Tariq entered the SSA top 1,000 list in 1991. Though it seems to have peaked in use in 1998, there were 200 Tariqs born in the United States in 2004, ranking it 867th on the SSA list. African-Americans also frequently use alternative spellings such as **Tariek, Tarik, Tarique, Teriek,** and **Terik** for this name.

Tarkan

Turkish "vizier." Turkish singer Tarkan has been wildly popular for more than a decade in both the Middle East and Europe.

Tate

Surname based on the Old English name *Tāt*, for which no meaning has been discovered. Though **Tait** is pronounced the same way, as a surname it comes from the Old Norse *teitr*, "cheerful," and is not related. Tate is much more common as a spelling of the given name in the United States. There was a minor vogue for Tate in the 1970s; it then vanished from the SSA top 1,000 list in the 1980s and returned in 1990. Since then it has marched up the popularity chart, ranking 354th in 2004 with almost 700 Tates born. The name's similarity in sound to **Nate** and **Jake** is undoubtedly helping its rise.

Tau

Tswana (Botswana) "lion."

Taylor

Old French *tailleur*, "tailor," a word brought to England by the Normans. As **Tyler** became popular for American boys, Taylor was pulled up along with it. From 605th most popular in 1975, Taylor rose to 64th place by 1990. But Taylor had even more of an upsurge as a girls name during the 1980s, rising from below the top 1,000 in 1978 to 46th in 1990, the first year more girls than boys were given the name. Taylor stalled at around 51st on the boys list until 1995, when it began to fall away dramatically. In 2004, it was 206th on the boys list, and six times as many girls were being named Taylor every year. Its decline is typical of how parents stop giving names to sons once they realize the same name has become common for girls. Famous name: Taylor Hackford (movie producer and director)

Tayshaun

African-American creation blending sounds from **Taylor** and **Sean.** Like many other basketball players, Tayshaun Prince has seen his name enter the SSA top 1,000 as a bonus to his successful career.

Teague

In England this is a Cornish surname from Cornish *tek,* "beautiful," and in Ireland it's a variation of **Tighe.**

Tecumseh

Shawnee "one who springs," connoting a panther. The famous Shawnee chief Tecumseh fought against the encroachment of American colonists upon tribal land.

Ted

Form of **Edward, Edwin,** or **Theodore.**
Famous names: Ted Koppel (broadcast journalist)
Ted Turner (business executive)

Terence

Latin *Terentius,* a Roman family name, possibly related to *Terensis,* the goddess of milling grain. This old name has never been very popular in the United States except in the African-American community, where it was quite popular between 1970 and 1995. Terrance is now the most common spelling.
Nicknames: **Tel** (British), **Terri, Terrie, Terry**
Other spellings: **Terance, Terrance, Terrence**
Variations: **Terenc** (Czech), **Terencio** (Spanish), **Terentiu** (Romanian), **Terenzio** (Italian), **Teresk** (Estonian), **Tero** (Finnish)

Terrell

Origin uncertain, but probably from the same Old French word as **Tyrell.** This rare British surname was a very popular name for African-American boys in the 1980s and 1990s, probably because it blends the sounds of **Terry** and **Darryl.** However, Terrell's prominence may also honor Mary Church Terrell (1863–1964), a founder of the NAACP and advocate for women's suffrage who led a fight to desegregate the restaurants and theaters of Washington, D.C. If this is the case, Mrs. Terrell holds the unique distinction of being a woman whose fame turned her last name into a first name for boys instead of girls.

Terry

Form of **Terence;** or Old French *Thierri,* a form of *Theodoric* (see **Derek**).

Famous name: Terry Bradshaw (sportscaster)

Tesloach

Nuer (southern Sudanese) "happy heart," one of the more common names being given to sons of Sudanese refugees now living in the United States.

Variations: **Teathloach, Tethloch**

Thabo

Probably Xhosa (South Africa) "happy."

Famous name: Thabo Mbeki (president of South Africa)

Thad

Short form of **Thaddeus.** Thad had a minor upswing in use during the same 1960s and 1970s period that **Tad** was in vogue, but it has since vanished.

Thaddeus

Aramaic name of unknown meaning, but possibly an Aramaic form of Greek *Theodotos,* "given by God." Thaddeus was one of the 12 apostles. The Puritans often named their sons Thaddeus, but in 2004 it was just 900th on the SSA list.

Nicknames: **Tad, Thad**

Variations: **Tadeo** (Spanish), **Tadeusz** (Polish), **Thaddaus** (German)

Thane

Old English *thegn,* "warrior," "soldier," or "free man."

Other spellings: **Thaine, Thayne**

Theo

Short form of **Theodore.** There was a minor vogue for Theo in the United States at the start of the 20th century, but it vanished by 1940. In 2004 **Théo** was the second most popular boys name in France. Theo is an excellent candidate for revival in English-speaking countries if similar names like **Leo** continue to increase in use. Art historians remember this name because of art dealer Theo van Gogh, the younger brother of Vincent van Gogh who was instrumental in preserving his brother's artistic legacy.

Theodore

Greek *Theodoros*, "gift of God," from *theo* [god] + *doros* [gift]. Because there are almost 30 saints named Theodore, it's surprising that the name was not used regularly in the United States until the 19th century. Victorian Americans were fond of this name, and it had a huge upward spike in use during the first decade of the 20th century while Theodore Roosevelt was president. In 2004 almost 1,000 newborn American boys were named Theodore, which made it the 283rd most common name. Children's writer Theodor Geisel was better known by his pen name, Dr. Seuss.

Nicknames: **Doro, Ted, Teddie, Teddy, Theo**

Variations: **Deodoro** (Portuguese), **Fedor** (Russian), **Feodor** (Slavic), **Fyodor** (Russian), **Teodor** (Polish and Serbian), **Teodoro** (Italian and Spanish), **Teuvo** (Finnish), **Theodor** (Danish, German, and Swedish), **Theodoros** (Greek), **Theodorus** (Dutch), **Tivadar** (Hungarian), **Todor** (Bulgarian)

Theron

Greek "a hunter." Though never very common, Theron did reach a minor high point around 1900 shortly after Harold Frederic's famous novel *The Damnation of Theron Ware* was published. The name had vanished by 1940, though it would seem to fit in with today's love for two-syllable boys names ending in *-n*.

Thomas

Aramaic "twin." The apostle Thomas came to be known as Doubting Thomas because he would not believe in the resurrection of Jesus until he had touched his wounds. Thomas shares his name with several other religious figures. To keep the church on his side, King Henry II of England appointed his friend Thomas Becket as the Archbishop of Canterbury. When Becket would not go along with what the king wanted because he was more loyal to his church than to his friend, Henry had Becket murdered on the doorstep of the cathedral. The 13th-century St. Thomas Aquinas was one of the great philosophers of the Middle Ages. St. Thomas More was executed when he refused to allow Henry VIII to interfere with the rulings of the church. Two literary Thomases are English novelist Thomas Hardy and American poet and 1948 Nobel Prize-winner Thomas Stearns Eliot. Thomas Jefferson was the third president of the United States and one of the framers of the

Constitution. Thomas has recently surged back into great popularity in England, where it was the number-one name during the 1990s and was still third in 2004. However, it has continued to drift downward in the United States, where in 2004 it was only the 45th most common name.

Famous name: Thomas Edison (inventor)

Nicknames: **Tam** (Scottish), **Thom, Tom, Tommie, Tommy**

Variations: **Domas** (Lusatian), **Foma** (Russian), **Tamas** (Hungarian), **Toma** (Romanian), **Tomas** (Irish Gaelic and Lithuanian), **Tomás** (Spanish), **Tomasz** (Polish), **Tomaz** (Slovenian), **Tommaso** (Italian), **Tomos** (Welsh), **Toms** (Latvian and German), **Tuomo** (Finnish)

Thor

Old Norse "thunder," name of the ancient Scandinavian and Germanic god of thunder, lightning, and war; Thursday is named after him. Thor was a favorite god of the ancient Vikings, probably because in Norse myths he is often presented as the god who sided with mortal men against the other Norse deities.

Famous name: Thor Heyerdahl (writer and adventurer)

Thorne

English surname, "dweller by the thorn bushes." This name has seen some sporadic use since the character Thorne Forrester began appearing on the television soap opera *The Bold and the Beautiful*.

Tibor

Hungarian form of Tiberius, the name of the second emperor of the Roman Empire, whose name simply means "of the Tiber River."

Tighe

Irish Gaelic *Tadhg*, "poet, bard, philosopher," in Ireland pronounced as the word "tiger" without the *r*.

Tim

Short form of **Timothy**. Tim has been an extremely popular name in both the Netherlands and Germany recently.

Famous name: Tim Allen (comedian)

Timothy

Greek *Timotheos*, "honor God." St. Paul's conversion of his friend St. Timothy gave this name Christian roots, but the name was not widely

used until the Reformation. Timothy was a leading name for boys in both England and the United States during the 1960s, but today it has fallen to 89th place in the United States and even lower in England.
Famous name: Timothy Hutton (actor)
Nicknames: **Tim, Timmie, Timmy**
Variations: **Timofei** (Russian), **Timot** (Hungarian), **Timotej** (Czech), **Timoteo** (Italian, Portuguese, and Spanish), **Timothee** (French), **Timotheos** (Greek), **Timotheus** (German), **Tymoteusz** (Polish)

Titus

Roman family name of unknown meaning, known both as the name of one of Paul's companions in the New Testament and of a Roman emperor. Shakespeare also wrote a play titled *Titus Andronicus*. Titus first entered the SSA top 1,000 list for boys in 1960 and for the next 40 years stayed on the list without ever rising above 650th place. Recently more parents seem to be discovering it as an alternative to other popular names beginning with the *Ty-* sound such as **Tyler** and **Tyson.** In 2004 it ranked 572nd on the SSA list, its highest level ever, with almost 400 American boys given the name.

Tobey, Toby

This short form of **Tobias** has been used as an independent name in England since medieval times. Between 1965 and 1989, Toby had a pronounced up-and-down movement of popularity, peaking in 1975, when it was among the 200 most popular names for American boys. Since 2000, Toby has begun another upswing and ranked 376th among boys names given in 2004. About 25 percent more boys are named Toby than Tobias every year.
Famous names: Tobey Maguire (actor)
Toby Keith (country singer)

Tobias

Greek form of Hebrew *Tobiah,* "God is good." This name became popular in the Middle Ages because of the Book of Tobit, which is in the Old Testament of Roman Catholic Bibles but is part of the Apocrypha for Protestants. Tobias has had a rather unusual history of popularity, since it resurfaced on the SSA list in the late 1960s after an 80-year absence. It peaked in use in the late 1970s, then receded, and since 1996 has been climbing up the popularity charts

again. In 2004 Tobias ranked 436th among names given to American boys, with more than 470 born that year.
Nicknames: **Tobey, Toby**

Todd

Old English *tod,* "a fox." Todd was a chief name of the baby boom and retained a good bit of its popularity until the 1980s. Since then it has plummeted in use and was only 535th on the SSA list in 2004.
Famous name: Todd Eldredge (figure skater)
Other spelling: **Tod**

Tom

Form of **Thomas.** Since medieval times most men named Thomas in English-speaking countries have been called Tom in everyday life. One of the most famous examples is the title character of Henry Fielding's novel *Tom Jones,* published in 1749. Modern examples include actors Tom Cruise, Tom Hanks, and Tom Selleck, writer Tom Wolfe, playwright Tom Stoppard, television anchor Tom Brokaw, and dozens of professional athletes. Tom is also a popular name in Israel because *tom* means "perfection, purity" in Hebrew.

Tomas

Spanish *Tomás,* form of **Thomas.** This name is still popular in the Hispanic-American community.

Tommie, Tommy

Forms of **Thomas.** English soldiers are called Tommies because the name "Thomas Atkins" is used in examples on the forms that soldiers are required to fill out.
Famous names: Tommy Hilfiger (fashion designer)
Tommy Lee Jones (actor)

Tony

Form of **Anthony.** Like Tom, this nickname has long been used independently.
Famous name: Tony Danza (actor)

Topher

Though this is still very rare as an independent name, the career of actor Topher Grace has gotten this unusual short form of **Christopher** noticed since 1998.

Trace

Short form of **Tracy.** Tracy is an English surname going back to place names in Normandy that originally meant "Thrasius's place." It became a boys first name in the 19th century and was used by Charles Dickens for a character in *The Pickwick Papers* in 1837. Tracy was steadily used as a male name in the United States, and then about 1932 it began a rise that made it one of the 100 most common boys names by 1966 and 1967. However, the film *The Philadelphia Story* starring Katharine Hepburn as Tracy Lord led parents to begin naming daughters Tracy, and its increase for girls was much steeper than that for boys. Once parents noticed that trend, the name declined swiftly for boys, finally leaving the SSA top 1,000 list in 2000. However, in 1990 Trace had entered the SSA top 1,000 list. Parents must have decided that Trace was a more "masculine" form of Tracy. Historical names such as The Natchez Trace also help to give Trace a rugged pioneer image. Though Trace seems to have peaked around 1998, in 2004 there were 443 boys given the name in the United States, ranking it 528th on the SSA list.

Famous name: Trace Adkins (country singer)

Travis

Middle English *travers,* "toll collector, crossing guard." This surname originally became a first name in Texas in honor of William Travis, the commander of the ill-fated American forces at the Battle of the Alamo in 1836. The majority of Travises born before 1950 probably had Texas connections. By 1975, Travis was a fashionable name in both the United States and Australia. The name held a position on the top 50 list of names given to newborn American boys between 1976 and 1993, but by 2004 it had fallen to 162nd place.

Famous name: Travis Tritt (country singer)

Trent

English river and village name, perhaps from a pre-Celtic word for "flooder." Trent has been used as a first name in the United States since the start of the 20th century. In the 1970s and 1980s, Trent became more popular, but after 1990 when its derivative **Trenton** passed it, Trent began to recede as an official name.

Famous name: Trent Lott (U.S. senator)

Trenton

Eighteenth-century American "Trent's Town," the name of the city in New Jersey founded by William Trent. According to George Stewart, author of *American Place-Names,* this was "one of the first instances of a developer naming a place after himself." Trenton does not seem to exist as an English place name or surname, but it has been used as a first name in the United States since the 1950s and is becoming more popular. This probably happened because Americans who heard the name **Trent** assumed that it must be short for Trenton in the same way that **Clint** was derived from **Clinton,** although in this case it was the other way around. Trenton was the 175th most common name given to boys born in the United States in 2004.

Trevin

Probably a blend of **Trevor** and **Kevin.** Trevin is a name that has been regularly used since the 1980s but has always been rare. It has bounced in and out of the bottom ranks of the SSA top 1,000 five times since 1987. In 2004 there were 167 Trevins born in the United States, ranking it 986th on the SSA list that year.

Trevion

Probably an African-American creation, but also a brand name for watches made in Switzerland. Trevion has been on the SSA top 1,000 list since 1999 but isn't showing much growth in popularity.

Trevor

Welsh *Trefor,* a place name from *tref* [home] + *mor* [great]. This Welsh surname became popular as a first name throughout Britain during the 1950s. Trevor has been used in the United States since 1975, although it never reached the heights of fashion that it did in England. After peaking at around 60th place on the list of names given to American boys in 1994, it dropped to 112th in 2004.
Nickname: **Trev**
Variation: **Trefor** (Welsh)

Trey

Latin *tres,* "three." This began as a prep-school nickname for a boy with "III" after his real given name. A few parents began turning Trey into an official given name during the 1960s, after Hollywood had used it for gambler characters in Westerns. Though Trey has risen in use considerably since the 1980s, its rise has been more erratic than that of most names, with unexplained peaks in both 1993 and 1999. More than 1,500 Treys were born in 2004, ranking it 211th.

Treyton

The first instance of this name seems to be as the surname of Clay Treyton, a character in a made-for-television movie called *Convict Cowboy,* which aired on the Showtime cable television network in 1995. However, the name may also have been independently created by parents who liked the sound of **Trey** but were reluctant to put a one-syllable form on a birth certificate. Treyton first entered the SSA top 1,000 list in 2002 but in 2004 was only 997th on that list, with 163 boys given the name.

Tristan

This version of **Tristram** is famous to music lovers because of Wagner's 1865 opera *Tristan und Isolde.* Tristan first entered the SSA top 1,000 list for boys in 1971, which is curious because that was the year before British veterinarian James Herriot's novel *All Creatures Great and Small,* featuring a character called Tristan, was published. For whatever reason, the name slowly increased in use during the 1970s, being more widely noticed after the television series based on Herriot's novel aired on PBS in 1978. Tristan peaked at 222nd on the SSA list in 1985 but fell to 452nd by 1994. During this period, Tristan was used mostly by college-educated parents. Then the film *Legends of the Fall,* starring Brad Pitt as Tristan Ludlow, became a huge hit in 1994. In 1996 there were more than 16 times the number of Tristans born as there had been in 1994, catapulting the name into the top 50 for boys. The alternate spellings **Tristen, Tristin,** and **Triston** appeared, and the name shifted its demographics to become especially popular with blue-collar parents. Though it's now receding in use, Tristan was still the 88th most popular name in 2004, with four-and-a-half times the popularity of its previous 1985 high point.

Tristram

Celtic *drystan,* "tumult" or "loud noise." This name dates back to the Arthurian romances but is perhaps best known through Laurence Sterne's 18th-century novel *Tristram Shandy.*
Nickname: **Tris**
Variations: **Drystan, Tristan, Trystan**

Troy

Middle English *Troie,* "from [French town of] Troyes"; or Irish Gaelic *troightheach,* "foot soldier"; or from the ancient city in Asia Minor made famous by the Trojan War. There is little doubt that Troy's huge success during the 1960s was due to movie actor Troy Donahue. By 2004 Troy had fallen to 219th on the list of names. Troy has been almost equally popular with both black and white parents.
Famous name: Troy Aikman (football player)

Truman

Middle English *Treweman,* "trustworthy man." Though many people assume this surname became a first name because of President Harry Truman, it was well established as a given name in the United States in the 19th century, perhaps because of its positive meaning. Its first peak of use was in 1913. There was another sharp spike in the use of Truman in 1945 and 1946, right after Harry Truman took office, but the name then fell quickly away. In 2003 it reached the SSA top 1,000 list for the first time in more than 30 years. With its fashionable sound (two syllables ending in *-n*) and the upswing in other presidential surnames, Truman's use may well continue to increase.
Famous name: Truman Capote (writer)

Tucker

Old English *tucian,* "to torment," through Middle English *touken,* "to stretch (cloth)." In medieval England a tucker's job was to sew folds in cloth. As a given name, Tucker first appeared on the SSA list in 1978. It has risen slowly but steadily ever since and was the 263rd most common boys name of 2004, with more than 1,000 Tuckers born.
Nickname: **Tuck**

Tucson

Papago "black base of the mountain." With **Phoenix** now a popular name, rare instances of boys named Tucson have also been noted.

Turner

Old French *tornour,* "one who turns wooden or metal objects on a lathe while making them." Turner was regularly used as a given name in the 19th century and then nearly vanished in the 20th. Since 1994 it has returned to regular use at a low level along with other occupational surnames, but its rate of increase has been very slow.

Ty

This short form of names like **Tyler** or **Tyrone** is the exception to the rule that American parents prefer longer forms. Ty has been used regularly in the United States since the 1960s. Around 1990 it began to increase rapidly, reaching 177th place in 2004 with more than 2,000 boys given the name. Ty Murray, "King of the Cowboys," retired in 2002 at age 32 from the professional rodeo circuit. Famous name: Ty Pennington (carpenter and television personality)

Tycho

Latin form of Greek *Tychōn,* "hitting the mark." Sixteenth-century Danish astronomer Tycho Brahe proved that comets were objects in outer space, not in the earth's atmosphere.

Tyehimba

Tiv (Nigeria) "we stand as a people."

Tyler

Old English *tygeler* or Old French *tieuleor,* both meaning "tile maker." This common occupational surname was rare as a first name until the 1970s, although it had occasionally been given since the 19th century, especially in the South, in honor of John Tyler, the tenth president of the United States. In the late 1970s, Tyler became fashionable, and it was among the top 20 names for boys in the Great Plains and Rocky Mountains by 1985. Its vogue quickly spread eastward; in 1992, Tyler reached the national top ten. Tyler's similarity in sound to fashionable names such as **Ryan** and **Kyle** made it appealing to parents looking for an alternative. Tyler was the 18th most common boys name of 2004. Nickname: **Ty**

Tyree

This is a Scottish surname, taken either from the island of *Tiree,* "land belonging to Iath," or a form of *McIntyre,* "son of the mason." Tyree became popular as a given name in the late 1970s, especially in the African-American community, as an alternative for **Tyler** and **Tyrone.** But it's been quickly falling in use since 1998.

Tyrell

Possibly from Old French *tirel,* "stubborn person." This Norman French surname (in the spelling **Tyrrell**) was the name of a prominent white family in the Carolinas, but in modern times it has become a popular name for African-American boys by blending the sounds of **Tyrone** and **Terrell.**

Tyrese

African-American creation expanding **Tyree.** Though this name has been heard for some time in the African-American community, often in other spellings such as **Tyreese** and **Tyriece,** it only entered the SSA top 1,000 in 1998, the year R&B singer Tyrese's self-titled debut album went platinum.

Tyrion

A name invented by author George R. R. Martin for Tyrion Lannister, a character in his *A Song of Ice and Fire* fantasy series. Tyrion, a dwarf son in a devious noble family, is a brave and intelligent character who is the favorite of many readers, and so he has spawned namesakes. The resemblance of the name to the Welsh female name *Tirion,* "gentle," is probably coincidental.

Tyrone

Irish Gaelic "Eoghan's territory," the name of a county in Northern Ireland. American matinee idol Tyrone Power was descended from a great-grandfather named Tyrone Power (also an actor) who was born in Ireland. Although the name Tyrone never caught on with white Americans, it was very successful in the African-American community from 1950 through 1980. Tyrone is now going out of style. Nickname: **Ty**

Tyshawn

This African-American creation blending **Ty** and **Shawn** has been on the SSA top 1,000 list since 1992. Around 175 boys have been named Tyshawn every year since.

Tyson

Old French *tison,* "firebrand." Modern Americans probably interpret the meaning of this name as "son of **Ty.**" Tyson entered the SSA top 1,000 list in 1966, and its use rose along with **Tyler**'s. However, the name dropped in use after 1987 as boxer Mike Tyson's public image became more unsavory. Since 1997, however, as memories of him fade, the name has taken an upswing again. In 2004 more than 1,000 Tysons were born in the United States, ranking the name 261st. Famous name: Tyson Chandler (basketball player)

Ubani

Omaha (Native American, Nebraska) "digging in the earth."

Ulises

Spanish version of **Ulysses.** This name has been increasing in use along with the Hispanic population. In 2004 there were more than 370 American boys named Ulises, ranking it 591st on the SSA list.

Ultan

Irish Gaelic *Ultán,* "man from Ulster." In Ireland, St. Ultan, the seventh-century Bishop of Ardbraccen, is the patron saint of children.

Ulysses

Latin form of *Odysseus,* meaning uncertain. In the *Iliad* and the *Odyssey,* Homer tells the story of Odysseus. The Irish writer James Joyce used *Ulysses* as the title of his famous book. Ulysses S. Grant led the Northern forces in the Civil War and was the 18th president of the United States. In modern times, Ulysses is the most common name that begins with the letter *U* for non-Hispanic-American boys, but it is still a very unusual name.
Variations: **Ulises** (Spanish), **Ulisse** (Italian)

Umtali

Shona (Zimbabwe) "river of ore."

Upton

English place name and surname, "farmstead or village higher up than others nearby." American writer Upton Sinclair (1878–1968) became famous after his novel *The Jungle,* an exposé of the Chicago meatpacking industry, was published in 1906. Reaction to the book led to the passage of the first federal Pure Food and Drug Act. In 1943 Sinclair won a Pulitzer Prize for his novel *Dragon's Teeth,* which described the rise of the Nazi Party in Germany.

Urban

Latin "the town." Eight popes have been called Urban. Though Urban was regularly used in the United States during the 19th century, it had almost completely vanished by 1930.

Variations: **Orban** (Hungarian), **Urbain** (French), **Urbano** (Italian and Spanish), **Urbanus** (German and Dutch), **Urpo** (Finnish), **Urvan** (Russian)

Uriah

Hebrew "God is light." In the Old Testament, King David deliberately placed the soldier Uriah in the front line of an army attack so he would be killed; David then married Uriah's widow, Bathsheba. The prophet Nathan later made David remorseful for his evil deed. Uriah is quite rare in the United States today. For unknown reasons it seems to be somewhat more common in Colorado and New Mexico than elsewhere.

Variation: **Urías** (Spanish)

Uriel

Hebrew "God is my light." Although it's not mentioned in the Bible, Uriel is traditionally the name of one of the four great archangels in Christian literature. Because it is still fairly popular with Hispanic-Americans, Uriel is now the most common name that starts with U for boys in the United States. There were 580 boys named Uriel born in 2004, making it 442nd on the SSA list.

Ursin, Urson, Ursyn

(See **Orson**.)

Utah

Name of the state, from the Ute nation of Native Americans. As is the case with most Native American tribes, "Ute" was not the group's name for themselves. It is from the Southern Paiute *yuuttaci*, perhaps meaning "people of the mountains." With **Dakota** first becoming a popular name, there have been several instances of American boys named Utah within the last decade.

Uttam

Sanskrit *uttama*, "best, excellent, greatest."

Vaden

American surname, origin unclear, but perhaps a form of French *Vaudon,* itself a form of *Gaudon,* from the same Germanic root word as **Waldo.** Vaden would be an excellent underused alternative for all the other names that rhyme with **Aidan.**

Val

Short form of **Valentine.**
Famous name: Val Kilmer (actor)

Valentine

Latin *Valentinus,* from *valens,* "strong, healthy." The third-century Roman St. Valentinus was martyred on February 14, which is his feast day. The ancient Roman fertility festival, Lupercalia, was celebrated on approximately the same day. By merging the two festival days, St. Valentine became associated with love and romance. The name is unusual in the United States, but it used to be popular in continental Europe.

Nickname: **Val**
Variations: **Ualan** (Scots Gaelic), **Valente** (Italian), **Valentijn** (Dutch), **Valentin** (French and German), **Valentín** (Spanish), **Valentino** (Italian), **Velten** (German)

Van

Dutch or German prefix "from," placed before a surname that is usually derived from a place name, or a short form of **Evan** or **Ivan.**
Famous names: Van Johnson (actor)
Van Morrison (musician)
Nickname: **Vanny**
Other spelling: **Vann**

Vance

Old English *fenns*, "marshes." The initial *V* of this name shows that it originated in southwestern England. Vance has never been a very popular name, but it has been regularly used in the 20th century, especially in the American South.

Varick

Dutch surname, originally *Van Varick*, "from the town of Varick." Other spellings: **Vareck, Varrick**

Varro

A Roman family name, probably from Latin *varo*, "hard, durable." Roman scholar Marcus Terentius Varro, known as Varro, lived in the first century B.C. and is credited with writing the first encyclopedia. Variation: **Varrón** (Spanish)

Vartan

Armenian, an ancient name of Iranian origin, but long associated with the Armenian word *vart*, "rose."

Vassar

English surname from Old French *vasseor*, "vassal." This name is, of course, best known today because of Vassar College.

Vaughan, Vaughn

Welsh *Fychan*, "small"; originally a nickname that became a surname. This name was most used from 1940 through 1960. Variation: **Von**

Ved

Sanskrit *Veda*, "knowledge; weaving together." The latter meaning is certainly appropriate for the Indian author Ved Mehta, who has written several autobiographical works weaving together the story of his life as a blind man with the history of modern India.

Velten

(See **Valentine**.)

Vembo

Shona (Zimbabwe) "juice of the fruit of the loquat tree." The loquat, native to China but now grown around the world, produces a pear-like fruit; its juice is very popular in Zimbabwe.

Vermont

Name of the state, created from the French words *vert,* "green," and *mont,* "mountain." (The correct word order in French would be "Montvert.") Vermont Connecticut Royster (1914–1996), an editor of *The Wall Street Journal* who won two Pulitzer Prizes, was named after his grandfather. His great-grandfather had named his sons Vermont, Iowa, Arkansas, Wisconsin, and Oregon, and his daughters Louisiana, **Virginia,** and **Georgia.**

Vernon

French place name from a Gaulish (ancient Celtic) word for "alder trees." This name is well known through George Washington's home, Mount Vernon, which was named for the original landowner, Vernon Washington. Vernon was among the top 100 boys names in the United States in the 1920s, but it vanished from the SSA top 1,000 list in 2004. It may stay gone for a long time if its image becomes dominated by Vernon Dursley, Harry Potter's nasty, overbearing uncle.
Famous names: Vernon Jordan (civil rights lawyer and executive)
                Vernon Presley (father of Elvis Presley)
                Vernon Reid (jazz and rock guitarist and songwriter)
Nicknames: **Vern, Verne, Verney**

Vic, Vick

Short form of **Victor.**
Famous name: Vic Damone (singer and songwriter)

Vicente

Spanish form of **Vincent,** still regularly used by Hispanic-Americans. In 2000, Vicente Fox was elected president of Mexico, the first from an opposition political party since 1910.

Victor

Latin "conqueror." Although this name dates back to at least the 13th century in England, it wasn't used regularly until the 19th century. Since then, Victor's popularity in the United States has remained remarkably consistent; for a century it has never been higher than 75th or lower than 125th on the boys list. In 2004, Victor was the 109th most common name given to American boys.
Famous names: Victor Hugo (French novelist)
                Victor Martinez (baseball catcher)

Nicknames: **Vic, Vick, Vico** (Spanish)

Variations: **Bictar, Vicho** (Mexican), **Víctor** (Spanish), **Vihtori** (Finnish), **Viktor** (German, Scandinavian, Czech, and Russian), **Viktoras** (Lithuanian), **Vitorio** (Portuguese), **Vittore, Vittorio** (Italian), **Wiktor** (Polish)

Viggo

A Latinized form of *Vigge,* an ancient Danish name based on the word *víg,* "war." A few years ago this name was unknown outside of Scandinavia, but today it is recognized worldwide because of Viggo Mortensen, the Danish-American actor who played Aragorn in the *Lord of the Rings* film trilogy. Viggo has had an upswing in use in Sweden during the last few years because of Mortensen's fame, but it is still rare in the United States.

Vijay

Sanskrit *Vijaya,* "victory, conquest, triumph."

Famous name: Vijay Singh (golfer)

Vince

Short form of **Vincent.** Country singer Vince Gill and actor Vince Vaughn are probably the main influences on this name's image today.

Vincent

Latin *vincens,* "conquering." In the 17th century, St. Vincent de Paul founded the Lazarists and the Sisters of Charity. The Dutch artist Vincent van Gogh is revered for his emotionally charged Post-Impressionist paintings. This name acquired new connotations through the late-1980s television series *Beauty and the Beast,* in which the beast Vincent was both gentle and ferocious. Like **Victor,** Vincent has been amazingly stable in its use, hovering between being the 65th and 125th most popular name for American boys for a century. Perhaps both these names retain a darkly handsome, slightly dangerous Mediterranean image that appeals to some parents but is a bit too exotic for the masses.

Famous name: Vincent Price (actor)

Nicknames: **Vin, Vince, Vinn, Vinnie, Vinny**

Variations: **Chento, Uinseann** (Irish Gaelic), **Vicente** (Spanish), **Vicko** (Croatian), **Vikent** (Ukrainian), **Vikentij** (Russian and Bulgarian), **Vincas** (Lithuanian), **Vincenc** (Czech), **Vincente**

(Italian and Portuguese), **Vincentiu** (Romanian), **Vincentius** (Dutch), **Vincenzo** (Italian), **Vinzenz** (German), **Wincenty** (Polish)

Vincenzo

Italian form of **Vincent**. Vincenzo appeared on the SSA top 1,000 list in 2004 at 928th place. This may be another sign that Italian-Americans are returning to their roots in the search for baby names.
Famous name: Vincenzo Bellini (opera composer)
Nickname: **Enzo**

Ving

Modern short form of **Irving**.
Famous name: Ving Rhames (actor)

Vinnie, Vinny

Forms of **Melvin** or **Vincent**.
Famous name: Vinny Testaverde (football player)

Virgil

Latin *Vergilius,* meaning unknown, but spelling altered in ancient times to conform with *virgo,* "maiden." The great Roman poet Virgil was the author of the *Aeneid.* Virgil became an American first name during the early 19th century while other classical names such as **Homer** were also in fashion.
Famous name: Virgil "Gus" Grissom (astronaut)
Nickname: **Virge**
Variations: **Vergil, Virgilio** (Italian and Spanish)

Vito

Italian, Spanish, and Portuguese form of Latin *Vitus,* "alive" or "lively."
Variations: **Veit** (German), **Wit** (Polish)

Vladimir

From Old Slavonic *volod* [rule] + *meri* [famous]. This Russian name is well known worldwide because of Vladimir Lenin, the first leader of the Soviet Union.
Famous name: Vladimir Guerrero (baseball player)

Von

(See **Vaughan**.)

Wade

Old English *Wada*, "to go," name of a sea giant in ancient Germanic legends; or Middle English *wade*, "ford." Wade became a fairly common first name in the American South after the Civil War because of Wade Hampton, a Confederate general who later became both the governor of South Carolina and a U.S. senator from that state. Now given to boys in all parts of the United States, Wade was the 522nd most popular name on the SSA list for American males born in 2004. Famous name: Wade Boggs (baseball player)

Wakili

Swahili "trustee, attorney."

Waldo

Old German *Wald*, "rule." The rare use of this name in the United States may have been inspired by admiration for the writer Ralph Waldo Emerson (1803–1882). Today, the name is best known from the children's picture books in which one must find Waldo in a drawing containing hundreds of different people.

Walker

Old English *wealcere*, "a fuller." A walker thickens cloth by gathering and pleating it. Walker was regularly used as a first name during the late 19th century, but by the end of the 1950s it was nearly obsolete. American parents began to rediscover it in the late 1980s as other occupational surnames like **Tyler** and **Spencer** became fashionable, and it rose steadily to 348th place by 2004.
Famous name: Walker Evans (photographer)

Wallace

Norman French *waleis*, "foreigner, Celt, Welshman." William Wallace was a 13th-century national hero of Scotland whose story was retold in fictionalized form in the film *Braveheart*. Wallace was first

used as a given name in Scotland in his honor, but it is rarely found in the United States today. Wallace (an inventor) and Gromit (his dog) are popular animated British film characters.
Nicknames: **Wallie, Wally**

Wallie, Wally

Form of **Oswald, Wallace,** or **Walter.**

Walt

Short form of **Walter.**
Famous names: Walt Disney (animator and film producer)
Walt Whitman (poet)

Walter

Old German *Waldhar* from *vald* [rule] + *harja* [people]. This name dates back to the Domesday Book in England. By the 16th century it had become well known through the exploits of Sir Walter Raleigh, who established one of the first English settlements in North America. In 1900 Walter was one of the top 15 names for American boys. There were 752 Walters born in the United States in 2004, which made it the 333rd most common name, but many of those boys were probably named after older relatives and will be called by a middle name in everyday life. *The Secret Life of Walter Mitty,* James Thurber's short story, which was made into a movie, is about the frustrations of day-to-day life. The association of the name Walter with the hapless hero of that story may partly explain its fall. However, with names like **Max** and **Oscar** now starting to come back, Walter may soon start to sound cool again.
Famous names: Walter Cronkite (TV newscaster)
Walter Payton (football player)
Walter Reed (pathologist)
Nicknames: **Wallie, Wally, Walt, Wat**
Variations: **Balto, Bhaltair** (Scottish), **Gauthier, Gautier** (French), **Gualterio** (Spanish), **Gualtiero** (Italian), **Gutierre** (Spanish), **Ualtar** (Irish), **Walgierz** (Polish), **Walther** (German), **Watkin**

Ward

Old English *weard,* "guard"; also, a form of **Howard.** Many baby boomers will associate this name with Ward Cleaver, the father in the 1950s television sitcom *Leave It to Beaver.*

Warner

Old German *Warinhari* from *Warin* [a tribal name of uncertain origin] + *hari* [army]. This name is more common as a surname, but mystery fans remember actor Warner Oland and the movies in which he played the famed Chinese sleuth Charlie Chan.
Variations: **Garner** (Old French), **Werner** (German, Scandinavian)

Warren

Old German *Warin,* a tribal name; also Norman French *La Varenne,* "the game park." This old name dates to the Domesday Book in England. Warren had a huge spike of popularity in the 1920s but had fallen to 532nd on the SSA list of names by 2004. Financier Warren Buffett is consistently ranked as the second-wealthiest person in the United States (after Bill Gates).
Famous names: Warren Beatty (actor)
Warren Burger (Chief Justice, U.S. Supreme Court)

Watkin

(See **Walter.**)

Wayland

Germanic, perhaps from *wig* [war] + *land* [territory]. In ancient Germanic legend, Wayland the Smith was king of the elves.
Variations: **Waylon, Wieland** (German)

Waylon

Modification of **Wayland.** Country singer Waylon Jennings has reported that his parents named him Wayland at birth, but while he was still an infant they changed it to Waylon. As Church of Christ members, they didn't want it assumed that he was named after Wayland Baptist University in Texas.

Wayne

Old English *waegen,* "cart, wagon," a nickname for either a driver or maker of carts. Between 1934 and 1958, Wayne was one of the top 50 names for boys born in the United States. Wayne was later exported to England, where it was one of the top 50 names for boys born between 1970 and 1986.
Famous names: Wayne Gretzky (hockey player)
Wayne Newton (singer)

Webster

Old English *webbestre,* "a weaver." This occupational surname was regularly used as a first name during the late 19th century, but it hasn't been among the top 1,000 names on the SSA list since 1940—not even between 1983 and 1989, when the television comedy *Webster* featured a cute kid with the name.

Wellington

English place name and surname, "town of *Wēola*'s people." This name will be forever associated with Arthur Wellesley, the Duke of Wellington, who led the forces that defeated Napoleon at the Battle of Waterloo in 1815.

Wendell

Old German *Wend* [a Slavic tribe living in eastern Germany]. Moderately used between 1900 and 1965, Wendell has now almost vanished as a name for newborns.
Famous names: Wendell Phillips (abolitionist)
 Wendell Wilkie (presidential candidate)
Variation: **Wendel** (German)

Wesley

Old English "west meadow." This surname became a first name in honor of John Wesley, the founder of Methodism. Wesley had ranked somewhere between 130th and 170th among American boys names for about a century when it suddenly doubled in use in 1977 and shot up to 66th place. This was probably a reaction to the character Wesley Jordache on the top-rated television miniseries *Rich Man, Poor Man.* The name stayed among the top 100 names for boys until 1990 but fell back to 178th place by 2004. Fans of *Star Trek* will associate this name with Wesley Crusher, the teenage character played by Wil Wheaton on *Star Trek: The Next Generation.*
Nicknames: **Lee, Wes**
Variations: **Westleigh, Westley**

Weston

Old English "west farm." This surname has been slowly growing in use as an American first name since the 1970s. It reached 347th on the boys list in 2004.
Nickname: **Wes**

Wiley

Old English *Wilig,* an ancient river name perhaps meaning "tricky stream" for a brook that often flooded.

Other spelling: **Wylie**

Will

Form of **William.** Referring to himself, Shakespeare wrote: "Make but my name thy love, and love that still/And then thou lovest me, for my name is Will." Through humorist Will Rogers and comic actors Will Smith and Will Ferrell, this name is associated with laughs and adventure today.

Willard

Old English *Wilheard* from *will* [desire] + *heard* [hardy, brave]. Willard has been used more in the United States than in Britain, though it's hard to find a baby with the name today.

Famous name: Willard Scott (TV weathercaster)

Willem

Dutch form of **William.**

Famous name: Willem Dafoe (actor)

Willi, Willie, Willy

Forms of **William.** *Steamboat Willie,* starring Mickey Mouse, was released in 1928. It was the first animated short film to receive wide notice for its music, dialogue, and sound effects.

Famous names: Willie Mays (baseball player)
            Willie Nelson (folk and country singer)
            Willie Shoemaker (jockey)

William

Old German *Wilahelm* from *wil* [will, desire] + *helm* [helmet]. For 700 years, between 1200 and 1900, William and John alternated between first and second place among names for boys in both Britain and the United States. This name came to England with William the Conqueror, who led the Norman Invasion. In the 11th century, William II, known as Rufus, came to the throne after his father. There was no other King William until William of Orange and his wife, Mary, were encouraged to depose James II. William IV briefly reigned after the death of his brother George IV and was succeeded by his niece Queen Victoria. Today Prince William is second in line to the British throne. There are many famous literary Williams, including the great dramatist William Shakespeare, poets William Wordsworth, William Blake, and William Butler Yeats, and American novelist William Faulkner. William Henry Harrison was the ninth president of the United States; William McKinley, the 25th; William Howard Taft, the 27th; and William Jefferson "Bill" Clinton, the 42nd. William was the 11th most popular name for boys nationally in 2004, but of all the top boys names its popularity shows the greatest regional differences. In Georgia, the Carolinas, Alabama, Mississippi, and Tennessee, William was the number-one boys name in 2004, but in California, Arizona, and New Mexico, it was not even among the top 30 names. William was the most popular boys name in Sweden in 2004.

Famous names: William Hurt (actor)
William Penn (founder of Pennsylvania)
William Rehnquist (Chief Justice, U.S. Supreme Court)
William Tell (Swiss hero)

Nicknames: **Bill, Billie, Billy, Liam** (Irish), **Will, Willi, Willie, Willy, Wim** (Dutch)

Variations: **Giermo, Guglielmo** (Italian), **Guillaume** (French), **Guillermo** (Spanish), **Gulielm** (Romanian), **Uilleam** (Scottish), **Uilliam** (Irish), **Vilem** (Czech), **Vilhelm** (Scandinavian), **Vilmos** (Hungarian), **Vilppu** (Finnish), **Wilhelm** (German), **Willem** (Dutch), **Willet, Wilmot**

Wilson

Middle English *Willeson,* "son of **Will.**" Wilson spiked sharply upward as a first name in the United States during World War I while Woodrow Wilson was president, showing that 90 years ago Americans had rather different ideas about politicians than they do today. The name then receded in use, but it began a modest rise again in 2001, perhaps under the influence of the popularity of two-syllable boys names ending in *-n.*

Famous name: Wilson Pickett (R&B singer)

Wim

Dutch form of **William.**

Famous name: Wim Wenders (film director)

Winn

Old English *Wine*, "friend"; also, a form of **Winston.**
Nicknames: **Winnie, Winny**
Other spelling: **Win**

Winston

Old English *Wynnstan* from *wynn* [joy] + *stan* [stone]; or Old English "Wine's village." The Churchill family made this name famous long before World War II brought the British prime minister to the attention of the world. In the 17th century, Sir Winston Churchill was the father of the first duke of Marlborough. More than 200 Winstons were born in the United States in 2004, ranking it 832nd on the SSA list.
Nicknames: **Win, Winn, Winnie, Winny**

Winthrop

Old English "Wynna's thorp," a place name, from *thorp*, "farm or village." This well-known New England surname conveys the idea of old wealth and colonial ancestors.
Nickname: **Win**

Winton

(See **Wynton.**)

Wolf

Wolf has been used as a "nature name" for thousands of years in Germany and Scandinavia, where the wolf has played an especially important part in myth and folklore. CNN news reporter Wolf Blitzer has made this name familiar around the world today, though few American parents have yet taken it up.
Variations: **Ulf** (Danish and Swedish), **Ulv** (Norwegian)

Wolfgang

From Germanic words meaning "wolf controversy." This name was made famous by Wolfgang Amadeus Mozart. Though Wolfgang has been used as a celebrity baby name and is known from chef Wolfgang Puck, it has yet to catch on with the general American public.

Woodrow

Old English "a row of cottages along a wood" from *wudu* [wood] + *raw* [row]. Woodrow Wilson was the 28th president of the United

States and won the 1919 Nobel Peace Prize. He was born Thomas Woodrow Wilson; Woodrow was his mother's maiden name. The use of Woodrow as a first name is due solely to Wilson's fame. Nicknames: **Wood, Woodie, Woody**

Woody

Form of **Woodrow** or other similar names. This name has become well known through musicians Woody Guthrie and Woody Herman, actor Woody Harrelson, and movie director and actor Woody Allen. Other spelling: **Woodie**

Wyatt

Middle English *Gwiot, Wiot,* a diminutive of **Guy.** This surname wouldn't be widely known as a given name if it weren't for the fame of Wyatt Earp. His gunfight at the O.K. Corral in Tombstone, Arizona, has been immortalized in countless books, movies, and television shows about the Old West. History tells us that Earp's posthumous reputation is much more heroic than his real life, but it is his legend that shapes perceptions of the name. The late 1950s–early 1960s television series *The Life and Legend of Wyatt Earp,* starring Hugh O'Brian, increased the number of Wyatts born during its run. The name then fell back a bit, holding steady at around 600th on the SSA list until 1986, when parents seem to have rediscovered it on their own. Wyatt's rise was accelerated by films in 1993 and 1994 in which Earp was played by Kurt Russell and Kevin Costner, but it's now soaring on its own momentum and reached 94th on the list of names given to American boys in 2004.

Wylie

(See **Wiley.**)

Wynton

Alternate spelling of **Winton,** an English place name from Old English *wynn* [pasture] or *withigen* [willows] + *tun* [village]. Wynton is now occasionally given to boys in the United States, probably due to admiration for jazz trumpeter Wynton Marsalis.

Xander

This modern short form of **Alexander** probably started to seem cool in 1996 when Treat Williams played the villain Xander Drax in the film *The Phantom*. Then, in 1997, the character Xander Harris started appearing on television's *Buffy the Vampire Slayer*. Xander first appeared on the SSA top 1,000 list in 1999. The alternative spelling **Zander,** which is nearly as common as the X- form, arrived on the list the next year. The name (with both spellings) exploded in popularity and was the 164th most popular boys name of 2004, with a total of almost 2,400 newborns given the name that year. Famous name: Xander Berkeley (actor)

Xavier

Spanish form of Basque *Etcheberria,* "the new house." Xavier became a first name in honor of St. Francis Xavier, who helped establish the Society of Jesus (the Jesuits). This name used to be confined to devout Roman Catholics, but it has become a common name with African-Americans because of the fame of basketball player Xavier McDaniel. Xavier was the 83rd most common name given to all boys born in the United States in 2004.
Famous name: Xavier Cugat (bandleader)
Variations: **Javier** (Spanish), **Xabiel, Xabier, Xaver** (Czech, German, Swedish, and Hungarian), **Xzavier, Zavier**

Xenos

Greek "stranger, foreigner."
Variation: **Xeno**

Xerxes

Probably a Greek form of Persian *Xshayârshan,* "ruler over heroes." This was the name of the ancient ruler of the Persian Empire who was defeated in battle when he tried to conquer Greece in 480 B.C.

Yahir

The Mexican equivalent of *American Idol* is called *La Academia*. In the first season of this program in 2002, a young singer who called himself Yahir (full name Yahir Othón Parra) was one of the top four finishers. In 2003 a program called *Desafío de Estrellas* featured a competition between the top singers from the first two seasons of *La Academia,* and Yahir came in first. His name was also an immediate winner with Hispanic parents in the United States. There were 1,267 American boys named Yahir born in 2003, and though, like many media-inspired names, it immediately dropped back a bit, there were still 940 Yahirs born in 2004, which ranked the name 290th for all boys born in the United States that year. Yahir is probably a Mexican respelling of *Jahir,* a rare Muslim name meaning "handsome" in Arabic. There have been several Arabic names introduced into Latin America by immigrants from Lebanon (see **Shakira** in the girls names for another example), and Hispanics often respell names that begin with *J* in English with *Y* instead.

Yair

Though this could be a Hispanic respelling of **Jair,** its pattern of use suggests that Hispanic parents see it as more of an alternative spelling for **Yahir.**

Yale

Welsh *ial,* "fertile upland." In the early 18th century, Elihu Yale donated books and money to a new college in Connecticut that then took his name.

Yarran

Aboriginal Australian, name of a species of acacia tree with wood that's good for firewood or making fence posts.

Yasir

Arabic "wealthy, easy."
Famous name: Yasir Arafat (Palestinian leader)

Yasunari

Japanese "becoming peaceful." Japanese novelist Yasunari Kawabata won the Nobel Prize in literature in 1968. His most famous novel, *Snow Country,* is the story of a disastrous love affair between a wealthy man from Tokyo and a provincial geisha.

Yelberton

Probably a form of *Yelverton,* English place name meaning "elder-tree ford village." This is the first name of Y. A. Tittle, who was inducted into the NFL Hall of Fame in 1971.

Yitzchak, Yitzhak

Modern Hebrew form of **Isaac.** Two prime ministers of Israel, Shamir and Rabin, have both had Yitzhak as a first name.

Yrjo

(See **George.**)

York

English place name and surname. The city in northern England was originally Celtic *Ebóracon,* "yew tree hill." The Anglo-Saxons altered this to *Eoforwic,* "wild boar town," in their own language. Scandinavian invaders altered that to *Iorvík,* and that finally became York in modern English. As a boys name, York is rarely used.

Yul

Form of **Julius.** Although the actor Yul Brynner, who was born in Vladivostok on the Pacific coast of Russia, liked to tell people that his first name came from a Mongolian word meaning "beyond the horizon," it was actually just a Russian version of **Jules,** the name of his Swiss-born grandfather.

Yuri

Russian and Ukrainian form of **George.** In 1961, Soviet cosmonaut Yuri A. Gagarin became the first person to orbit Earth.

Yusuf

Arabic form of **Joseph.** This name is now regularly found in the African-American community.

Yuuki

This was the top name given to boys born in Japan in 2004. *Yuu* can be written with characters that mean "excellent," "gentle," "eternity," or "male"; *ki* can mean "hopes," "tree," or "to shine." The second most popular name for Japanese boys in 2004 was Yuuta, which shows that Japanese parents are affected by fashionable sounds when choosing baby names, just as Americans are. A generic suffix for male names in Japan, *-ta* literally means "big and round."

Yvaine

(See **Evan.**)

Yves

French form of Germanic *iv,* "yew tree." In ancient times, this name reminded people of hunting or warfare because bows were normally made out of yew wood. Yves was a popular name in France from the 1930s through the 1960s, but it is now out of fashion there. Although this name has never been common in English-speaking countries, it is best known as a place name because of the nursery rhyme that begins, "As I was going to St. Ives, I met a man with seven wives." Famous names: Yves Montand (actor)

　　　　　　　Yves Saint-Laurent (fashion designer)

Variations: **Ives, Yvon**

Zac

Short form of **Isaac, Zachariah,** or **Zachary.**
Famous name: Zac Posen (fashion designer)

Zach

Short form of **Zachariah** or **Zachary.**
Famous name: Zach Braff (actor)

Zachariah

Form of **Zechariah.** In the King James Version of the Bible, this form
is used in the Old Testament for one of the kings of Israel, and the
Greek form **Zacharias** is used in the New Testament for the father
of John the Baptist. Even though more modern Bible translations call
these two men Zechariah, Zachariah is still the form more commonly given to American boys. In fact, as Zachary became fashionable, Zachariah also increased in popularity. But after reaching 309th
on the SSA list in 1992, Zachariah receded to 379th by 2004.
Nicknames: **Zac, Zach, Zack, Zak**
Variations: **Sahar** (Estonian), **Sakarias** (Finnish), **Zacarias** (Spanish),
　　　　　Zacario (Mexican), **Zaccaria** (Italian), **Zachar** (Bulgarian,
　　　　　Czech, Russian, and Ukrainian), **Zacharias** (German),
　　　　　Zachariasz (Polish), **Zacharie** (French), **Zachary, Zaharius**
　　　　　(modern Greek), **Zakarias** (Swedish and Hungarian),
　　　　　Zarko (Serbo-Croatian)

Zachary

Middle English form of **Zachariah.** Until the 1970s, parents almost
never chose this name for their babies, despite the fame of General
Zachary Taylor, "Old Rough and Ready," who was the 12th president
of the United States. But this name zoomed from obscurity into
prominence in the 1980s. It is now one of the top 25 names
for boys.

Nicknames: **Zac, Zach, Zack, Zak**
Other spellings: **Zacharie, Zachery, Zackary, Zackery, Zakary**

Zack

Form of **Zachariah** or **Zachary.**

Zaire

Kikongo *nzai,* "river." The country formerly called Zaire reverted to its original name of Democratic Republic of the Congo in 1997, but in 2004 African-Americans still named 171 sons Zaire.

Zak

Form of **Isaac, Zachariah,** or **Zachary.**

Zalman

A form of **Solomon.**

Zander

(See **Xander.**)

Zane

English surname of unknown origin. Since the Old English name *Saewine,* "sea friend," became *Sain* in Middle English, and all native English surnames starting with *Z* are forms of other names starting with *S,* perhaps Zane is a form of *Saewine.* Zane Grey was a New York dentist who wrote many best-selling Western adventure novels, including *Riders of the Purple Sage.* He was descended from the founders of Zanesville, Ohio, and his first published novel, *Betty Zane,* was based on the lives of his ancestors. Grey's fame is responsible for the regular use of Zane as a first name for American boys. In 2004 it was the 201st most popular name for newborn males.

Zebadiah

Hebrew "endowed by God." This is the name of nine different minor characters in the Old Testament.
Nickname: **Zeb**
Variation: **Zebedee**

Zebedee

New Testament Greek form of **Zebadiah.** Zebedee was the father of the apostles James and John.

Zebulon

Hebrew, perhaps "dwelling place." Zebulun was the sixth son of Jacob and Leah. Puritans began using this name in the 17th century.
Nickname: **Zeb**
Other spelling: **Zebulun**

Zechariah

Hebrew "the Lord has remembered." In the Bible, the prophet Zechariah was the author of one of the books of the Old Testament.
Variation: **Zachariah**

Zeke

Form of **Ezekiel.**

Ziggy

Form of **Sigmund.**
Famous name: Ziggy Marley (musician)

Zikomo

Ngoni (Malawi) "thank you." This name is a lovely way to give thanks for the birth of a child.

Zion

Hebrew *Tzion,* another name for the city of Jerusalem and, metaphorically, another name for all of Israel. When R&B singer Lauryn Hill and her husband, Rohan Marley, had their first son in 1997, they named him Zion in honor of his grandfather, famous reggae singer Bob Marley. Marley's nickname was Lion of Zion, a reference to his Rastafarian religious beliefs. When Hill's first solo album came out in 1998, it featured a song called "To Zion" for her son, which included the refrain "Now the joy of my world is in Zion!" The name Zion immediately caught the eye of many parents, especially African-Americans, and it quickly became as big a hit as the song. Zion was the 281st most common boys name in the United States in 2004, with almost 1,000 born. The fact that the name rhymes with **Brian** and **Ryan** helps to make it a perfect "different but not too different" choice.

Zubin

Persian "short spear; javelin." Although this name is still very rare, a few American parents who are fans of orchestra conductor Zubin Mehta have used it for their sons.

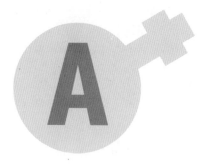

Aaliyah

Arabic *'Āliyah*, "sublime, elevated, outstanding." The parents of the singer and actress Aaliyah said they chose her name for its meaning when their daughter was born in 1979. Her first album was released in 1994, and her name immediately entered the SSA top 1,000 list for girls at 202nd place, one of the highest initial entry points ever. The alternate spelling **Aliyah** entered the list in 1994 at 358th place, and within a few years **Aleah, Alia,** and **Aliya** followed. The name remained popular in the African-American community for the next six years as Aaliyah's career blossomed. Then her life was tragically cut short by an airplane crash in August 2001. The five main spellings together accounted for the naming of 3,655 girls in 2000; 5,744 in 2001; and 7,281 in 2002. Aaliyah's influence on names reaches even further, because many other girls names ending in *–iyah,* such as **Jaliyah** and **Kaliyah,** became popular with African-Americans because of her fame. There were 5,933 girls named Aaliyah in 2004, ranking it 57th among all American girls.

Abbey, Abbi, Abbie, Abby

Short form of **Abigail**. In the 19th century, Abbie was the most common spelling of this name, but since its return to the SSA top 1,000 list in 1990 Abby has been the most frequent form. When all spellings are counted together, there were nearly 3,000 girls given this name in 2004, ranking it 124th.
Famous name: Abbey Lincoln (jazz singer)

Abigail

Hebrew *Avigayil,* "my father rejoices." In the Old Testament, Abigail was a wife of King David. This name was popular with the Puritans and remained in regular use until the late 19th century. Abigails were hard to find in the early 20th century, but use of the name slowly

revived in the 1950s. Since the 1970s it has risen steadily, being the eighth most popular girls name of 2004, with more than 16,000 American girls given the name. Abigail's revival began along the East Coast, but today it's popular everywhere in the United States.
Famous name: Abigail Adams (first lady)
Nicknames: **Abbey, Abbi, Abbie, Abby, Gail, Gale, Gayle**
Other spellings: **Abagail, Abbigail, Abigale, Abigayle**

Abra

Feminine form of **Abraham,** Hebrew "exalted father."

Abril

Spanish "**April.**" Both Hispanic-American parents and screenwriters have discovered Abril recently. There have been several minor characters in telenovelas with this name during the last decade. Abril first entered the SSA top 1,000 in 1998. In 2004, 289 girls born in the United States were called Abril, ranking it 839th on the SSA list that year.

Ada

Form of **Adelaide;** or Old German *adal,* "noble." George Gordon, Lord Byron, used this name in *Childe Harold's Pilgrimage.* Charles Dickens used the name in *Bleak House,* as did Vladimir Nabokov in *Ada.* The name Ada was quite popular in the 19th century, but it vanished almost completely by 1980. Its similarity to the very fashionable **Ava** has caused parents to rediscover it, and Ada returned to the SSA top 1,000 list in 2004 for the first time in 20 years.
Nicknames: **Adey, Adi, Adie**
Variation: **Adah** (Hebrew)

Adah

Hebrew *adah,* "ornament." In the Bible, Adah was the wife of Cain, one of Adam and Eve's sons. In modern times the name is treated as a spelling variation of **Ada.**

Addison

For origin, see Addison in the boys list. Parents looking for alternatives for **Madison** as a girls name began naming daughters Addison in the 1990s. It entered the SSA top 1,000 list in 1994 and soared upward. In 2004, nearly 2,300 girls were named Addison or **Addy-**

son, ranking the name 157th. By making the pet form **Addie** common again, Addison's popularity may inspire a revival of **Adelaide.**

Adela

Old German *athal,* "noble." William the Conqueror called one of his daughters Adela. The name was regularly used in the early 20th century but has been hard to find since the 1950s.
Nicknames: **Addie, Addy, Della**
Variations: **Adèle** (French), **Adelia, Adelina** (Latin), **Adeline, Adelle** (French)

Adelaide

Old German *Adelhaid* from *adal* [noble] + *heid* [rank]. Adelaide, wife of William IV, made this name popular in England and the Commonwealth in the 19th century. The capital of South Australia was named for her in 1836. The name was also regularly used in the United States in the 19th century, but it nearly vanished after 1950.
Nicknames: **Ada, Addie, Addy, Heidi** (German)
Variations: **Adelaida** (Spanish and Portuguese), **Adelheid** (German)

Adele

French *Adèle,* form of **Adela.**

Adeline

French diminutive of **Adela** or **Adele.** Adeline was fairly common in the 19th century and was one of the top 200 names in the United States until 1925. It vanished after 1950 but returned to the SSA top 1,000 list in 1999 and has grown in use, reaching 455th place in 2004, when 472 American girls were given the name. Barbershop quartets have been singing about Adeline for many years, paving the way for "Sweet Adelines," barbershop groups made up of women.
Nicknames: **Addie, Addy**
Variations: **Adelina** (Latin), **Adelinda, Alina, Aline**

Adria

Modern English short form of **Adrienne.**

Adriana, Adrianna

Spanish and Italian form of **Adrienne.** Use of this name has grown since the 1960s, and in 2004 Adriana reached 81st place on the popularity list, with more than 4,000 American girls given the name.

Adrienne

French feminine form of **Adrian,** Latin "from the Adriatic." Adrienne was popular in the 1980s, but **Adriana** is replacing it. Adrienne ranked 727th on the SSA list in 2004.
Famous name: Adrienne Rich (poet)
Nicknames: **Addie, Addy**
Variations: **Adria, Adrian, Adriana** (Italian and Spanish), **Adriane** (German), **Adrianna, Adrianne** (Spanish and Italian)

Agatha

Greek *agathos,* "good." This name was popular during the Middle Ages because of the third-century martyr St. Agatha of Sicily. The veil of St. Agatha is believed to have saved the city of Catania, Sicily, from the nearby volcano, Mount Etna. This explains why St. Agatha is the patron saint of fire protection. The name is best known today because of Agatha Christie, creator of the famous fictional sleuths Jane Marple and Hercule Poirot.

Agnes

Greek *hagnos,* "holy, pure." At the age of 13, St. Agnes was beheaded in Rome because she would not worship the goddess Minerva. She is the guardian of teenagers, and her symbol is the lamb. Agnes was one of the top 50 names for American girls born between 1887 and 1919, but it is rarely used today.
Famous names: Agnes de Mille (choreographer)
Agnes Moorehead (actress)
Nicknames: **Aggie, Aggy, Nessa, Nessie, Nesta, Nessy**
Variations: **Agnese** (Italian), **Agnessa** (Russian), **Agneta** (Swedish), **Agnieszka** (Polish), **Annis** (English), **Auno** (Finnish), **Inés** (Spanish), **Inês** (Portuguese), **Inez, Nancy** (medieval British)

Agnetha

This alternate spelling of **Agneta,** the Swedish form of **Agnes,** is known because of Agnetha Fältskog of the pop singing group ABBA.

Aida

Perhaps based on ancient Egyptian *Iiti,* "she is arriving." Verdi's opera *Aida* is about a slave girl in Egypt who is really the daughter of Amonasro, the king of Ethiopia. This name is sometimes used in the Hispanic-American community.

Aileen

Its popularity in the Hispanic community has made this the most common spelling of **Eileen** for newborns today. When all spellings are counted together, there were more than 1,000 Aileens born in 2004, ranking it 249th that year.
Variations: **Ailene, Aylin**

Aimee

French *Aimée*, "beloved," from Latin *amare*, "to love." This name has never been very popular in France, but it is regularly used in the United States and Britain as a spelling variation of **Amy,** which has the same Latin derivation.
Famous name: Aimee Mann (singer)

Ainsley

Scottish form of **Ansley.** Ainsley suddenly appeared on the SSA top 1,000 list in 2001 in 479th place, a fairly high initial entry point. That may have been related to the appearance of a bright, beautiful lawyer character named Ainsley Hayes (played by Emily Procter) on the television drama *The West Wing,* though since she was a minor character that's not a sure conclusion. Ainsley has more appeal on a national basis than Ansley, probably because it begins with the presently fashionable "long *a*" vowel. There were 756 Ainsleys born in the United States in 2004, ranking the name 341st.

Aisha

Arabic *A'isha,* "alive and well." Aisha was the third and favorite wife of the prophet Mohammed. This name has been well used by African-Americans since 1973. (See also **Iesha.**)
Famous name: Aisha Tyler (actress)
Variations: **Asha** (Swahili), **Ashia, Asia, Ayesha, Iesha**

Aki

Japanese "autumn" or "bright."

Alaina

This modern blend of **Alana** and **Elaine** is steadily growing more popular and was the 160th most common name for American girls born in 2004.
Variations: **Alaine, Alayna, Alayne**

Alamea

Hawaiian *alamea,* "precious."

Alana, Alanna

Usually a feminine form of **Alan;** occasionally from Irish Gaelic
a leanbh, "oh, child"; and in Hawaii sometimes from Hawaiian *alana,*
"awakening." Almost 2,500 Alanas were born in the United States in
2004, ranking it 145th.
Famous name: Alana Stewart (actress)
Variations: **Allene, Allyn, Lana, Lanna**

Alberta

Old German *athal* [noble] and *berhta* [bright]. This feminine form of
Albert is not a favorite with American parents, though it was fairly
common between 1900 and 1925.
Famous name: Alberta Hunter (jazz singer)
Nicknames: **Allie, Ally, Berta, Berti, Bertie, Berty, Birdie, Birdy**
Variations: **Albertina** (Portuguese, Spanish, and Swedish), **Albertine**
(French), **Elberta** (English)

Albina

Latin *albus,* "white."
Variations: **Alba, Albinia, Aubine**

Alda

Feminine form of **Aldo,** German "old" or "wise."

Alejandra

Spanish form of **Alexandra.** Alejandra was one of the most popular
names for Hispanic-American girls in the early 1990s, and though it's
receded a bit, it was still the 200th most popular name for all American girls born in 2004.

Alessandra

Spanish and Italian form of **Alexandra.** Alessandra has increased
quickly in use since 2001. Nearly 600 girls were given the name in
2004, ranking it 505th on the SSA list.

Alex

Short form of **Alexandra.** In the early 1990s it looked like Alex
might become popular as a girls name on its own, but it has since

receded and just barely managed to make the SSA top 1,000 list in 2004, at 990th place. It will be frequently heard as a nickname, though, for when all the girls who are being named **Alexa, Alexandra, Alexandria, Alexia,** and **Alexis** are added together, more than 30,000 American girls received an "Alex" name in 2004, which is 3,000 more than were named **Emily,** the top name of the year.

Alexa

This short form of the fashionable **Alexandra** is also common as an independent name, ranking 82nd for American girls born in 2004.

Alexandra

Feminine form of Greek *Alexandros,* "protector of mankind." In Russia, many princesses were named Alexandra. The name's association with royalty goes back to Roman times with Queen Alexandra of Judaea, who died in 69 B.C. In England, Queen Alexandra was the wife of Edward VII and great-grandmother of Queen Elizabeth. Since 1980, Alexandra and **Alexandria** have been fashionable names in the United States, and though they may have peaked around 1995, Alexandra was still 53rd on the list of names given to American girls in 2004, with more than 6,500 girls receiving the name.
Famous name: Alexandra Ripley (novelist)
Nicknames: **Alex, Alexa, Alix, Lexi, Lexie, Sandi, Sandie, Sandy, Sasha**
Variations: **Alejandra** (Spanish), **Aleka** (Greek), **Alessandra** (Spanish and Italian), **Alexa, Alexandria, Alexandrina, Alexandrine** (French), **Lexine, Sandra, Sondra, Zandra**

Alexandria

Form of **Alexandra.** Although both of these forms are popular with Americans from all ethnic backgrounds, the trend is for Alexandra to be more popular with whites while Alexandria is used more by African-Americans, perhaps because of the well-known African city of Alexandria, Egypt. Alexandria was the 133rd most popular name for American girls born in 2004.

Alexia

This was originally the feminine form of **Alexis,** which for non-Hispanic-Americans has itself become a predominantly female name. Alexia ranked 148th as an American girls name in 2004.
Famous name: Alexia (Italian singer)

Alexis

Greek *Alexios,* "helper, defender." Although it was originally a male name and is still popular for Hispanic-American boys, Alexis became extremely fashionable for girls during the 1980s. The name got a boost from the television series *Dynasty,* in which Joan Collins played the character Alexis, but its use had been increasing before and continued to grow after the series ended. At Alexis's peak in 1999, more than 19,000 girls were given the name. In 2004 it had decreased to about 14,000, ranking Alexis 16th for that year.

Alice

Old French *Adalis, Alis,* from Old German *Adalhaidis,* "of noble rank." This name developed in the 12th century as an abbreviated form of **Adelaide.** The best-known fictional Alice is the central character of Lewis Carroll's *Alice's Adventures in Wonderland* and *Through the Looking Glass.* These books may have been responsible for the popularity of the name in the late 19th century. Alice was a top ten name in the United States a century ago, but it steadily fell away until it bottomed out in 1995, when it was only given about 600 times. The name has inched up in use since then, but it's too soon to tell if Alice is about to have a revival or has just plateaued. Recently Alice has become fashionable again in England and Australia, but American parents still prefer to use **Alicia, Alison,** or **Alyssa.**

Famous names: Alice B. Toklas (writer)

Alice Walker (writer)

Nicknames: **Ali, Allie, Ally**

Other spellings: **Alis, Allyce, Alyce, Alys**

Variations: **Ailis** (Irish Gaelic), **Alicia** (Italian, Spanish, and Swedish), **Alisa** (Russian), **Alison, Alix, Alyssa** (French)

Alicia

Italian, Spanish, or Swedish variation of **Alice.** Alicia was very fashionable in the 1970s and 1980s. Though it's now receding, it was still the 116th most common name of 2004, with more than 3,000 Alicias born in the United States.

Famous name: Alicia Keys (R&B singer)

Nicknames: **Ali, Allie, Ally, Licia, Lisha**

Other spellings: **Alisha, Allycia, Alycia**

Alina

Medieval short form of **Adeline** or **Adelina.** This name is fairly common in the Hispanic-American community and ranked 221st as a name for all American girls born in 2004.
Other spelling: **Alena**

Alisa

Russian form of **Alice,** or a blend of the sounds of **Alicia** and **Lisa.** The name ranked 374th in the United States in 2004.

Alison

Old French form of **Alice** brought to England by the Normans. Chaucer used the name Alison in "The Miller's Tale." Alison was revived in the United States in the 1940s and grew steadily in use until it peaked around 1994 among the top 25 names. Now it's falling away slowly, but it was still the 34th most common girls name in 2004, with more than 9,000 Alisons born. Allison has been the most common American spelling of the name since 1963.
Famous name: Alison Krauss (singer)
Nicknames: **Ali, Allie, Ally**
Other spellings: **Allison, Allyson, Alyson**
Variation: **Allsun** (Irish Gaelic)

Alivia

Form of **Olivia.** Some Americans pronounce Olivia with an "uh" sound in the first syllable, but others use a definite "oh" and therefore consider Alivia to be a legitimate respelling. There were 945 Alivias born in the United States in 2004, ranking it 293rd on the SSA list.

Aliza

Modern Hebrew *Alizah,* "one who is merry and joyful." This Hebrew name is pronounced, and sometimes respelled, as **Aleeza.** It's hard to know how many American parents are giving daughters this modern Israeli name with that pronunciation and how many are thinking of Aliza as simply another spelling for **Eliza.** Aliza entered the SSA top 1,000 list in 2000 and has slowly but steadily increased in use. In 2004, 335 girls were named Aliza, ranking it 778th.

Alize, Alizee

French *alizé,* a tropical trade wind that blows from east to west. In the late 1980s, a cognac-based liqueur called Alizé was introduced in the United States and quickly became one of the fastest-growing products in its field. It seems that some parents then decided that Alize was a perfect new variation on **Alice,** and they began to give the name to their daughters. Alize is not the first baby name at least partly inspired by an alcoholic beverage: See **Brandy, Chardonnay,** and **Tia** for other examples. Alize entered the SSA top 1,000 list for girls in 1996, but after a minor peak at 713th in 1998, it has been fading. It only ranked 911th in 2004, when 262 girls were given the name. Use of Alize may well revive, however, if the alluring French singer Alizée, who released her first album in 2000, becomes popular in the United States. Alizée says that her parents chose her name because windsurfing was their favorite sport. The spelling with two e's was their way of feminizing the word. The name Alizée has skyrocketed in use in France since 2000. The singer's spelling is still rare in the United States, but parents who like the sound of this name might consider it as a way to lessen its alcohol associations.

Allegra

Italian "lively, cheerful, gay, sprightly."
Famous name: Allegra Kent (ballerina)

Allie, Ally

This pet form for any name starting with Al- was popular in its own right in the 19th century and revived during the 1980s when the television series *Kate and Allie* was on the air. It has continued to grow in use since and was the 184th most common girls name of 2004, given to more than 1,800 newborns.
Famous name: Ally Sheedy (actress)

Alma

Italian "soul"; Latin "nourishing, kind"; or Hebrew *almah,* "maiden." The Roman term *Alma Mater,* "bounteous mother," was used for several goddesses. In 1854, during the Crimean War, the British and French defeated the Russians in the Battle of Alma. The name was popular in England and the United States at the beginning of the 20th century, but then it fell away. There were still more than 440 Almas born in the United States in 2004, ranking it 608th on the SSA list. American soprano Alma Gluck (1884–1938) was the first female singer to make a phonograph record that sold more than a million copies.

Almira

Spanish "the woman from the city of Almira."

Alondra

Spanish "lark," though sometimes used by Hispanic parents as a short form of **Alejandra.** In 1995, popular Mexican actress Ana Colchero starred as the title character in the telenovela *Alondra,* the story of a provincial Mexican girl who, after many travails, escapes the clutches of a cruel aunt to start her own flower business in Mexico City. Alondra almost immediately became one of the top ten names for Hispanic-American girls, a position it has maintained since. In 2004, more than 2,100 girls were named Alondra in the United States, giving it a rank of 165th on the overall list.

Althea

Greek *Althaia,* perhaps "healing marsh plant."
Famous name: Althea Gibson (tennis player)

Alva

Irish Gaelic *Almha,* name of a legendary heroine of unknown meaning; or Scandinavian from Old Norse *alf,* "elf." Swedish author and diplomat Alva Myrdal won the Nobel Peace Prize in 1982 for her work on world disarmament.

Alyssa

Modern form of **Alice,** blending it with the sound of **Melissa.** Because the spelling Alyssa is 12 times more common than Alissa, American parents may also see this name as a feminine form of the flower named alyssum, which comes from Greek *alyssos,* "curing madness"; in medieval Europe, it was believed that this plant could cure rabies in dogs. In any event, Alyssa became hugely popular in the United States during the 1980s and 1990s. In 2004, it was 18th on the national list of names given to American girls, with nearly 13,000 born that year.
Famous name: Alyssa Milano (actress)
Other spelling: **Alissa**

Amabel

Latin *amabilis,* "lovable" or "loving." This name is much older than **Annabel,** but few parents choose it today.
Variation: **Mabel**

Amanda

Latin "worthy of love." In the 17th century, the writers of Restoration plays liked to invent pleasant names for their female characters, and Amanda is one of those names. It first became popular in the United States during the 1840s but then slowly went out of fashion. During the early 20th century, Amanda had an elderly and unattractive image. The name began to revive slowly in the 1950s, became very fashionable in England in the 1960s, and then soared in use in the United States during the 1970s, becoming one of the top five names for American girls born between 1979 and 1992. However, Amanda is now falling off rapidly and was only 79th in 2004. A factor in Amanda's revival may have been the fame of actress Amanda Blake, who played Miss Kitty on the long-running television Western *Gunsmoke*. Indeed, the name is a favorite among actresses, with Amanda Bearse, Amanda Donohoe, Amanda Peet, and Amanda Plummer all making names for themselves.
Nicknames: **Manda, Mandi, Mandie, Mandy**
Variations: **Amandine** (French), **Amenda, Mandita** (Mexican)

Amani

Swahili "peace," or Arabic *Amānī,* "aspirations." In East Africa, Amani is most often a male name, and a few American boys have received it, such as the football player Amani Toomer. Americans, though, have agreed with the Arabic-speaking world, where Amani is usually a female name. Amani entered the SSA top 1,000 list for girls in 1996 and has slowly increased in use since. In 2004, 457 girls received the name, ranking it 602nd on the SSA list.

Amara

Perhaps a feminine form of Arabic *A'mar,* "more populated, more flourishing." (Amara is also a masculine name in India from Sanskrit "immortal.") With similar names like **Amari, Amaya,** and **Samara** increasing in use, Amara obviously fits in with today's fashionable sounds. It first entered the SSA list in 2000 and has drifted upward in use. More than 450 girls received the name in 2004, ranking Amara 605th on the SSA list for that year.

Amari

Origin probably the same as the boys name Amari. This is a primarily African-American name for girls as well as for boys. In 2004,

632 boys and 690 girls received the name, which made it one of the least gender-specific names. Its rank for girls was 366th.

Amaris

Modern Hispanic creation, perhaps a short form of **Amaryllis** or based on Latin *amari*, "to be loved." Amaris ranked 825th on the SSA list in 2004, when 297 girls were given the name.

Amaryllis

Greek, perhaps from *amaryssein*, "to sparkle." In classical Greek and Roman poetry, this name was typically given to shepherdesses or other country maidens. In the 1780s, a newly discovered lilylike flower was named after one of these fictional maidens. The flower traditionally has the connotation of renewal. Most American girls now given this name have Hispanic parents.

Amaya

In 1879, Spanish author Francisco Navarro Villoslada published his historical novel *Amaya*, which was set in the Basque area of Spain during the eighth century. In the book, Amaya is a Basque princess who is instrumental in converting her people from paganism to Christianity. Navarro claimed that Amaya meant "the aim is the principle," implying that the aims of paganism were realized in the principles of Christianity, but whether that translation works in the Basque language is unknown. The novel remains in print in many Spanish-speaking countries, and Amaya has been used as a girls name since its initial publication, especially by those with Basque ancestry. The name was introduced to the general population in the United States when Amaya Brecher, who is of Spanish descent, was one of the stars of MTV's *The Real World: Hawaii* in 1999. Parents immediately seized upon Amaya as a cool new alternative for names like **Maya** and **Amanda,** and 702 Amayas were born that year, introducing Amaya to the SSA top 1,000 list in 397th place. By 2004, **Amya** had developed as an alternative spelling, and the two versions together were given to 2,305 American girls, ranking the name 156th for the year.

Amber

Arabic *anbar*, "amber," a pale yellow or green fossil resin used to make jewelry. Amber received some minor use in the late 19th and early 20th centuries when other jewel names such as **Pearl** and

Beryl were fashionable. It then disappeared until the controversial best-selling novel *Forever Amber* by Kathleen Winsor came out in 1944. Amber returned to the SSA top 1,000 list in 1945 and steadily grew in use until it was one of the top 20 names for girls born between 1981 and 1993. Amber then began to fall off rapidly, and it was only the 103rd most common name in 2004.

Famous name: Amber Tamblyn (actress)

Amelia

English form of German *Amalie*, probably from Old German *amal*, "work." This name was brought to England in the early 18th century when the German Hanoverian dynasty inherited the English throne. Since then, Amelia has been blended and confused with **Emily,** which has a different origin; the youngest daughter of King George III was called both Princess Amelia and Princess Emily, interchangeably. Amelia became generally popular when Henry Fielding used it for the title character of his popular novel *Amelia*. Although the name dropped greatly in use in the United States after 1900, it never vanished. Amelia was slowly revived in the late 1980s, probably spurred by the success of Emily, **Amy,** and similar-sounding names. It was the 110th most common girls name of 2004, with more than 3,300 Amelias born in the United States that year.

Famous name: Amelia Earhart (aviatrix)

Nicknames: **Mellie, Melly, Millie, Milly**

Variations: **Amalia** (Spanish, Italian, and Polish), **Amalie** (German), **Amalija** (Serbian and Bulgarian), **Amélie** (French), **Amelija** (Russian), **Ameline, Emeline, Emmeline**

Amelie

French *Amélie*, form of **Amelia.** American parents have recently discovered this name, perhaps because of the fame of tennis player Amélie Mauresmo, or from the charming 2001 French film *Amélie*. Amelie was the 841st name on the SSA list for girls in 2004, with nearly 300 born.

America

The name of two continents. Most experts believe that the continents of the Western hemisphere were named after the Italian navigator Amerigo Vespucci (1454–1512). There are competing explanations for the derivation of Amerigo: Some experts say it is an early Italian form of **Henry,** while others believe it is a form of **Amery.** Girls were regularly named America in the United States during the late 19th century, but this most patriotic name disappeared before 1910. It resurfaced on the SSA top 1,000 list in 1998, this time as a primarily Hispanic-American moniker. In 2004, 601 American girls were named America, ranking it 395th.

Amina

Arabic *Amina,* "honest, trustworthy," or *Āmina,* "feeling of safety." This is one of many cases where multiple Arabic names contribute to a single spelling in the Roman alphabet. With increasing Muslim and Arabic immigration to the United States, Amina entered the SSA top 1,000 list in 2000. There were 266 American Aminas born in 2004, ranking the name 898th on the SSA list. Tunisian-born singer and actress Amina Annabi is popular in the Arab world.

Amira

Feminine form of **Amir,** Arabic "prince"; or Hebrew "speech, utterance." This name is used by both Israelis and Palestinians. Amira entered the SSA top 1,000 list in 1998 and has steadily increased in use since then. In 2004, 407 Amiras were born in the United States; the name ranked 662nd on the SSA list that year.

Amity

Latin "friendship."

Amiya, Amiyah

Sanskrit *Amiya,* "full of tenderness," or an African-American creation blending the sounds of **Amina** or **Amira** with **Aaliyah.** Amiya has been used for both boys and girls in India, but for babies in the United States today it seems to be exclusively feminine. To make things more confusing, some African-American parents are pronouncing this name to rhyme with **Maya** rather than **Mia,** thus making it an alternative spelling for **Amaya.** In 2004, 658 girls received one of the name's two spellings, which ranked it 381st.

Amy

English form of Old French *Amee,* "beloved." This name was moderately popular during the 19th century. It's probably best known in the United States because of the sister named Amy in the childhood classic *Little Women* by Louisa May Alcott and the 1933 movie based on the novel. Actually, 1933 was the low point for the use of the name. It gradually increased during the 1960s and exploded in popularity during the 1970s, when it was second only to **Jennifer** as a name for American girls. Amy then began to fall almost as fast as it had risen and was only 105th on the list for girls born in 2004. Amy has recently revived in Great Britain, however. It was the fourth most common name in England and Wales in 2004 and the number-one name in Scotland.

Famous names: Amy Grant (singer and songwriter)
                  Amy Madigan (actress)
                  Amy Tan (novelist and screenwriter)

Other spellings: **Amee, Ami, Amye**

Variations: **Aime, Aimee** (French), **Amada** (Spanish), **Amata** (Italian, German, Swedish, Polish, and Hungarian), **Amatia** (Latin), **Amia, Ammy** (Norwegian)

Ana

Spanish form of **Anna** or **Anne.**

Anahi

Spanish *Anahí,* from the Guarani (Native American) for "voice of a bird." The Guarani were the original inhabitants of Paraguay, and they still form a large part of its population. In Guarani legend, Anahí was the daughter of a chief who battled the Spanish conquerors of his people. She was captured, abused, tied to a tree, and set on fire. The next day the tree was full of beautiful flowers never seen before. Anahí's legend and her name have now spread throughout Latin America. The name skyrocketed in popularity in the Hispanic-American community when the Mexican singer and actress Anahí (born Anahí Puente) released her first album in 1996. In 2004, 808 Anahis were born in the United States, ranking the name 331st.

Anais

French *Anaïs.* Anais is normally explained as simply a Catalan or Provencal variation of **Ana,** but perhaps it was originally a blend of **Ana** and **Isabel.** The name is known worldwide because of the fame of writer and diarist Anaïs Nin (1903–1977). Anaïs was extremely fashionable in France during the 1990s. The name may not have caught on strongly in the United States because of difficulties with its pronunciation. Though the standard French pronunciation is "ah-nah-EESE," many Americans pronounce the name as "ah-NYE-iss."

Anastasia

Feminine form of Greek *anastasis*, "resurrection." Books and movies have been made about the legendary Anastasia Romanov, daughter of Nicholas II. At least two women have claimed to be Anastasia. Each says that she escaped the massacre of the royal family by Bolsheviks during the Russian Revolution, but neither woman's claim has ever been proven. The name has become associated with royalty and romance. Use of Anastasia has risen slowly but steadily in the United States since the 1960s; in 2004 more than 1,000 Anastasias were born, ranking the name 261st that year.

Nicknames: **Anstey, Nastka** (Polish), **Nastya** (Russian), **Stacey, Stacie, Stacy**

Variations: **Anstice** (medieval English), **Nastasia, Nastassia, Nastassja** (Eastern European)

Anaya

Spanish surname, from Basque *anai*, "brother," best known through the New Mexican mystery writer Rudolfo Anaya. Lately, parents seem to have taken this up as a girls name blending **Anna** and **Amaya.** It entered the SSA top 1,000 list in 2000 and in 2004 already ranked 414th, with 560 girls given the name.

Andrea

Feminine form of **Andrew,** Greek "strong" or "manly." In Italian, Andrea is a form of Andrew and used for boys, but it became popular in the United States and England as a girls name in the second half of the 20th century. At its peak, around 1974, Andrea was one of the top 25 names for American girls. It is falling off fairly slowly but still ranked 70th in 2004, with nearly 5,000 Andreas born.

Famous names: Andrea Dworkin (feminist author)
Andrea Jaeger (tennis player)
Andrea Martin (comedienne)

Nicknames: **Andi, Andie, Andy**

Variations: **Andree** (French), **Andreina** (Italian), **Andresa** (Latvian), **Andria, Andrina**

Andromeda

Greek "ruler of men." In mythology, Andromeda was an Ethiopian princess saved by Perseus from a sea monster. A constellation was named after her, and within that constellation is the Andromeda Galaxy, the closest galaxy to our own Milky Way. Science fiction fans know *Andromeda* as a recent television series starring Kevin Sorbo. Harry Potter fans are familiar with Andromeda Tonks, the favorite cousin of Sirius Black and Nymphadora's mother.

Angel

This was formerly a male name in English, as it still is in Spanish. For most non-Hispanic-Americans, however, Angel has now become a name for girls. Angel has been steadily gaining popularity for three decades and in 2004 ranked 143rd on the list of names given to girls in the United States.

Angela

Greek *angelos*, "angel" or "messenger." Although a favorite name in Italy and Spain from early Christian times, Angela did not come into regular use in England and the United States until the 18th century, partly because the Puritans rejected it, regarding it as too sacred for use. Angela Merici founded the first order of female teachers, the Ursuline Order, but it wasn't until 1807, 300 years after her death, that Merici was canonized. Angela was a top ten name for American girls between 1965 and 1979. Its popularity has since declined, and it ranked 122nd in 2004.

Famous name: Angela Lansbury (actress)

Nicknames: **Ange, Angie**

Variations: **Aingeal** (Irish Gaelic), **Andela** (Czech and Croatian), **Andzela** (Latvian), **Anele** (Lithuanian), **Anelja** (Ukrainian), **Angele** (French), **Angelina** (Italian and Portuguese), **Angeline** (French), **Angelita** (Spanish), **Aniela** (Polish), **Anjela**, **Engel** (German)

Angeles

Spanish "angels." This name developed from "Our Lady Queen of Angels," one of the Virgin Mary's titles. This traditional Hispanic name entered the SSA top 1,000 list in 2003 and ranked 973rd in 2004, when 242 were born.

Angelica

Feminine form of Latin *angelicus,* "angelic." This name has a long literary history; it was used by William Congreve in *Love for Love* and by William Makepeace Thackeray in *The Rose and the Ring*. Angelica's popularity peaked in the mid-1990s. It is now falling off rapidly, ranking 179th in 2004, when 1,900 newborns were given the name. Variations: **Angelika** (German), **Angélique** (French), **Anjelica**

Angelina

Form of **Angela.** Angelina reached its first peak of use in the United States between 1910 and 1925, the period of greatest Italian immigration. Since 1997 the name has been booming, which probably reflects both the trend among Italian-Americans to revive their ancestral names, and the influence that actress Angelina Jolie has had on the rest of the American population. Almost 5,000 Angelinas were born in 2004, ranking it 71st on the SSA list.

Angelique

French *Angélique,* form of **Angelica.** Angelique first enjoyed moderate use in the United States in the late 1960s, reaching 301st on the SSA list in 1971. It then declined in use until it had a sudden increase in 1992 that almost brought it back to its 1971 level. Angelique is now decreasing again and ranked 607th on the SSA list in 2004.

Angie

This pet form of **Angela** was often used independently during the 1960s and 1970s, when Angela was popular. It declined along with Angela until 2000, when it suddenly started to increase in use again. This may have been due to the career of R&B and "neo-soul" singer Angie Stone, who released her first solo album in September 1999. Famous name: Angie Dickinson (actress)

Anissa

Probably a modern blend of **Anna** and **Melissa,** though there's an outside chance Anissa is related to *Anisia* (Greek "fulfillment"), the name of a saint martyred in Thessalonica around A.D. 300. Anissa has had two periods of frequent use. The first began in 1967, obviously a direct result of the appearance of child star Anissa Jones as Buffy on television's *Family Affair*. Anissa vanished from the SSA list in 1979 then reappeared in 1992, probably in response to wide media coverage of the story of Anissa Ayala, a 16-year-old California girl whose parents chose to have another child in hopes of creating a compatible blood-marrow donor to fight Anissa's leukemia. Anissa's peak came in 1993; in 2004, only 266 Anissas were born, ranking the name 899th on the SSA list.

Anita

Spanish form of **Anne.**
Famous name: Anita Roddick (founder of The Body Shop)
Variations: **Aneta, Nita**

Aniya, Aniyah

Probably a modern creation blending the sounds of **Anita** and **Aaliyah.** (**Annia** is an ancient Roman name of unknown meaning, but that is probably coincidental.) Aniya is one of the fastest growing of the newly created names based on Aaliyah. It entered the SSA top 1,000 list in 1999, and in 2004 there were more than 2,300 girls given one of the two main spellings, ranking Aniya 155th that year.

Anjelica

Variant spelling of **Angelica.**
Famous name: Anjelica Huston (actress)

Ann

English form of **Anne.** Ann was the original English spelling, but it is now less common than Anne, probably because the latter has been the form favored by the British royal family.
Famous name: Ann Landers (advice columnist)

Anna

Latin variation of **Anne** and **Hannah.** This is the standard form of Anne in most Slavic and Germanic languages. Anna was second only to Mary as a name for girls born in the United States between 1875 and 1899. It has never been as common in Britain. Anna dropped off to just under the top 100 rank for girls in the 1950s and 1960s, but around 1972 it began to get popular again. Since then Anna has had one of the steadiest rises in use of any girls name. More than 11,600 Annas were born in the United States in 2004, which ranked the name 21st that year. The tragic heroine of Leo Tolstoy's novel *Anna Karenina* is probably the best-known Anna in literature.

Famous names: Anna Kournikova (tennis player)
Anna Pavlova (ballerina)
Anna Quindlen (journalist and novelist)

Annabel, Annabelle

A medieval Scottish form of **Amabel,** probably modified to resemble **Anna** and **Belle** (French "beautiful"). Annabel was fairly common during the 1920s, but after 1950 it almost vanished until parents rediscovered it around 1995. It has risen steadily since and ranked 204th in 2004, when more than 1,500 were born.
Variations: **Anabel** (Spanish), **Annabèlla** (Italian)

Annabella

This Italian or Latinate form of **Annabel** entered the SSA top 1,000 list in 2001 and ranked 723rd in 2004.
Famous name: Annabella Sciorra (actress)

Anne

French and English form of Hebrew **Hannah,** "God has favored me." Anne with an "e" developed in France and was adopted in England in the 12th or 13th century. Tradition has it that St. Anne was the mother of the Virgin Mary, although she is not mentioned in the Bible. The name has long been used by royalty, including two wives of Henry VIII, Anne Boleyn and Anne of Cleves; Anne of Denmark, wife of James I; and Queen Anne, the last reigning Stuart. Princess Anne is the daughter of Queen Elizabeth II of England. *Anne of Green Gables* by L. M. Montgomery was published in 1908. Today, many celebrated American women share the name, including three prominent authors who have garnered both critical acclaim and best-selling status: Anne Morrow Lindbergh, Anne Rice, and Anne Tyler. Although Anne's popularity as a first name has diminished since 1960, it continues to be amazingly popular as a middle name. Probably one out of every ten American women alive today was given Anne or Ann as a middle name at birth. As a first name Anne ranked 259th in 2004, with more than 1,100 girls receiving it.
Famous names: Anne Archer (actress)
Anne Bancroft (actress)
Nicknames: **Anni, Annie, Anny, Nan, Nancy, Nannie, Nanny**
Other spelling: **Ann**

Variations: **Ana** (Spanish and Portuguese), **Anais** (Provencal), **Ane** (Danish), **Anica** (Romanian), **Aniko** (Hungarian), **Anilla** (Hungarian), **Anita** (Spanish), **Anka** (Croatian and Slovenian), **Anke** (German), **Anna** (Latin, Germanic, and Slavic), **Annah, Anneke** (Dutch), **Annette** (French), **Annick** (Breton), **Annika** (Danish and Swedish), **Annina, Anninka** (Russian and Czech), **Anula, Anusia** (Polish), **Anuska** (Czech), **Anya** (Russian), **Hannah, Nana, Nanette, Nina** (Italian), **Ninette, Ninon** (French), **Ona** (Lithuanian)

Annemarie

Combination of **Anne** and **Marie**. This name was well used during the 1960s and 1970s, especially by Roman Catholics, but it is rare today.
Variations: **Annmarie, Ann-Marie, Anne-Marie**

Annette

French variation of **Anne**. Annette was one of the 100 most common names for American girls between 1957 and 1967, coinciding with the height of actress Annette Funicello's career. There were 385 Annettes born in the United States in 2004, ranking it 693rd on the SSA list.
Famous name: Annette Bening (actress)

Annie

Form of **Ann** or **Anne**. This name began as a nickname for Anne, but it became a name in its own right in the 19th century, long before the 1976 Broadway musical *Annie*. Diane Keaton played the title character in Woody Allen's movie *Annie Hall* in 1977. Annie was one of the top 20 names for American girls until 1907 and one of the top 100 until 1948. In 2004 there were still almost 800 Annies born in the United States, ranking it 335th for the year.
Famous names: Annie Leibovitz (photographer)
Annie Potts (actress)
Annie Proulx (Pulitzer-prize-winning writer)
Other spellings: **Anni, Anny**

Annika

This Scandinavian form of **Anne** entered the SSA top 1,000 list in 1995 and rose steadily to become the 205th most common name for American girls in 2004, when more than 1,500 were born.
Famous name: Annika Sorenstam (golfer)

Ansley

English surname and place name, from Middle English *Anesteleye,* "hermitage clearing." Ansley is one of the few names that makes the SSA top 1,000 list by being popular in one state even though it's rare in the rest of the country. There were 410 Ansleys born in the United States in 2004, and 178 of those were born in Georgia, where the name ranked 51st that year while only ranking 654th on the national SSA list. Ansley Park is a tony neighborhood in Midtown Atlanta, which makes Georgians aware of the name and able to see it as a good alternative for **Ashley.** Ansley has been on the national SSA list since 1996 and is still increasing in use, but outside Georgia it's been quickly surpassed by its Scottish variation, **Ainsley.**

Anthea

Greek "flower." This name is the Greek equivalent of the Latin name **Flora** and the French name Fleur.

Antoinette

French form of **Antonia.** Like its male counterpart **Antoine,** Antoinette was especially popular among African-Americans throughout the 1980s, but it has become rare today. The Tony awards are named after Antoinette Perry, a Broadway actress, director, and producer.
Nicknames: **Nettie, Netty, Toni, Tonie, Tony**
Other spellings: **Antwanette, Antwonette**

Antonia

Feminine form of *Antonius,* Latin family name of unknown meaning. Antonia has been one of the most regularly used girls names in the United States for more than a century. Its rank of 771st on the SSA top 1,000 list in 2004 was its lowest ever. *My Antonia* is probably the most-read novel by American writer Willa Cather.
Nicknames: **Anya, Nia, Nina, Toni, Tonia, Tonie, Tony, Tonya**
Variations: **Andona** (Mexican), **Anete** (Latvian), **Antalka** (Hungarian), **Antane** (Lithuanian), **Antoinette** (French), **Antonetta** (Scandinavian), **Antonie** (Czech and German), **Antonietta** (Italian), **Antonina** (Italian, Russian, Polish, and Czech)

Anya

Russian pet form of **Anna** or **Antonia.** Anya entered the SSA top 1,000 list in 1998 and is still increasing in use. In 2004, 626 girls received the name, ranking Anya 389th. Readers of historical novels may remember Anya Seton (1906–1990), whose bestselling books were considered some of the better researched in that genre.

Aphra

Hebrew *Aphrah,* a biblical place name meaning "dust." Aphra Behn was the first female writer to make a living by her trade using her own name; she lived in the 17th century.

Apple

Gwyneth Paltrow and Chris Martin raised eyebrows in May 2004 when they named their daughter Apple, but they weren't the first parents to turn to fruit names. The same week their daughter was born, a novel by Plum Sykes was a bestseller. There are hundreds of women named **Cherry,** and recent examples of girls named Peach, Peaches, **Tangerine,** Strawberry, and Citrus have been observed.

April

Latin *aprilis,* the name of the month; perhaps from Latin *aperire,* "open to the sun," or from *Apru,* Etruscan name of the goddess Aphrodite. April is the most popular month name today, but it was almost never used before 1940. Between 1972 and 1985, April was one of the top 50 names for girls in the United States, but by 2004 it had receded to 254th place.
Variations: **Abril** (Spanish), **Apryl, Avril** (French)

Arabella

Possibly Latin *orabilis,* "able to be moved." This name was first recorded in Scotland in the 12th century. It is still rare in the United States, but it's getting some notice from parents looking for alternatives for **Isabella** and **Annabelle.** Arabella Figg was young Harry's chief babysitter in the *Harry Potter* novels.
Famous name: Arabella Steinbacher (violinist)

Araceli

Spanish form of Latin *ara coeli,* "altar of heaven." *Santa María de Araceli* is a title of the Virgin Mary that comes from a church dedicated to her on Rome's Capitoline Hill, which was called "altar of heaven" by the ancient Romans because it had been the site of a temple to the god Jupiter. As a girls name, Araceli is quite rare in Italy, but it has been regularly used in Spain. Araceli entered the SSA top 1,000 list in 1968 and has gradually increased in use among the Hispanic-American population. In 2004, 880 American girls were named Araceli or **Aracely,** ranking the name 306th overall.

Araminta

Created by playwright John Vanbrugh in 1705. Araminta Melifua is a *Harry Potter* character in favor of Muggle hunting.

Areli, Arely

The origin of this newly popular Hispanic-American name is unclear, but it may simply be a shortened form of **Araceli.** In 2004, 761 girls born in the United States were given one of these two spellings of the name, ranking it 339th.

Aretha

Possibly a form of Greek *arete,* "virtue." This name may stem from Arethusa, a nymph in Greek mythology who was transformed into a stream by the goddess Artemis.
Famous name: Aretha Franklin (soul singer)

Aria

In most cases a short form of **Ariana,** though some parents may be thinking of the word for an operatic solo, which is Italian for "air." Aria entered the SSA top 1,000 list in 2000 and has grown in use. In 2004, 394 Arias were born, ranking it 687th on the SSA list.

Ariana, Arianna

Latin form of Greek *Ariadne,* "very holy one"; in Greek mythology, the princess of Crete who helped Theseus escape from the Mino-taur. The two main spellings are almost equally used, with Ariana slightly ahead. Ariana first entered the SSA top 1,000 list for girls in 1978 and steadily ascended to 38th place by 2004, when more than 8,000 girls received the name. Ariana's similarity in sound to **Ariel** probably contributed to its quick success.
Famous name: Arianna Huffington (political commentator)

Ariel

Hebrew "lion of God." Shakespeare used this name for a magical spirit of the air in *The Tempest.* Although Ariel is a male name in both the Bible and Shakespeare's play, the creators of Disney's

popular 1989 animated film *The Little Mermaid* called their heroine Ariel because the mermaid has a beautiful singing voice, just like the Shakespearean air sprite. The idea that Ariel was an appropriate female name probably came from Ariel Durant, the American historian who, with her husband, Will, wrote many best-selling books. Though the name first entered the SSA top 1,000 list in 1978, the mermaid does seem to have inspired many parents, since 1990 to 1992 were the only years Ariel was among the top 100 names for American girls. By 2004 the name had dropped to 213th place, with about 1,500 female babies given the name.
Variation: **Arielle** (French)

Arielle

French feminine form of **Ariel.** This form was regularly used as a girls name in the United States before the name Ariel was given to girls. However, Arielle became popular only after Ariel took off in the late 1980s. Arielle was 183rd on the SSA list in 1991 but fell to the 635th spot in 2004.

Arlene

Form of **Arline,** a name invented by composer M. W. Balfe for the heroine of his 1843 opera *The Bohemian Girl.* Arlene was frequently given between 1910 and 1940, but it ranked only 985th out of 1,000 on the SSA list in 2004.
Variations: **Arleen, Arlena, Arleyne, Arlina, Arline, Lena**

Artemis

Ancient Greek goddess of the moon and the hunt. Artemis was the sister of Apollo and counterpart of the Roman goddess Diana.

Arwen

Name of an Elvish princess in J.R.R. Tolkien's *The Lord of the Rings,* played by Liv Tyler in the film trilogy based on that story. In Tolkien's invented Sindarin language, Arwen means "noble woman." Like the Welsh goddess **Rhiannon,** Arwen gives up immortality to marry a human, in her case Aragorn. Quite a few examples of American girls named Arwen have been noted lately.

Arya

A name created by George R. R. Martin for the younger, tougher, and more resourceful of two sisters caught between warring dynastic factions in his *A Song of Ice and Fire* series of fantasy novels. The name is pronounced "ARE-yuh," so it is not a form of **Aria**. Several examples of readers naming daughters after the character have been observed over the last decade.

Asha

Swahili form of **Aisha;** also, a Hindu name from Sanskrit *asa,* "wish, hope." Asha Bhosle is a popular singer who has sold more than 40 million records in India over a career spanning nearly 50 years.

Ashanti

The Ashanti are an Akan-speaking ethnic group who live in the southern and central part of Ghana. From the 16th until the 18th century, the Ashanti Confederacy they established was one of the most powerful nations of West Africa. A few African-American parents began to name daughters Ashanti in the 1970s, and the name first entered the SSA top 1,000 list in 1979. Like most names with true connections to the African continent, Ashanti was especially popular with college-educated African-American families. The name suddenly became popular in the general African-American community when the R&B singer Ashanti (born Ashanti Douglas in 1980) released her first album in 2002. There were 281 Ashantis born in the United States in 2001, and 2,923 were born in 2002— one of the most explosive increases of a name on record. Ashanti is already plummeting down from that peak, however; only 525 girls were given the name in 2004, ranking it 425th that year.

Ashley

Old English "meadow with ash trees." Before the 1960s Ashley was a name for boys, but since at least 1964, more girls have been given the name. Ashley was an aristocratic English surname with connections to the American South that were reinforced by the best-known fictional Ashley, the man who chose Melanie over Scarlett in *Gone With the Wind*. Upper-middle-class Southerners have long been accustomed to giving family surnames (including such unlikely ones as **Winston** and Langhorne) to daughters as well as to sons, so Ashley slowly became more popular as a name for girls in the South, where it was fairly common by 1975. The name then exploded in use all over the country, just as the similar Southern surnames **Shirley** and **Beverly** had done in previous decades. By the late 1980s, Ashley was the number-one name for girls in the United States, and though it is now receding in use it was still the tenth most common name of 2004, given to more than 16,000 girls that year. Remarkably, while Ashley was becoming successful for girls in the United States, it was becoming popular for boys in both Britain and Australia. In those countries, the spelling Ashley is considered masculine, while some girls are now being named Ashleigh.

Famous name: Ashley Judd (actress)

Other spellings: **Ashlea, Ashlee, Ashleigh, Ashlie, Ashly**

Ashton

For origin and history, see Ashton in the boys name list.

Other spellings: **Ashten, Ashtin, Ashtyn**

Asia

Name of the continent, from a Greek word meaning "east"; also, occasionally a form of **Aisha**. Asia first entered the SSA top 1,000 list for girls in 1979 and rose steadily until it peaked at 195th in 1997. In 2004 there were more than 1,200 Asias born in the United States, ranking the name 231st for the year. The name has been particularly popular in the African-American community.

Aspen

Old English *æsepn*, name of the tree. The use of this name for girls probably has as much to do with the ritzy image of the ski resort in Colorado as it does with its status as a "nature name." Aspen entered the SSA top 1,000 list in 1993. In 2004, 515 girls received the name, ranking it 430th that year.

Astra

Greek "star."

Astrid

Old Norse from *ass* [god] + *frithr* [beautiful]. This name used to be very popular in Scandinavia. Astrid made the SSA list in the United States in 2004 at 935th place. Like the male name **Axel**, it is a Scandinavian name that's been adopted by the Hispanic-American community today.

Famous name: Astrid Munoz (fashion model)

Athena, Athina

Greek "wise." In Greek mythology, Athena, the goddess of wisdom, was one of the most powerful deities. She was said to have sprung from the head of her father, Zeus. She was the patron goddess of Athens, which is named for her. Athena has been on the SSA top 1,000 list for girls since 1955, partly because it is widely used in the Greek-American community. Recently it seems to be inching upward in use as non-Greek parents discover it. Almost 600 American Athenas were born in 2004.

Famous name: Athina Onassis (heiress)

Variations: **Athene, Thena**

Atisa

Chamoru (Guam) "increase, brighten."

Atlanta

The capital city of Georgia received this name in 1845 because it was the terminus of the Western & Atlantic Railroad. As a girls name, Atlanta evokes images of both the Old and New South.

Aubrey

French form of Old German *Albirich* from *alfi* [elf] + *ric* [ruler]. Aubrey used to be a male name, especially popular in the American South, but since 1975 it has been growing fashionable for girls throughout the country. More than 2,400 girls were named Aubrey in the United States in 2004, ranking it 147th.

Famous name: Aubrey Collins (country singer)

Other spellings: **Aubree, Aubrie**

Audra

Usually a form of **Audrey,** but also a Lithuanian name meaning "thunderstorm." Though Audra was used regularly at a low level during the late 19th and early 20th centuries, its frequent use in the 1960s and 1970s is clearly traceable to the character Audra Barkley on the television Western *The Big Valley*. The series premiered in 1965, and Audra catapulted onto the SSA top 1,000 list in 1966 at 283rd place, after a 28-year absence. Audra's high point came in 1967, a year after it reappeared on the list, and it gradually declined afterward, leaving the SSA list again in 2002. Broadway actress and singer Audra McDonald won her fourth Tony Award in June 2004.

Audrey

Old English *Aethelthryth*, "noble strength." St. Audrey (originally St. Ethelreda) was a seventh-century Anglo-Saxon saint who founded a monastery at Ely in Britain. Edda Hepburn van Heelmstra became the actress Audrey Hepburn. Audrey was a popular name in the first half of the 20th century, peaking in 1929 and then gradually falling in use. It began to rise again in 1981, about a generation earlier than normally happens. In 2004 there were more than 3,800 Audreys born in the United States, and it ranked 94th, its highest showing since 1938. It's one of the few girls names that has returned to popularity while most of its earlier bearers were still alive.
Other spellings: **Audrie, Audry, Audrye**
Variations: **Audie, Audra**

Augusta

Feminine form of Latin *August*, "venerable." Roman emperors took the title Augustus, and their female relatives were honored with the title Augusta. Both names were often used by royalty in Germany during the 16th and 17th centuries. In England, Augusta was popular during the 18th and 19th centuries because it was used by the reigning Hanover family. The wife of George IV was named Caroline Amelia Augusta, and their daughter was Charlotte Augusta. In the United States, Augusta remained in regular use until the 1920s but has since been very hard to find. This may change if use of the boys names **August** and **Augustus** continues to increase.
Nicknames: **Gussie, Gusta**
Variations: **Aakusta** (Finnish), **Auguste** (German and Estonian),
      Avgusta (Russian)

Aurelia

Feminine form of Latin *Aurelius*, a Roman family name from *aureus*, "golden." Aurelia was regularly used in the 1890s but vanished during the 1940s. If **Aurora** continues to grow in popularity, adventurous parents may soon rediscover Aurelia.
Variations: **Aranka** (Hungarian), **Auli** (Estonian), **Aurélie** (French),
      Aurica (Romanian), **Aurilla, Oralie, Orelia**

Aurora

Latin "dawn." Aurora had a small upswing in popularity during the 1920s, and another one began around 1992. In 2004 there were almost 1,000 Auroras born in the United States, ranking it 286th, its highest spot yet.

Variations: **Aurore** (French), **Rora, Rory, Zora** (Slavic)

Autumn

Latin *autumnus,* the season. A few instances of this name were noted in the early 20th century, but Autumn wasn't used generally until 1969. In 2004 there were more than 3,800 Autumns born in the United States, ranking it 98th.

Ava

Possibly an Old German name of uncertain meaning, but more likely an American respelling of **Eva** to give the pronunciation in English that the name has in other European languages. Except for the years between 1973 and 1985, Ava has been on the SSA top 1,000 list for girls since 1880, but until recently its highest ranking was 331st (back in 1883). The name began to skyrocket in use around 1997, and in 2004 there were more than 8,500 girls named Ava born in the United States, ranking it 37th.

Famous name: Ava Gardner (actress)

Avery

For origin, see Avery in the boys list. It was probably inevitable after names like **Ashley** and **Bailey** became common for girls that parents would begin to see this formerly male name as perfect for their daughters. Avery entered the SSA top 1,000 list in 1989 and has steadily increased since. In 2004, more than 4,200 girls were named Avery or **Averie,** ranking the name 88th for the year.

Avril

French form of **April.**

Famous name: Avril Lavigne (singer)

Ayanna

The origin of Ayanna is still a bit mysterious, but it may be one of the few names whose introduction to the United States can be attributed to, of all things, a baby name book! *The Book of African Names* by Chief Osuntoki was published in 1970, one of the first such books available to African-American parents who were searching for "real African" names for their children. Ayanna is listed in that book as an "East African" name meaning "beautiful flower." Osuntoki seems to have been half right: **Ayana** is a name used for both males and females in Ethiopia, but its meaning is uncertain. Ayyänäw is a male Amharic name meaning "we saw him." *Ayana* is an Oromo word for the spirits believed to mediate between the high god, Waka, and human beings in the ancient indigenous religion of the Oromos, but it's unclear if either of those is related to the common Ethiopian name. In any event, it's easy to see how parents looking through Osuntoki's book would seize upon Ayanna as one of the few names included that fit in well with the look and sound of American names of the time. Ayanna first entered the SSA top 1,000 list in 1971, with its alternative spelling Ayana joining it in 1975. The name left the SSA list in 1978, seeming to go underground until it resurfaced in the early 1990s. Its use has been growing steadily since, with the variations **Iyana** and **Iyanna** also developing. The four spellings together accounted for more than 1,900 newborn girls names in 2004, ranking it 177th that year.

Ayla

When pronounced to rhyme with **Kyla,** Ayla is a Turkish name meaning "halo around the moon." When pronounced to rhyme with **Kayla,** it has occasionally been used by Jewish parents in the United States as a respelling of the modern Israeli name **Ela.** But neither of these is the major source of the name. That honor goes to Jean M. Auel's character Ayla, the heroine of novels set in prehistoric Europe. The first of these books, *Clan of the Cave Bear,* was made into a movie in 1986 starring Daryl Hannah in the role of Ayla, and the name leapt onto the SSA top 1,000 list in 1987 at 590th place. Though Ayla has not had a ranking that high again, it has never disappeared. There were 369 American Aylas born in 2004, ranking the name 712th on the SSA list.

Ayumi

Japanese "walking, stepping." Ayumi Hamasaki is one of the most popular singing stars in Japan.

Aziza

Swahili "precious."

Azure

The word, ultimately from Persian *lazhuward,* "lapis lazuli." This is one of the color names for girls gaining in use today.

Bahati

Swahili "luck."

Bailey

For the original meanings of this name, see Bailey in the list of names for boys. It's tempting to attribute the frequent use of Bailey for girls outside of the South to the *WKRP in Cincinnati* character Bailey Quarters, played by Jan Smithers, but it must be noted that the first year the name appeared on the SSA top 1,000 list for girls was 1983, the year after the program's prime-time run ended. The name grew quickly in use and peaked at around 60th place in 1998. In 2004 Bailey was the 87th most popular name for girls, with more than 4,000 born that year.

Barbara

Latin feminine form of Greek *barbaros,* "strange, foreign." St. Barbara was an early and possibly legendary Christian martyr whose devotion to her faith so enraged her father, Dioscurus, that he ordered her to be tortured. When she refused to renounce her religion despite her suffering, her father beheaded her, and he was struck by lightning and killed. St. Barbara became the patron saint invoked against thunder and lightning and the protectress of gunners and miners. Between 1927 and 1958, Barbara was a top ten name for American girls, ranking second only to **Mary** between 1937 and 1944. In 2004, however, only 395 American girls were named Barbara, ranking it 686th on the SSA list that year. Barbara McClintock won the 1983 Nobel Prize in medicine for her discovery of mobile genetic elements.

Famous names: Barbara Bush (first lady)
                      Barbara Stanwyck (actress)
                      Barbara Walters (broadcast journalist)

Nicknames: **Babbie, Babs, Barb, Barbie, Bobbi, Bobbie, Bobette**

Other spelling: **Barbra**

Variations: **Babette** (French), **Bairbre** (Irish Gaelic), **Barabal** (Scots Gaelic), **Barbe** (French), **Barbel** (German), **Barbora** (Czech), **Barbro** (Swedish), **Barica** (Slovakian), **Baruska** (Czech), **Basia** (Polish), **Borbala** (Hungarian), **Varenka** (Russian), **Varu** (Estonian), **Varvara, Varya** (Russian)

Barbra

Alternate spelling of **Barbara.**

Famous name: Barbra Streisand (singer, actress, and director)

Bathilda

Latinized form of Old English *Baldhild,* "bold battle." St. Bathilda was an Anglo-Saxon slave girl in medieval France whose great beauty attracted the notice of King Clovis, who married her in 649. When her husband died, Bathilda acted as regent for her young son. Not surprisingly for one born as a slave, she tried to suppress the slave trade and redeem captives. Her name is almost nonexistent today, but readers of the Harry Potter novels may recognize Bathilda Bagshot as the author of *A History of Magic,* one of the basic textbooks at Hogwarts School.

Beatrice

Latin *Viatrix,* "voyager," later altered to resemble *Beatus,* "blessed." St. Beatrix, a young Christian martyr during the Roman Empire, was killed because she rescued the bodies of her slain brothers, who were killed because of the greed of a neighboring landowner who used the excuse of their Christianity to abscond with their property. In literature, Beatrice guides Dante through Paradise in the *Divine Comedy.* The character was based on Beatrice Portinari, a young woman whom Dante met when he was a child. When she died at age 24, Beatrice became Dante's symbol of the ideal woman. One of Shakespeare's most memorable female characters is the witty and energetic Beatrice in *Much Ado About Nothing.* In the 19th century, the name was revived when Queen Victoria named her youngest daughter Beatrice. The name was among the top 50 for American girls born between 1902 and 1925, but it steadily declined in use thereafter, finally leaving the SSA top 1,000 list altogether in 2002.

There is little sign of a revival in spite of Prince Andrew of England and the Duchess of York, the former Sarah Ferguson, having named their first daughter Beatrice in 1988.

Famous name: Beatrice "Bea" Arthur (actress)

Nicknames: **Bea, Beattie, Bee, Trissie, Trix, Trixie, Trixy**

Variations: **Beatrisa** (Russian), **Beatrix** (German), **Beatriz** (Spanish), **Beitris** (Scots Gaelic), **Betrys** (Welsh), **Bice** (Italian), **Viatrix**

Beatrix

German form of **Beatrice**.

Famous names: Beatrix (queen of the Netherlands)
Beatrix Potter (children's writer)

Beatriz

Spanish form of **Beatrice**. Although Beatrice is now only rarely given in the United States, Beatriz is still somewhat used in the Hispanic-American community, though it's even fading there. In 2004 there were only about 250 newborns in the United States named Beatriz, half the number as in 1991.

Becky

Form of **Rebecca**. Becky was fairly common as an independent name in the 1950s and 1960s, but it left the SSA top 1,000 list in 1993. William Thackeray's heroine Rebecca Sharpe of *Vanity Fair* was known as Becky, and in the United States, Mark Twain created the character Becky Thatcher for *Tom Sawyer*.

Other spellings: **Beckie, Bekki**

Belen

Spanish *Belén*, "Bethlehem," the town where Jesus was born. Bethlehem means "house of bread" in Hebrew. Though Belen has long been used as a girls name in Spanish-speaking countries, it's only been on the SSA top 1,000 list in the United States since 2000. In 2004, it ranked 881st on that list, with 273 girls given the name.

Belinda

Origin unclear; perhaps from Old German *betlindis*, "dragonlike"; German *Berlinde* from *bero* [bear] + *linta* [linden wood shield]; or an Italian invention based on *bella*, "beautiful." Belinda's regular use began in the 17th century, partly because it was one of the pretty-sounding names that Restoration dramatists liked. For his famous 18th-century satire *The Rape of the Lock*, Alexander Pope most likely chose the name to mock the earlier plays, as well as to poke fun at society's petty rules and concentration on trivial matters. Belinda was one of the top 200 names for American girls born between 1959 and 1973, but it's rarely used today.

Famous name: Belinda Carlisle (pop singer)

Nicknames: **Bel, Binnie, Linda**

Variations: **Bella, Berlinda, Velinda** (Hispanic)

Bella

Latin and Italian *bella*, "beautiful"; also, a variation of **Isabel**. Bella was used moderately during the early 20th century but seemed to vanish after 1930. The recent success of **Isabella** has brought Bella back; it jumped onto the SSA top 1,000 list in 750th place in 2000, and there were more than 2,000 Bellas born in 2004, ranking it 235th for that year.

Famous names: Bella Abzug (politician and activist)
Bella Davidovich (pianist)

Variations: **Belinda, Belle**

Bellamy

English surname from Old French *bel ami*, "fair friend."

Bellatrix

Latin "female warrior," name of a bright blue-white star in the constellation Orion. If **Beatrice** is revived anytime soon, Bellatrix might start to sound good to parents as a blend between that name and **Bella,** unless the image of the sinister character Bellatrix Lestrange from the *Harry Potter* novels nixes that possibility.

Belle

French *belle*, "beautiful"; or a form of **Isabel**. The name Belle got a great deal of positive publicity in 1991 when the Disney studios used it for the heroine of the animated film *Beauty and the Beast*. This may counteract its previous associations with Belle Starr, the notorious Western outlaw. Even so, the name hasn't been in the SSA top 1,000 list since 1934.

Variations: **Bel, Bell, Bella**

Berenice

This original form of **Bernice** had a minor surge of popularity in the Hispanic-American community during the 1990s, but it has already fallen off in use once again.

Berit

Scandinavian form of **Bridget.**

Berkeley, Berkley

English place name and surname, "birch clearing." This name, best known to Americans through the University of California, Berkeley, is occasionally given to girls.

Bernadette

French feminine form of **Bernard.** The most famous Bernadette was the young girl who, in 1858, saw visions of the Virgin Mary at a spring near Lourdes. People went there to watch her pray, and many claimed that they were cured by drinking water from the spring. Bernadette said she was told to build a church at the site. In 1933, Bernadette Soubirois was canonized, although the church specifically recognized St. Bernadette for her faith, not her visions. In the United States, the name Bernadette was modestly popular, especially in Roman Catholic families, during the 1940s, but it then fell away and hasn't been on the SSA top 1,000 list since 1993.

Famous name: Bernadette Peters (actress)

Nicknames: **Bernie, Berny**

Variations: **Bernadine, Bernarda, Bernardette, Bernardina** (Italian), **Berneen** (Irish), **Bernetta, Bernharda** (German and Norwegian), **Bernita, Vernarda** (modern Greek)

Bernice

Ancient Macedonian form of Greek *Pherenike,* "bringer of victory," from *pheros* [bringer] and *nike* [victory]. This is a form of the ancient name **Berenice,** which was used widely in the Greek and Roman empires. In Egypt, many of the wives and daughters of the ruling Macedonian Ptolemaic pharoahs had this name. Between 1913 and 1927, Bernice was one of the top 50 names for American girls, but it is very rare today.

Nicknames: **Bernie, Berny**

Other spelling: **Berenice**

Variations: **Berenika** (Czech), **Berenike** (German), **Bernike** (Latvian), **Veronica**

Bertha

Old German *berhta,* "bright." Berchta, the name of a Teutonic goddess, was the original form of this name. Charlemagne's mother was named Berchta. Bertha was one of the top ten names for American girls born in the 1880s, being one of many medieval names that the Victorians revived. It is very unusual today because of its association with Big Bertha, a powerful German gun used to shell France in World War I. The cannon was named for industrialist Bertha Krupp, owner of the Krupp factory where the guns were made. Though Bertha Krupp was a pretty woman, Americans ever since have associated the name Bertha with obesity. In 1905, Baroness Bertha von Suttner was the first woman to win the Nobel Peace Prize.
Nicknames: **Berti, Bertie, Berty, Birdie, Birdy**
Variations: **Berta** (German, Italian, Slavic, and Spanish), **Berthe** (French), **Bertina** (German)

Beryl

Greek *beryllos,* a semiprecious stone. Like other jewel names, Beryl was first given to girls in the late 19th century. It then had a minor vogue between 1900 and 1930, but it is very rare today.
Famous name: Beryl Markham (aviatrix)

Bess

Form of **Elizabeth.** Bess may be most familiar to modern Americans through George Gershwin's opera *Porgy and Bess.*
Famous name: Bess Truman (first lady)

Beta

Greek; also a variation of **Elizabeth.** This is the second letter in the Greek alphabet.

Beth

Form of **Elizabeth;** also, Hebrew *Bethia,* "daughter of the Lord." Scots were the first to use this name independently, perhaps because of its connection with the Celtic word *beath,* "life." During the 1960s, Beth was one of the top 100 names given to American girls. Today it's rare as a first name, but it's still often used as a middle name.
Famous name: Beth Henley (playwright)

Bethany

Biblical name of a village near Jerusalem that Jesus visited more than once. The meaning of the place name is disputed; "house of figs" and "house of poverty" have been suggested. Bethany was the home of Mary and Martha, the sisters in the famous biblical episode where Martha complains that she is doing all the housework while Mary listens to Jesus. Jesus tells Martha that she is "distracted by many things" and that "Mary has chosen the better part." In England, Bethany is a rare name that is mostly used by Roman Catholics in honor of Mary of Bethany. In the United States, however, Bethany has probably been most often chosen by evangelical Protestant parents. Bethany wasn't regularly used as a girls name before 1950. It was one of the top 100 names between 1983 and 1988, but by 2004 it had slipped to 203rd place.

Betsy

Form of **Elizabeth**. This name is associated with Betsy Ross, who is said to have made the first American flag at the request of George Washington. Betsy was quite common as an independent name in the late 18th century and had another minor vogue in the 1940s and 1950s, but it's very rare today.
Other spellings: **Betsey, Betsie**
Variation: **Bets**

Bette

French form of **Elizabeth**. The final e is silent in the pronunciation of this French name, but many Americans use this form as another spelling of **Betty.**
Famous names: Bette Davis (actress)
Bette Midler (singer and actress)

Bettina

German variation of **Elizabeth** or Italian feminine form of **Benedict**. There was a minor vogue for Bettina in the 1960s, but today it is rarely used.

Betty

Form of **Elizabeth**. This popular nickname has often been used as an independent given name. It was incredibly popular between 1920 and 1950, ranking second behind **Mary** from 1928 to 1934. Today young Americans think of it as a grandmotherly name, and it's almost never given to infants. Betty Williams of Northern Ireland was cowinner of the 1976 Nobel Peace Prize.

Famous names: Betty Friedan (feminist writer)
            Betty Grable (actress)

Variation: **Bette**

Beulah

Hebrew "married." This name was used as a poetic name for the land of Israel in the Bible. Beulah came into regular use as an American name in the late 19th century after Augusta Evans Wilson published her bestselling novel *Beulah*. Between 1885 and 1917, it was one of the top 100 names for American girls. Since 1950, however, the name has become extremely rare.

Other spelling: **Beula**

Beverly

Old English *Beferlic*, "beaver stream." This is an aristocratic English surname that was sometimes used as a masculine name in the 19th century. Beverly's regular use as a girls name originated with George Barr McCutcheon's *Beverly of Graustark*, a now-forgotten best-selling novel from 1904, in which Beverly is a beautiful Southern girl who ends up marrying a European prince. Beverly first appeared in the SSA top 1,000 list in 1905. Between 1928 and 1957, it was one of the top 50 names. Beverly's popularity then faded away until it left the SSA top 1,000 list in 1999.

Famous names: Beverly Cleary (children's writer)
            Beverly D'Angelo (actress)
            Beverly Sills (operatic soprano)

Nickname: **Bev**
Other spellings: **Beverlee, Beverley**

Beyonce

The singer Beyonce Knowles's mother created her first name by altering her own maiden surname, *Beyince*. This rare surname is probably originally French, but its derivation beyond that is undiscovered. The name Beyonce bounced into the SSA top 1,000 list in 2001 and bounced right back out again. Probably nothing so illustrates the present African-American custom of creating new names for daughters as much as the fact that Beyonce's name has had so little impact. She may be admired, but it is now out of style in her own community for girls to be directly named after celebrities.

Bianca

Italian form of **Blanche.** Shakespeare named characters Bianca in both *The Taming of the Shrew* and *Othello.* Bianca first entered the SSA top 1,000 list in the United States in 1973, shortly after Bianca Jagger became famous as the wife of rock star Mick Jagger. Although the original meaning of this name is "white," since the 1980s it has been particularly popular in the African-American community. Bianca was the 29th most common name given to nonwhite girls born in the United States in 1991, when it was among the top 100 names for all girls on the SSA list. Since then it has receded, though it was still the 172nd most common name of 2004, with nearly 2,000 girls given the name that year.
Variations: **Beonca, Beonka, Bianka, Vianca**

Billie

Feminine form of **Billy** or form of **Wilhemina.** This name started out as a boys nickname, but by 1890 it was regularly being given to girls, especially in the southern part of the United States. Billie was among the top 100 names for girls between 1928 and 1934, but is rarely given today. It is often found in combinations such as Billie Jean or Billie Jo.
Famous names: Billie Holiday (jazz and blues singer)
              Billie Jean King (tennis player)
Variation: **Billy**

Birdie, Birdy

Forms of **Alberta** or **Bertha,** or a name invented from the word. Birdie was fairly common as a given name during the late 19th century, but it's flown far away since the 1940s.

Birunji

Luganda (Uganda) "pretty, perfect."

Blair

Celtic "plains." Blair was almost exclusively masculine until Blair Warner, a character on the television series *The Facts of Life* played by Lisa Whelchel, gave the name a pretty blonde "preppy" image.

Blair remained moderately common for girls during the 1980s, but it then receded and left the SSA top 1,000 list in 2001.
Famous name: Blair Brown (actress)

Blanca

Spanish form of **Blanche.** Blanca increased in use among Hispanic-Americans during the 1980s and 1990s, but it now seems to be going out of fashion. It ranked 858th on the SSA list in 2004.
Famous name: Blanca Uribe (concert pianist)

Blanche

Old French "white." The 12th-century French queen Blanche of Castile is the first historic bearer of this name; it also appears among members of the House of Lancaster in Britain. The most famous Blanche in literature is Blanche DuBois in Tennessee Williams's *A Streetcar Named Desire*. The creators of the television sitcom *The Golden Girls* must have had her in mind when they named a character in their series Blanche Devereaux. Neither of these characters helped the name's popularity; although Blanche was one of the top 100 names for American girls for the 50 years before 1920, it has almost vanished as a baby name today.
Other spelling: **Blanch**
Variations: **Bianca** (Italian), **Blanca** (Spanish), **Blanka** (Polish and Czech), **Bljanka** (Russian and Ukrainian)

Bliss

Old English *bliths,* "supreme happiness."

Blossom

Old English *blosma,* "flower of a plant." Though examples of Blossom occur as far back as 1880, it's always been a rare name. The early 1990s television series *Blossom,* where Mayim Bialik played the teenage title character, led to no discernible increase in its use.

Blue

This color name has started to turn up for girls a few times each year in the United States.

Blythe

Old English "blithe, joyous, carefree." Despite its cheerful meaning, and the positive notice given to it by actress Blythe Danner over the years, this name has never been common enough to make the SSA top 1,000 list.

Bobbie

Feminine form of **Bobby**; variation of **Barbara** and **Roberta.** As a girls name, Bobbie has a history similar to **Billie**'s. It peaked at 110th place on the SSA list in 1934 and vanished after 1998.
Famous name: Bobbie Gentry (singer and songwriter)
Other spellings: **Bobbi, Bobby**

Bonnie

This name stems from the Scottish word *bonnie,* which means "beautiful" with a connotation of goodness. According to an old ballad, "The child who is born on the Sabbath day is blithe and bonnie and good and gay." Bonnie was already in use as a girls name in the 1870s, and it steadily grew in use until it was one of the top 50 names for girls between 1940 and 1955. It then began its inevitable decline, finally leaving the SSA top 1,000 in 2004.
Famous names: Bonnie Blair (speed skater)
              Bonnie Hunt (comedian and actress)
              Bonnie Raitt (country singer)
Other spellings: **Bonni, Bonny**

Brandy

Origin uncertain; perhaps a feminine form of **Brandon** or from Dutch *brandewijn,* "burnt wine," the name of the alcoholic beverage. Brandy first entered the SSA top 1,000 list in 1967; the 1972 hit song "Brandy (You're a Fine Girl)" by the group Looking Glass seems to have accelerated the name's rise a bit, but it didn't start the fashion for it. At its peak, around 1978, the four main spellings combined were among the top 25 names for American girls; by 2004 the name had dropped to 328th place.
Famous names: Brandi Chastain (soccer player)
              Brandy Norwood (singer and actress)
Other spellings: **Brandee, Brandi, Brandie**

Bree

Irish short form of **Bridget.** There was a brief vogue for Bree in the United States in the late 1970s, but it's basically been a rare name since. It remains to be seen if the character Bree Van De Kamp on the television series *Desperate Housewives* will revive interest in the name. Bree Walker, a television news anchor in California, is nationally known as an advocate for the disabled because of her own experience as a person with ectrodactyly, a fusion of the toes and fingers. She played the role of Sabina on the HBO series *Carnivale* in 2005.

Breeze

The word used as a name. The English borrowed this word from Spanish *brisa*. Breeze has shown up occasionally as a "nature name" since the 1960s in both England and the United States, but as yet it hasn't become as popular a name with English-speakers as **Brisa** now is with Hispanic-Americans.

Brenda

Feminine form of Old Norse *Brandr*, "sword"; also, a feminine form of **Brendan.** Brenda got a slow start on the SSA list in the 1920s, but it suddenly exploded in the 1930s. Brenda was one of the top 50 names between 1940 and 1972—a very long run at the top for a formerly obscure name. Some commentators have connected this with the long-running cartoon strip *Brenda Starr*, but that first appeared in 1940, so its creator, Dale Messick, simply chose a name for his character that fit the tastes of the times. Though Brenda has fallen in use today, it was still the 197th most common girls name in 2004, given to more than 1,600 newborns. It is now particularly popular in the Hispanic-American community.
Famous names: Brenda Lee (singer)
Brenda Vaccaro (actress)

Brenna

Probably a 20th-century creation, either a simplification of **Brenda** or a feminine form of **Brennan.** Though Brenna entered the SSA top 1,000 list in 1971, five years after Brennan, from that point until 1991 there were more Brennas than Brennans born every year, which reflects parents' greater willingness to give girls "new" names than boys. Brenna peaked in use in 1995 and has been slowly receding since. In 2004, 955 American girls were given the name, ranking it 290th that year.

Bria

Probably a short form of **Brianna.** Bria had a sudden burst of popularity in the African-American community in the early 1990s, peaking at 175th on the SSA list in 1993. This may be an instance where a celebrity baby had a huge effect, since Bria is the name of Eddie Murphy's oldest child, who was born in November 1989. Bria has been slowly receding in use and only ranked 938th in 2004.

Briana, Brianna

Feminine form of Celtic **Brian,** "high, noble." Like **Brenda,** Briana is a name that rose from obscurity to great heights very quickly, but it was even more successful. The spelling Briana first entered the SSA top 1,000 list in 1973, with Brianna following in 1976. All the spellings combined made for a top ten name by 1996, ranking ninth by 2004 with more than 16,000 girls given the name. The variety of spellings that became popular separately shows that parents were primarily attracted to the sound of the name. The great majority of women and girls with this name rhyme the first syllable with "free," but a few, including soccer player Briana Scurry, prefer "fry." Brianna has increased its lead over the other alternative spellings the last few years and now accounts for more than half the girls given the name.
Variations: **Breana, Breanna, Breanne, Breonna, Brianne, Bryana, Bryanna**

Bridget

Celtic *Brigenti,* "the high one." This name was extremely popular in Ireland for hundreds of years, although it has now gone out of fashion there. Bridget is the name of the goddess of wisdom in Irish mythology and is associated with the female patron saint of Ireland, St. Bridget, also called St. Brigid and St. Bride. The sixth-century daughter of a Druid, she lived beneath an oak tree and devoted her life to charitable deeds. In Scandinavia, the name's popularity is based on the fame of St. Birgitta, the patron saint of Sweden. She and her husband, Ulpho, a Swedish prince, withdrew from their court and devoted themselves to pious lives. In the United States, the name is still most often given to girls with Irish ancestry. Bridget was most common in the 1970s. Though it's now receding in use, there were still more than 1,000 Bridgets born in the United States in 2004, ranking it 278th. Many young women today will associate the name with the novels *Bridget Jones's Diary* and *Bridget Jones: The Edge of Reason* by Helen Fielding and the films based on them.
Famous name: Bridget Fonda (actress)

Nicknames: **Biddie, Biddy, Bree, Bridie, Brie** (Irish)

Other spellings: **Bridgett, Bridgette**

Variations: **Berit, Birgit** (Scandinavian), **Birgitta** (Swedish), **Birte** (Danish), **Bregetta** (Dutch and Lithuanian), **Brid** (Irish Gaelic), **Bride** (Irish), **Brighid** (Gaelic), **Brigid** (Irish), **Brigida** (Italian, Portuguese, Russian, and Spanish), **Brigita** (Czech, Latvian, and Croatian), **Brigitte** (French), **Brita, Britt** (Swedish), **Britta, Brygida** (Polish and Ukrainian), **Pirkko** (Finnish)

Brielle

Probably a short form of **Gabrielle,** though in rare cases perhaps inspired by the town in New Jersey, which in 1881 was named after a town in the Netherlands. The Dutch town's name probably goes back to Celtic *brogilo,* "swampy area." Brielle entered the SSA top 1,000 list in 1990 and has continually increased in use, especially during the last few years. In 2004, 590 girls were named Brielle in the United States, ranking the name 402nd.

Briley

English surname of unknown origin, but perhaps a variation of **Brierley,** "briar clearing." This name is especially well known in Nashville, Tennessee, where Briley Parkway is a major thoroughfare. A few parents have begun to discover Briley as a "different but not too different" alternative for the androgynous name **Riley,** and alternative spellings such as **Brylee** are already showing up.

Brisa

This is the Spanish word for "breeze," but it may also be a short form of **Briseida.** There was a sudden whirlwind of Brisas born in the Hispanic-American community in 2000, probably because of a character with that name on the telenovela *Por Tu Amor* ("For Your Love"). There were 562 Brisas born in the United States that year, but by 2004 the number was down to 344, ranking the name 749th on the SSA list.

Briseida

Spanish form of Briseis, Greek "daughter of *Briseus.*" Briseus possibly meant "weighty, strong." In the Greek legends of the Trojan War, Briseis was a young Trojan widow taken as a spoil of war by Achilles. In romantic versions of the story, she is often presented as being in love with him. Though Briseida has never been a common name in Latin America, it has been used more often there than Briseis has been in English-speaking countries.

Britney

Form of **Brittany.**
Famous name: Britney Spears (pop singer)

Britt

Swedish form of **Bridget.** Also a short form of **Brittany.** The fame of Swedish actress Britt Ekland may have helped create the fashion for Brittany in the United States.

Brittany

French *Bretagne,* a region of France settled by Celtic refugees from Britain. The idea of turning this place name into a first name is purely American. It appeared rarely in the late 1960s, entered the SSA top 1,000 list in 1971, and then exploded in popularity during the 1980s. By 1989, Brittany was in a close race with **Ashley** for the top spot on the list of names given to American girls. It's possible that some parents saw Brittany as the full form of **Britt,** not realizing that Britt was actually a Swedish form of **Bridget.** The popularity of other names for girls ending in *-any* and *-anie,* combined with the fashion for similar names for boys such as **Brent** and **Brett,** also helped to spur the use of this name. Today the name is falling away almost as fast as it rose. In 2004 it only ranked 134th as a name for newborn American girls.
Famous name: Brittany Murphy (actress)
Other spellings: **Britanee, Britani, Britany, Britney, Britni, Britny, Brittani, Brittanie, Brittney, Brittni, Brittnie**
Variations: **Britt, Britta, Brittin, Britton**

Bronte

Greek "thunder." The father of the famous English novelists the Bronte sisters (Charlotte, Emily, and Anne) changed his surname to Bronte from *Prunty* (Irish Gaelic *Proinnteach,* "bestower, generous person"). His daughters made the adopted name famous. Bronte was fairly popular as a girls first name in Australia during the 1990s, and it is just starting to show up in the United States.

Bronwen, Bronwyn

Welsh from *bron*, "breast," and *gwen*, "white, fair, holy." In Wales this name is always spelled Bronwen because in Welsh *–wyn* is a masculine ending. Americans and Australians, however, are so used to girls names like **Carolyn, Kathryn,** and **Camryn** that when they use this name it's more likely to be spelled Bronwyn.

Brooke

Old English "brook, stream." The fame of the New York socialite and philanthropist Brooke Astor (born Roberta Brooke Russell) is probably what originally turned this formerly masculine name into a popular name for girls. Indeed, 1953, the year she married Vincent Astor and first received publicity, was also the first year Brooke appeared on the SSA top 1,000 list. The name's connotations of wealth and beauty have since been greatly reinforced by the image of actress Brooke Shields.

Famous names: Brooke Adams (actress)
　　　　　　　Brooke Valentine (R&B singer)

Variation: **Brook**

Brooklyn

American form of Dutch *Breukelen*, "broken land," name of the borough of New York City. It was probably inevitable after **Brooke** became popular that creative parents would seize upon Brooklyn as a "different but not too different" alternative. One of the first examples noted is disco singer Donna Summer's daughter, born in 1981. The name built up slowly at first, entering the SSA top 1,000 list in 1990, but since then it has steadily increased. The alternative spelling **Brooklynn,** which itself entered the SSA list in 1995, shows that many parents are interpreting the name as simply a blend of **Brooke** and **Lynn.** In 2004 the two spellings combined were given to more than 4,100 girls, ranking the name 90th for the year. Brooklyn is one of the best examples of a name that would have been thought eccentric a generation ago becoming commonplace within a few short years.

Brynn

Probably an alternate spelling of **Bryn,** a modern Welsh male name from the word *bryn*, "hill." Though Bryn is still a male name in Wales, as exemplified by the operatic bass Bryn Terfel, it has been over-whelmingly female in the United States since its introduction here, and Brynn has been the preferred spelling. The name seems to have been first brought to the attention of American parents by the actress Brynn Thayer, who began playing the character Jenny on the daytime soap opera *One Life to Live* in 1978. Brynn first entered the SSA top 1,000 list in 1980; it left after 1986, the year Ms. Thayer left the soap. Brynn's second upswing is one of the more remarkable in recent times. In 1998, the name suddenly reappeared on the SSA top 1,000 list at 720th place, when 306 girls were given the name, an increase of at least 56 percent over the number of Brynns born in 1997. The event that seems to have precipitated this was the murder in May 1998 of comedian Phil Hartman by his wife, Brynn, and her subsequent suicide. There is no better example of how media attention given to a name can cause an increase in its use, even when that attention is negative. Parents who named daughters Brynn in 1998 and 1999 would of course be appalled to think that they had named them after Brynn Hartman, but when so many people are constantly on the lookout for uncommon but well-known names, any recent publicity can make it more likely for parents to think of the name and therefore choose it, without consciously realizing where they heard it. Like most names inspired by singular media events, Brynn peaked the year after the event, in 1999, and then receded in 2000 and 2001. It probably would have continued to fall if it hadn't gotten a much bigger and more positive dose of media attention in 2002, when Brynn Smith was one of the stars of MTV's *Real World: Las Vegas*. In 2004, more than 1,100 American girls were named Brynn, ranking the name 264th.

Cadence

The word, meaning "the beat or flow of any rhythmic movement."
Cadence is one of the most explosively growing girls names today.
There are isolated examples of girls named Cadence in Australia
and the United States as far back as the 1920s. The heroine of
Armistead Maupin's 1992 novel *Maybe the Moon* was named
Cadence. But the name only entered the SSA top 1,000 list in 2002,
when 231 were born. In 2004, there were 3,140 girls named
Cadence, **Kadence,** or **Kaydence.** Characters named Cadence in
the 2001 film *Shallow Hal* and the 2003 film *American Wedding*
helped introduce the name to parents, but the boom in Cadences is
probably because the name is considered a feminine form of **Caden.**

Caitlin

Irish Gaelic form of *Cateline,* an Old French form of **Katherine**
brought to Ireland by the Normans. Caitlin is really the Gaelic spelling
of **Kathleen,** but Americans unfamiliar with Gaelic who saw the
name written out began pronouncing it as if it were a combination of
Kate and Lynn. After **Katie** became the most popular nickname for
Katherine in the 1970s, parents of Irish descent in the eastern United
States began to name their daughters Caitlin. The original spelling
first entered the SSA top 1,000 list in 1976; it was followed in the
1980s by **Caitlyn, Kaitlin, Kaitlyn, Kaitlynn, Katelin, Katelyn,** and
Katelynn. By 1990, all the spellings counted together were in the top
ten. Though the name may have just peaked, it was still the fifth most
common girls name of 2004, with more than 19,000 newborns given
one of the eight main spellings. Kaitlyn and Katelyn are now both
more common than the original form, with Caitlyn about equal to it.

Calista

Feminine form of Greek *kallistos,* "fairest, best." Calista was steadily
used during the 19th century but was fairly rare even then. It van-

ished except for scattered use by bold or creative parents after 1881 until actress Calista Flockhart appeared in the title role on television's *Ally McBeal* in 1997. Calista popped back onto the SSA top 1,000 list in 1998, though after reaching 519th place in 1999 it receded again, ranking only 873rd in 2004.

Callie

Originally a pet form of **Caroline,** but probably associated more today with **Calista** or other names starting with *Cal-.* Callie was common in the late 19th century but vanished during the 1960s only to re-emerge on the SSA top 1,000 list in 1971. It peaked around 1999 and in 2004 ranked 252nd, with more than 1,100 girls named Callie or **Kallie.**
Famous name: Callie Khouri (screenwriter and director)

Camila

Spanish form of **Camilla.** This name has been booming in the Hispanic-American community recently. There have been several Spanish-language television series featuring characters called Camila in the last decade, perhaps the most notable being *Nada Personal,* which starred Ana Colchero, one of Mexico's favorite actresses, in the role of Camila. That series began in 1996, the year before Camila first appeared on the SSA top 1,000 list. There were more than 1,000 Camilas born in the United States in 2004, ranking it 262nd for all girls born that year.

Camilla

Possibly Etruscan through Latin *camillus,* "acolyte" or "young ceremonial attendant." In Roman mythology, Camilla was an attendant to the goddess Diana. The image of this name is dominated today by Prince Charles's wife, Camilla, Duchess of Cornwall.
Nicknames: **Cami, Cammie, Cammy, Kami, Millie, Milly**
Variations: **Camila** (Spanish), **Camille** (French), **Kamila** (Polish and Czech), **Kamilla** (German, Hungarian, and Latvian)

Camille

French form of **Camilla.** Camille has always been much more popular in the United States than Camilla, perhaps because of Greta Garbo's role in the 1936 movie *Camille.* Over the last three decades it's been slowly inching up on the list of most popular names. More than 1,200 Camilles were born in 2004, ranking it 232nd.
Famous name: Camille Claudel (sculptor)

Campbell

Scottish surname from Gaelic *caimbeul*, "crooked mouth." Television reporter Campbell Brown became coanchor of the program *Weekend Today* in 2003, and the same year her name entered the SSA top 1,000 list for girls in 910th place. In 2004, it ranked 794th, with 317 born. Though that still makes Campbell a relatively uncommon girls name, it is now much more often used for girls than for boys.

Camry

Trade name of the automobile, an Anglicization of the Japanese word *kammuri*, "crown." Camry is probably the most popular automobile-inspired girls name after **Lexus**. Its similarity in sound to **Camryn** helps convince parents that it's an appropriate name for a child.
Other spellings: **Camree, Camrie, Kamrie, Kamry**

Camryn

Feminine spelling of **Cameron** (see the boys list for origins). Cameron entered the SSA top 1,000 list for girls in 1980. It grew steadily in use and began to accelerate around 1996. This was about the same time actress Cameron Diaz became popular. In 1997, the television series *The Practice* began, with Camryn Manheim being one of its stars. The spelling Camryn entered the SSA list that year, and in 1999, there were more girls named Camryn than Cameron. The spellings have run neck-and-neck since, with the top one shifting almost every year. In 2004, Camryn was ahead by about 200 births. Meanwhile, parents had also discovered the spelling **Kamryn,** which was a strong third choice in 2004. All three spellings combined accounted for more than 3,800 girls born that year, ranking the name 96th.

Candace

A title of the queens of ancient Ethiopia; meaning uncertain. In the 19th century, this name was often pronounced "can-DAY-suh," but in the 20th century, "CAN-diss" became the popular version and has led to many alternative spellings. All the spellings together were one of the top 100 girls names of the 1980s, when the name was especially popular with African-Americans, but the name has since faded.
Nicknames: **Candee, Candi, Candie, Candy, Dace, Dacey, Kandi, Kandie, Kandy**
Other spellings: **Candice, Candis, Kandace, Kandice, Kandis**

Candida

Late Latin *canditia,* "whiteness." English teachers are likely to identify this rare name with George Bernard Shaw's play *Candida.*
Variations: **Candy, Kandida** (Norwegian)

Candy

Form of **Candace** and **Candida;** or from the word.
Famous name: Candy Crowley (television journalist)

Capri

Name of the famous resort island in the Mediterranean. The origin of the place name is unclear, though Latin "goat" and Etruscan "burial place" have been suggested.

Cara

Form of **Kara.**

Carissa

Latin form of Greek *charis,* "grace," or Italian "dear little one." Because Carissa blends the sounds of the fashionable names **Carrie** and **Melissa,** it was fairly common in the late 1980s. In 2004 it still ranked 265th, with more than 1,000 born.
Variations: **Carisa, Charissa, Karisa, Karissa**

Carla

Feminine form of **Carlo;** or form of **Karla.** This name brings to mind Carla Tortelli, the caustic waitress played by Rhea Perlman in the long-running television sitcom *Cheers.*
Variations: **Carlene, Carline, Carly, Karla, Karlene, Karline**

Carly

Modern form of **Carla.** Carly's popularity is hidden by its great number of common spellings: **Carlee, Carley, Carli, Carlie, Karlee, Karley, Karli, Karlie,** and **Karly** were all separately on the SSA top 1,000 list in 2004. When all ten spellings are added together, there were more than 5,600 girls given the name, and it ranked 60th.
Famous names: Carly Patterson (gold-medal-winning gymnast)
Carly Simon (singer)

Carma

Sanskrit "destiny"; also, a variation of **Carmel.**
Variation: **Karma**

Carmel

Hebrew "the garden." In the 12th century, the order of the Carmelite nuns was founded on Mount Carmel in Israel. In the United States, the name is often associated with the beautiful village of Carmel on the Monterey peninsula in California.

Variations: **Carma, Carmela** (Italian), **Carmelina, Carmelita, Carmen** (Spanish), **Karmel, Karmela** (Polish), **Melina**

Carmen

Spanish form of **Carmel** modified in medieval times to resemble Latin *carmen*, "song." Carmen has been popular in both the Hispanic-American and African-American communities. There were more than 1,300 Carmens born in 2004, ranking it 226th. Many adults will think of the famous opera *Carmen* by Georges Bizet when they hear this name, but the computer geography game and television game show *Where in the World Is Carmen Sandiego?* will come to mind for most children.

Famous name: Carmen Miranda (Brazilian entertainer)

Variations: **Carmencita** (Spanish), **Carmina, Carmine, Carmita**

Carol

A shortened form of **Caroline,** also associated with French "song." It first appeared as an independent name in the late 19th century. Carol was a top ten name for American girls born from 1936 to 1950, but it's been falling ever since and was only 855th on the SSA list for girls born in 2004.

Famous name: Carol Burnett (entertainer)

Other spellings: **Carel, Carole, Carroll, Caryl, Karel, Karole**

Variation: **Carola** (Latin)

Carola

This feminine form of *Carolus*, the Latin form of **Charles,** has always been very rare itself, but it's the base from which **Carol, Carolina,** and **Caroline** were created.

Carolina

Spanish and Italian form of **Caroline.** Carolina has been growing in use among the Hispanic-American population and in 2004 reached 233rd on the popularity chart.

Famous name: Carolina Herrera (fashion designer)

Caroline

French and English form of **Carolina,** an Italian derivative of **Carola.**
Caroline began appearing frequently in 18th-century England after
Caroline of Anspach married George II and was crowned queen in
1727. Today, the name retains its association with royalty through
Princess Caroline of Monaco. Caroline has been one of the most
consistently used girls names in the United States. After being
among the top 100 names in the 19th century, it slowly slid down to
a low point of 329th on the SSA list in 1956, but then it began a
slow recovery that brought it to 85th in 2004, when more than
4,000 newborns were given the name.
Famous name: Caroline Kennedy Schlossberg (lawyer)
Nicknames: **Callie, Caro, Carol, Carrie, Carry, Lina, Line**
Variations: **Carline, Carolina** (Spanish, Portuguese, and Italian),
       Carola, Carolyn, Kara, Karolina (Polish and Russian),
       Karoline (German)

Carolyn

Variation of **Caroline.** Carolyn was one of the first names ending in
–lyn to become popular, already being used regularly in the 1870s. It
rose to tenth place in 1942 but in 2004 was ranked only 355th, its
lowest point in more than a century.

Carrie, Carry

Forms of **Caroline.** Carrie first appeared as an independent name in
the 19th century and became very popular, being one of the top 25
names in the 1880s. It declined to a low point of 241st in 1950 and
then rose again to top 25 status in the late 1970s. The last few years
it has declined precipitously and was only 813th on the SSA list in
2004. Carrie Underwood won the 2005 season of *American Idol.*
Famous name: Carrie Fisher (actress)
Other spellings: **Carey, Cari, Cary**

Carrigan

Form of Irish Gaelic *Corragáin,* perhaps based on *corr,* "spear." A few
parents have used this as an alternative for **Caroline.**

Carson

For origin, see Carson in the boys list. Readers of classic American
literature have long admired the work of Carson McCullers

(1917–1967), most famous for her novel *The Heart Is a Lonely Hunter*. It is undoubtedly her fame that led many parents to think of Carson as an appropriate name for girls. It's been in the SSA top 1,000 list since 1992, though it only ranked 992nd in 2004.

Casey, Casie

From Gaelic *Cathasach*, "watchful." This traditionally male name became fashionable for girls in the 1970s, ranking among the top 100 names in the late 1980s. It's now begun to fall off for both genders, ranking 211th for girls in 2004, but it's maintaining its unisex status.
Variations: **Caci, Kaci, Kacie, Kasey**

Cassandra

Greek, uncertain meaning. Cassandra was the unfortunate daughter of Priam and Hecuba, the king and queen of Troy. The god Apollo was attracted to her, and she agreed to a liaison in exchange for the gift of prophecy. When she spurned him, he sought revenge by making sure that his gift would be useless; he caused her to be believed by no one. Cassandra foresaw the fall of Troy but could do nothing to prevent it. This name was popular with African-Americans in the 1970s but was taken up by other ethnic groups in the 1980s. Cassandra's popularity peaked in 1990 when it was one of the top 50 names. It still ranked 121st in 2004, when more than 3,000 girls were given the name.
Famous name: Cassandra Wilson (jazz singer and songwriter)
Nicknames: **Cass, Cassie, Sandi, Sandra, Sandy**
Variations: **Cassandre** (French), **Kassandra** (Greek)

Cassidy

Irish surname from Gaelic *Caiside*, derived from *cas*, "curly." American parents discovered Cassidy around 1980 as an alternative to names like **Cassandra** and **Chastity**. Cassidy entered the SSA top 1,000 list in 1981 and grew to a peak in 1999, when it was among the 75 most popular names for girls. It ranked 136th in 2004, when more than 2,700 girls were named Cassidy or **Kassidy.**

Cassie

Form of **Cassandra**. Cassie was often given as an independent name while Cassandra was popular in the late 1980s, but it's receding even faster than its parent name. It was only 664th on the 2004 SSA list.

Catalina

Spanish form of **Katherine.** Catalina has been rising in use and ranked 764th on the SSA list in 2004. Colombian actress Catalina Sandino Moreno received an Oscar nomination for her role in the 2004 film *Maria Full of Grace.*

Catherine

French form of **Katherine.** Until 1972 this was the most common spelling in the United States. St. Catherine of Siena was a 14th-century saint who campaigned for the pope's return to Rome from Avignon and the resurgence of a devout life for all Christians. Catherine II, empress of Russia, was the wife of Peter III. She became known as Catherine the Great and is famous for both her decadent personal life and her long, impressive reign. Today Catherine is the name of many prominent actresses, including Catherine Deneuve, Catherine Oxenberg, and Catherine Zeta-Jones. More than 3,000 American girls were given this spelling of the name in 2004.
Nicknames: **Cat, Cath, Cathie, Cathy, Catie**
Other spellings: **Catharine, Cathryn, Katharine, Kathryn**

Cecilia

Feminine form of **Cecil.** St. Cecilia was a third-century Christian who is the patron saint of music and the legendary inventor of the pipe organ. Chaucer tells her story in *The Canterbury Tales,* while William Wordsworth, Alexander Pope, and John Dryden wrote poems in her honor to celebrate music. Cecilia has been one of the most steadily used girls names over the last century. It's been inching upward since the 1970s; more than 1,500 girls received the name in 2004, ranking it 208th for the year.
Famous name: Cecilia Bartoli (opera singer)
Nicknames: **Cece, Cele, Celie, Cissie, Cissy, Sissie, Sissy**
Other spelling: **Cecelia**
Variations: **Cäcilia** (German), **Cécile** (French), **Cecily, Cecylia** (Polish), **Celia, Cicelle** (Hungarian), **Cicely, Kikilia** (Russian), **Sheila, Sidsel** (Danish), **Síle** (Irish), **Sileas** (Scots Gaelic), **Sissel** (Norwegian)

Celeste

Latin *caelestis,* "heavenly." Celeste was regularly used but never very fashionable for more than a century, but it has recently become

more popular. Perhaps it appeals to parents who like its meaning but are looking for something more subtle and sophisticated than **Heaven** or **Nevaeh**. More than 1,600 Celestes were born in 2004, ranking it 198th for the year.
Famous name: Celeste Holm (actress)
Variations: **Celesta, Celestina, Celestine**

Celestina

Form of **Celeste**. In the 19th century a "celestina" was a small hand-cranked organ, and the word is also used for a stop on large pipe organs that gives a flute-like sound. As such, it is a fitting name for Celestina Warbeck, the singing sorceress in the *Harry Potter* novels.

Celia

Latin *Caelia*, perhaps from *caelum*, "heaven"; or a form of **Cecilia**. Celia was fairly common in the 1890s. It's been decreasing ever since, but at a very slow rate. Exactly 400 girls were named Celia in the United States in 2004, ranking it 675th on the SSA list.
Famous name: Celia Cruz (salsa singer)
Variations: **Celie, Celina** (Polish), **Céline** (French), **Zelia**

Celine

Form of **Celia**. French-Canadian singer Celine Dion is undoubtedly responsible for the regular use of this name in the United States. Celine entered the SSA list in 1994, had a mild peak in 1998, and in 2004 ranked 796th, with 315 girls given the name.

Chamique

African-American creation blending sounds from names such as **Shaniqua, Tamika,** and **Dominique.**
Famous name: Chamique Holdsclaw (basketball player)

Chana

Hebrew "gracious, merciful." Like **Chaya,** this original Hebrew form of **Hannah** probably owes its place on the SSA top 1,000 list to its use by the Orthodox Jewish community. In 2004, 243 Chanas were born in the United States, ranking the name 970th.

Chanel

French *chenal*, "canal." This French surname became a first name for girls in honor of Gabrielle "Coco" Chanel, the famous Parisian fashion designer for whom Chanel No. 5 perfume was named. The name was fairly common in the early 1990s, especially with African-Americans, and spawned many respellings, such as **Chanelle, Chenelle, Shanel, Shanell, Shanelle,** and **Shonelle.** Today the name is quickly fading away.

Chantal

Old French *cantal,* "stone," a place name that became a first name for girls in honor of St. Jeanne de Chantal, a widowed baroness who founded the Visitation Order of nuns in 1610.
Variations: **Chantel, Shantal**

Chantel

American variation of **Chantal.** This name seems to have been created for the Chantels, a 1950s female rock group. The French word *chanteur,* "singer," may have influenced their choice of a name. Chantel was much more successful as a first name in the United States than Chantal. With all its varied spellings, Chantel was among the top 150 names of the early 1990s, but its use has since receded.
Other spellings: **Chantell, Chantelle, Shantel, Shantell, Shantelle, Shontel, Shontell, Shontelle**

Chardonnay

From the white wine, made from a green-skinned grape grown near the village of Chardonnay in France. The place name meant "place covered with thistles." Chardonnay has been used sporadically as a girls name in the United States, especially by African-Americans.

Charity

The original religious meaning of *charity* was much broader than just "giving money to the poor," encompassing all forms of kindliness and consideration for others, inspired by God's love. It was this biblical meaning that moved the Puritans to use the name in the 17th century. Charity was in regular use throughout the 19th century, but it vanished during the 1920s. Its reappearance on the SSA top 1,000 list in 1968 may be linked to the popular Broadway musical *Sweet Charity,* which opened in 1967 and was made into a film in 1969. After its revival, Charity swiftly rose to a peak in 1975, when it ranked 182nd on the SSA list. It has been slowly receding ever since. In 2004, 489 Charitys were born in the United States, ranking the name 572nd for the year.

Charlene

Modern feminine form of **Charles,** Old German "a man." Most
people pronounce this name with the "Sh-" sound as in **Charlotte,**
but some Southerners prefer the "Ch-" sound of Charles. Charlene
was fairly common in the 1940s and 1950s but is rare today.
Other spellings: **Charleen, Charline**
Variations: **Charlaine, Charlie, Sharlene**

Charlie

Form of **Charlene** or **Charlotte.** Charlie has been among the top
100 names for girls in England and Wales recently, but as yet it
appeals to few American parents.

Charlize

This is a new feminine form of **Charles** created in 1975 by the
parents of South African–born actress Charlize Theron, who was
named after her father. When she won the Best Actress Oscar for
her role in the 2003 film *Monster,* parents immediately noticed her
name. It entered the SSA top 1,000 list in 2004, when 429 girls
received it, ranking the name 625th that year.

Charlotte

Feminine form of **Charles.** Charlotte was probably invented in the
Savoy region of the French Alps and spread to the rest of Western
Europe after Princess Charlotte of Savoy wed King Louis XI of
France in the 15th century. Between 1908 and 1952, Charlotte was
among the top 100 names on the SSA list. Charlotte has been
among the top ten names in England and Wales since 1990, and
Americans began to rediscover it around 2000. In 2004 there were
almost 2,000 Charlottes born in the United States, ranking it 174th.
Famous name: Charlotte Bronte (writer)
Nicknames: **Charli, Charlie, Lotta, Lotti, Lottie, Lotty**
Other spelling: **Charlot**
Variations: **Carlota** (Spanish, Portuguese, and Romanian), **Carlotta**
(Italian), **Charlene, Charlotta** (Finnish), **Karlotta, Searlait**
(Irish Gaelic)

Chase

For origin, see Chase in the boys list. This usually male name popped
onto the SSA top 1,000 list for girls in 1996, undoubtedly because

Nicole Kidman played Dr. Chase Meridian in the 1995 film *Batman Forever*. It left the list in 1999 but snuck in again at 998th place in 2004, when 233 girls were given the name.

Chasity, Chastity

In 1969 entertainers Sonny Bono and Cher had a daughter and named her **Chastity,** the title of the first film Cher had appeared in. Two years later, when Sonny and Cher began their successful variety program on television, they often featured their daughter in the closing credits. Other parents adopted the name, and Chastity entered the SSA top 1,000 list in 1972 at 675th place. From the beginning, however, some parents, either through mishearing or deliberate alteration, named their daughters Chasity, which was the 748th most common name of 1972. By 1975, there were more girls named Chasity than Chastity, and the variant form has widened its lead over the years. Chastity left the SSA top 1,000 list after 1993, but in 2004 there were still 360 Chasitys born, ranking it 730th.

Chaya

Hebrew "life, living." This name, which has been on the SSA top 1,000 list continuously since 1988, is extremely popular in the Orthodox Jewish community. There were 323 Chayas born in the United States in 2004, ranking the name 783rd on the SSA list.

Chelsea

English place name, "landing place for chalk," now a neighborhood of greater London. The idea of using Chelsea as a girls name seems to have begun in Australia. The name entered the SSA top 1,000 list in 1969. This was the same year Joni Mitchell's song "Chelsea Morning" was released, though that might be coincidental. The name was rising slowly in use until Jane Fonda appeared as the character Chelsea in the 1981 film *On Golden Pond*. Chelsea then boomed, peaking in popularity in 1992, when it was 15th on the SSA list. In 2004 Chelsea was the 169th most popular name given to American girls.
Other spellings: **Chelsey, Chelsi, Chelsie**

Cher

Variation of **Cherie, Cherilyn,** or **Cheryl**. Singer and actress Cher created her name from her given name, Cherilyn, which is a modern blend of Cheryl and **Carolyn.**

Cherie

French *chere*, "cherished, beloved." This name was well used in the 1960s and 1970s but is rarely given to babies now.
Variations: **Cher, Chere, Cheri, Cheryl**

Cherry

Greek *kerasion*, "cherry tree or fruit," or a nickname for **Cheryl**. Cherry was first used as a girls name at the end of the 19th century, when other names from plants and flowers, such as **Fern**, Pansy, Poppy, and **Viola**, were invented. Its high period was in the 1940s and 1950s, when similar-sounding names like **Terry** and **Sherry** were popular.

Cheryl

This name seems to have been created around 1900 as a blend of **Cherry** or **Cherie** with the gem name **Beryl**. One of the first examples noted is the Broadway producer Cheryl Crawford (1902–1986), who cofounded the famous Group Theatre in 1931. It may be a coincidence, but 1931 was the year Cheryl first entered the SSA top 1,000 list. The name had an incredibly fast rise and was one of the top 50 names for American girls between 1944 and 1971. Many parents probably saw it as being a perfect "different but not too different" alternative for **Carol**. Cheryl left the SSA top 1,000 list in 1998 and is rare as a baby name today.
Famous names: Cheryl Ladd (actress)
                Cheryl Miller (basketball player and coach)
Nicknames: **Cher, Cherie, Cherry, Sherry**
Other spellings: **Cheryll, Sharyl, Sherryl, Sheryl, Sheryll**

Cheyenne

Name of an American Indian nation, originally a Siouan word meaning "people who talk differently," referring to the Algonquian language the Cheyenne spoke. The initial use of Cheyenne as a first name seems to have been for the television character Cheyenne Bodie, who was featured in a Western series called *Cheyenne* that ran from 1955 through 1963. Despite the character's masculine image, when those who had watched the program as children grew up, they named more daughters than sons Cheyenne. This is probably because the name sounds like "shy Anne" and is accented on the second syllable, which for most Americans implies femininity. Cheyenne rapidly became fashionable in the early 1990s, peaking among the top 50 names in 1997. Since then it's been falling, but it was still the 108th most popular name of 2004, with more than 3,300 born. Other spellings: **Cheyanne, Shianne, Shyann, Shyanne**

Chikako

Japanese "wise, fragrant child."

Chinue

Ibo (Nigeria) "God's own blessing."

Chloe

Greek *kloe,* "green, young plant." This New Testament name was popular in the 19th century. It vanished from the SSA top 1,000 list in 1944 but resurfaced in 1982, quickly becoming fashionable. In 2004 Chloe ranked 36th, when more than 8,600 girls were given the name, making it more popular than it had been in 150 years.
Famous name: Chloe Sevigny (actress)

Christian

Though usually thought of as a male name, Christian has also been given to girls since medieval times. There have been enough girls named Christian in the United States for the name to have been on the SSA top 1,000 list since 1966, peaking in 1992 when it ranked 280th. In 2004 it ranked 821st, with exactly 300 girls given the name.

Christiana

This feminine form of **Christian** has been used in English-speaking countries since John Bunyan used it as the name of the wife of the hero Christian in his 1684 *Pilgrim's Progress.* Christiana has been on the SSA top 1,000 list since 1989, but after a minor peak at 695th place in 1996, it has been drifting downward. It only ranked 936th in 2004, when 254 girls received the name.
Famous name: Christiana Drapkin (jazz singer)
Nickname: **Tiana**

Christiane

German form of **Christina.** Biologist Christiane Nüesslein-Volhard was cowinner of the 1995 Nobel Prize in medicine for her work on how genes control embryonic development.
Famous name: Christiane Amanpour (news correspondent)

Christie

Variation of **Christina.**
Famous name: Christie Brinkley (fashion model)
Other spellings: **Christy, Kristi, Kristie, Kristy**

Christina

Feminine form of **Christian.** The third-century martyr St. Christina reportedly was shot to death with arrows after angels helped her survive drowning. Christina has not been off the SSA top 1,000 list since 1880, though it only ranked around 400th in the 1930s. It shot up in popularity during the 1960s and was one of the top 25 names for girls between 1972 and 1990. It's now receding but was still the 84th most common name of 2004, with more than 4,000 born.
Famous names: Christina Aguilera (singer)
                 Christina Rossetti (poet)
Nicknames: **Chris, Chrissie, Chrissy, Christie, Crissie, Crissy, Kirstie** (Scottish), **Kirsty, Kris, Kristy, Tina**
Variations: **Christa, Christiana** (French), **Christiane** (German), **Cristina** (Spanish, Italian, and Portuguese), **Christine** (French), **Chrystyna** (Ukrainian), **Kerstin** (Swedish), **Kirsten** (Danish), **Kirstin** (Scottish), **Krista** (German, Czech, and Estonian), **Kristen, Kristin** (Norwegian), **Kristina** (Czech and Swedish), **Kristine** (Lithuanian and Latvian), **Krisztina** (Hungarian), **Krystyna** (Polish), **Stina** (Swedish and Norwegian)

Christine

French form of **Christina.** Christine was a top 50 name between 1946 and 1987, but by 2004 it had dropped to 324th place.
Famous name: Christine Lahti (actress)
Nickname: **Chris**
Other spelling: **Kristine**

Chudier

Nuer (southern Sudan) "don't worry." This name is given to both girls and boys by Sudanese refugee parents in the United States.

Ciara

This is one of the most varied names as to both origin and pronunciation. In Ireland, Ciara is the original Gaelic spelling of **Keira,** and there are Irish-American parents who have given daughters the name using that pronunciation. However, in 1973 Revlon introduced a perfume with the trade name Ciara, pronounced "see-ARE-uh." Some parents have used that pronunciation. Finally, many parents, especially in the African-American community, have used Ciara as an alternative spelling for **Sierra,** which is how the R&B singer Ciara pronounces the name. Ciara entered the SSA top 1,000 list in 1982 and peaked in 1995, when it was among the top 200 names on the list. In 2004, 950 girls were named Ciara, ranking it 291st.

Cicely

Variation of **Cecilia.**
Famous name: Cicely Tyson (actress)

Cindy

Form of **Cynthia** or **Lucinda.** Cindy is falling away more slowly than many other names fashionable in the 1950s and 1960s. There were still more than 1,000 Cindys born in 2004, ranking it 274th that year.
Famous names: Cindy Crawford (fashion model)
Cindy Sherman (photographer)
Other spellings: **Cinda, Cindi, Cindie, Cyndi, Cyndie, Cyndy**

Cinnamon

Ultimately from Semitic *qinnāmōn,* the name of the spice. Cinnamon was on the SSA top 1,000 list for one year, in 1969, probably because of Barbara Bain playing the character Cinnamon Carter on the original *Mission: Impossible* television series. Though it's never become a regularly used name, one or two Cinnamons are born in most states in the United States every year.

Citlali

Nahuatl (Aztec) "star." This ancient Native American name has been on the SSA top 1,000 list since 2001 and is part of the fashion for Aztec and Mayan names for girls in the Hispanic-American community. There were 245 Citlalis born in the United States in 2004.

Clair, Claire

French form of **Clara.** There was a minor fashion for Claire in the 1920s. Surprisingly, it began to grow again in the 1970s, perhaps because it was the number-one name in England during that decade.

In 2004 Claire ranked 100th in the United States, with more than 3,700 girls given the name. Claire seems to be a name that appeals to parents who like both simplicity and sophistication.
Famous name: Claire Danes (actress)
Other spelling: **Clare**

Clara

From the Latin *clarus,* "bright, clear, famous." This name appears to date to the 13th-century saint who founded an order of nuns who emulated the Franciscan brothers. Clara was hugely popular among the Victorians, being a top ten name of the 1880s. It fell off greatly in the 20th century, though it never quite disappeared. The name began to inch up again in use around 1980 and seems poised to become one of the next revivals from Victorian times. More than 1,000 Claras were born in the United States in 2004, ranking it 285th.
Famous name: Clara Barton (founder of the American Red Cross)
Variations: **Chiara** (Italian), **Claartje** (Dutch), **Clair, Claire** (French), **Clare** (English), **Clarina** (Dutch), **Clarinda, Clarine** (German), **Clarita, Clary, Klara** (Slavic, Germanic, and Baltic), **Klare** (Danish)

Clare

Original English form of **Clara.**
Famous name: Clare Boothe Luce (playwright and politician)

Clarice

French form of Latin *Claritia,* "fame."
Variations: **Clarisa** (Spanish), **Clarissa** (English)

Clarinda

Variation of **Clara** created in 1596 by English poet Edmund Spenser for a character in his poem *The Faerie Queene.* Clarinda was a popular name in Restoration comedies.

Clarissa

English form of **Clarice.** Clarissa is the title character of Samuel Richardson's popular 17th-century novel. The name was common in the United States in the early 19th century but then faded. It revived a bit in the 1980s and 1990s when similar names like **Carissa** were popular, but it seems to be fading again as **Clara** rises.
Other spelling: **Klarissa**

Claudia

Feminine form of **Claude.** Claudia was fairly common in the 1940s and 1950s. It then faded in most parts of the United States, but it has been kept alive by its popularity with Hispanic-Americans. More than 1,000 Claudias were born in 2004, ranking it 246th.
Famous name: Claudia Schiffer (fashion model)
Variations: **Claudette** (French), **Claudina** (Spanish), **Claudine** (French), **Gladys** (Welsh), **Klaudia** (German and Polish)

Clementine

Feminine form of **Clement.**

Cleo

Greek *kleios,* "praise, fame." There was a minor fashion for Cleo in the early 20th century. The name's association with Cleopatra gives it an air of exotic beauty and mystery. With **Chloe** and **Leo** both returning to frequent use, Cleo could be ripe for revival.
Famous name: Cleo Laine (jazz singer)
Variations: **Clea, Clio**

Clover

Old English *clafre,* name of the flowering plant. Clover is still a rare name, but it's arousing some interest among young parents today.

Coco

French "coconut." Coco became the nickname of the famous French fashion designer and entrepreneur Gabrielle "Coco" Chanel when, as a young woman, she got a job singing in a nightclub. One of her favorite songs was about a lost dog named Coco, and young men who frequented the nightclub started calling her Coco as a result. Coco has aroused a lot of comment as an unusual celebrity baby name ever since Courteney Cox and David Arquette bestowed it on their daughter in June 2004.

Colette

Form of **Nicole.**
Variations: **Coleta** (Spanish), **Collette, Cosette**

Colleen

Irish Gaelic *cailin,* "girl." This Irish-American creation was popularized in the 1920s by silent film star Colleen Moore. Colleen was not

used as a name in Ireland until about 1980, but it's been popular since the 1940s with Americans and Australians of Irish descent. Colleen peaked in the United States in the late 1960s when it was among the top 100 names, but in 2004 fewer than 400 Colleens were born in the United States, and it ranked 701st on the SSA list.
Famous names: Colleen Dewhurst (actress)
Colleen McCullough (author)
Other spellings: **Coleen, Colene, Colline**

Concetta

Italian from Latin *conceptio,* "conception," a reference to the Immaculate Conception of the Virgin Mary. Concetta was the original name of the singers Connie Francis and Connie Stevens.
Variations: **Concepción** (Spanish), **Conchita** (Spanish), **Connie**

Connie

Form of **Concetta, Constance,** or **Consuelo.** Connie was a top 50 name between 1945 and 1960, but it is rarely given today.
Famous name: Connie Chung (broadcast journalist)

Constance

Latin *Constantia,* "constancy." The name Constantia was used in imperial Roman families, and it spread throughout the empire. Constance was one of the top 100 names in the United States from 1946 to 1953, but more parents chose Connie than the original form.
Nicknames: **Connie, Conny**
Variations: **Constancia** (Spanish), **Constancy, Constanta** (Romanian), **Constantia, Constanza** (Italian)

Consuelo

Spanish "consolation," from Our Lady of Consolation, a title of the Virgin Mary. Consuelo is one traditional Spanish name that is rare today, even among Hispanic-Americans.
Variations: **Connie, Consolata** (Italian)

Cora

Probably created by American author James Fenimore Cooper for the heroine of his 1826 novel *The Last of the Mohicans,* possibly from Greek *kore,* "girl." Cora was one of the top 20 names given to American girls born in the mid-19th century. It almost vanished in the 1980s but like its sister **Clara** has lately begun to revive. In 2004 almost 700 Coras were born, ranking it 371st.

Variations: **Coralie, Coreen, Corene, Coretta, Cori, Koren**

Coral

Latin *corallium*, "coral," a gem name regularly used in the 19th century and given sporadically since.

Variation: **Coralie**

Corazon

Spanish "heart."

Cordelia

William Shakespeare created this name for the tragic heroine of his play *King Lear* by "Latinizing" *Cordeilla*, a name first found in the writings of 11th-century author Geoffrey of Monmouth. There is no agreement on that name's origin, but Cordelia has often been associated with Latin *cordis*, "of the heart." Cordelia was used moderately in the United States during the 19th century, but it has been very rare as a baby name since the 1930s.

Coretta

Variation of **Cora**.

Famous name: Coretta Scott King (civil rights activist)

Variation: **Corette**

Cori

Female form of **Corey** or form of **Cora, Corinna,** or **Cornelia**. There was a moderate fashion for Cori during the 1970s and 1980s, but it left the SSA top 1,000 list in 1999. The variety of spellings used, however, means that if they were added together Cori might still be on the list.

Other spellings: **Corey, Corrie, Cory, Kori**

Corinna

Greek *Korinna*, probably a form of *kore*, "girl." This name had some use in the 1960s and 1970s but may have had its greatest popularity in the 17th century, when the name had several literary references. The best known is probably Robert Herrick's "Corinna's Going A-Maying," a poem that celebrates living life to its fullest.

Variations: **Cori, Corina** (Spanish), **Corine, Corinne** (French)

Corinne

French form of **Corinna.** Corinne has been regularly used in the United States since the 19th century and is a good example of a name that's always present but never gets extremely popular. There were 345 Corinnes born in 2004, ranking it 747th on the SSA list.

Corliss

British surname, perhaps from Old English "cheerful."

Cornelia

Latin feminine form of *Cornelius,* a Roman clan name probably from *cornu,* "a horn." Cornelia was moderately common in the 19th century but has been barely used since the 1960s.
Nicknames: **Cori, Corrie, Cory, Nelie, Nelleke** (Dutch)
Variations: **Cornela, Cornelie** (French), **Cornelle**

Cosette

This rare variation of **Colette** is the name of the orphan adopted by Jean Valjean in *Les Misérables,* now best known through the musical based on the novel by Victor Hugo.

Cosima

Feminine form of Greek *Kosmas,* "order, beauty."

Courtney

Middle English *de Curtenay* from *Courtenay,* French place name, "short one's manor." Like **Ashley,** Courtney is an aristocratic British surname that first became a name for girls in the American South. A 1977 psychological study found that a woman named Courtney was expected to be a smart, upper-class, attractive, strong-willed, and creative leader. It's no wonder then that Courtney boomed during the 1980s and was one of the top 25 girls names of the 1990s. It's now receding quickly, however, and only ranked 127th in popularity for newborns in 2004.
Famous name: Courtney Love (singer and guitarist)
Other spellings: **Cortney, Cortnie, Courteney, Kortney, Kortnie, Kourtney**

Cristina

Spanish form of **Christina.** Television talk-show host Cristina Saralegui is a huge celebrity in the Hispanic-American community.

Crystal

Greek *krystalos,* "rock crystal, clear ice." Crystal was one of the most popular names of the 1970s and 1980s. Its popularity has often been attributed to the character Krystle Carrington, played by Linda Evans, on the television series *Dynasty,* but the program didn't debut until 1981, when the name had been popular for years and was already among the top 20 names for girls. It probably was simply discovered by parents looking for "different but not too different" alternatives for **Christine** and **Christina.** Though the name is fading today, there were still more than 3,000 baby girls named Crystal in 2004, ranking it 115th.

Famous name: Crystal Gayle (singer)

Variations: **Christal, Chrystal, Kristal, Krystle**

Cyan

"Blue-green," from Greek *kýan,* "dark blue."

Cybil, Cybill

Variations of **Sybil.** Actress Cybill Shepherd has stated that her parents chose the unusual spelling of her name to honor her two uncles, Cy and Bill.

Cyndi

Form of **Cindy;** nickname for **Cynthia** or **Lucinda.**

Famous name: Cyndi Lauper (singer)

Cynthia

Greek *Kynthia,* a title of Artemis, the moon goddess. The title was from Mount Kynthos, on the Aegean island of Delos where, according to legend, Artemis was born. Cynthia was regularly used in the 19th century in the United States. It receded in the early 20th century, began to rise slowly in the 1930s, and then skyrocketed in the 1940s to end up as one of the top ten names given to American girls born between 1954 and 1966. By 2004, it had fallen to 215th place. Cynthia is somewhat more popular with Hispanic-Americans than with other parents today.

Famous name: Cynthia Rowley (fashion designer)

Nicknames: **Cindi, Cindie, Cindy, Cyndi, Cyndie, Cyndy**

Variations: **Cinthia, Cintia** (Spanish), **Cinzia** (Italian), **Cynthie** (French), **Cyntia** (Polish)

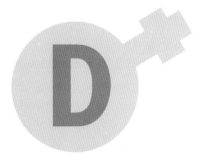

Dagmar

Danish, from Old Scandinavian *dag* [day] + *mar* [maid].

Daisy

Old English *daeges-eage,* "the day's eye," because the flower looks like the sun. Several literary heroines have this name, including Henry James's Daisy Miller; Daisy Buchanan, the girl pursued by Jay Gatsby in F. Scott Fitzgerald's *The Great Gatsby;* and the title character of *Driving Miss Daisy,* which won author Alfred Uhry the 1988 Pulitzer Prize. Daisy was one of the top 50 names for American girls in the 1880s. It receded until the 1980s, when it began to slowly rise in use again, and it is particularly popular with Hispanic-Americans today. More than 2,000 Daisys were born in the United States in 2004, ranking it 159th for the year.

Famous names: Daisy Fuentes (model and television host)

Daisy Lowe (founder of the Girl Scouts)

Other spellings: **Daisie, Daizy, Dazey**

Dakota

Name of a Native American nation. Dakota broke into the SSA top 1,000 list for girls in 1990, five years after its entry on the boys list. Until 2004 its use for girls paralleled that for boys, but now it seems to be increasing for girls while decreasing for boys. The rise of Dakota Fanning as a favorite child actress may finally be helping to shift the name to predominantly female status. More than 1,000 girls were named Dakota in 2004, ranking it 251st.

Dalia

Spanish form of **Dahlia,** the flower native to Mexico named after 18th-century Swedish botanist Anders Dahl. Dalia suddenly bloomed at 485th place on the SSA top 1,000 list in 1994, a very high initial entry. This was probably because of the character Dalia in the telenovela *Buscando el Paraíso* ("Looking for Paradise") played by Mexican actress Yolanda Andrade. The name has been receding since, and the 297 Dalias born in 2004 made the name 826th on the SSA list.

Damaris

Perhaps a form of Greek *Damalis,* "calf." Damaris is mentioned in the Bible as a woman converted to Christianity by St. Paul. Her name was used by the Puritans in the 17th century. Damaris became very rare but then developed some minor popularity in the 1990s, especially in the Hispanic-American community, where names ending in -*is* have been in vogue. There were 368 Damarises born in the United States in 2004, ranking it 715th on the SSA list.

Dana

Perhaps Old English "a dane." In Irish mythology, Dana or Danu is the mother of a race of demigods who ruled Ireland in a golden age. Dana has been more common for girls than boys since 1954. One of the top 100 girls names between 1963 and 1988, it dropped to 362nd place in 2004.
Famous name: Dana Delany (actress)

Dania

Latin form of Denmark, name of a Florida town; or a blend of **Daniele** and **Tanya**. Dania ranked 982nd on the SSA list in 2004. Other spelling: **Danya**

Danica

Form of *Danika,* a Slavic name meaning "morning star." There was a minor fashion for Danica during the 1980s, which was reinforced in the early 1990s by the appearance of actress Danica McKellar on *The Wonder Years,* but it left the SSA top 1,000 list after 1995.
Famous name: Danica Patrick (race car driver)

Daniela, Daniella

These Latinate feminine forms of **Daniel** are booming at the moment. They are especially popular with Hispanic- and Italian-Americans, but the recent general preference for girls names ending in -*a* is also a factor. More than 3,700 girls were given the name in 2004, ranking it 99th.
Famous name: Daniela Pestova (fashion model)

Daniele, Danielle

French feminine form of **Daniel,** Hebrew "God is my judge."
Danielle was the most common name for girls born in France
between 1944 and 1947. A few Americans began to use it in the
1940s, and then it soared during the 1970s to become one of the
top 25 names for girls between 1984 and 1995. Danielle has been
falling off slowly and ranked 106th in 2004.
Famous name: Danielle Steel (novelist)
Nicknames: **Dani, Danni, Dannie**
Variations: **Danelle, Danette, Daniela** (Spanish), **Daniella** (Estonian
and Italian), **Danila** (Serbian, Slovakian, and Slovenian),
Danita

Danna

Modern feminine form of **Dan.** Danna maintained a place in the
lower half of the SSA top 1,000 list from 1944 to 1978. It then
vanished, but it suddenly resurfaced in 2002. This may be because
the Hispanic-American community has taken up the name due to
Danna Paola, a wildly popular Mexican child actress and singer.
There were 421 Dannas born in the United States in 2004, ranking
it 638th on the SSA list.

Daphne

Greek "laurel tree." In Greek mythology, the nymph Daphne had
pledged herself to the goddess Artemis, and when the god Apollo
pursued Daphne, she prayed to Artemis to save her. The goddess
answered her request by transforming her into a laurel tree. The
American image that Daphne is a typically British name was reinforced by the character Daphne Moon (played by Jane Leeves)
on the long-running sitcom *Frasier.*
Famous name: Daphne du Maurier (English novelist)
Nickname: **Daffy**

Darci, Darcie, Darcy

French *d'Arcy,* "from Arcy," a place name perhaps meaning "Bear's
home"; or Irish Gaelic *O Dorchaidhe,* "dark one's descendant." This
formerly male name was moderately used for girls from 1950
through 1994, but it is now rare.
Famous name: Darci Kistler (ballerina)

Daria

Feminine form of **Darius,** Persian "maintaining goodness." This rare name snuck onto the SSA top 1,000 list from 1997 to 1999 while the cartoon series *Daria* was airing.

Darlene

Probably from Old English *deorling,* "darling." This name is a 20th-century creation. It was popular from the 1930s through the 1960s but is rarely given today.
Variations: **Darla, Darlyn**

Daryl

Feminine form of **Darryl.**
Famous name: Daryl Hannah (actress)

Dawn

Old English *dagian,* "daybreak." Aurora was the Roman goddess of dawn, and her name was occasionally used during the 19th century. The English translation of the goddess's name, Dawn, came into rare use as a given name sometime in the late 1800s, an early example being novelist Dawn Powell, born in 1896. But it wasn't until the 1950s that Dawn started to become popular. By 1971, Dawn was the 14th most popular name for girls. It then underwent a similarly spectacular decline and is rare for babies today.

Dayana

Usually a Hispanic respelling of **Diana,** though may occasionally be an independent invention with the first syllable pronounced as the word "day." Dayana has been independently rising on the SSA top 1,000 list since 2000. If it is counted separately from Diana, it ranked 630th on the SSA list in 2004.

Dayanara

In 1993, Dayanara Torres of Puerto Rico became the youngest woman ever to win the Miss Universe beauty pageant. She went on to have a film career in the Philippines and Puerto Rico and has remained one of the most widely known celebrities on her home island. Her name didn't enter the SSA top 1,000 list until 2003, after **Dayana** had paved the way, but it doubled in numbers in one year to rank 361st in 2004, with 700 girls given the name on the U.S. mainland. It's unknown how

Ms. Torres's parents chose her name, but it may simply be an alteration of **Deyanira** to give it a more fashionable sound.

Dayo

Yoruba (Nigeria) "joy arrives."

Deanna

Alteration of **Diana** or feminine form of **Dean**. When Canadian teenager Edna Durbin became a Hollywood star in 1936, she was renamed Deanna, and parents immediately began to name babies Deanna, too. It was one of the top 300 names for American girls until the year 2000, peaking at 88th place in 1969. There were still 661 Deannas born in 2004, ranking it 380th. The name is known to science fiction fans because of Deanna Troi, the psychological counselor played by Marina Sirtis on television's *Star Trek: The Next Generation*.

Debbie

Form of **Deborah**. Debbie occurred as an independent name only rarely before 1938. The name's quick rise thereafter is often attributed to actress Debbie Reynolds, but movie mogul Jack Warner didn't rename Mary Frances Reynolds as Debbie until 1948, taking the name from the infant daughter of a screenwriter friend. So instead of starting a baby name fashion, Debbie Reynolds was named after a baby. Of course her fame may have helped push the name to the top 25 status it achieved in the late 1950s. Debbie vanished from the SSA top 1,000 list after 1991.

Other spellings: **Debby, Debi**

Deborah

Hebrew "bee." The most famous biblical Deborah was a judge of Israel who called for an uprising against the Canaanites. The Song of Deborah, one of the oldest poems in the Bible, celebrates the victory of the Israelites. The Puritans frequently used this name, but it was barely present for the first three decades of the 20th century. In the 1930s it began to slowly increase, and then in the 1940s it became the most incredible success in American naming history. This is hidden by the fact that the spelling **Debra** was almost as popular as the original. Between 1952 and 1960, both Deborah and Debra were separately among the top ten names on the SSA list, and when their totals are added the name was the overwhelming first choice of the 1950s and the second most popular girls name of the 1960s. There doesn't seem to be any specific reason for Deborah's success; the careers of actresses Deborah Kerr and Debbie Reynolds both began after use of the name was already swiftly increasing. Of course this huge triumph was followed by the inevitable fall; in 2004 there were only 418 baby girls named Deborah in the United States, ranking it 645th on the SSA list.

Famous name: Deborah Norville (broadcast journalist)

Nicknames: **Deb, Debbie, Debby, Debi**

Other spellings: **Debora, Debra, Debrah**

Variations: **Deetsje** (Dutch), **Devora, Devorah, Dvora, Dvorah** (Israeli)

Debra

Alternate spelling of **Deborah**. Debra first appeared on the SSA list in 1934. Between 1956 and 1960, it was actually a bit more common than the traditional spelling. But it has fallen away even more quickly and left the SSA top 1,000 list in 1999.

Famous name: Debra Winger (actress)

Deirdre

Irish Gaelic *Derdriu*, possibly "chatterer." The heroine of an Irish legend, Deirdre fled with her lover to England, and when he was killed on their return, she died on his grave.

Other spellings: **Deidra, Deidre**

Deja

French *déjà*, "already," well known in English from the phrase "déjà vu," the illusion of having experienced something before that's actually happening for the first time. In 1987 R&B singers Starleana Young and Curt Jones formed the duo Deja, and their song "You and Me Tonight" was a number-two hit on the R&B charts that year. The group's name was also an immediate hit with African-American parents, who took it up as an alternative for **Asia** and quickly created respellings such as **Daja, Dasia, Dayzha,** and **Dejah.** The name seems to have gotten a boost in 1995 when Tyra Banks played the character Deja in the film *Higher Learning,* and it was one of the most popular names for African-American girls born in the late 1990s. It's receding today, but the two main spellings, Deja and Dasia, were given to 707 girls in 2004, ranking the name 359th in the United States.

Delaney

As an English surname, Norman French *Del Aunaie,* "from the alder grove"; as an Irish surname, from *Dubhshláine,* "black Slaney (River)." Delaney entered the SSA top 1,000 list in 1991 and has steadily increased since. No one person seems to have started the fashion for this name. Its ending is similar to **Brittany** and **Tiffany,** and it has the "long *a*" vowel sound that has been in vogue. Almost 2,000 Delaneys were born in 2004, ranking the name 171st for the year.

Delia

Greek "from Delos," a Mediterranean island.

Delight

This word has been used as a girls name on rare occasions since at least the 1940s.

Delilah

Biblical name of unknown meaning. The biblical Delilah robbed Samson of his power by cutting off his hair while he slept. It's not surprising that the name hasn't been very popular, but it has bounced in and out of the SSA top 1,000 list for 120 years. Delilah's ranking of 595th on that list in 2004 was one of its highest ever.
Other spelling: **Delila**
Variations: **Dalila, Lila, Lilah**

Della

Nickname for **Adela.**
Famous name: Della Reese (actress and R&B singer)

Delta

Greek; Delta is the fourth letter of the Greek alphabet.
Famous name: Delta Burke (actress)

Demi

Short form of *Demetria,* the feminine form of **Demetrius,** made famous by actress Demi Moore. Demi was in the SSA top 1,000 list between 1991 and 1998 but never rose higher than 612th place. In contrast, it was one of the top 100 names in Scotland and England during that period. This is probably because the name is normally pronounced to rhyme with Emmy in Britain, while Americans accent it on the second syllable, as Ms. Moore prefers.

Denali

Athabascan (Alaskan Native American) "the high one." This original name of Mt. McKinley, the highest peak in North America, is also the name of the national park that surrounds the mountain. It is given as a "nature name" to a few American girls every year.

Denise

Feminine form of **Dennis.** Denise was very popular in France in the 1920s, and it first turned up on the SSA top 1,000 list in the United States in 1926. Between 1950 and 1981 Denise was one of the top 100 American girls names, following the same trajectory as the male name Dennis about 15 years later. There were still almost 900 girls named Denise in the United States in 2004, ranking it 310th.
Famous name: Denise Austin (fitness expert)
Nicknames: **Deni, Denni**
Other spellings: **Denice, Denyce, Denyse**
Variations: **Dione, Dionisia** (Spanish and Italian), **Dionne**

Derartu

Oromifa (Ethiopia) "flower."

Desiree

French "desired one." This name originally expressed the parents' desire for a child, but in modern times it often implies that the bearer is "desirable" to men. Desiree peaked in use around 1983 but was still the 196th most popular name of 2004. The name especially appeals to blue-collar families.

Destiny

Middle English *destinee,* "fortune, fate," from Latin *destinata,* "established." This word was first used as a girls name in the United States around 1970. Some parents chose it with the idea that they were destined to have a daughter; perhaps others hope the name will ensure that their daughter is destined for great things. Destiny swiftly rose to great heights, peaking in 2001 as one of the top 25 names. Almost 7,500 Destinys were born in 2004, ranking the name 44th.
Other spellings: **Destany, Destinee, Destiney**

Devin, Devon

For the possible origins of this name, see Devin in the boys list. Although the trend is for Devon to be a somewhat more popular spelling for girls, both forms are regularly used for both sexes. These two spellings plus Devyn were, together, the 302nd most common name for girls in 2004.

Other spellings: **Devan, Deven, Devyn**

Deyanira

Spanish form of **Deianira,** perhaps Greek "destroyer of men." In Greek myth, Deianira was the second wife of Hercules. She was tricked by the dying centaur Nessus into giving Hercules a tunic dipped in Nessus's blood, which caused such excruciating pain that Hercules killed himself by fire. Deyanira has been regularly used in Latin America at a low level, though it only made the SSA top 1,000 list in the United States for one year, in 1993. It may be the base of the more recent Hispanic fashion **Dayanara.**

Diamond

Old French *diamant,* "diamond." This name was rare in the 19th century when other jewel names such as **Ruby** and **Pearl** were common, but it rapidly became fashionable with African-American parents in the 1990s. It's now just past its peak, but more than 1,000 Diamonds were born in 2004, ranking it 244th.

Diana

Greek *deus,* "god, divine," through Latin *dius.* Diana was the goddess of the hunt and the moon, the Roman counterpart of the Greek Artemis. Diana had minor use in the United States during the 19th century. During the 20th it enjoyed a slow, steady increase, becoming one of the top 100 names between 1942 and 1974. The name's recent popularity is linked to Diana, Princess of Wales. Diana increased in use by 70 percent after Charles and Di married in 1981, bouncing back into the top 100 names. It had begun to decrease again when Diana died in 1997; that led to another bounce of 30 percent, which was most evident in the Hispanic-American community. Hispanics often use the spelling Dayana to force Spanish speakers to use the English "eye" sound when pronouncing the name. More than 4,000 American girls were given the name in 2004, ranking it 89th for the year.

Famous name: Diana Ross (R&B singer)

Variations: **Dayana, Deanna, Di, Diane** (French), **Dianna, Kiana** (Hawaiian), **Tiana** (Cherokee)

Diane, Dianne

French variation of **Diana**. Diane became well known in the 16th century because of Diane de Poitiers, the famous mistress of Henry II of France. American parents only began to use it in the 20th century. Diane was one of the top 25 names during the 1940s and 1950s but has steadily fallen since. In 2004 it only ranked 904th on the SSA list.
Famous names: Diane Keaton (actress)
Diane Sawyer (journalist)
Other spellings: **Diahann, Dyan, Dyanne**

Dilys

Welsh "genuine, steadfast." This modern Welsh name has always been rare in the United States. In *Harry Potter and the Order of the Phoenix*, Dilys Derwent is described as one of the most celebrated of Hogwarts' former headmasters.

Dinah

Hebrew "judgment." In the Bible, Dinah was the beautiful daughter of Jacob and Leah. There was a minor fashion for Dinah in the 1940s and 1950s, but it's very rare today.
Famous name: Dinah Shore (singer)

Diya

Hindi "light." Diya is now one of the more popular girls names in the Hindu community in the United States. This is mostly because it fits in well with American names, but it's also due in part to the celebrity status of Bollywood actress and model Diya Mirza, who now spells her name "Dia" in the Roman alphabet. There were 279 Diyas born in the United States in 2004.

Dolly

Variation of **Dorothy**. Dolly was regularly used as an independent name until the 1940s, but it is almost never given to babies today.
Famous name: Dolly Parton (singer)
Nickname: **Doll**
Other spellings: **Dolley, Dollie**

Dolores

Latin *dolere*, "pain, sorrow." Virgen de los Dolores is a Spanish title for the Virgin Mary, and this name honors her. Dolores was amazingly popular in the 1920s and 1930s; if its variant spellings are added in, it was one of the top ten names of the era. Part of its success may have been due to the fame of silent film star Dolores Del Rio, but the name was already appealing to many parents in the United States before she arrived on the scene in 1925. It is the first example of a Spanish name becoming extremely common for non-Hispanic-American girls.

Variations: **Delores, Deloris, Dolorita, Doloroza** (Ukrainian and Hungarian), **Lola, Lolita**

Dominique

French feminine form of **Dominic.** Dominique became very popular in the African-American community right after Diahann Carroll began playing the part of Dominique Deveraux on the television series *Dynasty* in 1984. It stayed among the top 200 names in the United States until 1999, but in 2004 it had fallen to only 412th place, with 571 girls given the name. Perhaps the two most famous women with the name in recent years have been the American gymnasts Dominique Dawes and Dominique Moceanu, both Olympic gold medalists in 1996.

Donna

Italian form of Latin *domina,* "lady." This name sounds like a feminine version of **Don** or **Donald,** which helps explain why it was one of the top 20 names for American girls born between 1937 and 1966. Donna ranked 781st on the SSA list in 2004, with 325 born.

Famous names: Donna Karan (fashion designer)
Donna Summer (singer)

Variations: **Dona, Donella, Donnie**

Dora

Variation of **Dorothy.** Dora was fairly common as a name in its own right during the 19th century but was very rare by the 1990s. In literature, Dora is the wife of the title character in Charles Dickens's *David Copperfield.*

Nicknames: **Dori, Dorie, Dorrie, Dory**
Variations: **Doreen, Dorena, Dorette, Dorina**

Dorcas

Greek "gazelle." This New Testament name was used somewhat in the United States until the 1940s. It will be hard for it to revive, however, as long as the slang term "dork" (which appeared around 1967) stays in frequent use.

Doreen

Form of **Dora** or Irish Gaelic *Doireann,* "daughter of the fair hero." Doreen was a top ten name in Britain during the 1920s. It was never as common in the United States, though it was fashionable during the 1940s and 1950s. Today it is extremely rare as a baby name.
Other spellings: **Dorene, Dorine**

Doris

Greek "woman from Doris (central Greece)"; also the name of a mythological sea nymph. Doris was a top ten name between 1924 and 1934, but few parents choose it for their daughters today.
Famous name: Doris Day (actress)
Variation: **Doryda** (Polish)

Dorothea

Latin form of **Dorothy.** St. Dorothea was an early Christian martyr who refused to worship idols. Although Dorothea was a moderately common name around 1915, it has always been rarer than Dorothy, the traditional English form.
Famous names: Dorothea Dix (social reformer)
Dorothea Lange (photographer)

Dorothy

English feminine form of Greek *Dorotheus,* "gift of God." Dorothy was such a popular name in Shakespeare's time that its pet name **Doll** became the name for the children's toy. The name's second period of popularity began around 1900, the same year that L. Frank Baum chose Dorothy Gale as the name for his heroine in *The Wonderful Wizard of Oz.* Dorothy was a top ten name for American girls between 1904 and 1939; since then it's steadily declined. In 2004, there were only 281 Dorothys born, ranking it 859th on the SSA list. Dorothy C. Hodgkin won the 1964 Nobel Prize in chemistry for developing X-ray methods to determine biochemical structures.
Famous name: Dorothy Hamill (figure skater)
Nicknames: **Dee, Dodie, Doll, Dolly, Doro, Dot, Dottie**
Variations: **Darta** (Latvian), **Dora, Dorete** (Danish), **Dorla** (Czech), **Dorli** (Swiss), **Dorota** (Polish and Czech), **Dorotea**

(Italian, Spanish, Finnish, and Swedish), **Doroteya** (Russian), **Dorothea, Dorothée** (French), **Dorottya** (Hungarian), **Dorte** (Danish and Norwegian), **Dorthy, Dosia** (Polish), **Dosya** (Russian)

Dove

Old English *dūfe*, "diver." The name of this bird, a traditional symbol of peace, has shown up a few times as an American girls name in the last decade.

Drew

For origin, see Drew in the boys name list. The regular use of Drew as a girls name by American parents probably has to do with the fame of actress Drew Barrymore, though the ups and downs of the name don't quite parallel her career. Drew first entered the SSA top 1,000 list for girls in 1994, peaked at 613th place in 1999, and then fell away to 993rd in 2004, when only 234 girls received the name.

Drusilla

Latin *Drusus*, a Roman family name. This New Testament name has barely been used since the 19th century.

Dulce

Spanish form of *dulcis*, "sweet." This traditional name has been increasing in the Hispanic community recently. More than 600 Dulces were born in the United States in 2004, ranking it 385th.

Dusty

The idea of turning this former nickname into an official name for girls probably came from the career of English soul singer Dusty Spring-field, though its high point of use in the United States was from 1972 to 1981, after the high point of her career. In spite of its origin, the name has a Western cowgirl image for most Americans.

Dylan

For origin, see Dylan in the boys list. Like most predominantly male names, Dylan has also been given to girls. Dylan made the SSA top 1,000 list for girls in 1993 and 1994, and again starting in 2002. The latter entry may have something to do with Drew Barrymore playing Dylan Sanders in the 2000 film *Charlie's Angels*. In 2004, 615 American girls were named Dylan, ranking the name 391st.

Eartha

Old German *erde,* "earth, ground."
Famous name: Eartha Kitt (jazz singer)

Easter

Old English *eastre,* "spring."

Ebony

Middle English *hebeny* from Latin *ebenus,* "ebony wood." Ebony is a hard, durable wood from trees that grow in India and Sri Lanka. The most prized variety of this wood is a deep, lustrous black, so the word *ebony* has come to signify that color. Around 1970, African-American parents began to name their daughters Ebony. The name grew quickly in popularity; in the middle 1980s it was one of the top ten names given to African-American girls. There were 303 Ebonys born in the United States in 2004, ranking it 817th on the SSA list.
Famous name: Ebony Hoffman (basketball player)
Other spellings: **Ebeny, Ebonee, Eboni, Ebonie, Ebyni**

Ebun

Yoruba "gift."

Eden

Hebrew "pleasure," from the biblical Garden of Eden, though as an English surname Eden is a Celtic river name meaning "water." Regular use of Eden as a name may have been inspired by the character Eden Capwell on the soap opera *Santa Barbara.* Eden entered the SSA top 1,000 list in 1986 and has increased in use since. The 922 Edens born in the United States in 2004 ranked it 298th.

Edith

Old English *Eadgyth* from *ead* [riches, prosperity] and *gyth* [war]. St. Edith of Wilton, a tenth-century nun, was noted for her friendship with wild animals. Two Ediths were queens of England in the 11th century. The name was revived in Victorian times as part of that era's fascination with medieval chivalry, and Edith was one of the top 50 names for American girls from the 1870s until 1928. The name is now identified with the character Edith Bunker, played by Jean Stapleton, on the long-running television comedy *All in the Family*, and this may ensure that the lack of enthusiasm American parents have shown for this name since the 1940s will continue for another generation. The name hasn't completely vanished, however: Almost 400 Ediths were born in 2004, ranking it 681st on the SSA list.

Famous name: Edith Wharton (novelist)

Nicknames: **Eda, Ede, Edie, Eydi, Eydie**

Other spellings: **Edithe, Edyth, Edythe**

Edna

Hebrew *ednah,* "delight." Edna is the name of the wife of Tobit in the Book of Tobit, which is part of the Old Testament in Roman Catholic Bibles and of the Apocrypha in Protestant ones. The name became very popular in the United States in the 19th century because of Edna Earl, heroine of Augusta Evans Wilson's 1866 novel *St. Elmo*. The book remained a best seller for decades, and Edna was one of the top 25 names for girls between 1886 and 1919. Today, however, Edna is almost completely ignored by new parents.

Famous names: Edna Ferber (novelist)
Edna St. Vincent Millay (poet)

Edwina

Feminine form of **Edwin,** Old English "rich friend."

Effie

Form of Greek *Euphemia,* "well-spoken." Effie was traditionally popular in Scotland because it was used to Anglicize *Oighrig,* an ancient Gaelic name perhaps meaning "new freckled one." Effie was one of the top 100 names for girls in the United States in the late 19th century. It's been rare for 50 years, but with **Ellie** returning to popularity, it may start sounding good to modern parents again soon.

Eileen

Irish Gaelic *Eibhlin,* originally a form of **Evelyn,** although later also used as the Irish variation of **Helen.** Eileen was one of the 100 top

names for American girls born between 1920 and 1952. Today this traditionally Irish name is especially popular in the Hispanic-American community, usually with the spelling **Aileen.** Astronaut Eileen Collins was the first woman to pilot and command a Space Shuttle flight.
Famous name: Eileen Brennan (actress)
Other spellings: **Aileen, Ilene**

Ela, Elah

Hebrew "terebinth tree" or "goddess," a fairly common name in modern Israel.

Elaine

Old French form of **Helen.** Elaine was the wife of Sir Lancelot and the mother of Sir Galahad in Sir Thomas Malory's *Morte d'Arthur.* In *Idylls of the King,* poet Alfred, Lord Tennyson, introduced the name to a wide audience. Elaine was one of the top 50 names between 1936 and 1947, but by 2004 it had fallen to 657th place on the SSA list, with 410 girls given the name. Many modern Americans will identify the name with Elaine Benes, the character played by Julia Louis-Dreyfus on the 1990s television sitcom *Seinfeld.*
Famous name: Elaine May (film writer and director)
Other spellings: **Elain, Elane, Elayne**

Eleanor

Old Provencal *Alienor,* meaning uncertain; perhaps based on Greek *eleas,* "mercy," or Germanic *ali,* "foreign"; since medieval times, however, the name has often been used as a variation of **Helen.** Eleanor of Aquitaine, wife of Henry II, may have introduced the name to England. In the United States, First Lady Eleanor Roosevelt brought her own influence to the government and is considered one of the great humanitarians of the 20th century. Eleanor's greatest period of use in the United States was between 1911 and 1936, when it was among the 50 most popular names. Since 1990 Eleanor has slowly been growing in use again.
Nicknames: **Ella, Elle, Ellie, Elly, Nell, Nellie, Nelly, Nora, Norah**
Other spellings: **Eleanore, Elenore, Elinor, Elinore, Ellenor**
Variations: **Elenor** (Swedish), **Elenora** (Dutch), **Eleonora** (Italian, Polish, and Russian), **Eleonore** (French and German), **Elna** (Swedish and Norwegian), **Elnora, Lenora, Lenore, Leonor** (Spanish and Portuguese), **Leonora** (Italian)

Electra

Greek "amber." In Greek mythology, Electra was the daughter of Clytemnestra and Agamemnon. With her brother Orestes, she avenged the murder of their father. Eugene O'Neill used this myth as the basis for his trilogy of plays titled *Mourning Becomes Electra*.

Elena

Spanish, Italian, and Russian form of **Helen.** Elena is still quite common in the Hispanic-American community, and others are being attracted to it as an updated version of **Elaine.** More than 2,000 girls were named Elena or **Elaina** in 2004, making it the 161st most popular name that year.

Elfrida, Elfriede

Modern English and German forms of Old English *Ælfþryð*, "elf strength." In J. K. Rowling's *Quidditch Through the Ages,* Elfrida Clagg was the head of the Wizards' Council who, centuries ago, outlawed the use of live birds in quidditch. Austrian novelist and playwright Elfriede Jelinek won the 2004 Nobel Prize in literature.

Eliana

A name with two very different derivations: It can be the Spanish or Italian form of Latin *Aeliāna,* a saint's name ultimately from Greek *hēlios,* "sun," but it's also a modern Israeli name from Hebrew "my God has answered." In spite of the present fondness for **Elian** as a boys name in the Hispanic community, Eliana is now most popular with Jewish parents. It's been increasing fairly quickly since 1996. In 2004, almost 1,000 Elianas were born in the United States, ranking it 280th for the year.

Elisa

This Spanish or Italian short form of **Elizabeth** has never been hugely popular in the United States but is always in regular use. Almost 600 girls received the name in 2004, ranking it 403rd.

Elise

French form of **Elizabeth,** now frequently used in Germany and the United States. Elise's popularily has been growing for about 20 years. More than 1,800 girls received the name in 2004, ranking it 183rd. Other spelling: **Elyse**

Elissa

Phoenician name of Dido, the legendary queen who founded ancient Carthage; used in modern times as a form of **Elizabeth.** Other spelling: **Elyssa**

Eliza

This short form of **Elizabeth** has been used as an independent name since the 16th century. The most famous Eliza is Eliza Doolittle, the Cockney flower girl who is transformed into a lady in George Bernard Shaw's play *Pygmalion*. This story later became the basis for the Broadway musical *My Fair Lady*. Eliza briefly disappeared as an American baby name in the 1960s, but it has been slowly increasing since. Almost 1,000 Elizas were born in 2004, ranking the name 285th and making it more popular than it has been since 1917.

Elizabeth

Hebrew *Elisheba*, traditionally interpreted as "the Lord is an oath," although some modern scholars of ancient Hebrew believe "the Lord is good fortune" is a more accurate translation. The first biblical Elisheba was the wife of Aaron and the sister-in-law of Moses. But St. Elizabeth, the mother of John the Baptist, is better known. The most famous royal Elizabeth was the daughter of King Henry VIII of England and Anne Boleyn. Queen Elizabeth I gave her name to a golden age of English literature. Queen Elizabeth II is the current British monarch. Elizabeth has been the most consistently popular name in American history. During its lowest point, in the 1940s, it was never less than the 26th most popular name. Elizabeth maintains its huge popularity partly because it has so many pet forms, and the most common one of those changes across the generations: Elizabeths born in the 1930s were Bettys; those in the 1960s were Beths; and those in the 1990s are often Lizzies. With this variety of nicknames and a regal longer form, Elizabeth will be in style for many years to come.

Famous names: Elizabeth Arden (cosmetics entrepreneur)
Elizabeth Barrett Browning (English poet)
Elizabeth Cady Stanton (suffragist)
Elizabeth Dole (politician)
Elizabeth Taylor (actress)
Nicknames: **Bess, Bessie, Bessy, Bet, Beta, Beth, Bets, Betsy, Betta, Bette, Betty, Elsie, Libby, Liz, Liza, Lizzie, Lizzy**

Variations: **Babette** (French), **Bettina** (German), **Ealasaid** (Scots
Gaelic), **Eilis** (Irish Gaelic), **Eliisa** (Finnish), **Elisa** (Italian, Span-
ish, and Greek), **Elisabet** (Scandinavian), **Elisabeth** (French
and German), **Elisabetha** (Dutch), **Elisabetta** (Italian), **Elise**
(French), **Eliska** (Czech and Slovakian), **Elissa, Eliza, Eliza-
beta** (Latvian and Slovenian), **Elizaveta** (Russian and Bul-
garian), **Elli, Elsa** (Danish and German), **Elsbeth** (Swiss
German), **Elspeth** (Scottish), **Elza** (Bulgarian, Czech, and
Hungarian), **Elzbieta** (Polish), **Erzsebet** (Hungarian), **Ilsa, Ilse**
(German), **Ilze** (Latvian), **Isabel** (Spanish), **Liesl** (German),
Lillian, Lis (Scandinavian), **Lisa** (Italian and Scandinavian),
Lisbet (Swedish), **Lisbeth, Lise, Lisette, Lissette, Lizette**
(French), **Lizabeth, Lizette** (French), **Yelizaveta** (Russian)

Ella

Norman French form of Old German *ali*, "foreign"; or short form of
Eleanor. Ella was one of the top 25 names for American girls born in
the 1870s and 1880s. It then fell away and vanished during the 1980s.
Since 1990 Ella has made a triumphant return; parents looking for
"different but not too different" alternatives for **Emily** and **Emma**
have suddenly made it one of the fastest-growing names. In 2004
more than 8,000 American girls were named Ella, ranking it 40th, and
it will almost assuredly rise even further over the next decade.
Famous names: Ella Fitzgerald (jazz singer)
Ella Wheeler Wilcox (poet)

Elle

A short form of numerous names, including **Eleanor, Ellen,** and
Michelle. The first person to use this as a separate name was the
model Elle Macpherson (born Eleanor), who may have gotten the
idea from the fashion magazine *ELLE,* where photos of her
appeared in every issue for the first six years of her career in the
1980s. However, American parents didn't begin to routinely use Elle
as a birth certificate form until Reese Witherspoon starred as Elle
Woods in the 2001 film *Legally Blonde.* The name leapt onto the
SSA top 1,000 list in 612th place in 2002, and it increased 40 percent in two years to rank 405th in 2004, when 585 girls were given
the name. Elle's similarity to the presently "hot" name **Ella** is
undoubtedly another factor fueling its growth.

Ellen

English variation of **Helen.** Ellen was one of the top girls names for centuries and had a fashionable upswing in the 1940s and 1950s, especially in the northeastern United States. But it's fading today and in 2004 ranked below the top 400 names for the first time.
Famous names: Ellen Burstyn (actress)
　　　　　　　　Ellen DeGeneres (comedian and talk-show host)
　　　　　　　　Ellen Goodman (Pulitzer Prize–winning columnist)
Nicknames: **Elle, Ellie, Elly**
Other spellings: **Ellyn, Elyn**
Variations: **Elin** (Welsh and Swedish), **Elina, Ellette**

Ellie, Elly

Pet form of **Eleanor** or **Ellen.** Many Americans over the age of 40 have an unsophisticated rural image of this name from the old television sitcom *The Beverly Hillbillies.* They will be surprised to learn that Ellie was the number-two name for girls born in England and Wales in 2004 and that, like **Ella,** it's also booming as a baby name in the United States. Ellie returned to the SSA top 1,000 list for American baby girls in 1992 for the first time in more than 60 years, and in 2004 it ranked 190th, with nearly 1,800 Ellies born.

Elodie

French *Élodie,* form of Spanish *Elodia,* from Visigothic *ali* [foreign] + *od* [wealth]. St. Elodia was a ninth-century Spanish Christian martyr. Élodie was the top name for girls in France from 1988 to 1990.
Famous name: Elodie Lauten (composer)

Eloise

Modern French and English form of **Heloise.** There was a minor fashion for Eloise around 1920, but it is very rare in the United States today. For more than 50 years the image of this name has been shaped by Kay Thompson's children's books about the delightful young Eloise who lives at the Plaza Hotel in New York.
Variation: **Eloisa**

Elsa

Variation of **Elizabeth.**
Famous name: Elsa Schiaparelli (fashion designer)
Variations: **Else, Ilsa, Ilse**

Elsie

Variation of **Elizabeth,** originally a Scottish form, but extremely popular in the United States at the end of the 19th century. This name is rare today despite the success of the similar-sounding names **Kelsey** and **Chelsea.** But with **Ella** and **Ellie** having come back so strongly, in another decade or so **Elsa** and Elsie will probably sound good to young parents again.
Other spelling: **Elsy**

Elvira

Spanish form of Visigothic German *Alvera,* perhaps "noble guardian." Elvira was regularly used around 1910 but is rare today.

Emerence

Dutch and French form of *Emerentia,* name of an early Christian martyr in Rome, from Latin *ēmeréri,* "to earn, to merit." Emerence was regularly used in both Quebec and the Netherlands in the 19th century. It would make a good alternative for the very popular **Emma.**

Emerson

For the name's history, see Emerson in the boys list. Parents inspired by **Madison** have recently gotten the idea that Emerson would make a great "different but not too different" girls name. It ranked 905th on the SSA list in 2004, and the number of girls and boys given the name that year was essentially equal.

Emilia

This Latinate form of **Emily** has been ascending as parents search for variations. Since 1990 Emilia has tripled in use, ranking 390th in 2004.

Emily

English feminine form of *Aemilius,* an ancient Roman family name possibly from Latin *aemulus,* "rival." Emily was a rare name in England until the 18th century when the German Hanoverian dynasty began to use it as an English version of **Amelia,** a name that actually has a different origin. Emily was quite common in the early 19th century, but its use faded considerably after 1880, though it never fell out of the top 300 names for girls. In the late 1960s it began an incredible comeback that made it the number-one name in the United States by 1996, a status it maintained through 2004, when nearly 28,000

American Emilys were born. In 2003 and 2004 Emily was also the top name in England and Wales. Emily Bronte and Emily Dickinson give the name an intelligent literary image, while at the same time its -*ly* ending implies beauty and femininity. There's a good chance Emily will continue to be on top of the charts through 2010.

Nicknames: **Em, Emmi, Emmie, Emmy, Millie, Milly**
Other spellings: **Emely, Emilee, Emmalee**
Variations: **Emila** (Latvian and Ukrainian), **Emilia** (Spanish, Italian, and German), **Emilie** (French and Scandinavian), **Emilka** (Czech and Bulgarian), **Mila** (Serbo-Croatian and Czech), **Milka** (Slavic)

Emma

Old German "whole, universal." The first Queen Emma was the Norman wife of Ethelred II. Their marriage united parts of Britain with Normandy. After Ethelred died, Emma married his successor, Canute, becoming the only English queen to be married to two kings. Jane Austen's *Emma* is considered one of the finest novels in English literature. Emma Bovary is the tragic heroine of Gustave Flaubert's novel *Madame Bovary,* a classic in French literature. In the 19th century Emma became fashionable a generation after **Emily,** and it was a top ten name from 1870 until 1900. The fashion for Emily, combined with the celebrity of English actresses such as Emma Thompson and Emma Samms, began to revive interest in Emma in the United States during the late 1980s. Emma was the 172nd most popular name in 1989 and then reached second place behind Emily in 2003. In 2004 more than 21,000 American Emmas were born. Emma's popularity is widespread: It was the number-one girls name in 2004 in Ireland, Sweden, Denmark, and Norway.

Nicknames: **Em, Emmi, Emmie, Emmy**
Variation: **Ema** (Spanish, Bulgarian, Czech, and Lithuanian)

Emmanuelle

French feminine form of **Emmanuel.**

Emmeline

Norman French *Ameline.* Emmeline was introduced into England at the time of the Norman Conquest. Even then it was unclear whether the name was derived from **Amelia** or **Emma.** There was a minor vogue for Emmeline in the early 19th century while **Emily** was enjoying its first era of popularity, but despite today's renewed love for Emily and Emma, American parents have yet to rediscover Emmeline as an alternative.

Variations: **Emelina, Emeline** (French), **Emelyne, Emiline, Emmaline, Emmalyn**

Enid

Welsh, uncertain meaning, perhaps "pure." In the Arthurian romances, Enid was the saintly wife of Geraint. Although her fidelity was questioned, she passed every test of purity, and her husband came to regret his lack of faith in her virtue. There was a mild vogue for Enid in the 1920s, but it's almost extinct as a baby name today.

Eowyn

J.R.R. Tolkien probably created this name from the Old English words *éo*, "horse," and *wyn*, "joy" for the character of the princess of Rohan who disguises herself so she can fight as a warrior. Miranda Otto played her in the *Lord of the Rings* film trilogy. Several examples of this name being given to American girls have been recently noted.

Erica

Feminine form of **Eric,** possibly Old Norse "ever-ruler." Erica became common in the United States around 1970, about a decade after Eric had become a popular name for boys. It's probably no accident that Erica's rise began while *All My Children*'s Erica Kane, played by actress Susan Lucci, was becoming one of the most celebrated characters ever to appear on daytime television. Though Erica's fashion has begun to fade, it was still the 95th most popular name of 2004, when more than 3,800 girls received it.

Famous name: Erica Jong (writer)

Nicknames: **Ricki, Rickie, Rikki**

Other spellings: **Ericka, Erika** (Scandinavian), **Erykah**

Erin

Gaelic *Eireann*, perhaps "western island," a poetic name for Ireland. This is based on *Eriu*, the name of a legendary Irish goddess. Like **Colleen,** Erin is an example of an Irish word that is hardly ever used as a name in Ireland itself but became very popular in the United States. Erin was one of the top 25 names for girls born between

1976 and 1985, and though it's now receding, it was still 109th in 2004, when more than 3,300 girls were given the name.
Variations: **Erina, Eryn**

Erma

Variation of **Irma.**
Famous name: Erma Bombeck (humorist)

Ernestine

Feminine form of **Ernest.** Ernestine was moderately popular in the 1920s and 1930s, a generation after Ernest had hit its peak. The best-known Ernestine may be actress Lily Tomlin's comic character who comments from her switchboard on the ways of the world.

Esha

Sanskrit *Eśā,* "wish, aim, desire." This name seems to be becoming more popular with Hindu parents, partly because of Esha Deol, a star of Bollywood films.

Esmeralda

Spanish "emerald." Esmeralda has been booming in the Hispanic-American community recently. Part of this is related to a telenovela called *Esmeralda* that aired in 1997, with popular Mexican actress Leticia Calderon in the title role. Nearly 1,600 Esmeraldas were born in 2004, ranking it 202nd. Victor Hugo gave the name to the young woman who is adored by the hunchback of Notre Dame.

Esperanza

Spanish "hope." This traditional Spanish name ranked 750th on the SSA list in 2004, with 344 girls receiving it.

Essence

Though **Ebony** was probably not created as a girls name because of *Ebony* magazine, many African-Americans immediately think of the magazine when they hear the name. So after Ebony was established as a girls name, other parents got the idea that the name of the fashion magazine for African-American women, *Essence,* would make an elegant name for a daughter. Essence entered the SSA top 1,000 list in 1991, and though its vogue seems to have peaked in 1998, there were still 304 girls given the name in 2004, ranking it 815th on the SSA list.

Estefania

Spanish *Estefanía,* form of **Stephanie.** This traditional Spanish form
has been in the SSA top 1,000 list since 1991, though Hispanic-
Americans themselves now prefer Stephanie as a name for their
daughters. Estefania was 989th on the SSA list in 2004.

Estella

Latin or Italian form of **Estelle.** Though it hasn't broken into the SSA
top 1,000 list yet, this name is arousing a lot of interest now that
Stella has become voguish.

Estelle

French *estoile,* "star." Although this name was popular in the first half
of the 20th century, it is unusual today.
Famous name: Estelle Getty (actress)
Variations: **Estela** (Polish, Czech, and Spanish), **Estella** (Italian), **Estrela**
   (Portuguese), **Estrelita, Estrella** (Spanish), **Stella**

Esther

Possibly Persian *satarah,* "star, the planet Venus." Esther is one of two
feminine names used to title a book of the Bible, reflecting the great
honor given to the first Esther, a young Jewish slave who was made a
queen of Persia. Esther saved the Jews from the scourge of Haman,
an event that is remembered in the feast of Purim. In 1893 Esther
Cleveland became the only child of a U.S. president to be born in the
White House. Partly as a result, Esther was one of the top 50 names
for American girls born between 1893 and 1923, one of the few Old
Testament names to be fashionable then. Though the name has
declined in use since, it has plateaued at a level of about 1,000 girls
given the name every year since 1990. Esther ranked 275th in 2004.
Famous name: Esther Williams (swimmer and actress)
Nicknames: **Essie, Ettie, Etty**
Variations: **Esfir** (Russian), **Essi** (Finnish), **Ester** (Spanish), **Estera**
   (Polish, Czech, and Romanian), **Esteri** (Finnish), **Esterina**
   (Italian), **Eszter** (Hungarian), **Hester**

Estrella

Spanish form of **Estelle.** Estrella has recently grown more popular
with Hispanic parents. It entered the SSA top 1,000 list in 1997 and
in 2004 ranked 606th on that list, with 451 girls given the name.

Ethel

Old English *aethel,* "noble." Ethel was one of the top ten names of the 1890s but vanished about 30 years ago. Its popularity hasn't been helped by Ethel Mertz, seen regularly on *I Love Lucy* reruns. Famous name: Ethel Merman (singer and actress)

Etosha

Ovambo "place of dry water." The name of this famous national park in the southern African country of Namibia has recently been used as a girls name by some African-American parents.

Etta

Form of **Henrietta** or other names ending in *-etta.*
Famous name: Etta James (jazz singer)

Eudora

Greek "good gift," a modern name created from Greek elements.
Famous name: Eudora Welty (writer)

Eugenia, Eugenie

English and French feminine forms of **Eugene,** Greek "well born." Eugenia was fairly well used until the 1930s but is rare today. Eugenie is just as rare, in spite of its having been used to name Prince Andrew's younger daughter in 1990. Princess Eugenie was named after the wife of Napoleon III, Eugénie, empress of France. After her husband was deposed in 1870, she spent most of the rest of her life in England.
Nicknames: **Gena, Gene, Genia, Nia**
Variations: **Evgenia** (Russian), **Gina** (Italian)

Eunice

Greek *Eunike,* "good victory," from *eu* [good, well] + *nike* [victory]. In the Bible, Eunice was the mother of the apostle Timothy. Eunice was a fairly common name in the early 20th century but is rare today. Most of the few girls now being named Eunice are daughters of Korean immigrants; *Eun* is a common syllable in native Korean names.
Famous name: Eunice Kennedy Shriver (humanitarian)

Eustacia

Feminine form of Greek *Eustakhios,* "good grapes, fruitful." This name has never been popular, but its short form Stacy is well known.
Nicknames: **Stacey, Stacia, Stacie, Stacy**

Eva

Latin form of Hebrew *Chava*, "life." Eva was very popular in the 19th century and remained one of the top 100 names until 1934. As **Ava** boomed, Eva began to increase again around 1999. In 2004 more than 1,700 Evas were born in the United States, ranking it 195th, and it seems likely to rise further in the near future.

Famous names: Eva Longoria (actress)

Eva Marie Saint (actress)

Nicknames: **Evie, Evy**

Variations: **Ava, Eabha** (Irish Gaelic), **Eubh** (Scots Gaelic), **Eve** (English and French), **Evica** (Bulgarian), **Evita** (Spanish), **Ewa** (Polish), **Ieva** (Latvian and Lithuanian), **Zoe** (Greek)

Evangeline

Greek "messenger of good news."

Eve

English form of **Eva.** Eve was absent from the SSA top 1,000 list for more than a decade but returned in 1998 and has been growing along with Eva since, though almost four Evas were born for every Eve in 2004. Fans of classic films will associate this name with the scheming title character in *All About Eve.*

Famous name: Eve (rap singer and actress)

Evelyn

Modern English form of Norman French *Aveline,* a medieval name of unknown origin. In England this name was formerly used for boys, but today it is usually a girls name in all English-speaking countries. Evelyn was extremely popular in the early 20th century, being one of the top 25 names for girls until 1933. Though it greatly receded, Evelyn never totally disappeared like many other names of its era. It lowest point on the SSA top 1,000 list was 289th in 1987. Since then it has risen substantially again. More than 4,000 girls were named Evelyn in 2004, ranking it 91st that year. Hispanic-Americans are now especially fond of the name, but it's used by all ethnic groups.

Famous names: Evelyn Ashford (Olympic sprinter and gold medalist)

Evelyn Cisneros (ballerina)

Variations: **Aveline, Eileen** (Irish), **Eveleen, Evelina, Eveline**

Fabiola

Feminine diminutive form of Roman family name *Fabius,* from Latin *faba,* "bean." St. Fabiola lived in Rome in the fourth century and is said to have founded the first hospital as a retreat for pilgrims who became ill while visiting her city. Her name is regularly used by Hispanic-American parents today. There were 279 Fabiolas born in 2004, ranking the name 867th on the SSA list.

Fairuza

Farsi *Firūzah,* "turquoise."
Famous name: Fairuza Balk (actress)

Faith

Latin *fides,* "belief in God" or "trust," through Old French *feid.* The legendary St. Sophia's martyred daughters were Faith, Hope, and Charity, named for the three virtues. Faith was a common Puritan name, but it was rare during the 19th century. It had a long slow rise in use until about 1990, when it started to boom. More than 5,300 American girls were named Faith in 2004, ranking it 65th.
Famous names: Faith Ford (actress)
                Faith Hill (country singer)
Other spellings: **Fayth, Faythe**
Variations: **Fae, Fay, Faye**

Fallon

Irish Gaelic *Fallamhan,* "leader." This Irish surname became a first name for American girls because of the character Fallon Carrington on the television series *Dynasty.* In 1982 and 1983, it was one of the top 400 names for girls, but it left the SSA top 1,000 list after 1995.

Fannie, Fanny

Form of **Frances.** This nickname for Frances became an independent name in the 17th century. It was very common in the 19th century, but when "fanny" became a slang term for "buttocks" after World War I, it quickly vanished as a baby name.

Famous name: Fannie Flagg (comedienne and author)

Fantasia

The word, meaning "a musical composition with an irregular or fanciful form." Many modern Americans will identify this name with Walt Disney's classic 1940 animated film *Fantasia,* which illustrated works of classical music using Mickey Mouse and other cartoon characters. Fantasia has been used as a girls name in the United States on rare occasions at least since the film was released. The best-known bearer of the name today is Fantasia Barrino, winner of the 2004 season of television's *American Idol* contest.

Fante

(Ghana) "born on Friday."

Farrah

Perhaps a form of Arabic *Farah,* "joy, happiness"; the name of the wife of the late shah of Iran. However, the actress Farrah Fawcett has stated that her parents simply made up the name, so a blend of **Sarah** with the word *fair* may be the best explanation.

Fatima, Fatimah

Arabic "weaner, abstainer," a name implying both motherly care and chastity. Fatima is a common name in all Muslim communities because it was the name of the prophet Muhammad's favorite daughter, the mother of his only grandchildren. The name is also occasionally given by devout Roman Catholics in honor of the visions of the Virgin Mary that occurred at the village of Fatima in Portugal in 1917. Nearly 1,200 girls received the name in 2004, ranking it 247th for the year.

Variation: **Fatma**

Fawn

Middle French *faon,* "young deer," from Latin *feton,* "offspring." This rare "nature name" had a minor vogue around 1977.

Fay, Faye

Old French *faie,* "fairy"; also a variation of **Faith.** Both forms of this name were fairly common in the early 20th century. Today they're best known because of actresses Fay Wray and Faye Dunaway.

Fayola

Yoruba (Nigeria) "good fortune walks with honor."

February

Latin *Februarius,* "month of expiation." All the names of the months have been given to girls on occasion, but February is the most rare.

Feigel

Yiddish "bird." This name is commonly used by parents in Israel's Orthodox Jewish community.

Felicia

Feminine form of **Felix,** Latin "lucky, happy." Felicia had a long, slow rise for most of the 20th century, then briefly boomed during the 1970s and 1980s to become one of the top 100 names given to American girls. It was only 878th on the SSA top 1,000 list in 2004.
Variations: **Felia** (Dutch), **Felice, Felicie** (French), **Felicija** (Russian), **Feliksa** (Polish and Greek), **Felizia** (German), **Licia** (Hungarian), **Phylicia**

Felicity

English form of Latin *felicitas,* "good fortune." Though regularly used in Britain, Felicity was quite rare in the United States before the television program *Felicity,* starring Keri Russell in the title role, premiered in 1998. The name immediately jumped onto the SSA top 1,000 list and in 2004 ranked 710th.
Famous name: Felicity Huffman (actress)
Variations: **Felicata** (Russian), **Felicidad** (Spanish), **Felicita** (Italian, Czech, and Baltic), **Felicitas** (Dutch, German, Scandinavian, and Romanian), **Félicité** (French)

Fenella

Scottish form of Gaelic *Fionnguala,* "white shoulder."

Fern

Old English *fearn,* "fern." Fern peaked in 1916 and has been rare since 1961, but parents looking for "nature names" might consider it.

Fernanda

Feminine form of **Fernando.** Though Fernanda is much less common today than Fernando, it has enjoyed a minor boom lately. Almost 600 Fernandas were born in 2004, ranking it 408th that year.

Fesamay

Chamoru (Guam) "serious seedling."

Fidelia

Feminine form of Latin *fidelis,* "faithful." Fidelia was not uncommon in the United States during the early 19th century, but it has been practically nonexistent for more than a century now.

Finola

This is the Irish version of the same Gaelic name that becomes **Fenella** in Scotland.

Famous name: Finola Hughes (actress)

Fiona

Form of Scots Gaelic *fionn,* "white, fair." This name was invented by Scottish poet James Macpherson in the 18th century. In the 20th century, it became quite common in Scotland, England, and Australia. American parents have just begun to discover it, and it's rising quickly in use. In 2004 more than 950 Fionas were born in the United States, ranking it 289th for the year. Children will be likely to identify the name with the character of Princess Fiona from the *Shrek* animated films.

Famous name: Fiona Apple (singer and songwriter)

Flannery

Irish Gaelic *Flannabhra,* "red eyebrows."

Famous name: Flannery O'Connor (writer)

Flavia

Latin "golden yellow."

Flora

Latin *floris,* "flower." Flora was the Roman goddess of spring. Flora was common in the United States in the 19th century but is very rare today.

Variations: **Fiora, Fiorella** (Italian), **Fleur** (French), **Fleurette, Floora** (Estonian and Finnish), **Flor** (Spanish), **Flore** (French), **Florella, Florette, Floria, Florica** (Romanian), **Florinda, Florka** (Bulgarian), **Flower**

Florence

Latin *Florentia,* from *florens,* "flourishing, in the prime of life." This name is associated with Florence Nightingale, an English nurse who helped the wounded during the Crimean War. She was given the name Florence because she was born in the city of Florence, Italy. Between 1886 and 1904, Florence was one of the top ten names given to American girls, but it has practically vanished today.

Famous names: Florence Griffith Joyner (track athlete)
Florence Henderson (actress)

Nicknames: **Flo, Flori, Florrie, Florry, Floss, Flossie, Floy**

Variations: **Fiorenza** (Italian), **Florencia** (Spanish, Hungarian, and Dutch), **Florenta** (Romanian), **Florentia** (German and Finnish), **Florenza** (Italian)

Florida

Spanish "flowery," the name of the American state given to it in 1513 by Spanish explorer Ponce de Leon. This place name was fairly common as a girls name between 1870 and 1920.

Fonda

Origin unknown; perhaps a modern creation based on the word *fond,* "loving," from Middle English *fonned,* "foolish."

Frances

Feminine form of **Francis,** Latin "a Frenchman." The difference in spelling between the male and female forms of this name was not set until the 17th century. Frances was among the top 50 names for American girls born between 1875 and 1950, a very long run of popularity. The image of the name was enhanced by Frances Cleveland, wife of President Grover Cleveland. She was young and beautiful and was the first presidential spouse to be featured on her husband's campaign posters. In 2004, Frances had fallen to 639th place on the SSA list, with only 421 girls given the name.

Famous name: Frances McDormand (actress)

Nicknames: **Fannie, Fanny, Fran, Francie, Francy, Frankie, Franky, Frannie, Franny**

Variations: **Cecca** (Italian), **Fanchon** (French), **Francesca** (Italian), **Francine** (French), **Francisca** (Spanish), **Franciska** (Bulgarian, Danish, and Hungarian), **Franciszka** (Polish), **Francoise** (French), **Franka** (Russian and Norwegian), **Fransina** (Dutch), **Frantiska** (Czech and Greek), **Franuse** (Latvian), **Franzi, Franziska** (German), **Prane** (Lithuanian)

Francesca

Italian form of **Frances.** This name is now more popular in the U.S. Hispanic community than is **Francisca,** the Spanish form of Frances. The nearly 700 girls named Francesca in 2004 ranked it 363rd.

Francine

Variation of **Frances,** well used in the 1940s and 1950s.

Freda

French variation of **Frederika** or **Winifred.**
Other spellings: **Freida, Frieda**
Variation: **Frida** (Hungarian and Spanish)

Frederica, Fredricka

Feminine forms of **Frederick.**
Famous name: Fredricka Whitfield (television news anchor)
Variation: **Freda** (French)

Freya

Old Norse *Freyja,* name of the ancient Scandinavian goddess of love, fertility, and war, depicted as extremely beautiful and desirable. Freya has traditionally been a common name in the Shetland Islands north of Scotland, and recently its use has been booming in England and Wales. In 2004 Freya was among the top 50 names given to English and Welsh girls. As yet the name is practically unknown in the United States, but its similarity in sound to present American fashions like **Grace** and **Ava** would seem to indicate a bright future for Freya if and when American parents notice it.

Frida

This Spanish form of **Freda** is gaining popularity in the Hispanic-American community as Mexican artist Frida Kahlo (1907–1954) becomes a more celebrated cult figure. Salma Hayek produced and starred in the 2002 film based on Kahlo's life. There were 360 Fridas born in the United States in 2004, ranking it 731st on the SSA list.

Froma

Originally a short form of the German name *Frodemute,* from Old German root words meaning "intelligent" and "courage," Froma has also been used by Jewish families as a form of **Fruma,** a Yiddish name meaning "pious one."

Gabriela, Gabriella

Spanish, Polish, Italian, and Swedish form of **Gabrielle.** This name is
very popular in Latin America and in the U.S. Hispanic community. It
is now being used by other Americans as an alternative feminine
form for **Gabriel,** and Gabriella is part of the revival of Italian names.
The two spellings combined were given to more than 7,000 girls in
2004, ranking the name 49th that year. Chilean poet Gabriela Mistral
won the 1945 Nobel Prize in literature.
Famous name: Gabriela Sabatini (tennis player)

Gabrielle

French feminine form of **Gabriel,** Hebrew "man of God." This name
is not very popular in France, but it became fashionable in the
United States as Gabriel became more popular for boys. It's just
begun to recede a bit as **Gabriella** is now the more voguish form.
More than 4,300 Gabrielles were born in 2004, ranking the name
83rd for the year. The drawback to this pretty name is the nickname
Gabby, which has a negative connotation of "gossipy."
Famous name: Gabrielle Reese (beach volleyball player)
Nicknames: **Gabby, Gabie, Gaby**
Variations: **Gabra** (Czech), **Gabriela** (Spanish, Portuguese, and Polish),
Gabriele (German), **Gabriella** (Italian and Swedish),
Gabysia (Polish), **Gavraila** (Bulgarian), **Gavrina** (Romanian)

Gail

Form of **Abigail.** Gail was popular as an independent name from the
1940s through the 1960s in the United States, but it has disappeared
as present-day parents much prefer **Abby.**
Famous name: Gail Godwin (novelist)
Other spellings: **Gale, Gayle**
Variations: **Gayla, Gayleen**

Galatea

Greek, probably "milk-white." In Greek mythology, Galatea was a nymph whose beloved, Acis, was killed by a jealous Cyclops. She then turned Acis's blood into a river in Sicily. Galatea is also the name of a moon of the planet Neptune, discovered in 1989. In *Harry Potter and the Half-Blood Prince,* Galatea Merrythought is described as a former Defense of the Dark Arts professor at Hogwarts school.

Gali

Modern Hebrew "my ocean wave." In the 1980s, this was the most popular name for newborn girls in Israel.

Galilea

Feminine form of *Galileo,* Spanish and Italian form of Galilee, the region of northern Palestine where Jesus began his ministry. The place name is from a Hebrew word meaning "circuit." Galilea Montijo is a Mexican actress who hosts *Vida TV* ("Life Television"), one of the most popular family programs on Spanish-language television. The program began in 2001, and Galilea entered the SSA top 1,000 list in 2002. In 2004, 290 girls were given the name in the United States, ranking it 837th on the SSA list.

Garnet

Latin *granulum,* "granular, seedlike." This jewel name was mildly popular between 1890 and 1910.

Gaynor

(See **Guinevere.**)

Gazelle

Arabic "small antelope" or "gazelle."

Geena

Form of **Gena** or **Gina.**
Famous name: Geena Davis (actress)

Gemma

Italian *gemma,* "jewel, gem." In England in the mid-1980s, this became one of the top ten most popular names for girls. With **Emma** being such a big hit, and Italian-Americans now returning to Italian names, it's surprising that Gemma is still so rare in the United States.

Gena

Form of **Eugenia** or **Gina.**
Famous name: Gena Rowlands (actress)
Other spelling: **Geena**

Genesis

Name of the first book of the Bible, from Greek *génesis,* "origin." The sound similarity to **Jennifer** led parents to see Genesis as a good alternative, and it entered the SSA top 1,000 list in 1988. It has been particularly common in the Hispanic-American community, for whom names ending in *-is* have recently been fashionable. However, parents from other ethnic backgrounds use it, too. More than 1,800 girls in the United States were named Genesis in 2004, ranking the name 186th.

Geneva

French *Geneve,* possibly from Latin *janua,* "gateway." This Swiss place name has been used as a given name for more than 150 years, probably because some parents have seen it as an alternative form of **Genevieve.** It reached its peak around 1925 and is rare today, but perhaps parents attracted to **London** and **Paris** will revive it as another European city name for modern girls.

Genevieve

Probably a French form of *Genovefa,* Old German from *genos* [race of people] + *wefa* [woman]. St. Genevieve is the patron saint of Paris because she saved the city from an attack by Attila the Hun. Her name was one of the top 100 names for American girls born between 1909 and 1923. It's never gone completely out of fashion and lately seems to be slowly increasing. There were 744 Genevieves born in 2004, ranking it 343rd for the year.
Famous name: Geneviève Bujold (actress)
Nicknames: **Gen, Geni, Genni, Gennie, Genny, Jen, Jennie, Jenny**
Variations: **Genevie, Genna, Genovaite** (Lithuanian), **Genoveffa** (Italian), **Genoveva** (Spanish, Swedish, and German), **Jenovefa** (Czech and Greek)

Georgia

Form of **Georgiana;** name of the state. Georgia was popular in the late 19th century, and around 1990 it began to increase in use again. In 2004 more than 800 Georgias were born in the United States,

ranking it 321st. It is even more popular in England and Australia, where it's recently been among the top 50 names.
Famous name: Georgia O'Keeffe (painter)
Alternate spelling: **Jorja**

Georgiana

Feminine form of **George,** Greek "farmer." This name has hardly been used since the 1940s.
Nicknames: **Georgie, Gigi, Gina**
Variations: **Georgeanna, Georgeanne, Georgette** (French), **Georgia, Georgianna, Georgina, Georgine**

Georgina

Form of **Georgiana.** Although rare in the United States, Georgina was the most popular feminine version of **George** in Britain for two centuries. Though recently it's been eclipsed by **Georgia,** Georgina is still among the top 100 names in England.

Geraldine

Feminine form of **Gerald,** Old German "spear ruler." Geraldine was a top 50 name between 1928 and 1943 but is very rare today. Geraldine Ferraro was the first woman in U.S. history to be a vice-presidential candidate on a major party ticket.
Famous name: Geraldine Page (actress)
Nicknames: **Gerri, Gerrie, Gerry, Jeri, Jerri, Jerry**

Germaine

Feminine form of Late Latin *Germanus*, "brother."
Famous name: Germaine Greer (writer)

Gertrude

Old German *Gertrud* from *ger* [spear] + *trud* [strength]. In ancient Norse mythology, Gertrude was one of the goddesses who accompanied dead heroes to Valhalla. St. Gertrude of Nivelles is the patron saint of travelers, and St. Gertrude the Great was a mystic. The most famous fictional Gertrude is the mother of Hamlet in Shakespeare's play *Hamlet*. Gertrude was among the top 25 names for American girls in the late 19th century, being one of the medieval names that romantic Victorians revived. But it's been completely out of fashion for more than 50 years.

Famous names: Gertrude Elion (won 1988 Nobel Prize in medicine)
Gertrude Stein (writer)
Nicknames: **Gert, Gertie, Gerty, Truda, Trudi, Trudie, Trudy**

Gia

Short form of **Gianna** or of Italian names that end in -*gia,* such as *Remìgia,* from Latin "remedy." Along with Gianna, Italian-Americans have begun to revive this name, and it is also gaining interest because of its similarity to **Bria, Mia,** and **Tia.** Gia entered the SSA top 1,000 list in 2000 and ranked 753rd on that list in 2004.
Famous name: Gia Carangi (fashion model)

Gianna

Italian form of **Jane.** Gianna has been a chief beneficiary of the recent revival of Italian names in the Italian-American community. Nationally there were nearly 3,000 Giannas born in 2004, ranking it 126th for the year. But in New Jersey, with its large Italian-American population, Gianna was the 13th most common girls name of 2004.
Variations: **Gia, Giannina, Jeanna**

Gigi

Form of **Georgiana** or **Virginia.** The Lerner and Loewe musical *Gigi* was made into an Oscar-winning movie starring Leslie Caron in 1958. For eight years thereafter, enough girls were given Gigi as an official name for it to make the SSA top 1,000 list.

Gilda

Italian form of Old German *gild,* "sacrificed." In Verdi's opera *Rigoletto,* Gilda is Rigoletto's daughter.
Famous name: Gilda Radner (comedienne)

Gillian

Medieval English form of **Juliana.** This name was popular in the Middle Ages and enjoyed renewed popularity in Great Britain during the 1960s. It is starting to catch on in the United States, where **Jillian** is the preferred spelling. As a name for girls, Gillian is pronounced with a soft *g;* with a hard *g* it becomes a Scots Gaelic name for boys meaning "servant of St. John."
Famous name: Gillian Anderson (actress)
Variations: **Gill, Jill, Jillian, Jillie, Jilly**

Gina

Form of **Eugenia, Georgiana, Luigina,** or **Regina.** Americans began to use this name regularly around 1945, ten years before Italian actress Gina Lollobrigida became well known in the United States. Between 1963 and 1980, Gina was one of the top 100 names for girls. It's now fading away but was still the 448th most common name of 2004.
Famous name: Gina Gershon (actress)
Other spellings: **Geena, Gena**

Ginevra

This Italian form of **Guinevere** is reportedly the full given name of Ginny Weasley, Ron's younger sister in the *Harry Potter* novels.

Ginger

Latin *gingiber* from Greek *zingiberis,* "ginger spice"; also a variation of **Virginia.**
Famous name: Ginger Rogers (actress and dancer)

Giovanna

Italian form of **Jane.** Though not as popular as **Gianna,** Giovanna is also increasing in use and ranked 688th on the SSA list in 2004.
Famous name: Giovanna Garzoni (painter)

Giselle

French form of *Gisila,* Old German "pledge, hostage." *Giselle* is one of the most often performed ballets, with music composed by Adolphe Charles Adam. This traditionally French name is now especially popular in the United States with parents of Hispanic ancestry. It's booming in use; more than 2,300 Giselles were born in the United States in 2004, ranking it 153rd.
Famous name: Gisele Bündchen (fashion model)
Variations: **Gisela** (German, Dutch, Spanish, and Finnish), **Gisèle** (French), **Gisella** (Italian), **Gizela** (Polish)

Gladys

English form of Welsh *Gwladus,* meaning uncertain. This name may possibly be from an ancient Welsh word for "ruler," or it may simply be the Welsh form of **Claudia.** Gladys stormed out of Wales around 1890 and was one of the top 15 names for girls in both England and the United States by 1900. However, it was already falling out of

fashion again by 1930. It's probable that the vogue for Gladys was helped by the name's similarity to the flower name *gladiolus* (Latin "lily") and the common word *glad,* although there is no real etymological connection between the name and either of these words. Gladys is now extremely rare as a name for newborn girls.
Famous name: Gladys Knight (R&B singer)

Glenda

Probably a feminine form of **Glenn,** blending it with the sound of **Linda.** In Britain it is often interpreted as Welsh *glen* [clean, pure] + *da* [good]. In the United States, Glenda was fairly common in the 1940s, but it's rarely given today.
Famous name: Glenda Jackson (actress)

Glenn, Glenne

Celtic *gleann,* "wooded valley, glen." Despite the recent fame of actresses Glenn Close and Glenne Headly, this is still almost invariably a name for boys in the United States.

Gloria

Latin *gloria,* "glory." Gloria was a favorite name for American novelists writing in the 1890s, which seems to have started off its regular use as a baby name. This was greatly reinforced by the fame of actress Gloria Swanson, who began appearing in silent films in 1915. Gloria was one of the top 50 names for American girls born between 1923 and 1955. Although the name is much less popular today, it is still used regularly, especially by Hispanic-Americans. It ranked 346th in 2004, with more than 700 girls given the name.
Famous names: Gloria Estefan (pop singer)
Gloria Steinem (feminist writer)
Variations: **Glorea, Glori, Gloriana, Glorianna, Glory**

Glynis

Welsh "little valley."
Other spellings: **Glynnis, Glynys**

Golda

Yiddish and Old English "gold."
Famous name: Golda Meir (prime minister of Israel)
Variation: **Goldie**

Goldie

Form of **Golda.**

Famous name: Goldie Hawn (actress)

Grace

Latin *gratia,* "grace." In Greek mythology, the three Graces—Aglaia, Euphrosyne, and Thaleia—are associated with art and beauty. This name, however, appears to have been initiated by the Puritans, who used it to mean "favor and love of God." But Grace remained a common name after most other Puritan virtue names died out, which probably means that parents once again interpreted it as "beauty of form or movement." Grace was very popular in the late 19th century and only gradually declined in the 20th, reaching a low point in the late 1970s. It has since had a very strong comeback: More than 12,000 Graces were born in the United States in 2004, ranking it 20th, higher than it has been since at least 1908.

Famous name: Grace Kelly (actress and princess of Monaco)

Nicknames: **Gracie, Gracye**

Variations: **Gracia** (Spanish), **Graciela** (Spanish and Bulgarian), **Gratia** (German, Dutch, and Scandinavian), **Grazia, Graziella** (Italian)

Gracelyn

Modern creation combining **Grace** and **Lynn.** There are isolated examples of girls named Gracelyn going back to at least 1894 in both the United States and Australia, but it's only with the recent upsurge of Grace that Gracelyn finally made the SSA top 1,000 list for the first time in 2004, in 920th place.

Gracie

With **Grace**'s return to popularity, American parents began using this pet form as an official name again around 1997. Gracie has skyrocketed in use even faster than its parent name, rising to 130th place in 2004, with almost 3,000 girls given the name. It probably appeals to parents who think Grace sounds a bit formal for a baby.

Famous name: Gracie Allen (comedienne)

Graciela

This traditional Spanish form of **Grace** was used often enough in the Hispanic-American community to rank 863rd on the SSA list in 2004.

Grazia

Italian form of **Grace.** Sardinian novelist Grazia Deledda won the Nobel Prize for literature in 1926.

Greer

Scottish surname, form of **Gregory,** Greek "watchful." The general use of this last name as a first name for girls in the 20th century is due entirely to the fame of actress Greer Garson. Greer was her mother's maiden name.

Greta

Swedish variation of **Margaret.** Greta returned to the SSA top 1,000 list for girls in 1999 after a 16-year absence. It seems to be a name that the avant garde is starting to find "cool" again. There were 374 Gretas born in 2004, ranking it 704th on the SSA list.
Famous names: Greta Garbo (actress)
Greta Van Susteren (broadcast journalist)

Gretchen

Form of **Margaret.** This German diminutive for Margaret has become an independent name in Germany as well as the United States. There was a substantial upward spike in the use of Gretchen during the 1970s, but it has now retreated considerably. The name ranked 882nd on the SSA list in 2004.
Famous name: Gretchen Wilson (country singer)

Griselda

Old German *gris* [gray] + *hild* [battle]. This name was regularly used by Hispanic-Americans in the 1980s and 1990s, but now even they are abandoning it.
Variations: **Grizel** (Scottish), **Zelda**

Guadalupe

In Spain this is a place name originally from Arabic *wādī al-lubb,* "river of the wolf." It became a girls name because of the vision Juan Diego, a poor Mexican peasant, had in 1531 of the Virgin Mary on Tepeyac Hill near Mexico City. Calling herself Holy Mary of Guadalupe, she asked that a church be built on the hill. Many modern experts believe that "Guadalupe" was the closest Juan Diego could come in Spanish to some Aztec words that are now lost. Eventually his vision was accepted as a miracle by the Roman Catholic church, and Guadalupe came to be a popular name for girls in Mexico. In 2004, almost 1,200 American girls received the name, ranking it 241st.

Variations: **Lupe, Lupita**

Guinevere

Old French form of Welsh *Gwenhwyfar* from *gwen* [white, blessed] + *hwyfar* [soft, smooth]. In the Arthurian legend, Guinevere, the wife of King Arthur, falls in love with Sir Lancelot. Guinevere is very rare as a modern name, but its Cornish form, **Jennifer**, has been one of the most popular names for girls since the late 1960s.

Nicknames: **Guin, Gwynne**

Variations: **Gaynor, Ginebra** (Spanish), **Ginevra** (Italian), **Guenevere, Gwenore, Jennifer** (Cornish), **Vanora** (Scottish)

Gwen

Form of **Gwendolyn,** often used as an independent name in the 1950s and 1960s.

Famous name: Gwen Stefani (rock singer)

Gwendolyn

Welsh *Gwendolen* from *gwen* [white, fair, holy] + *dolen* [link, ring, bow]. This name was popular with some African-American parents during the 1950s and 1960s because of admiration for poet Gwendolyn Brooks. In 1950, she was the first African-American poet to win a Pulitzer Prize. Gwendolyn has recently had a slight revival; 467 were born in 2004, ranking the name 592nd on the SSA list.

Nickname: **Gwen**

Variations: **Guendolina** (Spanish), **Gvendolina** (Czech), **Gwenda, Gwendalina** (Polish), **Gwendolen, Gwendoline** (French)

Gwyneth

Experts disagree as to whether this is an alteration of the name of the ancient province of Gwynedd in northwestern Wales, or of the Welsh word *gwynaeth,* "bliss." It was not used as a girls name in Wales before the 19th century, originally popularized by Annie Harriet, the Welsh writer known by her pen name, Gwyneth Vaughan (1852–1910). Gwyneth crept onto the SSA top 1,000 list in 2004 at 960th place when 245 American girls were given the name, undoubtedly due to the influence of actress Gwyneth Paltrow.

Hadley

English place name and surname, "heather clearing." Ernest Hemingway's first wife, Elizabeth Hadley Richardson, went by her middle name and is well known to literary scholars. In the 1990s, the name's similarity to **Hailey** received some attention from scriptwriters on several minor films and movies, and parents began to use Hadley enough that it entered the SSA top 1,000 list in 1998. In 2004 it had risen to 689th place on the SSA list, with 390 girls given the name.

Hailey, Haley, Hayley

Old English *Hayley,* "hay clearing," a British place name and surname; in the 19th century, also a rare pet form of **Mahala.** The modern fashion may be related to the fame of actress Hayley Mills, though her name didn't rise in use until her childhood fans grew old enough to become parents themselves. Haley was originally the more popular American spelling, but since 2001 Hailey has been the favorite. With all spellings combined, there were more than 19,000 Haileys born in 2004, making it the fourth most popular name for girls. The variety of spellings used masks this on many popularity charts. Other spellings: **Hailee, Hailie, Haleigh, Halie, Haylee, Haylie**

Halle, Hallie

Form of **Harriet;** Hallie developed as a nickname for Harriet in the same way that **Hal** evolved as a nickname for **Harry.** This 19th-century name began to return to regular use in the late 1980s. In 2002 Halle Berry won an Oscar, and her formerly unusual spelling became the most common for American girls. Nearly 1,500 babies were named Halle or Hallie in 2004, ranking it 219th.

Hallel

Hebrew "song of praise." Formerly a male name, Hallel is now a popular name for girls born in Israel.

Hannah

Hebrew "the Lord has favored me." In the Bible, Hannah was the mother of the prophet Samuel. This name was common at the start of the 19th century but became rare by the 20th. In the 1970s Hannah rapidly returned to popularity in both England and the United States. By 1995, it was one of the top ten names for girls. Hannah was fifth on the SSA list in 2004, with more than 17,000 born.

Famous names: Hannah Hoch (artist)

Hannah Storm (television journalist)

Other spellings: **Hana, Hanna**

Variations: **Anna, Hanne** (Scandinavian and German), **Hannele** (German), **Hannie, Hanny**

Harley

Old English "hares' glade." Stumbling over her roommate's motorcycle, aspiring actress Susan Kozak decided that Harley Jane Kozak would be a perfect stage name. In 1983 she got a job playing Annabelle Reardon on the soap opera *Guiding Light*. She left the show in 1985, and the show's writers created the character Harley Davidson Cooper in 1987. Harley entered the SSA top 1,000 list in 1991 and has been one of the top 400 names for girls in the United States since 1993. In 2004, 869 girls received the name, ranking it 311th.

Harmony

Greek *harmonia*, "framework, agreement." The modern musical meaning of the word is probably more important in its use as a girls name. Harmony was first regularly used from 1975 to 1984. It left the SSA top 1,000 list but returned in 1997 and has been increasing in use. In 2004, 476 girls received the name, ranking it 453rd.

Harper

English surname, "harp player." Harper Lee won the Pulitzer Prize in 1961 for her classic novel *To Kill a Mockingbird*. But it wasn't until 2004, with the modern search for more unusual names and the prominence of other surnames starting with *H-* for girls, that Harper finally landed on the SSA list, in 889th place.

Harriet

Form of **Henrietta** created in 17th-century England. Harriet was a name of choice in the 18th and 19th centuries, but by the time the

television series *The Adventures of Ozzie and Harriet* began in 1952 it was falling rapidly, and it left the SSA top 1,000 list in 1971. Harriet has now returned to the top 100 names for girls in England and Wales, but so far American parents continue to ignore it.
Famous names: Harriet Beecher Stowe (author)
Harriet Tubman (civil rights activist)
Nicknames: **Halle, Hallie, Hattie, Hatty**

Hasna

Arabic *Hasnā'*, "beautiful."

Havana

Spanish *La Habana*. The origin of the name of the capital city of Cuba is disputed; some think it is based on the English word **Haven;** others think the town is named after Habaguanex, a Native American chieftain, or is a corruption of the word **Savannah.** In any event, Havana's similarity in sound to Savannah is undoubtedly what has inspired several parents to give the name to their daughters lately, often respelling it as **Havanna** or **Havannah.**

Haven

The word meaning "harbor" or "safe refuge." By blending the sounds of **Heaven** and **Hayden,** along with its positive meaning, Haven has become a cool new name for girls. Haven's been on the SSA list since 1996; in 2004 it was bestowed upon 404 girls, ranking it 670th.

Hayden

For origin, see Hayden in the boys list. Hayden's similarity in sound to **Hailey** is probably what gave parents and screenwriters the idea in the 1990s to use it as a girls name. It entered the SSA top 1,000 list in 1997 and in 2004 ranked 450th, with 483 girls given the name. That year there were still 11 boys named Hayden for every girl.

Hazel

Old English *haesel*, "hazel tree." Many Americans over the age of 45 were shocked when Julia Roberts named her daughter Hazel in November 2004. Not only do they think the name sounds elderly, but they're reminded of the cartoon series *Hazel* and its spin-off television show, in which actress Shirley Booth played an outspoken maid. But to adventurous parents today, Hazel sounds like the perfect cool "retro" name, a great alternative for the overly popular

Hailey. Hazel has been back in the SSA top 1,000 list since 1997 and increased every year since. There were 399 Hazels born in the United States in 2004, ranking it 676th on the SSA list.

Heather

Middle English *hathir,* "heather." This flower name first became popular in England in the 1950s. Heather became one of the top ten names for American girls born between 1972 and 1987. But by 2004 Heather ranked only 230th, with about 1,300 girls given the name that year.
Famous name: Heather Locklear (actress)

Heaven

One of the first prominent examples of this name is the title charac-ter of V. C. Andrews's 1985 novel *Heaven,* which seems to have been especially popular with teenage girls. Heaven entered the SSA top 1,000 list in 1990 and has risen steadily ever since. In 2004, almost 1,200 girls were given the name, ranking it 242nd.

Heidi

German form of **Adelaide.** The cheerful Swiss girl in Johanna Spyri's *Heidi* is responsible for the Americanization of this German name. It first appeared on the SSA top 1,000 list in 1939, two years after Shirley Temple starred in a film version of *Heidi.* The name's period of greatest use, however, was the 1970s, when it was one of the 100 most common names for American girls. More than 1,100 Heidis were born in 2004, ranking the name 257th for the year.
Famous name: Heidi Klum (fashion model)

Helen

Greek *Helene,* perhaps "bright, sunbeam." The legend of the beautiful Helen of Troy has led parents to choose this name for their daughters for thousands of years. In Homer's *Iliad,* Helen was the wife of Men-elaus, the king of Sparta. She was abducted by Paris, the son of the king of Troy, which began the Trojan War. Helen was "the face that launched a thousand ships." Helens also appear in Christopher Mar-lowe's *Dr. Faustus* and in Shakespeare's *A Midsummer Night's Dream* and *All's Well That Ends Well.* Between 1900 and 1920, Helen was second only to **Mary** as a popular name for American girls. More than 800 Helens were born in the United States in 2004, ranking it 316th.

Famous names: Helen Frankenthaler (painter)
Helen Hunt (actress)
Helen Keller (author and educator)
Variations: **Eileen** (Irish), **Elaine, Eleanor, Elena** (Italian, Spanish, Portuguese, Baltic, and Russian), **Eleni** (Greek), **Elin** (Scandinavian), **Elina** (Finnish), **Ellen, Helaine, Helena** (Latin), **Helene** (French, Latvian, and German), **Helenka** (Czech), **Ileana** (Romanian), **Ilona** (Hungarian), **Jelena** (Croatian and Slovenian), **Lena** (German, Dutch, and Scandinavian), **Lenka** (Slavic), **Lenuta** (Romanian), **Nell, Nellie, Olena** (Ukrainian), **Yelena** (Russian)

Helena

Latin form of **Helen.** St. Helena was the mother of Constantine the Great, the first Christian Roman emperor. Helena has been on the upswing lately and may soon surpass Helen in the United States. There were 505 Helenas born in 2004, ranking it 436th.

Helga

Old Norse *heilagr,* "prosperous, blessed."
Variations: **Elga** (Danish, Latvian, and Greek), **Ola** (Serbian and Slovenian), **Olga** (Russian, Polish, Spanish, Portuguese, and Italian), **Ollo** (Estonian)

Heloise

Origin unclear; perhaps a French form of Old German *Helewidis* from *haila* [healthy] + *vid* [wide].
Variations: **Eloisa, Eloise**

Henrietta

Feminine form of **Henry,** made famous by Henrietta Maria, wife of King Charles I of England. Henrietta was common in the 18th century but probably sounds old-fashioned to most Americans today.
Nicknames: **Etta, Ettie, Etty, Hettie, Hetty**
Variations: **Enrica** (Italian), **Enriqueta** (Spanish), **Harriet, Henriette** (French)

Hera

Greek "lady." In Greek mythology, Hera was the wife of Zeus and a powerful goddess in her own right.

Hermia

Latin feminine form of Greek *Hermes*, name of the god who served as Zeus's messenger.
Variation: **Hermione**

Hermione

Variation of **Hermia**. There are two legendary Hermiones: the daughter of Mars and Venus, who was turned into a serpent, and the daughter of Helen of Troy and Menelaus. Of course the best-known example today is Harry Potter's friend, Hermione Granger.

Hester

Variation of **Esther**. In Nathaniel Hawthorne's *The Scarlet Letter*, Hester Prynne was forced by her Puritan community to wear a badge of adultery. She is still the most famous bearer of this name.

Hestia

Name of the Greek goddess of the hearth. In the *Harry Potter* novels, the witch Hestia Jones is a member of Harry's advanced guard.
Variation: **Vesta** (Latin)

Hilary, Hillary

Latin *Hilaria*, form of *hilaris*, "cheerful." In medieval times, this was considered a male name, but it was revived in England around 1890 as a female form. Hilary was popular in Britain during the 1950s and 1960s. In the United States, Hilary began to be used regularly around 1960. The name grew more popular, and its combined spellings were among the top 100 names given to American girls in 1992. But with the arrival of Hillary Rodham Clinton as first lady, the name plummeted in use. Now that some of the Hilarys who were born in the 1970s and 1980s are becoming famous, such as actresses Hilary Swank and Hilary Duff, Hillary Clinton will not dominate its image, and more parents may consider it again. But that may partially depend on Hillary Clinton's political future. The 308 Hillarys born in 2004 ranked the name 805th on the SSA list.

Hilda

Latin form of Germanic *hild*, "battle." This name was popular around 1900 but is rarely given today.
Variations: **Hilde** (Norwegian and German), **Ildiko** (Hungarian)

Hina

Hawaiian goddess of the moon, in legend said to be an overworked woman who escapes her cruel husband by climbing a rainbow to her new home in the moon.

Holly

Old English *holegn,* "holly." Holly used to be a popular name for girls born around Christmas, but since it was one of the top 100 names for girls born between 1969 and 1992, it's clearly given to girls born at all times of the year. Holly is now receding, but there were still more than 1,000 girls given the name in 2004, ranking it 268th.
Famous name: Holly Hunter (actress)
Other spellings: **Holley, Hollie**

Honesty

The present fashion for names like **Destiny** and **Serenity** has recently inspired a few parents to bestow this name on their daughters.

Honor

Latin "honorable."
Variations: **Honora** (Irish), **Honoria, Nora, Norah**

Hope

Old English *hopian,* "hope." The Puritans liked to give their children names that they should live up to, and so they used Hope frequently in 17th-century England and America. It's been used as a name in the United States since, peaking in the 1970s, receding in the 1980s, and growing again since 1994. Hope and Faith were the most popular pair of names for female twins born in the United States in 2004.

Hortense

French feminine form of Latin *Hortensius,* a Roman family name, possibly meaning "gardener."

Hunter

This name has been on the SSA top 1,000 for girls since 1993 and is probably related to the career of actress Hunter Tylo, who was starring on the soap *The Bold and the Beautiful* at the time. It peaked for girls in 1998 at 304th place and is now waning, ranking 740th in 2004.

Hyacinth

Greek "blue larkspur." This flower name is very unusual.

Iantha, Ianthe
Greek "violet."

Ida
Old German *id,* "work, labor." The Normans brought this name with them to the British Isles when they invaded in 1066. Ida was one of the medieval names romantic Victorians loved. It was popularized through the 1849 poem "The Princess" by Alfred, Lord Tennyson. Ida was one of the top ten girls names of the 1870s and 1880s. It's almost never given today, but with **Ava** and **Ada** being revived, it's an excellent bet that Ida will be one of the next Victorian names to catch the eye of creative young parents.

Famous names: Ida Lupino (actress)
       Ida B. Wells (civil rights activist)

Idalia
From a title of Aphrodite, the Greek goddess of love. This is a form of *Idalion,* a town where there was an important temple of the goddess. The town's name is legendarily explained as being a contraction of the Greek phrase *eidon helios,* "I see the sun."

Iesha
American form of **Aisha.** In 1991 the American hip-hop singing group Another Bad Creation had a huge hit with the song "Iesha." The name Iesha immediately became as big a hit as the song, becoming the fifth most popular name given to nonwhite girls born in the United States in 1991. This was a classic example of a meteoric rise leading to a meteoric fall, however, for by 1997 the name was no longer found on the SSA top 1,000 list for girls.

Ifetayo
Yoruba (Nigeria) "love brings happiness."

Iliana

Probably a variation of **Ileana,** the Romanian form of **Helen.** Iliana has been regularly used in the Hispanic-American community since the 1980s and ranked 799th on the SSA list in 2004.

Ilona

Hungarian form of **Helen.**
Variations: **Elona, Ilka, Ilonka**

Ilsa, Ilse

German forms of **Elizabeth** or **Elsa.**

Imani

Swahili "faith." Imani is the name of the seventh and last day of the Kwanzaa celebration, and it has been a common name in the African-American community since 1990. Nearly 800 American girls were named Imani in 2004, ranking it 336th.

Imelda

Italian and Spanish form of Germanic *Irmhild* from *irmen* [whole, entire] + *hild* [battle].

Imogen

From Celtic *Innogen,* perhaps from *inghean,* "maiden." This unusual name first appeared in Shakespeare's play *Cymbeline.* Most experts believe that Shakespeare simply misread "Innogen" as "Imogen" when he consulted the written sources on which he based this play. Imogen is now among the top 100 names for girls in England, but American parents are not yet attracted to it.
Famous name: Imogen Cunningham (photographer)
Variation: **Imogene**

Imogene

Modern form of **Imogen,** blending it with the sound of **Jean.** Though Imogen has always been rare in the United States, this altered form was fairly common in the 1920s.
Famous name: Imogene Coca (comedienne)
Variations: **Emogene, Imogine, Imojean**

Independence

This patriotic name is inspired by the same motives as **Liberty.**

India

Sanskrit *sindhuh,* "river," name of the country. India has been well used, especially by African-American parents, since the 1980s. More than 600 girls received the name in 2004, ranking it 393rd.

Indiana

Though modern Americans may think of this as a male name because of the film character Indiana Jones, it was used as a girls name in the 19th century, both in the United States and in Norway, where the idea of using it may have been taken from letters written back home by Norwegian immigrants living in Indiana.

Indigo

The word, referring to a leguminous plant and the deep blue color of the dye derived from it. This word goes back to ancient Greek *indikón,* because the plant was thought to be native to India. Several instances of this name have been noted lately as part of the recent interest in "color names" for children.

Indira

Hindi *Indra,* "India."
Famous name: Indira Gandhi (prime minister of India)

Inez

Form of *Inés,* Spanish form of **Agnes.** This name may have been first popularized by *Inez: A Tale of the Alamo,* a romantic novel published in 1855 by Augusta Evans Wilson, who was the Danielle Steel of her day. *Inez,* her first book, was written when she was just 15. The name Inez was fairly common in the late 19th century and hit its high point of use about 1910, but it is quite rare today.
Other spelling: **Ines**

Ingrid

Old Norse *Ingfrid* from *Inge* [a Norse god] + *frid* [pretty]. Inge was the powerful god of the harvest in Norse mythology. The name Ingrid honored the god and also blessed the child to whom the name was given. The regular use of this Scandinavian name in the United States since 1940 is due to the career of film star Ingrid Bergman. During the last decade, Ingrid has been drifting upward in use again. More than 400 girls received the name in 2004, ranking it 622nd on the SSA list.

Variations: **Inga** (Swedish), **Inge** (Danish and German), **Inger** (Swedish)

Iola

Greek "cloud at dawn."

Iolanthe

From the Greek words *iole*, "violet," and *anthos*, "flower," evidently created in 1882 by Gilbert and Sullivan for the title character of their operetta *Iolanthe*.

Iona

Latin form of Old Norse *ey*, "island," the name of a famous island off the coast of Scotland where St. Columba founded a monastery; or a form of **Ione.**

Ione

Origin unclear; perhaps Greek "violet" or "one from Ionia," which is the ancient name for the western part of Asia Minor bordering the Aegean Sea.
Famous name: Ione Skye (actress)
Variations: **Iona, Ionia**

Ireland

The name of the country. Creative parents are starting to give this name to daughters even as the poetic name for Ireland, **Erin,** is falling out of fashion.

Irene

Greek *Eirene*, "peace." Eirene was the Greek goddess of peace, and Greek queens took this name at their coronations, as did some of the Russian empresses. Irene was one of the top 25 names between 1905 and 1927. It is still hanging on today in 428th place, with more than 500 girls given the name in 2004. Even today it's probably best recognized from the folk song "Good Night, Irene," made famous by a 1950 recording by the blues singer Leadbelly. Irene Joliot-Curie won the Nobel Prize in chemistry in 1935, following in her mother Marie Curie's footsteps.
Nicknames: **Rena, Rene, Renie, Rina**
Variations: **Eirene** (Greek), **Eirin** (Norwegian), **Ira** (Serbo-Croatian), **Irena** (Polish), **Irina** (Russian and Romanian)

Iris

Greek "rainbow." Though it was most popular in the 1930s, Iris is a name that has never faded away. Recently it has been especially popular in the Hispanic-American community. More than 800 Irises were born in 2004, ranking it 326th.

Variations: **Irida** (Bulgarian and Croatian), **Irisa** (Romanian)

Irma

Old German *irmen,* "whole, universal."

Variations: **Erma, Irmina** (Polish, Lithuanian, and Italian)

Iruka

Ibo (Nigeria) "the future is supreme."

Isabeau

Though still rare, this medieval French form of **Isabel** has seemed romantic ever since Michelle Pfeiffer played the heroine Isabeau in the 1985 fantasy film *Ladyhawke.*

Isabel

Spanish variation of **Elizabeth.** Isabel was exported through royal marriages from Spain to both France and England during the Middle Ages. Like **Isabella,** Isabel has been skyrocketing in use lately. Nearly 7,000 American girls were named Isabel or **Isabelle** in 2004, ranking the name 51st for the year.

Famous name: Isabel Allende (writer)

Other spellings: **Isabell, Izabelle**

Variations: **Belita, Bella, Belle, Isa** (Danish and German), **Isabeau** (French), **Isabelita, Isabella** (Italian and Swedish), **Isabelle** (French), **Isbel, Ishbel, Isobel** (Scottish), **Issie, Izzie, Izzy**

Isabella

Variation of **Isabel.** Isabella has been one of the most successful names of the last decade. More than 11 times as many Isabellas were born in 2004 as in 1994, and if the Isabellas and Isabels were counted together, they would have been the second most popular name. Like **Emily,** Isabella has an image that is strong and intelligent and yet very feminine. It also is being helped by the recent upsurge in other Italian names.

Famous name: Isabella Rossellini (actress)

Other spellings: **Isabela, Izabela, Izabella**

Isadora, Isidora

Greek "gift of Isis" from *Isis* [goddess of the Nile] + *dorus* [gift].
Famous name: Isadora Duncan (modern dancer)

Isis

Greek form of ancient Egyptian *Aset,* possibly "throne." Isis was the most important and powerful goddess in ancient Egypt. She was the sister and wife of Osiris, and she reassembled his body after the wicked god Set killed him. Osiris became the god of the underworld, and Isis gave birth to Horus, who avenged his father's death. Statues of Isis often depicted her nursing the infant Horus. The Egyptians saw Isis as being the perfect mother, as well as the goddess with the strongest magic, able to heal the sick and bring the dead back to life. During the time of the Roman empire, the worship of Isis spread throughout the Mediterranean, as is evidenced by the existence of Greek names such as **Isadora.** The name Isis entered the SSA top 1,000 list in 1993 and has steadily grown in use; in 2004, 524 Isises were born in the United States, ranking it 426th.

Isolde

Perhaps Celtic "beautiful" or Old German "ice rule." Isolde is the heroine of an often-told tale of tragic love that was incorporated into the Arthurian legend by Sir Thomas Malory and turned into the opera *Tristan und Isolde* by Richard Wagner.
Variations: **Isolda, Isotta** (Italian), **Yseult, Ysonde**

Itzel

Probably Mayan "evening star." This name has spread from the Maya areas of Yucatan and Guatemala throughout Mexico, Central America, and the Caribbean, and since 1993 it has been increasingly popular with Hispanic-Americans in the United States. In 2004, 860 Itzels were born, ranking it 315th.

Ivy

Old English *ifig,* "ivy." This plant was sacred to Bacchus and played a part in the religious ceremonies of the Druids. Ivy has climbed up the popularity charts recently and is now as common as it was at its previous peak in the 1880s. Almost 800 girls received the name in 2004, ranking it 334th.
Other spelling: **Ivie**

Jacey, Jacie, Jacy

Although some parents may interpret this name as a feminine form of
Jason, in many cases it is simply used because it blends fashionable
sounds, which is shown by the fact that Jaycee is now the second
most common spelling. There were 583 American girls named either
Jacey or Jaycee in 2004, and there were many more given spellings
that alone weren't common enough to make the SSA top 1,000 list.
Other spellings: **Jaicee, Jaicie, Jaycee, Jayci, Jaycie**

Jacinta

Spanish "hyacinth."
Variation: **Jacinthe** (French)

Jackie

Form of **Jacqueline.** This nickname has been used regularly as an
independent name since 1904, but it was definitely most popular in
the 1960s, when Jackie Kennedy was in the White House.
Famous names: Jackie Collins (author)
                     Jackie Joyner-Kersee (track athlete)
Other spellings: **Jacki, Jacky, Jacquie**

Jaclyn

Modern variation of **Jacqueline.** This name may have been deliberately created to provide a feminine form for the masculine name
Jack. Jaclyn became a popular alternative form of Jacqueline after
actress Jaclyn Smith became famous on television's *Charlie's Angels* in
1976, though it's losing ground today.
Other spellings: **Jacalyn, Jackeline, Jackelyn, Jacklyn, Jacklynn**

Jacqueline

Feminine form of **Jacques,** the French form of **Jacob** or **James.**
Jacqueline was one of the first French derivatives of a traditionally
masculine name to become popular for girls in the United States. It

was widely used by the 1930s. It had just started to dramatically fall away when Jacqueline Bouvier Kennedy became first lady in 1961. The number of Jacquelines born more than doubled between 1959 and 1961; it has slowly receded since. More than 4,600 were born in 2004, ranking it 75th that year.

Nicknames: **Jacki, Jackie, Jacky, Jacquie**
Other spellings: **Jacquelin, Jacquelyn, Jaqueline**
Variations: **Jaclyn, Jacobina, Jacquetta, Zakelina** (Czech)

Jada

Many modern parents probably interpret Jada as being a form of **Jade,** but there is an obscure male character in the Bible named Jada (from Hebrew "he knew"). The first sure female bearer of this name so far discovered is actress Jada Rowland who, starting in 1954, had a successful 20-year career, mostly on the soap opera *The Secret Storm.* Jada entered the SSA top 1,000 list in 1969, and it began a rapid increase after actress Jada Pinkett Smith started appearing on the sitcom *A Different World* in 1992. In 2004, more than 5,200 Jadas were born, ranking the name 66th. (*Jada* is an Arabic name meaning "gift" or "gain," but as its pronunciation is very different from Jada's this is probably a coincidence.)

Other spellings: **Jaida, Jayda**

Jade

Italian *giada,* "jade," from Spanish *piedra de ijada,* "stone of the bowels," because in medieval times jade was thought to protect its wearers from intestinal diseases. This name was very rare until Mick and Bianca Jagger named their daughter Jade in the late 1970s. It then began to climb in popularity and was among the top 30 names given to English girls by 1990. Although Jade's rise in the United States was slower, it has grown steadily. More than 3,000 Jades were born in 2004, ranking it 123rd for the year.

Jaelyn

Many parents have decided that if the newly popular male name **Jalen** was reinterpreted as **Jay** + **Lynn** it would make a wonderful name for a daughter, and they have tried a myriad of respellings to "feminize" the name. Though Jaelyn was the most common spelling in 2004, it only accounted for 21 percent of the total on the SSA list, where **Jailyn, Jalyn, Jalynn, Jaylen, Jaylin, Jaylyn,** and **Jaylynn** also appeared. The total for all eight spellings was 2,619 in 2004, ranking the name 138th.

Jahaira

This name, often respelled **Yahaira,** is regularly used in the Hispanic-American community. Its origin is unclear, but it may be based on the Arabic name *Jahír* and so related to the presently fashionable Hispanic male name **Yahir.** The possibility of an Arabic origin is reinforced by **Jaheira,** the name of an intelligent but demanding half-elf character in the popular computer role-playing game series Baldur's Gate and the novels based upon them. Even though the characters in these games are described as Druids, many of them have obviously Arabic names, like Jaheira's husband, Khalid.

Jaime

(See **Jamie.**)

Jakayla

Modern creation, *Ja-* + **Kayla.** Jakayla entered the SSA top 1,000 in 1999 and slowly increased to 760th place on the list in 2004, with 337 girls given the name.

Jaleesa, Jalisa

An African-American creation blending *Ja-* from names such as **Jamila** or **Janelle** with **Lisa.** This formerly rare name exploded in popularity in 1988, a year after the character Jaleesa Vinson Taylor was introduced on the television comedy *A Different World.* By 1991, Jaleesa was the 41st most popular name for African-American girls, but it disappeared by 1993.

Jaliyah

Perhaps a feminine form of the rare male Arabic name *Jaliy,* "clear, plain," but in many cases it may be an independent African-American creation based on **Aaliyah.** It's been in the SSA top 1,000 since 2002, ranking 786th on that list in 2004.

Jamaica

Arawak "island of springs," the Caribbean nation.

Jamie

Feminine form of **James.** Americans had been slowly increasing the number of daughters given this formerly male name since the 1940s, but when Lindsay Wagner started playing Jaime Sommers in 1976 on television's *The Bionic Woman*, the name exploded in use. Jamie in all its spellings was one of the most used girls names of the late 1970s and 1980s. Though it's dropping swiftly today, there were still almost 2,000 born in 2004, ranking it 173rd on the list.

Famous name: Jamie Lee Curtis (actress)

Other spellings: **Jaime, Jaimie, Jamee, Jami, Jayme, Jaymee, Jaymie**

Jamila

Arabic and Swahili "beautiful." This name is now regularly used in the African-American community.

Jamya

African-American creation blending names like **Jamila** and **Maya**. Jamya first entered the SSA top 1,000 list in 2001 and was up to 640th place by 2004, with 420 girls given the name that year.

Jan

Modern form of **Jane, Janet,** or **Janice.**

Jana

This form of **Jane** was moderately common in the 1960s and 1970s, though it's just hanging on today at 961st place on the SSA list.

Famous name: Jana Novotna (tennis player)

Janae

This is an American respelling of **Janet** to approximate the French pronunciation of that name. It's been regularly used since the 1970s and ranked 452nd in 2004.

Jane

Feminine form of **John.** Until the 16th century, the older form **Joan** was used more frequently in England than Jane. But after Henry VIII married his third wife, Jane Seymour, this name began to appear more often. In the 19th century, writer Jane Austen brought literary fame to the name. *Jane Eyre* by Charlotte Bronte began a line of fictional Janes that extends to Jane Marple, Agatha Christie's famous crime-solving detective. Jane is also a popular name for actresses, including Jane Alexander, Jane Curtin, Jane Fonda, Jane Seymour, and Jane Wyman. Sociologist Jane Addams won the 1931 Nobel Peace prize. Jane has always been well used in the United States; between

1932 and 1956 it was one of the top 50 names for girls. It is now dropping drastically; only 642 Janes were born in 2004, and its ranking of 386th was its lowest ever.

Famous names: Jane Goodall (primatologist)
Jane Pauley (television journalist)

Nicknames: **Janey, Janie, Jany**

Other spelling: **Jayne**

Variations: **Gianna, Giovanna** (Italian), **Hanka** (Frisian), **Ivana** (Czech and Russian), **Jan, Jana** (Czech), **Janelle, Janet, Janice, Janina** (Polish and Latvian), **Janine, Janka** (Hungarian), **Janna** (Dutch), **Jannike** (Norwegian), **Jean** (English and Scottish), **Jeanne** (French), **Jenna, Jenny** (Scottish), **Jensine** (Danish), **Joan, Joana** (Portuguese and Lithuanian), **Joanna, Joanne, Johana** (Czech and Slovakian), **Johanna** (German), **Johanne** (Norwegian), **Johnette, Johnna, Jonna** (Danish), **Jonnie, Jovanka** (Serbian), **Juana, Juanita** (Spanish), **Sheena** (Scottish), **Sian** (Welsh), **Zanna** (Polish)

Janelle

This modern form of **Jane** has been in use since the 1930s. At its peak around 1990 it was one of the top 200 names for girls in the United States, but by 2004 it had fallen to 431st.

Variations: **Janel, Janell, Janella**

Janessa

Modern creation blending **Janice** and **Vanessa**. For an invented name that doesn't seem to have any celebrity connection, Janessa has been remarkably successful. It entered the SSA top 1,000 list in 1984 and has lately enjoyed an increase in use. There were 536 Janessas born in 2004, ranking the name 421st for the year.

Janet

Variation of **Jane**. Janet was originally most common in Scotland, but it was one of the top 25 names between 1933 and 1957 in the United States. It ranked 379th in 2004, when 662 girls were given the name.

Famous names: Janet Evans (swimmer and Olympic gold medalist)
Janet Jackson (singer)
Janet Reno (Attorney General)

Variations: **Jan, Janae, Janette, Jannette, Jennet, Jessie, Seonaid** (Scots Gaelic), **Sinead** (Irish Gaelic)

Janiah

This modern blend of **Jan** with **Mariah** or **Shania** just entered the SSA top 1,000 list in 2004, in 951st place.

Janice

Variation of **Jane**. This name was created in 1899 for *Janice Meredith,* a novel by Paul Leicester Ford. He probably blended the sounds of **Janet** and **Alice** to come up with Janice. The novel was a bestseller in 1900, but the name didn't hit its peak of popularity until the 1950s. Today it's uncommon, ranking only 856th on the SSA list in 2004.
Other spellings: **Janis, Janise**

Janine

Form of **Jane**.
Famous name: Janine Turner (actress)

Janiya, Janiyah

African-American creation combining **Jan** with *-iyah* from **Aaliyah**. Like other names with this ending, Janiya has been booming lately. More than 1,300 were born in 2004, ranking the name 227th.

Jasmine

Persian *yasemin,* a flower name. Jasmine is often associated with passionate love. This name was fairly uncommon until it skyrocketed into first place for nonwhite American girls by 1991. Part of Jasmine's success can be attributed to actress Jasmine Guy, who began appearing in the television series *A Different World* in 1987. Several of the alternative spellings for the name show that many parents relate Jasmine to jazz music, although there is no historical connection between the two words. Jasmine is also popular with Hispanic-Americans and Asian-Americans. After Disney's *Aladdin,* with its character Princess Jasmine, was released in 1992, white parents increased their use of the name as it started to decline a bit with other groups. The result is that Jasmine has held about the same place on the national popularity chart for over a decade. More than 14,000 girls received the name in 2004, ranking it 14th.
Other spellings: **Jasmin, Jasmyn, Jazmin, Jazmine, Jazmyn, Jazzmin, Jazzmine, Jazzmyn**
Variations: **Jessamine, Jessamyn, Yasmin, Yasmine**

Jaya

Sanskrit *Jayā,* "victory, victorious." Hindu parents in the United States sometimes use this name because it fits in well with the sounds of today's popular American names.

Jaycee, Jaycie

Alternative spellings of **Jacey.** American gymnast Jaycie Phelps was named for her parents, Jack and Cheryl, who combined their initials. Similar motives may explain many instances of these names.

Jayden

Though all the **Aidan**-rhyming names have been given to girls on occasion, Jayden is by far the most popular in that role, probably because many parents see it as an expansion of **Jade.** Since 1998 Jayden has been booming for girls as well as boys, and though in 2004 there were more than three times as many boys given the name, the nearly 4,800 girls ranked it 72nd on the girls list. Jayden may well be on its way to replacing **Jordan** as the most popular "unisex" name. Other spellings: **Jaden, Jadyn, Jaiden, Jaidyn**

Jayla

Modern creation blending **Jay** and **Kayla.** Though there were isolated examples of this name in the 1980s, it's only been on the SSA top 1,000 list since 1995. More than 1,500 Jaylas were born in 2004, ranking the name 209th for the year.

Jaylee

Another creation blending **Jay** with other popular sounds, Jaylee entered the SSA top 1,000 list in 2004 at 921st place. Astronomer Jaylee M. Mead, who was born in the 1930s, shows that a few parents had the idea for this name quite a while ago.

Jaylene, Jayleen

Most names ending in *-lene* are now out of fashion, but the modern love of names starting with *Jay-* has this one rising instead of falling. There were 583 born in 2004, ranking this name 407th for the year.

Jazlyn

A modern creation blending **Jasmine** and **Jocelyn,** Jazlyn has been on the SSA top 1,000 list since 1996 and ranked 649th on that list in 2004, with 414 born.

Jean

English and Scottish variation of **Jane.** This name was a traditional favorite in Scotland, and the Scottish poet Robert Burns wrote a charming poem in Scots dialect to his wife called "I Love My Jean." Maggie Smith portrayed another Scottish woman named Jean as the title character in the movie *The Prime of Miss Jean Brodie,* based on a novel by Muriel Spark. Jean was one of the top 25 names in the United States from 1921 to 1937, but it left the SSA top 1,000 list in 1995.
Famous name: Jean Harlow (actress)
Other spellings: **Gene, Jeane, Jeanne**
Variations: **Jeanette, Jeanie, Jeannie**

Jeanne

French variation of **Jane.**
Variations: **Jean, Jeannette, Jeannine**

Jemima

Hebrew "dove." In the Old Testament, Jemima was the first daughter born to Job after his affliction. The name is well known through the pancake brand name and two fictional characters, Beatrix Potter's Jemima Puddle-Duck and Antonia Fraser's Jemima Shore, the liberated London broadcast journalist who doubles as a sleuth. Although Jemima is still regularly used in Britain, modern American parents almost never give the name to their daughters.

Jenna

Form of **Jennifer** or **Jane.** This name was around in the 1970s, but then it suddenly quintupled in use in 1984, a year after Priscilla Presley began playing Jenna Wade on television's long-running soap opera *Dallas.* Jenna has been one of the steadiest names in its popularity since, though it had a slight upswing in use in 2001, the year Jenna Bush's father entered the White House. More than 5,000 Jennas were born in 2004, ranking it 68th for the year.
Famous name: Jenna Elfman (actress)
Other spelling: **Genna**

Jennifer

Cornish form of **Guinevere.** Jennifer developed in Cornwall and then became popular throughout England in the mid-20th century. Educated American parents began to use the name around 1940,

and it was already one of the top 100 names for girls in 1957. Jennifer's success was probably because it was the one obvious shift from **Jane, Janet, Janice, Jean,** and **Joan,** which were all going out of fashion around 1970, when Jennifer became the number-one name for girls. Jennifer held that spot through 1984, a very long run at the top for a girls name. It is falling away slowly now, though its numbers are largely being maintained because Jennifer Lopez has made it hugely popular in the Hispanic-American community, the one segment of the population where it wasn't used much in the 1970s. More than 6,700 Jennifers were born in 2004, ranking it 52nd.
Famous names: Jennifer Aniston (actress)
Jennifer Higdon (composer)
Nicknames: **Genni, Gennie, Genny, Jen, Jenni, Jennie, Jenny**
Other spellings: **Gennifer, Jenefer, Jenifer, Jennefer**
Variations: **Jenna**

Jenny, Jennie

Forms of **Genevieve, Jane,** and **Jennifer.** In the 19th century, Jennie was very common, years before anyone had heard of Jennifer. Jenny is the more common spelling when this name is given independently today.
Famous name: Jenny Craig (weight-loss entrepreneur)

Jerusha

Hebrew "inheritance." In the Old Testament, Jerusha is the mother of King Jotham of Judah. In the 18th century, the Puritans in New England frequently named daughters Jerusha. The name is also well known from Jerusha Bromley Hale, a character in James Michener's novel *Hawaii* who was played by Julie Andrews in the 1966 movie based on that bestseller. Jerusha has never returned to regular use, in spite of the fact that it might seem to be a good alternative for names like **Jessica** and **Jennifer.** Jerusha Hess jointly wrote the script of the 2004 cult film *Napoleon Dynamite* with her husband, Jared.

Jessica

Feminine form of **Jesse,** Hebrew "God exists." Shakespeare, who probably invented the name, called Shylock's lovely daughter Jessica in *The Merchant of Venice.* Jessica rose to prominence during the 1970s as an alternative for **Jennifer;** between 1985 and 1995 it was in a close race with **Ashley** for the number-one spot. Since 2000, Jessica's decline has been rapid, and it only ranked 32nd in 2004.

Famous names: Jessica Lange (actress)
Jessica Simpson (pop singer)
Nicknames: **Jess, Jessie, Jessy**
Other spellings: **Jesica, Jesseca**

Jessie

Form of **Jessica** or **Janet.** As a name for girls, Jessie originated in Scotland, where it was a pet name for Janet. It was very popular as an independent name in the United States in the late 19th century. Jessie has once again become popular, although it has now become a pet form of Jessica.

Jetta

As **Jett** rises in popularity for boys, Jetta is starting to turn up more often for girls in the United States. In Germany and Sweden, Jetta is considered to be a pet form of **Henrietta,** but British name experts think it is a modern creation based on the word *jet* in its meaning of a lustrous black gemstone. Of course, in some instances it might be taken from the trade name of the automobile, and so be a sister of names like **Lexus** and **Camry** in its origin.

Jewel

Old French *jouel,* "jewel." Jewel was a moderately popular name a century ago, and since 1997 it has returned to the SSA top 1,000 list, probably under the inspiration of singer and poet Jewel, whose surname is Kilcher.
Other spellings: **Jewell, Jewelle**

Jill

Variation of **Gillian.** This name is well known from the nursery rhyme about Jack and Jill. Jill was popular in the 1960s and 1970s but has faded as an official name as **Jillian** has become the favored form.
Famous name: Jill Clayburgh (actress)
Variations: **Jillie, Jilly**

Jillian

Variation of **Gillian.** Jillian has become more common as **Jill** has disappeared. More than 2,600 Jillians were born in 2004, ranking it 137th.

Jina

Swahili "name."

Jo

Variation of **Joan, Joanna, Joanne, Joelle,** or **Josephine.** Jo is the strong-willed sister in Louisa May Alcott's *Little Women.*

Joan

Feminine form of **John,** Hebrew "the Lord is gracious." Joan dates back to at least the 12th century, when it is recorded as the name of a daughter of Henry II of England. Jeanne d'Arc, known in English as Joan of Arc, is the patron saint of France. She was a poor peasant girl, but after hearing the voices of saints, she donned armor and inspired the French forces in battle. After several initial successes, she was captured and turned over to the English, who had her burned at the stake as a witch in 1431. Joan had an incredibly swift boom during the 1920s and was a top ten name of the 1930s. It started to fall in the 1940s and 1950s, and today it's very rare.
Famous names: Joan Allen (actress)
Joan Crawford (actress)
Joan Jett (rock musician)
Nicknames: **Jo, Joanie, Joni, Jonie, Jonnie, Jony**
Variations: **Jane, Joana, Joann, Joanna, Joanne, Jodi, Jodie, Jody, Siobhan** (Irish Gaelic), **Siubhan** (Scots Gaelic), **Siwan** (Welsh)

Joanna

Variation of **Jane** or **Joan.** Joanna has been used since medieval times. It's generally been a name that never becomes wildly popular and yet never goes out of style, though it did have a peak in the mid-1980s, when it was briefly one of the top 100 names. Joanna ranked 210th in 2004, with more than 1,500 girls given the name.
Famous name: Joanna Cassidy (actress)
Variations: **Jo, Joana, Joann, Joanne, Jodi, Jodie, Jody, Joeanna**

Joanne

French form of **Joanna.** Joanne was one of the top 100 names for girls born in the United States between 1930 and 1960. Then between 1960 and 1985 Joanne was one of the top 25 names for girls born in England. The world's most famous Joanne, J. K. Rowling, was born during that time period.
Famous name: Joanne Woodward (actress)
Variations: **Jo, Jo Ann, Joann, Joanna, Joeanne**

Jocelyn

Norman French form of Old German *gautelen,* probably "of the Goths." Since 1948 this lovely old name has enjoyed a slow but steady rise that brought it to 69th place in 2004, with more than 5,000 born. Jocelyn is now quite fashionable with Hispanic-American parents, who evidently interpret it as a modern feminine form for **Jose.**
Nickname: **Joss**
Other spellings: **Joscelin, Joscelyn, Joselyn, Joslyn**

Jodi, Jodie, Jody

Variation of **Joan, Joanna, Josephine,** and **Judith.** This top 50 name of the 1970s is rare today in spite of the fame of actress Jodie Foster. Jody Williams won the 1997 Nobel Peace prize for her work in banning and clearing antipersonnel land mines.

Joelle

Feminine form of **Joel.** Something happened in 1966 to bring this name to the notice of young parents, because it jumped onto the SSA top 1,000 list from nowhere into 468th place. It has been receding ever since; in 2004 it was still hanging on at 932nd place.
Famous name: Joelle Wallach (composer)
Nickname: **Jo**

Johana, Johanna

Taken together, these two spellings accounted for more than 800 baby names in 2004, ranking the name 330th that year. The popularity of Johana in the 20th century has paralleled that of **Joanna.**

Jokudu

Bari (southern Sudan) "girl born while it is raining."

Jolie

Pet form of *Jolán,* the Hungarian form of **Yolanda.** This name was first brought to the attention of Americans by Jolie Gabor (1894–1997), the mother of actresses Eva and Zsa Zsa Gabor. Jolie was briefly on the SSA top 1,000 list in the 1970s and then disappeared. It suddenly reappeared in 2000 and has been growing swiftly in use. This is perhaps an instance of a celebrity's surname being turned into a first name, as Angelina Jolie's fame markedly increased at about the same time the name Jolie's popularity was renewed. Jolie ranked 620th on the SSA list in 2004, with 434 girls given the name.

Joni, Jonie

Form of **Joan.**

Famous name: Joni Mitchell (singer and songwriter)

Variations: **Jonnie, Jony**

Jonquil

This flower name has been given to girls in the United States on rare occasions since at least 1975.

Jordan

Hebrew *Yarden,* "descender," the name of the Palestinian river. Although Jordan was used for both boys and girls in medieval times, it disappeared as a feminine name for several centuries until its 20th-century revival. In 1925, F. Scott Fitzgerald chose Jordan as the name of a female character in his novel *The Great Gatsby.* In the 1980s Jordan quickly became fashionable for both sexes in the United States. Remarkably, Jordan peaked for both boys and girls in 1997 and has been receding at about the same rate for both. Jordan is therefore the popular name to most successfully maintain its "unisex" status in history. More than 6,200 girls were named Jordan in 2004, ranking it 54th that year. In 2005 the most famous female Jordan may be the fictional Dr. Jordan Cavanaugh, the medical examiner played by Jill Hennessy on the television drama *Crossing Jordan,* which began in 2001.

Variations: **Jordana, Jordanka** (Czech), **Jordanne**

Jorie

Short form of **Marjorie.**

Josephine

Feminine form of **Joseph,** Hebrew "the Lord added." The most famous royal woman to bear this name is Josephine Beauharnais, who became the wife of Napoleon and empress of France. In the United States, Josephine was a common name for most of the 19th century and grew even more so at the start of the 20th, peaking at 22nd place on the SSA list in 1917. Since 1990 it's been growing in popularity again; more than 1,300 girls were given the name in 2004, ranking it 228th for the year.

Famous name: Josephine Baker (dancer and singer)

Nicknames: **Jo, Jodi, Jodie, Jody, Josee, Josie**

Variations: **Fifi** (French), **Giuseppina** (Italian), **Josefa, Josefina** (Spanish), **Josepha** (German), **Josephina** (Portuguese), **Josette** (French), **Josypa** (Ukrainian), **Jozefa** (Polish), **Pepita** (Spanish), **Seosaimhin** (Irish Gaelic)

Josie

Form of **Josephine.** Josie began to rise in use a few years before Josephine and in the mid-1990s was briefly more common than the longer name. In 2004 more than 900 girls were given Josie as their official form, ranking it 288th that year.
Famous name: Josie Bissett (actress)

Journey

This word name has been in the SSA top 1,000 list since 1999, though it's never grown enough to get beyond the "uncommon but noticeable" level. In 2004 it ranked 941st on the SSA list, with 253 born. Perhaps the message parents give their daughters with this name is that "life is a journey."

Joy

Old French *joie,* "joy." This word has been regularly used as a name since 1890, and it had a very long run of moderate popularity between 1927 and 1981. It has receded since, but there were still 600 Joys born in 2004, ranking it 398th for the year.
Variation: **Joya**

Joyce

Norman French *Josce,* form of Breton *Iodoc,* "lord." In the Middle Ages, this was a male name, but since the 17th century it has been used for girls, probably because of its similarity in sound to **Joy.** Joyce boomed during the 1920s and was a top 25 name of the 1930s and 1940s, but then it dropped precipitously after that. It ranked 758th on the SSA list in 2004, with only 338 girls given the name.
Famous names: Dr. Joyce Brothers (psychologist/advice columnist)
　　　　　　　　Joyce Carol Oates (novelist)
Variations: **Jodoca** (Dutch), **Joice**

Juana, Juanita

Spanish forms of **Jane.** Juanita was frequently used by non-Hispanics during the mid-20th century, but today neither of these names is popular with parents from any ethnic background.

Judith

Hebrew "a Jewish woman." Judith had a spectacular rise and fall between 1930 and 1960. It was one of the top ten names of the 1940s, but its total of 542 in 2004 ranked it only 429th that year. Judith Martin is the real name of Miss Manners, who writes today's most popular etiquette advice column.
Famous names: Judith Leyster (artist)
Judith A. Resnik (astronaut)
Nicknames: **Jodi, Jodie, Jody, Jude, Judie, Judy**

Judy

Variation of **Judith.** This was the stage name of one of the 20th century's greatest performers, Judy Garland. Judy was almost as common as an official name during its 1940s heyday as Judith, but it has vanished completely today.
Famous names: Judy Blume (author)
Judy Collins (singer)

Julia

Feminine form of **Julius,** a Latin family name. Julia was a popular name during the 19th century. Though it receded during the 20th, especially while **Julie** was in vogue as an independent name, Julia never ranked lower than 143rd on the SSA list. It started climbing back up the charts in the late 1970s and was the 50th most common name of 2004, when more than 7,000 American girls received it. This history means that Julia is one of the few female names in the United States where it is difficult to guess the age of the bearer from the first name alone.
Famous names: Julia Child (food expert)
Julia Roberts (actress)
Nicknames: **Juli, Julie**
Variations: **Giulia, Giulietta** (Italian), **Juliet, Julieta** (Spanish), **Julie, Julietta, Juliette** (French)

Juliana, Julianna

Feminine form of **Julian.** St. Juliana got into trouble by rejecting the advances of a nobleman. According to legend, more than 500 people were converted after she was thrown into a furnace and the fire went out. Her name has increased in use considerably lately; more than 3,600 girls received it in 2004, ranking it 101st that year.

Famous names: Juliana (queen of the Netherlands)
Juliana Hatfield (guitarist and songwriter)
Julianna Margulies (actress)
Variations: **Gillian, Jillian, Julianne, Julina, Juline, Liana** (Italian), **Yuliana** (Russian and Bulgarian)

Julianne

This form of **Juliana** has been regularly used since the 1940s, though it has recently been surpassed by Juliana itself. It ranked 634th on the SSA list in 2004.
Famous name: Julianne Moore (actress)

Julie

French form of **Julia**. Between 1958 and 1978, Julie was one of the top 25 names for girls in the United States. It is now falling away as Julia is growing once again. Julie ranked 236th in 2004, with about 1,200 girls given the name. Julie Krone is the only female jockey to win a Triple Crown race, the 1993 Belmont Stakes.
Famous names: Julie Andrews (singer and actress)
Julie Kavner (actress)

Juliet

Form of **Julia**. William Shakespeare coined this name from the Italian name Giulietta for the famous tragic heroine of *Romeo and Juliet*. In the United States, the name has usually been current but never common for the last century. Its 651st ranking on the 2004 SSA list was the highest it's ever reached.
Other spelling: **Juliette**

Juliette

This French form of **Juliet** was 679th on the SSA list in 2004. Counted together, the two spellings would have been 331st on the list, with just over 800 girls given the names.
Famous name: Juliette Binoche (actress)

Julissa

Blend of **Julia** and **Isabel**. Julia Isabel de Llano Mecado is a Mexican rock singer and actress who is known professionally as Julissa. She first became famous in Mexico at age 14 in 1959. Her name was in the SSA top 1,000 list for several years in the 1970s and then disappeared

again until 1988, after which it grew rapidly until a peak in 1997, when more than 1,300 Julissas were born in the United States. In 2004, more than 1,000 girls received the name, ranking it 279th that year.
Other spelling: **Julisa**

June

Latin *mensis Junius,* name of the month. *Junius* was a Roman clan name, probably derived from the goddess Juno. This popular name of the 1920s hasn't been on the SSA top 1,000 list since 1986.
Variations: **Junette, Junia, Junie, Junine**

Junza

Tonga (Zambia) "tomorrow," a name given to children born at dawn.

Justice

This word name first entered the SSA top 1,000 list in 1994 at 362nd place, a remarkably high ranking for its first year. But if there was any specific cultural event that brought it to parents' attention, it remains a mystery. Justice is being used for both genders. In 2004 it was given to 581 girls, which ranked it 410th that year.

Justina

Feminine form of **Justin,** Latin "the just." The minor vogue for Justina in the 1980s and 1990s has already petered out.
Famous name: Justina Robson (science fiction author)
Variations: **Giustina** (Italian), **Justine** (French), **Justyna** (Polish, Czech, and Ukrainian), **Jusztina** (Hungarian)

Justine

French form of **Justina.** Justine has been in regular use as an American name for 150 years. It had a minor boom in the 1980s and 1990s but is now back to its average level for the past century, ranking 673rd on the SSA list in 2004.

Jyoti

Sanskrit *jyotī,* "light, brilliant, flamelike." In Vedic religious literature, this word was used metaphorically to denote both intelligence and liberation. It was not used as a name in ancient India but has been common in modern times. In the United States, women of East Indian descent with this name often go by **Jodi.**

Kairi

Japanese "ocean."

Kaitlyn

Form of **Caitlin**. In 2004 this was the most common spelling of the name, with almost 7,000 girls given it.

Kali

Sanskrit "dark goddess." Kali is the Hindu goddess of destruction, often pictured wearing a necklace of severed human heads. It's probable that although Kali is properly pronounced "KAH-lee," many American parents are using it as a spelling variation of **Kaylee**.

Kalila

Feminine form of Arabic *Khalil*, "close friend."

Kaliyah

African-American creation blending **Kalila** and **Aaliyah**. There were 358 girls born in the United States who received this name in 2004, ranking it 732nd on the SSA list.

Kalpana

Sanskrit *Kalpanā*, "imagination, idea, composition." Kalpana Chawla was an astronaut who died in the Columbia shuttle disaster in 2003.

Kamaria

Swahili "like the moon."

Kamilah

Feminine form of Arabic *Kamil*, "perfect."

Kanisha

African-American creation. Invented to rhyme with **Tanisha**, this name was popular in the 1990s for African-American girls. Respelled as **Kenisha** it's considered a modern feminine form for **Kenneth**.

Kansas

Name of the state, from the Kansa nation of Native Americans. Though rare, examples of Kansas as a girls first name were found all around the United States in the 19th century.

Kara

Form of Latin *cara,* feminine of *carus,* "dear"; or a form of **Caroline.** Kara was quite common in the 1980s but has since receded. More than 1,800 Karas were born in 2004, ranking the name 187th.
Famous name: Kara Walker (artist)
Other spelling: **Cara**

Karen

Danish form of **Katherine.** Karen began its rise to prominence around 1930 and was a top ten name for American girls throughout the 1950s and 1960s. Its popularity has been receding since then, though not as quickly as some other names of its era. There were more than 1,800 Karens born in 2004, ranking it 166th.
Famous name: Karen Carpenter (singer)
Other spellings: **Caren, Carin, Karyn**
Variations: **Kari** (Norwegian), **Karin** (Swedish), **Karina**

Karina

Latin feminine form of Greek *karinos,* "witty"; form of Italian *carina,* "dear one"; a 19th-century Swedish expansion of **Karen.** Recently this name has been especially popular in the Hispanic-American community, partly because it's been used to name characters in several different telenovelas during the last two decades. More than 2,000 girls were named Karina in 2004, ranking it 168th.
Other spellings: **Carina, Karena**

Karis

Greek *kharis,* "grace." This name found its way onto the SSA list for the first time in 2004, at 922nd place, with 259 girls given the name.

Karla

German feminine form of **Karl. Carla** used to be the more common spelling of this name in the United States, but Karla is now more than twice as popular. More than 2,300 girls were given one of the two spellings in 2004, ranking the name 150th.

Katarina

German and Scandinavian variation of **Katherine.** Katarina first made the SSA top 1,000 list in 1988, the year Katarina Witt won her second consecutive Olympic gold medal for East Germany in figure skating. After she became a professional, her name became moderately popular in the early 1990s. Now receding, Katarina was 852nd on the SSA list in 2004, with 284 girls given the name.

Kate

Variation of **Katherine.** William Shakespeare used this diminutive for his Katharina in *The Taming of the Shrew,* and the famous line, "Come on, and kiss me, Kate," inspired Cole Porter to write the Broadway musical *Kiss Me Kate.* Kate's image for most Americans is of a smart, ambitious, competent, and beautiful woman, which is why scholars of mystery novels have found that Kate is the most common name authors give a female detective. It's no wonder then that since 1995 the number of parents who name their daughters Kate has increased. Kate ranked 163rd in 2004, with more than 2,000 born.
Famous names: Kate Winslet (actress)
Kate Ziegler (swimmer)

Katharine

Form of **Katherine.** Because this spelling is the closest to the Greek word *katharos,* it has the best claim to a meaning of "purity." This spelling is still a distant fourth choice after **Katherine, Catherine,** and **Kathryn,** despite the fame of actress Katharine Hepburn.
Famous name: Katharine Graham (newspaper publisher)

Katherine

Greek *Aikaterine,* meaning unknown, possibly originally from an African language. The third-century St. Katherine of Alexandria was the first of many saints with this name. When the cult of St. Katherine became popular in Western Europe, Roman Catholic writers wrongly assumed that her name was from Greek *katharos,* "pure." This is how the original spelling of the name was altered to drop the first syllable and change "-ter-" to "-thar-." The Romans also made the usual substitution of Latin *C* for Greek *K.* This name has been popular since the Middle Ages because of its associations with purity, beauty, and grace. Katherine has consistently appeared among the top 50 most popular names for girls in the United States since colonial times. In England, the best-known Katherines are three of the wives of Henry VIII. Strong-willed literary Katherines appear in Shakespeare's *Love's Labour's Lost* and Ernest Hemingway's *A Farewell to Arms*. Well-known authors named Katherine include Katherine Mansfield, Katherine Anne Porter, and Katherine Paterson.

Nicknames: **Kat, Kate, Kathie, Kathy, Katie, Katy, Kay, Kaye, Kitty**

Other spellings: **Catherine, Katharine, Katheryn, Kathryn**

Variations: **Caitlin, Caitriona** (Irish Gaelic), **Catalina** (Spanish), **Catarina** (Portuguese), **Caterina** (Italian), **Catharina** (Dutch), **Catherine** (French), **Catrin** (Welsh), **Catrina** (Romanian), **Catriona** (Scottish), **Ekaterina** (Bulgarian and Russian), **Kaia** (Estonian and Scandanavian), **Karen** (Danish), **Kari** (Norwegian), **Karin** (Swedish), **Kasia** (Polish), **Katalin** (Hungarian), **Katarina** (German and Scandinavian), **Katarzyna** (Polish), **Katerina** (Czech, Russian, and Bulgarian), **Katharina** (German and Estonian), **Kathleen** (Irish), **Katina** (modern Greek and Bulgarian), **Katinka** (Russian), **Katri** (Finnish), **Katrien** (Dutch), **Katrina** (Latvian, German, Czech, and Scottish), **Katrine** (Norwegian and Danish), **Katrya** (Ukrainian), **Katuska** (Czech), **Katya** (Russian), **Kaya, Ketterle** (German), **Kotryna** (Lithuanian), **Krin** (German), **Rina, Trine** (Danish), **Yekaterina** (Russian)

Kathleen

Irish Gaelic *Caitlin,* variation of **Katherine.** Kathleen was one of the first traditional Irish names to become popular with all Americans. It was one of the top 25 names of the 1940s and 1950s. Though **Kaitlyn** has largely replaced it today, there were still nearly 1,000 Kathleens born in 2004, ranking it 284th.

Famous names: Kathleen Battle (opera singer)
Kathleen Turner (actress)

Other spelling: **Cathleen**

Kathy

This pet form of **Katherine** was popular as an independent name in the 1950s. It only ranked 876th on the SSA list in 2004.

Famous names: Kathy Bates (actress)
Kathy Griffin (comedienne)
Kathy Mattea (country singer)

Katie, Katy

This is the most common pet form of **Katherine** today. Katie was independently one of the top 50 names for girls in the 1980s. With more than 3,000 born in 2004, it ranked 119th.
Famous name: Katie Couric (newscaster)

Katlyn

Blend of **Kathryn** and **Caitlin.** It's unknown how many parents who use this name are pronouncing the first syllable as "cat" compared to those who may be using it as another spelling of Caitlin. Katlyn entered the SSA list in 1986; it peaked in 1995 and is now receding. The 508 girls who received the name in 2004 ranked it 433rd.

Katrina

Variation of **Katherine.** Katrina wasn't regularly used in the United States before 1940, but it became one of the top 100 names for girls in the 1980s. In 2004 it had dropped back to 258th place, with more than 1,100 born, but because of the publicity surrounding 2005's Hurricane Katrina, its numbers will likely rise again.
Nickname: **Trina**

Kay, Kaye

Form of **Katherine,** frequently given as an independent name in the 1940s but very rare today.

Kaya

Respelling of **Kaia,** a Scandinavian name that is used as a pet form of **Katherine** in Scandinavia, though it could also be a feminine form of **Kai.** This is a newly fashionable name that parents are hearing rather than seeing, as the spellings Kaya and Kaia both entered the SSA top 1,000 list for the first time in 2000, followed by **Kaiya** and **Kya** in 2001. In 2004, all four spellings combined were given to more than 1,500 American girls, ranking the name 207th.

Kayden

Feminine form of **Caden;** 741st on the SSA top 1,000 list in 2004.

Kayla

Modern American creation based on **Kay;** short form of **Michaela;** or Yiddish form of *Kelila,* a Hebrew name meaning "crown of laurel." Many Jewish immigrant women who came to the United States from Eastern Europe between 1880 and 1920 were called Kayla. However, Kayla first became popular with other Americans around 1970 in rural Western states such as the Dakotas, so it's unlikely that the Yiddish name was being copied. Although Kayla can be a nickname for Michaela, it's most likely a newly invented name. The similar creation **Gayla,** a variation of Gail, has been in use since at least the 1940s. Kayla's use was slowly increasing in 1982 when the character Kayla Brady was introduced on the soap opera *Days of Our Lives.* Seven times more Kaylas were born in 1982 as had been in 1981. Kayla's similarity in sound to previous 1980s fads such as **Kelly, Caitlin,** and **Casey** contributed to its swift rise. Kayla has been one of the top 25 names since 1988; it's just starting to slip back a bit, but in 2004 more than 10,000 Kaylas were born, ranking it 25th. Other spellings: **Cayla, Kaila, Kala, Kaylah**

Kaylee

Modern blend of **Kay** and **Lee;** form of *Cayley,* English surname from *Cailly,* French place name; or form of Kayley, Irish or Manx surname from Celtic words meaning "slender." Kaylee is an example of a name becoming popular because it's made up of fashionable sounds. This is shown by the variety of spellings being used; although Kaylee is the most common spelling in the United States, it accounts for less than half of all girls with this name. In England, where the name has also become popular since the mid-1980s, **Kayleigh** is the most popular spelling. Others frequently found spellings include **Kaeleigh, Kailee, Kaileigh, Kaily, Kaleigh, Kaley, Kali, Kalie, Kayley, Kayli,** and **Kaylie.** Counting all the spellings together, Kaylee was the 22nd most common name in 2004, given to more than 11,000 girls.

Kaylin

Modern blend of **Kay** and **Lynn;** or Irish Gaelic *Caelainn,* "slender lady." Kaylin has become popular recently because it starts with the fashionable "Kay" sound of **Kayla, Caitlin, Katie,** and so forth. In 2004 more than 2,700 girls were given the name, ranking it 135th. Other spellings: **Kaelyn, Kailyn, Kaylyn, Kaylynn, Kaylynne**

Keely, Keeley

Irish Gaelic *Caollaidhe,* from *caol,* "graceful." This Irish surname has been regularly used for girls in the United States since the 1970s and ranked 767th on the SSA top 1,000 list in 2004.

Keiko

Japanese "cinnamon child." This may seem like a name connected with food to Americans, but in Japan a "cinnamon crown" is equivalent to the ancient Greek laurel wreath, so this name implies something like "poet laureate child" in Japan.

Keira, Kiera, Kira

Modern feminine form of **Kieran.** In Ireland **Ciara** and Kiera are the common spellings, but Keira and Kira are preferred in the United States as they represent the pronunciation more clearly to Americans. Kira was the first spelling to become popular in the United States in the 1970s, but Keira exploded in use in 2003 after actress Keira Knightley became famous in the film *Pirates of the Caribbean,* and it was slightly ahead in 2004. More than 3,200 girls received one of the three main forms in 2004, ranking the name 114th. (See also **Kyra.**)

Keisha

Origin unknown. Although it's often claimed that Keisha is from an African language, it's not mentioned in existing works on native African names and is probably an American invention. Keisha was first used by African-American parents around 1970 and became very popular in the late 1970s and early 1980s. By 2004, it had vanished from the SSA top 1,000 list.
Other spellings: **Kecia, Keesha, Keshia, Keysha**

Kelly

Irish Gaelic *Ceallagh,* uncertain meaning, perhaps "churchgoer," "bright-headed," or "strife"; also, rarely, Cornish *celli,* "wood." Kelly's regular use for girls began in 1948; its growth in popularity was accelerated in 1957 when the teenage character Kelly Gregg appeared on the television sitcom *Bachelor Father.* Kelly was a top ten name during the 1970s. It's now slowly going out of style, but it was still the 140th most popular name of 2004, given to nearly 2,600 girls that year. The most famous Kelly today may well be singer Kelly Clarkson, winner of the 2002 *American Idol.*
Other spellings: **Kelley, Kelli, Kellie**

Kelsey

Probably Old English *ceol* [ship] + *sige* [victory]. Kelsey was an uncommon name and used predominantly for boys until 1977. It

then became one of the more fashionable names for girls. Kelsey's success was probably due to its combination of the sounds of **Kelly** and **Chelsea,** two names that were already in vogue. Kelsey's use peaked in 1992; in 2004 it was the 139th most popular name given to newborn American girls, just above Kelly.
Other spellings: **Kelci, Kelcie, Kelcy, Kelsi, Kelsie, Kelsy**

Kendall

For origin, see Kendall in the boys list. Kendall has been used sporadically for girls since at least 1960 but only solidified its place as a girls name after 1980. Since then it's slowly risen in use until nearly 2,900 girls received the name in 2004, ranking it 131st that year.
Other spellings: **Kendal, Kendel, Kendell, Kendyl**

Kendra

Probably originally a feminine form of **Kendrick;** now often given as a feminine form of **Kenneth.** Kendra has been in regular use in the United States since 1946. It peaked in 1987 at 77th on the SSA list; in 2004 it was in 245th place, with about 1,200 girls given the name.

Kennedy

For origin, see Kennedy in the boys list. The MTV vee-jay Kennedy (full name Lisa Kennedy Montgomery) and the character Kennedy on the sitcom *Blossom* helped introduce Americans to the idea of using this name for girls. Kennedy has been soaring since 1994. In 2004, more than 3,200 girls received the name, ranking it 111th. Kennedy is slightly more popular in the African-American community, but its geographical spread doesn't fit what many people would expect. The top three states for the name in 2004 were Louisiana, Iowa, and South Dakota, while it was much less common in New England than elsewhere.

Kenya

Kikuyu *kere-nyanga,* "mountains of whiteness," name of a country in East Africa. Kenya has been used as a name for American girls since 1968. Some parents interpret it as being a feminine form of **Kenneth.** In 2004 nearly 700 girls were given the name, ranking it 369th.

Kenzie

Short form of **Mackenzie,** on the SSA top 1,000 list since 1994 and still slowly increasing. There were 420 Kenzies born in 2004, ranking it 641st on the list.

Keri, Kerri, Kerry

"*Ciar's* people," Irish place name. *Ciar* itself meant "black." This name was especially popular in the late 1970s but is rare again today. Famous name: Kerri Strug (gymnast and Olympic gold medalist)

Keyla

Probably a modern creation blending the sounds of **Kayla** and **Sheila.** This name ranked 908th on the SSA list in 2004.

Kiana

Kiana is the Hawaiian language form of **Diana,** but it clearly began its career as a girls name in the mainland United States as an alternative spelling of **Qiana.** Qiana was an artificial silk-like fabric manufactured by DuPont. Its name was chosen from a list of words randomly generated by a computer to look glamorous and exotic, sound pleasant, and have no unfortunate meanings in any language. Qiana was heavily promoted in the late 1970s as a material for wedding gowns and elegant shirts, and both Qiana and **Quianna** entered the SSA top 1,000 list for girls in 1977, being especially popular with African-American parents. Kiana first made the SSA list in 1978, and many other spellings, such as **Keonna, Keyana, Keyonna, Kianna,** and **Kionna,** have also been used. All forms of the name were absent from the SSA list between 1986 and 1988. The name's reappearance in 1989 may be due to fitness expert Kiana Tom. Since she was born in Hawaii, the Hawaiian derivation is the explanation for her name, as it is for the Hawaiian-born novelist Kiana Davenport. The name peaked at 190th on the SSA list in 1996. In 2004, nearly 1,200 newborns in the United States were named Kiana or Kianna, ranking it 248th.

Kiara

Origin unclear, but probably a respelling of **Chiara,** a modern Italian form of **Clara.** Kiara was voguish in the African-American community in the early 1990s, began to recede, and then suddenly jumped to 78th place in 1999, higher than it had ever been. This was probably due to the release of the direct-to-video animated film *The Lion King II* in 1998, in which Kiara was the Lion King Simba's daughter. Along with the boys name **Koda,** Kiara is an example of an animated animal character affecting what human children are named. In 2004 almost 1,800 Kiaras were born, ranking it 189th.
Variations: **Chiara, Kierra**

Kierra

Probably a blend of the sounds of **Kiara** and **Sierra.** In regular use since 1987, it ranked 427th in 2004, with 524 girls given the name.

Kiersten

Many Americans pronounce **Kirsten** as it is in Scotland, with the first syllable rhyming with "fur." This form is used by parents who want to insure that their daughter's name is pronounced in the original Scandinavian way, rhyming with "fear." Kiersten has been in the SSA top 1,000 list since 1988. In 2004, it ranked 455th, with 653 girls receiving it. If Kiersten and Kirsten are considered the same name, their combined total would have ranked the name 194th in 2004.

Kim

Probably the same derivation as the boys name Kim, first used for a girl in Edna Ferber's 1926 novel *Show Boat.* The name wasn't regularly used, however, until the 1940s when actress Kim Hunter's career began. Although Kim is thought of as a nickname for **Kimberly** today, it was actually in regular use for girls before Kimberly became popular. Between 1955 and 1970, Kim was one of the top 50 names for girls, but it vanished from the SSA top 1,000 list in 1994.
Famous names: Kim Basinger (actress)
Kim Novak (actress)

Kimberly

Old English *Cyneburh-leah,* "Cyneburgh's meadow." Cyneburgh was a woman's name meaning "royal fort." Though Kim came first, Kimberly surpassed it in 1958 and was a top ten American name for girls from 1964 to 1977. Though it's now receding, there were still nearly 4,800 Kimberlys born in 2004, ranking it 73rd.
Nicknames: **Kim, Kimmie**
Other spelling: **Kimberley**

Kimora

This name was evidently created by the parents of model and fashion designer Kimora Lee Simmons. Though her mother is Japanese and her father is African-American, Kimora is not a Japanese name or word and so probably falls under the category of an African-American creation. Simmons' fame propelled Kimora onto the SSA top 1,000 list in 803rd place in 2004.

Kinsey

Old English *Cynesige,* "royal victory." This rare name is now well known because of Sue Grafton's best-selling mysteries about the adventures of Kinsey Millhone, a private investigator who lives and works in California.

Kira

(See **Keira** and **Kyra.**)

Kirsten, Kirstin

Danish and Scottish variations of **Christina,** regularly used in the United States since 1960. This name peaked in the 1990s, but there were still more than 1,000 Kirstens born in 2004, ranking the name 269th. (See also **Kiersten.**)
Famous name: Kirsten Dunst (actress)

Kirstie

Scottish form of **Christina.**
Famous name: Kirstie Alley (actress)

Kitty

Form of **Katherine,** common as an independent name in the 19th century and again in the 1940s.
Famous name: Kitty Wells (country music singer)

Krista

This German form of **Christina** was a top 100 name in the United States in the late 1980s. Krista and **Christa** combined had fallen to 340th place in 2004, with 757 born.

Kristen, Kristin

Norwegian forms of **Christian** and **Christina.** In Norway, Kristen is a male name and Kristin the female form; in the United States, both spellings are used for girls, and since 1973 Kristen has been more common. Americans began to discover Kristen as an alternative for **Christine** in the 1950s. The name was already a top 100 name for girls when it got an extra boost in 1980 from the character Kristin, played by Mary Crosby, on the television series *Dallas,* and briefly became a top ten name. In 2004 it had dropped to 191st place.
Famous name: Kristin Chenoweth (actress)
Other spellings: **Christen, Christin, Krysten, Krystin, Krystyn**

Kristi, Kristie, Kristy

Forms of **Christie.**

Famous name: Kristi Yamaguchi (figure skater)

Kyla

Modern feminine form of **Kyle,** gradually increasing since it first entered the SSA top 1,000 list in 1974. In 2004, more than 2,000 girls received the name, ranking it 170th.

Kylie

Probably a feminine form of **Kyle,** although in Australia, where the name was the third most popular for girls born in the mid-1970s, it is said to be an aboriginal Australian word for "boomerang." The alternative spellings Kiley and Kyley are also Irish surnames from Gaelic *cadhla,* "graceful." Something happened in 1978 to introduce Americans to Kylie, since it jumped onto the SSA top 1,000 list in 407th place that year. It then receded for a few years until the vogue for Kyle as a boys name started it rising again. Kylie has been steadily advancing the last few years and in 2004 reached 30th place, with more than 9,400 American girls given the name.

Famous names: Kylie Bivens (soccer player)
           Kylie Minogue (pop singer)

Other spellings: **Kiley, Kylee, Kyley**

Kyra

Russian and Ukrainian feminine form of *Kyros* (**Cyrus**). In Russia, this name is pronounced "Keera" and so can be an alternate for **Kira.** Actress Kyra Sedgwick uses that pronunciation. However, many other bearers of this name pronounce the first syllable as in **Kyla.** Kyra came into general use during the 1980s and increased until its peak in 1998, when it was among the top 200 girls names. Though it's now slowly receding, there were still more than 1,500 American girls given the name in 2004, ranking it 212th. If Kyra was counted as an alternate spelling of **Keira,** the combined name would have ranked 74th in 2004.

Lacey

Norman French surname from *Lassy*, French place name, "Lascius's estate." In the early 20th century, Lacey was primarily a male name popular in the South. Parents began to give the name to girls around 1975, and when the career of country singer Lacy J. Dalton began in 1980 it rose to become one of the 100 most popular names of the decade. It declined throughout the 1990s, and by 2000 the less common spellings had fallen off the SSA top 1,000 list. Then in December 2002 the Laci Peterson disappearance and murder case received nationwide publicity. All three of the less common spellings jumped back onto the top 1,000 list in 2003, with Laci, formerly the rarest spelling, now just behind Lacey. This is a striking example of how media attention can inspire some parents to use a name even when that publicity is negative. In 2004 the four spellings combined were given to more than 1,800 girls, ranking the name 185th. Other spellings: **Laci, Lacie, Lacy**

Laisha

The most popular women's fashion magazine in Israel is called *Laisha*, in Hebrew "For the Woman." One of the most popular young actresses in Mexico is named Laisha Wilkins. Whether her name has anything to do with the Hebrew phrase is unknown, but it's certain that her fame has led many Hispanic-American parents to name daughters Laisha lately. There were 320 Laishas born in the United States in 2004, ranking the name 789th on the SSA top 1,000 list.

Lakeisha

African-American creation, derived by adding *La-* to the name **Keisha.** Lakeisha is the most popular *La-* name, but other fashionable names formed in the same way include Laporsha, Laquisha, Lashay, Lashonda, **Latasha, Latisha,** Latonya, **Latoya,** and Latrice. *La-* names were particularly popular during the 1970s and 1980s; by 1990, however, *Sha-* had become a more fashionable prefix for newly created African-American names.

Lalia

Feminine form of Latin *Laelius,* "fair speech."

Lana

Variation of **Alana.** Lana is one of the names most clearly connected to the career of a particular film star. Lana Turner first received wide notice from her role in the 1938 film *Love Finds Andy Hardy,* and her name jumped onto the SSA top 1,000 list in 1939. Lana was moderately popular in the 1940s and then receded until it nearly vanished in 1995. It suddenly began to revive in 2001. By 2004 its use had almost tripled; it ranked 388th, with 632 girls receiving the name. Perhaps the huge popularity of **Ava** has inspired parents to search for other "Hollywood legend" names.

Other spelling: **Lanna**

Laney

Pet form of **Elaine** used independently. Laney entered the SSA top 1,000 list in 2000, and the variant spelling **Lainey** followed in 2003. There were 844 Laneys born in 2004, ranking the name 319th.

Lara

Form of **Larissa.** In 1965 when Julie Christie played Lara in the movie version of Boris Pasternak's *Doctor Zhivago,* and a song from the movie, "Lara's Theme," became a hit, this Russian name suddenly leapt onto the SSA top 1,000 list. Lara was moderately popular for the next decade, then slowly declined until 2001, when another film, *Lara Croft: Tomb Raider,* starring Angelina Jolie, caused a small reversal in this decline, though there are already signs that reverse may have been temporary. Lara ranked 734th on the SSA list in 2004, when 356 girls were given the name.

Larissa

Russian form of Latin *hilaris,* "laughing, cheerful." This name became well established in the United States in the 1970s, though it never grew hugely popular. In 2004 almost 700 girls were given the name, ranking it 375th. In 1991 a newly discovered moon of the planet Neptune was named Larissa.

Variation: **Lara**

Lark

Old English *lāwerce*, name of the bird. Lark has been sporadically used as a girls name for at least 120 years.

Latifah

Feminine form of Arabic *Latif*, "kind, gentle."
Famous name: Queen Latifah (singer and actress)

Latisha

Form of **Letitia,** respelled to conform to the pattern of *La-* names popular in the African-American community.

LaToya

In her autobiography, singer LaToya Jackson says that her mother simply made up this name. It was possibly formed by adding *La-* to **Toya,** a Mexican pet form of **Victoria.** The singer's fame made LaToya the third most popular name for African-American girls born in the early 1980s, but its use has now faded.

Laura

Feminine form of Latin *Laurus*, "laurel tree." Laura was a familiar name in England by the 12th century. In 1327, Petrarch caught sight of Laure de Noves in a church in Avignon. He maintained that seeing her made him a poet, and the famous sonnets Petrarch wrote for his beloved Laura immortalized the name. Laura was common in the 19th century but then receded until 1944, when it was in 119th place on the SSA list. That year the film *Laura* came out, in which actor Dana Andrews is mesmerized by the portrait of actress Gene Tierney, and use of the name revived. Between 1960 and 1989, it was again one of the 25 most common names for girls. It then began to diminish, and its 2004 ranking of 146th, with nearly 2,500 Lauras born, was its lowest ever.
Famous names: Laura Bush (first lady)
               Laura Dern (actress)
               Laura Ingalls Wilder (writer)
Nicknames: **Laurie, Lori, Lorie, Lorrie, Lorry**
Variations: **Laure** (French), **Lauretta, Laurette** (French), **Laurice, Lavra** (Czech and Greek), **Lora** (German), **Loretta, Lorette, Lorita**

Laurel

English form of Old French *lorer,* "bay tree, laurel." The ancient Greeks crowned winners of athletic games with laurel wreaths. Laurel was barely used in the 19th century when other flower names were common, but it had a minor vogue in the 1950s, when it was one of the 250 most common girls names. In 2004 it ranked 738th on the SSA list, with 353 born.

Lauren

Modern feminine form of **Lawrence.** This was a male name before Lauren Bacall's debut as a movie star in 1944 immediately caused it to become more common for girls. Use of Lauren grew slowly until around 1980 when it suddenly exploded. It has been one of the top 30 names for American girls since 1982, and although it peaked in 1989, its subsequent decline has been gradual. In 2004 Lauren was the 26th most popular name, given to more than 10,000 girls.
Famous names: Lauren Graham (actress)
　　　　　　　Lauren Jackson (basketball player)
Variations: **Laureen, Laurence** (French), **Laurentia** (Latin), **Laurina, Loren, Lorena, Lorene, Lorenza** (Spanish and Italian), **Lorine, Lourenca** (Portuguese)

Lavender

Name of an herb with sweet-smelling blossoms; often used today to describe the pale purple color of those flowers. Lavender Brown is a Hogwarts student in Harry Potter's class in J. K. Rowling's novels.

Lavinia

Lavinia is the wife of the Trojan hero Aeneas in Virgil's *Aeneid.* Lavinia Mannon is the heroine of playwright Eugene O'Neill's tragedy *Mourning Becomes Electra.* This 19th-century name is rare today.

Layla, Laila

Forms of **Leila.** Layla had a minor vogue in the 1970s when Eric Clapton's song "Layla" became a huge hit. It then vanished until the 1990s when parents rediscovered it as an alternative to names like **Kayla** and **Lacey.** The two spellings combined were given to more than 3,000 girls in 2004, ranking it 113th and making Layla one of the fastest-growing girls names of the new century.
Famous name: Laila Ali (boxer)

Leah

Origin unclear; perhaps Hebrew "languid" or "wild cow" or Assyrian "ruler." In the Bible, Leah is the sister of Rachel and the first wife of Jacob. Leah is a name that has always been present but never very common in the United States. Recently Leah has been growing in use, and in 2004 ranked 62nd, its highest placing ever, with more than 5,500 American girls given the name.
Other spellings: **Lea, Leia, Lia**

Leandra

Feminine form of *Leandros,* Greek *leon* [lion] + *andros* [man].

Leann, Leanne

Combination of **Leah** or **Lee** and **Anne,** or an English respelling of **Liane.** Mildly popular in the 1960s, this name has now faded.
Famous name: LeAnn Rimes (country singer)

Leanna

English form of **Liana,** reinterpreted as a blend of **Lee** and **Anna.** Until 2004 this was the most common spelling of the name in the United States, but Liana has now surpassed it.

Leda

Greek, meaning unknown. In Greek mythology, Leda is the mother of four famous children: Helen of Troy, Castor, Pollux, and Clytemnestra. Helen was the child of Leda and Zeus, who seduced Leda by appearing to her as a swan. Irish poet William Butler Yeats wrote the poem "Leda and the Swan" about this mythological event.

Lee

Old English *leah,* "glade, clearing, pasture." Lee can also be used as a nickname for any name ending with *-ley.*
Famous name: Lee Grant (actress and director)
Other spellings: **Lea, Leigh**

Leila

Arabic *Layla,* perhaps "dark night" or "intoxicating wine." This popular name in Middle Eastern countries has roots in Arabian romance literature. English poet George Gordon, Lord Byron, chose it for *Don Juan* and *The Giaour.* Leila was popular in the United States in the 19th century and recently has begun to increase in use; almost 900 girls were given the name in 2004, ranking it 307th. It can be pronounced either "Leela," "Layla," or "Lyla."

Famous name: Leila Josefowicz (violinist)

Variations: **Laila, Layla, Leilah, Lela, Lelah, Lelia, Lila**

Leilani

Hawaiian "heavenly garland." This common Hawaiian name spread to the mainland United States and Latin America by the song "Sweet Leilani." Introduced in the movie *Waikiki Wedding* (1937), the song won an Academy Award. A recording of it by Bing Crosby sold more than a million copies. Almost 1,000 Leilanis were born in the United States in 2004, ranking it 299th for the year.

Lena

Usually a variation of **Helen,** but also a form of **Arlene** or **Magdalena.** Lena was one of the top 50 names of the 1890s and has had an extremely slow decline ever since. More than 800 girls were given the name in 2004, ranking it 329th.

Famous names: Lena Horne (singer and actress)

Lena Olin (actress)

Other spellings: **Leana, Lina**

Lenore

Variation of **Eleanor** and **Leonora.** Edgar Allan Poe used this name in his often-memorized poem "The Raven."

Lenuta

(See **Helen.**)

Leona

Feminine form of **Leo** or **Leon,** Latin "lion." This name was at its height of popularity in 1905 but is rare today.

Variations: **Leone** (Lithuanian), **Leonella** (Italian), **Leonelle, Leonia** (Russian and Ukrainian), **Leonie, Leonne** (French)

Leonora

Italian form of **Eleanor.** In Beethoven's opera *Fidelio,* Leonora assumes the name Fidelio. Beethoven wrote four different overtures for this opera, and three are entitled "Leonora."

Variations: **Lenora, Lenore, Leonor, Leonore**

Lesley

British feminine form of **Leslie;** Scottish place name and surname, perhaps from Gaelic *leas celyn,* "court of hollies." Robert Burns wrote a poem about a bonny Scottish lass named Lesley, but this name was not regularly used for girls in England and the United States until the 20th century.

Famous name: Lesley Stahl (television newscaster)

Variations: **Lesli, Leslie, Lesly, Lezlie**

Leslie

Variation of **Lesley.** This is considered a masculine spelling in England, but in the United States it has been the most common spelling of the feminine name. Leslie rose swiftly during the 1940s and was one of the top 100 names for American girls born between 1953 and 1988. It then receded for a few years but began to grow in use again when Hispanic-Americans adopted it. This spelling yields identical pronunciations in both Spanish and English. More than 4,600 Leslies were born in 2004, ranking the name 78th.

Famous name: Leslie Caron (actress)

Leta

Latin *laetus,* "glad."

Letitia

Latin *laetitia,* "gladness."

Famous name: Letitia Baldrige (etiquette expert)

Nicknames: **Lettie, Letty, Ticia, Tish, Tisha, Titia**

Variations: **Laeticia, Laetitia, Latisha, Leticia** (Spanish), **Letizia** (Italian), **Lettice, Letycja** (Polish)

Lexi, Lexie

These pet forms of **Alexandra** are booming in popularity along with almost every other variation of the name. More than 1,500 were born in 2004, ranking the name 214th for the year.

Lexus

The trade name of the luxury automobile used as a girls name. Though Lexus is popular because it could be considered a short form of **Alexis,** the name of the car is obviously affecting parents' choices because the spelling Lexus is much more frequently found than **Lexis.** Lexus has been on the SSA top 1,000 list since 1992 and peaked at 450th on that list in 1996, when 555 girls received the name. In 2004, 244 girls were named Lexus, ranking it 968th.

Liana

Short form of **Juliana** or **Liliana,** or Romanian form of **Lillian.** This form of the name is rising as Leanna is falling. Some parents interpret this as a nature name since *liana* means "climbing plant or vine." Liana ranked 360th in 2004, with about 700 girls given the name.
Other spellings: **Leana, Leanna, Leeanna, Leighanna, Lianna**

Liane

French short form of *Eliane,* feminine form of Latin *Elianus* from Greek *helios,* "sun."
Other spellings: **Leanne, Lianne**

Libby

Variation of **Elizabeth.** Libby abruptly vanished around 1970 but returned to the SSA top 1,000 list in 2002. In 2004, 295 girls were given the name, ranking it 827th.

Liberty

Since 1880, this patriotic word name has entered the SSA top 1,000 list three times: first, in 1918, the year World War I ended; second, in 1976, the bicentennial year of the American revolution; and third, in 2001, as part of the modern vogue for word names ending in –y. Liberty has continued to increase in use since 2001. In 2004, 730 American girls were given the name, ranking it 347th.

Liesl

This German pet form of **Elizabeth** is probably still best known to Americans as the name of the Von Trapp daughter who was "sixteen going on seventeen" in the famous musical film *The Sound of Music.*

Lila

Form of **Delilah** or **Leila.** Like **Layla,** Leila, and **Lola,** Lila has been rediscovered by American parents recently. It ranked 404th in 2004.
Other spellings: **Lilah, Lyla, Lylah**

Lilia

This Latinate form of **Lily** is regularly used by Hispanic-Americans but is also found in central and eastern Europe. It ranked 948th on the SSA list in 2004.

Liliana, Lilliana

Spanish and Italian form of **Lillian.** This name is increasing in use; more than 1,900 girls were given the name in 2004, ranking it 178th.

Lilith

Hebrew "night monster" or "screech owl." In medieval Jewish folk-lore, Lilith was the first woman. Most people today will associate the name with the character Lilith, played by Bebe Neuwirth, on the television shows *Cheers* and *Frasier.*

Lillian

Origin unclear, but probably a medieval English and German varia-tion of **Elizabeth.** Lillian seems to be an older name in Britain than **Lily,** but this name has long been associated with the lily, which is a symbol for purity in Christian art. Lillian was a top ten name between 1890 and 1923. It fell to a low point in the 1980s but was always among the 500 most common names on the SSA list. Lately it has been rebounding; more than 5,000 Lillians were born in 2004, ranking the name 67th.

Famous names: Lillian Gish (actress)
               Lillian Vernon (entrepreneur)
Nicknames: **Lil, Lilie, Lillie, Lilly, Lily**
Other spelling: **Lilian**
Variations: **Liana** (Romanian), **Lili** (German), **Lilia, Liliana, Liliane**
          (French), **Lilias** (Scottish), **Lilli** (German), **Lilliana** (Italian,
          Spanish, and Slavic), **Lilyan**

Lily

Greek *leirion,* Latin *lilium,* and Old English *lilie,* "lily"; or a variation of **Lillian.** This name has been soaring for a decade and is now the most popular flower name after **Jasmine.** More than 7,300 girls received Lily as their name in 2004, ranking it 46th. If all the girls named **Liliana,** Lillian, and Lily were counted together, they would rank as the 14th most common name of 2004.

Famous name: Lily Tomlin (actress and comedienne)
Other spellings: **Lillie, Lilly**

Linda

Spanish "beautiful"; German *linde,* "weak, mild" or "linden-wood"; or a variation of **Belinda** or **Melinda.** This name was probably first derived from one of the many Germanic names ending in -linde or from one of the popular poetic names created in 17th-century England using the feminine suffix -inda, such as Melinda. But when Linda became widely popular around 1940, it was often assumed to be from the Spanish adjective "linda." However, this name wasn't used in Spanish-speaking countries until after it became popular in England and the United States. Whatever its origins, Linda had a meteoric rise and ranked as the number-one name between 1947 and 1952, the first name to replace **Mary** at the top of the girls list in centuries. More than 99,000 girls were named Linda in 1947 alone. In 2004, however, there were only 700 Lindas born, ranking it 357th.

Famous names: Linda Evans (actress)
                Linda Ronstadt (singer)
Other spelling: **Lynda**
Variations: **Lin, Lindy**

Lindsay, Lindsey

Old English place name "Lincoln's island" from linn [lake] + coln [Roman colony] + eg [island]. Both main spellings of this formerly masculine name entered the SSA top 1,000 list in 1974, the year before Lindsay Wagner began to star in The Bionic Woman. Perhaps audiences noticed her when she appeared in 1974 in the pilot for The Rockford Files, or perhaps her rise to fame and the name's rise to prominence are coincidental. In any event, Lindsay undoubtedly became popular in the 1980s because parents decided it was the perfect twist on **Linda,** no matter where they originally heard it. In 2004 there were more than 3,800 Lindsays born, ranking it 97th.

Famous name: Lindsay Lohan (actress)
Other spellings: **Lindsie, Lindsy**
Variation: **Linsey**

Linnea

Feminine form of Linne, Germanic "lime tree." This name has traditionally been most common in Sweden.

Lisa

Variation of **Elizabeth.** Lisa entered the SSA top 1,000 list in 1937 and steadily advanced to the top spot, which it held between 1962 and 1969. However, by 2004 fewer than 700 Lisas were born, ranking the name 364th for the year.

Famous names: Lisa Fernandez (softball player)
Lisa Kudrow (actress)
Lisa Loeb (singer and songwriter)
Other spellings: **Leesa, Lesa**

Lisette, Lissette, Lizette

French forms of **Elizabeth.** This name has been fashionable with Hispanic-Americans for three decades, though the most popular spelling has changed over the years. By 2004 **Lizeth** was the chief spelling ("th" is pronounced as "t" in Spanish). The combined spellings accounted for almost 1,000 births in 2004, ranking the name 282nd.

Litzy

In 1999 young Mexican singer and actress Litzy starred as the character Laura in *DKDA,* the same series about young rock musicians that made **Axel** a popular name for boys in the Hispanic community. Litzy's career has continued to flower, and her name is still on the SSA top 1,000 list, ranking 420th in 2004, with 538 born. The origin of Litzy is obscure, but it is possibly just a Hispanic pet form of **Elizabeth** influenced by the present vogue among Latinos for the *-itz* sound also found in names like **Itzel** and **Maritza.**

Liv

Old Norse *hlíf,* "defense." In modern Norwegian, *liv* is the word for "life," and many parents in Scandinavia have reinterpreted this ancient name to have that meaning. American actress Liv Tyler was named after Norwegian actress Liv Ullmann.

Livia

Possibly Latin *lividus,* "bluish." Livia was the first empress of Rome. In modern times, this name is also used as a variation of **Olivia,** which is probably why it entered the SSA top 1,000 for the first time in 2004, at 949th place.

Liza

Variation of **Elizabeth.**
Famous name: Liza Minnelli (singer and actress)

Lizbeth

It might surprise some non-Hispanics to learn that the English name **Elizabeth** has been quite fashionable in Latin America for more than a generation and that Spanish speakers use many short forms of it as official names. Lizbeth is now the most common of these. It entered the SSA top 1,000 list in 1988, and though it peaked in 2002, in 2004 it still ranked 222nd, with more than 1,400 girls given the name, the great majority of them Hispanic.

Lizzie

Form of **Elizabeth.**

Logan

For origin, see Logan in the boys list. Logan has been regularly given to girls as well as boys since the late 1980s. As the name has become a hit for boys, it's receded a bit for girls. In 2004, almost 15 boys were named Logan for every girl that received the name. Still, there were 886 girls named Logan that year, ranking it 304th.

Lois

Possibly Greek "the better." Lois was one of the top 25 names around 1930, probably seen by parents as an alternative for **Louise.** It vanished in the 1980s and hasn't returned, in spite of the many versions of the Superman story that feature his girlfriend, Lois Lane.

Lola

Form of **Dolores.** Lola was common a century ago, and it just re-entered the SSA top 1,000 list in 2002, rising to 418th place in 2004 with more than 500 girls given the name. Many older Americans may have a hard time seeing Lola as an appropriate baby name, as it has a somewhat bawdy image that's been reinforced in movies and songs such as "Whatever Lola Wants, Lola Gets" from the musical *Damn Yankees!*
Famous name: Lola Falana (singer)

London

For origin, see London in the boys name list. Great cities, like ships and planes, are often poetically referred to as "she," so perhaps it's no surprise that more than twice as many girls as boys were named London in the United States in 2004, ranking it 668th on the SSA list.

Lorelei

Old German "lookout rock." The Lorelei is a huge rock along the Rhine that creates a dangerous narrow. Experts disagree as to whether the early-19th-century German poet Clemens Brentano invented the story of a beautiful lovelorn maiden who leaps from the rock and becomes a siren luring boatmen to their deaths, or whether he was reviving an ancient tale. In either case, the Lorelei maiden is one of the most beloved figures in German literature. However, the name has been most often used in the United States, partly because of Anita Loos's classic 1925 novel *Gentlemen Prefer Blondes,* in which Lorelei Lee is a fun-loving gold digger. The story became a Broadway musical and a 1953 film starring Marilyn Monroe. Lorelei had been off the SSA top 1,000 list for nearly 40 years when it popped in again at 969th place in 2004. Perhaps that is related to the character Lorelai on the television series *Gilmore Girls.*

Lorena

Variation of **Lauren.** This name is especially common in the Hispanic-American community today. There were 464 girls named Lorena in 2004, ranking it 596th on the SSA list.

Loretta

Variation of **Laura;** also, a feminine form of *Loreto,* "laurels," name of an Italian town to which angels supposedly brought the Virgin Mary's house in the 13th century. Loretta's peak of use in the 1930s and 1940s seems to have coincided with the film career of Loretta Young. The name hasn't been on the SSA top 1,000 list since 1990. Famous name: Loretta Lynn (country singer)

Lori

Variation of **Laura** and **Lorraine.** Lori had one of the fastest rises and falls as a baby name in the 20th century. It was seemingly nonexistent before 1946, rose to top ten status in 1963, and then slid back down to disappear in 2001.

Lorna

This name was invented for the heroine of the popular 19th-century novel *Lorna Doone* by R. D. Blackmore. There was a minor vogue for Lorna from 1930 to 1960, but it vanished again after 1975.

Lorraine

French place name, derived from **Lothair,** Old German "loud army." Lorraine was a top 100 name from 1918 to 1948, but it's now rare. Variations: **Laraine, Lorain, Loraine, Lori, Lorrayne, Lorrie, Lorry**

Lottie

Form of **Charlotte**. In the 19th century, this nickname was so popular that it became an independent name, but few parents choose it today.
Other spellings: **Lottey, Lotti, Lotty**
Variations: **Lotta, Lotte** (German)

Louisa

Feminine form of **Louis,** Old German "famous warrior." This name has a lengthy history as a favorite name of royal women in Europe, but it was seldom used in England until the 17th century. Louisa of Mecklenburg-Strelitz, the wife of Frederick William, was the queen of Prussia in the 18th century. Americans are most familiar with the name of Louisa May Alcott, the author of *Little Women*. Louisa was extremely common in the early 19th century and is one of the few such names from that time period not yet revived by American parents. But with **Lucy** gaining ground and **Sophia** and **Isabella** so popular, Louisa would make a great "different but not too different" choice today.
Variations: **Lou, Louise** (French), **Lovisa** (Swedish), **Ludovica** (Danish and Romanian), **Ludwika** (Polish), **Luigina** (Italian), **Luisa** (Italian and Spanish), **Luise** (German)

Louise

French form of **Louisa.** Louise largely replaced Louisa at the end of the 19th century in the United States and was one of the top 50 names for girls between 1875 and 1937. It's almost never given as an American first name today, but it retains some popularity as a middle name. In England, however, Louise only started to become popular after 1960 and was at its peak around 1978 when Louise Brown, the world's first "test-tube baby," was born. In the 1990s Louise returned to regular use in its native France after having been rare there since 1920.
Famous names: Louise Erdrich (writer)
Louise Fletcher (actress)
Louise Nevelson (sculptor)
Variations: **Lou, Louisette, Luise, Lulu**

Luba

Polish and Bulgarian form of a Slavic name meaning "love."

Lucia

Spanish, Italian, Portuguese, and Scandinavian form of **Lucy.** St. Lucia (Lucy) has been especially popular in both Sweden and Italy, and both Swedish-American and Italian-American communities hold Santa Lucia festivals in her honor. Lucia is a name that has been regularly used but never very popular for more than a century. The last few years it has begun to gain some notice, and it may be primed to have a more fashionable period soon. More than 700 Lucias were born in the United States in 2004, ranking it 348th. Lucia was the number-one name for girls born in Spain in 2004.

Luciana

Feminine form of **Lucian,** Latin "bringing light."
Variations: **Lucienne** (French), **Lucina**

Lucille

French form of Lucilla. Between 1896 and 1937, Lucille was a top 100 name in the United States and was especially popular in the South. The name returned to the SSA top 1,000 list in 2003 after having been absent since 1976. Lucille Mulhall (1885–1940) was the first woman to compete in rodeo-riding and steer-roping events and is known as "the world's first cowgirl."
Famous name: Lucille Ball (actress)
Other spelling: **Lucile**
Variation: **Lucy**

Lucinda

Variation of **Lucy,** created by Spanish author Miguel de Cervantes in the 17th century for a character in his famous novel *Don Quixote.*

Lucretia

Feminine form of *Lucretius,* ancient Roman family name of unknown derivation. In the 15th century, Lucrezia di Borgia was a powerful member of the Borgia family of Italy. She was accused of poisoning her enemies.
Variations: **Lucrece** (French), **Lucrecia** (Spanish), **Lucrezia** (Italian)

Lucy

Feminine form of **Lucius,** a Roman family name, probably meaning "light." Although it seems that Lucy ought to be a derivative of

Lucille, it's actually the other way around. Lucy was quite popular in the 19th century and then faded. It revived strongly in England in the 1990s and in 2004 was one of the top ten names in England and Wales. American parents have also begun to notice Lucy again. In 2004 more than 1,600 girls were given the name, ranking it 199th for the year. It is, of course, difficult for many Americans over the age of 40 to hear this name and not immediately think of the comic persona created by Lucille Ball in several successive television series.

Famous names: Lucy Liu (actress)
Lucy Stone (suffragist)

Variations: **Liusaidh** (Scots Gaelic), **Luca** (Hungarian), **Luce** (French), **Lucetta, Lucette, Lucia** (Spanish, Italian, Portuguese, and Scandinavian), **Lucie** (Dutch, French, Czech, and German), **Lucilla, Lucinda, Lucja** (Polish), **Lukija** (Greek and Ukrainian), **Luzia** (Portuguese)

Lulu

Swahili "pearl"; also, a form of **Louise.**
Variations: **Lula, Lulita**

Luna

Name of the ancient Roman goddess personifying the moon. Luna was regularly used as a first name in the late 19th century, but it completely vanished in the 1920s. The name's long eclipse ended in 2003, and in 2004 there were 364 American girls given the name, ranking it 725th on the SSA list.

Luz

Spanish "light," a Marian devotion name from the title "Our Lady of Light." This traditional Hispanic name has been in the SSA top 1,000 continuously since 1950, ranking 601st in 2004.

Lydia

Greek place name *Lydios,* an ancient country in Asia Minor, which was once ruled by Croesus, a king who was noted for his great wealth. In the New Testament, Lydia is the name of a business-woman who converted to Christianity and entertained the apostle Paul in her home. Lydia was a common name in the 19th century, and though it faded in the 20th it never vanished like many other Victorian names did. Since the early 1980s it's been slowly but steadily increasing in use. More than 2,500 Lydias were born in 2004, ranking it 141st for the year.

Variations: **Liddy, Lidia** (Spanish, Polish, and Italian), **Lidija** (Russian), **Lyda, Lydie** (French)

Lynette

Old French form of Welsh *Eluned,* meaning uncertain. Lynette is often thought of as a modern variation of **Lynn,** but it's actually a much older name. In Arthurian legends, Gareth wins Lynette's love by rescuing her sister, held hostage by four renegade knights. Today the name is probably best known through the frazzled character Lynette Scavo on the television series *Desperate Housewives.*

Other spellings: **Linette, Lynnette**

Variations: **Linet, Linetta**

Lynn, Lynne

Old English *hlynn,* "stream." Lynn was considered a masculine name until the 20th century. It probably changed sexes after **Linda** became a popular name for girls and it was reinterpreted as a short form of that name. Lynn was one of the top 100 names for American girls between 1946 and 1968. It is rare as a first name today but remains one of the top middle names for American girls.

Famous name: Lynn Redgrave (actress)

Other spellings: **Lin, Linn, Lyn**

Variation: **Lynelle**

Lyric

In 1983, actor and aspiring songwriter Robby Benson named his daughter Lyric. Perhaps the screenwriters of the 1994 film *Jason's Lyric,* in which Jada Pinkett Smith played the title role, remembered that when choosing the name. In any event, 1995 was the first year enough parents named daughters Lyric for the name to enter the SSA top 1,000 list. Like many names introduced by films, Lyric peaked in use the year after (in 1996), although it hasn't yet vanished. There were 365 Lyrics born in the United States in 2004, ranking the name 722nd.

Mabel

Latin *amabilis*, "lovable, amiable." Mabel is an old variation of Amabel, dating to at least the 13th century. It was one of the top 25 names for American girls from about 1873 until 1903. It then declined and vanished during the 1960s. Although it hasn't returned to the SSA top 1,000 list, creative intellectual parents have already begun to name daughters Mabel again, and with **Hazel** returning to popularity, Mabel probably won't be far behind. In Spanish-speaking countries Mabel is often used as a short form of María Isabel, pronounced "mah-BEHL." Variations: **Amabel, Mabelle, Mable, Maible** (Irish), **Maybelle**

Mackenzie

Scots Gaelic "son of Kenneth." This name was rarely used for girls before 1975, when actress Mackenzie Phillips began appearing on the television series *One Day at a Time*. Mackenzie marched up the popularity charts after that and seems to have inspired parents to turn other surnames starting with *Mc-* into first names for girls. In 2004 more than 9,300 Mackenzies were born in the United States, ranking it 31st. Other spellings: **Makenzie, McKenzie**

Macy

English surname, either from a medieval pet form of **Matthew** or from a Norman French place name meaning "Maccius's place." Macy was used sporadically in the late 19th century, probably as a variation of **Maisie.** The beginning of its frequent use, however, came in 1990, almost surely as a result of the character Macy Alexander on the daytime soap opera *The Bold and the Beautiful*. Many Americans will associate this name with the department store in New York and its famous Thanksgiving Day parade, and since the soap opera deals with the New York fashion industry, there may have been a connection in the screenwriters' minds. Macy entered the SSA list at 641st place and has steadily risen in use since. In 2004, almost 3,000

American girls were given one of the name's four main spellings, ranking it 125th for the year.

Other spellings: **Macey, Maci, Macie**

Maddie

Variation of **Madeline** or **Madison**. Though Maddie will be often heard as a nickname in the future, it's rarely used as an official name.

Madeleine

French form of **Madeline**. Madeleine Albright was the first woman to serve as U.S. secretary of state. Madeleine L'Engle is author of the classic young adult novel *A Wrinkle in Time*.

Madeline

English form of *Magdalene*, "woman of Magdala"; or Greek form of Hebrew place-name *migdal*, "high tower." This became a popular name in medieval times in honor of St. Mary Magdalene. Madeline is the name of the heroine of John Keats's poem "The Eve of St. Agnes." Most modern Americans will remember it better, though, as the little Parisian heroine of the best-selling children's books by Ludwig Bemelmans. The first *Madeline* book was published in 1939 and has sold more than ten million copies worldwide. Bemelmans named the character after his wife, Madeleine. The name Madeline was moderately popular around 1914 and then declined. It was just beginning to creep up in use when the television series *Moonlighting* premiered in 1985 with its model-turned-investigator character Maddie, played by Cybill Shepherd, which gave it a huge boost. In 2004 there were more than 10,700 Madelines born, ranking the name 24th.

Famous name: Madeline Kahn (actress)

Nicknames: **Mada, Maddie, Maddy** (German)

Other spellings: **Madaline, Madelaine, Madolyn**

Variations: **Alena** (Czech), **Madailein** (Irish Gaelic), **Madalena** (Portuguese), **Madalene, Maddalena** (Italian), **Madel** (Norwegian), **Madeleine** (French), **Madelena, Madelina** (Dutch), **Madelon** (French), **Madlen** (German), **Madzia** (Polish), **Magdalen, Magdalena** (Spanish), **Magdalene** (German), **Magdalina** (Russian), **Magdalini** (Greek), **Magdolna** (Hungarian), **Magli** (Danish), **Makalonca** (Slovenian), **Malena** (German), **Malene** (Danish), **Malin, Malina** (Swedish), **Maudlin**

Madison

Middle English *Madyson,* either "son of Matthew" or "son of Maud."
Madison was exclusively a name for boys until 1984, when it was
used for the mermaid character played by actress Daryl Hannah in
the movie *Splash.* Even though the name was presented as a joke—
the character, asked her name, looks at a New York City street sign
and names herself after Madison Avenue—parents immediately
began giving the name to their daughters. Madison may have been
readily accepted as a name for girls despite its *-son* ending because
Maddie and **Madeline** were given a boost by *Moonlighting* the following year. In 2004, Madison was the number-two girls name in the
United States, with 22,584 girls given one of the five chief spellings.
Other spellings: **Maddison, Madisen, Madisyn, Madyson**

Mae

Variation of **May.** In September 1992 astronaut Dr. Mae C. Jemison
became the first nonwhite woman to go into space.
Famous name: Mae West (actress)

Maegan

Modern American variation of **Megan,** blending it with the sound of
Mae. This form was regularly used in the 1990s but is rare today.

Maeve

Irish Gaelic *Medb,* "intoxicating." The most famous Maeve in Irish
legend is Queen Maeve of Connacht. She was strong, beautiful, sexy,
and impetuous, and the story of her battle with Ulster to acquire its
famous Brown Bull is one of the most beloved Irish tales. Her name
seems to be gradually becoming more popular with Irish-Americans.
Maeve entered the SSA list in 1997, and 369 American girls
received it in 2004, ranking it 713th.
Famous name: Maeve Binchy (author)

Magda

Variation of **Magdalena.** This used to be a popular name in German-
speaking countries.

Magdalena

Form of **Madeline.** This is the main form of the name in Spain,
Portugal, Germany, the Netherlands, and Poland. In the United

States, use of this name has been growing recently among the Hispanic-American population. More than 300 Magdalenas were born in 2004, ranking it 804th on the SSA list.
Nicknames: **Lena, Magda, Maggie**

Magenta

The reddish-purple color, named after the 1859 Battle of Magenta, Italy, where Napoleon defeated the Austrians. This is one of the color names attracting creative parents today.

Maggie

Form of **Magdalena, Magnolia,** or **Margaret.** Maggie was common as an independent name in the 19th century. It then slid down the SSA list to a low point of 806th place in 1970, but since then it has had a slow and fairly steady increase. In 2004, more than 1,600 girls were given the name, ranking Maggie 201st that year. In Tennessee Williams's play *Cat on a Hot Tin Roof,* Maggie the Cat is a young wife stifled by her Southern in-laws. Rod Stewart popularized the song "Maggie May." And television today features a baby called Maggie on *The Simpsons.*
Famous names: Maggie Gyllenhaal (actress)
           Maggie Smith (actress)

Magnolia

New Latin "magnolia flower and tree," from Pierre Magnol, a French botanist. This name is best known from a character in the Broadway musical *Show Boat,* which was based on the novel of the same name by Edna Ferber. Though the name was never very common, there were enough Magnolias born to keep the name in the lower part of the SSA top 1,000 list from 1880 until 1940.
Variations: **Mag, Maggie, Maggy, Nola, Nolie**

Mahala, Mahalia

Forms of *Mahalath,* an Old Testament Hebrew name perhaps meaning "harp."
Famous name: Mahalia Jackson (singer)
Variations: **Haley, Mahalah, Mahalie**

Mairead

Gaelic form of **Margaret.** Mairead Corrigan shared the Nobel Peace prize (with Betty Williams) in 1976 for cofounding the Community for Peace in Northern Ireland.

Maisie

Scottish variation of **Margaret.** Henry James used this name for the child heroine in *What Maisie Knew.* Maisie has recently returned to popularity in England and Wales, ranking 58th there in 2004.

Maitland

British surname from Norman French *mautalent,* "bad disposition." It's unclear if this originally referred to someone's personality, or to someone from a village in France given the name because its soil was poor.

Maki

Japanese "true hope."

Malia, Maliyah

Malia is the Hawaiian language form of **Mary;** Maliyah is possibly from Arabic *Maliha,* "praising," but is more likely a respelling of Malia influenced by the fashion for *-iyah* names in the African-American community. Malia was so common in Hawaii between 1977 and 1984 that the name usually made the national SSA top 1,000 list in those years, though it never rose above 920th place. In the early 1990s parents all over the United States discovered it, and it has risen in use fairly steadily since. **Maleah** entered the SSA list in 2001, and Maliyah in 2002. The three spellings combined were given to nearly 1,200 girls in 2004, ranking the name 243rd.
Famous name: Malia Jones (champion surfer)

Mallory

Old French *malheure,* "unlucky, unhappy." Mallory is a classic example of a television-inspired name. Before 1982 it was quite rare as a given name and when found was usually male. Then the television comedy *Family Ties* premiered. Mallory was the name of the older teenage daughter, played by Justine Bateman. In 1983, Mallory catapulted onto the SSA top 1,000 list in 333rd place, a very high initial entry, and in the mid-1980s it became one of the top 100 names for American girls. Though the name has slowly declined since, it does not seem to be in any danger of vanishing soon. More than 1,800 Mallorys were born in 2004, ranking it 188th that year.
Other spellings: **Malerie, Mallori, Mallorie, Malorie, Malory**

Mame, Mamie

Forms of **Mary**. The novel *Auntie Mame* was made into a movie, a Broadway musical, and then a movie of the musical, with the title role played by actresses Rosalind Russell, Angela Lansbury, and Lucille Ball. Mamie was a top 100 name in the late 19th century and then swiftly dropped in use after 1912. Having Mamie Eisenhower in the White House as first lady in the 1950s did nothing to help the name, and it vanished in the 1960s.

Mamuranta

Chamoru (Guam) "to keep vigil over our own."

Mandy

Form of **Amanda**. Mandy was used as a given name in the 19th century but then disappeared until Amanda itself began to revive in the late 1950s. Barry Manilow's 1974 hit song "Mandy" pushed the name into the top 100 for a few years in the mid-1970s. But by 2004 it had fallen to 840th place on the SSA list, with fewer than 300 girls given the name that year.
Famous name: Mandy Moore (singer and actress)
Other spellings: **Mandi, Mandie**

Manisha

Sanskrit *Maniṣā*, "thought, conception, reflection." Nepali actress Manisha Koirala is a star of India's Bollywood film industry.

Manon

This French form of **Mary** was the number-one name in France in 1995 and 1996, but it is still exceedingly rare in the United States, in spite of opera fans' familiarity with *Manon Lescaut*.

Manuela

Feminine form of **Manuel**.

Mara

Hebrew "bitter." The name appears in the biblical Book of Ruth, when Naomi refers to herself as Mara to express her grief and bitterness over the death of her husband and sons. This name has been regularly used since the 1950s without ever becoming very common. There were 422 Maras born in 2004, ranking it 637th on the SSA list.
Famous name: Mara Liasson (radio news correspondent)

Marcela, Marcella

Spanish and Italian feminine forms of Latin *Marcellus*, "little **Marcus**." In *Don Quixote*, Marcela is a shepherdess who is described as "the most beautiful creature ever sent into the world."
Nicknames: **Marcie, Marcy**
Variations: **Marcelena, Marcelia, Marcelline**

March

The name of the month, originally Latin *Martius mēnsis*, "month of Mars."

Marcia

Feminine form of *Marcius*, Latin family name derived from Mars, the god of war. Most American women with this name pronounce it as Marsha, but a few insist on the original Latin "Mar-see-uh." Marcia was quite popular in the 1940s and 1950s but has now faded away as an American baby name.
Famous name: Marcia Cross (actress)
Nicknames: **Marcie, Marcy**
Variations: **Marca, Marchita, Marcile, Markita, Marquita, Marsha, Marsi** (Estonian), **Marzia** (Italian)

Marcie, Marcy

These short forms of **Marcella** or **Marcia** were moderately common as independent names in the 1960s but have vanished along with Marcia as baby names today.

Maren

This is the Danish form of **Marina**, but many American parents probably consider it a form of **Mary**. Maren is a name that's always present at a low level but usually not given enough times in a year to make the SSA top 1,000 list. It did manage this in 2004, however, reaching 946th place when it was given to 252 girls.

Margaret

Greek *Margarites*, form of *margaron*, "pearl." There are many saints named Margaret, but only St. Margaret, the maid of Antioch, is represented wearing pearls. Margaret Beaufort, the countess of Richmond, was the mother of Henry VII of England and was instrumental in putting him and the House of Tudor on the throne. The late Princess Margaret was the sister of Queen Elizabeth II. Margaret was one of the top ten names for girls through most of American history until 1940. Use of the name has slowly declined since. Though its ranking of 149th in 2004 was its lowest ever, there were still more than 2,400 girls given the name that year. The large number of variations of Margaret shows that it has historically been a favorite name in almost every European culture.

Famous names: Margaret Atwood (writer)
Margaret Cho (comedienne)
Margaret Mead (anthropologist)
Margaret Mitchell (novelist)
Margaret Thatcher (prime minister of Great Britain)

Nicknames: **Madge, Mag, Maggie, Maggy, Marge, Margie, May, Meg, Meggie, Midge, Peg, Peggie, Peggy**

Variations: **Gosia** (Polish), **Greet** (Dutch), **Greta** (Swedish), **Gretchen** (German), **Grete** (Danish and German), **Gretel** (German), **Mairead** (Irish and Scots Gaelic), **Maisie** (Scottish), **Maj** (Swedish), **Malgorzata** (Polish), **Maret** (Danish), **Marete** (Norwegian), **Marga, Margareta** (Swedish), **Margarethe** (German), **Margaretta, Margarette, Margarida** (Portuguese), **Margarita** (Lithuanian and Spanish), **Margherita** (Italian), **Margit** (Hungarian and Norwegian), **Margot** (French), **Margret, Margrethe** (Danish), **Margriet** (Dutch), **Marguerite** (French), **Mariquita** (Spanish), **Marjarita, Marjeta** (Slavic), **Marjorie** (Scottish), **Marketa** (Czech), **Marketta** (Finnish), **Megan** (Welsh), **Merete** (Danish), **Meta** (Norwegian), **Rita**

Margarita

Spanish form of **Margaret**. Margarita has been among the top 1,000 names on the SSA list since 1883, much longer than most Hispanic names. However, it is now decreasing in the Hispanic community just as Margaret is elsewhere. There were only 258 Margaritas born in 2004, and its ranking of 926th on the SSA list was its lowest ever. Nickname: **Rita**

Margo

Variation of **Margot.** There was a minor fashion for Margo in the 1940s, but it is quite rare today.

Margot

French variation of **Margaret.**
Famous name: Dame Margot Fonteyn (ballerina)
Other spellings: **Margaux, Margo**

Marguerite

French variation of **Margaret.** The French word *marguerite* means
"daisy." Marguerite was one of the top 100 names in the United
States between 1890 and 1921, but it's rare today.

Maria

Latin form of **Mary.** Maria is also the standard form of Mary in Italian,
Spanish, Portuguese, and most Germanic and Slavic languages. Maria
Theresa of Austria was empress of the Austro-Hungarian Empire
from 1740 to 1780, and was the mother of Queen Marie Antoinette
of France. In Leonard Bernstein's *West Side Story,* a Broadway musical
that re-creates the story of Romeo and Juliet, Maria is a young Puerto
Rican girl who falls in love with an American boy. "Maria," the song he
sings about her, is one of the best-known love songs in musical theater.
Maria Goeppert-Mayer was a cowinner of the 1963 Nobel Prize in
physics. Although Maria has been one of the top 100 names in the
United States since 1994, this traditional number-one name of Hispanic culture is receding just as Mary is receding in the general population; its highest point of use was in the 1970s. In 2004 more than
5,600 Marias were born in the United States, ranking it 59th.
Famous name: Maria Callas (opera singer)
Variations: **Mariah, Mia** (Swedish), **Mariela**

Mariah

This modern form of **Maria** is used to indicate that the name should
be pronounced "ma-RYE-uh," which was the way non-Hispanic-
Americans said "Maria" before the 20th century. Mariah entered the
SSA top 1,000 list in 1973 and grew slowly until 1990, when the
fame of singer Mariah Carey boosted it into the top 100 names for
girls. Though it's been receding since 1999, there were still more
than 2,900 Mariahs born in 2004, ranking it 129th for the year.

Mariam, Maryam

This is the Arabic form of **Mary** or **Miriam** and is used by both
Christians and Muslims with Middle Eastern ancestry. Use of this

name has increased in the United States since 1994. In 2004, 652 girls received it, ranking it 384th on the SSA list.

Marian

Modern form of **Marion.** Despite appearances, this name originally had no connection with **Mary Ann.**
Famous names: Marian Anderson (opera singer)
Marian McPartland (jazz pianist)

Mariana, Marianna

This blend of **Maria** and **Ana** has been growing in the United States among the Hispanic population. More than 2,300 girls received the name in 2004, ranking it 152nd that year.

Marianne

French blend of **Marie** and **Anne.** In France, the figure Marianne represents the spirit of the French Republic in much the same way that Uncle Sam and John Bull signify the United States and England.
Famous name: Marianne Moore (poet)
Variations: **Mariana** (Spanish and Russian), **Mariane, Marianna** (Polish, Latvian, Hungarian, and Italian), **Maryann** (English)

Maribel

Spanish blend of **Maria** and **Isabel.** Maribel boomed in the Hispanic-American community during the 1960s and 1970s but has been gradually declining since its peak in 1980. In 2004, 334 Maribels were born, ranking the name 768th on the SSA list.

Marie

This French variation of **Mary** has had some famous bearers throughout history, including the 16th-century Marie de Medicis, the queen regent of France, and Marie Antoinette, the ill-fated queen beheaded in the French Revolution. Marie Curie is one of the greatest scientists in history, having won the Nobel Prize in physics in 1903 and the Nobel Prize in chemistry in 1911. In 2004, Marie was the number-one name for girls born in Germany. In the United States, Marie was one of the top ten first names for girls born between 1895 and 1914. It has steadily declined since and ranked only 409th in 2004, but it remains popular as a middle name.
Famous name: Marie Osmond (singer)

Mariel

Variation of **Mary.**

Famous name: Mariel Hemingway (actress)

Mariela

This modern diminutive of **Maria** has been regularly used by Hispanic-Americans since 1990. There were 472 born in 2004, ranking it 586th on the SSA list.

Marilyn

Combination of **Mary** and **Lynn.** Marilyn seems to have been created around 1905. Between 1927 and 1955, Marilyn was one of the top 50 names for American girls. Marilyn Monroe became a big star in 1953 but couldn't stop the steady decline of her name. In 2004, 490 Marilyns were born, ranking it 444th.

Famous names: Marilyn French (writer)

Marilyn Horne (opera singer)

Variations: **Marilin, Marylin**

Marin

Spanish surname, form of *Marinus.* (See **Marina.**) Many parents are probably using this name as an alternate spelling of **Maren,** but others are accenting it on the second syllable and thinking of the California county. Marin County, across the Golden Gate Bridge from San Francisco, is known as one of the more expensive suburbs in the United States. The origin of the county's name is unclear, but it may have been named for a Native American chief who fought the Spanish invaders in the early 19th century. If so, Marin is the Spaniards' name for him, not his original Miwok name. There were 291 American girls named Marin in 2004, ranking it 835th on the SSA list.

Marina

Perhaps a feminine form of Latin *marinus,* "of the sea." Shakespeare used this name in his play *Pericles.* British actress Marina Sirtis played Counselor Deanna Troi on *Star Trek: The Next Generation.* Her fame may have influenced the minor fashion for the name in the 1990s because 1994, the year the series ended, was also the peak year for the name. In 2004 the 875 Marinas born in the United States ranked it 308th.

Variations: **Maren** (Danish), **Mari, Marna, Marni, Marnie, Marny**

Marion

Norman French variation of **Mary.** Maid Marion is the Queen of the May in traditional English May Day games. Maid Marion is also the beloved of Robin Hood. Marion was the normal spelling of this name for girls until the surname Marion began to be given to boys as a first name around 1800. Then some parents began spelling the name for girls as Marian to differentiate it from the masculine form. Marion, however, remained somewhat more common when the name revived during the early 20th century. It is rare again today. Other spelling: **Marian**

Marisa

Italian and Spanish blend of **Maria** with **Lisa** or **Isabel.** Although this name is usually pronounced to rhyme with Lisa, actress Marisa Tomei pronounces her name as if it were spelled Marissa. Her Oscar-winning performance in the 1992 film *My Cousin Vinny* had an impact, because the next three years were the name's high point of use. There were 940 Marisas born in 2004, ranking it 294th. Variations: **Maressa, Marissa**

Marisol

Spanish blended form of **Maria** and **Sol** (Spanish "sun"), which has been used as a girls name in Spain since the Middle Ages. Sol is very rare today, but Marisol has been common in the Hispanic-American community since the 1960s. There were 763 girls born in the United States who received the name in 2004, ranking it 338th. Famous name: Marisol Escobar (artist)

Marissa

Modern American blend of the sounds of **Marisa** and **Melissa.** This name has been among the top 100 names given to American girls since 1989. It had been receding since 1996, but it began an upswing again in 2004. Perhaps that is due to the character Marissa Cooper on the teen-oriented television drama *The O.C.* Nearly 4,000 Marissas were born in 2004, ranking it 93rd.

Maritza

The Maritsa or Maritza is the main river of southern Bulgaria; its name may come from Thracian *mari,* "swamp." **Mariska** and **Marica** are Slavic pet forms of **Maria** or **Mary.** Around 1920, novelists and screenwriters in western Europe and the United States seem to have gotten confused and started naming exotic women from an Eastern European background Maritza. For example, the Hungarian operetta *Marica Grófnõ* was translated as *Countess Maritza* when it made it to Broadway in 1926. Maritza became accepted as a form of Maria in Italy and the Spanish-speaking world, becoming especially popular in Latin America. In the United States, Maritza entered the SSA list in 1956 and has never left. In 2004, 725 Maritzas were born, ranking the name 349th. Maritza has inspired Hispanic-Americans to create similar names, such as Yaritza and Julitza.

Marjorie

Old French or Scottish variation of **Margaret.** Marjorie was extremely fashionable in the 1920s, but it is rare again today.
Variations: **Marge, Margery, Margie, Margory, Margy, Marje, Marjie, Marjory, Marjy, Marsaili** (Scots Gaelic)

Marlene

Form of *Marielene,* a German blend of **Maria** with either **Helene** or **Magdalena.** American parents began to discover Marlene in the 1920s, and when actress Marlene Dietrich moved to Hollywood from Germany in 1930, she ignited an explosion in the name. There were 130 Marlenes born in 1929; 2,581 born in 1931; and 5,332 in its peak year of 1936. Many parents saw Marlene as the perfect "different but not too different" shift from the already common **Arlene.** Marlene fell off quickly from its peak, but it hasn't vanished, and it's now particularly popular with Hispanic-Americans. There were 600 Marlenes born in 2004, ranking it 397th for the year.
Variations: **Marla, Marleen, Marlena, Marley, Marline**

Marley

As an English surname, Marley means "boundary clearing" or "merry clearing," but as a modern girls name it's best thought of as a pet form of **Marlene.** Marley has been increasing in use lately as similar names like **Carly** and **Harley** are also popular. There were 851 Marleys born in 2004, ranking the name 317th.

Marnie

Form of **Marina** or of *Marnina,* modern Hebrew "joyful."
Variations: **Marna, Marne, Marni, Marny**

Marquita

Variation of **Marcia.** This was a popular name in the early 1980s with African-American parents.

Marsha

Variation of **Marcia.** In the 1940s and 1950s, this spelling was almost as popular as the original, but it has vanished today.
Famous name: Marsha Mason (actress)

Martha

Aramaic feminine form of *mar,* "a lord." In the Bible, Martha, the sister of Lazarus and Mary, is admonished by Jesus for her sharp words about others. Martha Washington was the original first lady, and as a result, Martha has been more common in the United States than in England. Martha remained one of the 30 most popular names for girls until 1945. It dropped off steeply during the 1950s, and in 2004 the 560 Marthas born ranked the name 415th. Martha often turns up in popular culture as the name of a kindly elderly woman, one example being Martha Kent, the name of Clark Kent's (Superman's) adoptive mother. This image of course may have been somewhat altered lately by the special fame of Martha Stewart.
Famous name: Martha Graham (dancer)
Nicknames: **Mart, Martie, Marty, Mat, Mattie, Matty, Patty**
Variations: **Maarva** (Estonian), **Marfa** (Russian), **Marta** (Hungarian, Italian, Norwegian, and Swedish), **Martella, Marthe** (French and German), **Marthena, Marthine, Martita, Martta** (Finnish)

Martina

Feminine form of **Martin,** Latin "of Mars."
Famous names: Martina McBride (country singer)
　　　　　　　Martina Navratilova (tennis player)
Variations: **Marta, Martie, Martine, Tina**

Marva

Feminine form of **Marvin,** or form of **Marvel.**
Famous name: Marva Collins (educator)

Marvel

Old French *Merveille,* "miraculous."
Variations: **Marvela, Marvella, Marvelle**

Mary

English form of Hebrew Miriam, meaning unknown; "beloved" or "child we wished for" are possibilities. Mary is the most popular name for girls in European history because it is revered as the name of the mother of Jesus, the Virgin Mary. In England, two ruling Queens have been named Mary. Mary I, also known as Bloody Mary, was the first daughter of Henry VIII. Mary II deposed her father, James II, in the "Glorious Revolution" of 1688 and ruled with her husband, William III. The College of William and Mary in Virginia, the second oldest college in the United States, is named after them. Mary Shelley, wife of poet Percy Bysshe Shelley, created the most popular monster in the history of literature in her novel *Frankenstein*. A magical English nanny named Mary Poppins, played by Julie Andrews in the popular movie, is a favorite in children's literature. Mary was the number-one name in the United States until 1948. By 2004, Mary had fallen to 74th place on the list of names given to newborn girls, with 4,700 born. In England and Wales, Mary hasn't been among the top 100 names since 1970.

Famous names: Mary J. Blige (R&B singer)
Mary Cassatt (artist)
Mary Tyler Moore (actress)
Mary Wollstonecraft (political philosopher)

Nicknames: **Mame, Mamie, Mar, Mare, Mayme, Moll, Mollie, Molly, Poll, Polly**

Other spelling: **Mari**

Variations: **Maara** (Finnish), **Mair** (Welsh), **Maire** (Irish Gaelic), **Mairi** (Scots Gaelic), **Malia** (Hawaiian), **Malkin, Manette** (French), **Manica** (Slovenian), **Manon** (French), **Marella, Marelle, Maretta, Marette, Maria** (Italian, Latin, and Spanish), **Mariam** (Arabic), **Marica, Marie** (French), **Mariel, Mariella** (Italian), **Marietta, Mariette, Marika, Marinka, Marion** (French), **Mariquita** (Spanish), **Mariska** (Slavic), **Marita** (Spanish), **Marite, Marya, Maryam** (Arabic), **Maryse** (French), **Masha** (Russian), **Maura, Maureen** (Irish), **May, Mears** (Irish), **Minnie** (Scottish), **Miren** (Basque), **Miriam, Moira** (Irish), **Moire** (Scots Gaelic), **Moya** (Irish), **Muire** (Gaelic)

Masako

Japanese "correct child" or "elegant child." The second meaning is the correct one for Crown Princess Masako of Japan.

Mathilda, Matilda

Old German *maht* [might] + *hild* [battle]. The earliest form of this name was probably Mathilda, but by the time of the Norman Conquest of England, it was Matilda, the name of the wife of William the Conqueror who became the queen of England. The name was regularly used in the 19th century but is rare today.

Variations: **Maitilde** (Irish), **Matelda** (Italian), **Matelle, Mathilde** (French and German), **Matilde** (Spanish), **Mattie, Matty, Maud, Maude**

Mattie, Matty

This pet form of **Martha** or **Matilda** was common in the 19th century but became very rare until 1994, when it reappeared on the SSA top 1,000 list. It has been slowly drifting upward since. The 315 Matties born in 2004 ranked the name 797th on the SSA list.

Maud, Maude

Variation of **Mathilda.** A granddaughter of William the Conqueror, **Matilda,** was known as Maud, but the name became an independent name centuries ago. Although unfashionable today, Maud appears in popular culture as a name that connotes a rebellious woman, one who doesn't fit into the culturally accepted feminine mold. Actress Françoise Fabian is the intellectual freethinker in Eric Rohmer's movie *My Night at Maud's,* while a similar but older Maude was created by actress Ruth Gordon in the movie *Harold and Maude.* In the popular television comedy *Maude,* Bea Arthur played an independent woman who went against the conventions of the time.

Maura

Irish variation of **Mary** from Gaelic *Máire.* Maura has been used in the United States since the 1950s. It seems to be one Irish name that usually indicates Irish-American ancestry.

Famous name: Maura Tierney (actress)

Maureen

Irish variation of **Mary.** Maureen was a top 100 name in the 1940s and 1950s, but today it has been replaced by **Maura.**

Famous names: Maureen O'Hara (actress)

Maureen Stapleton (actress)

Variations: **Maurene, Moreen**

Maxine

Feminine form of **Max** or **Maximilian**. Between 1915 and 1930, this American creation was a top 100 name for girls, but in spite of today's love for Max as a boys name, Maxine hasn't been revived.

May

Latin *maius*, the month; also, a variation of **Margaret** or **Mary**. May was common in the 19th century but vanished as a first name after 1960.
Famous name: May Sarton (poet)
Variations: **Mae** (Portuguese), **Mai, Maye**

Maya

Probably a modern form of *Maia*, Greek "wet-nurse" or Latin "great, major." In Greek and Roman mythology, Maia was the mother of Hermes, or Mercury, the winged messenger god. Architect Maya Ying Lin designed the wall of names at the Vietnam Veterans Memorial in Washington, D.C. Maya has been soaring in use since 1992. In 2004 more than 7,600 girls received the name, ranking it 41st for the year. **Mya** is now a frequent spelling alternative.
Famous name: Maya Angelou (writer)

Mayra

This is a respelling of **Myra** to give the same pronunciation in Spanish that Myra has in English. Mayra has been used in Latin America for at least 50 years and was quite popular with Hispanic-Americans in the 1980s and 1990s, especially in Caribbean Hispanic cultures. Though now receding, Mayra ranked 600th on the SSA list in 2004.
Other spelling: **Maira**

McCall, McKell

Irish and Scottish surnames meaning "son of *Cathal* (battle mighty) or *Cathmáel* (battle chief)." Both of these names have been regularly given to girls in Utah recently, though they are still rare in the rest of the United States.

McKenna

Scottish Gaelic "son of *Cionaodha*." *Cionaodha* probably meant "beloved of Aodh (the god of fire)." When **Mackenzie** became popular, parents looking for a "different but not too different" alternative latched on to McKenna, which was especially attractive because of its feminine-sounding -a ending. McKenna entered the SSA top 1,000 list in 1991 and quickly rose up the ranks. Its alternative spelling **Makenna** entered the list in 1994, with **Makena** joining them in 2002. Together the three spellings accounted for almost 3,400 girls born in 2004, ranking the name 107th.

Meadow

From Old English *mædw*. This "nature name" was rare before the character Meadow, played by Jamie-Lynn DiScala, began appearing on HBO's critically acclaimed series *The Sopranos* in 1999. Meadow entered the SSA top 1,000 list in 2001; in 2004, it ranked 766th, with 335 born.

Mecca

Name of the city in Saudi Arabia, the birthplace of Islam and site of the pilgrimage all Muslims should make at least once in their lifetime.

Megan

Welsh variation of **Margaret.** John Galsworthy used this name for the heroine of his story *The Apple Tree.* Megan became extremely popular during the 1980s and was a top ten name between 1984 and 1997. The many respellings of this name are American attempts to make the name look Irish, but it is not an Irish name and has almost never been used in Ireland. The idea that it's Irish may have come from confusing it with the Irish surname *Meighan,* with which it has no connection. In 2004 the more than 8,600 Megans born ranked the name 35th.
Famous name: Megan Mullaly (actress)
Variations: **Maegan, Meagan, Meaghan, Meghan**

Melanie

French form of *melaina,* Greek "dark, black." Melanie is the long-suffering wife of Ashley Wilkes in Margaret Mitchell's 1936 novel *Gone With the Wind.* That book and the 1939 movie based on it clearly helped to popularize Melanie as a name in the United States. It rose steadily in use to become one of the top 100 girls names between 1968 and 1992. It then receded for a time but in 2002 began to revive again. In 2004 more than 4,000 Melanies were born, ranking the name 92nd for the year.
Famous name: Melanie Griffith (actress)
Nicknames: **Mel, Mellie, Melly**

Other spellings: **Melani, Melany, Melony**
Variations: **Melaine, Melania** (Greek and Polish), **Melina**

Melina

Perhaps a form of **Carmel, Melanie,** or **Melissa.** Melina has been regularly used in the United States since the 1980s. The 428 Melinas born in 2004 ranked it 627th on the SSA list.
Famous name: Melina Mercouri (actress)

Melinda

Created by 18th-century English poets, probably by blending **Belinda** and **Melissa.** Melinda was fairly popular in the 1960s and 1970s but is now rare again.
Famous name: Melinda Gates (philanthropist)
Variations: **Linda, Lindy, Malinda, Mindy**

Melisa

Spanish and Polish form of **Melissa.** This name should be pronounced to rhyme with **Lisa** and so be distinct from Melissa, but some parents may use it as a spelling variation of that name. Melisa's popularity almost exactly parallels Melissa's; its peak year of use was 1973, and in 2004 it had almost vanished, ranking 952nd on the SSA list, with 248 girls receiving the name.

Melissa

Greek *melissa*, "honey bee." In Greek myths, Melissa was a nymph who nursed the infant Zeus and taught humans the use of honey. Melissa became a popular name in the United States during the 1960s and was one of the top ten names for American girls born between 1967 and 1984. It is now falling out of fashion and was the 112th most common name of 2004, with almost 3,300 born.
Famous names: Melissa Etheridge (singer)
　　　　　　　 Melissa Gilbert (actress)
Nicknames: **Lissa, Mellie, Melly, Missie, Missy**
Variations: **Melessa, Melina, Melisa** (Spanish and Polish), **Melita, Melitta**

Melody

Greek *meloidia*, "choral singing." The idea of turning this word into a name seems to have first occurred to Americans around 1940. The newfound popularity of **Melanie** was undoubtedly part of the inspi-

ration. The name was moderately fashionable in the 1950s and 1960s. It has now begun to recede, but was probably part of the inspiration for **Harmony** and **Cadence**. Almost 1,000 Melodys were born in 2004, ranking the name 281st that year.
Other spelling: **Melodie**

Memory

This "word name" may seem like a modern creation, but there was a silent film released in 1919 called *Jacques of the Silver North* with a heroine named Memory Baird. Sporadic examples of girls named Memory have occurred all over the United States since 1990, sometimes respelled as **Memorie** or **Memree.**

Mercedes

Spanish "mercy, mercies" from *María de las Mercedes,* "Mary of Mercies." This is a popular Spanish name for girls. The Mercedes-Benz is named after Mercedes Jellinek, daughter of a financier of the German car company. The luxury image of the automobile seems to have been part of the inspiration for the many non-Hispanic parents who named their daughters Mercedes in the early 1990s, briefly making it one of the top 200 names for girls. In 2004 it ranked 295th.
Famous names: Mercedes McCambridge (actress)
　　　　　　　Mercedes Ruehl (actress)

Mercy

Mercy was a common name among the Puritans in New England.

Meredith

Welsh *Maredudd,* "magnificent lord." Meredith is a male name in Wales, but it has been used primarily for girls in both England and the United States since 1925. Meredith seemed to get a big boost in 1968 when the daytime soap opera *One Life To Live* premiered featuring a sweet, wealthy heiress named Meredith Lord as a character. The name was moderately popular in the 1970s and 1980s but slipped to 292nd place by 2004. Meredith has been more common in North Carolina than elsewhere, probably because of Meredith College, an exclusive women's school in Raleigh.
Famous names: Meredith Baxter-Birney (actress)
　　　　　　　Meredith Vieira (television host and journalist)
Other spelling: **Merideth, Meridith**

Merle

From the Latin *merula*, "blackbird." There was a minor fashion for Merle in the first two decades of the 20th century. The name was fading when actress Merle Oberon's fame briefly revived it in the 1930s, but it disappeared from the SSA top 1,000 list in 1957.

Merope

Greek, possibly "bee mask." There are at least five Meropes in ancient Greek mythology, including the foster mother of the unfortunate King Oedipus, and the only one of the seven nymphs, called the Pleiades, to marry a mortal. Because of that disgrace, Merope is the name of the faintest of the seven stars in the cluster that astronomers call the Pleiades. It is probably the latter story that makes Merope Gaunt an appropriate name for the character in *Harry Potter and the Half-Blood Prince*.

Merrill

Form of **Muriel** or an English place name meaning "merry hill." Merrill can also be used as a name for boys.
Famous name: Merrill Ashley (ballerina)
Other spelling: **Meryl**

Merry

Old English *myrige*, "pleasant, merry." This word name was briefly fashionable during the 1940s and 1950s, the same time period that Gay was also voguish. That makes sense given the frequent use of the phrase "merry and gay" at the time.
Other spellings: **Merri, Merrie**

Meryl

Form of **Merrill**. Actress Meryl Streep was born Mary Louise Streep, but her mother has called her Meryl since she was a child.

Meseret

Amharic *Mäsärät*, "a foundation, a base, an essence."
Famous name: Meseret Defar (Olympic runner)

Metaxia

Greek "silk." This is a modern Greek name, regularly used in Greece during the 20th century.

Mia

Swedish form of **Maria;** also, Italian "mine." Mia was quite rare until 1964 when actress Mia Farrow became well known through her role on television's *Peyton Place.* Her name vaulted onto the SSA top 1,000 list that year and never left. Since 1996, Mia has been soaring in popularity, perhaps as an alternative for **Maya.** Almost 7,300 Mias were born in 2004, ranking the name 47th.
Famous name: Mia Hamm (soccer player)

Micah

For origin, see Micah in the boys list. Though this is a male name in the Bible, some parents in the United States have used Micah as a feminine form of **Michael** since the late 1970s. Micah rose in use during the early 1990s and peaked as a girls name in 1998. In 2004, it ranked 759th on the SSA list.

Michaela

Latin feminine form of Michael. Michaela began to be sporadically used in the United States in the 1960s. It started to build in the 1970s and was common in Nebraska by 1980. Parents in other states soon discovered it, and the title character on *Dr. Quinn, Medicine Woman* gave Michaela a boost when the show premiered in 1993. Parents were primarily attracted to the name's similarity in sound to **Kayla,** which is shown by the fact that **Makayla** and **Mikayla** developed very quickly. Both these alternatives surpassed the original spelling in 1998, which is now a distinct third choice. The combined spellings were given to more than 10,000 American girls in 2004, ranking the name 27th for the year.
Nicknames: **Kayla, Micki, Mickie, Micky**
Other spellings: **McKayla, Micaela, Mikaela**
Variations: **Micaela, Michael, Michaele** (Italian), **Michaelina, Michaeline** (German), **Michaella** (Italian), **Michel, Michele, Michelina, Micheline, Michelle** (French), **Miguela** (Spanish), **Miguelita** (Spanish), **Mikaela, Mikelina** (Russian)

Michele, Michelle

French feminine form of **Michael.** Michelle entered the SSA top 1,000 list in 1938 and rose steadily. It was the 18th most popular name in 1965, the year before the Beatles song "Michelle" was

released, and then it jumped to first place on the popularity charts. Michelle was a top ten name until 1980 but has been receding since, ranking 77th in 2004 with more than 4,600 girls given the name.
Famous names: Michelle Akers (soccer player)
Michelle Pfeiffer (actress)
Michelle Shocked (singer and songwriter)
Nicknames: **Elle, Micki, Mickie, Micky, Shelley, Shelli, Shellie, Shelly**

Michiko

Japanese "beautiful, wise child." Empress Michiko was the first commoner to marry into the royal family of Japan.

Mignon

French "sweet, cute, dainty." Mignon was turned into a first name by the German poet Johann von Goethe in 1796. It is not used as a given name in France.
Variation: **Mignonette**

Miho

Japanese "enduring beauty."

Milbrey, Milbry

Old English *Mildburh*, "mild fortress." Milbrey was used in England until the 18th century. If **Millie** regains popularity in the United States soon, parents might find that Milbrey fits in with other modern names.

Mildred

Old English *mild* [gentle] + *thryth* [strength]. This very old Anglo-Saxon name was revived in Victorian times and was one of the top ten names given to American girls born between 1903 and 1926. In W. Somerset Maugham's 1915 novel *Of Human Bondage,* Mildred is the name of the callous waitress with whom the book's hero, Philip Carey, falls in love. In the movie *Mildred Pierce,* Joan Crawford played a mother obsessed with her daughter. Neither of these works helped the image of the name. It disappeared in the 1980s and is probably one of the names least likely to be revived before 2020. Dr. Mildred Dresselhaus of MIT is a physicist whose research on nanostructures and superconductivity have kept her on the cutting edge of modern technology.
Nicknames: **Mil, Millie, Milly**
Other spelling: **Mildrid**

Milla

Slavic *mil,* "grace, favor."

Famous name: Milla Jovovich (actress)

Millicent

Old German *amal* [work] + *swintha* [strength]. This name was introduced to England in medieval times by the Normans. In the United States it had a minor vogue in the 1920s, probably as an alternative for **Mildred,** but it vanished in the 1960s. Millicent probably has more chance of being revived than Mildred.

Nicknames: **Millie, Milly, Missie, Missy**

Variations: **Melicent, Melisande** (French), **Melisenda** (Spanish), **Mellicent, Milicent, Milissent, Millisent, Milzie**

Millie

Form of **Camilla, Emily, Mildred,** or **Millicent.** Millie was moderately common as a given name in the 19th century but vanished completely during the 1960s. It has returned strongly in Great Britain recently and was one of the top 25 names for girls born in England and Wales in 2004. As yet there are no signs of a revival in the United States, but one might happen when American parents realize that Millie can be an alternative for Emily as much as a short form of Mildred. Fans of movie musicals will associate this name with the 1967 film *Thoroughly Modern Millie,* in which Julie Andrews played the title character.

Other spelling: **Milly**

Mimi

Form of **Miriam.** Mimi is the heroine of Puccini's opera *La Boheme.* Between 1947 and 1967, Mimi was used as an independent name in the United States often enough to make the SSA top 1,000 list, but it was never very popular.

Mina

This short form of names like **Wilhelmina** or Guillermina (Spanish form of the same) made the SSA top 1,000 list for girls in 2004 at 890th place. Some of the girls being given the name may be from Hindu families, where the name is derived from *mina,* a Sanskrit word meaning "fish" that is the Indian name of the zodiac sign Pisces and the name of a daughter of Usha, goddess of the dawn.

Other spelling: **Meena**

Mindy

This short form of **Melinda** was regularly used in the 1970s while the similar **Mandy** was popular, and it was one of the top 100 names for girls in 1979, the year the television show *Mork and Mindy* became a hit. Mindy left the SSA top 1,000 list in 1997.

Minerva

Latin "wisdom." In Roman mythology, Minerva was the goddess of wisdom; she is the counterpart of the Greek goddess Athena. The name's connection with wisdom is probably why J. K. Rowling chose it for Minerva McGonagall, the Transfiguration teacher and head of Gryffindor House in the *Harry Potter* novels. Minerva was regularly used in the United States in the 19th century and, perhaps surprisingly, didn't leave the SSA top 1,000 list until 1974.
Nicknames: **Min, Minnie, Minny**

Minnie

Variation of **Minerva** or **Wilhelmina;** also, a Scottish variation of **Mary.** Minnie was one of the top ten names for girls in the United States during the 1880s but disappeared in the 20th century. Its association with Walt Disney's cartoon mouse may be too strong for it to revive any time soon.
Famous names: Minnie Driver (actress)
Minnie Pearl (country comedianne)
Other spelling: **Minny**

Mira

Like **Mina,** Mira only recently entered the SSA top 1,000 list, ranking 910th in 2004. It can have both Western and Hindu derivations. In Italy, Mira is either considered a short form of **Miranda** or the feminine form of *Miro,* the Italian form of **Myron.** Actress Mira Sorvino's name is an example of that derivation. As a Hindu name, Mira is from Sanskrit *mira,* "the sea," and was the name of an ancient poet. Film director Mira Nair's name is an example of that derivation.

Miracle

The word used as a name, expressing the joys of new parenthood. There are occasional news stories about babies named Miracle because they are born to previously infertile couples or as a result of very difficult pregnancies, but the name is now too common for that to be the explanation in most cases. Miracle entered the SSA top 1,000 list in 1995. In 2004, 594 Miracles were born in the United States.

Miranda

Latin "admirable." Miranda is Prospero's daughter in Shakespeare's *The Tempest*. Miranda was one of the top 100 girls names of the 1990s. It has just begun to fade; more than 2,500 girls received the name in 2004, ranking it 142nd that year.
Famous names: Miranda Lambert (country singer)
                     Miranda Richardson (actress)
Nicknames: **Randa, Randee, Randi, Randie, Randy**
Variations: **Mira, Mirella, Mirelle, Mirra**

Mireya

Spanish form of Provençal (southern France) *Mirèio,* from *mirar,* "to look," interpreted as "the admirable or beautiful one." This name became well known in France and Spain in 1859 when Frederic Mistral wrote his epic poem *Mirèio.* In 1861, Mistral's goddaughter was baptized with the name, and he lied and told the priest it was a form of **Miriam** so she could be baptized with a "Christian" name. There was a sudden upsurge in this name in the Hispanic-American community in 1996, bringing it into the SSA top 1,000 list and leading to a peak in 1997, when 567 girls were given the name. In 2004, 253 girls were named Mireya, ranking it 943rd. Between 1999 and 2004, Mireya Moscoso was the first female president of Panama.

Miriam

Hebrew form of **Mary.** This is the original form of the name Mary. In the Old Testament, Miriam is a prophetess and the sister of Aaron. Miriam was a fairly common name from 1906 through 1930, and though it then receded, it never disappeared like so many other names of its era, partly because Orthodox Jewish parents continued to favor it. Since 1997 it has shown signs of increasing slightly. More than 1,100 Miriams were born in 2004, ranking it 255th.
Variations: **Mimi** (French), **Mitzi** (German)

Misty

Misty is one of the first modern examples of a regular vocabulary word turned into a girls name. One of its early instances is a character in the 1942 film *Don Winslow of the Navy.* The name's vogue may have been inspired by Erroll Garner's classic romantic song "Misty," originally recorded in 1954 and since remade by many other famous singers. Misty entered the SSA top 1,000 list in 1960 and skyrocketed in use; it was one of the top 100 names for girls in the United States between 1973 and 1984. Misty left the SSA list in 2001.

Mitzi

Variation of **Miriam.** There was a minor vogue for Mitzi as an independent name around 1960, but it's rare again today.
Famous name: Mitzi Gaynor (actress)

Mohini

Sanskrit *Mohini,* "fascinating" or "jasmine blossom."

Moira

English spelling of *Máire,* Irish Gaelic form of **Mary. Maura** is a different Anglicization of the same name. Moira has been popular in Scotland as well as Ireland but, except for a brief period in the 1960s, American parents have avoided it.
Famous name: Moira Kelly (actress)
Other spelling: **Moyra**

Mollie, Molly

Form of **Mary.** During the Revolutionary War battle of Monmouth, Mary MacCauley carried water to exhausted and wounded colonial soldiers. In appreciation of her kindness, they renamed her Molly Pitcher. In literature, Molly Bloom is the heroine of James Joyce's *Ulysses.* Until recently Molly was a name that was used regularly without ever becoming really popular. In the 1970s it began to grow in use, and since 1987 Molly has been one of the top 120 names for girls. In 2004 more than 3,600 Mollys were born, ranking it 102nd.
Famous names: Molly Ivins (columnist)
Molly Ringwald (actress)

Momoka

Japanese, from *momo,* "peach" or "one hundred," and *ka,* "flower" or "fragrance." This was the top name for girls born in Japan in 2004.

Mona

Form of **Monica;** also, from Irish Gaelic *Muadhnait,* "noble." Some parents who name their daughters Mona believe they are naming her for the "Mona Lisa" of Leonardo da Vinci's famous painting, but in that case, Mona is not a first name but an honorary title, a contraction of the Italian *ma donna,* "my lady." After being in regular use since the 1880s, Mona vanished from the SSA top 1,000 list in 1987. Other spelling: **Monna**

Monica

Origin uncertain; possibly from Greek *monos,* "alone," Latin "advise," or of North African origin. St. Monica was the mother of St. Augustine. In the United States, Monica's most fashionable period was the 1970s, when it consistently ranked between 40th and 50th on the SSA list. It then began its inevitable fall. In 1994 *Friends* came on the air, and during the next three years there was a slight upward trend in the name, suggesting that the character on that show was slowing Monica's decline. But in 1998 Monica Lewinsky became infamous, and the name resumed its descent at a faster rate. (Monica Lewinsky was born in 1973, at the height of the name's vogue.) Monica hasn't been completely abandoned as a name yet; in 2004 there were almost 1,500 girls given the name, ranking it 217th for the year.
Famous name: Monica Seles (tennis player)
Variations: **Mona, Monca** (Irish), **Monika** (German and Polish), **Monique** (French)

Monique

French form of **Monica.** Monique was very popular in the African-American community in the 1980s, and though its vogue has passed, there were still more than 600 born in 2004, ranking it 387th.
Famous name: Monique Currie (basketball player)

Monserrat

Simplified form of *Montserrat,* Catalan place name from Latin *mons serrātus,* "jagged hill." Montserrat became a girls name in Catalonia because of a Benedictine monastery founded on a hill called Montserrat near Barcelona in the tenth century. The recent upswing in babies named Monserrat may have something to do with the Caribbean island of Monserrat being in the news because of the disastrous volcanic eruptions there. Monserrat entered the SSA top 1,000 list in 2000; in 2004, it ranked 708th on that list, with 372 American girls given the name.

Moriah

Hebrew, perhaps "seen by God" or "God teaches." In the Bible, Mount Moriah is the place where Abraham is told to go and sacrifice his son Isaac as a test of his faith; God provides another sacrifice, and Isaac's life is saved. The use of this name rose and fell along with **Mariah,** which shows that many parents think of it as a variation of that name, even though they have different origins and slightly different pronunciations. Moriah ranked 857th on the SSA list in 2004, with 283 girls given the name.

Morgan

Welsh, either *mor* [sea] or *mawr* [great] + *can* [bright]. In the Arthurian romances, Morgan le Fay, the queen of the Incubi, is the half-sister of King Arthur. Their incestuous relationship led to the birth of a child, Mordred. American parents began to give the name to daughters regularly in the 1970s, and it has steadily grown as an alternative to **Megan.** Between 1994 and 2000, Morgan was one of the top 25 names on the SSA list. Though it's now just past its peak, Morgan still ranked 48th in 2004, with more than 7,200 girls given the name.
Famous name: Morgan Fairchild (actress)
Variations: **Morgana, Morganne, Morgen**

Moxie

Magician and comedian Penn Jillette (of Penn and Teller) got national publicity for naming his daughter Moxie CrimeFighter in June 2005. Her first name probably comes from the slang word meaning "vigor, courage, nerve." That word comes from the trade name Moxie, the name of the oldest continuously sold carbonated drink in the United States, which was originally marketed in 1884 as a health tonic (like many other 19th-century soft drinks). Moxie is still sold in New England, and in 2005 it was declared the state beverage of Maine. The trade name in turn comes from the town and pond in Maine called Moxie. That is a Native American name, perhaps from Algonquian "dark water."

Moya

Along with **Moira** and **Maura,** Moya is one of many Irish versions of **Mary.** Science fiction fans, however, will recognize it as the name of the living starship on the television series *Farscape.*
Famous name: Moya Brennan (Irish singer)

Muriel

Old Celtic "sea-bright." During the 1850s, a popular novel by Dinah M. M. Craik, *John Halifax, Gentleman,* introduced this name. Muriel was fashionable in the 1920s but vanished from the SSA top 1,000 list in the 1960s and shows no signs of revival.
Famous names: Muriel Rukeyser (poet)
Muriel Spark (novelist)
Variations: **Meriel, Merril, Merrill, Muirgheal** (Irish)

Muteteli

Rwanda "dainty."

Myra

Invented by English poet Fulke Greville in the 16th century. No one knows how he came up with it, but theories include a variation of **Miranda;** Latin *myrra,* "myrrh"; or simply an anagram of **Mary.** There was a minor vogue for Myra from 1920 to 1950. It then slowly vanished in most parts of the United States. However, it was quite fashionable with Hispanic-Americans in the 1990s with the spellings **Maira** and **Mayra** (see Mayra).
Other spelling: **Mira**

Myrna

Irish Gaelic *Muirne,* "the loved one."
Famous name: Myrna Loy (actress)

Myrtle

Latin *myrtilla,* "myrtle tree." Myrtle was one of the top 25 names of the late 19th century but vanished more than 40 years ago. Along with her husband, Charles, Myrtle Fillmore (1845–1931) founded the religious denomination known as Unity. Modern children will know this name best through Moaning Myrtle, the ghost in the girls lavatory at Hogwarts in the *Harry Potter* novels.
Variations: **Mertice, Myrt, Myrta, Myrtia, Myrtice, Myrtis**

Mystery

Several instances of girls named Mystery have been noted since the year 2000.

Nadia

Ukrainian form of Russian *nadezhda*, "hope." Nadia vaulted onto the SSA top 1,000 list in 361st place in 1976, the year Romanian gymnast Nadia Comaneci became the star of the summer Olympics as the first gymnast ever to score a perfect 10. Since 1995 this name has been increasing in use again, and in 2004 more than 1,500 Nadias were born in the United States, ranking it 206th for the year.
Variations: **Nadine** (French), **Nadya**

Nadine

French variation of **Nadia.** Nadine was moderately common in the United States from 1915 to 1960 but left the SSA top 1,000 list in 2002. South African author Nadine Gordimer won the Nobel Prize in literature in 1991.

Naledi

Southern Sotho (South Africa) "star."

Nana

Variation of **Anne.** Emile Zola's novel *Nana* is considered a classic.

Nancy

Though Nancy may have started out in medieval times as a pet form of **Agnes,** which was then pronounced "Annis," it's also been used as a form of **Anne** for several centuries. Nancy was common in the late 18th century, faded somewhat in the 19th, and then came roaring back in the 20th to be one of the top ten names between 1934 and 1955. It's one of the most "American" names, not having been popular in England since 1800. Perhaps the American veneration of Nancy Hanks, Abraham Lincoln's mother, led to this difference. Though use of the name has fallen considerably, there were still more than 1,100 Nancys born in the United States in 2004, ranking it 266th that year.

Famous names: Nancy Kerrigan (figure skater)

Nancy Lopez (golfer)

Nancy Reagan (first lady)

Nicknames: **Nan, Nance, Nanni, Nannie, Nanny**

Other spellings: **Nancie, Nansie**

Variation: **Nanette**

Naomi

Hebrew "pleasantness." In the Bible, Naomi is the mother of Boaz and the mother-in-law of Ruth. The Puritans made this a popular name in the 17th century. It faded in the 18th, then was regularly used in the early 20th century. Since 1990 it has been growing in use again. In 2004 more than 2,200 Naomis were born in the United States, ranking it 162nd that year.

Famous names: Naomi Campbell (fashion model)

Naomi Judd (country singer)

Naomi Wolf (feminist author)

Variations: **Naoma, Noami, Noemi** (Spanish)

Natalia

Polish, Portuguese, and Spanish variation of **Natalie.** Natalia increased rapidly in the 1990s, especially with African-Americans and Hispanic-Americans. More than 2,200 were born in 2004, ranking it 158th.

Variation: **Talia**

Natalie

French form of Latin *natale,* "birthday." This name was originally given to girls born on Christmas Day. Natalie has been regularly used in the United States for more than a century. It has had a long, slow increase that began in 1955, the year Natalie Wood costarred with James Dean in *Rebel Without a Cause.* In 2004 there were more than 11,000 Natalies born in the United States, ranking it 23rd. Its slow build-up means it will probably be popular until at least 2015.

Famous names: Natalie Merchant (singer and songwriter)

Natalie Morales (television newscaster)

Natalie Portman (actress)

Variations: **Natala, Natalia** (Polish, Portuguese, and Spanish), **Natalina, Nataline, Natalya, Natasha** (Russian), **Nathalia, Nathalie** (French), **Natividad** (Spanish), **Noelle** (French), **Talia**

Natasha

Russian variation of **Natalie.** In the television cartoon series *Rocky and His Friends,* Natasha is the colleague of spy Boris Badenov. Though it's only been regularly used in the United States since 1965, Natasha was one of the top 100 girls names of the 1980s, being especially popular with African-Americans. It is now fading, but there were still more than 1,000 Natashas born in 2004, ranking it 272nd.
Famous name: Natasha Richardson (actress)
Nickname: **Tasha**

Nayeli

Probably Zapotec (Native American, Mexico) "I love you." This name has been growing in use in Mexico for some time, and it entered the SSA top 1,000 list in the United States in 2003. It had a moderate rate of growth until 2001, when the number of Nayelis suddenly more than quadrupled. This was undoubtedly because of the character Nayeli on the telenovela *Amigas y Rivales.* Nayeli swiftly receded from its high point, but in 2004 there were still 780 Nayelis born in the United States, ranking the name 337th.

Neema

Swahili "born into prosperous times."

Nellie, Nelly

Variation of **Eleanor, Helen,** or Nell. On stage and screen, Nellie Forbush was the popular heroine of the musical *South Pacific.* Nellie was a common name in the 19th century but is now quite rare. Swedish poet Nelly Sachs won the Nobel Prize in literature in 1966.
Variations: **Nela, Nelina, Nelita, Nell, Nella, Nelle**

Nevaeh

The word "heaven" spelled backwards. Reverse spellings of other names or words have been used as baby names many times in the past. In Russia during communism, Ninel was sometimes used as a girls name. **Semaj** is now fairly common for boys, and examples of girls named Nella, Sirron, Mada, Ronaele, and Neleh as backward spellings of relatives' names have also been noted. Nevaeh, though, is by far the most successful back-spelled name in history. In 1999, there were only eight girls in the entire United States named Nevaeh. Then in March 2000, Sonny Sandoval of the rock group P.O.D. named his daughter

Nevaeh. That fall, he was featured on the MTV program *Cribs*, where he introduced his daughter and explained her name. Other parents embraced the name immediately. There were 86 newborns in the United States named Nevaeh in 2000; by 2004 the number had shot up to 3,134, ranking it 120th on the list of all girls names. Nevaeh rose so quickly because its sound (neh-VAY-uh) fit in with the vogue for the long *a* vowel, and many parents thought it was a cool idea to give their daughter a name meaning "heaven" that wasn't quite so obvious. However, many people have the feeling that if you spell a word backwards, it also reverses the meaning. In fact, the creator of Tarzan, Edgar Rice Burroughs, once wrote a story titled "Minidoka" where Nevaeh was the name for the hell that abusers of animals were sent to.

Nia

This is a name with three very different origins. First, it is an African-American name from the Swahili word *nia*, "aim, intention, purpose." Nia is also used in Wales, where it is the Welsh counterpart to **Niamh.** Finally, Nia can be a short form of any name ending in *-nia*, such as **Antonia** or **Eugenia.** Screenwriter and actress Nia Vardalos, who became famous because of the 2002 film *My Big Fat Greek Wedding*, was given the full name Antonia Eugenia Vardalos. Nia has increased steadily in use in the United States since 1990. In 2004, there were 875 American girls named Nia, ranking it 309th.

Niamh

Irish Gaelic "brightness, radiance." This name is pronounced to rhyme with **Eve.** Niamh has been extremely popular in Ireland since the 1980s. It has yet to show up to any great extent in the United States, but if either of the Irish singers Niamh Parsons or Niamh Kavanagh, who are both very popular in Europe, develop a following in the United States, Irish-Americans may well yet discover it.

Nicola

Feminine form of **Nicholas.** Nicola was hugely popular in England during the 1970s, but it never caught on in the United States, where **Nicole** has always been preferred.

Nicole

French feminine form of **Nicholas.** Nicole was extremely popular in France during the 1940s. In 1950, it began to show up regularly on

United States birth certificates, and it exploded in popularity during the 1960s to become one of the top ten names for girls between 1972 and 1988. Nicole is now having its inevitable recession, but almost 6,000 girls were given the name in 2004, ranking it 56th.
Famous names: Nicole Kidman (actress)
Nicole Miller (fashion designer)
Nicknames: **Nickie, Nicky, Nikki**
Variations: **Colette** (French), **Nichola, Nicol, Nicola** (British), **Nicolette, Nicollette** (French), **Nicolina** (Greek), **Nicoline**

Nicolette, Nicollette

French diminutive of **Nicole**. Nicolette began to show up regularly in the United States in 1979 and grew as a "different but not too different" shift from Nicole. It peaked in the early 1990s and has receded swiftly since, ranking 849th on the SSA list in 2004.
Famous name: Nicollette Sheridan (actress)

Nikki

Short form of **Nicole**. Nikki actually paved the way for Nicole rather than vice versa. Nikki entered the SSA top 1,000 list in 1941, probably inspired by Nikki Porter, the secretary and love interest of detective Ellery Queen in several early 1940s films. Nikki peaked as a separate name in the early 1970s, just before Nicole hit the top ten. In 2004, 279 Nikkis were born in the United States, ranking the name 869th on the SSA list.
Famous name: Nikki Giovanni (poet)

Nina

Form of **Anne** or **Antonia**. Nina was fairly common in the 19th century, when its first syllable was often pronounced as "nine," and since then it has not fallen below 376th on the SSA list. In 2004 nearly 1,300 girls were named Nina, ranking it 229th for the year.
Famous names: Nina Simone (singer, songwriter, and pianist)
Nina Totenberg (legal affairs radio reporter)
Variations: **Ninetta, Ninette** (French)

Noelia

Spanish form of **Noelle**. In February 1999 the Puerto Rican singer Noelia (full name Noelia Lorenzo) released her first album, and her name immediately became popular with Hispanic-American parents.

Noelia is receding from its 1999 peak and only ranked 895th on the SSA list in 2004, when 267 girls received the name.

Noelle

Feminine form of **Noel.** This name has been regularly used since 1964. The 670 Noelles born in 2004 ranked the name 377th.
Variation: **Noelia** (Spanish)

Nora, Norah

Form of **Eleanor** or **Honor.** Nora was a top 100 name of the late 19th century; it then receded gradually, finally bottoming out at 501st on the SSA list in 2000. It has sharply increased since; almost 1,500 Noras were born in 2004, ranking the name 216th that year. Nora's simple but elegant image fits in with **Ava, Lana,** and **Ella,** so its immediate future is bright.
Famous names: Nora Ephron (screenwriter and novelist)
Norah Jones (singer and songwriter)
Variations: **Noreen** (Irish), **Norina, Norine, Norita**

Norma

Latin *norma,* "standard" or "pattern"; or feminine form of **Norman.** Norma was one of the top 50 names between 1922 and 1941 but is rare again today.
Famous name: Norma Kamali (fashion designer)

Nova

Latin "new," the word for a star that suddenly increases in brightness and then fades, as well as a part of many place names created from Latin such as Nova Scotia. Nova has been used as a girls name since the 19th century. It was on the SSA top 1,000 list between 1885 and 1938 but is rare today.

Novalee

A combination of **Nova** and **Lee.** This was the name of the pregnant teenage heroine of Billie Letts's 1995 novel *Where the Heart Is,* which was made into a film in 2000 starring Natalie Portman. It's unknown whether the name was created for the novel or whether Ms. Letts found the name in use in Oklahoma, where she lives and where the story is set. Since the film was released, Novalee has been turning up regularly as a girls name in the United States, though it's not yet common enough to make the SSA top 1,000 list.

Nya

Probably a modern creation blending the sounds of **Nia** and **Maya.** Nya entered the SSA top 1,000 list in 1999; in 2004, 349 girls received the name, ranking it 742nd.

Nyadet

Nuer (southern Sudan) "woman-goats." This name implies that the child's father owned many goats and sheep when she was born. The great majority of Nuer girls names begin with the syllables *Nya-* or *Nyi-*, signifying "female." Other examples are Nyanyoch ("girl born during a flood year"), Nyawech ("female village dweller"), and Nyibol ("second child born after the twins"). The *Ny-* in these names should be pronounced as in the word "canyon."

Nyasia

This name was created by the Latin freestyle singer Nyasia, whose birth name was Blanca Bautista. She has said that she formed it by "changing around" the name of a friend who had died of leukemia. Nyasia has been in the SSA top 1,000 list since 1999 without increasing greatly; in 2004, it ranked 934th.

Nyla

Probably originally created as a feminine form of **Neil** or **Niles,** Nyla has been in use for generations, though it was rare until recently. It has now begun to rise in use as parents search for "different but not too different" alternatives to names like **Kyla** and **Maya.** Nyla entered the SSA top 1,000 list in 2001 and in 2004 ranked 344th, with 742 girls given the name.

Nymphadora

This seems to be one of the few names of people in the *Harry Potter* novels that J. K. Rowling created herself. Nympha, a feminized form of the word "nymph," has been used on rare occasions as a girls name in English-speaking countries, and its Spanish form, Ninfa, has been regularly if not commonly used in Spanish-speaking ones. Rowling probably deliberately created Nymphadora to seem a bit silly and unwieldy, as her character Nymphadora Tonks despises her first name and wishes to be addressed as Tonks by her fellow wizards.

Ocean

This "nature name" has been used several times in the United States recently. In France, **Océane** has been one of the top ten names for girls since the year 2000. Interestingly, Océane has been most popular in the provinces of France that lie furthest away from the ocean.

Octavia

Latin "eighth." Octavia was the wife of Mark Antony, but she is not nearly as well known as his mistress, Cleopatra. In the 1980s it briefly seemed as if Octavia was about to become fashionable, but it vanished again after 1999.
Famous name: Octavia E. Butler (science fiction novelist)
Nicknames: **Tavi, Tavy**
Variations: **Octavie** (French), **Ottavia** (Italian)

Odessa

The name of the city on the Black Sea coast of Ukraine, founded in 1795 on the supposed site of the ancient Greek colony city of Odessos, whose original meaning is unknown. Odessa was regularly used as a girls first name in the United States from around 1870 through the 1950s. It is rarely given today.

Olga

Russian form of **Helga.** This is an old Russian name, brought to Russia and the Ukraine by Scandinavian settlers in the ninth century. Olga has been much more successful than Helga outside its homeland. It has been popular in Germany, Italy, and Latin America and has even been re-exported to Scandinavia, where it competes in fashion with Helga, the original name. Olga was moderately common in the United States until 1930, and some continuing use in the Hispanic community kept it on the SSA list until 1997.

Famous name: Olga Korbut (Olympic gymnast)
Variations: **Ola, Olenka, Ollo**

Olibama, Olivama

Spanish form of *Oholibamah,* Hebrew "my tent is in them"; In the Old Testament, one of the wives of Esau, Jacob's older brother, who Jacob tricked out of his birthright. This very rare name was used in the early 20th century within the small community of Hispanic-American Protestants.

Olina

Hawaiian *Olina,* "to make merry, joyous."

Olive

Form of **Olivia.** This common 19th-century name completely disappeared after 1950 and today is known primarily as the name of cartoon character Popeye's girlfriend. With Olivia hugely popular, and other "1920s-flapper-style" names like **Stella** and **Hazel** returning, bold young parents may revive Olive soon.

Olivia

Italian form of Latin *oliva,* "olive tree." Shakespeare used this name in his play *Twelfth Night,* in which Olivia is a rich and beautiful countess. Only moderately common in the 19th century, Olivia slowly receded to a low point of 543rd on the SSA list in 1971 and then quickly became fashionable, soaring into the top ten in 2001. Olivia's revival began with a character on television's *The Waltons;* the later characters called Olivia on *The Cosby Show* and *Law & Order: SVU* are results, not causes, of the modern love of this name. In 2004, nearly 16,000 American girls were named Olivia, ranking it 12th for the year. If the 945 girls named **Alivia** were added to the total, the name would rank 8th. It's remarkable that, in spite of Olivia's huge success, it was the only name starting with the letter *O* on the entire SSA top 1,000 list in 2004. Perhaps parents will soon see **Octavia, Olive, Olympia,** or **Oriana** as "different but not too different" alternatives.
Famous names: Olivia de Havilland (actress)
Olivia Newton-John (singer and actress)
Nicknames: **Livia, Livvie, Livy, Nollie, Ollie, Olly**
Variations: **Ola, Oliva, Olive, Olivette, Olivka** (Czech)

Olympe

French form of **Olympia.** With her knack for choosing appropriate names, J. K. Rowling called the half-giant headmistress of Beaux-batons Academy in the *Harry Potter* novels Olympe Maxime.

Olympia

Greek "heavenly," from Mount Olympus. Olympus was the mountain home of the gods and goddesses of Greek mythology. In Offen-bach's opera *Tales from Hoffman,* Olympia is one of the heroines.
Famous names: Olympia Dukakis (actress)
                Olympia Snowe (U.S. senator)
Variations: **Olimpia** (Italian and Portuguese), **Olympe** (French),
             Olympie (Czech)

Opal

Sanskrit *upala,* "gem stone." This jewel name was quite common in the early 20th century but is not often used today, perhaps because Hollywood screenwriters often seem to give the name to humor-ous, uneducated Southern characters.
Variation: **Opaline**

Ophelia

Probably a feminine form of Greek *Ophelos,* "help." This is the name of the mad, tragic character in Shakespeare's *Hamlet.* Today the name is probably best known through *Reviving Ophelia,* Dr. Mary Pipher's best-selling book on the psychology of teenage American girls. Ophelia was regularly used in the late 19th century but van-ished from the SSA top 1,000 list almost 50 years ago.
Variations: **Ofelia, Ophelie** (French)

Oprah

This name was unknown until the 1980s, when the success of talk-show host Oprah Winfrey made it a household word. She says that her parents intended to give her the biblical name **Orpah,** but when the clerk who filled out her birth certificate made a typographical error, they decided they liked the mistake better than their original choice. A few American parents have named their daughters Oprah since she became famous, but the name is still exceedingly rare.

Oriana

Perhaps a form of Latin *aurum,* "gold." The name Oriana was used by poets in verses celebrating both Queen Elizabeth I and Queen Anne of England.

Variation: **Oriane** (French)

Orla

Irish Gaelic *Órlaith,* "golden rulership, princess." Orla was a very common name in 12th-century Ireland and was the name of one of the sisters of the famous hero Brian Boru. Orla was quite popular again in Ireland during the 1980s and 1990s. It is now receding there, and Irish-Americans have never used it in any great numbers.

Orpah

Old Testament name of uncertain meaning. In the Book of Ruth, Orpah is Ruth's sister-in-law who remains in Moab when Ruth follows her mother-in-law Naomi back to Israel. Orpah has always been extremely rare, but in the late 19th century Orpha, which seems to be a blend of Orpah and the male name Orpheus from Greek mythology, was regularly found in the United States.

Variations: **Oprah, Orpha**

Otylia

Polish form of German *Ottilie* (a feminine form of **Otto**) or *Othild* (Germanic "rich war"). When Otylia Jedrzejczak won the first Olympic gold medal in swimming ever for Poland at the 2004 summer Olympics, Polish journalists dubbed the event the "Otyliad" instead of the "Olympiad."

Padma

Sanskrit "lotus." In Hinduism the lotus is important as a sacred symbol representing creation.

Paige

Greek *pais*, "child," through Italian *paggio*, "young servant." It's unclear how this surname became regularly used as a first name for girls. It entered the SSA top 1,000 list in 1952. A 1958 novel called *Parrish*, by Mildred Savage, and the 1961 film based on it helped to solidify the name but didn't initiate it. Since 1979 Paige has steadily grown in popularity; in 2004 nearly 5,400 girls received it, ranking it 64th. Paige Davis became famous as the host of the popular home-makeover television show *Trading Spaces*.

Paisley

Scottish surname and place name, medieval Scots *Passeleth*, possibly from Latin *basilica*, "church." Today Paisley is most associated with the colorful detailed fabric pattern named after the Scottish town. Paisley has occasionally been used as a girls name in Canada and the United States since at least the late 1950s, but it's always been rare.

Paloma

Spanish "dove." Paloma ranked 847th on the SSA list in 2004. Famous name: Paloma Picasso (jewelry designer)

Palycha

Hmong, *Pang* [flower] + *Ly* [moon] + *Cha* [new], "flower of the new moon." This name was created by Hmong immigrants in the United States by blending three traditional Hmong names used in Laos.

Pamela

Possibly Greek *pan-meli*, "all honey." In the 18th century, Samuel Richardson's novel *Pamela: Or Virtue Rewarded* boosted the popularity of this name, which dates to the 16th century, when Philip Sidney used the name in his novel *Arcadia*. In the 1940s Pamela skyrocketed in use to become one of the top 25 names between 1948 and 1970. Parents probably saw it as a perfect "different but not too different" shift from **Patricia.** In the early 1980s the name had a slight rebound while Victoria Principal played Pamela Ewing on the television soap opera *Dallas,* but it's receding quickly today. There were 531 Pamelas born in the United States in 2004, ranking the name 422nd.

Famous name: Pamela Anderson (actress)

Nicknames: **Pam, Pammie, Pammy**

Variations: **Pamelia, Pamella**

Pandora

Greek "all gifted" from *pan* [all, universal] + *dorus* [gift]. In Greek mythology, Pandora was the equivalent of the curious cat. She was warned not to open a box given to her husband by the gods, but she couldn't resist. All the troubles of the world escaped when she opened it, although she managed to shut the lid in time to retain the virtue of hope.

Pansy

The name of the flower, from Middle French *pensée,* "thought." Pansy was one of the flower names created in the 19th century and was on the SSA top 1,000 list between 1880 and 1952. Pansy Parkinson is a friend of Draco Malfoy in the *Harry Potter* novels.

Paola

Italian form of **Paula,** now common in the Hispanic-American community. More than 900 Paolas were born in the United States in 2004, ranking it 297th that year.

Paris

Name of the capital city of France, from the Gaulish tribe *Parisii;* also, in Greek legend, the name of the Trojan prince whose abduction of Helen precipitated the Trojan War. Perhaps because of the latter meaning, Paris was used as a boys name in the United States during the late 19th century. It returned as a boys name in the 1960s and slowly built up to a minor peak of use in 1991. Meanwhile, Paris had entered the girls SSA list in 1985 and quickly became more popular for girls than for boys. The romantic reputation of the city may have made the name seem feminine to many parents. Paris vanished as a boys name in 2001, just before the fame of Paris Hilton caused it to skyrocket in use for girls. In 2004, more than 2,100 American girls were named Paris, ranking it 167th.

Parker

For origin, see Parker in the boys name list. Parker entered the SSA top 1,000 list for girls in 1999 and has been slowly increasing. There were 410 girls who received the name in 2004, ranking it 658th. That year about one girl was named Parker for every seven boys given the name. It's been reported that actress Parker Posey was named after the fashion model Suzy Parker.

Parminder

Punjabi "god of gods, supreme goddess."
Famous name: Parminder Nagra (actress)

Parvati

Sanskrit *Pārvatī,* "of the mountains." In Hindu mythology, Parvati is the daughter of a Himalayan king who wants to marry the god Shiva. When she proves her determination and loyalty by undergoing severe penances and withstanding ridicule, Shiva does marry her. In the *Harry Potter* novels, Parvati Patil is a fellow resident of Gryffindor House, Harry's dormitory.

Patience

Latin "patience." Like **Charity** and **Hope,** this virtue name was popular in Puritan times. Sir Thomas Carew, speaker of the British House of Commons in the 17th century, named his four daughters Patience, Temperance, Silence, and **Prudence.** Patience returned to the SSA top 1,000 list in 1994 after a century's absence. There were 287 girls given the name in 2004, ranking it 844th on the SSA list.

Patricia

Feminine form of **Patrick,** Latin "member of the nobility." Between 1929 and 1966, Patricia was one of the top ten names for girls born in the United States, which was quite a long run of popularity for a female name. It has been falling out of fashion since the 1960s but is doing so slowly, still being 283rd on the list for American girls born in 2004, with nearly 1,000 girls given the name. After watching

Patricia Richardson on *Home Improvement* and Patricia Heaton on *Everybody Loves Raymond* between 1991 and 2005, many Americans must think that Patricia is the perfect name for an actress playing a long-suffering wife on a situation comedy.

Famous names: Patricia Barber (jazz singer and pianist)
Patricia Cornwell (mystery writer)

Nicknames: **Pat, Patsy, Patti, Pattie, Patty, Tricia, Trish, Trisha**

Variations: **Patrice** (French), **Patrizia** (Italian)

Paula

Feminine form of **Paul,** Latin "small." Paula was one of the top 100 names for American girls born between 1943 and 1974, but it had fallen to 661st place on the SSA list by 2004.

Famous names: Paula Abdul (pop singer)
Paula Zahn (television journalist)

Nicknames: **Pauly, Polly**

Variations: **Paola, Paolina** (Italian), **Paule, Paulette** (French), **Paulina, Pauline** (French), **Pavla** (Russian, Czech, and Bulgarian), **Pola** (Slavic)

Paulina

Variation of **Paula.** Paulina was rare before the 1990s but has now surpassed Paula for the affections of American parents.

Famous name: Paulina Porizkova (model)

Pauline

French variation of **Paula.** Pauline was the first feminine form of **Paul** to be popular in the United States and was a top 50 name from 1909 to 1929.

Famous name: Pauline Kael (movie critic)

Pearl

Latin *perna,* "sea mussel"; Middle English *perle,* "pearl." In the 19th and early 20th centuries, Pearl was by far the most popular jewel name, partly because of its use as the name of Hester's young daughter in Nathaniel Hawthorne's classic novel *The Scarlet Letter.* It has been very rare since the 1980s. American novelist Pearl S. Buck won the Nobel Prize in literature in 1938.

Famous name: Pearl Bailey (jazz and blues singer)

Variations: **Pearle, Pearline, Perla** (Spanish)

Peggy

Form of **Margaret.** Peggy was one of the top 50 names for girls between 1931 and 1954 but is quite rare today.

Famous names: Peggy Fleming (Olympic figure skater)
　　　　　　　Peggy Lee (singer)

Other spelling: **Peggie**

Penelope

Greek *penelops,* "duck." In Homer's *Odyssey,* Penelope was the wife of Odysseus. Penelope Clearwater is Percy's girlfriend and "head girl" of Hogwarts in the *Harry Potter* novels. Penelope was regularly used in the 1940s, and it has been back on the SSA top 1,000 list since 2000, ranking 642nd in 2004.

Famous names: Penelope Cruz (actress)
　　　　　　　Penelope Spheeris (movie director)

Nicknames: **Pen, Penny**

Penny

Variation of **Penelope.** In the mid-1960s Penny was one of the top 100 names, but it fell away quickly, and parents rarely use it today.

Famous name: Penny Marshall (movie director)

Perla

The name **Pearl** may be rare today, but Perla is booming with Hispanic-American parents. There were 867 girls given the name in 2004, ranking it 313th for the year.

Persephone

Experts agree that the first part of this name is from Greek "destroyer of," but they disagree as to whether the second part originally meant "murder" or "light." In Greek myth, Persephone is the daughter of the earth and fertility goddess, Demeter. She is stolen by Hades, the god of the underworld. Demeter's grief results in perpetual winterlike conditions. Hades eventually agrees to send Persephone back to her mother for part of the year, which is the Greek mythological explanation for the cycle of the seasons. A few bold parents in the United States have named their daughters Persephone recently.

Petrula

Probably a Greek feminine form of **Peter.**

Peyton

For origin and history, see Peyton in the boys name list. Like many aristocratic Southern surnames, Peyton has occasionally been given to girls in the South for several generations. But it wasn't until Rebecca De Mornay played the character Peyton in the 1992 film *The Hand That Rocks the Cradle* that parents all over the country decided it would be a good name for a girl. This is a classic example of how it is merely the sound of a name in a hit movie that attracts parents to it, since the character was an evil nanny. Both Peyton and **Payton** entered the SSA top 1,000 list for girls in 1992, and their combined total ranked them 364th that year, a very high initial entry. The name has continued to grow in use, with more than 4,400 girls receiving one of the two main spellings in 2004, ranking the name 80th for the year. The spelling Payton has consistently accounted for about 45 percent of girls given the name. In 2004, 15 percent more girls than boys were given this name.

Phaedra, Phaidra

Greek "bright one." In Greek mythology, Phaidra, or Phaedra, was the wife of Theseus. She fell in love with her stepson, and great tragedy resulted. Euripides used the story for his play *Hippolytus*.

Philippa

Feminine form of **Philip,** Greek "lover of horses." Philippa of Hainault was the wife of Edward III of England. Philippa is a well-known name in England, but it's always been rare in the United States.
Nickname: **Pippa**

Phoebe

Greek *Phoibe,* "the bright one." Like **Artemis, Diana,** and **Cynthia,** Phoebe is another name associated with the moon. In Greek mythology, she was the twin of Phoebus, or Apollo. Because the name appears in the New Testament, Phoebe was regularly used in the 19th century. It returned to the SSA list in 1989. The character of Phoebe Buffay on *Friends* seems to have accelerated its increase only slightly. In 2004 Phoebe ranked 346th on the list of American girls names.
Famous name: Phoebe Snow (singer and songwriter)
Variation: **Phebe**

Phoenix

For origin and history, see Phoenix in the boys name list. Phoenix entered the SSA top 1,000 list for girls in 2003, and in 2004, 274 girls received the name, ranking it 880th on that list. Phoenix was a well-used name for female characters in kung fu films made in Hong Kong.

Phyllida

Form of **Phyllis**. In the *Harry Potter* novels, Phyllida Spore is the author of *One Thousand Magical Herbs and Fungi*.

Phyllis

Greek *phullis*, "foliage, leafy." Phyllis, daughter of the king of Thrace, is the mythological source of the almond tree, or *philla*. She committed suicide after her lover did not return to her, and a tree grew over her grave. When he finally returned, the tree bloomed. Phyllis was a top 50 name between 1923 and 1949 but fell out of the SSA top 1,000 list in 1985.

Famous name: Phyllis Diller (comedienne)

Variations: **Phylicia, Phyllida**

Piper

Old English "pipe player." Piper was invented as a girls first name in 1950 when Universal Studios changed Rosetta Jacobs' name to Piper Laurie. In spite of her success as an actress, parents took no notice of the name until the television series *Charmed*, with a character named Piper Halliwell, premiered in 1998. Piper immediately entered the SSA top 1,000 list and flourished. More than 1,200 American girls were given the name in 2004, ranking it 240th. The same series has also made Piper a popular girls name in Australia.

Polly

Variation of **Mary** or **Paula**. Polly abruptly vanished from the SSA top 1,000 list in 1978 after being regularly used for more than two centuries.

Famous name: Polly Draper (actress)

Pollyanna

Combination of **Polly** and **Anne**. The heroine of Eleanor Porter's novel *Pollyanna* was the epitome of naïveté. Today, the name is ascribed to anyone who is foolishly naive.

Pomona

The ancient Roman goddess of fruit trees, usually depicted holding a cornucopia as a symbol of abundance. In the *Harry Potter* novels, the aptly named Pomona Sprout is the herbology teacher and head of Hufflepuff House.

Poppy

Latin *papāver*, the name of the flower. Poppy has been growing like a weed in England lately and is now among the top 50 names for girls there. American parents have not yet discovered it, and the more common use of "Pop" as a name for a father or grandfather in the United States may inhibit its transplantation here. However, that might change when the children growing up with Harry Potter become adults, since Poppy Pomfrey is the name of the Hogwarts school nurse, who Harry and his friends have had all too many occasions to see in J. K. Rowling's novels.

Portia

Latin family name *Porcius,* "pig farmers." In Shakespeare's *The Merchant of Venice,* Portia saves Antonio's life by cleverly outwitting Shylock. Portia was popular in the African-American community during the 1980s, although it is was usually spelled **Porsha** or **Porsche,** like the expensive German automobile.
Famous name: Portia de Rossi (actress)

Prairie

The word, originally French "meadow," used as a nature name.

Precious

The word, from Latin *pretiōs,* "costly, valuable." Precious entered the SSA top 1,000 list in 1978, the same year the British group Eruption, featuring Jamaican-born singer Precious Wilson, had their first international hit with the song "I Can't Stand the Rain." Precious quickly became fashionable in the African-American community and rose to a peak of 378th on the SSA list in 1996. Though the name is receding today, there were still 500 girls named Precious born in the United States in 2004, ranking it 441st. It's interesting that Precious has been a popular name not only in the West Indies and the United States with parents of African descent, but also in the English-speaking countries of southern Africa.

Presley

English surname, "dweller by the priest's clearing." With the great adulation of Elvis Presley, and the penchant of American parents for turning many other surnames ending in *-ley* into first names for girls, it's surprising that Presley didn't enter the SSA top 1,000 list until 1998. It has been rapidly increasing in use since, however. There were 504 girls named Presley in 2004, ranking the name 438th for the year.

Princess

This word name entered the SSA top 1,000 list in 1979 and has been regularly used since. Its highest ranking was 613th in 1986. Some parents may avoid the name because they fear it would encourage prima donna behavior in their daughters. It seemed as if Princess was vanishing in the middle 1990s, but it has slightly increased again since. In 2004, 345 Princesses were born in the United States, ranking the name 748th on the SSA list.

Priscilla

Latin *Priscus,* "ancient," a family name. In literature, Henry Wadsworth Longfellow immortalized the name in "The Courtship of Miles Standish." Priscilla had peaks of popularity in 1940 and again in 1985. In 2004 it ranked 300th, with 906 born.
Famous name: Priscilla Presley (actress)
Nicknames: **Cilla, Pris, Prissie**
Variation: **Piroska** (Hungarian)

Priya

Sanskrit *Priya,* "beloved, dear."

Prudence

Latin *prudentia,* "foresight, intelligence." Like other virtue names, Prudence was popular with the Puritans. It vanished from the top American names in 1949, and not even the magic of *Charmed,* with a character named Prudence Halliwell, has been able to revive it.
Nicknames: **Pru, Prudy, Prue**

Psyche

Greek "soul." In Greek mythology, Eros, the son of the goddess of love, Aphrodite, fell in love with a mortal woman named Psyche. Aphrodite did not approve, but after several failed attempts to end the relationship, she gave in because Eros had found his true love.

Quanisha

African-American creation, "Qua-" + "-nisha" from **Tanisha.** Quanisha was regularly used in the early 1990s but is now rare again.
Other spellings: **Quaneesha, Quanesha, Quaneshia, Quinesha**

Queen

Old English *Cwen,* "a queen." Queen was a moderately common name through the 1940s, but it vanished abruptly in 1960.
Variations: **Queena, Queenie**

Querida

Spanish "beloved."

Quinn

For the origin of the name, see Quinn in the boys list. Quinn popped onto the SSA top 1,000 list for girls in 1979, the year after child actress Quinn Cummings first appeared as Annie Cooper on the television drama *Family.* It then immediately dropped off the list and didn't reappear until 1995. Since then it has grown in use and ranked 680th on the SSA list in 2004, when 398 girls were given the name. That year there were still two-and-a-half times as many boys as girls named Quinn in the United States.

Quintana

Spanish "country home," Mexican place name.

Quintina

Latin "fifth."
Variations: **Quenta, Quentina, Quinta**

Quitterie

French form of Spanish *Quiteria,* from Greek *chiton,* "short tunic." This French version of an obscure Spanish saint's name has recently been popular with descendants of the old French aristocracy.

Rachel

Hebrew "ewe." In the Bible, Rachel was the wife of Jacob and the mother of many sons, including Joseph. As with many biblical names that had faded from use, this name was revived in 17th-century England by the Puritans. The name was a favorite of Sir Walter Scott, who used it in both *Waverly* and *Peveril of the Peak*. Between 1880 and 1967, Rachel was always between 100th and 200th on the SSA list. Then in the 1960s it abruptly started to soar. Between 1980 and 2002, it was one of the 25 most popular names for girls. It's just starting to decline, and the nearly 7,600 girls given the name in 2004 ranked it 42nd for the year. Rachel is a name with such historic depth that it will probably always be at least moderately in use.
Famous names: Rachel Carson (biologist)
                   Rachel Weisz (actress)
Nicknames: **Rachie, Rae, Ray**
Variations: **Rachael, Rachele** (Italian), **Rachelle, Rahel** (Hungarian and German), **Raquel** (Spanish)

Rachelle

Many people assume this is the French form of **Rachel,** but it is actually an American creation blending Rachel with **Rochelle.** Rachelle was a fairly popular name in the 1970s and 1980s, but it left the SSA top 1,000 list in 2004.

Rainbow

Though never very common, Rainbow is often considered one of the classic "hippy" names. It was used as such during the 1960s and 1970s and now is inspiring some new interest as a "nature name" for the 21st century. The idea of using the word as a name is older than the hippies, however. *Rainbow* was a silent film in 1921 about an orphan girl named Rainbow who inherits a copper mine.

Ramona

Feminine form of **Ramon,** a Spanish form of **Raymond.** In the early 20th century, Ramona was often used by non-Hispanic-Americans because of the long-term popularity of *Ramona,* Helen Hunt Jackson's 1884 novel about the plight of Native Americans in California. Film versions of the book were made in 1910, 1916, 1928, and 1936. Today people are more likely to associate the name Ramona with the children's book series by Beverly Cleary, but those books haven't helped the name, which has been very rare since 1988.

Randi

Feminine form of **Randall** or **Randolph,** Old English "shield-wolf"; also, a form of **Miranda.**
Other spellings: **Randie, Randy**

Rani

Hindu "queen."
Variation: **Ranee**

Raquel

Spanish form of **Rachel.** Before 1966 this name was largely confined to the Hispanic-American community, but the career of actress Raquel Welch changed that. Raquel was among the top 250 girls names in the United States until 1994. By 2004 it had slipped to 373rd place, with 680 girls given the name.

Rasheeda

Arabic "mature, rightly guided." This name was regularly given by African-American parents during the 1970s.
Other spelling: **Rashida**

Raven

Old English *hraefn,* "raven." Until recently, Raven was a very rare name. But after **Robin** became a popular name, some parents were inspired to give the names of other birds, such as **Lark** and Wren, to their daughters. Starting in 1976, the television soap opera *The Edge of Night* featured a character called Raven Alexander, and Raven flew onto the SSA top 1,000 list in 1978. The name exploded in popularity in the African-American community in the fall of 1989 after the child actress Raven-Symone began appearing as Olivia on

The Cosby Show. Raven became one of the top 150 names given to American girls born between 1990 and 1998. By 2004 it had receded to 239th place, with more than 1,200 girls given the name.

Ravenna

Name of the Italian city, so ancient the original meaning is unknown. This name is occasionally bestowed on American girls.

Rawan

Arabic "gold." This was the most popular girls name in Amman, Jordan, in 2005.

Reagan

For origin, see Reagan in the boys list. The idea that Reagan could be a girls name started when it was confused with **Regan,** even though the two names have different origins and often different pronunciations. Reagan was used sporadically as a girls name during Regan's first period of popularity in the late 1970s, but it vanished during Ronald Reagan's presidency, only to resurface on the SSA top 1,000 list in 1993. Since then it has grown rapidly in use and has developed the fairly common spelling variant **Raegan.** More than 2,800 girls received the name in 2004, ranking it 132nd that year.

Reality

Several instances of this "word name" have been noted lately, possibly inspired by the trade name of a perfume.

Reba

Variation of **Rebecca.** Reba was used in the 1920s and 1930s but, despite the fame of country singer Reba McEntire, is very rare today.

Rebecca

Hebrew *Ribqah,* uncertain meaning, perhaps "heifer" or "yoke." In the Bible, Rebecca was the wife of Isaac and the mother of Jacob and Esau. Like the name **Rachel,** Rebecca was popular among the Puritans. Rebecca is a central character in Sir Walter Scott's *Ivanhoe,* William Makepeace Thackeray's *Vanity Fair,* and Kate Douglas Wiggin's *Rebecca of Sunnybrook Farm.* In Daphne du Maurier's *Rebecca,* the haunting Rebecca is already dead when the novel begins. As the name of one of the biblical matriarchs, Rebecca, like Rachel, never fell below 200th place in the United States, even in the early 20th century when biblical names were unfashionable. It began to rise in the 1940s and was one of the top 25 names from 1971 to 1994. Though it's now receding, more than 6,000 Rebeccas were born in 2004, ranking it 55th.

Famous names: Rebecca De Mornay (actress)
                   Rebecca Lobo (basketball player)
Nicknames: **Becca, Beckie, Becky, Bekki, Reba, Reeba**
Other spellings: **Rebecah, Rebeka, Rebekah**
Variations: **Rebeca** (Spanish), **Rebecka** (Swedish), **Rebekka** (German), **Revekka** (Russian), **Rivka** (modern Hebrew)

Reem

Arabic *Rím,* "white antelope."

Reese

Welsh *Rhys,* "ardor." Like **Reagan** and **Riley,** Reese is a formerly male name that is suddenly booming for girls. This is due to the career of actress Reese Witherspoon. Reese was rare as a girls name before 2000, but in 2004, 1,220 girls received it (ranking it 237th) while it was given to only 688 boys. When the alternative spellings **Reece** and **Rhys** are added in, however, the boys are still slightly ahead.

Regan

The name of one of King Lear's daughters in Shakespeare's famous play. Its origin is unknown, although since the sources the play is based on go back to Celtic Britain, the name might have the same root as **Rhiannon,** but that is unproven. What is clear is that its modern use as a girls name can be traced to the 1973 film *The Exorcist,* because Regan first entered the SSA top 1,000 in 1974. After a minor vogue, it vanished again in 1982, reappearing in 1991, two years before **Reagan.** Many parents choose the spelling Regan because they want the first syllable to rhyme with *league,* but others pronounce it the same as Reagan. On its own, Regan ranked 351st in 2004 with 722 born; if Regan and Reagan were counted together, they would have been the 105th most common girls name of 2004.

Regina

Latin "queen." In the 19th century, this name was synonymous with the queen of England, referred to as Victoria Regina. In the 1960s, Regina was one of the top 100 names for girls, but in 2004 it was only 652nd on the SSA list.

Famous name: Regina King (actress)
Nickname: **Gina**
Variations: **Raina** (Belorusan), **Raine, Regine** (French), **Reina** (Spanish), **Reine** (French), **Reyna** (Spanish), **Riona** (Irish Gaelic)

Rehema

Swahili "compassion."

Reiko

Japanese "courteous child."

Renata

Latin "born again."
Famous name: Renata Tebaldi (opera singer)
Variations: **Renate** (German), **Renee** (French)

Renee

French form of **Renata.** In the 1960s and 1970s, Renee was one of the top 100 names. Its fashion as a first name has passed, but its pleasant rhythm has made Renee one of the most common middle names for American girls. It ranked 392nd as a first name in 2004.
Famous name: Renee Fleming (opera singer)
Other spellings: **Ranae, Renae, Rene**

Reshma

Sanskrit *Rsmā,* "moonbeam."

Reyna

Spanish form of **Regina.** This is now the most common spelling for Hispanic-Americans of the traditional **Reina.** Both spellings accounted for more than 1,300 girls named in 2004, ranking it 225th.

Rhea

Greek, perhaps "earth." Rhea was one of the ancient Greek goddesses and the mother of Zeus. In 2004, Rhea entered the SSA top 1,000 list for the first time in 36 years, at 903rd place.
Famous name: Rhea Perlman (actress)
Other spelling: **Rea**

Rhiannon

Name of a Welsh moon goddess who gave up her immortality to marry a human, probably derived from Old Celtic *Rigantona,* "great queen." This is a name whose popularity can be traced to a particular popular song: "Rhiannon" by Fleetwood Mac, which was released in 1975. The name burst onto the SSA top 1,000 list in 1976 and has never left, just waxing and waning a bit over the years. In 2004, 432 Rhiannons were born in the United States, ranking it 623rd on the SSA list. Rhiannon is also quite popular in Wales today.

Rhoda

Greek *rhodon*, "rose." This biblical name was regularly used in the 19th century and stayed on the top 1,000 list during the early 20th. The name was on its last legs when the sitcom *Rhoda* appeared in the fall of 1974. For the next two years there was a small increase in use of the name, but the character's divorce in the third season of the show coincided with the complete disappearance of the name.

Rhonda

Welsh, perhaps from *rhon* [lance] + *da* [good]. Between 1958 and 1971, Rhonda was a top 50 name for girls. Parents probably saw it as a feminine form of **Ronald**. It left the SSA top 1,000 list in 1995.

Rigoberta

Feminine form of **Rigoberto**.

Riley

For origin, see Riley in the boys name list. Since 1990 this has been one of the fastest-growing names for girls, joining **Ashley** and **Sydney** as a formerly male name ending –*y* that is now primarily female. The alternative spellings **Reilly, Rylee, Ryleigh,** and **Rylie** are all used enough to separately be on the SSA top 1,000 list. There were more than 9,200 girls given one of the five spellings in 2004, ranking Riley 33rd for the year.

Rina

Variation of **Irene** or **Katherine;** also, Hebrew "song."

Rinoa

This name was created for Rinoa Heartily, the beautiful leader of a resistance movement in the popular computer role-playing game Final Fantasy VIII, originally released in 1999. Rinoa is now voguish in Japan, and some American Final Fantasy fans have also bestowed the name on their daughters.

Ripley

English place name and surname, "strip-shaped woodland clearing." A few parents have used Ripley as a girls name since 1979, when Sigourney Weaver played the character Ripley in the movie *Alien*. In the sequels to that film, it's revealed that Ripley's first name is Ellen, but she remains more easily identified by her surname to science-fiction fans.

Rita

Form of **Margarita.** Between 1914 and 1960, Rita was a top 100 name in the United States, but it left the top 1,000 list in 2003. In 1986 Rita Levi-Montalcini was cowinner of the Nobel Prize in medicine and physiology for her discovery of nerve-growth factors.
Famous names: Rita Mae Brown (writer)
Rita Dove (poet laureate of the United States)
Rita Moreno (actress)

Roberta

Feminine form of **Robert.** Roberta was a top 100 name between 1935 and 1953 but vanished during the 1990s.
Famous name: Roberta Flack (singer)
Nicknames: **Bobbi, Bobbie, Bobby, Robbie, Robby**
Variations: **Roberte** (French), **Robertina** (Dutch and Hungarian), **Robin, Robina, Robine** (French), **Robinett, Robinette, Robinia, Robyn, Ruperta** (German)

Robin, Robyn

Variation of **Robert** or **Roberta.** Robin was first used for girls in the 1930s. It quickly climbed the charts and was one of the top 50 names between 1954 and 1969. The name is close to vanishing today. During its heyday Robin was the more popular spelling, but in 2004 there were exactly 245 girls each named Robin and Robyn. The combined total ranked the name 445th.
Famous name: Robin Wright Penn (actress)

Rochelle

French "little rock." This French place name was somehow brought to the attention of American parents around 1933. It remained in regular use until the 1990s but is rare today.
Nicknames: **Shelley, Shelli, Shellie, Shelly**

Rocio

Spanish *Rocío,* from *Maria de la Rocío,* "Mary of the Dew," a title of the Virgin Mary that comes from the symbolic connection between dew and the tears Mary sheds for the world. This traditional Hispanic-American name has been in the SSA top 1,000 list since 1972, though it's now receding and ranked 862nd in 2004.

Romaine

French feminine form of **Roman.**

Romilda

Italian, from the Germanic Lombard *hrôth* [fame] + *hiltja* [battle]. In *Harry Potter and the Half-Blood Prince,* Romilda Vane is a new Hogwarts student who has a crush on Harry.

Rosa

Latin form of **Rose.** Rosa Parks is considered the mother of the Civil Rights Movement in the United States. Her refusal to move to the back of a bus initiated a bus strike in Montgomery, Alabama, that eventually led to far-reaching social change. Rosa was one of the top 100 names of the 1880s but has been slowly receding ever since. It ranked 314th in 2004, when 719 girls received the name.
Famous names: Rosa Bonheur (artist)
           Rosa Mota (marathoner)

Rosalia

Italian variation of **Rose;** also, Latin "festival of roses."
Variations: **Rosalie** (French), **Roselie, Rozalie, Rozele** (Lithuanian)

Rosalind

Old German *hros* [horse] + *lind* [tender, soft]; reinterpreted in medieval times as Latin *rosa linda,* "pretty rose." The English poet Edmund Spenser revived this name, and Shakespeare made it popular with his play *As You Like It.* In the United States, Rosalind was regularly used in the 1940s but vanished before 1980.
Famous name: Rosalind Russell (actress)
Variations: **Rosaleen, Rosalinda, Rosaline, Rosalyn, Roselyn, Roz**

Rosalyn

Variation of **Rosalind** or **Rose.** Rosalyn Yalow was cowinner of the 1977 Nobel Prize in medicine.

Rosamund

Old Germanic *hros* [horse] + *mund* [protection].

Rosana, Rosanna

Form of **Rosanne.**

Famous name: Rosanna Arquette (actress)

Rosanne

Combination of **Rose** and **Anne.** This name is well known today, thanks to comedienne and actress Roseanne and to country singer Rosanne Cash.

Variations: **Rosana, Rosanna, Roseann, Roseanne**

Rose

English form of *rosa,* Latin "rose"; or Old German *Hrodohaidis,* "famous kind." The Germanic form was probably the original version of this name, but its similarity to the word *rose,* often considered the most beautiful flower, greatly increased its popularity. Rose was the first flower name used in Europe and probably inspired the many others that came later. St. Rose of Lima was the first person born in the New World to be canonized by the Roman Catholic church. Between 1890 and 1928, Rose was one of the top 25 names for girls, but it's been falling away since. There was a minor upswing in the name for a few years after *Titanic,* starring Kate Winslet as Rose, came out in 1997. The 867 Roses born in 2004 ranked the name 314th. Rose is very common now as a middle name.

Famous name: Rose McGowan (actress)

Nicknames: **Rosi, Rosie, Rosy**

Variations: **Rosa** (Dutch, Italian, Latin, Spanish, and Swedish), **Rosabel, Rosabella, Rosabelle, Rosaleen** (Irish), **Rosalia** (Italian), **Rosaline, Rosalyn, Rosel** (Swiss), **Rosella, Roselle, Roselyn, Rosetta** (Italian), **Rosette, Rosina** (Italian), **Rosine, Rosita** (Spanish)

Roselyn

Blend of **Rose** and **Lynn,** or a form of **Rosalind.** Roselyn is the only one of the Rose family of names to be increasing at the moment. It entered the SSA list in 2003 after an absence of 49 years and almost doubled in use to reach 610th place on the SSA list in 2004.

Famous name: Roselyn Sanchez (actress)

Rosemarie

Combination of **Rose** and **Marie**.

Rosemary

Combination of **Rose** and **Mary.** The herb rosemary is the symbol of remembrance. Between 1926 and 1949, Rosemary was one of the top 100 names for girls, but it's been decreasing in use ever since and ranked only 718th on the SSA list in 2004.

Rosmerta

Name of the ancient Celtic goddess of prosperity in Gaul, possibly connected with the word *ros,* "seed." The ancient Gauls considered Rosmerta to be the supplier of food, which makes her name appropriate for the waitress and bartender of the Three Broomsticks Pub in the *Harry Potter* novels.

Rowan

For origin, see Rowan in the boys name list. Rowan has been in the SSA top 1,000 for girls only since 2003, but it rose 50 percent in a year to rank 706th in 2004, with 373 girls given the name. Science-fiction fans may know this name from Anne McCaffrey's novel *The Rowan,* about a woman with incredible telepathic and teleportation abilities.

Rowena

Perhaps Old English *hrod* [fame] + *wynn* [joy]. Sir Walter Scott immortalized this name in *Ivanhoe.* J. K. Rowling chose it for the character Rowena Ravenclaw, one of the founders of Hogwarts School in the *Harry Potter* novels.

Roxana, Roxanna

Bactrian "little star" or Persian "shining." Roxana was the Bactrian wife of Alexander the Great. This name ranked 978th on the SSA list in 2004.
Variations: **Roxanne** (French), **Roxene, Roxine**

Roxanne

French form of **Roxana**. Roxanne is the heroine of *Cyrano de Bergerac* by Edmond Rostand. Comedian Steve Martin played a modern-day Cyrano in the 1987 movie *Roxanne.*
Nicknames: **Rox, Roxie, Roxy**
Other spellings: **Roxane, Roxann**

Ruby

Latin *rubinus lapis,* "red stone." Ruby was a top 30 name between 1905 and 1927. It then slid down to a low point of 403rd in 1986 but has since inched upward again. More than 2,500 Rubys were born in 2004, ranking it 144th.
Famous name: Ruby Dee (actress)
Variations: **Rubia, Rubye**

Rue

Name of a flowering herb (see **Ruta**) or a form of **Ruth.**
Famous name: Rue McClanahan (actress)

Ruta

Lithuanian *ruta,* "rue," a medicinal herb with yellow blossoms that is considered the national flower of Lithuania.
Variation: **Rue**

Ruth

Hebrew, perhaps "companion." In the Bible, Ruth is the daughter-in-law of Naomi, and their story is about the ideal of devotion. President Grover Cleveland's eldest daughter, born in 1891, was named Ruth. When he entered the White House for the second time in 1893, the press called the toddler "Baby Ruth"; the candy bar was named after her. Ruth was a top ten name from 1892 to 1930. It has decreased since; the 883 Ruths born in 2004 ranked it 305th.
Famous name: Ruth Bader Ginsburg (U.S. Supreme Court associate justice)
Nicknames: **Rue, Ruthie**
Variation: **Rut** (Spanish, Polish, and Scandinavian)

Ryan

For origin, see Ryan in the boys list. Ryan has been given to enough girls each year to make the SSA top 1,000 list since 1974, the height of Ryan's success as a boys name. For girls the name peaked at 340th and then receded; however, it began to rise again in the 1990s. In 2004, 689 girls were named Ryan, ranking it 367th that year.

Ryann

This alternate feminine form of **Ryan,** which shifts the accent to the second syllable, has been in the SSA top 1,000 list since 1997 and is increasing in use. It ranked 719th in 2004.

Sabina

Latin "of the Sabines." St. Sabina was a first-century Christian martyr.
The name was used sporadically in the United States in the early
20th century, but **Sabrina** seems to have replaced it.
Variations: **Sabine** (French and German), **Savina**

Sabrina

Name of the legendary goddess of the Severn River in England. This
name was introduced to American parents by the 1954 movie
Sabrina starring Audrey Hepburn. The name was briefly among the
top 100 names in 1977, when Kate Jackson played Sabrina on *Charlie's Angels*. Its high point of use, when it ranked 53rd on the SSA list,
was in 1997, the year after *Sabrina, the Teenage Witch* premiered on
television. Obviously, Sabrina has been one of the most Hollywood-
influenced names in American history. In 2004, more than 2,100
Sabrinas were born, ranking it 164th.
Variation: **Zabrina**

Sadie

Form of **Sarah**. Sadie was popular in the late 19th century but fell
off quickly during the 20th and left the SSA top 1,000 list in 1966.
However, it returned in 1974, much sooner than would normally be
expected, and has risen steadily since. The fashionable "long *a*" vowel
in the first syllable has probably has helped the name's revival. There
were more than 1,700 Sadies born in 2004, ranking it 194th.
Variations: **Sada, Sadye**

Saffron

Arabic *za'farān,* a yellow crocus and the condiment and color derived
from it. Fans of British television comedy will recognize the name
from Saffron Monsoon, the sensible daughter driven up the wall by
her mother's comic selfishness in the series *Absolutely Fabulous.*

Sage

This word of double meanings ("wise person" and "perennial herb") has been steadily increasing in use for girls since it entered the SSA top 1,000 list in 1993. In 2004, more than 1,200 girls were named Sage or **Saige,** ranking the name 238th. The name of the herb sage goes back to Latin *Salvia,* because of the healing properties it was thought to possess.

Sahara

Arabic *sahrā,* from *ashar,* "fawn-colored," the name of the world's largest desert, located in Northern Africa. A few American parents are choosing this name, perhaps as an alternative for **Sarah.**

Sakura

Japanese "cherry blossoms." This has been one of the most popular girls names in Japan since the 1990s.

Sally

Form of **Sarah.** No fictional Sally is as memorable as Sally Bowles, the creation of Christopher Isherwood in *The Berlin Stories.* She became well known when the book was made into a movie, *I Am a Camera,* with Julie Harris; a long-running Broadway musical, *Cabaret;* and then the film of the musical in which Liza Minnelli gained fame as the delightfully decadent Sally. This name was in the top 100 between 1930 and 1955, but in 2004 it only ranked 918th on the SSA list, receding as its sister **Sadie** takes over.
Famous names: Sally Field (actress)
Sally Mann (photographer)
Dr. Sally Ride (astronaut)
Other spelling: **Sallie**

Salma

Form of Arabic *salima,* "safe." This ancient Arabian name has been in the SSA top 1,000 list since 1997, probably propelled by the career of Mexican actress Salma Hayek, whose father is of Lebanese descent. In 2004 Salma ranked 811th on the SSA list.

Salome

Hebrew *shalom,* "peace." In the New Testament, Salome was the daughter of Herodias and the stepdaughter of Herod Antipas. Before she would dance for her stepfather's guests, she demanded the head of John the Baptist. Not surprisingly, this name has never been very popular.

Variations: **Salima** (Arabic), **Saloma, Salomea** (Polish), **Selima** (Turkish), **Selma** (German and Scandinavian)

Samantha

A colonial American creation, probably combining **Sam** with -antha, the feminine form of Greek anthos, "flower." This was an unusual name until 1964 when actress Elizabeth Montgomery began starring as Samantha, the witch-who-would-be-a-housewife on the television comedy Bewitched. The name steadily grew in use until it was one of the top ten names given to American girls between 1988 and 2001. In 2004, just starting to decline, Samantha ranked 17th, with more than 13,500 newborns receiving the name. Younger people may associate this name more with the character Samantha Jones on Sex and the City than with the character on Bewitched.

Nicknames: **Sam, Samanthy, Sami, Sammi**

Samara

The origin of this name is unclear, but it may be a form of Arabic Samārah, "soft, light" or Thamara, "benefit, gain." In botany, "samara" is also the term for the type of flat, papery, seed-bearing fruits found on elm or maple trees. Whatever the name's derivation, Samara first entered the SSA top 1,000 list in 1997. After the 2002 film The Ring featured a mysterious young character named Samara Morgan, the name more than tripled in use between 2002 and 2004. There were 845 girls given the name in 2004, ranking it 318th.

Samira

Arabic samira, "woman who regales with nighttime conversation." This name has just barely made the SSA top 1,000 list since 2002, ranking 996th in 2004 with 234 born. Samira is popular throughout the Arabic-speaking world.

Sanaa

Arabic Sanā' "brilliance, splendor." This name entered the SSA top 1,000 list in 2003. Its newfound vogue may be related to the career of actress Sanaa Lathan, who starred in the 2002 film Brown Sugar and then Alien vs. Predator in 2004. Almost 400 American girls were named Sanaa in 2004, ranking it 682nd on the SSA list.

Sandra

Form of **Alexandra** or **Cassandra**. Sandra boomed during the 1930s and became a top ten name between 1940 and 1952. It was just starting to decline when the career of actress Sandra Dee pushed it back into the top ten for a few years in the early 1960s. In 2004, more than 1,100 Sandras were born, ranking it 256th.

Famous names: Sandra Bullock (actress)

Sandra Day O'Connor (U.S. Supreme Court associate justice)

Nickname: **Sandy**

Sandy

Form of **Alexandra, Cassandra,** or **Sandra.** As an independent name, Sandy peaked at 126th on the SSA list in 1960, but it was still on that list in 2004, in 802nd place, with 312 born.

Famous name: Sandy Duncan (actress)

Other spellings: **Sandi, Sandie**

Saniya, Saniyah

Arabic *Saniyah,* "resplendent, brilliant, exalted." Saniya has been growing in use in the African-American community as part of the fashion for names ending in *-iyah.* There were 710 girls who received one of the two main spellings in 2004, ranking the name 358th.

Sanne

Dutch form of **Susan.** This was the most common name for girls born in the Netherlands in 2004. The name is also used in Scandinavia.

Sansa

Name of a character in George R. R. Martin's *A Song of Ice and Fire* series of fantasy novels. Martin probably created the name by altering *Sancha,* the feminine form of *Sancho,* itself a derivative of the Spanish name **Santos.** Several examples of readers naming daughters after the character have been noted.

Sanura

Swahili "civet cat."

Sapphire

Name of the gemstone or its deep blue color. This has always been a rare name, even when other gem names like **Ruby** were common.

Sarah

Hebrew "princess." In the Old Testament, Sarah was the wife of
Abraham and the mother of Isaac. Sarah was a very popular English
name by the 17th century. Sarah Jennings married John Churchill,
later duke of Marlborough. She was a close friend of Anne Stewart,
who became Queen Anne. The court was so jealous of the duchess
of Marlborough and her influence on the queen that "Queen Sarah"
became a common slur used against her. In the 19th century, actress
Sarah Bernhardt reigned on the stage. About 25 percent of parents
giving this name use the spelling Sara. If both main spellings are
counted together, Sarah has never ranked lower than 90th among
American girls names, a low point that was reached in 1959. Sarah
then rose swiftly to become a top ten name in 1977. In 2004 nearly
17,000 Sarahs were born in the United States, ranking it seventh.
Famous names: Sarah Brightman (soprano)
Sarah Jessica Parker (actress)
Variations: **Saara** (Finnish and Estonian), **Saartje** (Dutch), **Sadie, Sal,**
Sally, Sara, Sari (Hungarian), **Sarina** (Dutch), **Sarita**
(Spanish), **Sarra** (Russian), **Sassa** (Swedish), **Shari, Zadee,**
Zara, Zarah

Sarai

Hebrew, perhaps "contentious" or "my princess." In the Bible, **Sarah**
was originally called Sarai before her name was changed by God. For
unknown reasons, Sarai and its alternative spelling, **Sarahi,** have been
increasing in use in the Hispanic community since the late 1980s.
There were 889 girls given this name in 2004, ranking it 303rd.

Sariah

In the *Book of Mormon,* Sariah, wife of Lehi, is one of only two
women mentioned by name. Because of that, Sariah has been a
regularly used name in Utah for generations. During the last couple
decades, some non-Mormon parents in the United States have used
the name as an independent creation by blending **Sarah** and **Mariah,**
probably not realizing that the name has a Mormon connection.

Sasha

Russian form of **Alexandra.** This name has been on the SSA top
1,000 list since 1972. It peaked in 1988 at 147th and in 2004 ranked
322nd, with more than 800 girls given the name.

Saskia

Dutch, probably a Latinized feminine form of *Sachs*, "Saxon." This name has been used in the Netherlands since the Middle Ages and is well known to art lovers because it was the name of the painter Rembrandt's wife. Saskia is still quite rare in the United States, but there are signs that young parents are beginning to consider it.

Savannah

Taino (Caribbean Native American) *zabana*, "meadow," later given as a name to the river and city in Georgia. Savannah was used as a girls name in the South during the 19th century, but it vanished during the 1920s. It was revived throughout the United States in 1982 after the release of the comedy film *Savannah Smiles*. The name's similarity in sound to **Samantha** and **Hannah** made it a good alternative, and it's been one of the top 50 names since 1993. In 2004, more than 7,500 Savannahs were born, ranking it 43rd.
Variations: **Savana, Savanna, Vanna**

Scarlett

English "deep red." Before Scarlett O'Hara, the heroine of Margaret Mitchell's novel *Gone With the Wind,* no girls were named Scarlett. The name briefly appeared near the bottom of the SSA top 1,000 list in the early 1940s, but it was too bold a choice for most parents at the time and soon vanished again. The modern search for uncommon but well-known names brought it back in 1992. In 2004, 526 American girls were named Scarlett, ranking it 424th.
Famous name: Scarlett Johansson (actress)

Sedona

Like **Aspen**, Sedona is primarily used today because it's the name of a beautiful resort town in the American West, in this case Sedona, Arizona, famous for its artists' colony and beautiful canyon setting. Many people assume Sedona is a Native American word, but the town is named after Sedona M. Schnebbly, the wife of its founder. It's likely that Sedona is a variation of the 19th-century name **Sedonia,** which is a spelling variation of **Sidonia,** the feminine of Latin *Sidonius,* "man from Sidon," and the name of two early Christian saints. Sidonia was used in the Middle Ages, in England often in the form **Sidony,** which was frequently confused with **Sydney.** Sedona is a rare name, but two or three are born in most Western states every year.

Seema

Sanskrit *Sīmā,* "boundary, shore, horizon," or Arabic *Sīmah,* "sign, expression." Most critics consider Seema Biswas to be one of the more accomplished actresses in India's Bollywood film industry, and since her name has both Hindu and Muslim derivations, most of her fans can feel free to give it to their daughters.

Selena

Greek "the moon." Selena was regularly used in the 19th century, and it returned to the top 1,000 list in 1957, when Hope Lange played the character Selena Cross in the movie version of *Peyton Place.* The name's peak year, however, was 1995, when the tragic murder of the singer Selena made the name immensely popular with Hispanic-Americans and pushed it into the top 100 names overall for one year. It is now quickly receding, but in 2004 more than 1,400 Selenas were born, ranking the name 220th.
Variations: **Celena, Celina, Selene, Selina**

Selma

Possibly a form of Norse *Anselm,* "divine helmut," a German and Scandinavian form of **Salome,** or from a place name mentioned in James Macpherson's 18th-century Ossianic poems. Selma was a common name in Sweden in the 19th century, when Selma Lagerlöf, who in 1909 was the first woman to win the Nobel Prize in literature, was born. In the United States, Selma was regularly used in the 1940s but left the SSA top 1,000 list completely after 1956. Recently Selma has returned to fashion again in Sweden, and its similarity in sound to names like **Ella** and **Emma,** coupled with the recent fame of young actress Selma Blair, means that it will likely return to regular use in the United States within the next few years.
Variation: **Zelma**

Sequoia

Name of the giant redwood trees of northern California. The trees themselves were named after **Sequoyah,** who is credited with inventing the Cherokee alphabet and is one of the most famous Native Americans in history. The original meaning of his name is disputed. Most experts believe it is derived from the Cherokee word for "pig" and was originally a reference to a deformed or injured foot. However, others believe the name is from some other Native American language. In any event, modern parents who choose this name are thinking of the trees and consider it a "nature name" for girls.

Seraphina

Latin form of Hebrew *seraphim,* "burning ones." In the celestial hierarchy, seraphs, or seraphim, are the highest-ranked angels. St. Seraphina was a 15th-century saint. The name is unusual today.
Variations: **Serafina, Seraphine**

Serena

Latin feminine form of *serénus,* "calm." There was a legendary Christian saint named Serena described in early church writings as the wife of the Roman emperor Diocletian, but historians know he had no wife of that name. As an American baby name, Serena was regularly used in the late 19th century but disappeared from the SSA top 1,000 list after 1917. It popped in and out of the list during the 1930s and 1940s, then fitfully revived in the 1950s. Serena has been continuously present again since 1961. Its high point came in the year 2000, but it's been falling away since. The best-known Serena today is tennis player Serena Williams.

Serenity

The word, meaning "quality of being calm or tranquil." Serenity is the hot new "quality name" today. It entered the SSA top 1,000 list in 1997 and has bounded up the charts. More than 1,700 girls were blessed with this name in 2004, ranking it 192nd for the year.

Shakira

Arabic *Shākirah,* "grateful, thankful." Shakira had some use in the late 1980s in the African-American community as an Arabic name that fit in with the fashion for *Sha-* names. In the 1990s, it also became popular in the Hispanic-American community because of the Colombian singer Shakira, whose father is of Lebanese descent. The name suddenly vanished from the SSA top 1,000 list in 2004.

Shania

Country singer Shania Twain says that her stepfather, a member of the Ojibwe Native American nation, created her name to mean "I'm on my way." It's difficult to confirm this, but it may be largely correct. The phrase *ani-aya`aa* would seem to mean "someone moving away (from the speaker)" in the Ojibwe language, and it's reported, though not confirmed, that *sha-ni-yaa* or *zhi-ni-yaa* might mean "she is on her way" in the Ojibwe dialect of northern Ontario, where Shania Twain is from. It's also been suggested that Shania is related to *zhooniyaa,* the Ojibwe word for "money," but the pronunciation of the first vowel in that word makes that explanation less likely. In any event, the name's spelling and sound have obviously been altered to fit in with modern North American tastes. By blending the sounds of **Shannon** and **Mariah,** Shania gained mass appeal. It entered the SSA top 1,000 list in 1995 at 444th place, a very high initial entry, and was 171st the next year. In 2004 there were 798 Shanias born in the United States, ranking it 333rd.

Shanice

African-American creation. Shanice had a sudden burst of popularity in the African-American community in 1988 after singer Shanice Wilson (who prefers to be known as just Shanice) released her first hit album. Her name was in the SSA top 1,000 list until 1999, which made it the most popular of the invented *Sha-* names of the 1990s.

Other spellings: **Shaneice, Shaniece, Shanise**

Shaniqua

African-American creation. *Sha-* replaced *La-* as the most common prefix for newly created African-American names in the 1990s, and Shaniqua was the most popular such creation after **Shanice.** Other fashionable *Sha-* names included Shakisha, Shalonda, Shameka, Shanae, Shanika, and Shatara.

Other spellings: **Shaneequa, Shanequa, Shanikwa**

Shaniya

African-American creation blending the sounds of **Shania** and **Aaliyah.** Shaniya has been on the SSA top 1,000 list since 1999. There were 463 Shaniyas born in 2004, ranking the name 598th.

Other spellings: **Shaniea, Shaniyah, Shaniyya**

Shannon

For origin, see Shannon in the boys list. From 1969 to 1987, this was one of the top 50 names for American girls. In 2004, more than 1,200 Shannons were born, ranking the name 234th.

Famous name: Shannon Miller (gymnast and Olympic gold medalist)

Variations: **Shanna, Shannan, Shannyn, Shanon**

Shari

Form of **Sharon** or **Sherry;** also, an Americanized spelling of *Sari,* Hungarian variation of **Sarah.**
Famous names: Shari Belafonte (actress)
　　　　　　　 Shari Lewis (puppeteer)

Sharon

Hebrew "a plain," biblical place name. Sharon is a plain in Palestine famous for its fertility. In 1925 Adela Rogers St. Johns published a serial novel in *Cosmopolitan* magazine called *The Skyrocket.* The heroine, Sharon Kimm, is a poor young woman who becomes a big Hollywood star. It may be a coincidence, but 1925 was also the first year Sharon entered the SSA top 1,000 list, in 791st place. The name Sharon then skyrocketed, becoming a top ten name of the 1940s. It's gradually fallen away since; there were 501 Sharons born in 2004, ranking it 439th.
Famous name: Sharon Stone (actress)
Nicknames: **Shari, Sherri, Sherrie, Sherry**
Variations: **Shara, Sharona**

Shasta

Name of the volcanic mountain in northern California, a mecca for tourists and nature lovers. The mountain is most likely named after a Native American nation that lived in the area, but beyond that the meaning is unknown. Shasta entered the SSA top 1,000 list in 1976 then left after 1986, but it is still occasionally used by parents who are nature lovers or interested in New Age philosophies.

Shauna, Shawna

These feminine forms of **Sean** were common in the 1970s but are rare today.

Shayla

Probably a modern creation blending the sounds of **Kayla** and **Sheila.** Shayla first appeared in the 1970s. Its minor peak of popularity was in 1996, and it is now decreasing in use; 906 were born in 2004, ranking the name 301st for the year.

Shaylee

Modern creation blending **Shayla** and **Kaylee.** Shaylee entered the SSA top 1,000 list in 1997 and has been drifting upward since.

There were 325 born in 2004, ranking it 782nd. It's probable that several alternate spellings (**Shailee, Shailey, Shaley, Shalie, Shaylie,** etc.) are just below the SSA top 1,000 and would substantially raise the total number of girls with this name if they were added in.

Shayna

Yiddish "beautiful." This name ranked 812th on the SSA list in 2004. Variations: **Shaina, Shana**

Shea

Irish Gaelic *séaghdha*, "hawklike, fine, fortunate." Shea has been regularly used since the 1970s, though it has never ranked higher than 703rd on the SSA top 1,000 list. In 2004, 319 girls were named Shea, ranking it 790th.

Sheena

Scottish form of **Jane.** The career of Scottish singer Sheena Easton made this one of the flashiest "flash in the pan" names ever. Her only number-one hit, "Morning Train," was released in 1981. Sheena entered the SSA top 1,000 at 356th place in 1981 and was a top 100 name in 1984 and 1985. It left the SSA top 1,000 list in 1994. Variations: **Sheenagh, Shena, Sine** (Scots Gaelic)

Sheila

Irish Gaelic *Síle*, form of **Cecilia.** This traditional Irish name was in the top 100 from 1942 to 1972 but ranked only 807th in 2004. Famous name: Sheila E. (percussionist)
Other spellings: **Sheelagh, Sheelah, Sheilah, Shela, Shelagh**

Shelby

English place name, perhaps meaning "village on a ledge" or "willow village." This surname has long been used as a first name for boys in the American South and was given to Southern girls on rare occasions before 1935. That year Barbara Stanwyck played Shelby Barret Wyatt in the film *The Woman in Red,* and for the next four years Shelby was one of the top 200 girls names in the United States. It then declined until the early 1980s, when parents and writers began to notice it again, probably because of its similarity in sound to **Chelsea, Kelsey,** and **Shelley.** The name got another boost when Julia Roberts played the character Shelby in the 1989 film *Steel*

Magnolias, helping to make it a top 50 name from 1991 to 1998. More than 2,900 Shelbys were born in 2004, ranking it 128th.
Other spellings: **Shelbey, Shelbi, Shelbie**

Shelley

Old English *Selleg,* "clearing on a ledge," a place name; also, a variation of **Michele, Rachelle,** or **Rochelle.** Shelley became established as a girls name in the 1940s and was fairly common in the 1960s and 1970s, but it's rare today.
Famous name: Shelley Winters (actress)
Other spellings: **Shelli, Shellie, Shelly**

Shenandoah

Probably Algonquian "spruce stream." The name of this beautiful river and valley in Virginia, immortalized in the famous folk song, has been given to girls by a few adventurous parents since at least 1980.

Sherlyn

Blend of **Sheryl** and **Lynn.** The Mexican singer and actress Sherlyn (born Sherlyn Montserrat González Díaz) is one of the most famous stars of Spanish-language television, and her name is swiftly becoming popular in the Hispanic-American community. There were 483 Sherlyns born in the United States in 2004, ranking it 451st.

Sherry

Variation of **Cheryl** and **Sharon.** The wine takes its name from the town of Xeres, Spain, which was named for Caesar, but this name is probably more influenced by the French love word, *cherie.* Sherry entered the SSA top 1,000 list in 1925 and became one of the top 50 names between 1946 and 1975. It left the SSA list in 1976.
Famous name: Sherry Lansing (movie executive)
Other spellings: **Shari, Sheree, Sheri, Sherie, Sherri, Sherrie, Sherye**

Sheryl

Alternate spelling of **Cheryl.**
Famous name: Sheryl Crow (singer and songwriter)

Shirin

Farsi *Shirin,* "pleasant, sweet, exceedingly rare." In 2003, Iranian lawyer, writer, and activist Shirin Ebadi won the Nobel Peace prize for her efforts in protecting the human rights of women and children in Iran.

Shirley

Old English *Scirleah*, "bright forest clearing," a place name. Charlotte Bronte first used this name for a girl in her novel *Shirley*. The name gradually grew in use from the 1880s on, until it became a top ten name in 1927. It then plateaued and was probably about to recede when Shirley Temple became a huge star in the 1934 film *Little Miss Marker*. Shirley tripled in use the next two years to become the number-two name in 1935 and 1936. So, even though Shirley Temple didn't start the vogue for her name, there are surely thousands of women born in the late 1930s who would have been named something else if she hadn't become famous. Shirley is just barely visible today, ranking 984th on the 2004 SSA top 1,000 list.

Famous names: Shirley Horn (jazz pianist and singer)
Shirley MacLaine (actress)
Other spellings: **Shirlee, Shirlie**
Variations: **Shirl, Shirleen, Shirlene**

Shreya

Sanskrit *Śreyā*, "excellent, best, beautiful." Singer Shreya Ghosal is one of the biggest celebrities in India. Her fame comes primarily from being a "playback singer," one whose voice is used on the soundtrack of musical films while the main actress lip-syncs the songs. In Hollywood such singers usually remain anonymous, but in India they often become stars in their own right. Shreya Ghosal's fame may be part of the reason that Shreya is now one of the most common names for baby girls in the Hindu community in the United States. There were 284 American Shreyas born in 2004, ranking the name 853rd on the SSA list.

Sienna

The word, meaning a reddish-brown color originally derived from baking an iron-rich clay. The clay was named after the city of Siena, Italy, whose name comes from the ancient Senones, a Gaulish tribe whose own name may be from Gaulish *seno*, "old." The new popularity of "color" names, combined with Sienna's similarity in sound to **Sierra,** has led to its recent growth in popularity. Sienna first entered the SSA top 1,000 list in 1995. In 2004, 439 Siennas were born, ranking the name 616th on the SSA list.

Famous name: Sienna Miller (actress)

Sierra

Spanish "saw-toothed mountain range." Sierra began its regular use as a first name in the United States around 1970. It received a boost in 1985 when Sierra Esteban appeared as a character on the long-running daytime soap opera *As the World Turns*. The name quickly developed alternative spellings such as **Ciera, Cierra,** and **Seairra** and was particularly popular with African-American parents. At its peak in the late 1990s, Sierra was among the 50 most popular girls names. In 2004, the three main spellings were given to 4,664 girls, ranking the name 76th. Although *sierra* is a Spanish word, it is not used as a given name in Spanish-speaking countries.

Sigourney

French surname, from the village name *Sigournais,* origin undiscovered. Actress Sigourney Weaver changed her first name from Susan as a teenager after finding a male character named Sigourney Howard in F. Scott Fitzgerald's *The Great Gatsby*. Fitzgerald was probably thinking of the 19th-century religious poet Lydia Huntley Sigourney when he named the character.

Sigrid

Old Norse, from *sigr*, "victory," and *friðr*, "fair." Norwegian novelist Sigrid Undset won the Nobel Prize in literature in 1928.

Simone

French feminine form of **Simon.** Simone was very common in France in the early 20th century, but Americans barely noticed it until French actress Simone Signoret won an Oscar in 1960 for her role in the film *Room at the Top*. The name jumped onto the SSA list that year at 633rd place and has never left, though its highest rank was only 311th in 1988. In 2004, 603 Simones were born, ranking it 394th.
Famous name: Simone de Beauvoir (feminist philosopher)
Variations: **Simona, Simonette, Simonia, Ximena** (Spanish)

Siobhan

Irish Gaelic form of **Joan.** There was a minor fashion for this name in the 1980s, when it was often respelled **Shavon, Shavonne, Shevonne, Shivonne,** etc.

Siphokazi

IsiXhosa (South Africa), from *sipho*, "gift" and *-kazi*, a femininzing suffix.

Skye

Name of the largest island in the Hebrides off the west coast of
Scotland, derived from Gaelic *sgiath*, "winged," because from the
Scottish shore the ancient Gaels thought the island looked like a bird
in flight, as it has two large mountain ranges on its north and south
ends connected by lowlands in the center. Some modern parents may
think of Skye as a feminized spelling of **Sky**, but its first use as a girls
name seems to have been the title character of Phyllis A. Whitney's
1957 novel *Skye Cameron*, who is described as being named after her
father's Scottish birthplace. Substantial numbers of parents didn't
discover the name, however, until the character Skye Chandler began
appearing on the daytime soap opera *All My Children* in 1986. Skye
flew onto the SSA top 1,000 list in 1987 and is still winging higher; in
2004, 751 American girls were given the name, ranking it 342nd.

Skyla

This feminized form of **Skylar** has been attracting parents who are
afraid the original form seems too masculine. It entered the SSA top
1,000 list in 1998 and has continued to grow in use. There were
475 Skylas born in 2004, ranking the name 454th.

Skylar, Skyler

For origin, see **Schuyler** and Skyler in the boys list. With **Skye**
already being regularly used, it was probably inevitable that some
parents would begin naming girls Skylar during the 1990s. In 1989, a
major storyline on the daytime soap *All My Children* involved a baby
girl named Skylar, and 1990 was the first year both main spellings of
Skylar entered the SSA top 1,000 for girls at a fairly high level. The
name grew steadily during the 1990s and got another big push
when Minnie Driver played the character Skylar in the 1997 film
Good Will Hunting. The name's peak year was 1999, and it's been
gradually decreasing in use since. In 2004 there were still more than
3,100 Skylars born in the United States, ranking it 117th.

Solange

French form of Late Latin *Sollemnia*, from Latin *sollemnis*, "solemn,
pious." Solange was a common name in France around 1930 but is
rare for babies there today. In the United States it is receiving notice
because of the booming career of singer and songwriter Solange

Knowles. Meanwhile, in France the older forms **Solène** and **Solenne** have become fashionable.

Soledad

Spanish "solitude," a Marian devotion name from the title *Maria de Soledad*. This aspect of the Virgin Mary reminds Catholics of the virtue of removing oneself from the distractions of the material world.
Famous name: Soledad O'Brien (television news anchor)

Soleil

French "sun, sunshine."
Famous name: Soleil Moon Frye (actress)

Sonia, Sonya

Russian form of **Sophia.** Sonya is the heroine of Fyodor Dostoyevsky's novel *Crime and Punishment.* Sonia has been used regularly in the United States since the 1930s. It peaked in the 1970s and in 2004 ranked 553rd on the SSA list.
Famous names: Sonia Braga (actress)
Sonya Thomas (competitive eater)
Other spelling: **Sonja**

Sonica, Sonika

Sanskrit *Sonikā,* "with golden beauty."

Sonora

Name of a state in northwestern Mexico; uncertain derivation, but Opata (Native American) *Xunuta,* "in the corn," is a possibility.

Sophia

Greek "wisdom." St. Sophia was a third-century Christian saint. In 325, Constantine the Great built a huge church (now the Hagia Sophia mosque in Istanbul) dedicated to St. Sophia. The name was widely used among Byzantine royalty and appears to have first traveled to Europe through Austria. In the 17th century, when the house of Hanover inherited the English throne, the name became popular in England. Sophia Western is the heroine of Henry Fielding's novel *Tom Jones,* and Sophia Primrose is the heroine of Oliver Goldsmith's *The Vicar of Wakefield.* Sophia almost disappeared in the United States during the 1950s, but since 1996 it has exploded in use. More than 15,000 American girls were named Sophia in 2004, ranking it 13th.

Famous name: Sophia Loren (actress)

Nicknames: **Sophie, Sophy**

Variations: **Sofia** (Swedish), **Sofie** (Danish, Dutch, and German), **Sonia, Sonja** (Danish and Slavic), **Sonya** (Russian), **Sophie** (French), **Zofia** (Polish), **Zosia** (Polish)

Sophie

Variation of **Sophia.** Actress Bette Midler got her start in show business borrowing Sophie Tucker's jokes and voice, so it's no surprise that she honored her mentor by naming her daughter Sophie. In England and Wales, Sophie was among the top ten names for 2004. Sophie is also growing in popularity in the United States; in 2004 more than 2,300 girls were given the name, ranking it 151st.

Other spellings: **Sofie, Sophy**

Stacey

Form of **Anastasia.** or **Eustacia.** Stacey had one of the fastest rises in American history. Hardly used before 1950, in the early 1970s it was a top ten name if all four main spellings are counted. Its decline has also been swift. In 2004, Stacey and Stacy combined ranked 353rd.

Famous name: Stacey Earle (country singer)

Other spellings: **Staci, Stacie, Stacy**

Star, Starr

Star was used as a male nickname in the Middle Ages, resulting in the surname Starr. Starr has actually been the more common spelling for this modern girls "word name" in the United States. It is rare, but enough have been born for the name to have drifted in and out of the SSA top 1,000 list several times since 1946. For modern parents the Hollywood meaning of "star" may be as important as the astronomical meaning when they choose this name.

Famous name: Star Jones (lawyer and television host)

Starla

This blend of **Star** with names like **Carla** or **Darla** was regularly used between 1954 and 1984.

Starlyn

Blend of **Star** and **Lynn.** Unlike **Starla,** Starlyn has never been common enough to make the SSA top 1,000 list, but it is still occasionally used today, especially in the rural Midwest.

Stella

Latin "star." Stella was one of the top 100 names for American girls from 1870 to 1923. It then plummeted and left the SSA top 1,000 after 1987. Stella once had a vulgar image, reinforced by the 1937 movie *Stella Dallas* and Tennessee Williams's *A Streetcar Named Desire,* in which a drunken Stanley repeatedly shouting "Stella!" is a classic scene. But today's parents have overcome those associations, and with **Ella** booming, Stella has been revived as an alternative. Stella re-entered the SSA top 1,000 list in 1998 and in 2004 had shot up to 267th place with more than 1,100 girls given the name. Famous name: Stella McCartney (fashion designer)

Stephanie

French feminine form of **Stephen.** Stephanie boomed during the 1950s and 1960s and become a top ten name between 1972 and 1992. Though it's now receding, there were more than 5,400 Stephanies born in 2004, ranking the name 63rd. During the 1980s Stephanie was particularly popular with Hispanic-Americans. Famous name: Stephanie S. Tolan (children's book author)
Nicknames: **Steffi, Steffie, Steffy, Stevie**
Variations: **Estefanía** (Spanish), **Stefania** (Polish, Swedish, and Italian), **Stefanida** (Russian), **Stefanie, Stefanny** (Danish and Norwegian), **Stephania, Stevanka** (Serbian), **Tiennette** (French)

Stormy

This word has been used as a girls name for more than 80 years. The female lead character in the 1924 film *Silk Stocking Sal* was called Stormy, and Dale Evans's character in one of her Western films with Roy Rogers, *The Golden Stallion* (1949), was Stormy Billings. The name still has a cowgirl ambiance. There were enough Stormys born between 1991 and 1997 for the name to just make the SSA top 1,000 list, but its season seems to have passed for now.

Story

As a surname this was derived from Old Norse *Stori,* "big," though its modern use as a girls name seems to derive more from the word, originally a short form of Latin *historia,* "history." This might be a good choice for parents who love to read.

Sue

Variation of **Susan**. In the 1940s, Sue was independently one of the 100 most common names, but it's rare as a first name today.
Famous name: Sue Grafton (mystery writer)

Summer

Old English *sumar,* "summer." Summer entered the SSA list in 1971 and in 1977 was the 119th most common name, a very fast growth. Summer then receded until 1991, when it began to shine again. In 2004, more than 2,300 Summers were born, ranking it 154th.
Other spelling: **Sommer**

Sunshine

Sunshine has a reputation as the ultimate "hippy" name, and there may be some truth to that, particularly as the only years it was in the SSA top 1,000 list were from 1974 to 1981. But its history as a first name in the United States goes back to a best-selling novel of 1854, *Tempest and Sunshine,* by Mary Jane Holmes. In this tale, Tempest and Sunshine are two sisters whose given names are Julia and Fanny, but they are always called Tempest and Sunshine by their father, referring to their contrasting dispositions. This book remained in print throughout the 19th century, and there are examples of women born around 1900 who were named Sunshine because of it.

Susan

English form of Hebrew *shushannah,* "lily." Susan, along with **Deborah**, was a successful biblical revival name of the "baby boom" years. From a low point in the 1920s it rose to become one of the top ten names for girls between 1945 and 1968. Since then it's steadily fallen away and only ranked 442nd in 2004. The most famous bearer of this name in American history is Susan B. Anthony, the women's rights advocate. In 1979 her picture was placed on a new dollar coin, making her the first woman to ever appear on U.S. currency.
Famous names: Susan Sarandon (actress)
                Susan Sontag (writer)
Nicknames: **Sue, Sukey, Suki, Sukie, Susie, Suzie, Suzy**
Variations: **Sanna** (Finnish), **Sanne** (Dutch), **Schura** (Russian), **Shoshana** (Hebrew), **Shoshi** (Israeli), **Siusan** (Scots Gaelic), **Sosana** (Romanian), **Susa** (Italian and German), **Susana** (Spanish and Portuguese), **Susanna** (Italian and

Russian), **Susanne** (German), **Susetta** (Italian), **Suzana** (Romanian, Bulgarian, and Croatian), **Suzanne, Suzette, Suzon** (French), **Zosel** (German), **Zsa Zsa** (Hungarian), **Zuzana** (Czech), **Zuzanna** (Polish)

Susanna

Biblical form of **Susan.** The story of Susanna and the Elders is part of the Apocrypha in Protestant Bibles and the Old Testament in Catholic ones. The English forms of Susanna are very rare, but the Spanish version, **Susana,** ranked 848th on the SSA list in 2004.
Other spellings: **Susannah, Suzanna, Suzannah**

Suzanne

French form of **Susan.** Suzanne was one of the top 100 names in the United States from 1941 to 1973, but it is now rare.
Famous name: Suzanne Vega (singer)

Sybil

Greek *Sybilla,* "a woman prophet." There was a minor fashion for Sybil in the 1920s, but it's been rare since 1967.
Variations: **Cybil, Cybill, Sibilla** (Italian), **Sibyl, Sybille** (French)

Sybille

French form of **Sybil.** J. K. Rowling chose this fitting name for Sybille Trelawney, the Divination teacher in the *Harry Potter* novels.

Sydney

Feminine form of **Sidney;** the name of a city in Australia. Sydney has been one of the fastest-growing names for girls recently. In 2004, more than 10,000 girls received the name, ranking it 28th.
Other spellings: **Cydney, Sidney, Sydnee, Sydni, Sydnie**

Sylvia

Perhaps Latin *silva,* "wood." In Roman mythology, Rhea Silvia was the mother of Romulus and Remus, the founders of Rome. Sylvia was one of the top 100 names of the 1930s and 1940s. There were still more than 500 Sylvias born in 2004, ranking it 440th.
Famous names: Sylvia Earle (marine biologist)
Sylvia Plath (poet)
Other spelling: **Silvia**
Variations: **Silva** (Bulgarian), **Sylvie** (French), **Zilvia**

Tabitha

Aramaic "gazelle." Tabitha, also known as Dorcas, is mentioned in the Book of Acts in the New Testament. Tabitha was used by the Puritans but died out before the 20th century. The name was resurrected at 525th place on the SSA list in 1966 when it was used for Samantha's daughter on the popular television comedy *Bewitched.* Tabitha then increased until its peak in 1985 at 135th. In 2004, 671 Tabithas were born in the United States, ranking the name 376th. Variations: **Tabita** (Spanish and Polish), **Tabbi, Tabbie, Tabby**

Talia

Usually a form of **Natalia;** also, Spanish form of Greek *Thalia,* "plentiful," and modern Israeli name from Hebrew *tal,* "dew." After actress Talia Shire played Adrian in the 1976 film *Rocky,* Talia appeared at 708th on the SSA list. The name has been increasing in use since; the 933 Talias born in 2004 ranked it 296th, its highest spot ever.

Taliyah

African-American creation blending **Talia** and **Aaliyah.** This name has been on the SSA top 1,000 list since 2001 and ranked 683rd in 2004, with 397 born.

Tamar

Hebrew "palm tree." Three Old Testament women have this name. Variation: **Tamara** (Russian)

Tamara

Russian form of **Tamar,** much more popular in English-speaking countries than the original biblical form. American parents first noticed Tamara in 1939, and it became one of the top 100 names given to American girls from 1966 to 1977. Its popularity curve has fallen off since; 500 Tamaras were born in 2004, ranking it 443rd. Nicknames: **Tam, Tammie, Tammy**

Tamia

African-American creation, blending the sounds of names like **Tamika** and **Mia.** R&B singer Tamia's career began in 1995, and she had her first hit single with "Missing You" in 1996. The name Tamia leapt onto the SSA top 1,000 list at 497th place in 1996. In 2004, 824 girls were named Tamia in the United States, ranking it 325th for the year.

Tamika

African-American form of *Tamiko,* Japanese *tami* [people] + *-ko* [feminine suffix]. This name was inspired by singer Tamiko Jones, who released her first album in 1968, the same year both **Tamiko** and Tamika entered the SSA top 1,000 list. Because *-a* is a more common ending for girls names in English than *-o,* Tamika became the more common form within a few years. It was very popular with African-American parents during the 1970s and 1980s and inspired other African-American creations ending with the suffix *-ika.*
Variations: **Tameika, Tameka, Tamica, Tamiko, Tomika**

Tammy

Form of **Tamara** or Tamsin, British feminine form of **Thomas.** Tammy entered the SSA list in 1947 and was later propelled into the top 100 names by the 1957 movie *Tammy and the Bachelor,* in which actress Debbie Reynolds plays a country woman in love with an urban man. Tammy was a top ten name between 1964 and 1972, but it diminished swiftly and left the SSA top 1,000 list in 1999.
Famous names: Tammy Faye Bakker Messner (author and singer)
         Tammy Wynette (country singer)
Other spellings: **Tami, Tammi, Tammie**

Tamya

This African-American creation blending **Tamia** and **Maya** entered the SSA top 1,000 list in 2003 and ranked 953rd on that list in 2004.

Tangerine

The fruit named after the city of Tangier in Morocco. Some parents consider this a "color name."

Tanisha

This name first appeared in 1970 when the actress Ta-Tanisha appeared on the television series *Room 222.* It is unknown how she created her stage name, but it immediately appealed to African-

American parents, who created scores of respellings and made it one of their top names of the 1970s, 1980s, and 1990s.

Other spellings: **Taneisha, Tanesha, Taneshia, Taniesha, Tanishia, Tenecia, Teneisha, Tenesha, Teniesha, Tenisha, Tinisha**

Tanya

Russian short form of **Tatiana.** Tanya emigrated to the United States in the 1930s and rose to be one of the top 50 names between 1969 and 1981. It's fallen steadily since. More than 1,000 Tanyas were born in 2004, which ranked it 271st that year. Tania is now the more popular spelling, having overtaken Tanya in 1996.

Famous name: Tanya Tucker (country singer)

Other spellings: **Tania, Tanja** (German), **Tonya**

Tara

Gaelic "crag, high prominent rock"; or, in the Hindu community, from Sanskrit *tārā*, "star." Tara was a top 50 name for American girls from 1971 to 1984. In 2004, 961 Taras were born, ranking it 287th.

Famous name: Tara Lipinski (figure skater)

Other spellings: **Tarah, Tera, Terra**

Taryn

This name was invented in September 1953 by actors Tyrone Power and Linda Christian for their second daughter. It seems to be a blend of the shape and sound of **Tyrone** with **Karen** or **Sharon,** names popular at the time. Taryn barely made the SSA top 1,000 list in 1955 and 1956, then suddenly leapt back on in 1959, after Tyrone Power died of a sudden heart attack in November 1958, putting his children back in the news. After disappearing for almost 15 years, Taryn reappeared on the top 1,000 list in 1974. The name peaked in 1985 at 228th on the SSA list but has slowly fallen away since. In 2004, 717 American girls were named Taryn, ranking it 354th.

Tatiana, Tatyana

Feminine form of *Tatius,* Latin name of unknown meaning. Tatiana is popular in Greece, Russia, and Latin America. It's only been regularly used in the United States since the 1980s. In 2004, almost 1,500 Tatianas were born, ranking it 218th.

Famous name: Tatyana Ali (actress and R&B singer)

Variations: **Tanya, Tiana**

Tatum

English surname, from the place name *Tatham,* "Tate's homestead." (See **Tate** in the boys name list.) Tatum O'Neal won an Oscar in 1974 for her role in *Paper Moon* when she was only ten years old. Her name didn't appeal to parents at the time; its sound was too different from the fashions of the 1970s. After names like **Taylor** and **Peyton** paved the way, Tatum started sounding good in the 1990s, and the name entered the SSA top 1,000 list in 1994. In 2004, 808 girls received the name, ranking it 332nd on the popularity chart.

Taya

Probably a modern creation, though *Tayyā* is a rare Arabic name meaning "little one," and the name is sometimes used in Russian, where it is possibly a pet form of **Tatiana.** It's unknown how many parents who give this name pronounce it to rhyme with **Maya** or how many sound it more like **Taylor.** It entered the SSA list in 1997, but in 2004 only ranked 965th, with 245 born.

Taylor

Old French *tailleur,* "tailor." When Janet Miriam Holland Taylor Caldwell wrote her first novel in 1938, she used Taylor Caldwell as her pen name because she thought her book would be more successful if people thought it had been written by a man. Ironically, she soon became so celebrated as an author of best sellers that she no longer needed to hide her sex, and the American public came to think of Taylor as being an appropriate name for a woman. In 1979, Taylor entered the SSA top 1,000 list and exploded in use, becoming a top ten name for girls between 1993 and 2000. As with many names that rise very quickly, Taylor is starting to recede almost as fast. In 2004, more than 9,500 Taylors were born, ranking it 29th.

Teagan

Irish surname *Ó Tadhgáin,* "descendant of *Tadgh.*" (See **Tighe** in the boys list.) American parents began to give this name to daughters in noticeable numbers in 1999. Though some rhyme it with **Reagan,** the majority seem to pronounce the first syllable as the word *tea.* There were 543 girls who received the name in 2004, ranking it 417th.

Tempest, Tempestt

The word used as a name; for some of its history, see **Sunshine.**

Teresa

Variation of **Theresa.** This form is identified today with Mother Teresa of Calcutta, which may be part of the reason it's now the more common spelling.

Teri, Terri, Terrie

Feminine form of the male name **Terry** or a variation of **Theresa.**
Famous names: Teri Garr (actress)
                 Teri Hatcher (actress)

Tess

Form of **Tessa** or **Theresa.** *Tess of the D'Urbervilles,* a novel by Thomas Hardy, was published in 1891. Tess wasn't used regularly as a separate name until the 1980s, and it has never been very popular, perhaps because of its one-syllable form. In 2004, 418 girls were given the name, ranking it 647th on the SSA list.

Tessa

Form of **Theresa** or of Italian *contessa,* "countess." Tessa's regular use in the United States began in the late 1960s. It increased considerably after that, though there are signs that it's now just past its peak. In 2004, more than 1,100 Tessas were born, ranking the name 253rd.

Thalia

Greek *thallein* "to flourish," the name of the Muse of Comedy in Greek mythology. Thalia has been in the SSA top 1,000 list since 1992. About half of the girls being given the name are Hispanic-American, and in Spanish Thalia and **Talia** would be pronounced identically. In 2004, 489 Thalias were born, ranking the name 447th.

Thandiwe

Xhosa (South Africa) "a loving person."

Thea

Greek "goddess."

Thelma

This name was invented by Marie Corelli for her 1887 best seller, *Thelma.* When the hero first discovers the beautiful Thelma's name, he states it's "like a chord of music played softly in the distance." It's not surprising that Thelma soared in use; it was a top 50 name from 1903 to 1930. Today almost no babies receive the name.

Theodora

Feminine form of **Theodore,** Greek "gift of God." The sixth-century Byzantine empress Theodora was the wife of Justinian the Great. Theodora has been quite rare since the 1950s.

Variations: **Fedora** (Czech, Slovakian, and Ukrainian), **Feodora** (Russian), **Teodora** (Italian and Spanish), **Todora** (Bulgarian)

Theresa

Origin unknown, possibly "woman from Therasia," ancient name for two small Mediterranean islands. This name's Spanish heritage dates to at least the sixth century, but its popular use dates to the 16th-century Carmelite nun St. Theresa of Avila. Theresa was a top 50 name from 1953 to 1969. In 2004 it ranked 263rd, and almost two-thirds of the 1,100 born received the spelling Teresa.

Nicknames: **Teri, Terri, Terrie, Terry, Tess, Tessa, Tessi, Tessie, Tessy**

Other spelling: **Teresa**

Variations: **Resi** (German), **Terese** (Lithuanian), **Teresia** (Swedish), **Teresina** (Italian), **Teresita** (Spanish), **Teressa, Terez** (Hungarian), **Tereza** (Romanian and Portuguese), **Terezia** (Hungarian), **Terezie** (Czech), **Terka** (Bulgarian and Hungarian), **Therese** (French), **Theresia** (German), **Toireasa** (Irish Gaelic), **Tracy, Trexa** (Basque)

Thulani

Xhosa and Zulu (South Africa) "hush."

Tia

Spanish "aunt." This name may have arisen from parents misunderstanding the name of the liqueur Tia Maria, thinking "Tia" was a name rather than realizing its meaning. Today many people probably think of Tia as a short form of **Tiana** or **Tiara,** but it was in regular use as a girls name in the United States in the late 1950s, years before those other names appeared. The use of Tia has waxed and waned several times, with its latest peak occurring in the early 1990s. In 2004, 555 American girls were named Tia, ranking it 416th.

Famous name: Tia Carrere (actress)

Tiana, Tianna

Usually a short form of **Tatiana** or **Christiana,** though also the Cherokee language form of **Diana.** Tiana suddenly appeared on the

SSA top 1,000 list in 1975 at 634th place. It slowly grew until its peak in 1995, when more than 1,600 girls were named Tiana. More than 1,000 daughters received the name in 2004, ranking it 270th.

Tiara

Latin "headdress, jeweled coronet" from Greek word for "turban." Tiara was quite common as a name for African-American girls in the 1980s. But only 426 were born in 2004, ranking it 632nd on the SSA list. Variations: **Tiarra, Tierra**

Tierra

Spanish "earth" or "land."

Tiffany

Greek *Theophania*, "God appears." Tiffany was common in the Middle Ages, when it was often given to children born on Epiphany, January 6. The 1961 film *Breakfast at Tiffany's* reintroduced the name to American parents and associated it with the famous jewelry store in New York City. By 1982, Tiffany ranked 13th on the SSA list and was the top name for African-American girls. It then began an inevitable decline. In 2004 more than 1,900 Tiffanys were born, making it the 175th most common name.
Nicknames: **Tiff, Tiffie, Tiffy**
Other spellings: **Tifany, Tiffeny, Tyffany**

Tina

Form of names ending in *-tina,* including **Christina** and **Martina**. Tina was independently a top 25 name between 1966 and 1974. It's since diminished greatly; 344 were born in 2004, and its ranking of 751st on the SSA list was its lowest ever.
Famous name: Tina Turner (singer)

Tirunesh

Amharic "you are good."

Toni

Variation of **Antoinette** and **Antonia**. African-American novelist Toni Morrison won the Nobel Prize in literature in 1993. The name was moderately popular in the 1950s, 1960s, and 1970s but had receded by 2004 to 756th on the SSA list, with 339 Tonis born.
Other spellings: **Tonie, Tony**

Tori

Form of **Victoria.** Tori has been used regularly as an independent name since 1959. It grew somewhat more popular after 1990, the year when the careers of both actress Tori Spelling and singer Tori Amos took off. Now receding, it ranked 323rd in 2004.

Tovah

Hebrew "good," a common name for girls in modern Israel.

Tracy

Variation of **Theresa.** Tracy Samantha Lord was played by Katharine Hepburn in the 1940 movie *The Philadelphia Story* and by Grace Kelly in the 1956 musical version *High Society*. The first film revived the name and started its swift climb up the charts; by 1956, Tracy (along with the common alternative spellings Tracee, Tracey, Traci, and Tracie) had built up its own momentum and didn't need the second film's help. At its peak year, 1970, Tracy was the fifth most popular name for girls, but America's infatuation with it quickly evaporated during the 1980s. Tracy was the only spelling still in the SSA top 1,000 in 2004, at 944th place.
Famous names: Tracy Austin (tennis player)
                 Tracy Chapman (singer)
Other spellings: **Tracee, Tracey, Traci, Tracie**

Treasure

Isolated examples of girls given the "word name" Treasure have occurred since at least the 1940s, but it was only in 2004, with the recent search for new names, that Treasure finally made the SSA top 1,000 list, in 888th place.

Trinity

The word, from Latin *trīnitās,* referring to the Christian religious concept of the union of Father, Son, and Holy Spirit. Spanish-speaking cultures have used **Trinidad** for both boys and girls for centuries, but Trinity only began to be given to girls in English-speaking countries around 1970. Trinity first appeared on the SSA top 1,000 list from 1974 to 1979. It then vanished, but it reappeared in 1993 and slowly rose in use until 1999, the year the film *The Matrix* was released, with Carrie-Anne Moss playing the character Trinity. The name skyrocketed: 478 girls were named Trinity in

1998, and 4,269 received the name in 2000. More than 5,500 Trinitys were born in the United States in 2004, ranking it 61st.

Trisha, Tricia

These short forms of **Patricia,** counted together, were one of the top 100 names of the 1970s, but they are rare again today.
Famous name: Trisha Yearwood (country singer)

Trista

Feminine form of **Tristan.** Trista first entered the SSA top 1,000 list in 1970, the year before Tristan did on the boys list. It was probably an attractive alternate for **Trisha.** The name had a sharp upswing in 1983, when a character named Trista Evans Bradford was featured on the daytime soap opera *Days of Our Lives.* It then gradually declined until it left the top 1,000 list in 1992. It reappeared in 2002, when Trista Rehn became famous on television's *The Bachelor,* and increased markedly in 2003 when she was the star of *The Bachelorette.* In 2004, 531 Tristas were born, ranking the name 423rd.

Twyla

Origin unknown, but perhaps originally a Louisiana Cajun name from the French word *etoile,* "star."
Famous name: Twyla Tharp (choreographer)

Tyler

For origin, see Tyler in the boys list. In contrast to **Taylor,** there have never been enough girls named Tyler for them to seriously challenge its status as a predominantly boys name. Still, Tyler has been on the girls SSA top 1,000 list since 1984, peaking at 238th in 1993. In 2004, 484 American girls were named Tyler, ranking it 449th.

Tyne

Celtic *Tina,* "flowing," the name of an English river.
Famous name: Tyne Daly (actress)

Tyra

Probably a modern feminine form of **Tyrone** or **Tyree.** Tyra had a period of moderate use between 1968 and 1981. It resurfaced in 1993 under the influence of supermodel Tyra Banks. Tyra peaked in use in 1998 and ranked 707th on the SSA list in 2004.

Uilani

Hawaiian "youthful heavenly child." The syllable *lani* in native Hawaiian names means "heaven" or "heavenly" and also has connotations of royalty. Many names for girls still commonly used by native Hawaiian parents end in this syllable. Other examples include **Leilani**, Kanoelani ("the heavenly mist"), and Pualani ("heavenly flower").

Uma

Sanskrit "flax" or "turmeric." In the Upanishads, Uma is a goddess who mediates between the high god, Brahma, and the lesser gods. She is considered the personification of speech.
Famous name: Uma Thurman (actress)

Umayma

Swahili "young mother."

Una

Latin "one"; also, possibly Irish Gaelic *uan*, "lamb." This name was very common in medieval Ireland. In the first book of Edmund Spenser's *The Faerie Queene*, the heroine Una symbolizes truth.
Other spelling: **Oona**

Undine

English form of *undina*, "water sprite," from Latin *unda*, "wave." This word was coined in 1658 by the Swiss alchemist Paracelsus while he was writing in Latin about the magical female water spirits featured in Germanic myths.
Variation: **Ondine** (French)

Unique

The word, meaning "one of a kind." African-American parents began to give daughters this name in the 1990s, partly because its sound was similar to previous fashions like **Monique** and partly because it seemed like the ultimate choice of a name to help their child stand out from the crowd. Unique was among the top 1,000 names on the SSA list from 1993 through 2002, but its use has now decreased as parents realized it was not as unique a name as they had hoped.

Unity

English Puritans first created this "word name" to express their desire for spiritual unity with God. It's rare today and when given probably expresses patriotic rather than religious motives.

Urbi

Benin (Nigeria) "princess."

Ursula

Latin *ursa*, "female bear." The legend of St. Ursula was responsible for this name traditionally being the most popular name for girls beginning with *U* in European countries. Ursula was the daughter of a British noble who put a high price on her hand in marriage: a three-year pilgrimage accompanied by anywhere from 11 to 11,000 virgins (the number varies depending on the source) and enough ships to carry the group. It is said that a suitor complied and that Ursula and the virgins made their way toward Rome, but they met with Huns at Cologne and were slaughtered after refusing to submit. A church in Cologne has a stone inscribed to the saint, who is considered the patron of young women. Ursula was a fairly popular name in 17th-century England, and it had a minor revival in the 1960s and 1970s in the United States, but since then it's become rare in all English-speaking countries. Literary experts consider Ursula K. LeGuin to be one of the most important writers of science fiction and fantasy.
Famous name: Ursula Andress (actress)
Nicknames: **Sula, Ursa, Ursie, Ursy**
Variations: **Orsel** (Dutch), **Orsola** (Italian), **Ulla** (German), **Ursel** (Dutch and German), **Urska** (Croatian and Slovenian), **Ursley, Ursulina** (Spanish), **Uschi** (German)

Urvashi

Sanskrit *Urvaśī*, "widely extending." In the Hindu epic *Mahābhārata*, Urvashi is the most beautiful of all the celestial nymphs.

Uzuri

Ancient Basque name, perhaps a form of *Uzu*, "valiant, indomitable."

Valencia

Spanish place name based on *Valens*, a Roman given name from Latin *valere*, "to be strong." Valencia is regularly used as a first name in the southeastern United States.

Valentina

Feminine form of **Valentine**, Latin "healthy, strong." In June 1963, cosmonaut Valentina V. Tereshkova of the former Soviet Union became the first woman in space. This name, which used to be rare in the United States, began to rise in use in 1994. In 2004, 601 Valentinas were born, ranking the name 396th for the year.
Variations: **Val, Valentia, Valentine** (French and Norwegian), **Valja** (Estonian), **Vallatina** (Dutch)

Valeria

Spanish and Italian form of **Valerie**. Except for a few years around 1980, Valeria has been used enough in the United States to make the SSA top 1,000 list, and since 1992 it's been rising rapidly. More than 1,900 Valerias were born in 2004, ranking the name 176th, by far its highest point in history.
Famous name: Valeria Mazza (fashion model)

Valerie

French feminine form of *Valerius*, Roman family name probably from Latin *valere*, "to be strong." This French name became popular in England around 1930. The fashion for Valerie then crossed the Atlantic, and it was one of the top 100 American girls names from 1952 to 1987. Valerie is now decreasing in use as Valeria is rising. More than 1,800 Valeries were born in 2004, ranking it 181st.
Famous names: Valerie Bertinelli (actress)
　　　　　　　Valerie Harper (actress)
　　　　　　　Valerie Wilson Wesley (mystery writer)

Nickname: **Val**

Other spellings: **Valaree, Valarie, Valery, Valoree, Valorie**

Variations: **Valera** (Bulgarian), **Valeria** (Italian, Spanish, Portuguese, and Hungarian), **Valora, Walli** (German)

Vanessa

This name was created in 1713 by Irish author Jonathan Swift for his long poem *Cadenus and Vanessa*. The name honors his friend Esther Vanhomrigh. The *Van-* comes from her surname, and *Essa* is a nickname for Esther. A century later, a genus of butterflies was named after the character in the poem. Samuel Barber, who claimed he got the name from a book of babies names, won a 1958 Pulitzer Prize for his opera *Vanessa*. This name was almost unknown in the United States before 1950, but it was one of the top 200 names by 1953. It became one of the top 100 names in 1977. After 1982, Vanessa was especially popular with Hispanic-Americans because of a Spanish-language television series called *Vanessa* that starred Lucía Méndez, one of Mexico's favorite actresses, in the title role. It is receding slowly today; in 2004, there were about 4,300 Vanessas born, ranking it 86th for the year.

Famous names: Vanessa Bell (artist)

Vanessa Redgrave (actress)

Nicknames: **Van, Vanna, Vanny**

Other spellings: **Vanesa, Venessa**

Vanna

Possibly a form of **Savannah** or **Vanessa.**

Famous name: Vanna White (TV game show hostess)

Vashti

Persian "beautiful one," name of King Ahasuerus's first wife in the biblical Book of Esther. It's never been common, but both Vashti and its short form, **Vassie,** had enough sporadic use around 1900 to sometimes make the SSA top 1,000 list.

Veda

Sanskrit "knowledge."

Vega

Latinized form of Arabic *wāqi',* "falling," the name of a bright star in the constellation Lyra, the second brightest in the northern skies after Arcturus.

Velma

Probably an American form of **Wilhelmina.** From 1903 to 1917, Velma was one of the top 100 names for American girls, but it vanished from the SSA top 1,000 list after 1973. Perhaps the best-known Velma today is the fictional Velma Kelly, the singing murderess in the musical *Chicago.* Velma Dinkley is the smart, glasses-wearing character in the Scooby-Doo cartoon series.

Velvet

Middle English from Latin *velvetum,* "a soft fabric." The 1944 movie *National Velvet,* based on Enid Bagnold's sentimental novel about a young horsewoman, starred Elizabeth Taylor. But it wasn't until after 1960, when the television series *National Velvet* starring Lori Martin premiered, that enough Velvets were born to put the name on the SSA top 1,000 list for the following four years.

Venus

In ancient Italy, Venus was a goddess of gardens and the spring. Later the Romans identified her with the Greek goddess Aphrodite, and she also became their goddess of love and romance, as well as the name of the brightest planet in the sky. Venus has occasionally been given to girls in the United States since the late 19th century. The name was in the SSA top 1,000 list between 1958 and 1982, peaking at 662nd on that list in 1973. The recent fame of tennis player Venus Williams has not been able to revive her name, and it's rarely given today.

Vera

Russian "faith," or Latin *verus,* "true." Vera was a top 100 name between 1891 and 1929, but it's been quite rare since the 1980s. Famous name: Vera Wang (fashion designer)

Verena

Name of a third-century Swiss saint, meaning uncertain, but perhaps from Latin *vereri,* "fearful, shy."
Variations: **Vere, Verene** (French), **Verina, Verine**

Verity

English form of Latin *veritas,* "truth." Verity became a name for girls during Puritan times. It's still used in England but is almost nonexistent in the United States.

Veronica

Variation of **Bernice,** Greek "bringer of victory"; probably modified in ancient times to resemble Latin *vera icon,* "true image." According to legend, St. Veronica wiped the brow of Jesus as he carried his cross to Calvary. The image of his face was miraculously imprinted on the cloth. Between 1972 and 1992, Veronica was one of the top 100 names for girls. Though it's now receding, there were more than 1,700 Veronicas born in 2004, ranking it 193rd that year.

Famous names: Veronica Lake (actress)

Veronica Mars (fictional TV detective)

Nicknames: **Ronnie, Ronny, Vonnie, Vonny**

Variations: **Veronika, Veronique** (French), **Vonice**

Vesta

Latin form of **Hestia.** Vesta was the Roman goddess of the hearth in whose temple a perpetual flame was kept burning by priestesses known as Vestal Virgins.

Vicki, Vickie, Vicky

Form of **Victoria.** Vicki was very popular as an independent name during the 1950s, but today's parents much prefer using **Victoria.**

Famous name: Vicki Lawrence (actress and comedienne)

Victoria

Feminine form of **Victor.** St. Victoria was a third-century martyr, and the name became popular in Italy in the form of **Vittoria.** But not until Alexandrina Victoria, daughter of Edward, duke of Kent, and Princess Victoire of Saxe-Coburg-Saalfeld, was crowned queen of England did the name become known in the British Isles. Queen Victoria gave her name to the Victorian Era and was honored throughout the British Empire with the names of many places, including Lake Victoria in Africa, a state in Australia, and the capital of British Columbia in Canada. In the late 1990s, Victoria was one of the top 25 names for girls in the United States, the most popular the name has ever been. It is just now starting to recede; more than 8,100 Victorias were born in 2004, ranking it 39th.

Famous names: Victoria Bond (composer and conductor)

Victoria Jackson (comedienne)

Nicknames: **Tori, Vic, Vicki, Vickie, Vicky, Vikki, Vikky**

Variations: **Toya** (Mexican), **Victoire, Victorine** (French), **Vikte** (Lithuanian), **Viktoria** (German and Swedish), **Vita, Vitoria** (Portuguese), **Vittoria** (Italian)

Vida

Feminine form of **David,** Hebrew "beloved."

Viola

Variation of **Violet.** Viola is the heroine of Shakespeare's *Twelfth Night.* Between 1900 and 1911, Viola was one of the top 50 names for girls in the United States, but it's been extremely rare since the 1970s.

Violet

Latin *viola,* "violet." Although not as popular as **Rose,** this flower name was one of the 100 most used names for girls born from 1900 to 1926. It was rare in the 1970s and 1980s but has begun to grow again since 1998. There were 469 newborn Violets in 2004, ranking the name 590th on the SSA list. Children today will associate this name with Violet Baudelaire, the oldest of the three orphans whose adventures are recounted in the series of books by Lemony Snicket. Violet is noted for inventing clever devices that save her and her siblings from dangerous situations.
Nickname: **Vi**
Variations: **Fialka** (Czech), **Iolanthe, Vijole** (Lithuanian), **Viola, Violante, Violeta** (Spanish), **Violetta** (Italian), **Violette** (French), **Viorica** (Romanian), **Wioletta** (Polish), **Yolanda**

Virginia

Feminine form of *Verginius,* name of a Roman family of unknown meaning, but reinterpreted in ancient times as meaning "virgin-like." In North America, the colony Virginia was named by Sir Walter Raleigh in honor of Elizabeth I, the Virgin Queen. The first British child born in America was named Virginia Dare in the queen's honor. Virginia was one of the top ten names in the United States from 1916 through 1928. It's been gradually declining since but still ranked 370th in 2004.
Famous names: Virginia Madsen (actress)
Virginia Woolf (novelist)
Nicknames: **Gigi** (French), **Ginger, Ginnie, Ginny**
Variations: **Virga** (Estonian), **Virginie** (Dutch and French)

Vita

Latin *vita,* "life," or form of **Victoria.**

Viveca

Swedish form of Germanic *Wigburg,* "war-fortress."
Other spelling: **Viveka, Vivica**

Vivian, Vivien

From the Latin *vivus,* "alive." In many versions of the Arthurian legends, Vivian is the name of the "Lady of the Lake," an enchantress who lures Merlin. Here the Latin name seems to have been used to replace *Nimue* or *Niniane,* ancient Celtic names for lake goddesses. Between 1911 and 1934, Vivian was one of the 100 most popular names for American girls. In the 1990s, the name was particularly common in the Chinese-American community, probably because of Vivian Chow, a popular singer and actress from Hong Kong. In 2004 more than 1,400 Vivians were born in the United States, ranking it 223rd for the year.

Famous names: Vivian Vance (actress and comedienne)
              Vivian Vande Velde (children's author)
              Vivien Leigh (actress)
Nicknames: **Viv, Vivie**
Variations: **Viviana** (Spanish and Italian), **Vivienne** (French)

Viviana

Spanish and Italian form of **Vivian.** Four years before she starred in *Vanessa,* Mexico's Lucía Méndez starred in another telenovela called *Viviana* in 1978, and so she is responsible for popularizing two V names in the Hispanic-American community. In 2004, 691 Vivianas were born in the United States, ranking it 365th for the year.

Wallis

Old English "person from Wales."
Famous name: Wallis Simpson (duchess of Windsor)
Nicknames: **Wallie, Wally**

Wanda

Slavic name of uncertain meaning, perhaps a Polish form of *Wend*, name of a Slavic people living in eastern Germany. In the 1930s, Wanda was one of the top 50 names for American girls, but it left the SSA top 1,000 list after 1990.
Famous name: Wanda Sykes (actress and comedienne)
Variations: **Vanda, Wandy, Wenda**

Wangari

Kikuyu (Kenya) "leopard." In 2004, Wangari Maathai of Kenya was awarded the Nobel Peace prize for her work in founding the Green Belt movement, which advocates for environmental conservation and community development.

Wendy

Created by Sir James Barrie from the baby-talk phrase "friendy-wendy" for a character in his play *Peter Pan*; Wendy Darling may have been the first girl to have this name. Wendy was a top 50 American name between 1965 and 1977; in 2004 it ranked 277th.
Famous names: Sister Wendy Beckett (art commentator)
              Wendy Wasserstein (playwright)
Variations: **Wenda, Wendi, Wendie**

Whitley

English place name and surname, "white woodland clearing." Whitley Gilbert was the character played by Jasmine Guy on the television sitcom *A Different World*. As with **Jaleesa,** this name's popularity only ran from 1988 to 1993, almost the same run as the show.

Whitney

Old English "white island." Whitney was almost exclusively a male name until actress Whitney Blake appeared on the sitcom *Hazel* in 1961. Whitney immediately entered the SSA top 1,000 list and began to rise. The name took off in 1985 when singer Whitney Houston released her first album. Between 1985 and 1994, Whitney was one of the top 50 names for girls. However, in 2004 only 670 Whitneys were born in the United States, ranking the name 378th. Other spellings: **Whitni, Whitnie, Whittany**

Wilhelmina

Feminine form of **William,** Old German *wil* [will, desire] + *helm* [helmet]. This German name was regularly used in the United States in the late 19th century, but it has been rare since the 1950s.
Nicknames: **Billie, Billy, Minnie, Minny, Willa, Willie, Willy**
Variations: **Guglielma** (Italian), **Guillemette** (French), **Guillerma** (Spanish), **Helma, Helmine, Mina, Minna** (German), **Velma, Vilhelmina** (Swedish), **Vilma** (Estonian), **Wilhelma, Wilhelmine** (German), **Willamena, Willamina, Willemine** (Dutch), **Willetta, Willette, Wilma, Wilmette**

Willa

Form of **Wilhelmina.** The minor vogue for Willa in the 1920s and 1930s had completely vanished by 1963.
Famous name: Willa Cather (writer)

Willow

The word for the tree, from Old English *welig.* This nature name entered the SSA top 1,000 list in 1998, perhaps because of the character Willow Rosenberg on *Buffy the Vampire Slayer.* The 505 Willows born in the United States in 2004 ranked the name 437th.
Famous name: Willow Bay (television news anchor)

Wilma

Form of **Wilhelmina.** From 1912 to 1940, Wilma was one of the 100 most popular names for American girls. It disappeared in the 1970s, and since 1960 has probably been most identified with Wilma Flintstone, Fred's wife in the animated television series *The Flintstones.*
Famous name: Wilma Rudolph (Olympic track star)
Variation: **Vilma** (Czech and Hungarian)

Winifred

Welsh *Gwenfrewi,* probably "blessed reconciliation," but altered through confusion with the Old English male name *Winfred* from *wine* [friend] or *wynn* [joy] and *frith* [peace]. St. Winifred was a seventh-century Welsh woman who was martyred because she refused to marry a prince. The name Winifred remained fairly common in the United States through the 1930s but is rare today.
Nicknames: **Freda, Freddie, Freddy, Win, Winnie, Winny, Wynne**
Other spelling: **Winnifred**

Winnie, Winny

Form of **Winifred.** Winnie was used as an independent name in the late 19th century, but it vanished by 1958 and has shown no signs of revival, not even between 1988 and 1993, when it was the name of a popular character on the television series *The Wonder Years.*

Winona

Siouan "firstborn daughter." This Native American name was popularized in the United States during the 19th century by several poets, especially Henry Wadsworth Longfellow, who used the variation Wenonah as the name of Hiawatha's mother in his 1855 poem *The Song of Hiawatha.* Winona was used moderately around 1930, when parents probably saw it as a variation of **Winifred,** but like that name it vanished from the SSA top 1,000 before 1960.
Famous name: Winona Ryder (actress)
Variations: **Wenonah, Wynonna**

Winter

Winter has never been a frequent name, like **Summer** and **Autumn.** It made the SSA top 1,000 list in 1978 and 1979, while a character named Winter Austin was featured on the daytime soap opera *The Edge of Night.* A few Winters are born in most states every year.

Wislawa

Polish *Wislawa,* feminine form of an ancient Polish name from the Slavic roots *wito,* "lord, gentleman," and *slaw,* "glory." Polish poet Wislawa Szymborska won the 1996 Nobel Prize in literature.

Wynonna

Form of **Winona.**
Famous name: Wynonna Judd (country singer)

Xanthe

Feminine form of Greek *xanthus,* "yellow, bright."

Xenia

Greek "hospitality."
Variation: **Zenia**

Ximena

Origin uncertain, perhaps a medieval Spanish form of **Simone,** or perhaps from Basque *etxemendi,* "house on a mountain." In Pierre Corneille's *Le Cid,* the woman who marries the Cid is named Ximena. This name suddenly gained popularity in the Hispanic-American community in 2001. In 2004 almost 1,400 Ximenas were born in the United States, ranking the name 224th overall. The alternate spelling **Jimena** is almost as common as Ximena.

Xiomara

Probably a form of *Guiomar,* a medieval Spanish name from Germanic roots meaning "battle famous." Xiomara is becoming more common in the Hispanic-American community and entered the SSA top 1,000 list for the first time in 2004, in 828th place.

Xochitl

Nahuatl (Aztec) *xochitl,* "flower," a Native American word that has become a well-used name in Mexico and is sometimes found in Mexican-American families. The Aztec word was pronounced "show-cheat'l," but modern Spanish uses "so-cheel" or "so-chee." Other spellings: **Sochil, Xochil, Zochil**

Yadira

Perhaps a Hispanic feminine form of Arabic *Jadir*, "worthy." Yadira has been used in Mexico since at least 1945 and has been in the SSA top 1,000 in the United States since 1975. There were 508 Yadiras born in 2004, ranking the name 434th.

Yareli

Origin unknown; may be a recent Caribbean Spanish creation. Yareli is popular with Hispanic-Americans because of Mexican-born Cuban actress Yareli Arizmendi.

Yaritza

Probably a modern Latin-American creation based on **Maritza.** Yaritza ranked 979th on the SSA top 1,000 list in 2004, with 240 born.

Yasmin, Yasmine

Arabic forms of **Jasmine.** These names are now used by African-American and Hispanic-American parents, as well as by Muslim and Christian immigrants from Arabic-speaking countries. Almost 1,900 girls were given these names in 2004, for a combined rank of 180th. Famous name: Yasmine Bleeth (actress and model)

Yesenia

Yolanda Vargas Dulché (1926–1999) was a Mexican writer who became famous writing comic books and then became wealthy writing and producing telenovelas. One of her most successful stories was *Yesenia,* the tale of a poor gypsy girl who falls in love with a dashing army officer. The original series was shown in 1970, and the story was so popular it was remade in 1988. As a result, the name Yesenia became popular throughout Latin America and with Hispanic-American parents in the United States. No one knows how Yolanda Vargas created the name; some have speculated that she was thinking of **Jessenia,** the name of a type of South American palm tree, which has in fact often been used as an alternate spelling for this name, along with **Yessenia** and **Jesenia**. It's more likely that she created it herself to sound suitably exotic to her audience. Though not as common as it was in the 1990s, there were still more than 1,100 Yesenias born in the United States in 2004, ranking it 250th.

Yoko

This name illustrates how one must know the *kanji* characters a Japanese name is written in before one can know the meaning the parents intended. Yoko Ono's given name means "ocean child," but Japanese composer Yoko Shimomura's first name means "sunshine." Many other meanings would also be possible.

Yolanda

English form of a medieval French name of unknown origin, perhaps an obscure Germanic name blended with a Greek form of **Violet.** Yolanda was popular with African-American parents around 1970 because of the publicity given to Yolanda King, the eldest daughter of Martin Luther King, Jr., and Coretta Scott King. Yolanda is rare today.
Variations: **Iolanda, Jolán** (Hungarian), **Jolie, Yolande** (French), **Yolanthe**

Yuki

Japanese "noble and precious."

Yuliana

Russian and Bulgarian form of **Juliana,** popular with Hispanic-Americans because of Yuliana Peniche, one of the hosts of the popular Spanish-language family variety show *Vida TV*. Yuliana ranked 870th on the SSA list in 2004, with 279 born in the United States.

Yvette

Form of **Yvonne**. There was a minor fashion for this name in the 1960s, and it is still frequently found in the Hispanic-American community. Yvette ranked 791st on the SSA list in 2004.

Yvonne

Feminine form of **Yvon,** (a variation of **Yves**) French form of Germanic *iv*, "yew." This name was well used from the 1930s through the 1960s, but it is rare again today.
Other spelling: **Evonne**
Variations: **Ivonne** (French), **Vonnie, Vonny, Yvette**

Zainab, Zaynab, Zeinab

All three of these spellings are used by Muslim immigrants in the
United States for Arabic *Zaynab,* "fragrant plant" or "ornamented
tree." This was the name of one of the prophet Muhammad's
daughters, two of his wives, and one of his granddaughters.

Zanazan

Armenian "different, various."

Zaria

A city in northern Nigeria, said to have been founded by Queen
Bakwa Turunku about 1536 and named for her younger daughter. The
name is possibly a Hausa variation of Arabic *Zahra,* "flower." Zaria
became popular with African-Americans in 1997 because of the
character Zaria Peterson on the television series *The Parent 'Hood.* In
2004, Zaria ranked 669th, with 405 girls given the name.

Zariah

It's unclear if this is a spelling variation of **Zaria** or a separate name
blending it with the sound of **Mariah.** Zariah entered the SSA top
1,000 list in 2004 at 966th place, when 245 girls received the name.

Zelda

Form of **Griselda.** There was a minor fashion for Zelda at the
beginning of the 20th century. Though it's rare today, many people
are familiar with it through the videogame series Legend of Zelda.
Famous name: Zelda Fitzgerald (writer)

Zelia

Perhaps a form of **Celia** or a creation based on the word *zeal.*

Zella, Zelma

A century ago these names were even more popular than **Zelda,**
but they have nearly vanished today.

Zenobia

Feminine form of Greek *Zénobios*, "Zeus-life." Queen Zenobia of Palmyra, who lived in the third century, is famous for her beauty, ambition, and ruthlessness in expanding her empire.

Zergun

Turkish *Zergûn*, "goldlike."

Zillah

Hebrew *zillah*, "shadow." In the Bible, Zillah is the mother of Tubal-Cain, the blacksmith.

Zina

Swahili "beauty," occasionally chosen by African-American parents; also, form of Zinaida, Russian feminine form of Greek *Zenais*, "follower of Zeus," the name of two first-century martyrs revered by the Orthodox church.

Zoe

Greek "life." This name was used in Alexandria, Egypt, to translate the biblical name Eve. Zoe was at the height of fashion in England during the 1970s, when American parents were still ignoring it. It was discovered in the United States in the late 1980s, and it quickly grew in use. By 2000, it was among the top 100 names for American girls. In 2004, more than 7,400 Zoes were born in the United States, making it the 45th most popular name that year.

Zora

This is the word for "dawn" in southern Slavic languages such as Serbian and Bulgarian. Zora became a fairly popular name in the 19th-century United States. It has been rare since the 1940s, but with **Cora** and **Zoe** both rising in use, Zora may soon be seen as an alternative. Famous name: Zora Neale Hurston (author)

Zuleika

Variation of Arabic *Zulaikha*, "amazingly beautiful." A novel by Max Beerbohm, *Zuleika Dobson*, made this name familiar in England, but Byron had also used the name in *The Bride of Abydos*.
Variation: **Zula**

Zuwena

Swahili "small and beautiful."

References

Al Ja'fari, Fatimah Suzanne. *Digest of Muslim Names*. Beltsville, MD: Amana Publications, 1997.

Awde, Nicholas and Emanuela Losi. *Armenian First Names*. New York: Hippocrene Books, 2001.

Bahlow, Hans. *German Names,* trans. Edda Gentry. Madison, WI: University of Wisconsin Press, 2002.

Bowder, Diana (Ed.) *Who Was Who in the Roman World*. New York: Washington Square Press, 1980.

Bowder, Diana (Ed.) *Who Was Who in the Greek World*. New York: Washington Square Press, 1982.

Campbell, Mike. *Behind the Name: The Etymology and History of First Names,* 2005. *www.behindthename.com*

Farmer, David Hugh. *The Oxford Dictionary of Saints*. New York: Oxford University Press, 1987.

Gandhi, Maneka and Husain Ozair. *The Complete Book of Muslim & Parsi Names*. New Delhi: Penguin Books India, 2004.

Gandhi, Maneka. *The Penguin Book of Hindu Names*. New Delhi: Penguin India, 1992.

Gruffudd, Heini. *Welsh Personal Names*. Talybont, Wales: Y Lolfa, 1980.

Hanks, Patrick and Flavia Hodges. *A Dictionary of Surnames*. New York: Oxford University Press, 1992.

Hanks, Patrick. (Ed.) *Dictionary of American Family Names*. New York: Oxford University Press, 2003.

Internet Movie Database, 2005. *www.imdb.com/search*

Lieberson, Stanley. *A Matter of Taste: How Names, Fashions, and Culture Change*. New Haven: Yale University Press, 2000.

Lorenz, Brenna E. *The Pacific Islander's Book of Names*. Mangilao, Guam: Three Furies Press, 1996.

MacLysaght, Edward. *The Surnames of Ireland*. Dublin: Irish Academic Press, 1985.

Mills, A.D. *A Dictionary of English Place-Names*. New York: Oxford University Press, 1991.

Moss, Jennifer. The Babynames.com message boards, 2005. *http://www.babynames.com/boards/*

Musere, Jonathan. *Traditional African Names*. Lanham, MD: Scarecrow Press, Inc, 2000.

Ó Corráin, Donnchadh and Fidelma Maguire. *Irish Names*. Dublin: Lilliput Press, 1990.

Osuntoki, Chief. *The Book of African Names*. Baltimore, MD: Black Classic Press, 1970.

Reaney, P. H. and R. M. Wilson. *A Dictionary of English Surnames*. New York: Oxford University Press, 1997.

Room, Adrian. *African Placenames*. Jefferson, NC: McFarland, 1994.

Room, Adrian. *Placenames of the World*. Jefferson, NC: McFarland, 1997.

Root, Eileen M. *Hawaiian Names—English Names*. Kailua, HI: Press Pacifica, 1987.

Sidi, Smadar Shir. *The Complete Book of Hebrew Baby Names*. San Francisco: HarperCollins, 1989.

Stewart, George R. *American Place-Names*. New York: Oxford University Press, 1970.

U.S. Social Security Administration, 2005. Popular given names. *www.ssa.gov/OACT/NOTES/note139/note139.html*

Woods, Richard D. *Hispanic First Names*. Westport, CT: Greenwood Press, 1984.

Yemane, Elias. *Amharic and Ethiopic Onomastics*. Lewiston, NY: The Edwin Mellen Press, 2004.

Zawawi, Sharifa M. *What's in a Name? Unaitwaje?* Trenton, NJ: Africa World Press, Inc., 1993.